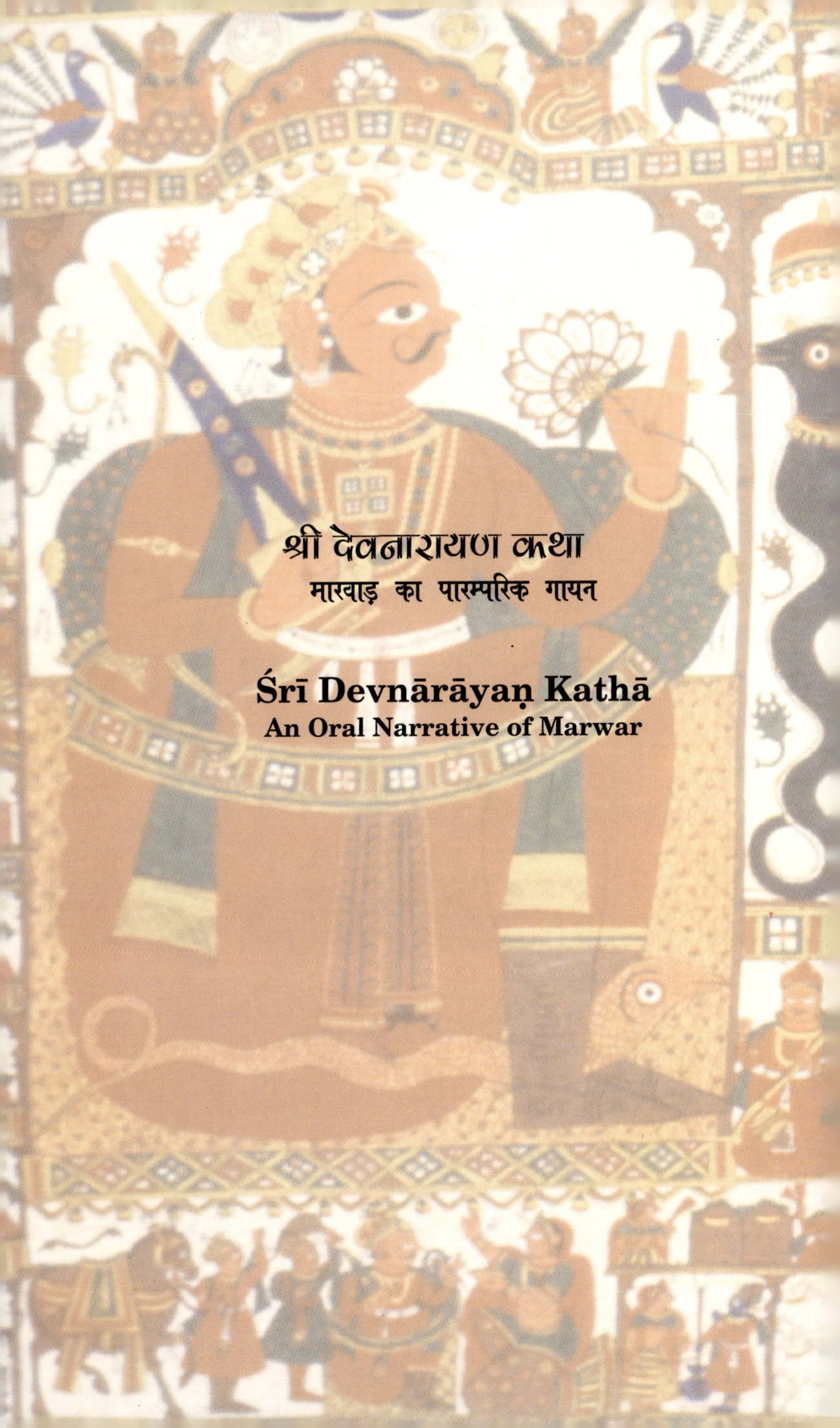

श्री देवनारायण कथा

मारवाड़ का पारम्परिक गायन

Śrī Devnārāyaṇ Kathā

An Oral Narrative of Marwar

Śrī Hukmārām Bhopā, the best singer of Śrī Devnārāyaṇ Kathā
श्री हुक्माराम भोपा, श्री देवनारायण कथा के सर्वश्रेष्ठ गायक

Śrī Devnārāyaṇ Kathā

An Oral Narrative of Marwar

Singers

Hukmaram Bhopa

Motaram Gujar

Editor

Aditya Malik

D.K. Printworld (P) Ltd.

New Delhi

SOUTH ASIA INSTITUTE, NEW DELHI BRANCH
HEIDELBERG UNIVERSITY

SOUTH ASIA STUDIES NO. XLII

श्री देवनारायण कथा

मारवाड़ का पारम्परिक गायन

गायक

श्री हुक्माराम भोपा
श्री मोटाराम गूजर

संपादक

आदित्य मलिक

डी॰ के॰ प्रिंटवर्ल्ड (प्रा॰) लि॰
नई दिल्ली – 110 015

Cataloging-in-Publication Data — DK

Bhopā, Hukmārāma.

Śrī Devanārāyaṇa kathā / gāyaka, Hukmārāma Bhopā, Moṭārāma Gūjara; sampādaka, Āditya Malika.

(South Asia studies / South Asia Institute, New Delhi Branch, Heidelberg University ; no. 42).

In Hindi.

Includes bibliographical references (p.)

1. Devnārāyaṇa (Hindu deity) — Oral narrative and songs. 2. Devanārāyaṇa (Hindu deity) — Cult — India — Rajasthan. 3. Folk songs, epic, Marwari. I. Gūjara Moṭārāma. II. Malika, Āditya. II. Series: South Asia studies / South Asia Institute, New Delhi Branch, Heidelberg University ; no. 42

ISBN 81-246-0225-5

प्रथम संस्करण, 2003

(दक्षिण एशिया अध्ययन शृंखला संख्या, XLII)

मूल्य : 680.00 रुपये

प्रकाशक एवं मुद्रक :

डी॰ के॰ प्रिण्टवर्ल्ड (प्रा॰) लि॰

पंजीकृत कार्यालय: 'श्री कुञ्ज', एफ-52, बाली नगर,
नई दिल्ली - 110 015
दूरभाष : (011) 2545 3975, 2546 6019
फैक्स : (011) 2546 5926
ई-मेल : dkprintworld@vsnl.net

Contents / विषय-सूची

Prefatory Note	vii
प्राक्कथन	ix
Acknowledgements	xi
आभार	xiii
Map of Rajasthan with locations from the narrative	xv
कथा से सम्बन्धित स्थानों सहित राजस्थान का मानचित्र	xvi
Introduction	1
श्री देवनारायण कथा – एक परिचय	45
श्री देवनारायण कथा	89
Glossary	385
परिभाषिक शब्द कोश	395
Bibliography	405
सन्दर्भ ग्रन्थ-सूची	407

In the memory of
Śrī Hukmārām Bhopā

श्री हुक्माराम भोपा
की निर्मल स्मृति को
सादर समर्पित

Prefatory Note

THE transcription of Śrī Devnārāyaṇ Kathā provided here is based on the recordings of recitations done by Śrī Hukmārām Bhopā and his partner Śrī Moṭārām Gūjar. The recordings were done by me at different localities including Śrī Hukmārām Bhopā's home in a village on the northern boundary of the district of Nagaur (Rajasthan) during the month of May in 1991. The total time for the recitation of the narrative came to about twenty-four hours. The language spoken by the singers belongs to one of the major 'dialects' spoken in Rajasthan, namely Mārvāḍī.[1] While their language can be identified from earlier surveys as falling within the cultural and political region of Mārvāḍ,[2] it must be noted that there can be considerable variation even within such a linguistic area. As the well-known Mārvāḍī phrase says: *bārāṁ kosāṁ bhāsā badle, tīsāṁ kosāṁ mausim* ('language changes every twelve *kos*, weather every thirty').[3] Thus the location of the singers' village in the north or south of Mārvāḍ can result in linguistic variation. For example, Śrī Hukmārām Bhopā's usage of the genitive postposition is different to that of 'Standard Mārvāḍī': instead of *ro*, *rā*, *rī*, he uses *ko*, *kā*, *kī* which is similar to Hindi. However, since it is not the aim of the present study to provide an analysis of the singers' language, these and other variations have not been dealt with here. The interested

1. See Grierson (1908), Magier (1992), Smith (1992) for general and specific sureys of Rājasthānī dialects.
2. On Rajasthan as a political and cultural region, see Lodrick (1994).
3. Magier (1992: 339); one *kos* equals about 3.2 km.

reader is therefore referred to studies on Rājasthānī dialect, language, and grammar found in Grierson (1908); Allen (1957, 1960); Behl (1980); Smith (1976, 1992); Magier (1992).

The voice of Śrī Moṭārām Gūjar has been placed in round brackets so as to distinguish it from that of Śrī Hukmārām Bhopā's. In contrast to the translation, the sung sections of the text in verse *gāv* have been provided here in full detail.* The narrative begins with an invocation of different deities before moving on to the story itself, which begins with the circumstances just prior to Devnārāyaṇ's birth. The narrative ends after Devnārāyaṇ's son Bilā acceeds to his father's wish of becoming a priest in Devnārāyaṇ's first shrine on the hill of Demālī. At the end of the narrative Devnārāyaṇ departs to Baikuṇṭh.

New Delhi / Christchurch
May 2002

Aditya Malik

* For a comprehensive study and full-length translation in English, readers are referred to my forthcoming monograph with Oxford University Press, New York (in press).

प्राक्कथन

देवनाराण की कथा का यहां प्रस्तुत प्रतिलेखन श्री हुक्माराम भोपा और उनके सहयोगी श्री मोटाराम गूजर द्वारा किए गए सस्वर पाठ की रिकॉर्डिंग पर आधारित है। यह रिकॉर्डिंग विभिन्न स्थानों पर की गई थी। जिनमें जिला नागौर (राजस्थान) की उत्तरी सीमा पर एक गांव में स्थित श्री हुक्माराम भोपा का घर भी शामिल है, जहां मई 1991 में रिकॉर्डिंग की गई थी। कथा का सस्वर पाठ लगभग चौबीस घंटों में पूरा हुआ। गायकों द्वारा बोली जाने वाली भाषा राजस्थान में बोली जाने वाली प्रमुख 'बोलियों' में से एक से सम्बन्ध रखती है जिसे मारवाड़ी कहा जाता है।[1] जहां उनकी भाषा की पहचान पूर्ववर्ती सर्वेक्षणों में मारवाड़ के सांस्कृतिक और राजनैतिक क्षेत्र के भीतर बोली जाने वाली भाषा के रूप में की जा सकती है,[2] वहां यह भी अवश्य ध्यान रखना चाहिए कि इस एक भाषाई क्षेत्र में भी विचारणीय भिन्नताएं हो सकती हैं। जैसाकि मारवाड़ी की विख्यात सूक्ति भी है – बारां कोसां भासा बदले, तीसां कोसां मौसिम (बारह कोस पर भाषा और तीस कोस पर मौसम बदल जाते हैं।)[3] इस प्रकार गायकों के गांव की स्थिति मारवाड़ के उत्तर या दक्षिण में होने से भाषाई भेद हो सकते हैं। उदाहरण के लिए, श्री हुक्माराम भोपा का शब्द की उत्पत्ति के बाद उसका उपयोग 'मानक मारवाड़ी' से भिन्न है। वे रो, रा, री, की अपेक्षा हिन्दी के समान को, का, की का उपयोग करते हैं। तथापि, क्योंकि इस अध्ययन का उद्देश्य गायकों की भाषा का विश्लेषण प्रस्तुत करना नहीं है, इसलिए इन और अन्य भिन्नताओं को यहां व्यवहार में नहीं लाया गया है। इन्हें जानने के इच्छुक पाठक राजस्थानी बोली, भाषा और व्याकरण पर किए गए अध्ययन – ग्रीसन (1908); एलेन (1957, 1960); बेहल (1980); स्मिथ (1976, 1992) और मागिर (1992) को देख सकते हैं।

श्री मोटाराम गूजर की आवाज को गोल कोष्ठकों में रखा गया है ताकि इसे श्री हुक्माराम भोपा की आवाज से पृथक् किया जा सके। अनुवाद से अलग हटकर गाव (पद्य) में कथावस्तु के गेय खण्डों को पूर्ण विस्तृत विवरण प्रदान किया गया है।* कथा का प्रारम्भ, सीधे ही कहानी शुरु करने की अपेक्षा विभिन्न देवी-देवताओं के आह्वान से किया गया है। कहानी

---

* विस्तृत अध्ययन हेतु अंग्रेज़ी भाषा में मेरे द्वारा पूर्णतया अनुवादित एवं ऑक्सफोर्ड युनिवरसिटी प्रेस, न्यूयार्क द्वारा शीध प्रकाशित होने वाली पुस्तक देखें।

देवनारायण के जन्म से ठीक पहले की परिस्थितियों में शुरु होती है। कहानी का अंत देवनारायण के पुत्र बीला द्वारा अपने पिता की इच्छानुसार देमाली पर्वत पर स्थित देवनारायण की प्रथम समाधि में पुरोहित बनने के साथ होता है। कथा के अंत में देवनारायण बैकुण्ठ की ओर प्रस्थान कर जाते हैं।

आदित्य मलिक

संदर्भ

1. राजस्थानी बोलियों के आम और विशेष सर्वेक्षण के लिए देखिए ग्रीसन (1908), मागिर (1992), स्मिथ (1992)।
2. राजनैतिक और सांस्कृति क्षेत्र के रूप में राजस्थान पर देखिए – लांड्रिक (1994)।
3. मागिर (1992 : 339); एक कोस लगभग 3.2 कि॰मी॰ के बराबर होता है।

Acknowledgements

THE process of completing this transcription of the oral narrative of Lord Devnārāyaṇ began in 1991, when I first visited Rajasthan to record the narrative. I was fortunate to meet Śrī Hukmārām Bhopā, the singer of the narrative whose wit, brilliance and sincerity was a great source of inspiration. As one of the outstanding singers of the tradition it was he that opened up the countless dimensions of the narrative for me. He died before this book was completed. Its publication fulfils the commitment that he had in having the story of his deity, Lord Devnārāyaṇ listened to and known. This book is dedicated to his memory.

I was welcomed and supported by many people in Rajasthan especially Pusanath Dangi and his family in Pisangan; Nathu Lal Solanki in Pushkar who assisted me with the tedious work of transcribing the narrative from audio recordings; Laburam Bhopa and his family in Dhaneriya; Shyam Singh Rathor of Kharwa and Dilip Singh Rathor of Bhawanipura; the Mahants of the Brahmā temple and the temples of Devnārāyaṇ and Savāī Bhoj in Pushkar, as well as numerous other individuals I met in the villages and towns I visited. I am also most grateful to Shri Shrilal Joshi for his patience in explaining the intricacies of the *paḍ* and for providing the line-drawing of the *paḍ* published here.

In Heidelberg I received the support of my teachers, colleagues and friends at the South Asia Institute. The fact that I undertook this project at all is a reflection of the inspiration and guidance provided by my teacher Günther-Dietz Sontheimer (*d.* 1992) who opened my eyes to the richness of the subject. I am extremely fortunate to have received all the academic training I did from him.

Monika Horstmann has over many years and in many ways been a most patient and committed support. Hermann Berger was gracious to sponsor the project with the German Research Council after its being initially sponsored by Günther-Dietz Sontheimer. Heidrun Brückner and Anne Feldhaus provided encouragement and advice through the many stages of completion of this work. I am also particularly thankful to Bahadur Singh of the University of Hamburg for his suggestions and for patiently listening to the recordings.

Generous funding for research and writing was provided by grants of the *Deutsche Forschungsgemeinschaft* (German Research Council) over a period of more than five years between 1991-93 and 1996-98. I am extremely grateful for their support.

The reassurance of my parents, Subhash Chandra Malik and Zarine Malik began well before this project, and continues after its completion. It is through them that I first experienced how enduring knowledge is transmitted through spoken words.

My wife, Bele, has persistently believed in the possibility of this book. At times she has expressed more commitment to its completion that I myself have shown. Her constant encouragement has made writing this book an exercise in joy that is matched only by being in the presence of our daughters Renuka-Maria and Ambika-Diana.

Mr. B.L. Dhiman of Jind has translated in Hindi the beginning pages, introduction, glossary and bibliography for which I would remain grateful. Finally, I am grateful to Susheel Mittal of D.K. Printworld for his patience and friendly support, and to the South Asia Institute of the University of Heidelberg, for publishing this volume in the South Asia Studies series. In this context I would particularly like to thank the staff of the branch office of the South Asia Institute in New Delhi, Shri Gabar Singh Chauhan, Shri Parasnath Chaudary, Shri Jainuddin Baksh, Shri Sohan Pal as well as Shri Ratan Lal and Shri Mehboob Ali for their kindness and support during my stay in New Delhi during 1999-2001.

Aditya Malik

आभार

भगवान देवनारायण की इस कथा के प्रतिलेखन का कार्य 1991 में शुरु हुआ था, जब मैंने इस कथा को रिकॉर्ड करने के लिए राजस्थान की यात्रा की तो सौभाग्यवश मेरी भेंट इस कथा के गायक श्री हुक्माराम भोपा से हुई जिनकी समझबूझ, प्रतिभा और सरलता प्रेरणा का महान् स्त्रोत थीं। इस पारम्परिक कथा के श्रेष्ठ गायक के रूप में उन्होंने मेरे समक्ष इसके असंख्य आयाम खोल दिए। इस पुस्तक का लेखन कार्य पूर्ण होने से पहले ही वे स्वर्ग सिधार गए। इसके प्रकाशन से उनकी वह प्रतिज्ञा पूर्ण होगी कि वे अपने देवता भगवान् देवनारायण की कथा को विख्यात कर देंगे। यह पुस्तक उनकी स्मृति को समर्पित है।

राजस्थान में अनेक लोगों ने मेरा स्वागत और समर्थन किया है जिनमें मुख्य हैं – पिसांगन निवासी पुसानाथ डांगी और उनका परिवार ; पुष्कर निवासी नाथूलाल सोलंकी, जिन्होंने इस कथा की रिकॉर्डिंग से इसके प्रतिलेखन के दु:साध्य कार्य में मेरा सहयोग किया; धनेरिया निवासी लाबुराम भोपा और उनका परिवार; खरवा के श्याम सिंह राठौर और भवानीपुरा के दिलीप सिंह राठौर ; पुष्कर में ब्रह्मा मन्दिर और देवनारायण व सवाई भोज मन्दिरों के महन्तों के साथ.साथ अनेक अन्य व्यक्ति जिनसे मैं गाँवों व नगरों के भ्रमण के दौरान मिला। इसके अतिरिक्त मैं आभारी हूँ श्री श्रीलाल जोशी जी का, जिन्होंने बहुत ही धर्य के साथ मुझे फड़ की बारीकियों का ज्ञान करवाया और फड़ का बृहद रेखा-चित्र, जोकि इस पुस्तक में उपलब्ध है, बनाया।

हैडेलबर्ग में मुझे दक्षिण एशिया संस्थान के अपने अध्यापकों, सहकर्मियों और मित्रों से काफी सहायता मिली। मेरा मानना है कि यह कार्य मेरे शिक्षक गुन्थर-डिट्ज सोंथेइमर (मृत्यु 1992) द्वारा दी गई प्रेरणा और मार्गदर्शन का प्रतिबिम्ब है। वे मुझे इस विषय की पूर्ण गहराई तक ले गए। उनसे शिक्षा प्राप्त करना मेरा परम सौभाग्य है। मोनिका हॉर्स्टमन से मुझे कई वर्षों से अनेक प्रकार की सही और ठोस सहायता मिली है। प्रारम्भ में इस कार्य को गुन्थर-डिट्ज सोंथेइमर द्वारा प्रायोजित करने के बाद हर्मन बर्गर ने उदारतापूर्वक इसे जर्मन रिसर्च कौंसिल से प्रायोजित करवाया है। हेड्रइन्न ब्रुकनर और अन्ने फेल्डहोस ने इस कार्य को पूरा करने में विभिन्न स्तरों पर मुझे उत्साहित किया और परामर्श दिया है। मैं हम्बर्ग विश्वविद्यालय

के बहादुर सिंह का विशेष आभार प्रकट करता हूं, जिन्होंने इस कथा की रिकॉर्डिंग को सुना और कई सुझाव दिए।

ड्यूटसे फॉर्सगंस्गेमेनशाफ्ट (जर्मन रिसर्च कौंसिल) ने 1991-93 और 1996-98 के बीच पांच वर्षों से भी अधिक की अवधि के दौरान अनुसंधान और लेखन के लिए उदारतापूर्वक अनुदान प्रदान किया है। मैं इस सहायता के लिए अत्यन्त आभारी हूं।

मेरे माता-पिता, सुभाषचन्द्र मलिक और ज़ेरिन मलिक का आर्शीवाद इस कार्य को शुरु करने से पहले और बाद में भी मेरे साथ है। मैंने पहली बार उन्हीं से सीखा कि प्राप्त ज्ञान को वाणी के माध्यम से कैसे प्रकट किया जाता है।

मेरी पत्नी बेले को इस पुस्तक की सफलता में दृढ़ विश्वास है। अनेक बार उन्होंने इसे पूरा करने में मेरे से भी अधिक दृढ़ता का परिचय दिया है। उनके उत्साहवर्द्धन से इस पुस्तक का लेखन बहुत सरल हो गया और यह कार्य हमारी बेटियों – रेणुका-मारिया तथा अम्बिका-डायना की उपस्थिति में अधिक रोचक बन गया।

जींद निवासी श्री बी०एल० धीमान ने पुस्तक के प्रारम्भिक तथा अन्तिम पृष्ठों का हिन्दी में अनुवाद करने में अद्वितीय भूमिका निभाई है इसके लिए मैं उनका हार्दिक धन्यवाद करता हूँ। अंत में मैं डी० के० प्रिण्टवर्ल्ड के निदेशक सुशील मित्तल का उनके धैर्य व सहायता के लिए तथा हैडेलबर्ग विश्वविद्यालय स्थित दक्षिण एशिया संस्थान का जिसने इस पुस्तक को दक्षिण एशिया अध्ययन श्रृंखला में प्रकाशित किया है, धन्यवाद प्रकट करता हूँ। इस संदर्भ में दक्षिण एशिया संस्थान, दिल्ली शाखा में कार्यरत सहयोगियों : श्री गबर सिंह चौहान, श्री पारसनाथ चौधरी, श्री जैनुदीन बक्श, श्री सोहनपाल, श्री रतन लाल एवं श्री महबूब अली को मैं धन्यवाद देता हूँ जिन्होंने 1999 से 2001 के बीच मेरे दिल्ली प्रवास के दौरान हर संभव सहयोग दिया तथा उदारता दिखाई।

नई दिल्ली/क्राईस्टचर्च **आदित्य मलिक**

मई 2002

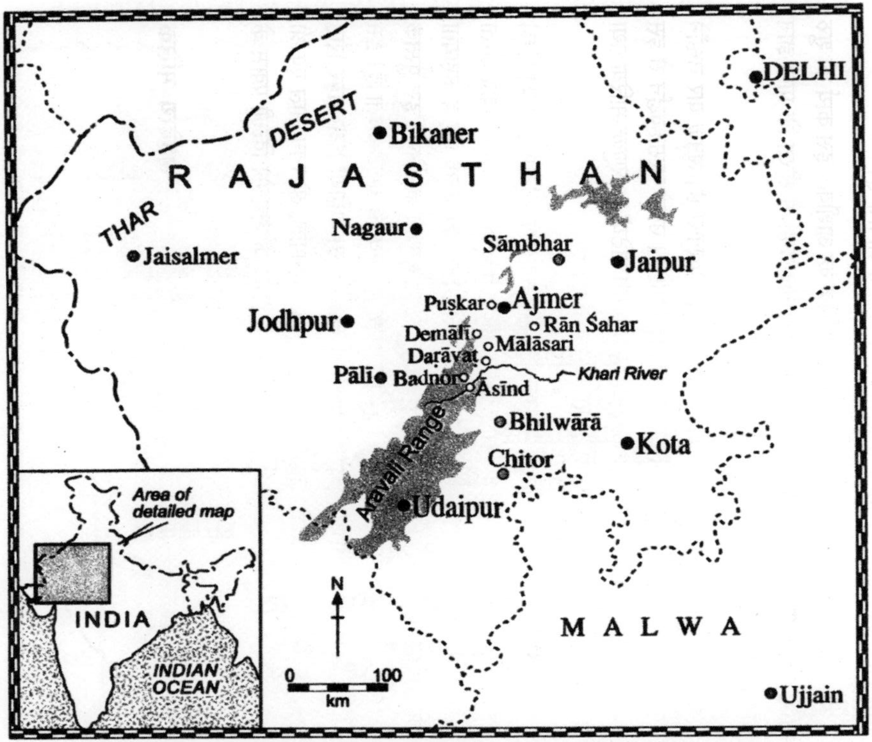

Map of Rajasthan with locations from the narrative

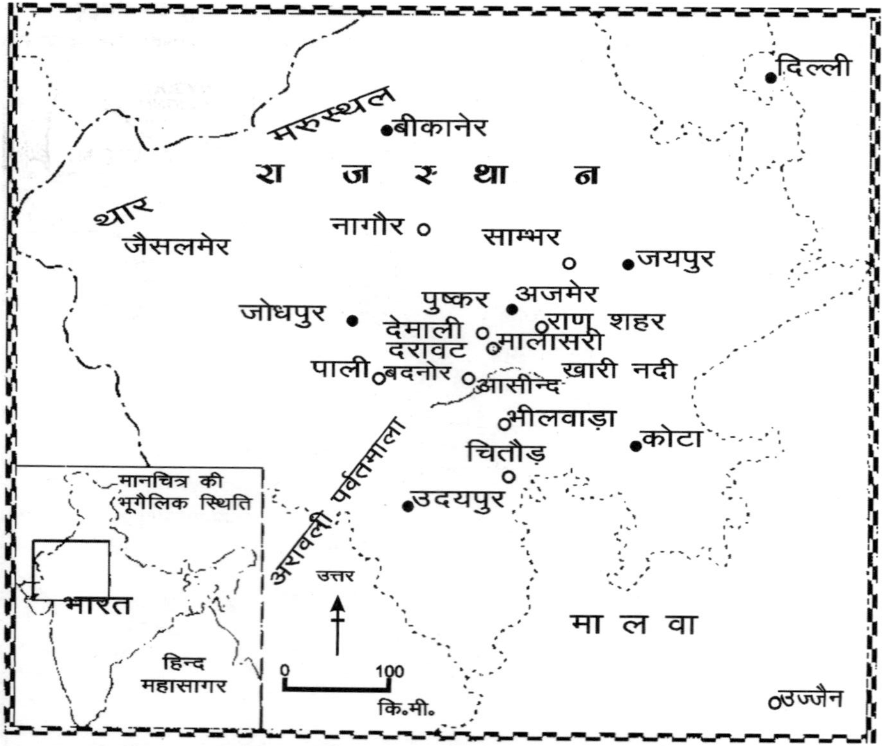

कथा से सम्बन्धित स्थानों सहित राजस्थान का मानचित्र

Introduction

THE narrative of Devnārāyaṇ — which has frequently been classified as an 'epic'[1] — is one of the most well-known folk narratives in Rajasthan.[2] The narrative and Devnārāyaṇ's cult covers a large area extending over most of Rajasthan and Malwa, the north-western region of Madhya Pradesh. Together with the 'epic' narratives of Pābūjī, Gūgājī, Tejājī, Rāmdevjī, Gopī Cand and Bharthari, it belongs to a rich and significant corpus of oral narratives current in Rajasthan today.[3] The current work is based on a telling of the narrative recorded from Śrī Hukmārām Bhopā and his companion Śrī Moṭārām Gūjar.[4] The recordings of the two parts of the narrative were done alternatively in the town of Sujangarh (Churu District), in the villages of Agunta and Kharesh (Nagaur Dist.), and in the pilgrimage town of

---

1. See, for example, Blackburn (1989), Malik (1993b), Miller (1994), Singh (1993), Smith (1991). Blackburn furthermore classifies the narrative under the category of so-called 'martial epics' in India that emphasise 'group solidarity' and are 'concerned with power, social obligation, and social unity; they turn on themes of revenge, regainning lost land, or restoring lost rights. . . . Martial epics celebrate external — often military or political — conflict and a warrior ethic'. (1989: 5)
2. A synopsis of the contents of the narrative that has two main parts is offered at the end of this introduction.
3. See Binford (1976), Blackburn (1989), Gold (1992), Lapoint (1978), Smith (1991).
4. Śrī Hukmārām Bhopā was accompanied by Śrī Moṭārām in 1991, and by his nephew Śrī Kiṣnārām in 1994 when the recording of the Bagaḍāvat Bhārat was made.

   NOTE: In the transcription the voice of Śrī Moṭārām has been placed in round brackets so as to distinguish it from the voice of Śrī Hukmārām.

Pushkar (Ajmer Dist.). The total number of hours of recording time came to about forty-six hours: the first part of the narrative dealing with the lives and deeds of Devnārāyaṇ's ancestors, the Bagaḍāvats, spanned some twenty-two hours; the second part which focuses on Devnārāyaṇ resulted in twenty-four hours of recitation. In addition to this, recordings amounting to roughly another one hundred hours were made. These consisted of interviews with other singers and devotees of Devnārāyaṇ, shorter narratives related to the main narrative, and various details regarding the content of the narrative as well as its visual counterpart, the *paḍ*.[5] All together approximately twelve months were spent in Rajasthan collecting materials on the narrative on three different occasions between 1991 and 1994.

The task of transcribing and translating the twenty-four hour long part of the narrative dealing with Devnārāyaṇ, that forms the centre-piece of this monograph, was completed in spring 1996, resulting in around seven hundred pages of Mārwaḍī text and English translation. Apart from recordings of the narrative, field trips were also conducted to the important centres of the cult of Devnārāyaṇ in the districts of Ajmer, Bhilwara, and Chittor. Many of the shrines and temples that were visited are mentioned in the narrative, and are connected to specific events and actions related either to the Bagaḍāvats or to Devnārāyaṇ. Thus for instance, the hill-top shrine of Demālī is considered to be the very first place of worship that was founded by Devnārāyaṇ himself, or the temple of Savāī Bhoj that commemorates the battle-field upon which the Bagaḍāvats lost their lives in the *Mahābhārata* against their arch-enemy, the Rāṇā of Rāṇ City, or the hill of Mālāsarī where Devnārāyaṇ was born to his mother Sāḍū Mātā, and so on.[6]

---

5. The narrative is performed in front of a painted scroll depicting Devnārāyaṇ together with hundreds of other items such as courts, towns, individual characters, deities, animals, birds, trees, water reservoirs, weapons, musical instruments, etc.
6. These and other locations are part of a 'sacred geography' that is exemplified through the narrative as well as the *paḍ*.

The present introduction deals primarily with questions relating to the verbal narrative which is transcribed here. Specifically, I look at how performance is defined; how the oral narrative structure of the text is shaped; how the communicative context of the narrative is composed of epistemological categories such as 'remembrance' on the one hand, and aspects of 'speech genres' such as 'repetition', 'dialogue', and 'reported speech' on the other.

Thus one of the chief concerns of any study of a folk narrative is not only to understand the structure and content of the narrative and the context in which it is performed, but also to understand and appreciate the notion of text and performance that is offered from within the cultural framework of the narrative. How are text and performance defined and perceived? Are there distinct and articulate notions of what constitutes a text and performance? Do these notions perhaps depart from a notion of text and performance derived from the researcher's own cultural framework?

In the following sections I successively examine the categories of performance, remembarance and memory, song and declamatory chant, repetition, dialogue and reported speech. Each of these features individually and collectively build the context for the communicative act of telling and listening to the oral narrative of Devnārāyaṇ. Taken together they also form the framework for the rationale for why the narrative is told, which is to elicit the *presence* of Devnārāyaṇ.[7] Thus the notion of 'text' (both oral and visual) here is bound to a larger context. Unlike the case of the 'written text' neither the oral nor the visual narrative exist as self-contained objects.[8]

---

7. There is no doubting the fact that performances are held for a number of reasons, such as a fulfilment of individual vows or during religious festivals. However, the binding feature of all performances beyond individual or group motivations is the celebration of the deity's presence. Without this the fulfilment of vows and other religious observances do not make sense.

8. As Kersenboom (1995: 16) with reference to the 'Tamil Text' observes: 'While the nature of the Western text is static, an object

Performance

The narrative of Devnārāyaṇ, or more precisely, sections from the narrative are performed in religiously determined contexts. Most usually a performance is part of a *jāgraṇ* or 'night-wake'.[9] The purpose of a *jāgraṇ* is to evoke the presence (*prakāś*) of Devnārāyaṇ.[10] Performances are called *paḍ vācṇo* ('speaking/ reading the *paḍ*') implying the use of an elaborately structured 8.5 × 1.5 mt painted scroll on which characters and scenes of the narrative are depicted. Performances of this kind take place in three distinct places: (a) the home of a devotee, (b) in front of a Devnārāyaṇ or Savāī Bhoj temple, (c) in front of the community

→ of analytical abstraction, and takes the form of a document, the Tamil Text is organic in nature, a process of synthetic absorption, living a reality of performance. The application of both differs as well: while the document adds to a database that eventually will produce the ultimate interpretation as truth, the performance offers a becoming, an embodiment of life, here and now. These extremes are substantiated in their material representations.'

9. Thiel-Horstmann (1985) provides a complete documentation of the *jāgraṇa* in the context of worship conducted by the north Indian *bhakti* sect, the Dādūpanth. In the preface she notes that the *jāgraṇa* is temporally speaking, the most extended form of worship that occurs in front of the community. During the course of a *jāgraṇa* a number of texts are either sung or declaimed. The purpose of these texts is to 'awaken' the devotee, and to motivate him or her to be free of *saṁsāra*. She also notes that the documentation in published form denies the reader many other components of the night-wake such as '. . . . die musikalisch-ästhetischen Freuden der Veranstaltung, ihre zeitliche Geschlossenheit, das Milieu des *satsaṅga* und den verdienstlosen Triumph einer doch glücklich überstandenen Nachtwache. . . .' (*ibid*., p. 10). Again the implication here is that the texts are embedded in a larger aesthetic, 'performative' situation, in which their meaning unfolds, thereby motivating singers and listeners.

10. Since my intention here is to provide an understanding of the 'concept' of performance, I do not describe the performance itself in great detail. The main features are summarised below. A complete documentation of a single night's performance would, as Theil-Horstmann's study mentioned above shows, entail a monograph in itself. For details on the performance situation of Devnārāyaṇ, see further Miller (1980 and 1994).

meeting place (*hathāi*). Performances can take place any time of the year except for the period called *caumāsā* or the rainy season. During the time Devnārāyaṇ (and other Hindu deities) are supposed to be asleep. Performances begin on the 11th day of the bright half of the month of *Kārttik* which falls in October-November. During the *caumāsā* period the painted scroll called *paḍ* which is a central element in perfomances, is never unrolled. Narratives and songs may be sung, but in the so-called seated posture (*baiṭho gāṇo*) without the use of the *paḍ* and other dance techniques operative during 'regular' performances. Thus as Śrī Hukmārām Bhopā pointed out:

> The fact of the matter is this — now either the temple of Bhagavān — some people recite praises of him in front of the temple. And, some [people] who worship and honour Bhagavān, what does Bhagavān do for them? He is beneficial to them. So such a [person] is understood to be a *bhagat* of Dev. In his home, *jātī*s — pure *jātī*s would receive water from his hand. So, in some of their homes it is recited. At our village, it is recited in the [homes] of Jāṭs; And even [in the homes] of Rājpūts it is recited — even now. There is the Khātī community — it is recited [in their homes]. So, Brāhmaṇs, Paṇḍits, they too have it recited even today. And, whoever honours Bhagavān is his favourite. And, in his home Bhagavān's story is recited. There's nothing wrong with that. But, in lanes and alleys in such places it is not recited. When the full-moon night of Kārttik arrives — when Dev awakes on the 11th — from that time on, in the evening of the 11th, [the recitation] begins. During [the month of] Āṣāḍh, Dev sleeps. For four months all the *devatā*s go to the place of Rājā Baḷ. In earlier times there was this powerful king, who would give the gods strength. They go there to work. We say the gods have gone to sleep. But what should gods sleep for? They don't sleep! They go abroad to Rājā Baḷ's place to do 'duty' for four months. Thus the work of Chatrīs and gods is stopped. It is wrong to open Bhagavān's door for four months. If the door is not opened, and only *jāgraṇ* is done just sitting, then it is possible to tell the story. The *paḍ* can't be opened. Then after that on the 11th day of the bright half of Kārttik open it and start [recitations] — there's no harm or hindrance in that.

The space marked by the scroll when it is unfolded and stood up is 'sacred'. The scroll itself is considered to be a 'portable' temple in the centre of which there is the life-size figure of Devnārāyaṇ seated together with his four brothers in his royal court (*darbār*). A makeshift altar is set-up in front of his image. Here incense sticks are burnt, and offerings of grain and money are made. Each time an offering from a member of the audience is made the Bhopā or his co-singer blows a conch (*śaṅkh*) and proclaims the devotee's name and the quantity and item offered by him. The performance is interrupted here. Besides such interruptions there are other pauseds during which the singers are offered tea or tobacco and are asked to be seated. Such pauses can be relatively frequent so that from a total time of about nine hours, six are spent in narrating and performing the story. The singers wear a particular costume (*bāgā*) and use a stringed instrument called *bīṇ* or *jantar*. This double gourd instrument is worn by the main singer who plays on it while singing the narrative and pointing to corresponding sections of the scroll. His partner carries an oil lamp which illuminates the scroll during the performance that involves a series of movements back and forth along the length of the scroll and between the two singers. The main singer may also undertake a series of pirouette-like steps at specific moments during the recitation. There is a considerable amount of interaction between singers and the audience. The audience members often comment on the episode concerned or the singers' performance itself. The singers are also apt to comment on the audience's degree of attentiveness and wakefulness. Audience members may also claim to know more than the singer who must claim and reclaim his authority as a 'specialist' by successfully answering 'critical' questions. At times, during pauses, members of the audience may also entertain the audience by performing a few lines themselves.

The first term that provides us with a correspondence to 'performance' is *paḍ vā̃cṇo*. Thus, the external description of song, narrative, dance, pointing to the *paḍ*, audience participation, etc., is — for Bhopās and devotees *bhakta*s alike — simply called 'speaking/reading the *paḍ*'. Thus the performance is not — as one might expect from a textual perspective — described as 'narrating or telling Devnārāyaṇ's story'. The focus here is not on the 'text' as such, but on the scroll, which is an icon of the deity, and of the text. However, the scroll is not self-explanatory: it needs to be 'spoken' or 'read', i.e., it needs to be 'decoded' and rendered meaningful by specialist, namely the singer. Each performance thus involves a deconstruction of the entirety of images on the *paḍ*, and a simultaneous reconstruction of its meaning. The meaning of the images becomes distinct or rather emerges through the juxtaposition of spoken and sung narrative together with visual images located on the *paḍ*. The *paḍ*, therefore, is not spoken or read like a picture-book, it is read, on the contrary, through a narrative which manifests on account of its own recitation. The Bhopā does not decode the images on the *paḍ* according to his own interpretation like an art historian may do, he is bound by the interpretation of the images encoded in the narrative. The *paḍ*, according to the definition provided by the term *paḍ vā̃cṇo*, is not, therefore, simply an illustration of verbal, narrative content. It is, in fact, that which gets revealed through the interpretative framework provided by the narration. It would appear then that the imagery and iconicity of the *paḍ* is much more central to a performance than is the narration itself. This iconic emphasis can also be traced in sentences such as *paḍā̃ kā lekh*, meaning 'writing of the *paḍ*', that the singer Śrī Hukmārām Bhopā used to prove the existence and authenticity of specific passages and episodes from the narrative. Thus the *paḍ* was 'proof' of the oral text, and not vice versa. Visual imagery and iconicity are thus considered primary to verbal expression. But without verbal expression, the meaning(s) of the images do not reveal themselves.[11]

---

11. Similarly Smith (1991: 17) writing on the related 'picture story-telling' tradition of Pābūjī points out that '. . . use of the phrase 'reading the *paḍ*' is a valuable indication of the way in which *bhopos* conceptualise their work. They do not speak of 'singing an epic'; they refer not to singing or narrative but to performance, and their term for performance invokes the cloth-painting. . . . We approach Pābūjī through his *paḍ*, and we approach the *paḍ* through the *bhopos* 'reading' of it.'

REMEMBRANCE

In this section I briefly examine the meaning of the act of *remembering* with which a recitation always begins. Rather than regard this preliminary segment of the narrative situation as a 'formulaic', and therefore insignificant, recurrent beginning, my intention is to relocate it as a primary source of knowledge. My contention is that this source, which is almost unintelligible or unimaginable to the rationalised users of the printed word, is of prime importance to a wide variety of expressive traditions in India, ranging from story-telling to dance, theatre, and music. Similarly, the efforts of scholars — who themselves no longer cognise through the oral and aural — to understand oral narratives in terms of 'mental texts', 'memorisation', 'formulaic language', etc., are drastic attempts at making orality intelligible. Nevertheless, by virtue of being cut off ourselves from the source of creative inspiration as it is perceived of in different expressive traditions, we tend to gloss over its validity and authencity.

Typically, the narration of Devnārāyaṇ begins with an invocation of different benevolent and auspicious deities that are also present on the *paḍ*. In the invocation, the deities are revered and remembered. The verb used here is *siṁvarṇo* which is cognate with Hindi *sumiraṇ* or *smaraṇ* and means 'remembering', 'recollecting', 'calling to mind', 'memory'.[12] The deities

12. This is very similar to the oral poetry of the Hāṭkar Dhangars of Maharashtra who begin compositions (*ovīs*) with *sumbārana māṇḍilā* or *sumbārana devācā* ('the rememberance is set', 'the rememberance of god') (Sontheimer 1989:9).

The oral narrative of Devnārāyaṇ involves memory in two senses. One sense, of course, is that in which the singer himself sings from 'memory' (although this is not what singers claim. More frequently a singer talks of being 'inspired' by Sarasvatī or Devnārāyaṇ). The other sense is that in which the singer is involved in recreating and re-expressing the past in the present. When concerned with the meaning of the narrative it is also imperative to look into his latter aspect of 'memory' and 'rememberance', although from the point of view of oral transmission the first sense of memory is equally important. Memory in the sense of the recreation of history brings us squarely onto one of the central concerns of the narrative, namely, a discourse on historicity.

invoked during the invocatory section are Devī Śāradā, Gaṇeśa, Devnārāyaṇ, Bhairūnāth, Sarasvatī, and one's *guru*. The deities are invoked in order to provide protection, learning, wisdom. Thus, for example, two lines tell us that without one's *guru* there is no 'knowledge', and without Mother Sarasvatī there is no song or voice. By remembering Śāradā (a name of Sarasvatī or Durgā), the singer begins by saying she will always reside in the heart. The goddess Sarasvatī also resides in the singer's voice (*kaṇṭh*; literally: 'throat'), inspiring him to sing. By remembering Gaṇpat or Bināyak one gains happiness and satisfaction. And, again, whoever reveres Devnārāyaṇ, the god worshipped in the form of bricks (*ĩṭh*),[13] will never have a scarcity of milk or cereals. The important point here is not only of course that the protective and inspirational qualities of different deities are being invoked, but also that they are being 'remembered'. There is an invitation to remember. In other words, the singer is 're-membering' or 're-attaching' himself to the source from which the recitation flows.

In fact the reference to remembrance at the beginning of the narrative marks out the very nature of the work of narrating which is an excercise in bringing forth from an epistemological domain presided over by the goddess of learning, creativity, and wisdom. It is not, from the point of view of the singer, an exercise in bringing forth from memory, in the sense of an internalised, 'mental' act of the retrieval of knowledge. The domain of knowledge and inspiration from which a singer draws out the song is in a sense *external* to him. It is an 'objectified', phenomenological sphere that grants him knowledge. This understanding of oral narration is, from an epistemological point of view, contrary to the understanding that oral narration is the result of complex process of learning and memorisation. Thus, for example, Finnegan (1992: 114-17) in her chapter on composition, transmission and memory, points out that in earlier models narratives were 'pictured as coming down automatically

13. The aniconic representation of Devnārāyaṇ is in the form of a row of large upright bricks.

irrespective of human agency', but that later critical studies move 'away from the idea of storing verbatim memories to one of the people reconstructing and organising on the basis of what they know and do, so that remembering means not drawing on rote memory but a *creative* and organisational activity by the user'. The emphasis in more recent work is, thus, in 'memory as a social process'. Some of the questions that are put in this context are:

> What kinds of processes and ideologies are recognised for the preservation of records and memories without writing, and how are they valued and sanctioned? Are there recognised ways in which people are explicitly or implicitly trained to remember or to forget? What kinds of mechanisms are involved, and memory of what? Are such devices — and the content of what is remembered — necessarily all verbal or are there other media, images, and/or active performances additionally or alternatively involved, and if so what is the interaction between these? (*ibid.*, p.116)

This set of questions in the context of Devnārāyaṇ relates to how Bhopās learn and transmit their knowledge, and how this knowledge is culturally sanctioned. To begin with, it is important to point out that the office of a Bhopā is not necessarily hereditary. An apprentice may or may not learn the trade from his father. Of fundamental importance is the 'call' (or attitude) that an individual feels towards Devnārāyaṇ and learning the narrative. Many individuals may, in fact, function as an assistant to a Bhopā, but not all finally become Bhopās. Those who do become Bhopās do not receive any formal training. On the contrary they 'pick up' their trade by listening to the Bhopā at performances, and by occasionally joining in the performance. The text is thus learnt in a process analogous to the learning of natural language. Besides 'picking up' the text itself through instructional prose narratives, the apprentice pays attention to other features of the performance such as *nāc* (dance), *vāṇo* (pointing out picturing), *gāv* (verse), *arthāv* (explanation), and *maskarī* (jokes). The performance itself, therefore, involves a wide range of 'transmission media': the *paḍ*, dance, narration, song, jokes, gestures, instrumental music, costumes, riddles, lighting, etc. Above all, of course, it should not be forgotten that the performance is a religiously determined event that serves in the worship of Devnārāyaṇ, the deity of the majority of audience members.[14]

But while the questions posed by Finnegan above are important from the researcher's perspective, they nevertheless tend to overlook the cultural categories used by singers and performers to describe their own activity. Thus

> . . . the Indian notions of *smara* (Sanskrit) and *marapu* (Tamil) combine love, memory, tradition and worship. They refer to reverential acts of ritual attendance, and also to the passionate longing of love. . . . *Smara*, 'memory', 'love', 'worship' constitute 'tradition' that which is handed down from one generation to the next (Skt. *parampara*). The heritage one receives from the elders is kept alive and fostered in love, for its beauty, value and concrete 'indexicality'.[15]

Moreover, the Sanskrit category of *smṛti* refers to the rememberance of revealed knowledge *śruti*. Mārwarī *siṁvarṇo*, Hindi *sumiraṇ*, and Sanskrit *smara* in the context of oral narratives and written texts, thus all refer to the *source* of religious literature. In the case of Devanārāyaṇ it is also this source that allows the oral narrative to manifest itself. The invocation of deities at the beginning of a recitation need not

14. The question that needs to be asked here is why a religious event requires such an elaborate 'performance' context. Supposing we were to take the notion of *prakāś* (presence, light, radiance) as the central feature about which all the other performative elements are oraganised? Since the purpose of a performance is, from the singers' and the audience's point of view, to bring forth, make possible the *prakāś* of Devnārāyaṇ we need to understand how and why the entire range of audio-visual and other sensory experience created by the 'transmission media' are geared toward bringing forth *prakāś*, and of expressing the audience's devotion towards Devnārāyaṇ. We would have to understand that the narrative performance, which is about Devnārāyaṇ, and his ancestors, is linked to different sensory elements and lives within framework of the deity's presence.

15. Kersenboom (1995: 19 and 94f).

therefore be reduced to a matter of 'formula' or ritual prescription of some kind. It is a matter becoming 're-connected' to a sphere of inspiration and knowledge.

Song and Declamatory Chant

Let us now turn to the formal structure of the narrative, while keeping in mind that the formal structure, by virtue of also being a reflection of what the singers do, provides us with an insight into the larger communicative framework of the narrative. As mentioned above, the Bhopā begins the narrative with an invocation (*rememberance*) of various deities, most notably Śāradā and Sarasvatī, the goddesses of learning, music, wisdom, speech and creative inspiration. Following this he begins with the narrative *per se*. The narrative itself is a weave of verse and prose on the one hand, and song and declaimed speech, on the other. In addition to the interaction between these textual forms and delivery modes, there is the interaction between the main singer and his partner. The dialogic form of the delivery is furthermore also to be found in the narrative itself, which proceeds through a series of dialogues between different characters or voices. Before turning to this central element of the narrative, let me first deal with the verse and prose sections.

GĀV AND ARTHĀV

The verse sections of the text, which incidentally are also called *gāv*,[16] on account of their being sung, consist of four lines and a refrain. In some cases the sung sections comprise more than four lines. These exceptions will be discussed below. The *gāv* is sung by both singers simultaneously. In many instances they begin with an extended vowel 'on-line': '*e*. . .'. The first line ends with ạn extended *auvū̃ rai* or simply *rai*. The last word in the second and the fourth lines invariably rhyme, but not the first and third lines. The refrain usually consists of (*bhalā̃ jī bhalā̃*) *dev bhalā̃* [Very good, sir. Very good, Dev]. When not referred to in terms of song (i.e., *gāv*), the verse sections are called *kaḍī*

16. From the verb *gāvṇo*: 'to sing'.

which literally means link in a chain, 'connection', or 'sequence'. Thus the verse sections are understood to be links in the narrative chain. And, in fact, the narrative moves from one set of *kaḍīs* to the next. Each set of *kaḍīs* contains a short, compressed monologue spoken by a particular character. In the prose section following a verse, this 'monologue' is almost repeated verbatim. The difference of course lies in the form of delivery which is now 'declamatory'. The prose sections which are declaimed are called *arthāv* literally meaning 'explanation' or 'meaning' (Hindi: *arth*). In contrast to the verse sections, here there is a definite spacing of the singer's voices. While the lead singer begins the sentences, his partner may rejoin in a number of alternative ways: (a) he may complete a sentence ended half way by the lead singer, (b) he may simply repeat the lead singer's text, (c) he may add a line of his own, and (d) he may simply acknowledge the lead singer's text with remarks such as *mhe* or *vāh vāh*.

After the lines of the verse section have been faithfully repeated in the declaimed prose section, the singer and his partner continue the narrative in the dialogic manner mentioned above, till it is time to sing another *kaḍī*. The declaimed section invariably ends with lines such as, *lets see what news x has to 'say/says'* and *by saying it, know it, lets see*. These lines denote (1) that a person is about to speak and (2) whatever is to be *known* is to be revealed by saying it or by speaking it. The word used for 'news' is *samcār*.[17] Thus *x* always begins his speech to *y* in the form of a first person sung 'news'. Logically then, that which is to be known through *x*'s speech, and by implication the continuation of the narrative, becomes apparent in telling it/ saying it/speaking it aloud. The emphasis on the connection between speaking and knowing is significant because it underlines the oral nature of the narrative. The singers do not say, for example, *know it, by reading it* or *know it by understanding what is written*. The reference throughout is to speaking and telling. This aspect importantly underscores the emergent nature of *knowledge* for this particular oral tradition. Since there is no

17. This term is discussed in more detail below.

knowing before someone speaks, we cannot take recourse to 'frozen' receptacles of knowledge such as scriptures, inscriptions, plam leaves, book, etc., preserve and reveal knowledge.

Conversational Discourse

The dialogic interaction between the lead singer and his partner is matched on an internal level by the dialogical structure of the narrative. By this I mean very specifically that the narrative is fundamentally nothing more than a series of conversations or dialogues between different voices.[18] There are hardly any extended third person descriptions of events or scenes offered by the singers themselves. Whatever happens in the narrative takes place through the voices of various characters. Thus, the narrative both in its internal structure as well as external expression comes closest to the speech genre of *conversation*. The analysis offered here and in the subsequent sections on repetition, dialogue, and reported speech, therefore, focuses primarily on the nature and occurrence of *utterances* as a fundamental unit of *speech*, rather than on linguistic features such as grammar, or even 'formulaic' language in order to understand the oral composition of the narrative.

While describing the features of conversational discourse in everyday situations,[19] Tannen (1994: 25f) points out that

> . . . conversational discourse frequently represents what others have said ('reported speech') as dialogue ('direct speech' or 'direct quotation') rather than third-person report ('indirect speech'), and that 'direct speech' is more vivid, more effective. But why is dialogue more vivid? I believe it is because the creation of voices occasions the imagination of a scene in which characters speak in those voices, and that these scenes occasion the imagination of alternative, distant, or familiar worlds, much as does artistic creation. Finally, the casting of ideas as the

18. These may involve humans, gods, demons, animals, and even trees.
19. On discourse and conversational analysis, see also Goodwin (1981), Gumperz (1982), Wardhaugh (1985).

speech of others is an important source of emotion in discourse.[20]

Whereas the conversations in the narrative are situated in the present, giving us a scene of a current event, the commentary offered by the singers is situated in the past. For example, such a commentary may be inserted between dialogues to spell out time and place:

> The time they reached Sindhbaḍā (mhe), both Bhairavnāths took hold of the trunk. They shook the trunk./ The Jogiṇīs were sitting on the leaves./ One by one they all tumbled and fell down. (sir said.)/ By Darbār's command, there was a well nearby. (mhe) They all went and fell into the well./Bhairavnāth said 'Śrī Mahārāj'.

Verbs involves saying or telling are most frequently used. These are almost always in the present tense, facilitating the usage of direct speech. One example has already been given above in the case of the line preceding a verse section (*let's see what news x has to say / says*). Other examples are to be found in sentences preceding actual 'direct speech'. Thus 'Bhairavnāth said', 'Dev Mahārāj said', 'He or she said'. Sometimes simply 'said' is used. In such cases the speaker can be determined by the foregoing sentences. In addition to these usages of the verb 'said' at the beginning of a spoken sentence, the second singer makes use of 'said' to end his lines: *came and fell down, sir said*. Thus while the lead singer introduces a character's speech by saying '*x* said', the second singer ends his version of the text also by saying 'he or she said'. The second singer's usage of 'he or she said' in fact facilitates the repetitive nature of his delivery. Not only is the content thus repeated but also the fact of the direct speech being spoken by *x* is re-emphasised and repeated. Repetition and dialogicity thus together form a fundamental aspect of both narrative delivery and narrative style.

---

20. In the following sections, under the headings of repetition, dialogue, and reported speech, I examine the 'conversational' nature of the narrative both from the point of view of its internal structure, and the exchange between the two singers.

Repetition

Finnegan (1977: 90) states that 'the most marked feature of poetry is surely repetition'.[21] Furthermore, she observes that:

> . . . repetition in some form is a characteristic of oral poetic style: repetition of phrases, lines or verses; the use of parallelisms; recurrent formulae. Oral poetry is necessarily ephemeral. Repetition has a real point in such circumstances. It makes it easier for the audience to grasp what has been said and gives the speaker/singer confidence that it has understood the message he is trying to communicate. In antiphonal forms, refrains, choruses or the direct repetition of a leader's lines, repetition offers an opportunity for an audience to take part with ease in the act of performance, to a degree not possible without some measure of repetition. (*ibid.*, p. 129[22])

The oral style of Devnārāyaṇ's narrative is repetitive on many levels. One obvious form of repetition is the verbatim declamation of sung sections. Then there is the refrain at the end of each verse section, and the use of certain stock descriptions to mark 'battle scenes'. In addition there is repetition in the case of certain passages where a specific action is repeated by different people. Thus, for example in the search for Bhūṇā, each family member, in consecutive sung sections entrust Chochū Bhāṭ with a letter of Bhūṇā. Here we find a degree of repetition in the phrases used, which describe, as mentioned, the same act carried out by different persons. The use of repetition here adds to the emotional and poetic quality of the moment which in terms of the narrative bears the promise of a reunion with a family member. Whereas these examples relate to the poetic structure of the narrative, the kind of repetition mentioned above involving the singers, can be said to relate to the style of delivery. In this case it is not that lines from the sung sections are repeated in the declaimed section, but that lines in declaimed sections are repeated by the

21. Cited in Tannen (1994: 20).

22. Notwithstanding the common occurrence of repetition in oral forms of poetry, Finnegan concludes, however, that 'the exact significance of repetition in oral poetry is not, therefore, clear.' (*ibid.*, p. 132).

lead singer's partner. 'Internal' repetition is thus paralleled by 'external' repetition. And, the 'internal' dialogue of the narrative as a series of spoken encounters between different characters is paralleled by the 'external' dialogue of the singers.

But repetition even in this case is quite varied and may involve a wide range of possibilities. However, given the nature of repetition itself as something that is not necessarily produced but 'reproduced', this would mean that even though there may be many options available to the singer, the ultimate choice of utterance is determined by the first singer's speech. Creativity on the part of the second singer then lies in choosing from a range of given responsive modes. But the second singer's response is not limited to repetition. He also may bring in his own text, which is either a commentary on the foregoing line or an addition that propels the narrative forward.

EXAMPLES OF REPETITION

In the context of conversational discourse Tannen (1994: 54) distinguishes between different forms of repetition:

> First, one may distinguish self-repetition and allo-repetition (repetition of others). Second, instances of repetition may be placed along a scale of fixity in form, ranging from exact repetition (the same words uttered in the same rhythmic pattern) to paraphrase (similar ideas in different words). Midway on the scale . . . is repetition with variation, such as questions transformed into statements, statements changed into questions, repetition with a single word or phrase changed, and repetition with change of person or tense . . . patterned rhythm, in which completely different words are uttered in the same syntactic and rhythmic paradigm as a preceding utterance.

Before turning to the function of repetition in the narrative I would like to first present some examples of different forms of repetition as a sub-category of rejoinders offered by the second singer. In discussing the repetition involved in the second singer's utterances, I am primarily focusing on what Tannen calls 'allo-repetition' or the repetition of others (in this case of the first singer).

Example 1: Exact Repetition

In the cases of exact repetition, most frequently only a part of the phrase is repeated verbatim by the second singer.[23] It is apparent that the second singer uses verbatim repetition almost always to emphasise the last one, two, or even three words spoken by the lead singer. Rarely is a whole line repeated unless this itself is fairly short. Once the words are repeated by the second singer, he may extend the phrase on his own, thereby either adding new information, or again, re-emphasising the foregoing line through a re-formulation.

Kīyo: Hā̃ śrī mahārāj ***mharai kannai hī hai***
(*hā̃* ***'mharai kannai haī'*** *hai*)

Aurū̃ māvo ***baṭhai hi karā̃***
(*hā̃* ***'baṭhai hī karā̃'*** *cālo sāge hī cālū̃*)

syāl tū̃ hviyo
(***'syāl tū̃ hai'*** *kīyo*)

paḍihār ko nā̃v liyo jarā̃ bhāṭ ke eḍī kī cāṭī jaḷ ***lāgī*** *jī jāḷā*
(*hā̃* ***'lāgi'*** *kīyo*)

ābā dey bhai dev kā ghar kī bajarśilā māthā par ***āḍi hai***
(***'āḍi hai'*** *kīyo*)

jiyān jūjaḷo nai marai jatī ṭaim hi koni lagāvai ***hāthi nai mārtā̃***
(***'i hāthi nai mārtā̃'*** *kīyo*)

tanai ***cir āvai kā̃i***
(*hā̃* ***'cir āvai'*** *kīyo 'o bābā bhāṭ'*)

ā̃panai darbār ke mā̃yanai ek ***sūṇi rahavai***
(*hā̃* ***'sūṇī rahavai'*** *kīyo*)

---

23. These sections have been emphasised in the following examples for the lead and the second singer's phrases. The second singer's lines are given in parenthesis.

Example 2

In the following examples there is a transposition of words while the meaning of the phrase is retained. In some cases words have been replaced by their synonyms producing a different phrase with the same semantic content. In this case, where the second singer does not just identically repeat the lead singer's lines, the phrases are longer, spanning more than only a few words as in the examples provided above. Apparently the freedom the second singer has in reproducing the lines in 'his own words' also facilitates the production of more text than does a faithful reproduction.

> *Darbār kā hukamū̃ Bagaḍāvatā̃ ko bhāṭ* ***manavār ko hi liyoḍo kadai koni ho***
> (*hā̃* ***'manavār ko kadai hi liyo koni ho'***)
>
> ***Kanai*** *to pisiyo lagābā* ***nai eka hi***
> (***'i mhārai kanai hai koni'***)
>
> *darbār kā hukamū̃ lāl mẽ to nīmā* ***thārai jaṇā āyo bhai***
> (*hā̃* ***'i vāstai āyoḍa hū̃'***)
>
> *jaṇā* ***kā̃ dorā hai bhai***
> (*hā̃* ***'ki dorā koni bā mẽ to'***)
>
> *kiyo dhūliyo ekānai hojā bhai kā̃var* ***khāṇḍerāv kī asavāri ab kī āri hai***
> (hā̃ ***'kā̃var khāṇḍerāvjī padhār riyā hai'*** *kīyo*)
>
> *bhūṇojī o kīyo bhāṭ man mẽ dekhiyo thārā dhaṇī nai* ***surgyāṇī suṇayo***
> ('*paṇ* ***surgyāṇi jarūr hi hai***' *kīyo*)
>
> *Mhānā bāp dādā ko nā̃v* ***jāṇai koni***
> (*hā̃* '*tū̃* ***jaṇai koy nī kā̃i' kīyo***)
>
> *man mē dekhiyo kā̃i bāt hui* ***māthā nai kāmaṇāvū̃ bā̃dh lyo***
> (*hā̃* ***'māthā nai*** *kāṭ* ***bā̃dh liyo' kiyo 'jādūvū̃'***)
>
> ***tanai ṭhā hviyo koni hviyo***
> (*hā̃* ***'tanai ṭhā paḍiyo koni paḍiyo'***)

MONOSYLLABIC REJOINDERS

In addition to the two recurrent kinds of repetition mentioned above, there is the repetition of particular monosyllabic words or interjections which the second singer uses as a response. These words are repeated extensively during a recitation at those intervals where the second singer does not repeat, reformulate or add phrases or words to the first singer's lines. In a sense they amount to an almost formless or meaningless kind of response. Śrī Moṭārām, the second singer, uses *vāh vāh* and *mhe* as a 'formless' response. It is difficult to determine a structure in the instrumentation of this kind of response. *Mhe* which is much shorter than *vāh vāh* is used at times like an exclamation mark or interjection or even for the kind of spacing provided by the use of a comma. Thus for example:

Nīmde kīyo 're Mū̃gtā' (*mhe*)
'Jagīśayā' (*mhe*)

kīyo 'Dhūliyā' (*mhe*)
darbār kā hukamū̃ kīyo 'Bhāṭ' (*mhe*)
nīgevān siradārā̃ kīyo 'Śrī Mahārāj' (*mhe*)

kīyo 'Nimā' (*mhe*)
kīyo 'Bhairavanāth' (*mhe*)
kanāt ke mā̃yanai baḍ siradār kīyo 'Śrī Mahārāj' (*mhe*)

muṇḍ agalā sirdār kīyo 're bhāī Dhūliyā' (*mhe*)
'are Jagīśayā' (*mhe*)
'are Siradārā̃' (*mhe*)

In the above examples we can see that *mhe* appears regularly after a person's name has been spoken out at the beginning of direct speech. It functions as a form of punctuation used after one person has been addressed by another. But this is not the only placement of *mhe*. The other placements are varied, and a pattern is difficult to discern. Some examples are given below to illustrate its varying usages:

'are amaldār ādamī hū̃' (*mhe*)
'ke koy jamānā mē̃ Bagaḍāvat hviyā' (*mhe*)

to bhaṭ man mẽ dekhiyo 'ke moharā̃ to ladhī' (*mhe*)

dev ko nā̃v ley (*mhe*)
dev ko nā̃v lay ar dhūl mẽ bhar ḍhāl nai (*mhe*)
kīyo 'bhāī ghaṇā din hviyā suṇiya ī nai' (*mhe*)

In the above examples we see that *mhe* is used interchangeably at the end of a section of direct speech or even at the end of a section which does not involve direct speech.

Let us now examine some extended examples of the narrative to determine where *mhe* and *vāh vāh* are used:

are amaldār ādamī hū̃ (*mhe*)/ *mẽ suṇayoḍi bāt hai bhāī Nimā re* (*hā̃ 'dekhyoḍī konī' kīyo*)/ *ke koy jamānā mẽ Bagaḍāvat hviyā* (*mhe*)/ *pāñcatolī moharā̃ kācā tārā̃ mẽ poy poy* (*ar*) *aṭīkar ghoṛā ke galai* (*'mẽ rāḷ rāḷ dapaṭāyā batāve hai' kīyo*)/ *kah batāvai bai moharā̃ bhāī re ṭūṭ ṭūṭ ar* (*hā̃ 'paḍī bajār mẽ'*)/ *mẽ dekhū̃* (*mhe*)/ *ek hi mhanāī mohar* (*'āj lādh jāve'*)/ *āj āj ko amal pāṇī* (*'mhāre ho jāve' kīyo*)/ *mẽ dekhū̃ bhagavān kharco de mhanai* (*vāh vāh*)/*Nimade kīyo 're Mū̃gtā* (*mhe*)/ *kuṇa deś ko hāī bol'* (*'kuṇso deś ko ayo tū̃ kīyo*)/ *kīyo 'sāt samandrā pār ko hū̃* (*hā̃ 'sāt samandrā pār kā hū̃'*)/ *'kuṇ log hai'* (*'jaki batā'*)/ *kīyo 'rājāvō̃ ko baī ko bhāṭ hū̃'* (*vāh vāh*)/ *'Nā̃v' 'sẽsārī duniyā jagīśyo kah ar batalāvai'* (*hā̃ 'jagīśyo kah ar batalāyā karai' kīyo*)/

The passages cites above involves a conversation between Chochū Bhāṭ and Rājā Nīmade, the Rāṇā's younger brother. Chochū Bhāṭ begins the dialogue with *are amaldār ādamī hū̃*. This is followed by *mhe* which is followed by a further remark spoken by Chochū Bhāṭ. Chochū Bhāṭ's speech continues till *mẽ dekhū̃ bhagavān kharco de mhanai*. The end of his speech is marked by *vāh vāh*. With the exception of one instance where *mhe* is used [*mẽ dekhū̃* (*mhe*)], Chochū Bhāṭ's speech is not punctuated by Śrī Moṭārām. On the contrary the lines spoken by Śrī Hukmārām are supplemented and extended by Śrī Moṭārām in his response. After the first occurrence of *vāh vāh* Nīmde begins his section of the dialogue. Here again *mhe* is used as a punctuation mark after Nīmde addresses Chochū Bhāṭ: *re mū̃gtā* (*mhe*). *vāh vāh* is inserted after Chochū Bhāṭ has ended his speech *rajāvō̃ ko baī ki bhāṭ hū̃* (*vāh vāh*)/.

In the passage quoted above we find that *mhe* is used us a form of punctuation within a single character's speech. *vāh vāh* on the other hand is used to mark the end of one character's speech, and the beginning of another character's speech. *mhe* and *vāh vāh* in these examples thus mark off elements of speech belonging to one character and the speech of different characters. However, while this description may give the impression of a patterned usage, there are also examples in which *vāh vāh* is used internally within a series of spoken lines belonging to one character in the same way as *mhe* is. In such examples we find that *vāh vāh* is placed as a punctuation within a particular character's speech. Conversely *mhe* is placed at the end of a character's speech. On the whole, however, there is a greater frequency with which *mhe* is used within speech and *vāh vāh* to mark its end. In addition *vāh vāh* is used regularly at the end of the sentence introducing the person who speaks a *gāv* section. Thus for example:

> *darbār kā hukumū̃ bhūṇojī bole (vāh vāh)/kā̃ī samcār kahavai dekhā̃ . . .*
>
> *to bhāṭ bole (vāh vāh)/kā̃ī ghoḍīmātā nai samcār kahavai dekhā̃ . . .*
>
> *mīr bole (vāh vāh)/kā̃ī samcār kā̃ī bhāṭ nai kahavai dekhā̃ . . .*
>
> *kalāḷī bole (vāh vāh)/kā̃ī samcār kahavai dekhā̃ . . .*

Here it is apparent that *vāh vāh* is not being used to induce a pause in speech, but as an interjection involving the original sense of the word *vāh* which may be translated as 'great', 'wonderful', or 'splendid'.

SAMCĀR

The above lines also make it clear that the *gāv* passages always consist of 'packets' of direct speech spoken by a particular character usually in response to another character's speech. These 'packets' of direct speech are referred to as *samcār*, a word translatable as 'news, message, report, or information'. It can also have the sense of 'dialogue' (*saṁvād*). In the context of the narrative tradition of Devnārāyaṇ, *samcār* has an almost 'technical' status as a dialogue marker within the narrative. Thus singers or listeners may inquire of a given passage 'whose *samcār* is it?' or simply 'which *samcār* is it?' in order to determine up to which point the narrative has progressed or from which point it should be taken up. Sometimes the singer may also ask 'who said this *samcār*?' immediately after he has sung the *samcār*. This sort of question (and its answer) reinforces the *samcār* speaker's identity in the singer's and audience's mind. Thus, the narrative progresses not only through interchanges between song (*gāv*) and declamatory prose (*arthāv*) but also through a series of 'messages', 'reports', 'newses' or 'dialogues' which constitute the content of the sung passages. The meaning of the term *samcār* as a concept used to describe fundamental units of the narrative, once again highlights the 'dialogic' conception of the narrative. Not only is the narrative in its declaimed sections built up of dialogues between characters, the sung sections too are understood as being units of direct speech that constitute a 'reply' within the parameters of a foregoing dialogue.

In addition to the concept of *samcār* which is most frequently used before beginning the four-lined verse section of the *gāv*, the singer Śrī Hukmārām also variously uses the term *vārtā* which means 'story', 'conversation', 'occurrence/truth/reality/fact', 'speech', 'talk', 'short tale', 'narration' or 'report'. The pre-verse line in this case is usually *kāī vārtā ban jāvai dekhā̃*. This does not, as in the case of *samcār* imply that someone is speaking, rather that an event or a scene is about to be described in the following song sections. The song sections that fall under the category of *vārtā* are considerably longer than the sections described as *samcār*. Thus, a *vārtā* may contain nine lines (of which the last words of the second and third lines rhyme). Each line itself also contains more syllables than the line belonging to the *samcār* sections. Besides the nine line *vārtā*s there are also long sung sections describing a preparation for battle or a clash between two parties. These descriptions are fairly standarised and contain ten or eighteen sung lines. Here too each individual line contains more syllables than the verse sections characterised as *samcār*.

THE FUNCTION OF REPETITION

Tannen (1994: 47f) while analysing repetition in conversation asks the following fundamental question:

> Why is there repetition in conversation? Why do we waste our breath saying the same thing over and over? The various purposes simultaneously served by repetition can be subsumed under the categories of production, comprehension, connection, and interaction. The congruence of these functions of discourse provides a fourth and overarching function in the establishment of coherence and interpersonal involvement.

In the case of production, she points out that

> repetition enables a speaker to produce language in a more efficient, less energy-draining way. It facilitates more language, more fluently. (*ibid*., p. 48)

Comprehension is facilitated by repetition

> by providing semantically less dense discourse. If some of the words are repetitions, comparatively less new information is communicated than if all words uttered carried new information. (*ibid*., p. 49)

Connection is established through repetition because

> it serves a referential and tying function. Repetition of sentences, phrases and words show how new utterances are linked to earlier discourse, and how ideas presented in the discourse are related to each other. (*ibid*., p. 50)

Tannen continues to point out that the function of repetition in relation to production, comprehension, and connection

> refer(s) to the creation of meaning in conversation. But repetition also functions on the interactional level of talk: accomplishing social goals, or simply managing the business of conversation. (*ibid*., p. 51)

Having so far discussed the various possibilities of repetition within the narrative, let us now turn to the function and role of repetition under the four headings stated above. The first category is that of 'production'. Repetition in this case facilitates 'more language, more fluently'. Certainly this feature is apparent in the *arthāv* sections where the second singer repeats parts of the first singer's lines. Undoubtedly 'more language' is created here by using more of the same words while providing information. As a whole the narrative is enlarged and extended through repetition, and, the production of 'more language' does actually also contribute to its lengthy 'epic' dimension. However, the production of more language here, is closely linked to the second category, namely comprehension. Thus the repetition of the *gāv* passages in the *arthāv* sections facilitates as better under standing of the sung verses. In fact, the term *arthāv* which means 'explanation', 'meaning', 'commentary', itself implies that the repetition of verse in declaimed prose is meant to provide a clearer comprehension of the former.

Here again we find that a term is used that suggests a conceptual, metalevel perception of the narrative and its narration from within the tradition. Thus, the passages following the *gāv* sections are not called 'prose' as against 'song', but significantly 'meaning' or 'explanation'. This distinction enables us to again visualise how the narrative is conceptualised. According to the terms used, the narrative of Devnārāyaṇ in this case consists of sung sections, which are then laid out and 'explained'.[24] Of course this form of 'explanation' does not involve answers to 'how and why' questions. It does not 'explain' the sung sections in different words. Rather it explains by repeating the same words in a different mode of delivery. It is repetition itself, as Tannen observes, that lays bare the meaning of the

24. This system of terse, compact verse followed by a commentary reminds one of Indian philosophical and literary schools which reproduce texts verse by verse each of which are followed by a longer, detailed commentary. The distinction between such philosophical and literary commentaries and the oral narrative of Devnārāyaṇ, lies of course in the fact that in the latter case the narrative (also) progresses in the *arthāv* sections which themselves anticipate the next *gāv* and so on.

words and sentences, since in the initial lines of the *arthāv* practically no new information is supplied. New information is supplied in subsequent lines. But here too there is repetition, as a consequence of which it is easier to comprehend the import of the first singer's utterance. But more than facilitate simple semantic comprehension, repetition within the *arthāv* — which often involves only some, select words — functions as an instrument of emphasis. Thus the few words that are repeated (sometimes the whole line in transposed form) carry within them the core of what the first singer intended to mean in his speech. Thus, repetition involving the *arthāv* and sections within it, facilitate and serve not only comprehension, but also emphasis.[25]

Tannen's third category is 'connection':

> Repetition of sentences, phrases, and words show how new utterances are linked to earlier discourse, and how ideas presented in the discourse are related to each omther.
>
> (*ibid*., p. 50)

This category it would appear is more linked to everyday conversation than it is to the situation relating to the narration of Devnārāyaṇ, in which there is less of ideas and more of scenes and events that are presented and linked with one another. The linkage of scenes and events is, of course, partially created through repetition, but more so this is afforded by the structure of plots and subplots in the narrative.

As Tannen points out, these three functions ultimately relate

> . . . to the creation of meaning in conversation [and] accomplishing social goals, or simply managing the business of conversation. (*ibid*., p. 52)

It is quite evident that repetition in the special case of the narrative, also relates to the production of meaning. The creation of meaning is guided in this case not towards the singers themselves, but towards the audience which listens to the

25. This beccomes easier to comprehend when actually listening to the second singer's spoken style of repeating the first singer's lines.

performance of the narrative. However, meaning does not emerge only at a purely linguistic or semantic level. It emerges here also at an 'experimental' level through the 'bringing-forth' of the content of the narrative which revolves about the life and deeds of Devnārāyaṇ, and the devotees' participation in the evocation of his power. Thus, the various forms of repetition inherent to the narrative and its telling, are transformed from being literary features to partaking in the realm of *praxis*. Together with the various other aspects of the whole performance they too take on a causal character in the production of meaning as an interplay of semantic, sensory, cultural, and religious elements.

Dialogue

As pointed out above, the narrative is 'repetitive' on (at least) two levels: the level of form (verse and prose) and the level of the delivery (lead singer and the second singer). Furthermore, it became clear, that the narrative is also 'dialogic' in two senses: the sense in which the dialogue between characters occupies a central position as a narrative strategy and the sense in which the singers are engaged in a dialogue with one another (and of course also with the audience producing a third sense of dialogue). Thus, as indicated previously, a full understanding of the narrative as a communicative event would not only involve an understanding of its language, but also an understanding of the nature and relationship of *utterances* as a vehicle for constructing oral narrative structure,[26] and also for the dialogic structure of the *world* presented in the narrative.

Given the centrality of the fact that the narrative delivery of Devnārāyaṇ is essentially constituted by two voices who spin

26. The distinction between language and utterance is comparable to the distinction between *language* and *parole* made by Saussure. Thus '. . . the language, thought of an abstract pattern or scheme, and speech (to adopt the usual, somewhat unsatisfactory, translation of *parole*) or individual uses of language on particular occasions' (Turner, G.W. 1987: 14).

out the narrative content through an exchange of utterances, it is worthwile to examine the nature of this dialogue. As pointed out above, it is possible to locate this form of dialogue within the umbrella category of speech genres we call *conversation*. Naturally, the kind of conversational dialogue which occurs during a narration of Devnārāyaṇ is contextually distinct from the kind of conversational dialogue which may occur in 'everyday life'. Whereas conversations of everyday life are centered around a variety of subjects and may develop in a variety of forms, the conversation occurring during a narrative of Devnārāyaṇ is focused and determined by the content of the narrative. Also, the form of the conversation or exchange between the singers is quite regularised. It is to be limited to a set of options which have been discussed above.[27] Above all, however, the conversational nature of the exchange between the singers has a distinguishing feature that 'everyday' conversation (fortunately) does not possess. Whereas in everyday conversation there is always the possibility that the respondent will become speaker, and the speaker take the place of respondent, in the case of the narrative, the identity of the respondent is always fixed. The second singer is one who provides the rejoinder to the first singer's utterances and not vice versa. The role of listener and speaker is, therefore, predetermined by the narrative style. Although the dialogue between the singers thereby involves a certain level of inflexibility, it also provides a set of options in terms of which the second singer's rejoinder may be expressed.

At this point it should be noted that the narrative tradition of Devnārāyaṇ itself has a notion of 'rejoinder'. This is called *hũkāro* (*hũkāriyo* for the person) and means a verbal expression of assent or of comprehension and agreement, of urging the narrator to carry on speaking. Thus, there is a conceptual awareness here of the fact that a speaker always requires a listener. In other words human communication is considered to be essentially 'dialogic' rather than monologic. The speaker or singer cannot express himself in a vacuum. It is the active

27. See section on 'Repetition'.

comprehension of the listener expressed through the *hũkāro* that draws out the singer's lines and ultimately facilitates the progress of the narrative. This notion of the active listener or respondent come close to Bakhtin's understanding of speech communication:

> . . . when the listener perceives and understands the meaning (the language meaning) of speech, he simul-taneously takes an active, responsive attitude toward it. He either agrees or disagrees with it . . . , augments it, applies it, prepares it for execution, and so on. Any understanding of live speech, a live utterance, is inher-ently responsive, although the degree of this activity varies extremely. Thus all real and integral understanding is actively responsive, and constitutes nothing other than the initial preparatory stage of a response (in whatever form it may be actualised). (1986: 68-69)

Given the importance of a response for all 'live speech', it is not surprising that the narrative tradition of Devnārāyaṇ with its focus on orality should involve a lead singer and his respondent. It is remarkable that such a notion should in fact be formalised to such a degree.[28]

So far we have pointed out the role of the dialogue, and of speaker and respondent in relation to the actual narration of the narrative. But what implications, if any, does such a narrative form have on the structure of the text? How is a text constructed through a series of utterances (and not 'sentences')? What kind of text emerges in this way? Thus, given the spoken nature of the narration as a series of utterances, the text is composed of a body of sometimes complete and sometimes only partially complete sentences, (in the case of *arthāv*) of exclamations, of

28. This notions is also found in other narrative traditions of Rajasthan (Pābūjī, etc.). In fact, it would be worthwhile to examine the notion of speaker and respondent in other performative traditions relating not only to narratives but also to music and dance. A comparative study would perhaps reveal the centrality of 'dialogue' in Indian expressive traditions and the arts. It may also reveal something about the way in which 'reality' is constructed.

monosyllabic rejoinders, etc. The text as a whole is made up of grammatically fragmented linguistic units (such as the sentence). These broken units only make sense due to the fact that they are utterances in an oral narrative and not written sentences in prose. The oral nature of the narrative allows for the *incompleteness* of the grammatical structure of the text. And, as has been pointed out above, within the chain of 'incomplete' sentences there is a chain of grammatically incomplete repetitive utterances created through the second singer's response to the lead singer's words. Thus, the text contains within itself a repetition of itself. As a series of dialogic utterances, it responds to and imitates itself. Thus, the 'text' created by the second singer does not lay importance on being 'autonomous' or 'original'. It is caught up in a perfect 'intertextual' flow with the text of the first singer. In other words, it exists on the boundaries of the lead singer's text by referring to and in fact reproducing it.[29]

REPORTED SPEECH

It was mentioned above that the delivery of the narrative and the narrative itself are dialogic in two different senses. The first sense is in which the recitation proceeds on the basis of an interchange between the two singers. This interchange — a communicative event situated in a performance setting — is directed at setting up and establishing a corpus of meaning for the audience who listens (and also interacts) with the singers. The second sense of dialogue involves the construction of the narrative in terms of dialogues between characters of the story. Thus it was shown that the central sections of the story (*gāv*) are units of speech or conversation uttered by one character and directed towards another character. Given these two senses of dialogue one could state that the 'inner' dialogue of the narrative occurs within the 'outer' dialogue of the singers, which in fact provides the frame for the narration. But in what sense

29. This results in a kind of 'inner' intertextuality. There exists, therefore also at the level of text (*qua* the notion of an inter/intratext) a notion of dialogue — of telling and responding — that interrelates the first and second singer's texts with each other.

are we to understand the relationship between the 'outer' and 'inner' dialogues? How is the inner dialogue part of or built into the outer dialogue? Once again the line of inquiry I will take up here rests on the assumption that the recitation of the narrative is a particular speech genre that comes closest to that of 'everyday' conversation following an interchange between two speakers. But before proceeding with this inquiry, I shall refer to an understanding of what in lingustic terms can be called a dialogue. A dialogue, in the sense Bakhtin refers to, arises from the fact that all utterances are in fact *polyphonic* in nature:

> Utterances are not indifferent to one another, and are not self-sufficient; they are aware of and mutually reflect one another. . . . Each utterance is filled with echoes and reverberations of other utterances. (1986: 91)

A special form of dialogic utterance is an interchange which involves the reporting of another's speech. 'Reported speech' can have two forms.[30] One which involves a direct quotation such as 'He/she said:' 'I did that'. The other which involves an indirect quotation such as 'He/she said that he/she did that/ had done that'. The assumption behind reported speech as 'direct quotations' is that the utterance of one person can be faithfully repeated by someone else in a content other than the original one in which the utterance was spoken. Thus there is the belief that the utterance and its meaning content can remain untouched regardless of speaker and spoken content.

However, Tannen (1994: 133) points out:

> 'reported speech' is a misnomer, an abstraction with no basis in the reality of interaction. When speakers cast the words of others in dialogue, they are not reporting so much as constructing dialogue. . . . Dialogue is not a general report; it is particular, and the particular enables listeners (or readers) to create their understanding by drawing on their own history of associations. . . . The constructing of dialogue for framing as

30. On reported speech and code-switching see, for example, Gumperz (1982).

> reported speech reflects the dual nature of language, like all human behaviour, as repetitive and novel, fixed and free, transforming rather than transmitting what comes its way.

From the point of view of the narrative of Devnārāyaṇ, we find that what the singers are doing — at least on the surface — is to continuously 'report' what characters in the narrative said (to one another). By inserting the name of the person who speaks before each dialogue the singer identifies his/her voice. The singers do not, for example, personify characters to speak in the first person as characters might do in theatre. On the contrary they are involved in reporting to the audience or listeners what went on or what was spoken. In this sense it is the singer who claims access to the scenes and events of the narrative, just as a third person who witnesses a conversation between two people, and then reports the conversation to a fourth. However, as Tannen points out 'reported speech' is not just repetition but also construction. How does the singer's activity of reporting dialogue involve construction? If it does involve construction is this the same as saying that the singers 'improvise' while narrating? What consequences follow if we begin to view the 'constructed' nature of the narrative rather than its 'improvisational' nature? Supposing we were to perceive the singers' task not as 'recitation' but as 'reporting'? How would our understanding of the communicative event alter from this perspective? Would our search for fixity (formula, repetition) and free play ('creativity/ improvisation') be altered? Thus, for example, as Tannen argues

> . . . the construction of dialogue represents an active, creative, transforming move which expresses the relationship not between the quoted party and the topic of talk but rather the quoting party and the audience to which the quotation is delivered.

In other words it is the context in which the act of reporting is done that determines the sense which the 'quoted' speech is to take. If reported speech does involve the creative and transforming aspect Tannen refers to, then it would seem obvious that singers alter what they say according to who they perceive the audience to be, and the relationship they have to the audience. A simple example of this alteration or, in fact, choice in telling can be seen in terms of the episode a singer 'reports' to the audience. He does not always 'report' episodes of his own choice, but also those wished for by the audience. By placing the communicative act of singer and audience within the framework of 'reported speech' we can conceptualise the process of selectivity involved in a different way. Selectivity in reporting is not just a question of desires or wants, but also of being in rapport with the 'listening' of the audience, just as a speaker reports what he/she has heard selectively depending on the intention he/she has in 'reproducing' an utterance in a specific social or interpersonal context. But what exactly is meant by 'listening'? How is listening different from verbal response? Listening, we may state, is an internal state of the listener that provides the context for the speaker's utterance to unfold and make sense. Therefore, it is a non-verbal *activity* that engenders speech.[31] The activity of singing and speaking is not solely bound to the singers' agency, but to the audience's particular agency evoked through listening. Thus, depending on this inter-relationship between audience and singer, the singer would tend to 'report' the narrative in varying ways. This would explain why performances are never exactly the same. However, it would also shift the emphasis from 'improvisation', i.e., an explanation of variation in terms of a singer's individual capability, to 'construction', or the creative building up of narrated dialogue in a specifically interactive situation in which listening plays a vital role. In such a situation it would be natural that there is a movement between fixity, i.e., the use of 'formula' and 'free play' (or creativity?). Thus the problem of formulaic language and improvisation during a performance need not refer solely to the

---

31. Listening is in the sense distinguishable from Bakhtin's notion of dialogic response. Whereas listening is certainly a crucial element of all dialogue, it is not manifest in the form of a response. It is the *pretext*, so to speak, of speech; the attentive field within which all speech arises. On the idea and consequences of listening, see, Fuimara (1990) and S.C. Malik (1995).

phenomenon of 'memorisation', and 'improvisation', etc., but to the question of 'construction', and the 'interaction' based on listening.

By viewing a performance or recital of the narrative as an example of extended 'reported speech', we can also begin to appreciate the nature of the singer's work. The singer's work is thus not simply to sing, recite or perform the narrative, rather it is to mediate or report what happened and what was said to the audience. Thus implict in the singer's work is a knowledge of past events which are then passed on as in a specific content as dialogue in the present to the audience. It is the singer's privilege then to have 'overheard' or gained knowledge about Devnārāyaṇ that is then communicated to his devotees.

EXAMPLES OF REPORTED SPEECH

The phenomenon of reported speech is found in a number of other textual examples. Amongst written genres, the most common use of reported speech is in epics and Purāṇas. In many Purāṇas (and *māhātmya*s) it is the bard or *sūta* who reports what has happened to group of interested listeners (mostly *ṛṣis*). The bard's reporting of what has happened invariably follows questions that have been put to him from the 'audience'. Thus, in Purāṇic (and epic) texts, the bard is very explicitly asked to narrate or report on what he has seen or knows. In a sense by inserting the voice of the bard and the audience into the text, the text in fact describes both the 'performance' (narrational) situation and that which is narrated or reported. The text is thus a 'report' on both: the setting and that which is being reported. Both levels are in a sense inscribed into the written text. In the oral narrative situation of Devnārāyaṇ, the first level of 'reporting', i.e., about the setting itself non-existent. This is because the setting involves an event that occurs in the present. The reporting is, like in the case of Purāṇas and epics, of events or dialogues that have occurred in the past. However, there are other basic differences in the construction of dialogue between written texts and the narrative of Devnārāyaṇ. For example, the dialogues contained in Sanskrit epic and Purāṇic texts are frequently quite lengthy, bordering on monologues. Moreover, they are placed within the parameters of Sanskrit poetic conventions, appearing in verse form. The dialogues reported in the narrative of Devnārāyaṇ, are on the other hand, short. Excepting for the *gāv* sections, they are formulated in the language of everyday situations, lacking poetic or literary embellishments. Their shortness coupled with the frequency with which voices change give the overall impression of a dialogue as we may encounter it in everyday conversation. The simplicity of language and the rapidness of exchange all heightens the sense of an actual dialogue with its dramatic overtones:

> (The Bhāṭ said:) 'Hey, Śrī Mahārāj when did I ever quarrel?' (Yes, 'I'm frightened of frightening a lion,' [he] said)/ [Dev Mahārāj] said: 'Then come close Bhāṭ!' (vāh vāh)/ 'I'll protect you!' (vāh vāh)/ [The Bhāṭ said:] 'How are you going to do that, Śrī Mahārāj?' (Yes, 'tell me that!)/ [Dev Mahārāj said:] 'Bābā Bhāṭ, [I'll] tie you down on top this rock'. (Yes, 'keep sitting up there')/ [The Bhāṭ said:] 'Great, great, hey, my lord, you thought good!' (vāh vāh)/ [Dev Mahārāj] said: 'Pāliyā, (mhe)/protect the Bhāṭ up there!' [Yes, 'tie his arms firmly to the rock and come back!' [he] said.)/ 'By God's command, tie the Bhāṭ up on to the branch' (mhe)/ [He] took the sash, wrapped it around the branch (vāh vāh)/and knotted it./

In this short example there are two main voices: Chochū Bhāṭ and Devnārāyaṇ. The interchanges are rapid, one person's part not lasting more than a maximum of two sentences. Often the speaker's name is not even explicitly referred to. The speaker's identity is deduced from the context. Sometimes only 'said' is used to convey that one of the persons is about to speak. Otherwise one utterence follows the other without being interrupted by any markers from which to judge the speaker's identity. There is a vivid sense conveyed of the Bhāṭ's fear of the lion, and the irony and sceptical tone of his response to Devnārāyaṇ. The singer himself adds only a single line at the end of the passage, which steps out of the dialogic situation (by adding a descriptive sentence in his own voice). The dramatic character of the interchange in the oral delivery is, however, watered down, for example, in the printed version of the narrative. In one case of the printed text, the narrative begins to assume a form similar to a Purāṇic text. The major difference, is of course, that the dialogues are now composed of grammatically 'complete' sentences rather than simply utterances which may or may not entail complete sentences. The dialogues are lengtheir and have the form of spoken passages, rather than spoken lines. Besides this, the element of repetition, so crucial to the oral rendering, is virtually absent from the printed text:[32]

> Many eons went by. Because of their great *sat* Brahmā, Viṣṇu and Śiva's thrones began quivering. The three gods rode on their celestial chariots and arrived at Mount Meru. But even after the three gods arrived there, those two didn't come out of *samādhi*. The gods spoke to them. 'O Suvāī Manu, O Śatarūpā, you've done a great amount of flawless penance. Termites crawl all over you. Your blood and flesh have been eaten away. Only bones remain. And still you haven't stopped uttering Rām's name. We're extremely pleased with you. We want to grant you all your desires: a kingdom, unending wealth or even a place in Vaikuṇṭh.' Hearing this Suvāī Manu and Śatarūpā replied: 'Go home Brahmā, go home Viṣṇu, go home Śaṅkar! There's nothing we want of you!' Perplexed Śaṅkar asked: 'Whose name are you repeating anyway?' Suvāī Manu replied: 'We're repeating Rām's name'. Then Śaṅkar exclaimed: 'Well, who's this other Rām besides us? Isn't it good enough that the three gods have appeared in front of you?' 'Well, none of you are Rām,' they said, 'It's true that you're the three subs-tances contained in Rām (*satoguṇ*, *rajoguṇ* and *tamoguṇ*), but we're worshipping that Rām who gave birth to the three of you. Now that Rām is Pārbrahm Parameśvar!'

In the above passage there are a number of evident differences to the passage from the oral rendering. First, there are longer sections inserted in the narrator's voice which describe a situation leading up to the actual dialogue between characters. The dialogues themselves are on the whole relatively lengthy, giving

32. The printed text is entitled 'Bagaḍāvat Bhārat, Śrī Devnārāyaṇ Kī Kathā' (Arcanā Prakāśan, Ajmer).

one more of the sense of an idea being expressed in the form of a dialogue, rather than an exchange between two parties as in everyday life. Second, the speakers are introduced in a commented form. For example, 'Hearing this . . . replied' or 'Perplexed Śaṅkar said' or 'Then Śaṅkar exclaimed'. In the oral rendering we simply learn whose voice it is, without commenting on the inner state of the speaker. The inner state of the speaker is left wholly to the utterance he speaks and not to a comment on part of the singer. Later on in the written text we also encounter passages that have the character of prophecies.

> 'O Lord, O Rām! Tell us at least when you'll appear as an *avatār*? When will our desire be fulfilled?' 'Look, Suvāī Manu, there'll come a time when Rāvaṇ will appear. He'll be so mighty that Indra will fetch water for him, Baimātā will feed his horses, and Pavan will sweep the rubbish. Listen, Suvāī Manu, there'll be a town called Ayodhya on the banks of the Sarju River where a king named Raghu from the solar dynasty will rule. Suvāī Manu you'll be born in Raghu's clan. In that birth you'll have to split yourself into two bodies. Through one you'll become a king called Daśarath. Your wife Śatarūpā will be Kauśalyā. Listen, O Suvāī Manu it's then that I will manifest myself as your child'!

This form of a lengthy dialogue embodying a prophecy is virtually absent from the oral rendering. In fact, the idea of different time cycles coupled with the birth of mythic-religious figures like Rāmā and Rāvaṇa does not arise. The only exception is in the prose beginning of the narrative in which the circumstances of the rebirth of 24 sages in the form of the 24 Bagaḍāvats is described. Once again in the 'reported' speech of the written text, the dialogue tends to convey the sense of an idea being expressed, rather than a living conversational interchange. The reported speech of the oral rendering through its short, simple dialogues similar to those of everyday situations, heightens a sense of being present at the actual event for the audience. Whereas the singers might engage in presenting what they know or have 'overheard', the audience experience 'hearing' the event in the present.

Synopsis of the Narrative

The narrative is composed of two main parts. These are recognised by singers as being distinct halves, and are called *Bagaḍāvat* or *Bagaḍāvat Bhārat* and *Śrī Devnārāyaṇ Kathā*. The first half deals, as its title suggests, with the Bagaḍāvats or the Twenty-Four Brothers who are the ancestors of Devnārāyaṇ. The second half, as is also clear from its title, deals with Śrī Devnārāyaṇ. While both halves of the narrative extoll the heroic deeds of the Bagaḍāvats and Devnārāyaṇ, they also articulate different sets of values. Above all, this is apparent in the sources of sacred power that each give prominence to. In the first half, sacred power flows from the devotional, self-sacrificial deeds of the twenty-four brothers. In the second half, it issues directly from the divine acts of Devnārāyaṇ, an *avatār* of Bhagavān.

BAGAḌĀVAT BHĀRAT

The first half of the narrative called the Bagaḍāvat Bhārat, has a time-frame spanning two world-ages. The beginning of the narrative is situated in the *satya yuga* at a time when Brahmā is performing a Vedic sacrifice (Rājasthānī: *jug*) in Pushkar, the famous pilgrim town in Rajasthan.[33]

> Brahmā invites all the gods and *ṛṣis* to his sacrifice in Pushkar. Among them is a group of twenty-four *ṛṣis* living in the Nāg Pahāḍ (Serpent Mountain), a mountain chain running parallel to Pushkar. These *ṛṣis* are disciples of Śaṅkar. When Śaṅkar hears of the invitation, he forbids them from attending the sacrifice. But they insist on going because they have been called by Brahmā. All of a sudden Śaṅkar grows ravenously hungry. The *ṛṣis* suggest he eat the fruits growing in the forest in which they live. But Śaṅkar claims this will not satisfy his hunger. He requires more than plain fruit. But what else is available in the forest? There is no cereal or grain either. So what does Śaṅkar do? He turns to his disciples and demands they offer their bodies to him. He com-mences consuming them one after another.[34] After he has eaten them and satiated his

33. Brahmā's performance of a *yajña* also the central theme of the eulogistic work on the origins of the pilgrim town in Sanskrit called the *Puṣkara-Māhātmya*. See Malik (1993a).

34. On Śiva as an Aghorī in the Bagaḍāvat, see B. Singh (1993: 415).

> hunger, he then takes it upon himself to visit Brahmā's sacrifice. The sarifice comes to a halt because of the misdeed Śaṅkar has commited.[35] He asks Brahmā how he should atone for his misconduct. Brahmā lets him know that the only means would be to offer the *ṛṣis* his own body in a future existence, in which the *ṛṣis* are to be born as the 24 sons of a single father.

After this relatively brief spoken (not sung) prelude, the temporal frame of the narrative abruptly shifts to the *kali yuga*. The geographical location has not changed. It is the reign of the legendary medieval king, Rājā Bīsaldev of Ajmer.

> The populace in the kingdom of Rājā Bīsaldev is being terrorised by a lion. In order to curb rampant killings, the king orders that one person offer himself as food for the lion every night. On one particular night, a Rājpūt called Hari Rām,[36] who is travelling through the ill-fated kingdom, offers to take the place of a boy from the Kumhār community whose turn it is to be eaten by the lion. He tricks the lion by placing a figure made of dough at the place where it feeds. When the lion attacks the figure of dough, Hari Rām comes out of his hide-away and beheads it. Then in order to wash the blood off his sword, and to cleanse himself of the impurity of slaughter, he goes to the holy lake of Pushkar carrying the lion's head on his shoulder.[37] It is full moon night (*pūnam*). Exactly at the same time on the opposite bank a Brahman girl called Līlā Sevrī who has taken a vow never to look at a man is performing ablutions and bathing in the lake. While bathing, she sees the reflection of a man's body with the head of a lion on the surface of the lake. Not only is her vow broken, she also conceives upon seeing the image

35. A close parallel to this motif is also found in the *Puṣkara-Māhātmya* where Brahmā's ritual activity is disrupted by Śiva. Appearing in the form of a naked, skull-bearing ascetic, here he magically lets his impure 'begging-bowl' replicate itself to the extent that the entire sacrificial awning is inundated with polluting human skulls. See Malik (1993a: 69-74; 284-88). Śiva's interference with Brahmā's sacrifice, echoes the ancient myth of Śiva and Dakṣa's rivalry. In the myth, Śiva, after having been excluded from Dakṣa's sacrifice, proceeds to destroy it and to kill Dakṣa.
36. In one varient, Hari Rām is supposed to be a Gūjar who is later given the title of 'Siṁh' from King Bīsaldev because of his selfless act of slaying the man-eating lion. See also, Malik (1993b: 381ff.).
37. On the *paḍ* Hari Rām is shown carrying the lion's head facing the lake of Pushkar.

on the water surface. She insists that Hari Rām marry her now, but he vacillates saying that such a marriage is not possible because she is a Brahman and he a Kṣatriya. Finally, they receive permission from King Bīsaldev who wants to reward Hari Rām in any way that he wishes. After nine months a son is born to Hari Rām and Līlā Sevrī. He has the head of a lion and the body of a man, and is named Bāgh Siṁh or Bāgh Rāvat. Bāgh Siṁh is abandonded at birth. But the trees in the grove where he was been begin to turn green and blossom, signalling that he has a godly nature. The king adopts him. But because of his frightening appearance he is placed in a garden under the care of a Brahman teacher and cook. Later when he grows up, his unusual features once again stand in the way of his finding a bride. He continues to live his solitary existence in the garden attended by his Brahman cook. One day, on the festival of swings (*sāvan tīj*), a number of young girls of various castes come to the garden attracted by Bāgh Siṁh's silken swing. The Brahman allows them to use the swing on the condition that each of them circumambulate Bāgh Siṁh. While they are doing this, he performs the necessary engagement rites. Thus, unknowingly, they are all engaged to Bāgh Siṁh. Later Bāgh Siṁh marries twelve of them. Each of his wives gives birth to two sons who are collectively called the Bagaḍāvats.

The Bagaḍāvats, whose mothers belong to different castes, are all married to Gūjar women. Of the 24 Bagaḍāvats, Savāī Bhoj is the most well-known and courageous. Each day Savāī Bhoj takes the Bagaḍāvats' cattle herds to graze on the slopes of Nāg Pahāḍ. One of the cows regularly leaves the herd and returns on its own in the evening. One day Savāī Bhoj follows the cow and discovers that it is being milked by the ascetic Rūpnāth. As compensation for milking their cow, Rūpnāth gives Savāī Bhoj a sack full of grain. But the brothers have no use for the small quantity of grain, so they feed it to birds. The next morning, they discover that the few grains left sticking to the seam of the sack have turned into gems.[38] They realise their folly. Savāī Bhoj returns to the ascetic to become his disciple. One day Rūpnāth has Savāī Bhoj heat a cauldron of oil. When the oil is boiling he asks Savāī Bhoj to go around the cauldron, while he himself follows. While they are encircling the cauldron, the ascetic tries pushing Savāī Bhoj into the boiling oil, but Savāī Bhoj — who has been forewarned of Rūpnāth's intentions — leaps

38. This incident and the one following it in which Rūpnāth's body turns into gold, are typical of the large corpus of legends extolling Nāth Yogīs' miraculous powers. See Gold (1992).

over it with the help of his cowherd's staff.[39] In the next round, Savāī Bhoj follows the ascetic and pushes him into the cauldron. Not so agile, the ascetic falls into the boiling oil. Instantly his body turns into solid gold. While Savāī Bhoj stands there repenting his crime, the ascetic reappears in the hermitage as though nothing had taken place. He explains that the golden image is a gift that will grant the Bagaḍāvats unending wealth for a period of twelve years after which both wealth and life (*māyā-kāyā*) shall come to an end. He also gives Savāī Bhoj the gifts of a mare, a cow, and an elephant, all of which have special powers.[40] Savāī Bhoj returns to his home. The brothers ask Tejājī, the eldest among them, what they should do with their newly acquired wealth. Tejājī, whose mother is a Banyā, advises them to bury the money in the ground and hoard it.[41] Nevājī, one of the youngest brothers counters this idea by suggesting that they do good deeds with the money, i.e., build wells and temples, distribute the wealth, and make a name for themselves because both the wealth and their lives is to end after twelve years. The brothers choose the latter alternative, Soon their fame spreads far and wide. In due course, they meet their future enemy, the Rājpūt chieftain of Rāṇ City whose name is Rāṇā (or Rāvjī). The Rāṇā and the Bagaḍāvats become *dharam*-brothers. In one extended drinking session, they overturn jars laden with alcohol onto a hillside flooding the earth to such an extent that the alcohol actually flows down into the kingdom of Bāsak Nāg, the serpent lord of the underworld. Angered, Rājā Bāsak deposits the Earth temporarily on a bull's horns and goes to Bhagavān's court to complain about the Bagaḍāvats. But neither Bāsak, nor Hanumān, nor Bhagavān can do anything to remedy the situation, not only because the Bagaḍāvats are so powerful, but more so because they are fervently devotional towards the gods. Finally, Bhagavān assumes the form of a mendicant (*jogī*) and visits Sāḍū Mātā, the wife of Savāī Bhoj, begging for alms. Sāḍū, who has just completed performing ablutions and bathing, appears in front of the mendicant covered only by her long tresses. Struck by her devotion, the mendicant grants her a boon, Sāḍū Mātā desires that Bhagavān be born as her son. Bhagavān promises to be born as her son on the 13th day after the Bagaḍāvats have been slain.

---

39. See also B. Singh (1993: 414).
40. The mare, in fact, is a manifestation of Śakti. The cow is none other than Kāmadhenū, the 'wish-fulfilling' cow. The elephant, too, is a form of the goddess. For variants on this, see B. Singh (*ibid.*, p. 414).
41. Banyā is the name of a caste of merchants and traders more known for their dealings with trade, commerce and money.

After his return, Bhagavān requests Śaktī, who agrees, to go to Earth to fulfil the task of destroying the Bagaḍāvats. She manifests herself as an infant girl in a forest where she is discovered by the King of Bhūāl, who adopts her. Exactly at the time of her birth, her maidservant Hīrā Dāsī is born in the house of a Mahājan. Śaktī grows up unusually fast. And, soon brāhmaṇas are sent out to find a suitable bridegroom for her. She insists that they find someone belonging to a family in which one father has twenty-four sons. After a long and frustrating search the brāhmaṇas find the Bagaḍāvats. They arrange to have the queen married to Savāī Bhoj. But because they are already married, the Bagaḍāvats suggest that the queen be married to their *dharam*-brother, the Rāṇā.[42] Thus arrangements are made for the Rāṇā to marry Rāṇī Jaimatī, as the queen is called. When the marriage procession sets out, Savāī Bhoj instead of the Rāṇā, leads it. In the meanwhile Rāṇī Jaimatī orders the marriage emblem (*toraṇ*) to be hung in a high place that the Rāṇā, who is old and feeble,[43] cannot reach up to. Instead of the Rāṇā, Savāī Bhoj strikes down the emblem. When the marriage procession arrives, the queen pretends she has high fever. She asks her maidservant to fetch Savāī Bhoj's sword that is supposed to have healing powers. In the inner chambers of the palace she then circumambulates the sword, thereby secretly marrying Savāī Bhoj. In public, however, she marries the Rāṇā. At the end of the ceremonies, when she is to accompany the Rāṇā to her new home, she insists on staying with the Bagaḍāvats. The Bagaḍāvats coax her into going with the Rāṇā, promising to fetch her after a period of six months. Upon arriving in the Rāṇā's palace, however, the queen says she will not play dice with the Rāṇā till he has constructed a new palace for her.[44] The construction of the palace, of course, takes a long time, and six months are soon over. In the meanwhile, the Bagaḍāvats — against the advice of her wives — prepare to fetch the queen. The queen elopes with the Bagaḍāvats. The Rāṇā is patient, advising the Bagaḍāvats in a brotherly manner to send the queen back to him. But the Bagaḍāvats stick to their decision. Finally, the Rāṇā gathers together the armies of fifty-two forts on the banks of the Khārī river.[45] Rāṇī

42. Rāṇā is a title carried by the Rājpūt chiefs of Mewar.
43. The Rāṇā is supposedly 120 years old!.
44. 'Playing dice' is a euphemism for sexual activity. See Gold (1992: 99, fn. 66).
45. The number fifty-two denotes the vast extent of the Rāṇā's military dominion. The number is used elsewhere also in order to convey

Jaimatī, who now has assumed her true form as Bhavānī, promises to accompany the Bagaḍāvats only on the condition that they fight the Rāṇā's army one at a time. She also demands that the brothers offer their head to her. The Bagaḍāvats willingly agree to her grotesque demands. A great war (*mahābhārat*) is fought on account of Rāṇī Jaimatī (or Bhavānī). In the battle, some of the brothers continue fighting even after their heads have been severed by the Goddess's discus. In the end all of them are slain and the Rāṇā is victorious. The Goddess assumes her awesome, terrifying form. Amidst the corpses of slain warriors, she squats on the battle ground, dripping with blood, stringing a necklace of the Bagaḍāvats heads and arms. After their deaths, the heroes' wives with the exception of Savāī Bhoj's wife, Sāḍū Mātā, commit *satī*. Four infants survive the carnage. These are Bhāṅgījī, Medūjī, Madnājī, and Bhūṇājī, each of whom are raised by step-parents.

ŚRĪ DEVNĀRĀYAṆ KATHĀ

The part of the narrative concerned with the life of Devnārāyaṇ is, in terms of time-frames, also situated in the *kali-yuga*. While the first part climaxes in the great bloody battle, the second part begins in the aftermath of the war. In the midst of this cataclysmic setting the birth of Devnārāyaṇ ushers in a new era of renewal and well-being.

Sāḍū Mātā practices severe *tapas* on a hill near the battle-field. After eleven days, when her honour and life is about to be threatened by the Rāṇā, she calls out to Bhagavān, who has promised to be born as her son. Devnārāyaṇ, who is playing a game of dice at the time with Rājā Bāsak, lord of the underworld, rises up on a stream of water that splits apart the rock on which Sāḍū is seated. Carried on that jet of water in a lotus blossom, the infant Devnārāyaṇ falls into Sāḍū Mātā's lap.[46]

Threatened by the Rāṇā again, Sāḍū Mātā decides to flee to her natal home in Malwa. Devnārāyaṇ spends his childhood there

---

→ greatness. See, for example, the 'fifty-two' *ghāṭ*s of Pushkar (Malik 1993a: 7) or the 'fifty-two' forts of the epic hero Pābūjī's kingdom of Koḷū (Smith 1991: 289).

46. The symbolism of this event can be compared with images of the womb and birth, fertility and victory found in the myth of Indra who slays the serpent demon Vṛtra and splits open the 'mountains' bellies', freeing the waters (*Ṛgveda*, 1.32-1ff).

without any knowledge of past events. One day Chochū Bhāṭ, the bard and genealogist of the 24 Bagaḍāvat brothers comes to Malwa in search of Devnārāyaṇ. Sāḍū Mātā who knows of his intentions tries getting him killed, but Devnārāyaṇ revives him. Chochū Bhāṭ then informs him of the battle between the Bagaḍāvats and the Rāṇā. Devnārāyaṇ then decides, against his mother's will, to return to his father's ancestral land and take revenge on the Rāṇā. While returning to the region of Bhilwara and his capital town of Causlā Kheḍā, Devnārāyaṇ marries three princesses, first, the daughter of a demon king (*dait rāj*), second, the niece of an underworld serpent king, and third, the daughter of the Rājpūt ruler of Ujjain. The latter is Queen Pīpalde who features most importantly than the other queens in the cult and narrative. While returning, Devnārāyaṇ also meets with his four cousins Medū, Madnā, Bhāṅgī, Bhūṇā, who likewise have grown up unaware of each other's existence. Whereas Medū and Madnā have been adopted by the Rāṇā's ally — the king of Ajmer — Bhāṅgī has grown up as a Nāth Jogī in the company of the Bagaḍāvat's *guru* Bābā Rūpnāth. Bhūṇā, whose name has been changed to Khāṇḍerāv, has been adopted by the Rāṇā himself. But once the cousins realise their true origins, they join Devnārāyaṇ to launch an assault against the Rāṇā. Before the final encounter takes place, Devnārāyaṇ releases his herd of 980,000 cows and buffaloes into the royal fields in order to destroy the Rāṇā's crops. In the end the cousins catch up with the Rāṇā who is trying to escape. He is beheaded by Devnārāyaṇ's bow-string. But when Devnārāyaṇ sees that Bhūṇā is sad over the death of his foster father, he revives the Rāṇā only after Chochū Bhāṭ has extracted the Bagaḍāvats' revenge from the Rāṇā's stomach. Devnārāyaṇ then retracts the title of 'Rāṇā' giving him the title of Sisodiā. Thereafter, Devnārāyaṇ instructus the revived Rāṇā to establish the city of Udaipur, which according to the narrative is named after one of Devnārāyaṇ's names, Ud.

After Devnārāyaṇ has taken revenge on the Rāṇā, he decides to depart to heaven. But his queen Pīpalde requests him not to leave her childless. A boy Bīlā and a girl Bīlī are born to her. Bīlī is quick to realise her father's divinity. But Bīlā is stubborn and refuses to acknowledge his father's authority. After many unhappy incidents including having leprosy befall him, Bīlā begins to realise the divine power of his father. He then agrees to look after Devnārāyaṇ's very first shrine and become Devnārāyaṇ's first priest from which the lineage of priests follow. Then, having established a place of worship, a lineage of priests, and a community of devotees, Devnārāyaṇ finally returns in his celestial chariot to Baikuṇṭh.

श्री देवनारायण कथा
एक परिचय

देवनारायण की कथा को बहुधा "महाकाव्य"[1] की श्रेणी में रखा जाता है। यह राजस्थान में सर्वाधिक विख्यात लोककथाओं में से एक है।[2] यह कथा और देवनारायण सम्प्रदाय अधिकांश राजस्थान राज्य में और मध्य प्रदेश के उत्तरी-पश्चिमी क्षेत्र मालवा में प्रचलित है। पाबूजी, गूगाजी, तेजाजी, रामदेवजी, गोपीचन्द व भृतृहरि की "महाकाव्य" कथाओं के साथ-साथ यह कथा आजकल राजस्थान में प्रचलित मौखिक कथाओं की समृद्ध तथा अति महत्त्वपूर्ण परम्परा से सम्बन्धित है।[3] वर्तमान कार्य 1991 और 1994[4] में विभिन्न अवसरों पर कई-कई दिनों तक श्री हुक्माराम भोपा और उनके साथी श्री मोटाराम गूजर व श्री किसनाराम गूजर द्वारा गाई गई कथा पर आधारित है। कथा के दो भागों की रिकॉर्डिंग क्रमशः सुजानगढ़ नगर (जिला चुरु), गांव अगुन्ता व खरेश (जिला नागौर) और तीर्थ-यात्रियों के नगर पुष्कर (जिला अजमेर) में की गई थी। यह रिकॉर्डिंग लगभग छियालीस घंटे की है। कथा का प्रथम भाग बाईस घंटे का है तथा यह देवनारायण के पुरखे बगड़ावतों के जीवन और कार्यों से सम्बन्धित है। द्वितीय भाग देवनारायण पर केन्द्रित है और यह चौबीस घंटों के सस्वर पाठ का परिणाम है। इसके अतिरिक्त लगभग सौ घंटों की और रिकॉर्डिंग की गई है। इसमें देवनारायण कथा, प्रमुख कथा से सम्बन्धित गौण कथाओं के अन्य गायकों व श्रद्धालुओं के साक्षात्कार और कथा के दृश्य भाग

---

1. उदाहरण के लिए देखिए ब्लैकबर्न (1989), मलिक (1993b), मिलर (1993), सिंह (1993), स्मिथ (1991)। यही नहीं ब्लैकबर्न ने इस कथा को भारत में ख्यात "वीरगाथाओं" की श्रेणी में रखा है जो "समूह की परस्पर निर्भरता" पर बल देती है और "सत्ता, सामाजिक दायित्व तथा सामाजिक एकता का चिन्तन करती हैं। वे प्रतिशोध की भावना, गंवाई गई भूमि या गंवाए गए अधिकारों की पुनः प्राप्ति के उद्देश्य के इर्द-गिर्द घूमती हैं। वीरगाथाओं में प्रायः सैनिक या राजनैतिक विवाद और किसी युद्ध नीति का स्पष्ट वर्णन है।" (1989:5)
2.. इस परिचय के अंत में दो प्रमुख भागों वाली इस कथा के अंशों का सिंहावलोकन किया गया है।
3. देखिए बिनफोर्ड (1976), ब्लैकबर्न (1989), गोल्ड (1992), लापॉइन्ट (1978), स्मिथ (1991)।
4. हुक्माराम के साथी 1991 में श्री मोटाराम और 1994 में उनके भतीजे किसनाराम थे। ध्यान दें – प्रतिलेखन में श्री मोटाराम की आवाज गोल कोष्ठकों में रखी गई है ताकि इसे श्री हुक्माराम की आवाज से पृथक् किया जा सके।

फड़[5] के साथ-साथ इसके अंशों से सम्बन्धित विभिन्न विवरण हैं। कुल मिलाकर इस कथा पर सामग्री एकत्रित करने के लिए राजस्थान में 1991 और 1994 के बीच भिन्न-भिन्न अवसरों पर लगभग बारह मास लगाए गए।

देवनारायण से सम्बन्धित कथा के चौबीस घंटे लम्बे भाग के प्रतिलेखन और अनुवाद का काम 1996 की बसन्त ऋतु में पूरा हुआ था। यह भाग इस पुस्तक का केन्द्रीय भाग है। इससे मारवाड़ी मूल ग्रन्थ और अंग्रेज़ी अनुवाद के लगभग सात सौ पृष्ठ बन गए। कथा की रिकॉर्डिंग के अतिरिक्त जिला अजमेर, भीलवाड़ा और चित्तौड़ में देवनारायण धर्मक्षेत्र के महत्त्वपूर्ण केन्द्रों की यात्राएं भी की गईं। जिन समाधियों और मन्दिरों के दर्शन किए गए उनमें से अनेक का वर्णन कथा में किया गया है और उनका सम्बन्ध बगड़ावतों या देवनारायण से सम्बन्धित विशिष्ट घटनाओं और कार्यो से जोड़ा गया है। उदाहरण के लिए पर्वत की चोटी पर स्थित देमाली की समाधि के विषय में माना जाता है कि यह वह प्रथम पूजा-स्थल है जिसकी स्थापना स्वयं देवनारायण ने की थी, या फिर सवाई भोज का मन्दिर जिसे उस युद्धक्षेत्र के रूप में याद किया जाता है जिसमें हुए "महाभारत" में बगड़वतों ने अपने प्रमुख शत्रु राणशहर के राणा के विरुद्ध लड़ते हुए वीरगति प्राप्त की थी, या मालासरी की पहाड़ी जहां देवनारायण की साडूमाता ने उसे जन्म दिया था। इसी प्रकार के और भी उदाहरण हैं।[6]

वर्तमान परिचय में उस मौखिक कथा से सम्बन्धित प्रश्नों को मुख्य रूप से समाविष्ट किया गया है जिस कथा का प्रतिलेखन किया गया है। इसमें विशेष रूप से मैंने इस बात पर ध्यान दिया है कि प्रस्तुति को स्पष्ट कैसे किया जाए; पुस्तक का मौखिक कथा-ढांचा कैसे आकार ग्रहण करे, कैसे कथा के संवादशील प्रकरण ज्ञानशास्त्रीय श्रेणी – जैसेकि एक तरफ "स्मरणीयता" और दूसरी तरफ वाक्‌शैली के पहलुओं – "पुनरावृत्ति", "संवाद" और "संवादित भाषण" – के क्रम में रखे जा सकें।

इस प्रकार किसी लोककथा के अध्ययन का एक प्रमुख उद्‌देश्य न केवल कथा के ढांचे और अंशों तथा जिसमें यह कथा घटी है उस परिस्थिति को समझना है, बल्कि कथा के सांस्कृतिक ढांचे के भीतर से प्रस्तावित कथावस्तु और उसकी प्रस्तुति के अभिप्राय को समझना और उसकी प्रशंसा करना भी है। कथावस्तु और उसकी प्रस्तुति कैसे स्पष्ट और विदित हो? कथावस्तु और उसकी प्रस्तुति किससे बनती है, क्या इसकी निश्चित और व्यक्त धारणाएं हैं? क्या ये धारणाएं अनुसंधानकर्त्ता के अपने सांस्कृतिक ढांचे से निकले कथावस्तु और उसकी प्रस्तुति के अभिप्राय से अलग होती हैं?

---

5. कथा एक चित्रित लिपटे हुए ऐसे कपड़े के सामने प्रस्तुत की जाती है जिस पर देवनारायण के साथ-साथ अन्य सैंकड़ों वस्तुओं; जैसेकि दरबारों, नगरों, व्यक्तियों, देवताओं, पशुओं, पक्षियों, वृक्षों, तालाबों, हथियारों, वाद्ययंत्रों आदि के चित्र बने होते हैं।

6. ये और अन्य स्थान उस "धर्म-क्षेत्र" के भाग हैं जिसके दृश्य कथा के साथ-साथ फड़ में भी चित्रित किए गए हैं।

निम्नलिखित खण्डों में मैने प्रस्तुति, स्मरणीयता व स्मृति, गीत और आलंकारिक भजन, पुनरावृत्ति, संवाद और संवादित भाषण की श्रेणियों की सफलतापूर्वक जांच की है। इनमें से प्रत्येक लक्षण अकेला भी और सामूहिक रूप से भी देवनारायण की मौखिक कथा को सुनाने और सुनने के संवादशील कार्य के लिए परिस्थिति बनाता है। कुल मिलाकर ये लक्षण उस मूल कारण के लिए ढांचा भी बनाते हैं जिसके लिए कथा कही जाती है, जो देवनारायण[7] के उपस्थित होने का आह्वान है। इस प्रकार यहां "कथावस्तु" (मौखिक और दृश्य दोनों) का अभिप्राय व्यापक परिस्थिति में निहित है। इससे भिन्न "लिखित कथावस्तु" के मामले में मौखिक और दृश्य कथा स्वयं निर्धारित लक्ष्यों के रूप मे अस्तित्व नहीं रखतीं।[8]

प्रस्तुति

देवनारायण की कथा या कथा के खण्ड धार्मिक ढंग से सुनिश्चित परिस्थितियों में सम्पन्न हुए हैं। बहुधा एक प्रस्तुति जागरण या "जगराता"[9] का भाग है। जागरण का उद्देश्य देवनारायण की उपस्थिति

---

7. इस बात में कोई सन्देह नहीं कि कथा की प्रस्तुतियां अनेक कारणों से की जाती हैं, जैसेकि किसी का व्रत पूरा होने पर या धार्मिक उत्सवों के दौरान। तथापि, व्यक्तिगत या सामूहिक कारणों से परे, सभी प्रस्तुतियों का संयुक्त स्वरूप देवता की उपस्थिति का अनुष्ठान है। इसके बिना व्रत या अन्य धार्मिक कर्मकाण्ड पूरे नहीं होते।

8. जैसाकि "तमिल ग्रन्थ" के संदर्भ में कर्सेनबूम (1995: 16) अनुभव करते हैं – "पश्चिमी ग्रंथ की प्रकृति स्थिर, एक विश्लेषणात्मक उधेड़बुन का विषय है, और वह एक दस्तावेज का आकार ग्रहण करता है, लेकिन तमिल ग्रन्थ की प्रकृति सहज है, एक कृत्रिम समावेशन की प्रकिया है, प्रस्तुति की वास्तविकंता में रहती है। दोनों के प्रयोग में भिन्नता है; जैसेकि दस्तावेज एक स्वीकृत सत्य को बताता है जो किन्हीं हालात में यह निर्णायक व्याख्या प्रस्तुत करेगा कि यही सच है। जबकि प्रस्तुति यहां और अब कुछ होने या घटने, जीवन के एक दृश्य या स्वरूप को पेश करती है। ये अतियां अपने भौतिक चित्रण में प्रमाणित हैं।"

9. थील-हार्सट्मन (1985) ने उत्तर भारतीय भक्ति सम्प्रदाय दादू पंथ द्वारा की जाने वाली पूजा के संदर्भ में जागरण का पूर्ण अध्ययन प्रस्तुत किया है। प्रस्तावना में उन्होंने कहा है कि जागरण लौकिक वचन, पूजा का सर्वाधिक विस्तृत रूप है, जो समाज के सामने किया जाता है। जागरण के दौरान धर्मग्रन्थों के अनेक उद्धरण गाए जाते हैं या उन पर जोरदार चर्चा होती है। इन उद्धरणों को गाने का उद्देश्य स्त्री या पुरुष भक्त को जाग्रत करना और उसे संसार से मुक्त होने के लिए प्रेरित करना है। थील हार्सट्मन ने यह भी देखा कि प्रकाशित दस्तावेज पाठक को जगराते के अन्य कई अवयवों से वंचित रख देते हैं। पुनः उलझन यह है कि ग्रन्थों में अधिक सौंदर्य, अधिक प्रस्तुति के गुण निहित हैं, जिनमें उनके अर्थ विस्तार ग्रहण करते हैं और उसके द्वारा गायकों और श्रोताओं को प्रेरित करते हैं।

(प्रकाश) का आह्वान करना है।[10] प्रस्तुति को फड़ "वाचणो" (बोलना / फड़ पढ़ना) कहा जाता है। फड़ बड़े यत्न से बनाए गए 8.5 × 1.5 मीटर आकार के चित्रित लिपटे हुए कपडे पर उकेरी होती है तथा इस पर कथा के चरित्रों और दृश्यों के चित्र बने होते हैं। इस प्रकार की प्रस्तुतियां तीन अलग-अलग स्थानों पर की जाती हैं – (क) श्रद्धालु का घर, (ख) देवनारायण या सवाई भोज मन्दिर के सामने, (ग) सामुदायिक भवन "हथाई" के सामने। कथा की प्रस्तुति "चौमासा" या वर्षा ऋतु को छोड़कर किसी भी समय की जा सकती है। चौमासे के दौरान देवनारायण (और अन्य हिन्दू देवी-देवता) सुप्तावस्था में माने जाते हैं। प्रस्तुतियां कार्तिक मास में शुक्ल पक्ष की एकादशी से शुरु होती हैं जो अक्तूबर-नवम्बर मास में पड़ता है। चौमासे के दौरान चित्रित लिपटे हुए कपड़े को, जिसे फड़ कहा जाता है तथा जो प्रस्तुति का केन्द्रीय तत्त्व है, कभी भी खोला नहीं जाता। चौमासे में कथाएं और गीत तो गाए जा सकते हैं लेकिन नियमित प्रस्तुतियों के दौरान उपयोग किए जाने वाले फड़ और अन्य नृत्य भंगिमाओं का उपयोग किया जाता है तथा गाने का कार्य बैठकर (बैठो गानो) किया जाता है। इस बारे में श्री हुक्माराम ने बताया था –

> वास्तविकता यह है कि अब कुछ लोग भगवान के मन्दिर के सामने उसकी प्रार्थना का सस्वर पाठ करते हैं और कुछ लोग भगवान की पूजा व प्रतिष्ठा करते हैं, भगवान उनके लिए क्या करता है? वह उनके लिए हितकारी है। ऐसे व्यक्ति को देव का भक्त माना जाता है । उसके घर में शुद्ध (सवर्ण) जातियां उसके हाथ से पानी ग्रहण करती हैं। इसलिए उनके कुछ घरों में कथा का सस्वर पाठ किया जाता है। हमारे गांव में यह जाटों के घरों में गाई जाती है; और राजपूतों के घरों में भी इसका सस्वर पाठ होता है। खाती जाति के लोगों के घरों में भी इसका सस्वर पाठ होता है। इसलिए ब्राह्मण, पण्डित वे भी अब इसका सस्वर पाठ करते हैं । और, जो भगवान की प्रतिष्ठा करता है वह उसका प्रिय होता है। और उसके घर में भगवान की कथा का सस्वर पाठ होता है। इसमें कुछ भी गलत नहीं है। लेकिन पतली और तंग गलियों में, कुछ स्थानों पर इसका सस्वर पाठ नहीं होता। जब कार्तिक मास में पूर्ण चन्द्र उदय होता है, जब एकादशी को देवता जागते हैं, तबसे, अर्थात् एकादशी की शाम से कथा का सस्वर पाठ शुरु हो जाता है। आषाढ़ मास में देवता सो जाते हैं। चार मास के लिए सभी देवता राजा बल के स्थान पर चले जाते हैं। प्राचीन काल में वह एक शक्तिशाली राजा था, जो देवताओं को शक्ति प्रदान करता है। वे वहां काम करने के लिए चले जाते हैं। हम कहते हैं कि

---

10. क्योंकि यहां मेरा उद्देश्य प्रस्तुति की धारणा को समझाना है। अतः मैं स्वयं प्रस्तुति का वर्णन अधिक विस्तार से नहीं कर रहा। इसके मुख्य लक्षण नीचे संक्षेप में दिए गए हैं। एक रात की प्रस्तुति का एक पूर्ण दस्तावेज स्वयं में एक पुस्तक बन जाता है, जैसाकि थील-हार्सट्मन के ऊपर दर्शाए गए अध्ययन में वर्णन किया गया है। देवनारायण की कथा की प्रस्तुति की स्थिति की विस्तृत जानकारी के लिए देखिए – मिलर (1980 और 1994)।

देवता सोने के लिए चले गए। लेकिन देवता किसलिए सोएं? वे सोते नहीं हैं । वे दूर राजा बल के स्थान पर चार मास के लिए कार्य करने चले जाते हैं। इस प्रकार छत्रियों (क्षत्रियों) और देवताओं का कार्य रुक जाता है। भगवान का द्वार चार मास के दौरान खोलना गलत है। यदि द्वार नहीं खुला है और केवल जागरण किया जाता है तो यह केवल बैठकर किया जाता है, बैठकर कथा को कहना सम्भव है। इस स्थिति में फड़ को नहीं खोला जा सकता। केवल कार्तिक मास के शुक्ल पक्ष की एकादशी को ही इसे खोला जा सकता है और कथा का सस्वर पाठ किया जा सकता है। तब इसमें कोई हानि या अड़चन नहीं होती।

जब लिपटे हुए कपड़े को खोला जाता है और खड़ा किया जाता है तो उसके द्वारा घेरी गई जगह पवित्र हो जाती है। लिपटा हुआ यह कपड़ा स्वयं में एक चलता- फिरता मन्दिर है जिसके मध्य में अपने शाही दरबार में बैठे देवनारायण और उसके चार भाईयों का चित्र होता है। देवनारायण के चित्र के सामने एक अस्थायी वेदी बनाई जाती है। इसमें धूपबत्ती जलाई जाती है और यहां अनाज तथा धन भेंट किए जाते हैं। जब कोई भी श्रोता चढ़ावा चढ़ाता है तो भोपा या उसका सहगायक शंख बजाता है तथा श्रद्धालु के नाम और उसके द्वारा चढ़ाए गए चढ़ावे की मात्रा की घोषणा करता है । इस बीच कथा गाना रुक जाता है। इस तरह की रुकावटों के साथ-साथ कुछ अन्य अंतराल भी होते हैं जिनके दौरान गायकों को चाय या तम्बाकू पिलाए जाते हैं और बैठने के लिए कहा जाता है। इस प्रकार के अन्तराल बार-बार आते रहते हैं। यहां तक कि कुल नौ घंटे के समय में से चार घंटे ही कथा कहने और कहानी सुनाने में लगाते हैं। गायक एक विशेष पोशाक (बागा) पहनते हैं और तार वाले वाद्ययंत्र का उपयोग करते हैं जिसे "बीन" या "जन्तर" कहा जाता है। बड़े तुम्बे वाला यह वाद्ययंत्र मुख्य गायक के पास होता है जो कथा गाते समय और लिपटे कपड़े (फड़) पर उससे सम्बन्धित भागों को दर्शाते हुए इस वाद्ययंत्र को बजाता है। उसका साथी तेल का दीया लिए होता है जिससे कथा की प्रस्तुति के दौरान लिपटे कपड़े पर उजाला होता है तथा कपड़े की लम्बाई के साथ और दो गायकों के बीच पीछे और आगे चलने का सिलसिला होता है। कथा गाते समय मुख्य गायक विशिष्ट क्षणों मे नाचने का आभास देने वाले कदम भी भरता है। गायकों और श्रोताओं के बीच अत्यन्त तारतम्य स्थापित हो जाता है। प्रायः श्रोता सम्बन्धित उपाख्यान या गायक के गायन की सराहना करते हैं। कुछ श्रोता गायक से अधिक जानने का दावा भी करते हैं जो "विवादास्पद" सवालों के सफलतापूर्वक उत्तर देकर विशेषज्ञ होने का दावा-प्रतिदावा करते हैं। कभी-कभी अन्तराल के समय कुछ श्रोता स्वयं कुछ पंक्तियां गाकर श्रोताओं का मनोरंजन करते हैं।

"प्रस्तुति" के समनुरूप पहला शब्द है "फड़ वाचणो"। इस प्रकार गीत, कथा, नृत्य, फड़ को निर्दिष्ट करना, श्रोताओं की भागीदारी आदि को साधारणतया "फड़" बोलना / पढ़ना कहा जाता है जिसे भोपा और श्रद्धालु भक्त समान रूप से पसन्द करते हैं। इस प्रकार प्रस्तुति का स्वरूप – जैसाकि कोई पुस्तकीय दृष्टिकोण से उम्मीद कर सकता है – देवनारायण की कहानी को "कहना या बताना" भर नहीं है। यहां हम "कथावस्तु" पर उसी रूप में ध्यान केन्द्रित नहीं कर रहे बल्कि लिपटे कपड़े

(फड़) पर ध्यान केन्द्रित कर रहे हैं जो देवता और कथावस्तु का प्रतिरूप है। तथापि, लिपटा कपड़ा स्वयं व्याख्यायित नहीं है। इसे "बोले जाने" या पढ़े जाने की आवश्यकता होती है अर्थात् इसे एक विशेषज्ञ नामतः गायक द्वारा अर्थपूर्ण ढंग से "प्रकट करने" या "वर्णित करने" की जरुरत होती है। इस प्रकार प्रत्येक प्रस्तुति में फड़ पर बनी आकृतियों की सम्पूर्ण व्याख्या और इसके अर्थों का समकालीन पुनर्निर्माण शामिल होते हैं। आकृतियों का अर्थ फड़ पर बनी दृश्य आकृतियों के साथ एक ही समय में कथा को बोलने और गाने के माध्यम से स्पष्ट या अधिकतर जाहिर हो जाता है। इसलिए फड़ किसी तस्वीरों वाली पुस्तक की तरह बोली या पढ़ी नहीं जाती, बल्कि यह एक कथा के माध्यम से पढ़ी जाती है जो स्वयं के सस्वर पाठ द्वारा व्यक्त होती है। भोपा किसी कला इतिहासकार की तरह फड़ पर बनी आकृतियों की व्याख्या अपने निष्कर्ष के अनुसार नहीं करता। वह आकृतियों की कथा में निहित व्याख्या से बंधा होता है। "फड़ वाचणो" शब्द द्वारा दी गई परिभाषा के अनुसार फड़ इसलिए सामान्यतः मौखिक कथा आयामों का दृष्टान्त नहीं है। वास्तव में यह वह है जो कथा द्वारा प्रदान किए गए व्याख्यात्मक ढांचे के माध्यम से व्यक्त होती है। इससे स्पष्ट होता है कि फड़ की कल्पना सृष्टि और मूर्त्तता किसी प्रस्तुति में स्वयं कथा से भी अधिक आकर्षण का केन्द्र होती है। इस मूर्त्त प्रभाव को वाक्यों में भी उतारा जा सकता है; जैसेकि – "फड़ां का लेख", जिसका अर्थ है "फड़ का लिखना" जिसका उपयोग हुक्माराम भोपा कथा के किसी विशिष्ट परिच्छेद और उपाख्यान के अस्तित्व व उसकी प्रामाणिकता को सिद्ध करने के लिए करते थे। इस प्रकार फड़ मौखिक कथावस्तु का प्रमाण है न कि इसके विपरीत। इस प्रकार दृश्य आकृति और चित्र को मौखिक अभिव्यक्ति से पहले होना आवश्यक माना गया है। लेकिन मौखिक अभिव्यक्ति के बिना आकृतियों के अर्थ स्वयं ही उद्घाटित नहीं होते।[11]

स्मरण

इस खण्ड में मैने स्मरण के अर्थ का संक्षेप में वर्णन किया है जिससे सस्वर पाठ सदैव शुरु होता है। कथा के इस प्रारम्भिक अवयव पर एक "सूत्रबद्ध" रूप में गौर करने और इसलिए एक महत्त्वहीन, आवृत्तियुक्त शुरुआत करने की अपेक्षा मेरी मंशा इसे ज्ञान के प्रारम्भिक स्त्रोत के रूप में पुनः स्थापित करने की है। मेरा दावा है कि यह स्त्रोत, जो कि प्रायः जाने-माने लेखकों के लिए अबोध्य या अकल्पनीय रहा है, भारत में अभिव्यक्ति परम्परा की उन व्यापक किस्मों के लिए अत्यधिक महत्त्वपूर्ण है जो

---

11. इसी प्रकार स्मिथ (1991: 17) ने पाबूजी की "चित्रकथा सुनाने" की परम्परा पर लिखते हुए स्पष्ट किया है कि : " . . . फड़ पढ़ते हुए सूक्ति का उपयोग उस मार्ग का अमूल्य संकेत है जिसमें भोपा अपना कार्य धारणीय बनाते हैं।" वे "एक महाकाव्य को गाना" नहीं कहते; वे गाने या कथा कहने को महत्त्व नहीं देते बल्कि प्रस्तुति को महत्त्व देते है, और अच्छी प्रस्तुति के लिए उन्होंने कपड़े पर चित्र बनाकर उनसे सहायता ली। . . . हम पाबूजी तक उनकी फड़ के माध्यम से पहुंचते हैं, और हम फड़ तक भोपाओं द्वारा इसे पढने के माध्यम से पहुंचते हैं।"

कि कहानी सुनाने से शुरु होकर नृत्य, थिएटर और संगीत तक जाती है। इसी प्रकार बुद्धिजीवी – जोकि मौखिक और श्रव्य के आर-पार स्वयं अधिक सचेत नहीं रहते – लेकिन मौखिक कथाओं को "मानसिक कथावस्तु", "स्मृति", "सूत्रबद्ध भाषा", इत्यादि के द्वारा समझने के लिए उन्हें मौखिक रूप से सुबोधगम्य बनाने पर किए गए उनके प्रयास बहुत ही प्रबल प्रयास हैं। तथापि, सृजनात्मक प्रेरणा के स्त्रोत से स्वयं कटे रहने के कारण से – जैसाकि अभिव्यक्ति की विभिन्न परम्पराओं में यह विदित है – हम इसकी वैधता और प्रामाणिकता की व्याख्या करने की ओर प्रवृत्त होते हैं।

आदर्श रूप में, देवनारायण की कथा विभिन्न परोपकारी और मांगलिक देवी-देवताओं के आह्वान से शुरु होती है, जो फड़ पर उपस्थित होते हैं। आह्वान में देवी-देवताओं के प्रति सम्मान प्रकट किया जाता है। यहां प्रयोग किया गया शब्द "सिमरणो" है, जो हिन्दी के "सुमिरन" या "स्मरण" का पर्याय है और इसका अर्थ है – "याद करना", "पुनः संग्रह करना", "मन में बुलाना", "स्मृति"।[12] आह्वान के दौरान बुलाए जाने वाले देवी-देवता हैं – देवी शारदा, गणेश, देवनारायण, भैरवनाथ, सरस्वती और गायक का गुरु। देवी-देवताओं का आह्वान सुरक्षा, ज्ञान, बुद्धि प्रदान करने के लिए किया जाता है। उदाहरण के लिए दो पंक्तियों में कहा जाता है कि गुरु के बिना "ज्ञान" नहीं। शारदा (सरस्वती या दुर्गा का नाम) के स्मरण द्वारा गायक कहना शुरु करता है कि वह उसके हृदय में सदैव निवास करे। देवी सरस्वती गायक के स्वर (कंठ, शब्द – शब्दः "गले") में निवास करे और उसे गाने की प्रेरणा दे। गणपत या विनायक का स्मरण करके कोई भी खुशी और संतुष्टि पाता है। और पुनः जो भी देवनारायण में श्रद्धा रखता है उसे दूध या अनाज की कभी कमी नहीं होती। देवनारायण वह देवता है जिसे ईंटों के आकार में पूजा जाता है।[13] वास्तव में यहां महत्त्वपूर्ण बिन्दु केवल यह नहीं है कि विभिन्न देवी-देवताओं के सुरक्षात्मक और प्रेरणात्मक गुणों का आह्वान किया जाता है, बल्कि यह भी महत्त्वपूर्ण है कि इन्हें "याद" किया जा रहा है। याद करने में एक निमंत्रण

---

12. यह महाराष्ट्र के हाटकर धंगर की मौखिक कविता के बहुत समान है, जो "सुम्बराना माण्डील" या "सुम्बराना देवाचा" ("स्मरण सत है", "देवता का स्मरण") से रचना की शुरुआत करते हैं। (सोंथिमर 1989: 9)।

    देवनारायण की मौखिक कथा में स्मृति दो अर्थों में शामिल है। एक अर्थ वास्तव में वह है जिसमें गायक स्वयं "स्मृति" से गाता है। (यद्यपि यह वह नहीं है जिसका दावा करता है। गायक तो सरस्वती या देवनारायण द्वारा "प्रेरित होने" या "शक्ति पाने" की बात करता है।) दूसरा अर्थ वह है जिसमें गायक भूतकाल को वर्तमान में पुनर्सर्जित करने और पुनः अभिव्यक्त करने में लगा होता है। जहां तक कथा के अर्थ का सम्बन्ध है, यह भी आवश्यक है कि इस "स्मृति" और "स्मरण" वाले बाद के पहलू पर भी ध्यान दिया जाए। यद्यपि मौखिक संचरण के दृष्टिकोण से स्मृति का पहला अर्थ भी समान रूप से महत्त्वपूर्ण है। इतिहास के पुनर्सर्जन के अर्थ में स्मृति हमें सीधे ही कथा के केन्द्रीय विषयों में से एक, नामतः, ऐतिहासिकता पर वार्तालाप, पर ले आती है।

13. देवनारायण की समाधि लम्ब रूप में खड़ी ईंटों की लम्बी पंक्ति के रूप में बनी है।

है। दूसरे शब्दों में गायक उस स्त्रोत को याद कर रहा है, स्वयं को उससे "पुनः" जोड़ रहा है, जिससे सस्वर पाठ बहता है।

वास्तव में कथा की शुरुआत में स्मरण का किया जाना कथा कहने के कार्य की सत्य प्रकृति को निर्दिष्ट करता है जो कि ज्ञान की देवी की अध्यक्षता वाले ज्ञान- शास्त्रीय विचार-क्षेत्र से सृजनात्मकता और विवेक को प्रकट करने का अभ्यास है। गायक के दृष्टिकोण से यह ज्ञान के पुनर्लाभ के आन्तरिक "मानसिक" कार्य के अर्थ में स्मृति से प्रकट करने का अभ्यास नहीं है। ज्ञान और प्रेरणा का विचार-क्षेत्र, जिससे गायक गीत को बढ़ाता है एक अर्थ में उसके के लिए बाह्य क्षेत्र है। यह एक "इन्द्रियगोचर" चमत्कारिक मण्डल है जो उसे ज्ञान प्रदान करता है मौखिक कथा की यह समझ ज्ञानशास्त्र के दृष्टिकोण से इस बात से भिन्न है कि मौखिक कथा अध्ययन और याद करने की जटिल प्रकिया का परिणाम है। उदाहरण के लिए फिन्नेगन (1992: 114-17) ने अपने रचना, संचरण और स्मृति अध्याय में स्पष्ट किया है कि पुराने समय की कथाएं "ऐसे चित्रमय होती थी जैसेकि वे मानव के माध्यम के बिना स्वतः ही प्रकट हो रही हों", लेकिन इसके बाद के छिद्रान्वेषी अध्ययनों में इस विचार को त्याग दिया गया कि लोग जो कुछ जानते और करते हैं उसके आधार पर पुनर्निर्माण और संगठन करते हुए एक व्यक्ति स्मृतियों का पदानुपद भंडारण करे, ताकि याद करने का अर्थ रट्टा मारकर याद करना न रहे बल्कि यह उपयोगकर्त्ता की एक सृजनात्मक और संगठित गतिविधि हो। इस प्रकार अधिक आधुनिक कार्य में "एक सामाजिक प्रकिया के रूप में स्मृति" को महत्त्व दिया गया है। इस संदर्भ में रखे गए कुछ प्रश्न इस प्रकार हैं –

> अलिखित रिकॉर्ड और स्मृतियों की प्रस्तुति के लिए किस प्रकार की प्रक्रिया और विचारधारा को मान्यता दी जाए, और वे मूल्यांकित तथा स्वीकृत कैसे हों? क्या ऐसे मान्य उपाय हैं जिनसे लोग याद करने या भूल जाने के लिए निःसंदेह व स्पष्टतया प्रशिक्षित हो सकते हों? किस प्रकार की तकनीक अपनाई जाए और किसकी स्मृति हो? क्या ऐसे उपाय – और जो कुछ याद किया गया है उसके अंश – आवश्यक रूप से सभी मौखिक हैं या क्या अतिरिक्त अथवा वैकल्पिक रूप में अन्य माध्यम, आकृतियां और / या सक्रिय प्रस्तुतियां शामिल हैं, और यदि ऐसा है तो इनके बीच परस्पर क्या सम्बन्ध है? (*वही*, पृष्ठ 116)।

देवनारायण के प्रसंग में प्रश्नों का यह समूह इस बात से सम्बन्ध रखता है कि भोपा कैसे याद करते हैं और अपने ज्ञान को कैसे अभिव्यक्त करते हैं और कैसे यह ज्ञान सांस्कृतिक रूप से स्वीकृत हो चुका है। प्रारम्भ में ही यह बता देना काफी महत्त्वपूर्ण है कि भोपा का कार्य आवश्यक रूप से पैतृक नहीं होता। कोई भी प्रशिक्षु इस कार्य को अपने पिता से अथवा किसी अन्य व्यक्ति से सीख सकता है। आधारभूत महत्त्व की बात आह्वान (या रुख) है जिसे कोई देवनारायण के इर्द-गिर्द और कथा को सीखने के दौरान अनुभव करता है। वास्तव में काफी लोग भोपा के सहायक के रूप में कार्य करते हैं, लेकिन अन्ततः सभी भोपा नहीं बन जाते। जो भोपा बनते हैं वे कोई औपचारिक प्रशिक्षण

ग्रहण नहीं करते। वे अपना व्यवसाय भोपा द्वारा गाई गई प्रस्तुतियों को सुनकर और यदा-कदा कथा गाने में शामिल होकर सीखते हैं। इस प्रकार कथावस्तु को प्राकृतिक भाषा सीखने के ही समान प्रक्रिया में सीखा जाता है। शिक्षा-सम्बन्धी गद्य कथाओं के द्वारा स्वयं कथावस्तु "ग्रहण करने" के अतिरिक्त प्रशिक्षु प्रस्तुति के अन्य पहलुओं; जैसेकि – नाच (नृत्य), वाणो (चित्र के बारे में बताना), गाव (गद्य), अर्थाव (व्याख्या), और मस्करी (मजाक), पर ध्यान देता है। इस प्रकार प्रस्तुति में "संचरण माध्यमों" की विस्तृत श्रृंखला शामिल होती है – फड़, नृत्य, कथा, गीत, हंसी-मजाक, हाव-भाव, वाद्ययंत्रों का संगीत, पोशाक, पहेलियां, प्रकाश, आदि। कुल मिलाकर यह नहीं भूलना चाहिए कि प्रस्तुति धार्मिक रूप से दृढ़निश्चित वृतान्त है जो बहुसंख्यक श्रोताओं के देवता देवनारायण की पूजा में प्रस्तुत की जाती है।[14]

लेकिन फिन्नेगन द्वारा ऊपर उठाए गए प्रश्न अनुसंधानकर्ताओं के लिए महत्त्वपूर्ण हैं, तथापि वे गायकों और कथा प्रस्तुत करने वालों द्वारा अपनी गतिविधियों का वर्णन करने के लिए उपयोग की जाने वाली सांस्कृतिक श्रेणियों की अनदेखी करने की प्रवृत्ति रखते हैं। इस प्रकार "... स्मर (संस्कृत) और मरपु (तमिल) की भारतीय धारणाएं प्रेम, स्मृति, परम्परा और पूजा का मिश्रण हैं। वे धार्मिक उपस्थिति में श्रद्धापूर्ण कार्यों की ओर संकेत करती हैं और प्रेम की निरन्तरता को भी उत्कट करती हैं। ... स्मर, "स्मृति", "प्रेम", पूजा, सृजन, "परम्परा" एक पीढ़ी दूसरी पीढ़ी को सौंपती है (संस्कृत परम्परा)। पूर्वजों से प्राप्त विरासत को जीवित रखा जाता है और इसकी सुन्दरता तथा उपयोगिता के लिए इसका प्यार से पालन-पोषण किया जाता है।"[15] यही नहीं संस्कृत में स्मृति द्वारा उद्घाटित ज्ञान, श्रुति के स्मरण का उल्लेख किया गया है। मौखिक कथाओं तथा लिखित ग्रन्थों के संदर्भ में मारवाड़ी का सिमरनो, हिन्दी का सुमिरन और संस्कृत का स्मर – ये सभी धार्मिक साहित्य के स्रोत की ओर संकेत करते हैं। देवनारायण के मामले में भी यही वह स्रोत है जो मौखिक कथा को स्वयं व्यक्त होने की अनुमति देता है। इसी सस्वर पाठ की शुरुआत में देवी-देवताओं के आह्वान को किसी "फार्मूले" या किसी प्रकार के कर्मकाण्डीय नुस्खे तक सीमित करने की आवश्यकता नहीं है। यह प्रेरणा व ज्ञान के मण्डल से "पुनः जुड़ जाने" का मामला है।

---

14. यहां जो प्रश्न पूछा जाना चाहिए वह यह है कि धार्मिक वृतान्त को ऐसे विस्तृत वर्णन वाले "प्रस्तुति के" प्रकरण की क्यों जरूरत होती है। मान लीजिए हम प्रकाश (उपस्थिति, रोशनी, दीप्ति) की धारणा को केन्द्रीय लक्षण के रूप में लेते है, जिसके बारे में सभी अन्य प्रस्तुति सम्बन्धी तत्त्व संगठित किए गए हैं। क्योंकि, गायकों और श्रोताओं के दृष्टिकोण से प्रस्तुति का उद्देश्य देवनारायण के प्रकाश को प्रकट करना, संभव बनाना है, अतः हमें यह समझने की जरूरत है कि "संचरण माध्यम" द्वारा उत्पन्न की गई समूची दृश्य-श्रव्य श्रृंखला और अन्य मस्तिष्क सम्बन्धी अनुभव "प्रकाश" को प्रकट करने, और देवनारायण के प्रति श्रोताओं के समर्पण को अभिव्यक्त करने के लिए गतिमान हैं। हमें यह समझना होगा कि देवनारायण और उसके पूर्वजों की कथा की प्रस्तुति विभिन्न मस्तिष्क- सम्बन्धी तत्त्वों से जुड़ी है और यह देवी-देवताओं की उपस्थिति में होती है।

15. कर्सेनबुम, 1995:19 और 94 अगला।

गीत और उद्‌घोषणात्मक भजन

आइए अब कथा के औपचारिक ढ़ांचे की तरफ मुड़ते हैं। हम यहां यह ध्यान में रखें कि औपचारिक ढांचा, गायक जो कुछ करता है उसका प्रतिबिम्ब भी होने के कारण, हमें कथा के विशाल संवादशील ढांचे के भीतर एक सूक्ष्मदृष्टि प्रदान करता है। जैसाकि ऊपर वर्णन किया गया है, भोपा कथा का आरम्भ विभिन्न देवी-देवताओं के आह्वान (स्मरण) से करता है, जिनमें मुख्य हैं – शारदा और सरस्वती, जो ज्ञान, संगीत, बुद्धि, भाषण और सर्जन की प्रेरणा की देवी हैं। इसके बाद वह स्वतः कथा का आरम्भ करता है। कथा स्वयं में एक तरफ पद्य और गद्य की रचना है और दूसरी तरफ गीत व उद्‌घोषित संवाद की रचना है। इन दो रूपों और भाषण करने के ढंगों के बीच परस्पर तालमेल के अतिरिक्त मुख्य गायक और सहगायक के बीच आपसी तालमेल रहता है। इससे भी आगे भाषण करने का संवादशील रूप स्वयं कथा में भी पाया जाता है जो विभिन्न चरित्रों या आवाजों के बीच संवादों की श्रृंखलाओं के माध्यम से आगे बढ़ता है। कथा के इस केन्द्रीय तत्त्व की तरफ मुड़ने से पहले आइए पद्य और गद्य भागों पर विचार करें।

गाव और अर्थाव

कथावस्तु के पद्य भाग, जिसे उसे गाए जा सकने के कारण "गाव"[16] भी कहा जाता है, में चार पंक्तियां और एक ध्रुवपद (टेक) होते हैं। कई बार गाए जाने वाले भाग में चार से अधिक पंक्तियां भी होती हैं। इन अपवादों पर विचार-विमर्श नीचे किया जाएगा। "गाव" को दोनों गायक एक साथ गाते हैं। पहली पंक्ति एक लम्बे स्वर : "ए"... से शुरु करते हैं। पहली पंक्ति एक लम्बे "औवूं रे" या केवल "रे" के साथ समाप्त होती है। दूसरी और चौथी पंक्ति में अंतिम शब्द समान तुकान्त वाले होते हैं, लेकिन पहली और तीसरी पंक्ति में ऐसा नहीं होता। ध्रुवपद (टेक) में प्रायः "(भलां जी भलां) देव भलां" {बहुत अच्छा जी, बहुत अच्छा देव} कहा जाता है। जब पद्य भाग गीत (अर्थात् गाव) के रूप में नहीं होता तो इसे "कड़ी" कहा जाता है, जिसका साहित्यिक अर्थ है – एक श्रृंखला, संयोग, क्रमवार जुड़ा हुआ। इस प्रकार समझा जाता है कि पद्य भाग कथा श्रृंखला में जुड़े होते हैं। और वास्तव में कथा कड़ी के एक समूह से अगले समूह में चलती है। कड़ी के हर समूह में एक संक्षिप्त, सटीक स्वगत भाषण (आत्म-वक्तव्य) होता है जो किसी एक पात्र द्वारा बोला होता है। गद्य भाग में एक पद्य के बाद यह "स्वगत भाषण" प्रायः शब्दशः दोहराया जाता है। वास्तव में अन्तर अभिव्यक्ति के ढ़ंग में निहित होता है जो अब उद्‌घोषणा है। गद्य भाग, जो कि उद्‌घोषित किए जाते हैं; "अर्थाव" कहलाते हैं जिनका साहित्यिक अर्थ "व्याख्या" या "अर्थ" (हिन्दी का अर्थ) होता है। पद्य खण्डों के विपरीत, यहां गायकों की आवाजों का निश्चित अन्तराल होता है। जब मुख्य गायक वाक्यों को शुरु करता है तो उसका साथी कई वैकल्पिक ढंगों से उसके साथ मिल जाता है – (क) वह मुख्य गायक द्वारा आधा गाया गया वाक्य पूरा कर सकता है। (ख) वह मुख्य गायक की शब्दावली को

---

16. यह शब्द क्रिया 'गावनो' से संबंधित है।

दोहरा सकता है। (ग) वह अपनी पंक्ति जोड़ सकता है और (घ) वह मुख्य गायक की बात को टिप्पणियों; जैसेकि "म्हे" या 'वाह वाह" से समर्थन दे सकता है।

उद्घोषित गद्य भाग में पद्य भाग की पंक्तियां पूरी तरह दोहराए जाने के बाद गायक और उसका साथी ऊपर वर्णित संवादपूर्ण ढ़ंग से कथा को तब तक जारी रखते हैं जब तक दूसरी कड़ी गाने का समय नहीं हो जाता। उद्घोषित भाग सदैव कुछ पंक्तियों के साथ समाप्त होता है; जैसेकि, – "आइए देखें 'क' क्या समाचार कहता है" और "इसके कहने द्वारा, इसे जानिए, आइए देखते हैं" ये पंक्तियां बतलाती हैं – (1) कि व्यक्ति बोलने वाला है और (2) जो कुछ भी जाना जाएगा वह यह कहने द्वारा या बोलने के द्वारा उद्घाटित होगा। "न्यूज" के लिए उपयोग किया जाने वाला शब्द है – 'समचार"[17]। इस प्रकार 'क' द्वारा 'ख' के लिए अपना भाषण इस तरह शुरु किया जाता है जैसेकि पहली बार कोई व्यक्ति "समचार" गाकर सुनाता है। तर्कसंगत रूप से तब, 'क' के भाषण द्वारा और कथा की निरन्तरता की जटिलता द्वारा जो कुछ ज्ञात किया जाना है, वह कथा को बताने / कहने / जोर से बोलने में स्पष्ट हो जाता है। बोलने और जानने के बीच सम्बन्ध पर जोर देना भी महत्त्वपूर्ण है क्योंकि यह कथा की मौखिक प्रकृति को रेखांकित करता है। गायक यह नहीं कहते कि "इसे पढ़कर इसे जानिए" या "जो कुछ लिखा है उसे समझकर इसे जानिए"। शुरु से लेकर अंत तक जो चर्चा होती है वह केवल बोलने और कहने में होती है। यह पहलू इस विशिष्ट मौखिक परम्परा के लिए ज्ञान की आकस्मिक प्रकृति को महत्त्वपूर्ण ढंग से रेखांकित करता है। क्योंकि किसी के बोलने से पहले कुछ जाना नहीं जाता, अतः हम ज्ञान को "जमा रखने" वाले पात्रों; जैसेकि – धर्मग्रन्थों, अभिलेखों, ताड़ के पत्तों, पुस्तकों का सहारा ज्ञान को सुरक्षित रखने व प्रकट करने के लिए नहीं ले सकते।

वार्तालाप सम्बन्धी संभाषण

मुख्य गायक और उसके साथी के बीच हुआ संवादशील आदान-प्रदान कथा के संवादपूर्ण ढ़ांचे द्वारा आन्तरिक स्तर पर मिल जाता है। यह कहने से मेरा विशेष अभिप्राय यह है कि मूल रूप में कथा विभिन्न आवाजों के बीच वार्तालाप या संवाद की शृंखलाओं के अतिरिक्त कुछ भी नहीं है।[18] गायक स्वयं मुश्किल से ही किसी तीसरे व्यक्ति को घटनाओं या दृश्यों का वर्णन करने की पेशकश करते हैं। कथा में जो कुछ भी होता है वह विभिन्न चरित्रों या पात्रों की आवाजों के माध्यम से होता है। इस प्रकार कथा अपने आन्तरिक ढांचे के साथ-साथ बाह्य अभिव्यक्ति, दोनों में ही, वार्तालाप की भाषण शैली के बहुत करीब आ जाती है। पुनरावृत्ति, संवाद और वर्णनात्मक भाषण पर यहां प्रस्तुत और बाद के खण्ड़ों में किए गए विश्लेषण में इसीलिए कथा की मौखिक रचना को समझने के उद्देश्य से भाषा-विषयक अंगों; जैसेकि – व्याकरण या "सूत्रबद्ध" भाषा पर ध्यान केन्द्रित करने की अपेक्षा

---

17. इस शब्द पर नीचे अधिक विस्तार से विचार-विमर्श किया गया है।
18. इसमें मानव, देवता, दैत्य, पशु और यहाँ तक कि पेड़ भी शामिल हो सकते हैं।

भाषण की सारभूत इकाई के रूप में उच्चारण की प्रकृति और उसके होने पर प्राथमिक रूप से ध्यान केन्द्रित किया गया है।

प्रतिदिन की परिस्थितियों में वार्तालाप सम्बन्धी संभाषण के अंगों का वर्णन करते हुए[19] टन्नेन (1994: 25 एफ.) ने कहा है –

> . . . वार्तालाप सम्बन्धी संभाषण तीसरे व्यक्ति के विवरण ("अप्रत्यक्ष भाषण") की अपेक्षा स्पष्ट रूप से यह प्रस्तुत करता है कि दूसरों ने संवाद ("प्रत्यक्ष भाषण या प्रत्यक्ष उद्धरण") के रूप में क्या कहा ("वर्णनात्मक भाषण") है, तथा वह "प्रत्यक्ष भाषण" अधिक स्पष्ट, अधिक प्रभावी है। संवाद अधिक स्पष्ट कैसे है? मेरा विश्वास है कि यह इस कारण से है कि आवाजों की उत्पत्ति उस दृश्य की कल्पना को घटित करती है जिस दृश्य में पात्र उन्हीं आवाजों में बोलते हैं और यह कारण भी है कि ये दृश्य विकल्प, दूरी या जाने-पहचाने शब्दों की कल्पना को घटित कर देते हैं, जैसाकि कलापूर्ण रचना में होता है। निष्कर्ष रूप में दूसरों के भाषण के अनुरूप विचारों को ढ़ाल लेना संभाषण में मनोभावों का महत्त्वपूर्ण स्त्रोत है।[20]

कथा में वार्तालाप ताजा घटना का दृश्य प्रस्तुत करते हुए वर्तमान काल में स्थित होते हैं जबकि गायकों द्वारा प्रस्तुत की जाने वाली व्याख्या भूतकाल में होती है। ऐसी व्याख्या कथा में समय और स्थान के परिवर्तन के लिए संवादों के बीच में प्रस्तुत की जाती है –

> जिस समय वे सिंधबडा पहुंचे (म्हे) तो दोनों भैरवनाथों ने तने को पकड़ लिया / उन्होनें तना हिलाया / जोगिणी पत्तों पर बैठी थीं / एक के बाद एक सभी नीचे गिर पड़ीं / (श्रीमान जी कहा है) / दरबार के निकट एक कुआं था / (म्हे) वे सब वहां गईं और कुएं में गिर गईं / भैरवनाथ ने कहा "श्री महाराज" /

कहना या बताना क्रियाओं का उपयोग पूरी स्पष्टता के साथ किया जाता है। ये शब्द प्रायः वर्तमान काल में होते हैं ताकि प्रत्यक्ष भाषण करना सुविधाजनक रहे। पद्य खण्ड से पहले की पंक्ति ("आइए देखते हैं "क" क्या समाचार कहता है।") के विषय में एक उदाहरण ऊपर दिया जा चुका है। अन्य उदाहरण भी वास्तविक "प्रत्यक्ष भाषण" के पूर्ववर्ती वाक्यों में पाए जा सकते हैं। जैसेकि – "भैरवनाथ ने कहा", "देव महाराज ने कहा", "उसने कहा", कभी-कभी केवल "कहा" का उपयोग किया जाता है। ऐसे मामलों में पूर्वोक्त वाक्य द्वारा वक्ता को निश्चित किया जा सकता है। बोले जाने वाले वाक्य

---

19. संभाषण और वार्तालाप सम्बन्धी विश्लेषण पर गुडविन (1981), गुम्पेर्ज (1982), वार्डहाग (1985)।

20. पुनरावृति, संवाद और वर्णनात्मक भाषण शीर्षकों के तहत निम्नलिखित खण्डों में मैने कथा की "वार्तालाप सम्बन्धी" प्रकृति का निरीक्षण इसके आन्तारिक ढ़ांचे और गायकों के बीच परस्पर विनिमय, दोनों दृष्टिकोणों से किया है।

के प्रारम्भ में "कहा" क्रिया के इन उपयोगों के अतिरिक्त दूसरा गायक "कहा" का उपयोग अपनी पंक्तियों की समाप्ति के लिए भी करता है – " 'आई और गिर पड़ी', श्रीमानजी कहा।" इस प्रकार मुख्य गायक किसी पात्र के संवाद को "क ने कहा" कहकर शुरु करता है तो दूसरा गायक "उसने कहा" कहकर अपना विवरण समाप्त करता है। दूसरे गायक द्वारा "उसने कहा" का उपयोग वास्तव में उसके वक्तव्य की पुनरावृत्ति की प्रकृति के लिए सुविधाजनक है। न केवल एक अंश इस प्रकार दोहराया जाता है बल्कि क द्वारा बोले गए प्रत्यक्ष भाषण पर भी पुनः बल दिया जाता है और दोहराया जाता है। पुनरावृत्ति और संवादशीलता इस प्रकार मिलकर कथा कहने और कथा की शैली, दोनों के सारभूत पहलू बनाते हैं।

पुनरावृत्ति

फिन्नेगन (1977: 90) ने कहा है, "कविता का सर्वाधिक श्रेष्ठ लक्षण पुनरावृत्ति है"[21] आगे उन्होंने अनुभव किया है –

> . . . पुनरावृत्ति एक प्रकार से मौखिक कविता की शैली का गुण है – सूक्तियों, पंक्तियों या छन्दों की पुनरावृत्ति सादृश्यता का उपयोग; आवर्तक सूत्र। मौखिक कविता अनिवार्यतः क्षणभंगुर है। ऐसी परिस्थितियों में पुनरावृत्ति में एक स्थावर बिन्दु है। यह स्थावर बिन्दु, जो कुछ कहा जा रहा है, उसे समझना श्रोता के लिए आसान बना देता है और वक्ता / गायक को यह दृढ़ विश्वास दिलाता है कि वह जिस संदेश को देने की कोशिश कर रहा है, वह समझा जा रहा है। पारी-पारी से गाने के रूप में, ध्रुवपद (टेक) गाना, कुछ पंक्तियां मिलकर गाना या मुख्य गायक की पंक्तियों की प्रत्यक्ष पुनरावृत्ति, ये सब पुनरावृत्तियां श्रोता को उस हद तक सुगमतापूर्वक प्रस्तुति में भाग लेने का अवसर प्रदान करती हैं जिस हद तक पुनरावृत्ति जैसे साधन के बिना भाग लेना संभव ही नही है"। (*वही*, पृष्ठ 129)[22]

देवनारायण की कथा की मौखिक शैली कई स्तरों पर पुनरावर्त्तक है। पुनरावृत्ति का एक स्पष्ट रूप गाए गए भाग को पुनः शब्दशः जोर से गाना है। इसके अलावा हर पद्य भाग के अंत में ध्रुवपद (टेक) की पुनरावृत्ति होती है, और "युद्ध के दृश्यों" को चित्रित करने के लिए कुछ संचित विवरणों का उपयोग किया जाता है। इसी प्रकार कुछ ऐसे परिच्छेदों में भी पुनरावृत्ति होती है जिनमें भिन्न-भिन्न व्यक्तियों द्वारा एक विशिष्ट कार्य को दोहराया जाता है। उदाहरण के लिए भूणा की खोज में परिवार का हर सदस्य भूणा के लिए एक पत्र छोछू भाट को विश्वासपूर्वक सौंपता है और

---

21. टन्नेन (1994:20) में कहा गया है।
22. इसके बावजूद कविता के मौखिक रूपों में पुनरावृति का सामान्य उच्चारण होने पर फिन्नेगन ने निष्कर्ष निकाला है कि मौखिक कविता में पुनरावृति का सही महत्त्व स्पष्ट नहीं है। (*वही*, पृष्ठ 132)

सम्बन्धित खण्डों को क्रमानुसार गाता है। यहां हम उपयोग किए गए वाक्यांशों में पुनरावृत्ति की मात्रा पाते हैं, जिसमें ऊपर जिक्र किए अनुसार, विभिन्न व्यक्तियों द्वारा किए गए एक ही कार्य का वर्णन है। यहां पुनरावृत्ति के उपयोग से उस क्षण की भावनात्मक और काव्यात्मक गुणवत्ता बढ़ जाती है, जिसमें कथा के अर्थों में परिवार के एक सदस्य के साथ पुनर्मिलन का वादा निहित है। हालांकि ये उदाहरण कथा के काव्यात्मक ढांचे से सम्बन्धित हैं लेकिन गायकों को शामिल करते हुए ऊपर वर्णित पुनरावृत्ति की किस्म का भाषण करने की शैली को बतलाने वाली कही जा सकती है। इस मामले में ऐसा नहीं है कि गाए हुए खण्डों की पंक्तियां, उद्घोषित किये जाने वाले खण्ड में दोहराई जाती हों, बल्कि जो पंक्तियां उद्घोषित किये गए खण्डों में हैं वे मुख्य गायक के साथी द्वारा दोहराई जाती हैं। इस प्रकार "आन्तरिक" पुनरावृत्ति "बाह्य" पुनरावृत्ति के समानान्तर होती है। और विभिन्न पात्रों के बीच शृंखलाबद्ध बोले गए कथा के "आंतरिक" संवाद गायक के "बाह्य" संवाद के सदृश्य होते हैं।

लेकिन इस मामले में भी पुनरावृत्ति काफी भिन्न होती है और अनेक संभावनाएं इसमें शामिल रहती हैं। तथापि, स्वयं पुनरावृत्ति की प्रवृत्ति उस चीज के रूप में जो आवश्यक रूप से उत्पन्न नहीं होती बल्कि "पुनः उत्पन्न होती हैं" देते हुए इसका अभिप्राय यह होगा कि हालांकि गायक के पास कई विकल्प उपलब्ध हो सकते हैं लेकिन उच्चारण का निर्णायक चयन पहले गायक के भाषण द्वारा सुनिश्चित होता है। दूसरे गायक के हिस्से की सृजनात्मकता तब दिए गए अनुक्रियात्मक ढंगों की शृंखला से चयन करने में निहित होती है। लेकिन दूसरे गायक की अनुक्रिया पुनरावृत्ति तक ही सीमित नहीं होती। वह अपनी स्वयं की कथावस्तु भी उत्पन्न कर सकता है, जो या तो पहले कही गई पंक्तियों की व्याख्या हो सकती है अथवा कोई अतिरिक्त कथन हो सकता है जो कथा को आगे बढ़ाता है।

पुनरावृत्ति के उदाहरण

वार्तालाप सम्बन्धी संभाषण के संदर्भ में टन्नेन (1994: 54) ने पुनरावृत्ति की विभिन्न किस्मों के बीच भेद किया है –

> प्रथम, कोई अपनी पुनरावृत्ति और दूसरों की पुनरावृत्ति में भेद कर सकता है। द्वितीय, पुनरावृत्ति के दृष्टान्त, आकार में स्थिरता के पैमाने पर रखे जा सकते हैं जो बिल्कुल सही पुनरावृत्ति (किन्हीं शब्दों का समान लयबद्ध पद्धति में) से भावानुवाद तक (विभिन्न शब्दों में समान विचार) क्रमबद्ध होते हैं। पैमाने के बीचोंबीच . . . विभिन्नताओं के साथ पुनरावृत्ति है; जैसेकि प्रश्न कथनों में बदल जाते हैं; कथन प्रश्नों में परिवर्तित हो जाते हैं, एक शब्द या वाक्यांश बदल जाने से पुनरावृत्ति होना और व्यक्ति या काल बदल जाने से पुनरावृत्ति होना . . . अनुकरणीय लय, जिसमें पूर्ववर्ती उच्चारण के रूप में पूर्णतया भिन्न शब्दों का उच्चारण समान वाक्य रचना और लय में किया जाता है।

कथा में पुनरावृत्ति का क्या काम है, इस बात की तरफ मुड़ने से पहले मैं पुनरावृत्ति के कुछ भिन्न-भिन्न उदाहरण प्रस्तुत करना चाहूंगा जो दूसरे गायक द्वारा प्रत्युत्तर की उपश्रेणी के रूप में पेश किए गए हैं। दूसरे गायक के उच्चारण में शामिल पुनरावृत्ति पर विचार-विनिमय करते हुए मैं पहले उस बात पर ध्यान केन्द्रित करूंगा जिसे टन्नेन ने "दूसरों की पुनरावृत्ति" (पहले गायक के मामले में) कहा है।

उदाहरण 1 : हूबहू पुनरावृत्ति

हूबहू पुनरावृत्ति के मामले में दूसरे गायक द्वारा वाक्यांश के केवल एक भाग को शब्दशः दोहराया जाता है।[23] यह स्पष्ट है कि दूसरा गायक शब्दशः पुनरावृत्ति को प्रायः मुख्य गायक द्वारा बोले गए एक, दो या तीन शब्दों पर बल देने के लिए करता है। पूरी पंक्ति की पुनरावृत्ति बहुत ही कम होती है और वह भी तब जब यह काफी छोटी होती है। दूसरा गायक एक बार शब्दों को दोहराकर स्वयं वाक्यांश को आगे बढ़ा सकता है और इसके द्वारा या तो नई जानकारी को जोड़ता है या पूर्ववर्ती पंक्ति को पुनः व्यवस्थित करके पुनः जोर देकर बोलता है।

> कीयो : हाँ श्री महाराज म्हारै कनै ही है
> (हाँ "म्हारे कन्नै है" कीयो)
> औरूँ मावो बठै ही कराँ
> (हाँ "बठै ही कराँ चालो सावो ही चालूँ")
> स्याल तूँ ह्वियो
> ("स्याल तूँ है" कीयो)
> पडिहार को नाँव लियो जराँ भाट के एडी की चाटी जळ लागी जी जाळा
> (हाँ "लागी" कीयो)
> आबा देय भई देव का घर की बजरशिला माथा पर आडी है
> ("आडी है" कीयो)
> जीयान जूजळो नै मरै जति टैम हि कोनि लगावै हाथि नै मारताँ
> ("इ हाथि नै मारताँ" कीयो)
> तनै चिर आवै काँई
> (हाँ "चिर आवै" कीयो "औ बाबा भाट")
> आपनै दरबार के माँयनै एक सूणी रहवै
> (हाँ "सूणी रहवै" कीयो)

23. मुख्य और दूसरे गायक के काव्यांशों के लिए इन खण्डों को निम्नलिखित उदाहरणों में महत्त्व दिया गया है। दूसरे गायक की पंक्तियां कोष्ठक में दी गई हैं।

उदाहरण 2

निम्नलिखित उदाहरणों मे शब्दों का क्रम परिवर्तन है, जबकि वाक्यांश का अर्थ वही रहता है। कुछ मामलों में शब्दों के स्थान पर उनके पर्यायवाची शब्दों का प्रयोग करते हुए उसी आकार का भिन्न वाक्यांश बना दिया जाता है। इस मामले में, जहां दूसरा गायक मुख्य गायक की पंक्तियों को हूबहू नहीं दोहराता, केवल कुछ और शब्दों को जोड़कर वाक्यांश अधिक लम्बे हैं, जैसाकि ऊपर दिए गए उदाहरण में है। स्पष्टतया दूसरे गायक की "अपने स्वयं के शब्दों" में पंक्तियों को प्रस्तुत करने की स्वतंत्रता भी विषय को आगे बढाने में एक विश्वसनीय या हूबहू पुनरावृत्ति से अधिक; पुनरावृत्ति को प्रस्तुत करने में सुविधाजनक है –

दरबार का हूक्मूँ बगड़ावतां को भाट मनवार को हि लियोड़ो कदै कोनि हो
(हां "मनवार को कदै हि लियो कोनि हो")
कनै जो पिसियो लगाबा नै एक हि
("इ म्हारै कनै है कोनि")
दरबार का हुक्मूँ लाल में तो नीमा थारै जणा आयो भइ
(हां "इ वास्तै आयोड़ा हूं")
जणा कांइ देरा है भइ
(हां "कीं देरा कोनि बा में तो")
कियो घूलियो एकानइ होजा भइ कंवर
खाण्डेराव की असवारि अब की आरी है।
(हां "कंवर खण्डेरावजी पधार रिया है" कीयो)
भूणोजी ओ कीयो भाट मन में देखियो
थारा धणी नै सुर्गयाणी सुणयो
("पण सुर्गयाणी जरूर है" कीयो)
म्हाना बाप दादा को नांव जाणै कोनि
(हां "तूं जाणै कोय नी कै" कीयो)
मन में देखियो कांई बात हुइ माथा नै
कामणावूं बांध ल्यो
(हां "माथा नै काट बांध ल्यो" कीयो "जादूवूं")
तनै ठा ह्रियो कोनि ह्रियो
(हां "तनै ठा पड़ियो कोनि पड़ियो")

एकाक्षरीय पुनर्योजक

पुनरावृत्ति की ऊपर वर्णित दो आवर्तक किस्मों के अतिरिक्त विशिष्ट एकाक्षरीय शब्दों या विस्मयादिबोधकों की पुनरावृत्ति होती है जिसे दूसरा गायक अनुक्रिया के रूप में उपयोग करता

है। ये शब्द प्रवचन के दौरान उन अन्तरालों में दोहराए जाते हैं जिनमें दूसरा गायक मुख्य गायक की पंक्तियों को नहीं दोहराता, पुनः व्यवस्थित नहीं करता या वाक्यांश अथवा शब्द नहीं जोड़ता। एक तरह से वे प्रायः आकारहीन या अर्थहीन किस्म की अनुक्रियाएं मानी जाती हैं। दूसरे गायक श्री मोटाराम "वाह वाह" और "म्हे" का उपयोग इसी "आकारहीन" अनुक्रिया के रूप में करते हैं। इस प्रकार की अनुक्रिया का वाद्य रचना में एक ढांचा सुनिश्चित करना काफी कठिन है। "म्हे" शब्द "वाह वाह" से बहुत छोटा है और इसका उपयोग विस्मयादिबोधक चिह्नों या विस्मयादिबोधक शब्दों के समय या अल्पविराम के उपयोग द्वारा उत्पन्न अन्तराल तक को भरने के लिए किया जाता है। उदाहरण के लिए –

नीमदे कीयो "रे मुंग्ता" (म्हे)
"जगीशया" (म्हे)
कीयो "धूलिया" (म्हे)
दरबार का हुक्मूं कीयो "भाट" (म्हे)
निंगेवान सिरदारां कीयो "श्री महाराज" (म्हे)
कीयो "नीमा" (म्हे)
कीयो "भैरवनाथ" (म्हे)
कनात के मांयनै बड़ सिरदार कीयो "श्री महाराज" (म्हे)
मुण्ड अगला सिरदार कीयों "रे भाई धूलिया" (म्हे)
"अरे जगीशया" (म्हे)
"अरे सिरदारां" (म्हे)

उपरोक्त उदाहरणों में हम देख सकते हैं कि "म्हे" जो कि एक व्यक्ति के नाम के बाद नियमित रूप से उपयोग किया जाता है वह प्रत्यक्ष भाषण की शुरुआत में बोला जाता है। यह एक व्यक्ति द्वारा दूसरे को सम्बोधित किए जाने पर बाद में विराम-चिह्न के रूप में कार्य करता है। लेकिन "म्हे" का केवल यह उपयोग नहीं है। अन्य कई प्रकार के प्रयोग भी हैं और इसके उपयोग सम्बन्धी कोई एक नियम या पद्धति का निर्णय करना कठिन है। इसके भिन्न-भिन्न उपयोगों को समझाने के लिए कुछ उदाहरण नीचे दिए गए हैं –

"अरे अमलदार आदमी हूं" (म्हे)
"के कोय जमाना में बगड़ावत ह्विया" (म्हे)
तो भाट मन में देखियो "के मोहरां तो लधी" (म्हे)
देव को नांव लेय (म्हे)
देव को नांव लेय अर धूल में भर ढाल नै (म्हे)
कियो "भाई घणा दिन ह्विया सुणियां ई नाइ" (म्हे)

उपरोक्त उदाहरणों में हम देखते हैं कि "म्हे" का उपयोग अपरिवर्तनीय रूप से प्रत्यक्ष भाषण

के एक खण्ड के अंत में या एक ऐसे भाग के अंत में भी किया गया है जो प्रत्यक्ष भाषण में शामिल नहीं है।

आइए अब यह सुनिश्चित करने के लिए कि "म्हे" और "वाह वाह" का उपयोग कहां होता है, कथा के कुछ विस्तृत उदाहरण देखते है –

> अरे अमलदार आदमी हूं (म्हे) / मैं सुणयोडि बात है भाई नीमा रे (हां "देखियोड़ी कोनी" कीयो) / के कोय जमाना में बगड़ावत ह्िया (म्हे) / पंचतोली मोहरां काचा तारां में पोय पोय (अर) अटीकर घोड़ा के गलै ("में राळ राळ दपटाया बतावै है" कीयो) / कह बतावै बै मोहरां भाई रे टूट टूट अर (हां "पड़ी बजार में") / मैं देखूं (म्हे) / एक हि म्हनै मोहर ("आज लाध जावे") / आज आज को अमल पाणी ("म्हारै हो जावे" कियो) / मैं देखूं भगवान खर्चो दे म्हनै (वाह वाह) / नीमदे कीयो "रे मूंगता (म्हे) / कुण देश को है बोल" ("कुणसो देश को अयो तूं" कीयो) / कीयो सात समन्द्रा पार को हू (हां "सात समन्द्रा पार का हूं") / "कुण लोग है" ("जकि बता") / कीयो "राजावों को बई को भाट हूं" (वाह वाह) / "नांव" "सेंसारी दुनिया जगीशयो कह अर बतलावै" (हां "जगीशयो कह अर बतलावै करै" कीयो)।

उपरोक्त परिच्छेद में छोछू भाट और राणा के छोटे भाई नीमदे के बीच वार्तालाप है। छोछू भाट संवाद की शुरुआत "अरे अमलदार आदमी हूं" से करता है। इसके बाद "म्हे" कहा जाता है तथा उसके बाद छोछू भाट द्वारा आगे कही गई टिप्पणी है। छोछू भाट का कथन "मै देखूं भगवान खर्चो दे म्हनै" तक चलता रहता है। उसके कथन के अंत में "वाह वाह" कहा गया है। एक बार जहां "म्हे" का उपयोग {मैं देखूं (म्हे)} किया गया है, को छोड़कर चोचू भाट के कथन को श्री मोटाराम द्वारा विराम नहीं दिया गया। दूसरी तरफ श्री हुक्माराम द्वारा बोली गई पंक्तियों में श्री मोटाराम द्वारा अपनी अनुक्रिया में कुछ जोड़ दिया गया है अथवा उन्हें विस्तार दे दिया गया है। "वाह वाह" के प्रथम उच्चारण के बाद नीमदे अपने हिस्से का संवाद बोलना शुरु करता है। यहां नीमदे द्वारा चोचू भाट को "रे मूंगता (म्हे)" सम्बोधित किए जाने में "म्हे" का उपयोग अंत में विराम-चिह्न के रूप में किया गया है। "वाह वाह" का उच्चारण तब किया गया है जब छोछू भाट ने अपना कथन "राजावों को बई को भाट हूं" (वाह वाह) / समाप्त कर दिया।

ऊपर उद्धृत परिच्छेद में हम पाते हैं कि "म्हे" का उपयोग एक पात्र के कथन के भीतर विराम-चिह्न के रूप में किया गया है। "वाह वाह" का उपयोग, दूसरी तरफ, एक पात्र के कथन की समाप्ति और दूसरे पात्र के कथन के प्रारम्भ को चिह्नित करने के लिए किया गया है। इस प्रकार "म्हे" और "वाह वाह" का उपयोग इन उदाहरणों में एक पात्र से सम्बन्धित कथन के अंशों और विभिन्न पात्रों के कथन को चिह्नित करने के लिए किया गया है। यद्यपि इस विवरण में (म्हे और वाह वाह का) एक पद्धतियुक्त उपयोग का आभास मिलता है, लेकिन ऐसे उदाहरण भी हैं जिनमें "वाह वाह" का उपयोग आन्तरिक रूप से एक पात्र से सम्बन्धित बोली गई पंक्तियों के भीतर वैसे ही किया गया

है जैसेकि "म्हे" का उपयोग किया गया है। ऐसे उदाहरणों में हम पाते हैं कि "वाह वाह" का उपयोग एक पात्र विशेष के कथन के भीतर विराम-चिह्न के रूप में किया गया है। इसके विपरीत "म्हे" का उपयोग पात्र के कथन के अंत में किया गया है। हालांकि कुल मिलाकर बारम्बार ऐसा हुआ है जिसमें "म्हे" का उपयोग कथन के भीतर और "वाह वाह" का उपयोग अंत को चिह्नित करने के लिए किया गया है। इसके अतिरिक्त "गाव" खण्ड को बोलने वाले व्यक्ति का परिचय कराने वाले वाक्य के अंत में "वाह वाह" का उपयोग नियमित रूप से किया गया है। उदाहरण के लिए –

> दरबार का हुक्मूं भूणोजी बोले (वाह वाह) / कांई समचार कहवै देखां . . . तो भाट बोले (वाह वाह) / कांइ घोड़ीमाता नै समचार कहवै देखां . . . मीर बोले (वाह वाह) / कांई समचार कांई भाट नाइ कहवै देखां . . . . कलाळी बोले (वाह वाह) / कांई समचार कहवै देखां

यहां यह स्पष्ट है कि "वाह वाह" का उपयोग कथन में विराम उत्पन्न करने के लिए नहीं किया गया है बल्कि वाह शब्द के मूल अर्थ को उपयोग में लाते हुए एक विस्मयादिबोधक शब्द के रूप में किया गया है, जिसका अर्थ है – "बहुत अच्छे" "आश्चर्यजनक" या "भव्य"।

समचार

उपरोक्त पक्तियां यह भी स्पष्ट कर देती हैं कि "गाव" परिच्छेद में सामान्यतः दूसरे पात्र के कथन की अनुक्रिया में किसी पात्र विशेष द्वारा बोले गए प्रत्यक्ष भाषण की "पोटलियां" (पैकेट) होती हैं। प्रत्यक्ष भाषण की इन पोटलियों का उल्लेख "समचार" के रूप में किया जा सकता है। इस शब्द (समचार) के अर्थ हैं – "न्यूज", संदेश, "रिपोर्ट" या सूचना। इसमें "संवाद" का अर्थ भी छिपा हो सकता है। देवनारायण की कथा परम्परा के घटकों में "समचार" को प्रायः कथा के भीतर संवाद को चिह्नित करने वाला एक "तकनीकी" दर्जा दिया गया है। इस प्रकार गायक या श्रोता एक दिए गए परिच्छेद के विषय में पूछ सकते हैं, "यह किसका समचार है?" या साधारणतया "कौन-सा समचार है?" ताकि यह सुनिश्चित किया जा सके कि किस बिन्दु तक कथा पहुंच चुकी है या किस बिन्दु से इसे लिया जाना चाहिए। कभी-कभी गायक भी समचार गाने के तुरन्त बाद पूछ सकता है "यह समचार किसने कहा?" प्रश्न करने (और इसका उत्तर देने) का यह ढंग समचार कहने वाले की पहचान को गायकों तथा श्रोताओं के मस्तिष्क में, पुष्ट करता है। इस प्रकार कथा न केवल गीत (गाव) और उद्घोषणात्मक गद्य (अर्थाव) के बीच आदान-प्रदान के माध्यम से आगे बढती है बल्कि गाए गए परिच्छेद की मात्रा को बनाने वाले "संदेशों", "रिपोर्टो" "समाचारों" या "संवादों" के माध्यम से भी आगे बढती है। एक धारणा के रूप में "समचार" शब्द का अर्थ कथा की सारभूत इकाईयों का वर्णन करने के लिए उपयोग में लाया जाता है, एक बार फिर यह कथा की "संवादशील" रूपरेखा को उजागर करता है। न केवल कथा अपने जोश के साथ गाए जाने वाले खण्डों में पात्रों के बीच बोले जाने वाले

संवादों से बनी होती है, बल्कि गाए जाने वाले खण्ड भी प्रत्यक्ष भाषण की इकाईयों के रूप में समझे जाते हैं जो पूर्ववर्ती संवाद के पैमानों के भीतर एक "उत्तर" बनाते हैं।

गाव के चार पंक्तियों वाले पद्य भाग को शुरु करने से पहले बारम्बार प्रयोग किए जाने वाले "समचार" की धारणा के अतिरिक्त गायक श्री हुक्माराम भी भिन्न प्रकार से "वार्ता" शब्द का उपयोग करते हैं जिसका अर्थ है 'कहानी", "वार्तालाप", "वृतान्त / सच्चाई / वास्तविकता / तथ्य", "भाषण", "बात", "छोटा किस्सा", "कथा", रिपोर्ट"। इस मामले में पूर्व-पद्य पंक्ति सामान्यतः है – "कांई वार्ता बन जावै देखां" जैसाकि समचार के मामले में होता है, इससे ऐसा अर्थ नहीं निकलता कि कोई बोल रहा है, बल्कि ऐसा अर्थ निकलता है कि निम्नलिखित गीत खण्डों में एक घटना या एक दृश्य का वर्णन होने को है। गीत खण्ड जोकि वार्ता की श्रेणी में आते हैं "समचार" के रूप में वार्णित खण्डों से काफी हद तक लम्बे होते हैं। इस प्रकार, एक वार्ता में नौ पंक्तियां हो सकती हैं। (जिसकी दूसरी और तीसरी पंक्तियों के अंतिम शब्द तुकान्त हैं।) हर पंक्ति में "समचार" खण्डों से सम्बन्धित पंक्ति की अपेक्षा अधिक सारांश होता है। नौ पंक्तियों की वार्ता के अलावा दो पार्टियों के बीच युद्ध या विवाद की तैयारियों का वर्णन करते हुए गाए जाने वाले लम्बे खण्ड भी होते हैं। ये विवरण शुद्ध रूप से मानक हैं और इनमें दस या अठारह पंक्तियां होती हैं। यहां भी हर एक पंक्ति में "समचार" के रूप में प्रतिष्ठित पद्य खण्डों की अपेक्षा अधिक सारांश होता है।

पुनरावृत्ति का कार्य

टन्नेन (1994: 47 एफ) ने वार्तालाप में पुनरावृत्ति का विश्लेषण करते हुए निम्नलिखित आधारभूत प्रश्न किए हैं –

> वार्तालाप में पुनरावृत्ति क्यों होती है? हम एक ही बात को बार-बार कहकर अपनी ऊर्जा क्यों गंवाते हैं? पुनरावृत्ति के विभिन्न उद्देश्यों को एक साथ उत्पादन, ज्ञानशक्ति, संयोजन और पारस्परिक प्रभाव उपश्रेणियों के अन्तर्गत रखा जा सकता है। संभाषण के इन कार्यों की अनुरूपता संगति और अन्तर्वैयक्तिक अन्तर्गतता की स्थापना में अत्यन्त प्रमुख कार्य प्रदान करती है।

उत्पादन के मामले में टन्नेन ने स्पष्ट किया कि "पुनरावृत्ति वक्ता को कम ऊर्जा खर्च करके अधिक समर्थता से भाषा उत्पन्न करने में सक्षम बनाती है। यह अधिक भाषा अधिक धाराप्रवाहिता को सुसाध्य बनाती है।" (*वही,* पृष्ठ 48) पुनरावृत्ति "कम घने संभाषण द्वारा ज्ञानशक्ति को सुसाध्य बनाती है। यदि बोले गए सभी शब्द नई जानकारी रखते हैं और उनमें से कुछ ही शब्द दोहराए जाएं तो अपेक्षाकृत कम जानकारी का संचार होगा।" (*वही,* पृष्ठ 49)। पुनरावृत्ति के जरिए सम्बन्ध जुड़ जाता है क्योंकि "यह सम्बन्ध जोड़ने और बांधने का कार्य करती है। वाक्यों, वाक्यांशों और शब्दों की पुनरावृत्ति दिखाती है कि कैसे नए उच्चारण पूर्ववर्ती संभाषण से जुड़े हैं और कैसे संभाषण में प्रस्तुत किए गए विचार एक-दूसरे से जुड़े हैं।" (*वही,* पृष्ठ 50) टन्नेन यह स्पष्ट करना जारी रखती हैं कि

उत्पादन, ज्ञानशक्ति और संयोजक के सम्बन्ध में पुनरावृत्ति का कार्य "वार्तालाप में अर्थ उत्पन्न करने में सहायता करना है। लेकिन पुनरावृत्ति सामाजिक उद्देश्यों को संपादित या सामान्यतः वार्तालाप के कार्य को व्यवस्थित करते हुए वार्ता के पारस्परिक प्रभाव के स्तर पर भी कार्य करती है।" (*वही*, पृष्ठ 51)।

कथा के भीतर पुनरावृत्ति की विभिन्न संभावनाओं पर इतना विचार-विमर्श करने के बाद आइए अब ऊपर कहे गए चार शीर्षकों के अन्तर्गत पुनरावृत्ति के कार्य तथा भूमिका की तरफ मुड़ें। इन शीर्षकों में पहली श्रेणी है – "उत्पादन"। इस विषय में पुनरावृत्ति "अधिक भाषा (वाग्व्यवहार), अधिक धाराप्रवाहिता" को सुसाध्य बनाती है। निश्चित रूप से यह लक्षण अर्थाव खण्डों में प्रकट होता है जहां दूसरा गायक पहले गायक की पंक्तियों के भाग दोहराता है। निःसंदेह, जानकारी देते समय अधिक समान शब्दों के प्रयोग से यहां अधिक भाषा (वाग्व्यवहार) उत्पन्न होती है। कुल मिलाकर पुनरावृत्ति के जरिए कथा लम्बी और विस्तृत हो जाती है, और "अधिक भाषा (वाग्व्यवहार)" का उत्पादन भी वास्तव में इसके (कथा के) लम्बे महाकाव्यात्मक विस्तार में योगदान करता है। तथापि अधिक भाषा (वाग्व्यवहार) का उत्पादन यहां दूसरी श्रेणी, नामतः ज्ञानशक्ति से गहरा जुड़ा हुआ है। इस प्रकार अर्थाव खण्डों में गाव परिच्छेदों की पुनरावृत्ति गाए जाने वाले पद्यों को बेहतर ढंग से समझना आसान बना देती है। वास्तव में अर्थाव शब्द – जिसके अर्थ हैं "स्पष्टीकरण", "अर्थ", "व्याख्या" – स्वयं संकेत करता है कि संभाषित गद्य में पद्य की पुनरावृत्ति पहले कही गई बात को अधिक स्पष्ट ज्ञानशक्ति देने का अर्थ रखती है।

पुनः यहां हम पाते हैं कि उपयोग की गई शब्दाबली परम्परा के भीतर कथा और इसे कहने की मनोभावना सम्बन्धी, बहुस्तरीय अनुभूति का सुझाव देती है। इस प्रकार खण्डों के पीछे के परिच्छेद "गीत" के विपरीत गद्य नहीं कहे जा सकते, बल्कि इनका अभिप्राय "अर्थ" या "स्पष्टीकरण" से है। यह भेद हमें पुनः यह देखने में समर्थ बनाता है कि कथा की अवधारणा कैसे बनती है। उपयोग की गई शब्दावली के अनुसार देवनारायण की कथा इस विषय में गेय खण्डों में समाहित है, जो बाद में प्रदर्शित और "स्पष्ट" किए गए हैं।[24] निःसंदेह "स्पष्टीकरण" के इस रूप में "कैसे और क्यों" प्रश्नों के उत्तर शामिल नहीं होते। यह गेय खण्डों को विभिन्न शब्दों में "स्पष्ट" नहीं करता। इसकी अपेक्षा यह भाषण करने के एक भिन्न ढंग में समान शब्दों की पुनरावृत्ति द्वारा स्पष्ट करता है। टन्नेन ने अनुभव किया है कि यह स्वयं पुनरावृत्ति ही है जो शब्दों और वाक्यों के अर्थों को तब तक खाली

---

24. संक्षिप्त, सुगठित पद्य – जिसके पीछे इसकी व्याख्या रहती है – की यह पद्धति भारतीय दार्शनिक और साहित्यिक विधाओं में से एक विधा की याद दिलाती है जो कथावस्तु को पदानुपद पुनः प्रस्तुत करती है तथा जिसमें प्रत्येक पद के बाद एक लंबी, विस्तृत व्याख्या रहती है। ऐसी और सहित्यिक व्याख्याओं और देवनारायण की मौखिक कथा के बीच भेद निःसन्देह इस तथ्य में निहित है कि बाद में कथा (भी) अर्थाव खण्डों में चलती है जो स्वयं अगले गाव का पूर्वज्ञान प्रदान करते हैं और आगे इसे प्रकार चलता रहता है।।

छोड़ देती है जब तक कि अर्थाव की प्रारम्भिक पंक्तियों में विशेष रूप से कोई नई जानकारी नहीं दी जाती। नई जानकारी बाद की पंक्तियों में दी जाती है। लेकिन यहां भी पुनरावृत्ति होती है जिसके परिणामस्वरूप पहले गायक के उच्चारण का महत्त्व समझना आसान होता है। लेकिन अर्थाव के भीतर पुनरावृत्ति – जिसमें प्रायः केवल कुछ, चयनित शब्द होते हैं – साधारण ज्ञानशक्ति को सुसाध्य बनाने से अधिक बोलने में शब्दों पर जोर देने के उपकरण के रूप में कार्य करती है। इस प्रकार जिन नए शब्दों की पुनरावृत्ति होती है (कभी-कभी पूरी पंक्ति बदले हुए क्रम में), वे अपने भीतर वह अर्थ समाहित रखते हैं, जो पहला गायक अपने भाषण में कहना चाहता है। इस प्रकार पुनरावृत्ति अपने भीतर अर्थाव और इसके खण्डों को शामिल रखते हुए, न केवल ज्ञानशक्ति बल्कि बोलने में शब्दों पर जोर को सुसाध्य बनती है / पैदा करती है।[25]

टन्नेन की तीसरी श्रेणी "संयोजन" है – "वाक्यों, वाक्यांशों और शब्दों की पुनरावृत्ति" दिखाती है कि कैसे नए उच्चारण पूर्ववर्ती संभाषण से जुड़े हैं, और कैसे संभाषण में प्रस्तुत विचार एक-दूसरे से सम्बधित हैं।" (*वही,* पृष्ठ 50) ऐसा लगता है कि यह श्रेणी देवनारायण की कथा से सम्बन्धित स्थिति – जिसमें विचार कम हैं और दृश्य तथा घटनाएं अधिक हैं, जो एक-दूसरे से जुड़े हैं – की तुलना में प्रतिदिन के वार्तालाप से अधिक जुड़ी है। दृश्यों और घटनाओं का संयोग, निःसंदेह, आंशिक रूप से पुनरावृत्ति के माध्यम से विकसित किया गया है, लेकिन इससे भी अधिक यह कथा में खण्डों और उपखण्डों के ढांचे द्वारा उत्पन्न किया गया है।

जैसाकि टन्नेन ने कहा है, ये तीन कार्य अन्ततः "वार्तालाप में अर्थ पैदा करने (और) सामाजिक उद्देश्यों का सम्पादन करने या सामान्यतः वार्तालाप के कार्य को व्यवस्थित करने से संबधित हैं।" (*वही,* पृष्ठ 52) यह पूर्णतया स्पष्ट है कि कथा के विशिष्ट विषय में पुनरावृत्ति अर्थ पैदा करने से भी सम्बंध रखती है। इस मामले में अर्थ की उत्पत्ति स्वयं गायकों की ओर निर्देशित नहीं की जाती, बल्कि श्रोताओं की ओर निर्देशित की जाती है, जो कथा की प्रस्तुति को सुनते हैं। तथापि, केवल एक शुद्ध भाषायी स्तर पर अर्थ उत्पन्न नहीं होता। यहां यह देवनारायण के जीवन और कार्यों और उनकी शक्ति के आह्वान में भाग लेने वाले भक्तों के इर्द-गिर्द घूमने वाले कथा के परिमाण को "प्रकट करने" के द्वारा "अनुभव के" स्तर पर भी उत्पन्न होता है। इस प्रकार, कथा और उसको कहने में अन्तर्निहित पुनरावृत्ति के विभिन्न रूप साहित्यिक लक्षण से आकार बदलकर अभ्यास के कार्यक्षेत्र में सम्मिलित होते जाते हैं। समूची प्रस्तुति के विभिन्न अन्य पहलुओं के साथ-साथ वे भी मस्तिष्क-सम्बन्धी सांस्कृतिक और धार्मिक तत्त्वों की अनन्य क्रिया के रूप में अर्थों को उत्पन्न करने में एक औपचारिक चरित्र ग्रहण कर लेते हैं।

---

25. जब पहले गायक की पंक्तियों की पुनरावृत्ति में दूसरे गायक की बोलने की शैली को सही रूप में सुना जाता है तो इसे समझना आसान हो जाता है।

संवाद

जैसाकि ऊपर कहा गया है कथा कम-से-कम दो स्तरों पर "आवर्त्तक" है – एक है आकार का स्तर (पद्य और गद्य आदि) और दूसरा है भाषण का स्तर (मुख्य गायक और दूसरा गायक)। इससे भी आगे यह स्पष्ट हो जाता है कि कथा दो प्रकार से "संवादपूर्ण" है – पहले प्रकार में पात्रों के बीच के संवाद कथा योजना के रूप में केन्द्रीय स्थिति ग्रहण कर लेते हैं। दूसरे प्रकार में गायक परस्पर संवाद में लगे होते हैं (और निःसंदेह संवाद का तीसरा रूप पैदा करते हुए श्रोताओं के साथ भी संवाद में लगे होते हैं।) इस प्रकार, जैसाकि पहले संकेत किया गया है, एक संवादशील घटना के रूप में कथा की समझ न केवल इसकी भाषा को समझने में होती है बल्कि मौखिक कथा-ढांचे[26] और कथा में प्रस्तुत संसार के संवादशील ढांचे को भी बनाने के लिए वाहन के रूप में उच्चारणों की प्रकृति और संबंध को समझने में भी होती है।

इस तथ्य को केन्द्र में रखते हुए कि देवनारायण की कथा की प्रस्तुति अनिवार्य रूप से दो आवाजों द्वारा बनी है जो उच्चारणों के आदान-प्रदान से कथा के अंगों को बुनती है, यह उचित होगा कि इस संवाद की प्रकृति का परीक्षण किया जाए। जैसाकि ऊपर कहा गया है, संवाद के इस रूप को बोलने की शैली, जिसे हम बातचीत कहते हैं, की श्रेणी के भीतर रखना संभव है। स्वाभावतः देवनारायण की कथा के दौरान होने वाले वार्तालाप सम्बन्धी संवाद की किस्म "प्रतिदिन के जीवन" में होने वाले वार्तालाप सम्बन्धी संवाद की किस्म से भिन्न है। यद्यपि दिन-प्रतिदिन के जीवन के वार्तालाप विषयों की किस्म के इर्द-गिर्द केन्द्रित होते हैं और विभिन्न आकारों में विकसित हो सकते हैं, लेकिन देवनारायण की कथा के दौरान हुआ वार्तालाप कथा की परिभाषा द्वारा केन्द्रित और सुनिश्चित है। गायकों के बीच वार्तालाप या आदान-प्रदान का रूप भी पूरी तरह सुव्यवस्थित है। यह विकल्पों के एक समूह में सीमित है जिस पर विचार-विमर्श ऊपर किया जा चुका है।[27] कुल मिलाकर गायकों के बीच आदान-प्रदान की वार्तालाप सम्बन्धी प्रकृति का भिन्न आकार है, जो प्रतिदिन के वार्तालाप में सम्भव नहीं है। प्रतिदिन के वार्तालाप में सदैव यह संभावना बनी रहती है कि अनुक्रिया करने वाला (श्रोता) वक्ता बन जाए और वक्ता श्रोता बन जाए, लेकिन कथा में श्रोता की पहचान सदैव निश्चित बनी रहती है। दूसरा गायक भी पहले गायक के उच्चारण में पुनर्योजक मिलाता है न कि पहले गायक के उच्चारण का जवाब देता है। इसलिए कथा-शैली द्वारा श्रोता और वक्ता की भूमिका पूर्व निश्चित कर दी जाती है। यद्यपि इससे गायकों के बीच संवाद में कुछ लोचहीनता आ जाती है लेकिन इससे दूसरे गायक के पुनर्योजकों को अभिव्यक्त करने के लिए विकल्पों का एक समूह

---

26. भाषा और उच्चारण के बीच भेद की तुलना सासुरे द्वारा बनाए गए लैंग और पॅरोल के बीच भेद से की जा सकती है। इस प्रकार ". . . भाषा, सम्पूर्ण पद्धति या योजना और भाषण (सामान्य, जो कुछ असंतोषजनक है, पॅरोल का अनुवाद है) का विचार है या अवसर विशेष पर भाषा का व्यक्तिगत उपयोग है" (टर्नर 1987:14)।

27. देखिए "पुनरावृति" पर खण्ड।

भी प्राप्त हो जाता है।

इस बिन्दु पर यह ध्यान दिया जाना चाहिए कि देवनारायण की कथा परम्परा स्वयं में "पुनर्योजक" की धारणा पर आधारित है। इसे हूंकारों (हूंकारियों एक व्यक्ति है) कहा जाता है और इसका अभिप्राय लेखक को बोलते रहने के लिए प्रेरित करने की सम्मति या ज्ञानशक्ति और सहमति की शाब्दिक अभिव्यक्ति है। इस प्रकार यहां इस तथ्य के प्रति धारणात्मक जागरूकता है कि वक्ता को सदैव एक श्रोता चाहिए। दूसरे शब्दों में मानव संचार अनिवार्य रूप से "संवादशील" माना जाता है न कि स्वगत भाषण। वक्ता या गायक अपनी अभिव्यक्ति शून्य में नहीं कर सकता हूंकारों के द्वारा अभिव्यक्त श्रोता की सक्रिय ज्ञानशक्ति ही गायक की पंक्तियों को बाहर निकालती है और अन्ततः कथा की प्रगति को आसान बनाती है। सक्रिय श्रोता या प्रतिवादी की धारणा भाषण संचार की भक्तिन की समझ के काफी करीब है –

> ... जब श्रोता भाषण के अर्थ (भाषा के अर्थ) को समझता है तो वह उसी समय इसके इर्द-गिर्द एक सक्रिय, अनुक्रियात्मक दृष्टिकोण अपना लेता है। वह इससे या तो सहमत होता है अथवा असहमत होता है . . . इसमें वृद्धि करता है, इसका आशय स्थापित कर लेता है, इसे निष्पादन के लिए तैयार कर लेता है, आदि, आदि। जीवन्त भाषण, एक जीवन्त उच्चारण की कोई समझ स्वभावतः अनुक्रियात्मक होती है, यद्यपि इस सक्रियता की मात्रा पूर्णतया भिन्न-भिन्न होती है। इस प्रकार वास्तविक और सम्पूर्ण समझ सक्रिय रूप से अनुक्रियात्मक है और अनुक्रिया की प्रारम्भिक तैयारी की अवस्था के अतिरिक्त कुछ नहीं बनाती (जिस भी रूप में यह निश्चित होती है।) । (1986: 68.69)

समूचे "जीवन्त भाषण" के लिए अनुक्रिया के महत्त्व को बताते हुए यह आश्चर्यजनक नहीं है कि देवनारायण की कथा परम्परा में मौखिकता पर केन्द्रित है और इसमें एक मुख्य गायक और उसका प्रतिवादी होता है। यह ध्यान देने योग्य है कि ऐसी धारणा वास्तव में इतनी ही मात्रा तक बननी चाहिए।[28]

अभी तक हमने कथा की वास्तविक प्रस्तुति के संबंध में संवाद, वक्ता और प्रतिवादी की भूमिका का वर्णन किया है। लेकिन कथावस्तु के ढांचे पर किसी ऐसे कथारूप में क्या तात्पर्य होते हैं? एक कथावस्तु उच्चारणों की शृंखला द्वारा कैसे बनती है ("वाक्यों" से नहीं)? इस प्रकार किस तरह की

---

28. यह धारणा राजस्थान का अन्य कथा परम्पराओं (पाबूजी आदि) में भी पाई जाती है। वास्तव में अन्य कथनीय परम्पराओं में वक्ता और श्रोता की धारणा का परीक्षण करना उचित होगा जो न केवल कथाओं से सम्बन्धित है बल्कि संगीत और नृत्य के सम्बन्ध में भी है। एक तुलनात्मक अध्ययन संभवतः भारतीय अभिव्यक्ति परम्पराओं और कलाओं में भाषण की सुनिश्चितता को उद्घाटित करेगा। यह उस मार्ग के बारे में भी कुछ उद्घाटित कर सकता है जिसमें "यथार्थ" का निर्माण होता है।

कथावस्तु बनेगी? इस प्रकार, कथा की कथनीय प्रकृति को उच्चारणों की शृंखला के रूप में देते हुए कथावस्तु कभी पूर्ण और कभी आंशिक रूप से पूर्ण वाक्यों (अर्थात के विषय में), विस्मयादिबोधकों, एकाक्षरी पुनर्योजकों आदि का शरीर बन जाती है। कुल मिलाकर कथावस्तु व्याकरण की दृष्टि से गढ़ी गई भाषाविषयक इकाईयों (जैसेकि वाक्य) से बनी है। ये टूटी हुई इकाईयां केवल इस तथ्य के कारण अर्थ बनाती हैं कि वे एक मौखिक कथा में उच्चरित हुई हैं न कि गद्य में लिखे गए वाक्य हैं। कथा की मौखिक प्रकृति कथावस्तु के व्याकरण-सम्बन्धी ढांचे को "अपूर्णता" की अनुमति देती है। और जैसाकि ऊपर बताया गया है "अपूर्ण वाक्यों की शृंखला" के भीतर व्याकरण की दृष्टि से अपूर्ण आवर्तक उच्चारणों की शृंखला होती है जो मुख्य गायक के शब्दों के प्रति दूसरे गायक की अनुक्रिया द्वारा पैदा होती है। इस प्रकार स्वयं कथावस्तु में स्वयं की ही पुनरावृत्ति होती है। संवादित उच्चारणों की शृंखला के रूप में यह स्वयं का उत्तर देती है और स्वयं का ही अनुकरण करती है। इस प्रकार दूसरे गायक द्वारा उत्पन्न की गई कथावस्तु "स्वायत्त" या "मूल" होने का महत्त्व नहीं रखती। यह पहले गायक की कथावस्तु के साथ एक "अन्तर्कथावस्तु सम्बन्धी" प्रवाह में बंध जाती है। दूसरे शब्दों में यह मुख्य गायक की कथावस्तु का उल्लेख करके और वास्तव में इसे पुनः उत्पन्न करके उसी कथावस्तु की सीमाओं में विद्यमान रहती है।[29]

संवादित भाषण

ऊपर वर्णन किया गया है कि कथा का कहा जाना और स्वयं कथा, दो भिन्न-भिन्न अर्थों में संवादित है। पहला अर्थ वह है जिसमें सस्वर पाठ दो गायकों के बीच परस्पर विनिमय के आधार पर चलता है। यह परस्पर विनिमय – जो कि एक प्रस्तुति के सुनियोजन में स्थित संवादशील घटना है – उन श्रोताओं के लिए सीधे ही अर्थों के समूह का सुनियोजन और स्थापन करता है, जो गायकों को सुनते हैं और उनसे आदान-प्रदान करते हैं। संवाद के दूसरे अर्थ में कहानी के पात्रों के बीच संवादों की शक्ल में कथा का निर्माण शामिल है। इस प्रकार यह दिखाया गया है कि कहानी (गाव) के केन्द्रीय खण्ड उस भाषण या बातचीत की इकाईयां हैं जो एक पात्र द्वारा उच्चरित हैं और दूसरे पात्रों के इर्द-गिर्द लक्षित हैं। संवाद के इन दो अर्थों से कोई भी कह सकता है कि कथा का "आन्तरिक" संवाद गायकों के "बाह्य संवाद" के भीतर घटता है, जो वास्तव में कथा के लिए सांचा प्रदान करते हैं। लेकिन हम "आन्तरिक" और "बाह्य" संवाद के बीच संबंध को किस अर्थ में समझें? आन्तरिक संवाद कैसे बाह्य संवाद का भाग है अथवा कैसे बाह्य संवाद में बना है? एक बार फिर मैं जांच-पड़ताल की दिशा को यहां उस धारणा पर विश्राम देता हूं कि कथा का सस्वर पाठ एक विशेष भाषण-शैली है जो "प्रतिदिन" की उस बातचीत के काफी करीब आ जाती है जिसके पीछे दो वक्ताओं के

---

29. इसका परिणाम एक प्रकार की "आन्तरिक" अन्तर्कथावस्तु है। इसलिए यहां कथावस्तु के स्तर पर कहने और अनुक्रिया करने रूपी संवाद की धारणा (एक आन्तरिक/भीतरी कथावस्तु की धारणा के रूप में) विद्यमान है जो पहले और दूसरे गायक की कथावस्तु से परस्पर सम्बन्ध रखती है।

बीच परस्पर विनिमय होता है। लेकिन इस जांच-पड़ताल को आगे बढ़ाने से पहले मैं उस समझ का उल्लेख करूंगा जिसे भाषायी अर्थों में हम संवाद कह सकते हैं। भक्तिन के अनुसार एक संवाद इस सच्चाई से निकलता है कि सभी उच्चारणों की प्रकृति वास्तव में बहुस्तरीय है : "उच्चारण एक-दूसरे के प्रति उदासीन नहीं हैं और आत्मनिर्भर नहीं हैं; वे एक-दूसरे के प्रति चेतन हैं और एक-दूसरे को प्रतिबिम्बित करते हैं। . . . प्रत्येक उच्चारण अन्य उच्चारणों की गूंज और प्रतिध्वनियों से भरा होता है।" (भक्तिन 1986: 91) संवादपूर्ण उच्चारण का एक विशेष रूप परस्पर विनिमय है जिसमें दूसरों के भाषण का विवरण शामिल होता है। "संवादित भाषण" के दो रूप हो सकते हैं।[30] एक वह रूप है जिसमें एक प्रत्यक्ष उद्धरण शामिल होता है, जैसेकि – "उसने कहा : मैने ऐसा किया" दूसरे रूप में एक अप्रत्यक्ष उद्धरण शामिल होता है; जैसेकि – "उसने कहा कि उसने ऐसा किया / ऐसा कर लिया था।" "प्रत्यक्ष उद्धरण" के रूप में संवादित भाषण के पीछे की धारणा यह है कि एक व्यक्ति का उच्चारण किसी दूसरे द्वारा विश्वसनीय ढंग से एक मात्रा में दोहराया जा सकता है, सिवाय उस मौलिक मात्रा के जिसमें उच्चारण बोला गया है। इस प्रकार यह विश्वास बनता है कि उच्चारण और इसके अर्थ का परिमाण वक्ता और बोले गए परिमाण से उदासीन रहकर अछूता रह सकता है।

जैसाकि टन्नेन (1994 : 133) ने कहा है –

> संवादित भाषण एक अपसंज्ञा (मिथ्यानाम), एक कल्पना मात्र है, जिसमें पारस्परिक प्रभाव की वास्तविकता का कोई आधार नहीं है। जब वक्ता दूसरों के शब्द संवाद में ढ़ालता है तो वे इतने अधिक विवरणयुक्त नहीं होते जितने कि बनाए गए संवाद होते हैं . . . संवाद एक सामान्य वर्णन नहीं हैं, यह विशेष वर्णन है और यह विशेषता श्रोताओं (या पाठकों) को उनके अपने इतिहास के चित्रण द्वारा अपनी समझ पैदा करने के लिए समर्थ बनाती है। . . . संवादित भाषण की रचना के लिए संवाद का बनाया जाना समूचे मानवीय व्यवहार की तरह भाषण की दोहरी प्रकृति – आवर्तक और नवीन, सुनिश्चित और स्वतंत्र, जो कुछ असके मार्ग में आता है उसके प्रेषण की अपेक्षा परिवर्तनीय – को प्रतिबिम्बत करता है।

देवनारायण की कथा के दृष्टिकोण से हम पाते हैं कि गायक जो कुछ कर रहे हैं – कम-से-कम एक धरातल पर – यह निरन्तर वह "वर्णन" है जो कुछ कथा में पात्र कहते हैं (एक-दूसरे को)। जो व्यक्ति हर संवाद से पहले बोलता है, उसका नाम शामिल करके गायक उसकी आवाज की पहचान करता है। उदाहरण के लिए गायक चरित्रों का मानवीकरण नहीं करते और न ही प्रथम पुरुष में बोलते हैं, जैसा कि थियेटर में पात्र करते हैं। वे विपरीत वे श्रोताओं के सामने इस बात का वर्णन करते रहते हैं कि क्या हो रहा था या क्या बोला गया था। इस अर्थ में यह गायक ही

---

30. संवादित भाषण और कोड़-स्विचिंग पर उदाहरण के लिए देखिए – गुम्पेर्ज (1982)।

है जो कथा के दृश्यों और घटनाओं तक पहुंचने का दावा करता है, ठीक ऐसे ही जैसे कोई तीसरा व्यक्ति जो दो व्यक्तियों के बीच के वार्तालाप का गवाह हो – उस वार्तालाप का वर्णन चौथे व्यक्ति के समक्ष करे। तथापि, जैसाकि टन्नेन ने कहा है "संवादित भाषण" केवल पुनरावृत्ति नहीं है बल्कि निर्माण भी है। गायक का संवाद कहने का कार्य निर्माण में कैसे शामिल होता है? यदि इसमें निर्माण शामिल हो तो क्या यह वही होता है जो गायक कथा कहते समय तत्काल कविता करते हैं? क्या परिणाम होगा यदि हम कथा की "तात्कालिक कविता वाली प्रकृति की अपेक्षा "निर्माण" की प्रकृति का अवलोकन करना शुरु कर दें? कल्पना कीजिए कि हम गायक के काम को "सस्वर पाठ" न मानकर "वर्णन" मान रहे हैं? इस परिदृश्य से हमारी संवादशील घटना की समझ कैसे बदलेगी? क्या स्थायित्व (सूत्र, पुनरावृत्ति) और स्वतंत्र नाटक ("सृजनात्मकता / तात्कालिक कविता") के लिए हमारी जांच-पड़ताल में परिवर्तन होगा?

उदाहरण के लिए, जैसाकि टन्नेन ने कहा है "... संवाद का निर्माण एक सक्रिय, रचनात्मक, रूपान्तरित गति प्रस्तुत करता है जो उद्धृत पार्टी और बातचीत के विषय के बीच संबंध को अभिव्यक्त नहीं करता, बल्कि उद्धृत पार्टी और जिनके लिए उद्धरण कहा गया है उन श्रोताओं के बीच के संबंध को अभिव्यक्त करता है।" दूसरे शब्दों में यह संदर्भ ही है जिसमें वर्णन का कार्य किया जाता है, जो "उद्धृत" भाषण से सम्बन्धित दृश्य को निर्धारित करता हैं। टन्नेन कहती हैं कि यदि संवादित भाषण में रचनात्मक और रूपान्तरणीय पहलू शामिल हैं तो यह स्पष्ट जाहिर होगा कि गायक जिन्हें श्रोता समझते हैं उनके अनुसार और गायकों का श्रोताओं के साथ जो संबंध होता है उसके अनुसार जो कुछ भी कहते हैं; उसे ही परिवर्तित करते हैं। कहने में इस परिवर्तन या वास्तव में चयन का एक साधारण उदाहरण गायक द्वारा श्रोताओं के सामने "वर्णन किए" गए उपाख्यान (वार्ता) के अर्थों में देखा जा सकता है। वह सदैव अपनी पसन्द के उपाख्यानों का "वर्णन" नहीं करता बल्कि उनका वर्णन भी करता है जिनकी इच्छा श्रोताओं द्वारा व्यक्त की जाती है। "संवादित भाषण" के सांचे में गायक और श्रोताओं के संवादशील कार्य को रखकर हम भिन्न-भिन्न ढंग से की जाने वाली चयन-प्रक्रिया को एक धारणा में पिरो सकते हैं। वर्णन में चयनात्मकता इच्छा या चाह का प्रश्न मात्र नहीं है बल्कि श्रोताओं के "सुनने" से तारतम्य रखने का भी है, ठीक ऐसे ही जैसे एक वक्ता वर्णन करता है कि उसने विशिष्ट सामाजिक या अन्तर्वैयक्तिक परिस्थिति में एक उच्चारण को "पुनः प्रस्तुत" करने में अपनी मंशा पर निर्भर रहते हुए चयनात्मक रूप से क्या सुना है। लेकिन "सुनने" से वास्तव में क्या अभिप्राय है? सुनना मौखिक अनुक्रिया से कैसे भिन्न है? हम कह सकते हैं कि सुनना श्रोता की आन्तरिक अवस्था है जो वक्ता के उच्चारण को फैलने के लिए और अर्थ बनाने के लिए परिस्थिति उपलब्ध कराती है। इसलिए यह गैरज़बानी कार्यकलाप है जो भाषण पैदा करता है।[31] इस

31. इस अर्थ में श्रवण भक्तिन की संवादपूर्ण अनुक्रिया की धारणा से पृथक् करने योग्य है। जहां श्रवण निश्चित रूप से सभी संवादों का निर्णायक तत्त्व है। वहीं यह अनुक्रिया के रूप में व्यक्त नहीं होता। इस तरह भाषण को बोलना ध्यान का वह क्षेत्र है जिसके भीतर सभी भाषण उत्पन्न होते हैं। श्रवण के विचार और महत्त्व पर देखिए – फुईमारा (1990) और मलिक, एस॰सी॰ (1995)।

प्रकार गाने और बोलने की गतिविधि अकेले गायक रूपी एजेंसी से नहीं बंधी है, बल्कि सुनने के माध्यम से श्रोता की एजेंसी विशेष से बंधी है। इस प्रकार श्रोता और गायक के बीच इस अन्तर्सम्बन्धता पर निर्भर रहते हुए गायक कथा को विभिन्न ढंगों से कहता है। इससे यह पता चलता है कि प्रस्तुति कभी भी एक समान क्यों नहीं होती। यद्यपि, यह बोलने में कुछ शब्दों पर विशेष दबाव को "तात्कालिक कविता" अर्थात् गायक की व्यक्तिगत सक्षमता के अर्थों में विभिन्नता की व्याख्या, से "निर्माण" या एक विशिष्ट परस्पर विनिमय की स्थिति में, जिसमें सुनना (श्रवण) महत्त्वपूर्ण भूमिका निभाता है, कहे गए संवाद की रचनात्मक रचना में परिवर्तित कर देता है। ऐसी स्थिति में यह स्वाभाविक होगा कि स्थायित्व अर्थात् "सूत्र" के प्रयोग और "स्वतंत्र रचना" (या रचनात्मकता) के बीच एक गति होती है। इस प्रकार प्रस्तुति के दौरान सूत्रबद्ध भाषा और तात्कालिक कविता की समस्या का "स्मरण करने" और "तात्कालिक कविता" आदि के आभास मात्र में आरोपित करने की आवश्यकता नहीं है, बल्कि इसे "निर्माण" के प्रश्न और श्रवण पर आधारित "पारस्परिक विनिमय" में आरोपित किया जाता है।

एक विस्तारित "संवादित" भाषण के उदाहरण के रूप में कथा की प्रस्तुति या सस्वर पाठ का अवलोकन करने से हम गायक के कार्य की प्रकृति की भी प्रशंसा कर सकते हैं। इस प्रकार गायक का कार्य मात्र गाना, सस्वर पाठ करना या कथा कहना नहीं है, बल्कि जो कुछ हुआ था और श्रोताओं को जो कुछ कहा गया उसकी मध्यस्थता करना या उसका वर्णन करना है। इसी प्रकार निःसंदेह गायक के कार्य में बीती हुई उन घटनाओं का ज्ञान अन्तर्निहित है जो तब एक विशिष्ट परिमाण में संवाद के रूप में श्रोताओं के सामने घट रही होती है। तब यह गायक का विशेषाधिकार है कि उसने देवनारायण के बारे में जो कुछ "सुन रखा है" या ज्ञान प्राप्त किया हुआ है, उसे श्रोताओं को सुनाए।

संवादित भाषण के उदाहरण

संवादित भाषण का आभास कथावस्तु के अनेक अन्य उदाहरणों में मिलता है। लिखित ग्रन्थों के बीच संवादित भाषण का सर्वाधिक उपयोग महाकाव्यों और पुराणों में किया गया है। कई पुराणों (माहात्मयों) में कवि या सूत जिज्ञासु श्रोताओं (अधिकांशतया ऋषियों) के सामने वर्णन करता है कि क्या हुआ था। जो कवि यह बताता है कि क्या हुआ था, उसके सामने पहले "श्रोताओं" की तरफ से प्रश्न रखे जाते हैं। इस प्रकार पौराणिक ग्रन्थों (और महाकाव्य) में कवि से बहुत स्पष्ट रूप में आग्रह किया जाता है कि वह उसे कहे या उसका वर्णन करे जो कुछ उसने देखा है अथवा जो कुछ वह जानता है। एक प्रकार से कवि और श्रोता की आवाज को कथावस्तु में शामिल किया जाता है और कथावस्तु में वास्तव में "कथा कहने" की स्थिति और जो कुछ कहा या वर्णित किया जाए, दोनों का वर्णन किया जाता है। इस प्रकार कथावस्तु स्थापन और जो कुछ वर्णित किया जा रहा है, दोनों का विवरण है। दोनों ही स्तर, एक प्रकार से, लिखित ग्रंथ में अन्तर्निहित हैं। देवनारायण की मौखिक कथा की स्थिति में "वर्णन करने" का पहला स्तर अर्थात् इसका जमाव विद्यमान नहीं है। इसका कारण यह

है कि जमाव में एक ऐसा तत्त्व विद्यमान होता है जो वर्तमान काल में ही घटता है। विवरण में जैसाकि पुराणों और महाकाव्यों में होता है – भूतकाल में घटी घटनाओं या संवादों का वर्णन होता है। यद्यपि संवाद के निर्माण में लिखित ग्रन्थों और देवनारायण की कथा के बीच अन्य मूलभूत भेद हैं। उदाहरण के लिए महाकाव्यों और पौराणिक ग्रन्थों में संवाद काफी लम्बे हैं तथा स्वगत भाषण जैसे लगते हैं। इससे भी आगे वे पद्य रूप में संस्कृत काव्य अभिसमय के मानदण्डों के भीतर रखे जाते हैं। दूसरी तरफ देवनारायण की कथा में वर्णित संवाद छोटे हैं। 'गाव' भाग को छोड़कर, वे दिन-प्रतिदिन की स्थितियों की भाषा में गढ़े गए हैं तथा उनमें काव्यात्मक या साहित्यिक अलंकरणों की कमी है। उनकी संक्षिप्तता आवृत्ति से युक्त है जिससे आवाजों का परिवर्तन कुल मिलाकर संवाद का ऐसा आभास छोड़ता है, जैसाकि हम प्रतिदिन की बातचीत में महसूस करते हैं। भाषा की साधारणता और परस्पर आदान-प्रदान की तीव्रता सभी एक वास्तविक संवाद के दृश्य को इसके नाटकीय स्वरूप में उजागर करते हैं –

> भाट ने कहा "हे श्री महाराज मैं कब सदैव झगड़ता था?" (हां मैं सिंह को ड़राने से ड़रता हूं, [उसने कहा] / [देव महाराज ने कहा] "तब भाट नजदीक आ जा।" (वाह वाह) / "मै तुम्हारी रक्षा करूंगा" (वाह वाह) / [भाट ने कहा] "आप ऐसा कैसे करने जा रहे हैं, श्री महराज" (हां, मुझे वह बताइए) / [देव महाराज ने कहा:] "बाबा भाट [मैं] तुम्हें इस चट्टान के शिखर पर बांध दूंगा।" (हां "वहां ऊपर बैठे रहना") / [भाट ने कहा] "महान, महान, हे मेरे भगवान, आपने अच्छा सोचा।" (वाह वाह) / [देव महाराज ने कहा] "पालिया, [म्हे] / भाट की रक्षा ऊपर करना। ("हां उसकी बाजुओं को चट्टान के साथ मजबूती से बांधिए और वापिस आइए।"[उसने कहा]) "भगवान की आज्ञा से, भाट को ऊपर शाख पर बांध दे" (म्हे) / [उसने] रूमाल लिया, उसे शाख के इर्द-गिर्द लपेटा (वाह वाह) / और इसकी गांठ बांध दी। /

इस छोटे से उदाहरण में दो मुख्य आवाजें हैं, जो छोछू भाट और देवनारायण की हैं। आदान-प्रदान इतनी तेजी से होता है कि एक व्यक्ति का संवाद अधिकतम दो वाक्यों में पूरा हो जाता है। प्रायः वक्ता के नाम तक का भी स्पष्ट उल्लेख नहीं होता। वक्ता की पहचान को प्रसंग से काट दिया जाता है। कभी-कभी यह बताने के लिए कि कोई व्यक्ति बोलने वाला है केवल "कहा" का उपयोग किया जाता है। अन्यथा वक्ता की पहचान का निर्णय करने वाले किसी चिह्नक द्वारा कोई रुकावट डाले बिना एक के बाद एक उच्चारण चलता रहता है। सिंह के प्रति भाट के भय और देवनारायण के प्रति उसकी अनुक्रिया के व्यंग्यात्मक व संशयात्मक स्वर को प्रस्तुत करने वाला दृश्य बड़ा सजीव है। अनुच्छेद के अंत में गायक केवल एक पंक्ति जोड़ता है जिसे संवादात्मक स्थिति का डग भरना कहा जाता है (स्वयं की आवाज में एक वर्णनात्मक वाक्य जोड़कर)। तथापि मौखिक वक्तव्य में परस्पर आदान-प्रदान का नाटकीय गुण फीका पड़ जाता है; उदाहरण के लिए कथा के मुद्रित विवरण में ऐसा ही होता है। मुद्रित कथावस्तु में कथा एक पौराणिक ग्रंथ का आकार ग्रहण करना शुरु कर

देती है। वास्तव में मुख्य भेद यह है कि अब (अर्थात् मुद्रित ग्रंथ में) संवाद व्याकरण के अनुसार "पूर्ण" वाक्य बनाए जाते हैं न कि साधारण उच्चारण मात्र, जो पूर्ण वाक्य हो भी सकते हैं अथवा नहीं भी। अब संवाद लंबे हैं और बोली गई पंक्तियों की अपेक्षा अनुच्छेदों का रूप धारण कर लेते हैं। इसके साथ-साथ पुनरावृत्ति का तत्त्व, जो कि मौखिक वर्णन के लिए अत्यन्त आवश्यक है, मुद्रित ग्रंथ में पूरी तरह अनुपस्थित रहता है।[32]

> अनेक युग बीत गए। उनके महान् सत से ब्रह्मा, विष्णु और शिव के सिंहासन कांपने लगे। तीनों देवता अपने-अपने दैविक रथों पर सवार होकर मेरु पर्वत पर आ गए। लेकिन तीनों देवताओं के वहां आने के बाद भी उन दोनों ने समाधि नहीं खोली। देवता उनसे बोले : "ओ सुवाई मनु, ओ सतरूपा तुमने घोर तपस्या की है। दीमक तुम्हारे ऊपर रेंग रही हैं। तुम्हारा रक्त और मांस खाया जा चुका है। केवल हड्डियां ही बची हैं। और अब भी तुम राम नाम जप रहे हो। हम तुमसे अति प्रसन्न हैं। हम तुम्हारी सब कामनाएं – राज्य, अपार धन-दौलत या वैकुण्ठ में स्थान तक – पूरी करना चाहते हैं।" यह सुनकर सुवाई मनु और सतरूपा ने उत्तर दिया – "ब्रह्मा अपने धाम जाइए, विष्णु अपने धाम जाइए, शंकर आप भी अपने धाम जाइए। हम आपसे कुछ नहीं चाहते।" परेशान होकर शंकर ने पूछा – "आप किसके नाम का जाप कर रहे हैं?" सुवाई मनु ने उत्तर दिया – 'हम राम के नाम का जप कर रहे हैं। तब शंकर ने कहा – "अच्छा, हमसे अलग यह दूसरा राम कौन है? क्या यही काफी नहीं है कि तीनों देवता आपके सामने प्रकट हो गए है?" "ठीक है, लेकिन आपमें से कोई भी राम नहीं है", उन्होंने कहा "यह सत्य है कि आप तीन तत्त्व हैं जो राम में समाहित हैं (तीन तत्त्व – सतोगुण, रजोगुण, तमोगुण), लेकिन हम उस राम की पूजा कर रहे हैं जिसने आप तीनों को जन्म दिया है। अब वह राम पारब्रह्म परमेश्वर है।

उपरोक्त अनुच्छेद में मौखिक वर्णन से इसे भिन्न करने वाले अनेक स्पष्ट भेद हैं। प्रथम, कथा कहने वाले की आवाज में लम्बे खण्ड शामिल हैं, जिनमें पात्रों के बीच वास्तविक संवाद तक की स्थिति का वर्णन है। कुल मिलाकर, संवाद अपेक्षाकृत लम्बे हैं जो इस बात का एक और प्रमाण हैं कि वे संवाद के ही रूप में अभिव्यक्त किए गए हैं, न कि वे दो पार्टियों के बीच का दिन-प्रतिदिन होने वाला वार्तालाप है। द्वितीय, वक्ताओं का परिचय समीक्षात्मक ढंग से कराया गया है। उदाहरण के लिए, "यह सुनकर . . . उत्तर दिया" या "परेशान शंकर ने कहा" या "तब शंकर ने कहा"। मौखिक वर्णन में हम वक्ता की आन्तरिक स्थिति पर कोई टिप्पणी किए बिना ही साधारणतः यह जानते हैं कि यह आवाज किसकी है। वक्ता की आन्तरिक दशा पूर्णतया उस उच्चारण पर छोड़ दी जाती है जिसे वह स्वयं बोलता है और गायक की तरफ से उस पर कोई टिप्पणी नहीं की जाती। बाद में लिखित ग्रंथ में हमें ऐसे अनुच्छेद भी मिलते हैं जिनमें भविष्यवाणी के लक्षण होते हैं –

---

32. मुद्रित ग्रन्थ का शीर्षक है – बगड़ावत भारत, श्री देवनारायण कथा, अर्चना प्रकाशन, अजमेर।

"ओ भगवान, ओ राम। हमें कम-से-कम यह बताइए कि आप कब अवतार के रूप में प्रकट होंगे? कब हमारी इच्छा पूरी होगी?" "देखो, सुवाई मनु, एक समय आएगा जब रावण जन्म लेगा। वह इतना शक्तिशाली होगा कि इन्द्र उसके लिए पानी भरेगा, बेमाता उसके घोडों को दाना डालेगी, और पवन उसकी धूल पोंछेगी। सुनो, सुवाई मनु, सरयू नदी के किनारे पर एक नगरी होगी, जिसका नाम अयोध्या होगा, जहां सूर्यवंश का राजा रघु राज करेगा। सुवाई मनु तुम रघु के कुल में जन्म लोगे। उस जन्म में तुम्हें अपने आपको दो शरीरों में बांटना होगा। एक शरीर से तुम राजा दशरथ बनोगे। तुम्हारी पत्नी सतरूपा कौशल्या बनेगी। सुनो, ओ सुवाई मनु तब मैं तुम्हारे पुत्र के रूप में प्रकट होऊंगा।"

भविष्यवाणी से युक्त लंबे संवाद के इस रूप में मौखिक वर्णन अनुपस्थित है। वास्तव में राम और रावण जैसे पौराणिक धार्मिक चरित्रों के जन्म से जुड़े विभिन्न समय-चक्रों का विचार उत्पन्न नहीं हुआ। कथा के प्रारम्भिक गद्य में केवल एक अपवाद हैं जिसमें 24 बगड़ावतों के रूप में 24 संतों के पुनर्जन्म की परिस्थितियों का वर्णन है। एक बार फिर लिखित ग्रन्थ के "संवादित" भाषण में एक जीवन्त वार्तालाप सम्बन्धी आदान-प्रदान की अपेक्षा एक विचार अभिव्यक्त किए जाने के अर्थ को प्रकट करता है। जबकि मौखिक वर्णन का संवादित भाषण अपने छोटे, साधारण संवादों के माध्यम से प्रतिदिन की उन परिस्थितियों के समान है जो श्रोताओं के लिए वास्तविक घटना प्रस्तुत होने के अर्थ को बढ़ावा देती हैं। चूंकि गायकों को यह प्रस्तुत करने में अवश्य लीन होना चाहिए कि जिस घटना को वर्तमान में श्रोता "सुनकर" अनुभव कर रहे हैं उन्हें (गायकों को) उस बारे में क्या पता है या क्या सुना है।

कथा का सिंहावलोकन

कथा दो मुख्य भागों से बनी है। इनकी पहचान गायकों ने पृथक्-पृथक् दो समभागों में की है। उन्हे बगड़ावत या बगड़ावत भारत और श्री देवनारायण कथा कहा जाता है। पहले अर्ध में जैसाकि शीर्षक से मालूम पड़ता है, बगड़ावतों या चौबीस भाईयों, जो देवनारायण के पुरखे हैं – का वर्णन है। दूसरे अर्ध में – जैसाकि यहां भी शीर्षक से स्पष्ट है – श्री देवनारायण से सम्बन्धित है। हालांकि कथा के दोनों समभागों में बगड़ावतों और देवनारायण के ऐतिहासिक कार्यों की प्रशंसा की गई है लेकिन वे विभिन्न मूल्यों को भी व्यक्त करते हैं। कुल मिलाकर यह स्पष्ट है कि पवित्र शक्ति के स्त्रोतों में से प्रत्येक को प्रमुखता दी गई है। पहले अर्ध में, पवित्र शक्ति चौबीस भाईयों के ईश्वरीय, आत्मबलिदानी कार्यों के माध्यम से बहती है। दूसरे अर्ध में यह देवनारायण, जो भगवान का अवतार है, के दैवीय कार्यों से सीधे ही जारी होती है।

बगड़ावत भारत

कथा का पहला अर्ध, जिसे बगड़ावत कहा गया है, दो युगों की समयावधि में फैला है। कथा की

शुरुआत सतयुग में होती है। यह वह समय है जब ब्रह्मा राजस्थान के प्रसिद्ध तीर्थ पुष्कर में एक वैदिक यज्ञ (राजस्थानी में जुग) कर रहे हैं।[33]

> ब्रह्मा ने सभी देवताओं और ऋषियों को पुष्कर में अपने यज्ञ में आमंत्रित किया है। उनमें चौबीस ऋषियों का एक दल पुष्कर के समानान्तर पर्वत-शृंखला नाग पहाड़ पर रहता है। ये ऋषि शंकर के अनुयायी हैं। जब शंकर ने आमंत्रण की बात सुनी तो वह उन्हें यज्ञ में भाग लेने से मना करता है। लेकिन वे जाने पर अड़े रहते हैं क्योंकि उनको ब्रह्मा ने आमंत्रित किया है। अचानक शंकर को बहुत ज्यादा भूख लगती है। ऋषि उसे सुझाव देते हैं कि वह उस वन के फल खा ले जिसमें वे रहते हैं। लेकिन शंकर कहता है कि इससे उसकी भूख शांत नहीं होगी। उसने और अधिक फलों की मांग की। लेकिन वन में और कुछ भी बचा नहीं है। रत्तीभर अनाज भी नहीं है। इसलिए शंकर क्या करें? वे अपने शिष्यों के पास जाते हैं और मांग करते हैं कि वे उन्हें अपने शरीर प्रस्तुत करें। वे उन्हें एक के बाद एक करके खाना शुरु कर देते हैं।[34] उन्हें खाकर अपनी भूख शांत करने के बाद वे स्वयं ब्रह्मा के यज्ञ में जाने का निर्णय करते हैं। शंकर के इस कार्य के कारण यज्ञ कुछ समय के लिए रोक दिया गया है।[35] शंकर जी ब्रह्मा से पूछते हैं कि उन्हें अपने इस दुष्कर्म का प्रायश्चित्त कैसे करना चाहिए। ब्रह्मा जी बताते हैं कि प्रायश्चित्त का एकमात्र उपाय यह है कि वे भविष्य में अपना शरीर ऋषियों को प्रदान करें, जब वे ऋषि एक ही पिता के 24 पुत्रों के रूप में जन्म लेंगे।

तुलनात्मक रूप से संक्षेप में कही गई (गाई गई नहीं) इस भूमिका के बाद कथानक अकस्मात् कलियुग में पहुंच जाता है। भौगोलिक स्थिति नहीं बदलती। यह पौराणिक मध्यकालीन अजमेर के राजा बीसलदेव का शासन है।

> राजा बीसलदेव के राज्य के नागरिकों को एक शेर का भय सता रहा है। अधिक मौतों को रोकने के लिए राजा ने आदेश दिया है कि हर रात एक व्यक्ति शेर के भोजन

---

33. ब्रह्मा का यज्ञण कार्य भी संस्कृत में तीर्थ-यात्रियों की नगरी कहे जाने वाले पुष्कर के उद्‌भव पर की गई स्तुति का मुख्य उद्‌देश्य है। देखिए – मलिक (1993ए)।

34. अघोरी के रूप में शिव पर देखिए – सिंह, बी (1993: 415)।

35. इस बात के बहुत ही सदृश्य बात पुष्कर माहात्म्य में भी पाई जाती है, जहां ब्रह्मा के यज्ञ को शिव द्वारा भंग कर दिया गया। एक नग्न, कपालधारी संन्यासी के रूप में प्रकट होकर, उसने जादुई ढ़ंग से अपने भिक्षापात्र को इस तरह उंड़ेल दिया कि समूची यज्ञशाला दूषित मानव कपालों से आच्छादित हो गई। देखिए – मलिक (1993ए 69-74; 248-88)। ब्रह्म के यज्ञ में शिव द्वारा बाधा डालने से शिव और दक्ष की शत्रुता वाली पौराणिक कथा की पुनरावृत्ति होती है। इस पौराणिक कथा में दक्ष द्वारा यज्ञ से वंचित रखे जाने पर शिव उस यज्ञ को भंग करने और दक्ष को मारने गए थे।

के लिए स्वयं उसके सामने जाए। एक रात को हरिराम नामक राजपूत[36] स्वयं को प्रस्तुत करता है जो उस पीड़ित राज्य से गुजर रहा होता है। वह कुम्हार जाति के एक लडके के स्थान पर स्वयं को प्रस्तुत करता है। उस दिन शेर का भोजन बनने की बारी उस लड़के की है। हरिराम उस स्थान पर गूंथे हुए आटे की एक आकृति रख देता है जहां आकर शेर भोजन करता है जब शेर आटे की आकृति पर आक्रमण करता है तो हरिराम अपने छिपने के स्थान से बाहर आता है और शेर का सिर काट डालता है। तब वह अपनी तलवार से रक्त साफ करने और वध की अपवित्रता से स्वयं शुद्ध होने के लिए पुष्कर की पवित्र झील पर जाता है। वह शेर का सिर अपने कंधे पर लिए हुए है।[37] वह पूर्णिमा (पूनम) की रात है। ठीक उसी समय सामने के किनारे पर एक ब्राह्मण कन्या लीला सेवरी आती है। उसने प्रण कर रखा है कि वह कभी भी झील में प्रक्षालन करते और स्नान करते हुए पुरुष को नहीं देखेगी। स्नान करते समय वह शेर के सिर के साथ एक मानव शरीर का प्रतिबिम्ब झील के तल पर देखती है। न केवल उसकी प्रतिज्ञा भंग हो जाती है बल्कि पानी के तल पर आकृति को देखने से वह गर्भवती भी हो जाती है। वह हठ करती है कि अब हरिराम उससे शादी करे। लेकिन वह यह कहते हुए मना कर देता है कि यह शादी नहीं हो सकती, क्योंकि वह ब्राह्मण कन्या है और मैं (हरिराम) क्षत्रिय हूं। अन्ततः वे राजा बीसलदेव से विवाह की अनुमति प्राप्त करते हैं, जो हरिराम को मुंहमांगा पुरस्कार देना चाहता है। नौ मास बाद हरिराम और लीला सेवरी के घर पुत्र का जन्म होता है। जन्म के समय उसका सिर सिंह का और शेष शरीर मनुष्य का है। उसका नाम बाघ सिंह या बाघ रावत रखा जाता है। बाघ सिंह को जन्म के समय ही त्याग दिया जाता है, लेकिन उपवन में पेड़ हरे होने शुरु हो जाते हैं और उनमें कोंपले फूटने लगती हैं, जो इस बात का संकेत है कि वह देव प्रकृति का मानव है। राजा उसे अपना लेता है। लेकिन उसकी डरावनी शक्ल के कारण उसे एक बाग में ब्राह्मण गुरु व रसोइए की देख-रेख में रखा जाता है। बाद में जब वह बड़ा होता है तो उसकी असामान्य शक्ल एक बार फिर उसके लिए दुल्हन पाने के रास्ते में रोड़ा बन जाती है। वह ब्राह्मण रसोइए के साथ बाग में एकान्तवास करता रहता है। एक दिन तीज के त्यौहार पर विभिन्न जातियों की काफी लड़कियां बाघ सिंह के रेशमी झूले से आकर्षित होकर वहां आती हैं। ब्राह्मण उनको इस शर्त पर झूलने की अनुमति देता है कि वे बाघ सिंह की परिक्रमा करेंगी। जब वे ऐसा करती हैं तो ब्राह्मण सगाई की रस्म पूरी कर देता है। इस प्रकार अनजाने में उन सबकी सगाई बाघ सिंह से हो जाती है। बाद में बाघ सिंह उनमें से

36. एक पाठान्तर में, हरिराम को गूजर बताया गया है जिसे बाद में राजा बीसलदेव से "सिंह" की उपाधि मिल गई थी, क्योंकि उसने नरभक्षी सिंह का वध करने का स्यार्थरहित कार्य किया था। देखिए – मलिक (1993 बीः 381 अगला)।

37. फड़ पर हरिराम को पुष्कर की झील के सामने से शेर का सिर ले जाते हुए दिखाया गया है।

बारह लडकियों के साथ विवाह कर लेता है। उसकी हर पत्नी दो पुत्रों को जन्म देती है और उन सबको बगड़ावत कहा जाने लगता है।

बगड़ावत, जिनकी माताएं विभिन्न जातियों की हैं की शादियां गूजर कन्याओं से की जाती हैं। चौबीस बगड़ावतों में से सवाई भोज सर्वाधिक विख्यात और साहसी है। सवाई भोज प्रतिदिन नाग पहाड़ की ढलानों पर बगड़ावतों के पशुओं को चराने के लिए जाता है। एक गाय प्रतिदिन झुण्ड से निकलकर चली जाती है। और शाम को लौट आती है। एक दिन सवाई भोज गाय का पीछा करता है और पता लगाता है कि उसे रूपनाथ संन्यासी द्वारा दुह लिया जाता है। उसकी गाय को दुहने के बदले में रूपनाथ सवाई भोज को अनाज से भरा एक बोरा देता है। लेकिन सब भाईयों के लिए इतने कम अनाज का कोई महत्त्व नहीं है। इसलिए वे उसे पक्षियों को खिला देते हैं। अगले दिन सुबह वे देखते हैं कि कुछ दाने, जो बोरे की सीवन में फंसे रह गए थे, मणियों में बदल गए हैं।[38] उन्हें अपनी गलती का अहसास होता है। सवाई भोज संन्यासी का शिष्य बनने के लिए उसके पास लौट जाता है। एक दिन रूपनाथ और सवाई भोज एक कड़ाहा तेल गर्म करते हैं। जब तेल उबलने लगता है तो रूपनाथ सवाई भोज को कड़ाहे का चक्कर लगाने को कहता है और स्वयं उसके पीछे चलता है। जब वे कड़ाहे का चक्कर लगा रहे होते हैं तो रूपनाथ सवाई भोज को कड़ाहे के उबलते हुए तेल में धकेलने की कोशिश करता है। लेकिन सवाई भोज पहले ही रूपनाथ की मंशा को भांप लेता है और वह गायों के झुंड को हांकने वाली लाठी की मदद से कड़ाहे को लांघ जाता है।[39] अगले चक्कर में सवाई भोज संन्यासी के पीछे चलता है और उसे कड़ाहे में धकेल देता है। साधु उतना चुस्त नहीं था, अतः वह उबलते तेल में गिर जाता है। उसका शरीर तुरन्त ठोस सोने में बदल जाता है। जब सवाई भोज अपने अपराध पर पछताने लगता है तो संन्यासी अपनी कुटिया में पुनः प्रकट हो जाता है जैसे कुछ हुआ ही नहीं। वह बताता है कि स्वर्ण आकृति एक उपहार है, जो बगड़ावतों को बारह सालों की अवधि के लिए समाप्त न होने वाली धन-दौलत देगी और उसके बाद धन और जीवन (माया-काया) का अंत हो जाएगा। वह सवाई भोज को एक घोडी, एक गाय और एक हाथी उपहार स्वरूप देता है जो सब विशेष शक्तियों से युक्त हैं।[40] सवाई भोज अपने घर लौटता है। सभी भाई अपने

---

38. यह घटना और इसके बाद की घटना, जिसमें रूपनाथ का शरीर सोने में बदल जाता है, उन पारम्परिक कथाओं के प्रतीक हैं जिनमें नाथ योगियों की चमत्कारिक शक्तियों का गुणगान किया गया है। देखिए – गोल्ड, 1992।

39. और भी देखिए – सिंह, बी॰, 1993:414।

40. घोडी, वास्तव में शक्ति का प्रकटीकरण है। गाय कामधेनु है, जिसे "सब इच्छाएं" पूर्ण करने वाली गाय कहा जाता है। हाथी भी देवी का रूप है। इस पर और अधिक देखिए – सिंह, बी॰, *वही,* पृ॰ 414।

बड़े भाई तेजाजी से पूछते हैं कि उन्हें प्राप्त नई धन-दौलत का क्या करना चाहिए। तेजाजी, जिसकी माता बनिया[41] जाति से है, उन्हें सलाह देता है कि धन को भूमि में गाड़ दें और गुप्त रखें। छोटे भाईयों में से एक नेवाजी इस विचार से असहमति जताता है और सुझाव देता है कि उन्हें इस धन से अच्छे काम करने चाहिएं, अर्थात् कुएं और मन्दिर बनवाने चाहिएं, धन को बांट देना चाहिए और नाम कमाना चाहिए, क्योंकि धन और जीवन दोनों का बारह सालों के बाद अंत हो जाना है। भाईयों ने इस बाद वाली सलाह को मान लिया। शीघ्र ही उनकी प्रसिद्धि दूर-दूर तक फैल जाती है। इस बीच उनकी मुलाकात अपने होने वाले शत्रु रणनगरी के राजपूत राजा से होती है जिसका नाम राणा (या रावजी) है। राणा और बगड़ावत धर्म-भाई बन जाते हैं। मदिरापान के एक लम्बे दौर में वे मदिरा से भरे मर्तबान पहाड़ पर उंड़ेल देते हैं जिससे धरती पर मदिरा की इतनी बाढ़ आती है कि मदिरा पाताल-लोक के सर्प स्वामी बासक नाग की राजधानी में बहने लगती है। क्रोधित राजा बासक थोड़े समय के लिए धरती को एक बैल के सींग पर रख देते हैं और बगड़ावतों की शिकायत करने के लिए भगवान् के दरबार में जाते हैं। लेकिन न तो बासक, न हनुमान जी, न ही भगवान् जी इस स्थिति को सुधारने के लिए कुछ कर पाते हैं। इसका कारण केवल यह नहीं है कि बगड़ावत इतने अधिक शक्तिशाली हैं, बल्कि यह भी है कि वे पूरी तरह देवताओं के प्रति समर्पित हैं। अन्ततः भगवान् जोगी का वेष धारण करते हैं और भिक्षा मांगने के लिए सवाई भोज की पत्नी साडूमाता के पास जाते हैं। साडूमाता ने अभी प्रक्षालन और स्नान किया ही है। वह अपने लम्बे केशों से ढ़की हुई ही भिखारी के समक्ष आ जाती है। उसकी इस अगाध भक्ति भावना से प्रसन्न होकर भिखारी उसे वरदान मांगने को कहते हैं। साडूमाता इच्छा व्यक्त करती है कि भगवान् उसके पुत्र के रूप में जन्म लें। भगवान् वचन देते हैं कि बगड़ावतों की मृत्यु के बाद तेरहवें दिन वे उसके पुत्र के रूप में जन्म लेंगे।

लौटने के बाद भगवान् शक्ति से प्रार्थना करते हैं, जो बगड़ावतों को नष्ट करने के लिए सहमत हो जाती हैं। वह वन में एक शिशु कन्या के रूप में प्रकट होती है जहां भूआंल का राजा उसे पाता है और गोद ले लेता है। ठीक उसके जन्म के समय उसकी नौकरानी हीरा दासी भी एक महाजन के घर जन्म लेती है। शक्ति असाधारण तेजी से बढ़ती है और शीघ्र ही उसके लिए उपयुक्त वर की तलाश के लिए ब्राह्मणों को भेजा जाता है। वह हठ करती है कि वे ऐसे वर की तलाश करें जो ऐसे परिवार से हो जिसमें एक पिता के चौबीस पुत्र हों। एक लम्बी और थका देने वाली खोज के बाद ब्राह्मण बगड़ावतों

---

41. बनिया सौदागरों और व्यापारियों की एक जाति का नाम है जो अपने व्यापार और वाणिज्य तथा धन-दौलत के लिए विख्यात हैं।

को पाते हैं। वे कन्या की सगाई सवाई भोज से करना चाहते हैं, लेकिन वह पहले ही विवाहित है। इसलिए बगड़ावत सुझाव देते हैं कि कन्या की शादी उनके धर्म-भाई राणा[42] से कर दी जाए। इस प्रकार राणा का विवाह रानी जैमती से करने के प्रबंध किए जाते हैं। जब बारात आती है तो राणा की अपेक्षा सवाई भोज इसके आगे चलते हैं। इस बीच रानी जैमती आदेश देती है कि तोरण को इतना ऊंचा लटकाया जाए कि बूढ़ा और कमजोर[43] राणा उस तक पहुंच न सके इसलिए राणा की अपेक्षा सवाई भोज तोरण को तोड़ते हैं। बारात के आने पर रानी बहाना करती है कि उसे बहुत ज्वर है। वह अपनी नौकरानी को कहती है कि वह सवाई भोज की तलवार लेकर आए, जिसमें स्वस्थ कर देने की शक्तियां हैं। महल के भीतरी कक्ष में वह तलवार की परिक्रमा लेती है और इस प्रकार द्वारा गुप्त रूप से सवाई भोज से विवाह कर लेती है। हालांकि सार्वजनिक रूप से वह राणा से शादी करती है। विवाह की रस्म पूरी हो जाने पर जब वह अपने नए घर में राणा का साथ निभाने जाती है तो वह बगड़ावतों के साथ ठहरने का आग्रह करती है। बगड़ावत उसे 6 मास के बाद ले आने का वचन देकर राणा के साथ जाने के लिए राजी कर लेते हैं। राणा के महल में आने पर रानी कहती है कि वह तब तक राणा के साथ पासे नहीं खेलेगी जब तक वे उसके लिए नया महल नहीं बना देते।[44] वास्तव में, महल के निर्माण में लम्बा समय लगता है और 6 मास शीघ्र पूरे होने को हैं। इस बीच अपनी पत्नियों की इच्छा के विरुद्ध बगड़ावत रानी को लाने के लिए तैयार हो जाते हैं। रानी बगड़ावतों के साथ भाग जाती है। राणा धैर्यवान है और वह भाईचारे के ढंग से बगड़ावतों को सलाह देता है कि वे रानी को वापिस भेज दें। लेकिन बगड़ावत अपने निर्णय पर अड़ जाते हैं। अन्ततः राणा बावन किलों[45] की सेना एकत्रित करके खारी नदी के किनारे आ जाता है। रानी जैमती, जिसने अब भवानी के रूप में अपना रूप धारण कर लिया है, बगड़ावतों को वचन देती है कि वह उनका साथ इस शर्त पर देगी कि उनमें से एक समय में एक ही राणा की सेना से युद्ध करेगा। वह यह भी मांग करती है कि सब भाई अपने सिर देंगे। बगड़ावत उसकी इस विलक्षण मांग से सहमत हो जाते हैं। रानी जैमती (या भवानी) के लिए भयंकर युद्ध (महाभारत) होता है। युद्ध में कुछ भाई देवी

42. राणा एक अपाधि है जिसे मेवाड़ के मुखिया राजपूत धारण करते हैं।

43. राणा की आयु अनुमानतः 120 वर्ष है।

44. "पासे खेलना" यौन क्रिया के लिए मंगलभाषित है। देखिए – गोल्ड, 1992:99, संदर्भ 66।

45. बावन की संख्या राणा के विशाल सैन्य आधिपत्य को सूचित करती है। इस संख्या का उपयोग महानता प्रदर्शित करने के लिए भी किया जाता है। उदाहरण के लिए देखिए – "पुष्कर के बावन घाट" (मलिक 1993 ए: 7) या पौराणिक नायक पाबूजी की राजधानी कोलू के बावन किले (स्मिथ, 1991:289)।

के चक्र द्वारा सिर काटे जाने के बाद भी लड़ते रहते हैं। अंत में सभी भाई मारे जाते हैं और राणा की विजय होती है। देवी अपना विस्मयकारी भयंकर रूप धारण कर लेती है। मारे गए योद्धाओं के शवों के बीच खून से लथपथ हुई युद्धक्षेत्र में पालथी मारकर बैठ जाती है और वह बगड़ावतों के सिरों और बाजुओं का हार पिरोती है। बगड़ावतों की मृत्यु के बाद सवाई भोज की पत्नी साडूमाता को छोड़कर सभी योद्धाओं की पत्नियां सती हो जाती हैं। इस नरसंहार के बाद चार शिशु जीवित रहते हैं। इनके नाम हैं – भांगीजी, मेदूजी, मदनाजी और भूणाजी। इनको इनके सौतले माता-पिता पालते हैं।

श्री देवनारायण कथा

कथा का देवनारायण से सम्बन्धित दूसरा भाग काल की दृष्टि से कलियुग में स्थित है। पहले भाग का उत्कर्ष रक्तरंजित युद्ध है तो दूसरा भाग युद्ध के बाद की स्थिति से शुरु होता है। इस तबाही के बीच देवनारायण का जन्म नवीनीकरण और शान्ति के नए युग से परिचय कराता है।

साडूमाता युद्ध क्षेत्र के निकट पर्वत पर तप करती है। ग्यारह दिनों बाद जब उसके सम्मान और जीवन का अंत करने की धमकी राणा द्वारा मिलती है तो वह भगवान् का आह्वान करती है, जिसने उसके पुत्र के रूप में जन्म लेने का वचन दिया था। देवनारायण उस समय पाताल लोक के राजा बासक के साथ पासे खेल रहे थे। वे पानी की एक लहर पर सवार होते हैं जो उस चट्टान से टकराकर बंट जाती है, जिस पर साडूमाता तप कर रही होती है। पानी की उस लहर द्वारा लाए गए एक खिले हुए कमल के फूल के रूप में शिशु देवनारायण साडूमाता की गोद में गिर पड़ते हैं।[46]

राणा द्वारा पुनः धमकी दिए जाने पर साडूमाता मालवा में अपने मायके जाने का निर्णय करती है। देवनारायण का बचपन वहां पिछली घटनाओं की किसी भी जानकारी के बिना बीतता है। एक दिन चौबीस बगड़ावत भाईयों की वंश-परम्परा जानने वाला कवि छोछू भाट देवनारायण की तलाश में मालवा आता है। साडूमाता उसकी मंशा को भांप लेती है और वह उसे मरवाने की कोशिश करती है। लेकिन देवनारायण उसे बचा लेता है। देवनारायण तब अपनी माता की इच्छा के विरुद्ध अपने पिता की पैतृक भूमि पर लौटने और राणा से बदला लेने का निर्णय करता है। भीलवाड़ा राज्य और उसकी राजधानी चौसला से गुजरते हुए देवनारायण तीन राजकुमारियों से विवाह करता है। पहली राजकुमारी दैत्यराजा की बेटी, दूसरी पाताल-लोक के राजा की भतीजी और तीसरी

---

46. इस घटना के प्रतीक की तुलना गर्भाशय और जन्म, जन्मशक्ति और विजय की प्रतिकृति से की जा सकती है, जो इन्द्र की कथा में पाई जाती है, जिसने सर्प दैत्य वृत्र का वध किया था और पर्वतों की घाटियों में पानी में मिल जाने के लिए बिखरा दिया था। (*ऋग्वेद,* 1.32.1 अगला)।

रानी पीपलदे है, जो इस धर्म सम्प्रदाय व कथा में अन्य रानियों की अपेक्षा महत्त्वपूर्ण मानी जाती है। लौटते समय देवनारायण अपने चार चचेरे भाईयों – मेदु, मदनो, भांगी और भूणा – से भी मिलता है। वे उसकी तरह एक-दूसरे से अनभिज्ञ रहते हुए बड़े हुए हैं। मेदु और मदनों को राणा के मित्र – अजमेर के राजा – ने गोद ले रखा है। भूणा को स्वयं राणा ने गोद ले रखा है उसका नाम बदलकर खाण्डेराव रख दिया गया है। भांगी बगड़ावतों के गुरु रूपनाथ के सांनिध्य में नाथजोगी के रूप में बड़े हुए हैं। लेकिन जब चचेरे भाईयों को अपनी असलियत का पता चलता है तो वे राणा के खिलाफ लड़ने के लिए देवनारायण के साथ मिल जाते हैं। अंतिम भिड़न्त शुरु होने से पहले देवनारायण राणा की फसलों को नष्ट करने के लिए शाही खेतों में 9 लाख 80 हजार गायों और भैंसो का झुण्ड छोड़ देता है। अंत में चचेरे भाई राणा को पकड़ लेते हैं जो बचने की कोशिश कर रहा होता है। देवनारायण उसका सिर धड़ से अलग कर देता है। लेकिन जब देवनारायण देखता है कि भूणा अपने पालक पिता की मृत्यु पर उदास है तो छोछू भाट द्वारा राणा के पेट से बगड़ावतों का बदला लेकर संतुष्ट होने पर देवनारायण उसे (राजा को) पुनर्जीवित कर देता है। देवनारायण तब उससे "राणा" की उपाधि वापिस ले लेता है और उसे "सिसोदिया" की उपाधि प्रदान करता है। इसके बाद देवनारायण राणा को उदयपुर नगर बसाने का आदेश देता है। कथा के अनुसार उदयपुर का नाम देवनारायण के एक नाम उद पर रखा गया है।

देवनारायण राणा से बदला लेने के बाद स्वर्ग वापिस जाने का निर्णय करता है, लेकिन उसकी रानी पीपलदे उससे अनुरोध करती है कि वह उसे निःसंतान छोड़कर न जाए। वह एक पुत्र बीला और एक पुत्री बीली को जन्म देती है। बीली शीघ्र ही अपने पिता की दिव्यता को अनुभव कर लेती है। लेकिन बीला हठी है और अपने पिता की शक्ति को पहचानने से इन्कार कर देता है। अनके दुःखद घटनाओं के बाद, जिनमें उसको कोढ़ लग जाना भी शामिल है, बीला अपने पिता की दिव्य-शक्ति को महसूस करता है। वह तब देवनारायण की प्रथम समाधि की देख-रेख करने और उसका पुजारी बनने पर सहमत हो जाता है जिससे पुजारियों की वंशावली चलती आई है। तब एक पूजास्थल की स्थापना कर, पुजारियों की वंशावली, भक्तों के सम्प्रदाय की स्थापना कर देवनारायण अंत में अपने दैवी रथ में सवार होकर बैकुण्ठ लौट जाते हैं।

श्री देवनारायण कथा

ए सदा सिंवरूं तो जी भाग भवानी देवी शारदा रे।
धूंधाळा देव के जी गणपत लागू पाय।
गजानन्द देव नै सिंवरियावूं सुख सांपते।
शारदा नै सिंवरियां जी हिरदै हूं बिराजै आय।
(भलां जी भलां) देव भलां

सदा ई सिंवरूं भाई भवानी शारदा (म्हे) । धूंधाळा देव के गणपत लागा (पाय)। गजानन्द देव नै सिंवरियावूं सुख सांपतै (वाह वाह)। शारदा नै सिंवरियां हिरदै बिराजै (आय)। दान्त दिसूसळ गे कंवळ बिनायक देव के शीश मुकुट गल (हार)। ओ जद टूटै गंवरी का लाडला (म्हे)। खोलेलो भगवान विद्या को भरयोड़ो ई (भंडार)।

ए निवण गरू तो जी जो निवण बिनायका रे।
निवण करूं सब देई देवता कीरोड़ ।
पण निवण करूं भाग भवानी देबी शारदा।
संकट पड़िया सूं दुर्गा ये संकट राळो तोड़।
(भलां जी भलां) देव भलां

निवण तो भाई गरू (म्हे)। निवण बिनायका निवण करां सब देई देवता (कीरोड़)। निवण करूं ये अबार भवानी देबी शारदा (म्हे)। संकट पड़िया सूं दुर्गा तूं संकट राळो (अब तोड़)।

ए इजगर आयगी तो जी ए ई भगवान के बैसणै औवूं रे।
मुण्डा के करै जी पदम नाग फूंकार ।
साडू खटाणी की दरबार झोळिया खेल गा ।
गोठां में धारयो जी कंवळ के फूल लियो औतार।
(भलां जी भलां) देव भलां

इजगर तो आई देव के बैसणै (म्हे)। मुण्डा के करै भगवान के पदम नाग (फूंकार)। साडू गूजरी खटाणी की झोळिया खेलिया भगवान (वाह वाह)। गोठां में धारयो रे भाई कंवळ का फूल में (औतार)। कंवळ का फूल में देव महाराज (औतार लीन्यो)। साडूमाता के झोळिया में (खेलिया जी कीयो)।

ए ईंठा का लेवांला जी ए ई देव का अवारणा रे।
ए तो भाई जी ईंठां बिराज्या ऊद।

ज्यांकै दुआवै रे काळी मांजरियां।
रीझया ठाकर माजी सुखड़िया पावै दूध।
(भलां जी भलां) देव भलां

ईंठां की पूजन हुई भगवान की (वाह वाह)। ईंठां का लेवां भाई देव का अवारणा (म्हे)। ईंठां में बिराज गा (ऊद)। ज्यांकै दुआवै काळी मांजरियां (वाह वाह)। रीझावूं ठाकर भगवान सुखड़िया घणा पाय (दूध)। देव नै भजै पूजै नै (म्हे)। जकां के दूध को धान को टोटो कदै ई (नैइ रहवे)।

ए कुचीपलै कुंचरै तो जी जो थाणा भैरूंनाथ का रे।
कीज्यै जी मण्डोवर मोटी ओट।
नर नारी जोड़ै निवण करै धरती के ऊपरे।
सांचो बिराज गो जामीजी मिण्धारी मारोट।
(भलां जी भलां) देव भलां

कुचीपलै कुचरै थाणा भैरूंनाथ का (म्हे)। कीज्यै मण्डोवर मोटी (ओट)। अरै नर नारी जोड़ै निवण करै धरती के ऊपरै (वाह वाह)। सांचो बिराज गो भगवान मिण्धारी (मारोट)।

ए देव नै भज्यासें तो जी ए ई दालद भाज्वै औवूं रे।
साप देव नै रटियावूं रे चली जायली भूख।
संकट धूणी बिराज्यो नारायण देवजी।
नका पर ठामी जी चार कूण्ट नौ दीप।
(भलां भी भलां) देव भलां

देव नै भज्यासें दालद भाजै (वाह वाह)। साप देव नै भज्यासूं चली जायली (भूख)। ए संकट धूणी बिराज्यो नारायण देवजी (वाह वाह)। नका पर ठाम्री चार कूण्ट नौ (दीप जी कीयो)।

सुर बिनै कोनी मिलै तो जी ए ई माता सुरसतियां रे।
कोनी मिलै जी गरू बिन ग्यान।
अन्न बिनै जोधरो हंसा ही उड चले।
जळ बिनै भाई रे चलता रहवै पीराण।
(भलां जी भलां) देव भलां

सुर बिनै नैइ मिलै माता सुरसती (वाह वाह)। कोनी मिलै गरू बिने (ग्यान)। अन्न बिनै जोधारी हंसा ही उड चलै (वाह वाह)। जळ बिनै मिनखा देही तजै (पीराण)। सुर देवै माता सुरसती। गरू बतावै (ग्यान)। अरै जळ तो राजा इन्द पूरवै है (म्हे)। अन्न देबाळा ई (ए भगवान)।

ए धूजी तारो पहली सिंवरज्यो जी गोठालां राजवियां रे।
सिंवरणी कीरतियांवाली जोड़।
पण धरमराजा देव को लीलागर बछेरो पहली सिंवरणा।

पियांळां में राजा जी बासक बांध्या मोड़।
(भलां जी भलां) देव भलां

धूणी तारो पहली सिंवरणो भाई (म्हे)। सिंवरज्यो कीरतियांवाली (जोड़)। ए धरमराजा देव को लीलागर बछेरो पहली सिंवरणा (म्हे)। पियांळां में राजा बासक बांध्या के (मोड़)। तूं तो तूं म्हारा दाता तूं तूं तो देव के निरजन तूं तूं तो तूं म्हारा दाता तूं म्हारा दाता तूं

दान्त दिसूसळ के जी जो गे कंवळ बिनायक देव के औवूं रे।
कीज्यै आप के जी केवळ भरणा कान।
तूं जान मूं पाछो पधारज्यां गुणेश देवता।
तूं चाल्या सूं म्हारी रे भूंडी लागै जान।
(भलां जी भलां) देव भलां

भगवान की बरात में सब देवातण चड़िया (वाह वाह)। तो बूझणा करी रे भाई आपणी बरात में कुण तो जानी फूटरो अर कुण (हां कफूटरो है कीयो)। सगळा जानी कीयो श्री महाराज और जानी है जका नाहाया धोया फूटरा फराह (सगळा है कीयो)। बिनायकजी महाराज अड़बड़ सूं ख्याल माण्डा में आपणी हेंसी (जांवता ही करां देवेला कीयो)। ई बिनायक नै पाछो (सीख दिरा द्यो)। दरबार का हुकमूं (म्हे)। भगवान बूझणा (करी है)। दान्त दिसूसळ गे कंवळ बिनायक के देव के केवळ भरणा (कान)। बरात मूं पाछा पधारो गुणेश देवता (म्हे)। भगवान के आप चाल्या से बहुत बिरंगी (म्हारी जान)। गुणेश देवता (पाछा पधारो कीयो आप)। बिनायकजी मन में देखियो (म्हे)। अरै सगळा म्हनै देवता (हां आपांणै ही बरतिया कीयो)। आज भगवान ही बरात में कोनी ले जांवै तो सेंसारी दुनिया लाखां ही (तनै मानेली कोनी जी कीयो)। दरबार का हुकमूं (म्हे)। आप का रूप मूसा पैदा (कर दिन्या)। मूसा जमीन नै पोळ अर (बगा दी जी कीयो)। भगवान का रथ अर घोड़ा ठौड़ का ठौड़ ही (रोप ग्या)।

पूठी टूट गा जी ए ई गाड़ा कर पाचरा रे।
भगवान की जाना में जी धुरियां बळ खायो रे।
श्री भगवान के जानया नै बूझणा।
आपांणी जान में रे कुणसो देव रीसायो रे।
(भलां जी भलां) देव भलां

पूठी टूट गा भाई गाड़ा का पाचरा (वाह वाह)। धुरियां बळ (खायो)। श्री भगवान करै जानया नै बूझणा (म्हे)। आपणी बरात में कुणसो (देव रीसायो)। अरै इतो बड़ो देवातण कुण है भाई (हां जको रीसाय ग्या गा ठौड़ (की ठौड़ जाना ढब गी कीयो)। कीयो श्री महाराज ए काम तो देखो ए बिनायकजी का है (हां बिनायकजी महाराज का है कीयो)। ए देखो बिनायकजी का रूप है जका ऊंधरा ही फिरता (हां दीखै कोनी आपणे)। बिनायकजी नै मनावो तो बरात आगा नै (चालेली)। नैइ जरां तो लाखां (नेइ चालै कीयो)। तो कांई भगवान बिनायकजी के लेरै मनावा नै जावै (म्हे)। कांई जांतां ही समचार

कहवै देखां (कीआवूं जाणज्यो भोपाजी महाराज अब कीआवूं)। अबार कहवां भगवान देव का ई का हुकमूं कह द्यां (वाह वाह जी वाह वाह)।

दान्त दिसूसळ के तो जी जो गे कंवळ बिनायक देव के औवूं रे।
कैज्ये आप के जी केवळ भरणा कान।
तूं बरात में पधारै गुणेश देवता।
तूं चाल्यावूं म्हारी रे सदा सुरंगी जान।
(भलां जी भलां) देव भलां

दान्त दिसूसळ गे कंवळ बिनायकजी देव के (वाह वाह)। थारै केवळ भरणा (अब कान)। बरात में चाल गुणेश देवता (म्हे)। भगवान के तूं चालियावूं सूं सदा सुरंगी (म्हारी जान)। बिनायकजी महाराज (हां जान में पधारो कीयो)। बिनायकजी महाराज जीकारो करियो जी (साबास)। ओ जीकारो की को (हां सामै जीकारो औरूं क्यां का कीयो)। कीयो सा मरदा मरदी का है (हां मरदा मरदी को है)। थै ई तो बरात नै ले गा तो म्हानै पहली (हां इतियार पहली ले ग्यावै कीयो)। मैं बरात में चांलां तो म्हांकी करामातूं (चांलां कीयो)। कीयो करामात नै सागै लियो (हां अर पधारो)। कीयो श्री महाराज खानै पीनै की पहली खोलो जरां (हां अठै ई बोथ लेवूं म्हांवूं तो)। कीयो खोला कांई बरात के सागै जिमायज्यो (बरात के सागै पाछै आजाज्यो)। कीयो नी श्री महाराज बे डावड़ा दूजा (हां म्हांको तो दस्येरो न्यारो ही लागै है कीयो)। कीयो अड़बड़ ख्याल (म्हे)। न्यारो कत्तो (लागै आप के)। कीयो सौ मण चावल अर सुवा सौ मण मूंग (म्हे)। शक्कर अर घीरद ऊपर गलावो अरै इताका तो मैं करज्यावूं कलेवो (हां)। दूजा माण्डावूं कद भेरी (जान के सागै जिमण नै बुलावो)। ओ जिमण कोनी है (हां म्हारो कलेवो है कीयो)। भगवान कीयो ए भैइ अड़बड़ ख्याल (म्हे)। आज तो म्हारो घर है तूं कांई जका थोक म्हनै (हां पूरज्यासूं)। सेंसारी दुनिया लाखां ही इतो भोग (हां तनै नैइ पूरवै कीयो)। कीयो श्री महाराज जको सगस तोरण पर आई (म्हे)। जका सगस नै मार गोठावूं (ले लेवूं कीयो)। थारो बांध्योड़ो दसियो छोड़ूं कोनी (हां तूं बांध दे कीयो)। कीयो जा भाई एक घरूं पूरवेला कोनी (म्हे)। सुरजी महाराज आंतै उगै बती दूर में (वाह वाह)। सुवा सेस मण को भोग रोजीना (थारै लागी कीयो)। सुवामणी करै तो मानी (वाह वाह)। पांच सेर परसाद का तो ही (मान लीज्यो)। हेंर सुवा पीसा भी नै छोड़ै (बो ही मान करीज्यो)। लियो अब चाल (पधारो कीयो)। बिनायकजी देखियो रे आज भगवान को ब्याज हुई सावो तो बड़ो ही है (हां सावो मोटो है)। ई सावा में थारा ई पलेटा हो जावै तो जरूरी (हां थारा ब्याव हो जाय तो हो जाय नी दोयता की (भूखी तनै बेटी कोय नैइ देवै जी)। कीयो श्री महाराज में बरात में कोनी चालूं (म्हे)। क्युं (हां) कीयो आप तो बैठा बैठा खाओ फैरा (अर मैं बैठियो बैठियो देखूं)। मैं कांई दुआगन लुगाई को जलमियोड़ो थोड़ो जको बैठो बैठो (हां देखबो करूं)। म्हारो ब्याव करावो पहली (जणा चालूं नी तो कोनी चालूं कीयो)। तो भगवान महाराज तो रुकमणीजी एक (परणीजा)। बिनायकजी महाराज नै रीध सिध दो बहना (परणाई जी कीयो)। रीध सिध को दातार महाराज बिनायकजी (कीवाया)। बींद पहली कांकण डोरड़ो बिनायकया के (बन्धाया जी कीयो)। ब्याव को धणी कुण है (महाराज बिनयाकजी)।

ए भैरूं बुरज के कांगरै तो जी बिराज गो राव मण्डोवरो रे।
लीना भाईजी काळू मीर दीया नै बुलाय।
कठै रह गो भोज को अटूट पोरसो।
की जागां रह गी भोज की ए तोरण सींगी गाय।
(भलां जी भलां) देव भलां

भैरूं बुरज को कांगरै बिराज्यो राव मण्डोवरो (वाह वाह)। लियो भाई काळू मीर दीया जोधका नै (बुलाय)। अरै भाई दीया की जागां रह गो भोज को देख अटूट पोरसो (म्हे)। की जागां रह गी भोज की तोरण सींगी (अब गाय)। सुण रे काळू मीर दीयाजी (म्हे)। के बगड़ावतां का घर में तीन ही चीज ही (हां तीनयो चीज आपनै लूट में आई कोनी)। आपनै लूट में आई कोनी महाभारत हो गो तो महाभारत में अरै सब चीजां निंगै में हा पण ए तीनो चीजां निंगै के नैइ आई भाई (वाह वाह)। तो आपां ल्यायां ई कांई बोलो (म्हे)। शंकर को दियोड़ो हो पोरसो जको भी रह गो अर शंकर की गाय दियोड़ी घी की जागां दूध है जो काम आतो बी को तो भी बा आपनै नी आई (बा ई कोनी आई)। ए साडू सतवंती ही तो बी को ही ग्यान कोनी ही सब गूजरियां सतीवाड़ै गी बी को पत्तो नी (वाह वाह)। दरबार का हुकमू दीयो जोधका बूझणा (करी है)। श्री महाराज (म्हे)। के पोरसा नै तो म्हानै ठा है तेजोजी लेय अर रीछोर का परबत भाज गो (हां ऊंचो चड़ ग्यो)। दरबार का हुकमू रावजीवूं छोटो भाई नीमदे जको बूझणा करी श्री महाराज (म्हे)। मैं पोसो कोस लियो (हां) नावड़ियो सात कोस पर पापड़ा काट नाकिया म्हारा कोस ले गो (हां पाछो कोस अर ले ग्यो कीयो)। तेजाजी कोनी दे लाखां ही (वाह वाह)। कीयो एक साडू बेपत्तै है (हां बी को ठा कोनी)। बी को पत्तो नी है (वाह वाह)। हेंर गायां है जकी चराबा नै गुआल ले गा जको बै ई पत्तो नी है की जागां है (हां की जागां है अर की जागां नैइ है जकी ठा कोनी)। तो जरां कीयो सिरदारां इसो काम करो भाई (म्हे)। कोय लूट नैइ आई आपणा बगड़ावतां की घर की (वाह वाह)। ए तीनो चीजां नी आई नै जरां कोय लूट नी आई (हां की कोनी आई चड़ाई पाछी कराय)। दूजा चड़ाई करावो जी जागां गाय भी है (हां) बटोवूं पकड़ कर ल्यायो (वाह वाह)। तो रावजी सा बावन गढ हा जींयां का जींयां दूजा चड़ाई करा दी (वाह वाह)। तो बांकै मांयनै रावजी साय का सिरदार हा आमेराव का खड़क सिंग निरवाण सिंग दो भाई कचावा (वाह वाह)। तो पांच पांच से तो घोड़ो हो बांकन (म्हे)। पांच पांच से असवार हा (वाह वाह)। तिनका रावजी साय देता (हां रावजी की नौकरी करतां बे)। कोय जमाना में जो भोज के कन्नै जाय (म्हे)। हेंर आंकै प्रेम बन गो अर धरम का भाई होया (वाह वाह)। ए बिचार करियो रे भाई के आपणो दोन्यो भाइयां का जाबा को धरम नी हो बांकन (हां गायां नै ल्याना का धरम कोनी है)। क्युं के आंपां तो दूध खा लियो बां गायां को (म्हे)। अब बां गायां नै आंपां पकड़बा जांवां आपणो धरम तो कठै रियो (वाह वाह)। तो आपणै तो बा गायां के वास्तै आपणो फौज नै ओ जो सांस देनो है डील को (म्हे)। जको मुण्डा के मर जावै जो आपनै तो बस धरम हे जको रह जाय (हां आपणो धरम तो) (रह जाय गायां नै जाण द्यां रावजी कन्नै)। दरबार का हुकमू ए दोन्यो भाई फौजां टाळ अर गांव के गोरवें फौजां के रावजी के साय आडा फिर गा (वाह वाह)। कीयो देखो

भाई के जो बगड़ावतां के गायां नै पकड़बा नै जावै नै (म्हे)। पहली झगड़ो मावूं ही हो (हां पहलो झगड़ो मावूं करे)। रावजी का अमराव कीयो भाई समंदर के मांयनू चिड़ी चांच पर ले जावै समंदर को पाणी घटै थोड़ो ही होवै (हां निवड़ै थोड़ो ई है)। अर आ फौज है रावजी की जकी समंदर है (म्हे)। थै चिड़िया हो (थांको थाक ई कांई लागै है कीयो)। कीयो भला ई कुछ भी हो म्हानै तो मरणो है (वाह वाह)। ई बात पर हुवै तो रावजी साय की फौजां अटेक करियो दरबार का हुकम बां दोन्यो भाइयां की फौज पलटन काम (हां गायां के मुण्डा के आयगी जी कीयो)। हेंर सिरदारां हां जकी नकी काम आयगा (वाह वाह) तो रावजी का अमराव गोरम के भाखर जाय (म्हे)। अर गाय के घेरो ले लियो (वाह वाह)। आ गुआलां नै ठा नी की भाई आपणै लेरै बगड़ावतां को महाभारत हु गो है (हां आंनै ठा ही कोनी)। ए चराबा गायां चराबा गियोड़ा हा बाहरें (म्हे)। तो गुआल कांई करियो के रावजी का अमरावांवूं दरबार का हुकम कोय बातावूं बख में नी बैठी (म्हे)। तो रावजी को अमराव औरूं बगड़ावतां के कोय के सैन्धो-मैन्धो हो रिशतेदारी में हो (म्हे)। जको कीयो रे भाई कुण के पाछै लड़ो थै (हां थांका धणी काम आई ग्या है कीयो)। हेंर मैं दरबार का हुकम दूजा चड़ाई व्हिया (वाह वाह)। थांकै नी तो गायां रहवेली (म्हे)। थै तो इस्यो काम करो के एक भोज की अस्त्री है साडूमाता बा सतीवाड़ै कोनी गी (हां बीको पत्तो लगार बीनै ले जाओ)। बीनै लुको द्यो थै (वाह वाह)। तो नी जरां मैं रावजी का अमराव पकड़ ले जां सेंसारी दुनिया बात आ हुई की रावजी की राणी तो ले गा बगड़ावत (म्हे)। हेंर रावजी की राणी तो ले गा बगड़ावत अर बगड़ावतां की राणियां ही (वाह वाह)। जकियां नै रावजी ले गो (पकड़ पकड़ पाछी ले ग्यो कीयो)। बरोबर की बात हो गी (वाह वाह)। तो दरबार का हुकमूं नापोजी गुआल हो देव महाराज को सिरायत (म्हे)। बीनै बूझणा करी ले नपा भैइ तूं जा अब (हां तूं पत्तो लगां गायां के आडा मैं हां)। तो नापो दरबार का हुकमूं रावजी का अमराव कीयो थें गायां की घेरो ई राखो भलां ई पर गायां थानै मैं ले जाबा द्यूं कोनी (हां द्यां तो एक ही आत)। क्युं के थांकै वास्तै पांच पांच से घोड़ा पांच पांच से असवार कचावा सिरदारां कांई बै ई मर गा थांकै कांई बिचार है (हां थांकै कांई टाक लागे)। पदमू दरबार का हुकमूं गुआल सिरायत हो नै (म्हे)। जको कांई करियो के गायां कन्नु घोड़ो हांक दियो (वाह वाह)। दरबार का हुकमूं गोठां के जमीन में गियो नै (वाह वाह)। बी टैम में जागां जागां खारी नंदी का डावा पर सेला फिरै (म्हे)। बो देखियो माठो बात तो की आ तो जकी रचना हो गैइ (हां हो तो गी रचना तो)। सवाई भोज का सेवा कन्नै जार ग्यान करियो (वाह वाह)। तो मालासर की डूंगरी में साडूजी के जी टैम में हाथी हो नै गजमंगलो (म्हे)। जको चारूंमेर परिकरमा दे रियो (हां चारूंमेर परिकरमा दे रियो)। ओ हाथी घूम्तो गुआल नै (दीखियायो)। मन में देखियो बी जागां हाथी है जी जागां मिनख को विश्वास जरूर होवै (हां जरूर बठै ही हो सकै भुवाजी)। घमसाय घोड़ो (म्हे)। के ओ कांई करियो है की दरबार का हुकम गोरम के भाखर मालासरी डूंगरी में पूगतो (हो ग्या)। तो साडूमाता भगवान का भजन तो कर री ही (वाह वाह)। हेंर बिखराळरूप के मायंनै बैठा बी टैप में (म्हे)। गुआल मन में देखियो रे भुवाजी को चित ऊठ गो भाई भुवाजी को चित ऊठ गो भाई (हां चित खराब होय ग्यो)। क्युं के बगड़ावत जातां रियां इस्या मानवी है जका तो इको डील ठाणै कोनी रियो (हां अब ग्यान कोनी रियो कोनी)। गुआल कांई करियो के हो लियो से जार कीयो भुवा साय (म्हे)। आप ईंयां से

ऊठो रावजी का अमराव आयगा आपणै पकड़बा के लियै (हां चालां कीयो)। भुवाजी बोलै (वाह वाह)। कांई समचार भतीजा नै कहवै देखां (अब कीआवूं जाणज्यो देखां कींयां कहवे)। अबार कहवां धणी देव भगवान का ई का हुकमूं देखां (वाह वाह सा)।

ए राणो चड़तो जी राजवी चड़ियावो रे गुआल गाय का रे।
चड़ियावो भाई रे धरती का पहली भूप।
मांह मांह के महीनै मालासरी तापसियां।
तापस्यूं गुआल रे कर राकस का रूप।
(भलां जी भलां) देव भलां

राणो चड़ भलां ही राजवी चड़ियावो (वाह वाह)। चड़ियावो धरती पहला (भूप) अरै मांह मांह के महीनै तो ए मालासरी में ई तापूं (म्हे)। कर राकस का (अब रूप)। भतीजा (म्हे)। म्हारी भगवान से अबार निरा लाग्योड़ी है (वाह वाह)। छुड़ा मत भाई (हां छेड़ मन्ना कीयो)। गुआल मन में देखियो रे भुवाजी देखिया (हां चित खराब हो ग्यो नै आंको)। आंको तो हो गो बांतां करै ने एरी बेरी के भगवान की लोलसिया है (वाह वाह)। कीयो माजी सा कांई के भगवान तनै अब (म्हे)। कीयो भगवान के अर म्हारै देख रे भतीजा कौल बचन है भाई (हां कौल बचन हियोड़ा है कीयो)। भोज नै जकै दिन तेंहर दिन हो जाय (जकै दिन म्हारै द्वारै भगवान पधारसी)। कीयो मानी बात पधारी (वाह वाह)। क्युं के बगड़ावत बियां का मानवी हां शंकर का चेला हा (जका तो गिया)। एक भगवान थारै घर आंजाय (हां बारणै आसी कीयो)। कीयो रे गुआल जरूर ही आयी कीयो (वाह वाह)। कीयो मैं तो कोनी मानू (हां ई बात नै मानू कोनी भुवाजी कीयो)। के तो दरबार का हुकमूं इयां से ऊठजा (म्हे)। नी जरां देख रावजी का अमरावां नै पकड़बा तनै कोनी ले जाबा द्यूं (हां पकड़ कोनी ले जाण द्यूं कीयो)। माथो काट (वाह वाह)। फूंफांजी के दरबार का हुकमूं सियाळा के मांयनै नाक द्यूं भेळै दाग हो जाय (हां थारो सतीवाड़ो सागै ईंयां करूं कीयो)।।

ए राणो चड़तो जी राजवी चड़ियावो रे गुआल गाय का रे।
चड़ाज्यो भलां ही रे धरती पहला भूप।
मांह के महीनै तो मालासरी में तापसियां।
बाळा देव नै रे खेंस्यां गूगळ घूप।
(भलां जी भलां) देव भलां

भलां ही राणो चड़ राजवी चड़ो कीयो (म्हे)। चड़ जावो धरती पहला ही (भूप)। अरै मांह के महीनै तो मालासरी तापूं भाई (म्हे)। बाळा देव नै खेवूं गूगळ (अब धूप)। कीयो मानी बात बाळो देव भगवान थारै बारणै आई (म्हे)। कीयो गुआल आई (वाह वाह)। दरबार का हुकमूं गुआल खाय रीस (म्हे)। तरवार ई कन्नै के तरवार सूंती (हां ले कीयो)। ले भाई भगवान भुवाजी भगवान है तनै अब दरबार का हुकमूं ले कीयो सवाई भोज का सियाळा में नाका अब (वाह वाह)। तरवार सूंती साडूमाता भगवान नै अरदास करी (म्हे)। के ले भाई भगवान थारै अर म्हारै कौल बचन हा की झोळिया में खेलूं (हां

तेंहरवां दिन का कौल बचन हा)। तेंहरै दिन तो गुआल होबा दे कोनी (हां होबा दे कोनी थारा बचना को कांई होसी कीयो)। म्हारै बी झोळिया में आज ग्यारह दिन ही है (आज ही पधारो अबें ही)। तीन तिलोकी को नाथ भगवान बासक नै चौपड़ (नीचै खेल रिया तेंहरवीं पियांले)। कीयो रे बासक राजा म्हांकै तो सती नै सताली कोय (म्हे)। म्हानै जाणो पड़ी भाई (अब ठहरां नैइ)। तेंहरवीं पितालू दरबार बी जागां से बिदा व्हिया नै (म्हे)। बी जागावूं धरतीमातावूं कांई करियो पतालू एक जळ की धार (चाली)। डूंगर फूट (म्हे)। हेंर जळ की धार आर साडूमाता की गोदियां में पड़ी (वाह वाह)। बी धार में कंवळ का फूल (औतार हां लीन्या आपड़ी1या)। कंवळ का फूल में देव महाराज तीन तिलोकी का नाथ आपो आप (हां औतार हां जी कीयो)। कीयो ले भतीजा तूं कौ के (म्हे)। की भगवान कींयां आई अर कठूं आई (ए आयग्या कीयो)। कीयो भैइ माजी साय तूं माळागर की भोम में रियोड़ी है माळवा के मांय बिद्या है (म्हे)। बिद्या से कोय बचियो (पेदा जादूवूं बना दिया)। कीयो गुआल जादूवूं बनायोड़ो ओ कोनी भाई (हां आपो आप ही है कीयो भगवान है)। कीयो आपा आप है जरां भाई थारा भगवान नै कह जको कोय परच्यो (हां म्हनै दिरा कीयो)। कीयो गुआल ओ बचियो अबार कांई परच्यो दे भाई (हां जकी बता ओ तो बच्चो) (है कीयो बाळक है)। कीयो सुण ए भुवाजी (म्हे)। स्यांप का बच्चा कोय छोटो-मोटो नी होवै (हां की छोटो अर की मोटो ओ तो एकसार ही है बड़ो है तो)। भगवान ही है जरां तो छोटो है कोनी (म्हे)। हेंर नी भगवान है तो सगळो छोटो ही है (हां छोटो ही है तूं पैदा करियो जादू जणा)। तीन तिलोकी को नाथ के होंकारो (करियो)। कीयो माता डर मत (हां मांग कांई गुआल थारो परच्या मांगै है कीयो)। कीयो रे गुआल बोल जरां भाई (हां कांई को परच्यो देवै है कीयो)। कीयो ओई परच्यो मांगां (म्हे)। बगड़ावत तो मारिया गिया जका राणीजी नै ल्यायां जरां मारिया गिया (हां मारिया गिया)। बानै अब पाछा अब कांई मांगां (हां अब मांगनां का कोनी बै तो गिया)। आमेराव का खड़क सिंग निरवाण सिंग दो भाई कचावा (म्हे)। ए बगड़ावतां का बारां में एरी सारड़ आज काम आया (हां वै गायां के मुण्डै आज मर ग्या)। बांकी फौजां जिन्दी हो जावै (अर बै दोन्यो भाई जिन्दा होवे)। गायां के अर गुआलां के सामिल आजावै (सामिल आजावै अर गायां को घेरो छूट जाय)। औतार जरूर जरां मानू (जणा थारा भगवान औतार है नी तो कठै कोय नी कीयो)। तो दरबार गोदियां में हा (म्हे)। कीयो होंकारो (करियो)। होंकारा के समचै राण शहर के गोरवें दोन्यो सिरदारां की फौजां है जकी बैठी हो गैइ (वाह वाह)। बैठी दरबार का हुकम होय (म्हे)। गोरम के भाखर गुआलां के सामिल (हां आय ऊबा रिया)। कीयो गुआलां सांठा रीज्यो भाई (हां अब की कोनी बिगड़ै कीयो गायां (नी जा)। अता दिन सत्ता दूजी ही (म्हे)। हेंर अब सत्ता है जकी आपणी (दूसरी है कीयो)। तो तीन तिलोकी को नाथ भगवान ओतार होतां ईं परच्यो देतां पहली (म्हे)। आमेराव का सिरदारां की फौजां बैठी (पाछी हुंवती)। गायां का घेरा (छुटता)। जय बोलो श्री देवनारायण की जय बोलो भाई छोटा अर मोटा ई से।

हांजी दाता मांह को तो महीनो ये पख चाण्दनो।
खटाणी मांह को तो महीनो ये पख चाण्दनो जी।
म्हारै छट ये थावर का रूड़ा बार नारायण आया पांवणा जी। हांजी दाता

सूखोड़ा भाखर में हरिया होय गा जी।
ओ म्हारा सिरजन सूखोड़ा भाखर तो हरिया होय गा जी।
जा में मोरिया करै नै मलहार भक्तां रे भीड़ी औतार लियो जी। हांजी दाता

पत्थर फूटियो भर जळ भर नीकलयो जी।
जीयै खटाणी पत्थर तो फूटियो ए जळ भर नीकलयो जी।
जळ में नीकलायो कंवळ के रो फूल फूलां में देव औतार लियो जी। हांजी

जिण दिन इजगर का घालिया म्हारा दाता बैसणो जी।
खावण इजगर का घालिया म्हारै दाता बैसणो जी।
बांकी सेवा में लागयाया बासक नाग भक्तां रे भीड़ी औतार लियो जी। हांजी

जिण दिन काळोड़ी भंवर नै लीला चूंग रिया जी।
ओ म्हारा दाता काळोड़ी भंवर नै लीला चूंग रिया जी।
म्हारी साडू की झोळिया में साळगराम
भक्तांलो भीड़ी औतार लियो जी। हांजी वीरां धिन धिन ये धिन

मालासरवाली डूंगरियां जी।
जी बळी हारी धिन धिन ये धिन मालासरवाली डूंगरियां जी।
थामै देव लियो ये परकाश फूलां में देव औतार लियो जी। हांजी मालक

परवण नै भुला दी ऊंडा समंदरा जी।
भाई भाई परवण नै भुला दी ऊंडड़ो समंदरा जी।
म्हारै फूली जी मितवालां री बेल भक्तां रे भीड़ी औतार लियो जी। हांजी

बीरां सपना रे दे दीज्यो घरवाला भाट नै जी।
भाई भाई सपना रे दे दीज्यो नारद भाट नै जी।
नारद कह दे नै सपनावाली बात साडूजी कर ले बूझणा जी। हांजी साडू

बैरां में रमतोड़ा देखियाया देव नै जी।
जीयै खटाणी बैरां में रमतोड़ा देखिया देव नै जी।
बांकी छट जी थावर का रूड़ा बार भक्तां रे भीड़ी औतार लियो जी। हांजी

बीरां मंगल ये गावो नै गोठांली गूजरियां जी।
थै तो मंगल जी गावो नै गढवाली कामणियां जी।
थै तो गावो ये सिरजन का मंगलाचार बधावो जी गावो देव रा जी। हांजी

भाई भाई नाद पचाईणी गोठां बाजिया जी।
को म्हारा दाता नाद रे पचाईणी गोठां बाज रिय जी।

ए तो घर घर में बाजिया भाई सोहन थाळ बधावा गावो देव रो जी। हांजी

भाई भाई मालन्की मनावै मरवा केवड़ो जी।
जिण दिन मालन्की मनावेली मरवा केवड़ो जी।
ओतो नाई को बांधेलो बांधरवाल गोठां में देव औतार लियो जी। हांजी

किषना चन्दन रे काटो ने घड़ लियावो पाळणा जी।
भाई भाई चन्दन जी काटो ने घड़ लियाजो पाळणो जी।
तूं तो ल्यायै बना द्यो दरबार गोठां में देव औतार लियो जी। हांजी माजी

आंखियावूं आंधो मैं पगलियांवूं पांगलो जी।
ये खटाणी आंखावूं आंधो में पगलियांवूं पांगलो जी।
म्हानी देही में जरै छै रिगचा कोढ कींयां तो ल्यावां पाळणो जी। किषना

आगो तो आजा भाई हरवल सामना जी।
कारीगर आगो तो आजा भाई हरवल सामना जी।
थारी होंकारै झाड़ेळा रिगचा कोढ घड़ ल्याज्यो हर के पाळणो जी। हांजी

कारीगर आगो तो आयो भाई हरवल सामना जी।
किषनो आगो तो आयो भाई हरवल सामना जी।
ईंकी होंकार झाड़ी हो रिगचा कोढ घड़ ल्यांवां हर के पाळणा जी। हांजी

साडू के लख ये घड़ ल्यांवां उड़्नी चिड़कलियां जी।
जीयै खटाणी के लख तो घड़ ल्यांवां उड़्नी चिड़कलियां जी।
मैं तो के लख ये बागांलां दादर मोर घड़ ल्यावां री हर के पाळणो जी।
हांजी किषना नौलख तो घड़ ल्याज्यो उड़्नी चिड़कलियां जी।

कारीगर नौलख तो घर ल्याज्यो घड़ उड़्नी चिड़कलियां जी।
तूं तो आया जी पायां पर दादर मोर घड़ ल्याज्यो रूड़ो पाळणा जी। हांजी

किषनो खांधा पर कवाड़ी बण में नीकलयो जी।
कारीगर कान्धा पर कवाड़ी बण मांयी नीसरयो जी।
ओ तो बाढन नै लाग्यो भाई चन्दन रूंख घड़ ल्यायो रूड़ा पाळणो जी।
हांजी मांजी की जागां बनया द्यूं हरवल पाळणो जी।

ये खटाणी की जागां बनया द्यूं हर का पाळणा जी।
मैं तो की जागां बांधोला रेशम डोर घड़ ल्यायो हर के पाळणो जी। हांजी

किषना पोळ में बनया द्यो हरवालो पाळणा जी।
कारीगर मोळिया में बनया द्यो जी हरवालो पाळणो जी।

तूं तो लीलागर के बांधो रेशम डोर नारायण हींडै पाळणै जी। हांजी भाई

भाई खातण ने उडा द्यो बाळा चूंदड़या जी।
जीयै भाटजी खातण नै उडा द्यूं मोहन चूंदड़या जी।
कारीगर के सोहन मुरकी कान नारायण हींडै पाळणे।
खातण नै घड़ावो टिमणो टेवटो कारीगर के पचरंग पाग नारायण हींडै पाळणे।
जय बोलो श्री देव महाराज की जय।

गुआल कांई करियो है (म्हे)। बी जागावूं डूंगर परूं घोचा चूगी (वाह वाह)। हेंर दरबार परच्यो दियो जरां हाथां ई पाळणो बनायर माथा पर मेल और गोठां में ल्याया (वाह वाह)। दरबार का हुकमूं देव महाराज औतार व्हियो नी बी टैम में (म्हे)। रावजी साय के परच्या पूग गा (वाह वाह)। के मतै ई तो दरबार का हुकमूं दरबार में तरवार और चालबा लागी (म्हे)। हेंर हाथीड़ा तलवा चूरमा (छोड़ दिन्या)। घोड़ा जका रातब घास (हां छोड़ दिन्यो)। रावजी सा बूझणा करी सिरदारां (म्हे)। आ बात आज ईंयां कींयां (हां हुई है कीयो)। रावजी सा को ढोलियो जको धूजबा लाग (गियो)। तो कीयो महाराज पिण्डतां नै बुलावो (वाह वाह)। तो पिण्डता नै बुलार दरबार का हुकमूं टिपणा दिखाया है (हां बूझणा कर लीनी)। कीयो पिण्डतां ओ भाई गेबावूं तरवार कींयां चाली म्हारै दरबार में (हां मतै ई तरवार चाली है (गढ का कांगरा तीन टूटर (मतै ई पड़ ग्या कांई बात है कीयो)। कीयो श्री महाराज (म्हे)। जो थै गायां पकड़बा गिया नै (वाह वाह)। हेंर बगड़ावतां को महाभारत करायो बांको बैर लेबालो भगवान औतार ले लियो (हां भगवान बांकै घरां आज औतार व्हिया है कीयो)। जो बै थामूं बैर नी काढी बगड़ावतांला (वाह वाह)। कीयो जरां भाई कोय बीनै कोय दरबार का हुकमूं मारबाळा सकस है (हां है कांई कीयो)। तो काशी का पिण्डत हां जका कीयो महाराज खरचो घणो लागै (हां मार तो देवां पण)। होमविदि में होम दियां (म्हे)। अर पहली मैं राण शहर को राज देयो आधो (जणा तो मैं . . .)। नाश मैं करियावां रावजी साय कीयो लियो बिरामणा आधो राज दे देवूं जरां (हां आधो राज कीयो समूधो ही ले लियो नै)। चार पिण्डत बी जागां से (विद्या व्हिया है)। तो साडूमाता दड़ावट में ले जार पाळणा नै बांधियो (म्हे)। साडूमाता नै बै बिरामणा जका पूगता (व्है ग्या जी कीयो)। जार बूझणा करी माजी सा थारै बच्च्यो हे (म्हे)। तो बच्च्या का नांव ठांव भाई (हां म्हरा कन्नु कढावां नांव कढ दिया कीयो)। कीयो रे बिरामणा (म्हे)। जलम की बांझड़ी हूं दीखै कोनी थनै बिचार (में?) (हां क्यें को नांव काढो कीयो)। कीयो भाई माता मैं तो बच्च्यो सुणियो है थारो व्हियोड़ो (हां जणा आया है कीयो)। कीयो नी भाई म्हारै तो कोय बच्च्यो व्हियो न तो कोय नांव न ठांव की कोनी लाडी (हां नांव नूं कढाना ही क्युं)। रसोई पाणी करणी होवै (म्हे)। तो मैं करां द्यूं (हां आ बात हो सके)। कीयो माता ई पाणी से रसोई पाणी मैं करां कोय नी (म्हे)। तो काचा कळस के मायं जळ आवै बी जळ से करां (हां बी जळूं करां थारै जळूं पाणीवूं करां कोनी)। क्युं काशी का पिण्डत हां नै मैं (म्हे अचूतो पाणी चावूं)। तो साडूमाता तो भगवान की भगत ही (म्हे)। कीयो देवता बैठो भाई जरां (हां पाणी मैं लेर आस्यूं)। साडूमाता तो जळ नै बावड़ी पर पूगती हु गी (वाह वाह)। कुमहारां के जार काचो कळस ले लियो (म्हे)। हेंर भगवान का आधार पर बा तो जळ नै आपके पूगती हुई (गैइ है)। लेरावूं

बिरामणो कांई करियो ओ लियो अब घर को समालो (हां लेवां ही बाळक कठै कांई है)। तो पहली बिरामण पाळणो पूगतो (व्हियो हैं)। दुसाळो ऊपर उडायोड़ो पाळणो झोल रियो है (म्हे)। तीन तिलोकी को नाथ दरबार का हुकमूं सरप का रूप कर लिया बी टैम में (वाह वाह)। बिरामण जार कांई करियो दुसाळा ने एकाना करतां जेज लागी सेंस नाग सुतो मांय (हां सरप के फण करियो)। फण करियो बो तो पाछो ही आपको बी नै दुसाळा नै ओड़ार भाग छूटियो (हां आयग्यो कीयो बाळक कोनी)। बिरामणा नै आर कीयो रे भाई बाळक कोनी अठै तो म्हनै तो खाजातो बा सरप दीखै हां सरप है बठै तो)। कीयो व्हिया व्हिया तूं तो बै (ठ) जा दूजो बिरामण पाळणै पूगतो (हां औरूं व्हिया है जी कीयो)। बी टैम में भगवान कांई करियो ओ (म्हे)। के बिसा सौ की ऊमर में हु गा (हां डेण हो गया सफा)। हेंर दरबार का हुकमूं घड़ी पलक में पीराण जाबालो सौ रूप कर दियो (वाह वाह)। बिरामण देवता मन में देखियो भाई ईनै आपां मार पाप में क्युं डोबूं (हां अठै कठै सरप है ओ तो सौ बरसां (के मांयनै डेण है)। बे मतै ही खतम हुई (हां खतम होणाळो है कीयो)। ओ जार कीयो भाई सरप नी है बठै (हां सरप तो कोनी पाळणै में तूं झूटो है)। बिसा सौ बिका आरबळ में है जो मानवी है (म्हे)। डेण है मरबालो है भाई (हां नाड़ टूटवा ही चाले)। के तूं ही झूटो है साव ही मैं सरप नै छोड़ आयूं अबार (म्हे)। बै (ठ) जावो भाई दोन्यु ही एक जगा तीजो बिरामण पाळणै पूगतो (औरूं व्हिया जी कीयो)। बी टैम मैं भगवान पाळणा नै खाली रूप दिखाळ दियो बिरामण नै (हां खाली झोटा खाय जी कीयो)। बो कीयो भाई नी तो सरप है (म्हे)। नी डेण है (वाह वाह)। पाळणो अबार की टैम मैं खाली है (एकदम खाली झोला खाय पाळणो)। कीयो तूं ही झूटो है भैइ (वाह वाह)। चोथो बिरामण के पाळणो पूगतो (हां औरूं व्हिया जी कीयो)। बी टैम में भगवान बच्च्या बाळक तो बन मेलिया (म्हे)। हेंर आपको पगालो ऊंगूठो हो जको मुण्डा में बोबा की जगा चंस रिया (हां चूंस रिया चसकड़का लिया)। दिसालो उठाय देखियो तो बच्च्यो सुतो मांयनै (वाह वाह)। पाछो आर बिरामण देवता कांई करियो (म्हे)। खोल पावड़ी (वाह वाह)। हेंर बामणां के पावड़ी की देबा लागी (हां ठोकण लाग्यो)। बीको चट्टो तो बीका हाथ में बीको चट्टो (बीकै हाथ में जी कीयो)। साडूमाता जळ लेर पूगती (पाछा व्हिया)। कीयो बिरामण देवता ईंयां कींयां भाई (हां ईंयां क्युं लड़ो भाई के कीयो)। रसोई पाणी करो और दखिणा देहां दखिणा लियो कीयो माजी सा मैं तो दखिणा ही ले लिया पूरा (म्हे)। हेंर रसोई धाप गा भाई (हां काटा धापयोड़ा है माजी सा म्हानै तो थे)। राण शहर को गेलो बताय देयो (बो बतावो जको म्हांका पाछा पूगता हुवां हाथ जोड़ूं)। कीयो रे क्युं भाई (हां आं कांई हुई कीयो)। कीयो ताणो बच्च्यो है जको माजी सा बहुत ही कळावान है वो (हां कळाकारी है कीयो)। दरबार का हुकमूं तूं कहवै बच्च्यो कोनी (म्हे)। मैं तो आया नांव काढबा हां पण तूं तो म्हांको नांव काढ दियो (हां म्हांको नांव पहली काढियो है)। दरबार का हुकमूं पिण्डत तो आया जींयां ही पाछा (बावड़ता)। हेंर रावजी सा नै जार कीयो श्री महाराज म्हांवूं तो बा बिचार कोनी बनै (म्हे)। फैर रावजी सा बिड़ो (हां फैरियो है)। कोय भाई बी बच्च्या नै मारबालो सकस हे (जको पैदा है तो बतावो कीयो)। तो दरबार का हुकमूं दूती बोलि श्री महाराज मैं मारियावूं (हां मैं मार आज्यावूं अबार कीयो)। तो राकसनी को रूप धार आ दूती (म्हे)। हेंर साडूमाता की बहन बन (वाह वाह)। आई पूगती (हां दड़ावट हुई है)। साडूमाता नै बूझणा करी हे बाई कित्ता दिना को तो भाण्यो व्हियो कित्ता दिना का नैइ व्हियो

(हां जकी बताय ए बाई कीयो)। आपां तो देख काका की बाबा की बहना हां (हां दोन्यु बहना है काका बाबाई)। तनै तो जांच तो है कोनी इता दिन तो ही कोनी (म्हे)। हेंर म्हनै बाई निंगै है थारावूं बडी हू मैं (वाह वाह)। कीयो बाई म्हानै जांच ही कोनी कीयो मैं तो भाण्यो व्हियोड़ो सुणियो थारै (हां जणा आई)। खिलाबा नै आई (वाह वाह)। खिला बाई तो साडूमाता अटवूं गोदियां में ले भगवान नै (म्हे)। दैतणी कांई करियो जहर घाल लेगी बोबा में (वाह वाह)। तो देव महाराज नै आपको जहर को बोबो देय (दियो)। देव महाराज चसकड़को लेंतां जेज लागी दैतणी का आंतड़ा उजड़ा काढ (सगळा खेंच अर काढ लिया जी कीयो) दैतणी पूरी (काम आई)। साडूमाता कीयो रे भाई आपणो रहणो तो कोनी होवै अब अठै (हां अठै कोनी होवे)। पहली तो बिरामणा नै काढियां (म्हे)। हेंर आ दूती जको फैर आयगी (वाह वाह)। ए रावजी का अमराव औरूं ले अर कर अर आया (हां आया रहसी अठै देव महाराज नै जीणतो कोनी)। तो साडूमाता पीर के मांयनै कागज पूगता कर दिया (वाह वाह)। सला मला भील नै कागज दे दिया (म्हे)। हेंर आमो अर निमो भाई हां जका नै कागज (दे दिया)। दरबार का हुकमूं रात नै विदा भगवान नै लेय (म्हे)। हेंर रात नै विदा (हां साडूमाता व्हिया है जी कीयो)। तो बी टैम में देव महाराज को औतार व्हियो नै (म्हे)। बी टैम में लीला घोड़ा को साथ औतार (हां व्हिया)। औतार होतां ही लीला के देव महाराज के बचन (हां व्हिया जी कीयो)। कीयो सुण रे भाई घोड़ा (म्हे)। तूं तो आपणै बोबो ले ले ई देख काळवी घोड़ी को (म्हे)। हेंर मैं ई माता गूजरी को (हां लेवूं कीयो)। साडूमाता के चड़बाली घोड़ी ही काळी (म्हे)। बी में लीलागर घोड़ो बोबो चूंगवा लाग (गियो जी कीयो)। दरबार का हुकमूं पांच कोस गिया दस कोस गिया बी टैम में भाई हां जका साडूमाता का सामा आयगा (वाह वाह)। कीयो ए भुवा सा (म्हे)। भगवान को पलणो म्हनै दे दे भाई (हां म्हानै ऊंचाओ कीयो म्हांको की कायदो पिछाण लेवै कीयो)। कीयो थै ले लियो भाई (हां थै ले लियो भाइयां)। साडूमाता आगा बह रही गायां का गुआल हा जका साडू के मुण्डा के (आगै चाल रिया)। पाळणो लिया भगवान को मामा हां जका माथा पर ऊंच विदा हुई (गिया जी कीयो)। देव महाराज मन में बिचार (कर लीन्यो)। कीयो देखां मामा की करामात तो देखां (हां आंकी करामात तो देख लियां किसी कांई है)। बिरामण को रूप धार (म्हे)। अकेला बिराजमान (हां हो ग्या जी कीयो) आगै रूप बिरामण को दीखियो जरां मामा देव महाराज का मन में देखियो रे बाई के इसी टैम में भाण्यो व्हियो (म्हे)। तो बठै कठै तो बिरामण हां (कठै तो बिरामण हां अर कठै हा आंको टेवो तो बूझल्यां (किसा कांई नकत्रा जलमियां है)। कीयो बिरामण दादा टीपणा को काम करो कीयो म्हांकै तो ओ ई धनदो है भाई (हां और धनदो किस्यो करां कीयो)। कीयो म्हांकै बाई के भाण्यो औतार व्हियो जको निंगै करो (हां किस्यो कांई नकत्रा)। ई टैम को अर ई घड़ी को जलम है ई को (म्हे)। बिरामण कीयो मैं झूट कोय नी बोलूंलां (हां सांची कहवांला)। दरबार का हुकमूं देव महाराज बूझणा करी (म्हे)। सुणो भाई म्हारा पत्रां में ईंयां को जोग है (वाह वाह)। कीयो जलमत्यां दादेरा नै (खायायो)। हेंर नानेरो खाबा नै औरूं ही (हां ओ बाळक जावै है कीयो)। ईंयां को जोग पत्रां में (हां बतावै जी कीयो)। देव महाराज का मामा मन में विचार करियो अरे बिरामण दादो तो देखबा तो गियो कोनी बठै (म्हे)। ए कहवै जकी बात तो सही हो गी (हां पत्रो देख रे तो बताई है)। अर कह जकी बात आगै आपां में बा ई हुई (बा की बा होसी आपां नै तो जांतां ही खासी)। तो आपणै तो ईंयां को भाण्यो

चावां कोनी आपां नै (म्हे)। नंदी नाळा बहवा मोकळा (वाह वाह)। बण के मांयनै (म्हे)। पाळणा देव महाराज का नै मामा तो दी आपके खाळा के मांयनै ऊंडो थरका दियो (हां हां फैंक दिन्यो आ ल्यो साय कीयो (आपणै तो ईंयां को भाण्यो की जरूरत कोनी)। बठै गिया पछै दरबार का हुकमूं नाहरी ही बी बणबास में (म्हे)। देव का पाळणा के छाती देर देव के मुण्डा में बोबो (हां चूंगाबा लाग ग्या जी कीयो)। लीला के बचन हो नी की मैं साथ लेयावो (हां बोबो सागै को सागै लेवांला)। तो लीलागरी घोड़ो आडो फिर घोड़ी के (म्हे)। हेंर बोबो काळवी घोड़ी को मुण्डा में (चूंगण लागगियो)। माजी सा ताजणा की (हां दिनी)। देव के थारै कांई कौल बचन हो भई (हां सागै बोबो लेनै का हां तूं पहली बोबो (कींया लेवै कीयो)। कीयो माजी साय (म्हे)। म्हांको नैम मत घटा (हां नैम तोड़ै मनवा का)। थारो देव अबार बोबो चूंग रियो है (हां जणा नैम तो चूंगण लागगियो)। जको म्हारो तो नैम तो म्हनै पूरो तो करबा दे (वाह वाह)। कीयो रे भाई म्हारी मां बी नै मां तो मैं बीकी अठै हूं (म्हे)। म्हारै बिन बोबो देबाळो (हां दूसरो कुण है बीने)। कीयो सुण ये माता (बीकै मावा मोकळी)। थारै जियान की मावा मोकळी है बीकै (लारै घणी)। निंगै कर (वाह वाह)। माजी सा घमसाय घोड़ी नै पाछी मुड़ी (म्हे)। भाई तो खाली (हां पाळणो हो कठै खाली खाली बहवै भाई तो)। कीयो रे भाइयां पाळणो कठै है भगवान को (म्हे)। कीयो किस्या भगवान हां मैं तो पलणो राळयाया हे ई बी देश नंदी में ही (बठै फैंकयाया कीयो)। कठै भगवान अठै (भगवान कोनी हो कोनी नकत्रा चोखो कोनी हो बाई)। कीयो जलम कर दिया भाई (वाह वाह)। साडूमाता घमसाय घोड़ी अर बी दरबार का हुकमूं नंदी कन्नै पूगती हुई है (वाह वाह)। तो खाळा के मांयनै पाळणो पड़ियो हो (म्हे)। नाहरी छाती देर ऊबी देव महाराज बोबो नाहरी को चूंगा (चूंग रिया)। साडूमाता देखिया तीरां से अबार डरां देयां आगी जाय (हां आगी जाय कीयो)। जिता तीर बाणा जिता बाह दिया (म्हे)। नाहरी सरकी कोनी (हां नाहरी बी जगावूं नी हल्ली)। दरबार का हुकमूं नाहरी बूझणा करी गूजरी ईंयां तीर भलां ही मोकळा बाह (हां ईंयां मत मार बो म्हारो (टाबर है जको तनै देनो तांई कोनी)। दरबार का हुकमूं साडूमाता कीयो भाई धरम की बहन हूं (म्हे)। तो कांचळी के मांयनै बच्चा नै म्हनै (हां पाछो दे कीयो)। कीयो देख जद देवूं के आज फैर कोयको विश्वास नैइ करणो (म्हे)। हेंर दूजा नै कोय नै सूंपना (हां करणी नैइ)। तूं तो एकर बोबो चूंगार धणी बन गी (म्हे)। मैं थारा देव नै अबकै सातवां बोबो (हां आज दियो हूं कीयो)। बहन को नांव लियो तो जरां नाहरी छोड़ देव नै (म्हे)। हेंर बनबास में आपकी बिदा होय (गैइ जी कीयो)। देव महाराज को पाळणो साडूमाता आपको पाछो मेल माथा पर छाबड़ा में (म्हे)। फिर बिदा (व्हिया है)। तीन तिलोकी को नाथ माळवै पूगता (म्हे)। नाहरी कन्नु दरबार का हुकमूं साडूमाता मांगता (मांगता जी कीयो)। जय बोलो श्री देवनारायण भगवान की (जय)। तो तीन कोस के दूड़िया खेड़ा से उरै दूधी नीमड़ी ही एक (म्हे)। भगवान को पाळणो कह बतावै बी जागां मतै उतर गो बठै (नीमड़ी के हेटै ही उतर गी)। जतै माळवै में गेला में देव रिया नै (म्हे)। जिता दिन ताणी तो गूजरी को बोबो (चूंगता रिया)। हेंर बी नीमड़ी पर पाळणो उतरिया पछै कह बतावै की बता दिन चूंगियो (हां आगै कोनी चूंगियो)। बी नीमड़ी नै चूंसता (वाह वाह)। तो बगड़ावतां की महादेवी कांजरी ही जकी बगड़ावतां नै जांचबा नै आयी है नै (म्हे)। जी दिन बगड़ावत कांई करियो के दोवड़ा बीनै गहणां का बनाया (म्हे)। हेंर कीयो जा भाई देश में दातारां नै जांचियां (जांचियां कीयो)। मांवूं दूणो दान

देबाळो होवै (म्हे)। तो म्हांको नांव (छोड़ देयी)। अर आगला को (नांव लेबा लाग जायज्यो)। आ देश के मांयनै दातारां नै जांचबा नै नीकल गैइ (म्हे)। लेरावूं बगड़ावतां को जो महाभारत (हां हु ग्यो काम आग्या जी कीयो)। दरबार का हुकमूं काम आयगा जर पाछी आई (वाह वाह)। शंकरवूं अब कौल बचन कर गैइ की के भाई बगड़ावत में पाछी आवूं नै (जितै अखै मिलणा चाहीज्ये)। शंकर बी टैम में ज्यादा नशा में हो (म्हे)। कहनी आयगो जावो चण्डी अखै मिलै गा (पाछा आजाज्यो अखै लाधी बगड़ावत)। कुछ नी बिगड़ै गो (वाह वाह)। तो शंकर कन्नै आर आपकी बगड़ावतां नै मांगबा लागी है (म्हे)। हेंर शंकर कीयो देख बांका तो वादा पुराणी बांतां ही जको वादा आयगा भाई (हां वादा पूरा हो ग्या)। तो अब इन्द्रासान का गियोड़ा है (म्हे)। जेज छै महीना तक लागी (वाह वाह)। तो बिजोरी कांजरी तेजाजी कन्नै जाय रीछोर के परबत (म्हे)। तेजाजी बगड़ावतां नै जांच (वाह वाह)। नागौर कानै बिदा (हुई है)। नागौर में ओ भाट है जको नानेरा गिया बगड़ावत मरियो जर (म्हे)। ओ आपको गूंगो व्हियोड़ो मुलक में फिरयाया (हां गूंगो व्हियोड़ो रहवै अमल कठै)। धणी तो मर गा तो दरबार का हुकमूं बिजोरी बूझणा करी रे भाट अठै देश में क्युं फिरै ई मैं (हां ई देश में कींयां फिरै रे कीयो)। कीयो भाई धणी जातां रिया तो मतेई फिरां (हां मतेई रुळियोड़ा हां)। कीयो धणी गिया कोनी (म्हे)। धणी के पछै बै भगवान तीन तिलोकी को नाथ औतार लियो (वाह वाह)। औतार होतां ही देव महाराज माळवै जातां रिया जा भाट भगवान नै माळवाऊं ल्यावो (माळवाऊं पाछा बुलाय अर लेवाओ कीयो)। गोठ खेड़ा बसावो पछै (वाह वाह)। कीयो बिजोरी बात तो तनै ठा तो जांच तो पूरी हे कीयो हां भाई (हां फोड़ा मत घाली न म्हने)।

ए नागौर से तो जी भाट बगड़ावतां को बिदा व्है ग्या रे।
पूग गो भाटजी रे नंदिया के निवाण।
आपां चालां मांजी ये माळागर की भोम में।
चालां ठाकर ये देव के जी दिवाण।
(भलां जी भलां)। देव भलां

नागौर से बगड़ावतां को भाट। (म्हे)। पूगो भाट नंदिया के (निवाण)। आंपां चालां देळूमाता माळागर की भोम में (वाह वाह)। ठाकर देव के (दिवाण)। जकै दिन भाट की मां ही जकी साथ ही (म्हे)। तो घणा दिन हो गा सपरा पूग ग्या जी टैम में (वाह वाह)। देळूमाता बूझणा (करी है)। कीयो रे भाट (म्हे)। कती दूर तो आयगा कतीक दूर माळवो रियो भाई अब (हां अब कतीक दूर है माळवो है कीयो)। कीयो माता ए मणमूं हाल पाव ही कोनी पीसीज्यो (हां थोड़ी सी ही दूर चालियां कीयो)। माळवो तीन सौ कोस हे अटवूं (हां नेड़ो ही कोय नी)। कीयो रे भाट जो म्हारा तो बारा दिन गेलो में हुई भाई जरां (हां गेला में ही हो जय के मैं माळवै तो क्यें को)। के तूं माळवै पूग जाय (म्हे)। पाछो कोनी पूगै (पाछो आणै को नैइ है)। तो रुदन कर देळूमाता (म्हे)। और बो भाट बगड़ावतां को दरबार का हुकमूं सपरा नंदी पर शीला ही एक जको बी शीला पर मां बेटो सोय गा (हां दोन्यु मां बेटो सोयगा)। हेंर घोड़ो हो नै (बी शीला के बांध लियो)। दरबार का हुकमूं तीन तिलोकी को नाथ दूधिया नीम पै बिराजमान हो मेलियो भैरूंनाथ ने बूझणा (करी है)। के भैरूंनाथ (म्हे)। म्हारो बैइ

को भाट दुख पावै भाई (हां बीनै जाय अर लेयावो कीयो)। सपरा नंदी पर सुतो है (वाह वाह)। मूठी का देवातण हा (म्हे)। हां दरबार का हुकमूं आंख जपै बती दार में आयगा (वाह वाह)। सपरा नंदीवूं शीला नै अधर के अधर उठाई (म्हे)। काळियोदे तळाव हो माळवा की भोम में (हां बठै ल्यार छोड़ दिया। (हां जियान का जियान ही छोड़ दिया)। परभात की टैम देळू भाटणी ऊठी (वाह वाह)। तो बो पाणी तो बहतो हो (म्हे)। बो पाणी पड़ियो हो (तळाव भरियोड़ो ही पड़ियोड़ो हो)। देळूमाता बूझणा करी रे छोछू (म्हे)। ऊठ भाई रात सुता हा जकी जगां (बा कोय नी कीयो)। भाट ऊठ अर कीयो माता (म्हे)। माळवा की भोम तो आयगी भैइ (हां आंपां तो माळवै ही आ पूग गी कीयो)। कीयो रात तो तूं के छै महीना लागी (म्हे)। अर तीन सौ कोस है सुता सुता माळवो कींयां आयो (हां ओ कींयां आयो रे भाई कीयो)। कीयो भगवान आपणो देव महाराज लियायो (वाह वाह)। तो ई म्हनै सवाई भोज की जान में आयो मैं ई (म्हे)। जी दिन सवाई भोज को सुसरो म्हनै को घोड़ो दियो (हां एक घोड़ो दिन्यो)। बो म्हारै दाय कोनी लाग्यो (वाह वाह)। काट पूंछड़ो (म्हे)। ई काळियादे में रळ गियो मैं बीनै (अठै छोड़ग्यो)। बो काळियोदे है कीयो (ओ है कीयो)। साडूमाता कांई करियो के गायां ही ने बगड़ावतां की (म्हे)। बांकै लेरै बगड़ावतां का गुआल हां जका ने घर के धंधै (दूसरै धंधै लगा दिया घरां)। हेंर दरबार का हुकमूं पीर का भाइयां का टाबार हां जका नै गायां का लेरै (गुआल खिना दी जी कीयो)। मां नै कीयो रे भाई (म्हे)। एक म्हांकै ईंयां को दुश्मन लागयोड़ो है लेरै (लारै है कीयो)। बीकी निंगै राखज्यो आजाय तो (अठै आगै नै मत आण दीज्यो रस्ता में ही मार दीज्यो)। भुवाजी कांई ऐनाणा-सैनाणा है (हां जकी बता द्यो)। कीयो फूलरियो तो घोड़ो है चड़बा नै (म्हे)। बूड़ी बी की मां सागै (है कीयो)। मोटा मोटा गला में राखै (तूंबा)। जी टैम में बो आवेलो नी (म्हे)। जी टैम में आ गाय (म्हे)। हेंर बो मिनख बा बतां करै जियान (करेला कीयो)। परभात की टैम गायां भगवान की काळियादे पर पूगती (हुई है)। गायां दीखी नै भाट नै (म्हे)। सुरबीण नै घाल गाला में (बजावण लाग्यो)। बैइ को भाट बोलै कांई समचार गायमाता ने कहवै देखां (कीआवूं जाणज्यो भोपाजी महाराज कीआवूं देखां)। अबार कहवूं भगवान देव का हुकमूं देखां (वाह वाह सा)।

जळ खड़ तो जी यो देश में मोकळा र।
नागलीमाता ये भंवरा रिया भरणाट।
बैइ को भाट करै थानै बूझणा।
नागलीमाता ये दूबली किस्यै गुणाय।
(भलां जी भलां) देव भलां

जळ खड़ तो माता देश में मोकळा है (वाह वाह)। भंवरा रिया (भरणाट)। बैइ को भाट करै बूझणा (म्हे)। नागलीमाता थै दूबली किस्यै (गुणा कीयो)। दूबली क्यूं भाई (हां अती दूबली कींयां हो कीयो)। जळ इतो घणो (म्हे)। खड़ (हां खानै नै मोकळो है)। भंवरा भरणावै बेटी का बाप नै (वाह वाह)। तो सुरेमाता बोलै (म्हे)। कांई समचार देखां भाट नै (कहवै पाछा देखां कीआवूं जाणज्यो कीआवूं)। अबार कह द्यां देव का हुकमूं जरां। (वाह वाह सा)।।

ए जळ खड़ तो जी ए ई देश में मोकळा रे।
भाट नारदी रे भंवरा रिया भरणाट।
जासा को निरपाल उछरियो कोय ने।
धूपट भेळ दे तो रे बदशाहियां का माल।।
(भलां जी भलां) देव भलां

जळ खड़ घणा ही ई देश में (म्हे)। दरबार का हुकमूं भंवरा रिया (भरणाट)। दरबार का हुकमूं जासां का निरपाल उछरियो कोनी (म्हे)। कदै ई धूपट भेळतो रे बदशाही का ही (माल कीयो)। सुण रे भाट (म्हे)। ओ दुख है भाई म्हानै (हां ऊनाळो साखा) गहूं चन्ना की जींवती (बै म्हांकै हाथ नैइ लागे)। मैं जांवां तो आथूणी मन म्हांको है (म्हे)। अरै देख उघाड़ा माथाला गुआल सींगां के ठोक कर अगूणी ले जावै (हां अगूणी घालै है कीयो ठोक कर)। सुरेमाता भाट के घरै ले लियो (वाह वाह)। देव का गुआल गायां का लेरली मुरी में के ऊंचा पाळ पर (चड़िया है)। कीयो ए गुआलां (म्हे)। बो भुवाजी कीयो है नै जको आदमी आज आयो है (हां ओ आज आयो है म्हांकालो बैरी)। ले ले गेडियां दरबार का हुकमूं भाट के चारूंमेर (हां बारो कर फिर रिया है जी कीयो)। तो सुरेमाता भाट के घेरो गुआलां को छुड़ा दियो (वाह वाह)। नागली गाय दूधै नीम जार दरबार नै अरदास करी (म्हे)। श्री महाराज बैइ को भाट आयो है गुआल मारै (हां बै थांका गुआलिया मारै है भुवाजी लियाला जी)। दरबार का हुकमूं भैरूंनाथ नै बूझणा करी भैरवानाथ (म्हे)। गुआल की जात है भैइ (वाह वाह)। ईकी मां नै भाट नै तो खतम हो जावै (हां लियावो कीयो)। जावो अठै ही लियावो (वाह वाह)। तो काळो गोरो भैरूंनाथ आं कन्नै पूगता (व्हिया है)। गुआलां का जितै कांई करियो गुआल भाट के पकड़ भाट नै (म्हे)। गोढालकड़ी दे काळियादे के मांय गुड़ा दियो (वाह वाह)। भैरूंनाथ खुलाय गोढालकड़ी (म्हे)। हेंर कीयो लियो भाटजी थांका धणी कन्न ले चांलां (चालो पधारो कीयो)। दूधीयै नीम भाट नै छोड़ियो बी टैम भाट बगड़ावतां को जातो ही आसका दीनी है (भगवान नै)। दरबार का हुकमूं बैइ को भाट है न बगड़ावतां को (म्हे)। जको आसका दियो (वाह वाह)। कीयो आद राजा आद का जुगाद राजा जुगाद का काछब काछब का रणधोळ (म्हे) रणधोळ का कजळी कजळी का मण्डळी (म्हे)। अर मण्डळी का हरीरामजी (वाह वाह)। हरीरामजी का बाघ जलमिया बाघ का भोज व्हिया अर भोज का देव (व्हिया जी कीयो)। अगणकुण्ड का ऊपनिया अर कुली बड़ा हो (चुहाण)। अरै पगतळी पदम बिराजै खुंवा राजा (खेम)। ऊंका है नागर (बेल)। लीला की एम से पताल में हेमजळ गाजियो (वाह वाह)। डूंगरा हो गाय (व्यवार)। देव का औतार व्हिया जकै दिन धरती बीचै आबा बीचै बन्या (उजास)। अरै भोज का उदल (म्हे)। पड़ता आबा (झेळ)। कीयो आओ भाटजी आओ (पधारो)। ईंयां की आसका तो आज ताणी तो म्हानै तो कहबालो (हां मिलियो कोनी)। हेंर औरूं मिलतो ही (दीखै कोनी कीयो)। कांई भाट बोलै (म्हे)। हेंर भगवान नै बतलावै देखां (कीआवूं जाणज्यो देखां अब कीआवूं)।

खंक ऊनाळो जी बाजै रे गोठालां राजवियां रे।
बाजै अन्नदाता रे सुरिया और पिरवाई रे।

गोठां में पधारो जी धरमराजा देवजी।
अबें रे अन्नदाता रे रितू मेवा की आई तो।
(भलां जी भलां) देव भलां

खंक ऊनाळो बाजै आज (म्हे)। गोठां का राजवी बाजै सुरिया और (पिरवाई) गोठां मैं पधार नै पधार नै पधार धरमराजा देवजी (म्हे)। अरै रितू मेवा (अब आई जी कीयो) अन्नदाता गोठां पधारो (हां अब अठै मत रहो)। आवो भाट अब आवो (वाह वाह)। मात खटाणी नै गुआलिया जार बूझणा करी ले भाई भुवाजी (हां बो आया तो गियो थांकालो समालो)। दरबार का हुकमूं साडूमाता मन में देखियो ए कुबदियो भाट आयग्या नै (म्हे)। जरां देव नै छोड़ै कोनी ले जाय (हां ले तो जाय अटवूं छोड़ै तो कोनी)। दरबार का हुकमूं भाट ताणी तो साडूजी जहर का कांसा (बनाया है)। देव महाराज ताणी अमरत का (कांसो बनाया जी कीयो)। जावो ए दासियां (म्हे)। तो दरबार नै तो देआओ अमरत को कांसो (वाह वाह)। बी भाट नै (ओ जहराळो कांसो ले जार सिरका दीज्यो)। दरबार का हुकमूं कुबदियो मर जावै तो पाप कठ जाय (वाह वाह)। चौईस भाई बगड़ावत हां जका नै ही दुश्मन रावजी खाई गो (म्हे)। आंको तो मगदूर ही (हां कांई है कीयो)। देव महाराज देख कांसा नै (म्हे)। मन में विचार करियो रे डोकळडी दगो कर दियो (हां ई भाट नै मारसी)। अमरत को कांसो जको तो भगवान के मुण्डा के हां दियोड़ो हो जको भाट के मुण्डा के सिरका दियो (म्हे)। हेंर जहर को कांसो भाट कन्नै जको आप (थोड़ा सरका लियो) ।साडूमाता महलां में ऊबी ऊंची निंगै (हां कर लीनी)। कांई हेटी आवे महलांवूं (म्हे)। कांई भोजाई नै बतलावै देखां (कीआवूं जाणज्यो देखां कीआवूं)।

खण चड़ै तो जी जो साडू खण हेटा उतरै औवूं रे।
खण खण आतो जी भाइयां के आंगण जाय।
जहर करियो भोजायां कुबदिया भाट ने।
म्हानू नानियो ये ऊद निगेलियां जाय।
(भलां जी भलां) देव भलां

खण चड़ै माजी सा खण हेटा ही उतरै (वाह वाह)। खण खण भाइयां के आंगण (अब जाय)। जहर करियो ये हीड़ागर दासियां कुबदिया भाट नै (म्हे)। ओ ठाकर ऊद निगेलियां (अब जाय जी कीयो)। भोजायां जावो रे भाई उठावो भाजो कोय (हां देवजी जहरवालो कांसो जीमे)। कीयो के माजी साय (म्हे)। तूं जाणै थारो भगवान जाणै (म्हानै ई बात को ठा कोनी कीयो)। तो तीन तिलोकी को नाथ जहर को कांसो जीम (म्हे)। के खेंखारो (करियो)। बीण दिन बी जहर का बीछू पैदा (करिया जी कीयो)। काळा खोड़ियाळा बीछू भगवान की सेवा में (लाग ग्या)। बैइ को भाट आपका धणी कन्नै जातां (म्हे)। देव महाराज अमरत को कांसो भाट नै देतां (वाह वाह)। जय बोलो श्री देवनारायण की (जय)। अब भगवान बूझणा करी (म्हे)। कीयो भाटजी (वाह वाह)। ठीक है थांकाळो देश में तो चालां ही (म्हे)। पण बसी का लोगां सागा आय साडूमाता के जका नै ई भाई सूचना देयो (हां बां नै समचार दे दियो जको बीर हुऐ चालां)। आपणै गाड़ा के पूठी पाचरा नारां ने तियार कर लियो भाई (वाह

वाह)। तो भाट बगड़ावतां को कांई बसी लोगां कन्नै जावै (म्हे)। कांई समचार कह दियो देखां (कीआवूं जाणज्यो देखां कीआवूं)।

> खड़ाऊं पहरिया तो जी ए ई पगां में मोचड़ा रे।
> फिर फिर बसी का लोगां कन्नै जाय।
> कोय चालै रे जलम भोम का देश में।
> माळागरूं देव तो पाछी हांकै गाय।
> (भलां जी भलां) देव भलां

खड़ाऊं पहर लिया भाटजी पगां में मोचड़ा (वाह वाह)। फिर फिर बसी का लोगां कन्नै (जाय)। अरे कोय चालै भाई देश का आपका जलम भोम का देश में (म्हे)। दरबार माळागरूं आज पाछी हांकेला (गाय)। बसी का लोगां (म्हे)। गाड़ां नै तियार करो भाई (हां पाछा चालो)। साडूमाता नै बूझणा करी माजी साय (म्हे)। थै भाइयां कन्नै सीख मांगो (हां सीख मांग लियो अर चालण की तियारी करो)। कीयो आओ जी भाटजी आओ घणा दिना उडीकता अब आया थें (वाह वाह)। म्हानै तो बांटां नाळतां ने घणा दिन (हां बोहळा दिन हो ग्या म्हूं कहवै आवै जणा ही चालां)। तो इसियो काम करो मैं ई तियार हूं (म्हे)। पण मैं जिण दिन आई नै अठै (वाह वाह)। जिण दिन भगवान की नांव से ए सिन्ध-बड़ा की सुवा रुपिया की सीरणी बोल्योड़ी है (हां सीरणी बोल्योड़ी है बा जार चड़ाई आओ)। पाछो आजावो (पाछा आजावो चांलां कीयो)। तो भाट नै कोड लाग्यो जणा तो काम सिधो है भैइ (हां माजी तो एकदम तियार ही बैठिया हैं)। कीयो रे माजी साय लेयावो (वाह वाह)। मात खटाणी सुवा रुपिया की तो भाट के पल्लै परसादी बांध दी (वाह वाह)। कीयो भाटजी ईयां कह दीज्यो (हां जांवतां ही)। कीयो भाई साडूमाता थानै भोग दियो है ने जको तियार ले लियो (हां ले लियो)। भाट नै तो परसादी बांध रवाना कर दियो (वाह वाह)। साडूमाता लेरूं पाणी की सात कड़छी डाल दी जोगणियां के नांव से (हां आ ल्यो ए जोगणियां अब)। मिनख आवै म्हारो (बी आंतां ही भख जाईज्यो)। मिनख को भख है म्हारो ले लीज्यो (वाह वाह)। दरबार का हुकमूं सिन्धबड़ा बगड़ावतां को भाट पूगतो (व्हियो है)। जाय बड़ के हेटै बैठ (म्हे)। कीयो लियो भाई जोगणियां (म्हे)। साडूमाता जको भोग दियो जको ओ लियो तियार थांको ले लियो (हां तियार है ले लियो कीयो)। कहतां जेज (लागी)। तो जोगणियां किरकाड़ पड़ी जको भाट की तो बोटी बोटी पाती (हां आई एक एक बोटी हाथ आई कोनी)। दरबार का हुकमूं भाट को सागार कर गी जोगणियां (वाह वाह)। दिन तीन हु गा (म्हे)। भाट की माता गियोड़ी नी देळूजी सागै (वाह वाह)। बा बसी का लोगां नै बूझै रे भाई सिन्धबड़ा कुण है (हां सिन्धबड़ा कठै है गौभाई कीयो)। कीयो डोकरी थारै कांई करणो है (हां थारै कांई काम है कीयो)। कीयो म्हारो बेटो गियो दिन तीन हु गा भाई (हां पाछो आयो कोनी औरूं कीयो)। कीयो सुण ये माता (म्हे)। सिन्ध-बड़ा गांव नी है (हां गांव कोय नी बठै है)। जोगणियां का बख है बी जागां (वाह वाह)। बठै गियोड़ो पाछो नी आवै (हां पाछो आणै को मानवी कोनी कीयो बो तो कोनी आवे)। देळूमाता बी जागावूं रोई रो रुदन करबा लागी कांई देव के दुलीचै (जावे)। कांई भगवान नै अरदास करै देखां (जांवता ही कांई ओळमा दे देखां)।

ए बीको भोलायो तो जी ए ई नागौर की भोम में औवूं रे।
कागद लियायी मैं तो ए मेदू कन्नु कन्नै से जाय।
धाई दुगाणी रे अन्नदाता थाणी लाख की।
म्हनै नै अन्नदाता रे आई जिसी खिनाय।
(भलां जी भलां) देव भलां

दरबार का हुकमूं के बीको भोलायो मैं नागौर की भोम में (म्हे)। कागज लियायी मेदू कन्नै (जार)। अरै धाई दुगाणी अन्नदाता थानी लाख की (म्हे)। म्हनै आई जिसी तो (पाछी खिनाय कीयो)। श्री महाराज आई तो दुगाणी नी ही में (म्हे)। दुगाणी धाई थारी मैं (वाह वाह)। दोन्यो मां बेटो साथ आया पण आयी जियान पाछी खिना दी (हां बियां की बियां पूगावो कीयो)। देळूमाता कांई रुदन करै कांई भगवान नै समचार कहवै देखां (कीआवूं जाणज्यो देखां कीआवूं)।

ए बीको भोलायो तो जी ए सुहावळ की भोम में औवूं रे।
कागद लियायी मैं तो जी अजमेरां से जाय।
धाई दुगाणी अन्नदाता थानी लाख की।
चाली म्हाना रे छोछू जियान का रतन गमाय।
(भलां जी भलां) देव भलां

मैं बीको तो भोलायो देख सुहावळ की भोम में (म्हे)। कागद लेयाई मेदू कन्नै से अजमेरां सूं (जार)। धाई दुगाणी अन्नदाता लाख की (म्हे)। मैं चाली म्हारा छोछू जियान का रतना (गमार)। छोछू जियान का रतना हा म्हारा (हां बी नै गमा दियो म्हारो)। अन्नदाता दुगाणी आगड़ी की (वाह वाह)। तीन तिलोकी को नाथ भगवान बोलै अब (म्हे)। कांई देखां देळू भाटणी नै समचार कहवै (कीआवूं भोपाजी महाराज कीआवूं)। अबार कहवूं देव का हुकमूं ले तूं (वाह वाह सा)।

ए रोय रोय तो जी जो रुदन मत करियै देळू भाटणियां रे।
तूं तो माता ये हां घड़ेक पलमूं सार।
लीलागर जीण करूं रे देळू भाटणियां।
एक होंकारा थारा जी छोछू कर द्यूं चार।
(भलां जी भलां) देव भलां

रोय रोय माता तूं रुदन मत कर (म्हे)। देळू भाटणी थोड़ो घड़ेक पलमूं (अब सार)। लीला पर अबार जीण करा द्यूं (म्हे)। एक होंकारा में छोछू करूं (थारा चार)। एक गमियो है की थारो (हां एक ही गमियो है कांई)। अन्नदाता भूखो धायां (पतीजै)। म्हनै चार की जरूरत कोनी (हां म्हारो सागै एक ही तो लेयावो)। तो माता थोड़ी नेठाव राख (वाह वाह)। पहल पोत माळागर की भोम में कांई लीलागर बिछाण भगवान पिलाणै (म्हे)। हेंर कांई देखां भाट की सरजींवत करबा की चड़ाई कर दियां देखां (कीआवूं जाणज्यो देखां अब कीआवूं)। अबार कहवां भगवान का हुकमूं (वाह वाह जी वाह वाह)।।

पाला ही फूंक पिलाणज्यो कर लीलागर बाहरें बेगो ही आण।
लीलो चाल्या धरतीमाता धर हरै बासक डरै पियांळ।
लीलो परणालिया गियो धरमराजा देवजी दिलै हला दी बाग।
खेम करो गोठां का राजवी और पिलावूं दूधां धायां काबरिया टार।
मकेरिया नै माथो मार दे पालासानी पड़ी चरण दे लाप।
पिलाण लेय काळी जायो लीलड़ो बैरियां में घाला अंवळी संवळी जांप।
लीलो ऊपरी नारायण को बैसणो जिण पर देव बिराज्यो आण।
नौसरी खरां पर पाखर पड़िया रे।
काळका देवी करै रे भैरूं नै बूझणा।
आसांगांवूं लंका भेळी देव की रे कुनै हुई चड़ाइया रे।
(भलां जी भलां) देव भलां

पालासानी भाई फूंक पिलाणो (म्हे)। कस लीलागर के बाहरें बेगो (आण)। लीलो चाल्या धरतीमाता धर हरै (वाह वाह)। बासक डरै (पियांळ)। लीला तो परणालिया गियो धरमराजा देवजी की (म्हे)। लीलै हला दी (बाग)। हुकम करो बाळा ठाकर देवजी (म्हे)। औरूं पिलाणूं दूधां धायां काबरिया (अब मैं टार)। मकेरिया नै माथै मार दे पालासानी पड़ै चरण दे (लांप)। अरै पिलाण भाई काळी जायो लीलड़ो (म्हे)। बैरियां में घाला अंवळी संवळी (जांप)। लीला ऊपरै नारायण को बैसणो जी पर देव बिराज्यो (आण)। नौसर खरां पर पाखर (पड़िया)। काळका देवी करै भैरूं नै बूझणा (म्हे)। आसांगांवूं लंका नै भगवान भेळी (म्हे)। आ थारी इता देव की कोनु हुई (औरूं . . . . ?)। तो दरबार का हुकमूं सिन्ध-बड़ा की चड़ाई कुण कुण करी (म्हे)। के काळो तो गोरो भैरवानाथ (वाह वाह)। अर देव महाराज अर पालोसानी (हां चारो जना चड़ाई करी जी कीयो)। देव महाराज तो गैलै गैलै बहवै घोड़ो चड़ियोड़ा (म्हे)। भैरवानाथ उजड़ चालै (वाह वाह)। दरबार का हुकमूं देव महाराज बूझणा करी भैरवानाथ (गैलै आजावो कांटां में उजड़ क्यूं भाजो कीयो)। कीयो श्री महाराज कोय कुबद सीखा (वाह वाह)। कात्तिक को महीनो जकै दिन (म्हे)। जको झाड़ कांकै बै बोरियां लाग्या करै नै पीला पीला (वाह वाह)। कात्तिक को तो महीनो हो झाड़ की बोरियां सब भरी (काटा भरियोड़ी ही)। तो लूंकड़ी जानवर होवै जको आय (पूंछड़ै को दे आंटो)। ए खळ खळी (दिनी)। बोरियां सारा जमी पर (आंतां पड़िया जी कीयो)। लूंकड़ी बा बोरियां नै चुगबा लागी (वाह वाह)। भैरवानाथ बूझणा करी श्री महाराज एक कुबद सीख ग्या (हां एक तो सीख लीनी)। कांई (म्हे)। कीयो बा लूंकड़ी है बी के मांयनै जको पोध में खड़ी है नी (म्हे)। जकी की जकी मैं जार सिन्धबड़ा में (जोगणियां में करालां कीयो)। तो सिन्धबड़ा में पूगिया बी टैम में (म्हे)। भैरवानाथ दोन्यो जणा पोड़ पकड़ लियो (वाह वाह)। पकड़ पोड़ के खळ खळी (दिनी)। पान पान में जोगणियां (बैठी ही)। तड़क तड़क तड़क तड़क सगळी हेटी (आर पड़ी जी कीयो)। दरबार का हुकमूं सारै बावड़ी ही (म्हे)। बावड़ी के मांयनै (जार पड़ गी)। भैरवानाथ बूझणा करी श्री महाराज मैं तो दोहरी पटकी बावड़ी में पड़ गी रांडां (हां थें आडा कोनी फिरया कीयो)। कीयो एक जागां भेळी हुई है भैइ (हां कठै जाय कोनी आ)। भैरवानाथ तो ले कोरड़ा अर पाणी में

बड़ गा (हां बावड़ी के मांयलै छेड़ै बड़तां व्हिया)। के जोगणियां नै सरकाई (वाह वाह)। जोगणियां ऊंची भाजी (म्हे)। ऊंची भाजी तो पेड़ी के ऊपर भगवान तीन तिलोकी को नाथ ऊबा (हां मुण्डा के ऊबा हां जी कीयो)। बूझणा करी रे बेटी का बाप काळिया दांगी नू भगवान (म्हानै मरावै क्युं है तूं)। कीयो बैइ को भाट आयो है बो कठै है (बो देवो जको मैं तो अबार छुड़ा देस्यूं)। अरै श्री महाराज दिन तीन हो गा गिळ गी मैं तो (हां बी नै खाय गी कीयो)। कीयो बैइ डूबै म्हारी (म्हे)। जको बीनै पाछो ऊगेलो थें (हां ऊगेल अर पाछो राळो थें)। म्हारा धणी गल गो (म्हे)। कीयो गलिया बळिया नै भी राळो पाछो (हां पाछो राळया सरी)। तो जोगणियां घाल घाल गोतड़ा में आंगलियां (म्हे)। झूटयानी उलटियां (पाछी करी है)। देव महाराज कांई करियो की बी के नक्षो बना दिया (वाह वाह)। बी में दो चीज मिली कोनी (म्हे)। एक तो पांसली नी मिली (वाह वाह)। बी पांसली को मांस (हां ऊपरलो मिलियो कोनी)। कीयो जोगणियां (म्हे)। दो चीज मिली कोनी भाई (हां दो मिली कोनी बै औरूं बतावो)। कीयो मावूं में दो कोनी (वाह वाह)। कठै गी (बतावो)। कीयो गूंगी पड़ गी पताला अर गेली चड़ गी (आकाश)। तीन तिलोकी को नाथ पेड़ी छोड़ (वाह वाह)। फैर बिदा पूगता (व्हिया जी कीयो)। बासक राजा नै कीयो रे बासक राजा चोर आयग्यो म्हारो (म्हारो चोर आयो जका नै सूंप)। कीयो आयग्यो महाराज (म्हे)। पण शरणा की जागां है आ (वाह वाह)। शरणो ले लियो अब चोर अठै आयोड़ो द्यू कोनी भाई (हां पाछो मैं थानै ईंयां कोनी देवूं)। हार जीत करणी होवै तो म्हारावूं (हां करो अर हारा जावूं जण ले जावो)। बासक कांई जीत करां मैं (हां जकी बतावो)। कीयो मैं हार जावूं जर म्हारो माथो काटो (म्हे)। हेंर तूं हार जावै (वाह वाह)। थारो माथो (काट लेवूं)। तीन तिलोकी को नाथ तेंहरवीं पिताल बासक से चौपड़ रमबा लागा (वाह वाह)। बासक राजा राळै जका तो दरबार का हुकमूं काना ही काना (पड़ै जी कीयो)। हेंर जो देव महाराज राळै (म्हे)। पो बारा पच्चीस (पड़ै है)। तीन बारी के मांयनै देव महाराज (हां जीत ग्या)। बासका नै बूझणा करी रे बासक कांई बात है (म्हे)। कीयो जीत गियो महाराज तूं (हां जीत ग्या)। सेंस फण है जका मूं चोखी लागै जकी काटलै (एक फण काटलै कीयो)। कीयो नैइ (हां बै दूसरा)। ए तो डाळा है ऊपरूं (म्हे)। पोड़ एक है (हां पोड़मो लिया कीयो)। बासक कीयो भाई महाराज ईंयां मत कर भाई (वाह वाह)। शीश के मांयनै जो आपकी किन्या परणा दे जर बैर उतर जावै (हां बैर पूरा हो जायां करे)। तेंहरां बरस की नागकिन्या हे म्हारै लड़की (म्हे)। जकी आप नै (परणा देस्यूं)। कीयो किसी तूं कुली को नाग है भाई (जकी बता)। मैं तो हूं गोग चुहाण (म्हे)। क्युं मैं ले लियो चुहाणा का औतार बोल (हां थारी बेटी अर म्हारै संबन्ध होवै कींयां)। कीयो श्री महाराज (म्हे)। नागां की कुली नौ है (वाह वाह)। नौ कुली का नाग हां मैं (म्हे)। म्हारा साळा की लड़की और है म्हारै कन्नै (बी नै परणा द्यूं)। तो तेंहरवीं पिताल बासक राजा की साळा की बेटी से भगवान की पहलो ब्याव (व्हिया है)। देव को शादी हुई (वाह वाह)। पिताल में (म्हे)। ब्याव कर भगवान पाछा बावड़िया (वाह वाह)। भैरवानाथ बूझणा करी श्री महाराज चोर लियावा नी गियो तूं (हां तूं तो ब्याव करतो फिरै कीयो)। कीयो भैरवानाथ मतै ई कुदरती हु गो भाई (वाह वाह)। पण भाई भाट का कांई करां (जकी बतावो)। कीयो चोर तो कोनी हाथ लागै (म्हे)। केर रूंख ऊबो हो बी नै कीयो जावो केर बो काट लियावो एक घोचो (हां ईको एक लकड़ी काट लियावो)। केर बोल्यो श्री महाराज तूं ही काट दुनिया कींयां छोड़ी म्हानै (हां दुनिया म्हनै लाखां

ही छोड़ेली कोनी कीयो) । कीयो जो म्हनै धोकी (म्हे) । जको टालो तो तनै काटै भी कोनी (वाह वाह) । जै काट लेवै (म्हे) । चुला में बाळ दे तो दरबार का हुकमूं आ सोगण है म्हारी जकै दिन परसादी करै बी दिन थारो कांटो ही (बळ जावे) । तो में मानू ही कोनी (हां बा सुवामणी अगत) (ही जावे मैं नैइ मान्यता करूं बी की) । आज तूं म्हनै साथ दे दे (हां साथ तो तनै देनो पड़ी) । तो पछै आ थारा टाल ही है (वाह वाह) । दरबार का हुकमूं हिरण नै जार कीयो हिरण को मांस काट लियो भाई (वाह वाह) । हिरण कीयो श्री महाराज तूं ही कटाई दुनिया कीयां छोड़ी (हां दुनिया म्हनै लाखां ही कोनी छोड़ेली) । कीयो मारबो घणी चीज है म्हनै धोकी (म्हे) । जको तने तो आंगलीवूं कोनी बतावै (आंगलीवूं कोनी बतावै कठिनै गियो) । कांई बैइ का भाट नै भगवान सरजींवत करै (म्हे) । अर कांई वारता बनजावै देखां (कीआवूं जाणज्यो देखां अब कीआवूं) । अबार कहवां देव का हुकमूं ईकावूं (वाह वाह वाह वाह) ।।

ए केर की बनाई तो जी जो दरबार पांसलियां रे।
घालियो भाट के जी हिरणयांवूं वालो मांस।
सरजींवत कीयो बैइ का भाट ने।
इबी दिन भगवान रे मुखां बजायो बांस ।।
(भलां जी भलां) देव भलां

केर की बनाई भगवान भाट की पांसली (वाह वाह) । अर हिरणिया केरो (मांस) । सरजींवत कीयो रे बैइ का भाट नै (म्हे) । जकै दिन भगवान मुखां बजायो (बांस) । बांस की भोगली लेय (म्हे) । अर फूंक (भगवान नै दिनी) । भाट अरड़ कान्को बैठो (व्हिया जी कीयो) । ए श्री महाराज कांची निंदा मूं जगा दियो (हां नींद मीठी घणी आवै म्हनै कीयो) । कीयो भाट नींद तो आई जिसी आई भाई (वाह वाह अब तो ऊठ चालां) । पहली ब्याव भगवान को पिताल में नागकिन्या से व्हियो (वाह वाह) । जी दिन सरजींवत करबा गियो नै बैइ का भाट नै (म्हे) । तो भाट नै भगवान सरजींवत करतां हेंर पहली भगवान को ब्याव (होंवतां) । जय बोलो भाई श्री देवनारायण की (जय) । बोलो छोटा अर मोटा (अब स) ।। दरबार का हुकमूं भाट बगड़ावतां का नै सरजींवत कर भगवान (म्हे) । हेंर पाछा पूगता (व्हिया जी कीयो) । कीयो देळूमाता ले भाई समाल (हां ओ लेयो थारो भाट कीयो) । सागै को सागै है कोनी (हां) अरै श्री महाराज धणी तो मोटो हो भैइ जरां म्हारा नै तूं जींवतो करियो (वाह वाह) । पण श्री महाराज दुगाणीवूं धापयोड़ी हूं (म्हे) । म्हनै तो सीख दिरा द्यो (वाह वाह) । कीयो देळूमाता सागै ही चालां (वाह वाह) । भाट जी माजी कन्नै जाओ बाइयां कन्नू सीख मांगै (हां चालां कीयो) । हेंर मैं माळवै आया पछै मांमियां कन्नै हाल गियो कोनी (वाह वाह) । जो मांमियांवूं भाई दो बात तो करियावूं बांकी (हां मिल तो लियां पछा चालां जको) । तो भगवान तीन तिलोकी को नाथ कांई मांमियां के रावळै जावै कांई जातो ही मांमियां नै समचार कहवै देखां (कीआवूं देखां भोपाजी महाराज अब कीआवूं) । अबार कहवां भगवान देव का हुकमूं देखां (वाह वाह जी वाह वाह) ।।

ऐ सोरा रिया तो जी सुख पाया मांमी ए ताणै माळवै रे।
म्हारी मांमी ये सोरी चरी बा गाय।

काळ मत पड़ जियो ताणा देश में।
घणी निपज्यो मामी धोलती खोड़ियाली जुवांर।।
(भलां जी भलां) देव भलां

सोरा घणा रिया सुख पाया मैं (म्हे)। सोरी चरी म्हारी (गाय)। काळ मत पड़ जियो मामी थारा देश में (म्हे)। आ घणी निपज्यो ए खोड़ियाली धोलती (जुवांर)। ले भाई मामी सोरा रिया (वाह वाह)। काळ कदै मत पड़ज्यो (हां थारा देश में काळ मामी)। बचन है म्हारो (वाह वाह कोनी पड़े)। मामी बोलै कांई समचार देव नै कहवै देखां (कीआवूं जाणज्यो देखां कीआवूं)।।

ए सोरा रिया तो जी सुख पाया मामी का नाणदा रे।
ताणी दरबारजी सोरी चरी मैं गाय।
पांतरै ही काळ पड़ज्यो रे ही ताणा देश में।
थारै जियान को पांवणो म्हारै जी नितका आवै बार।।
(भलां जी भलां) देव भलां

सोरा रिया सुख पाया मामी का नाणदा (म्हे)। सोरी चरी आपकी (गाय)। काळ पांतरै पड़ीज्यो थारा देश में (म्हे)। थारै जियान को पांवणो म्हारै नितका आवै (बार)। कीयो मामी रुळा दिया भाई अबकै (वाह वाह)। थोड़ी बोली फैरूं (म्हे)। कीयो नौ कूंटी मारवाड़ है (म्हे)। एक कूंट में तो जरूरी (काल पड़ेला)। बचन है म्हारा ही (देव भूमी कीयो)। देव महाराज कीयो सुण भाई मामी साय कीयो घणो ही निपज ही पण पगां में तो पगरखिया पहरज्यो (म्हे)। हेंर ऊबाणा ही (फिरीज्यो)। म्हारा देश में एक एक घर में सेर सेर सोनो मिली (हां पहरियां फिरी कीयो)।

गाड़ां के दिरावो जी ए ई पूठी रे पाचरा रे।
हंकती करज्यो जी माळागर सूं गाय।
कोय चालै जलम भोम का देश में।
माळवा सूं भाई रे पाछी हांका गाय।।
(भलां जी भलां) देव भलां

दरबार का हुकमूं ओ समचार भगवान कीयो है गाड़ीवान नै (म्हे)। गाड़ां के दिरावो रे भाई पाछा पूठी पाचरा (वाह वाह)। हंकती करो आपणै देश नै (गाय)। कोय चालै भाई जलम भोम का देश में (म्हे)। अरै भगवान माळागरूं पाछी हांकेला (आज गाय)। सागै ही जाणू है (म्हे)। बिदा हो जावो (वाह वाह)। मात खटाणी नै बूझणा करी है माजी साय (म्हे)। तूं ही भाइयां कन्नु सीख मांग (चालां कीयो)। कीयो लाल सिधारूं (हां कोनी चालूं है कीयो)। दरबार का हुकमूं तूं भाट को कीयो करै (म्हे)। अरै चौईस भाई बगड़ावत हां (जका नै ही कळह कर कर ओ मरा दिया)। थें पांच तूंतड़ा थांको थाक ही (काही लागी बठै)। कीयो माजी साय (म्हे)। गोठ खेड़ा बसाया बिनै जुगत बैठै कोनी (वाह वाह)। तो दरबार का हुकमूं माजी सा म्हनै तो जाणी पड़ी भाई (वाह वाह)। कीयो लाल दोहरो मालियो दोहरो मोटो करियो जाबा द्यूं कोनी (हां जाण द्यूं कोनी कीयो) ईंयां जावै (म्हे)। इता दिन दूध चुगायां

तनै (जको म्हारो दूध तो दे जावो)। पछै जा बो गेलो पड़ियो (हां रस्तो पड़ियो पधारो)। तीन तिलोकी को नाथ भगवान कर ओबड़ (म्हे)। हेंर साडूमाता को दूध चूंगियो जिस्यो को जिस्यो तलाई भर दी मुण्डा के (हां पाछी तलाई भर दिनी)। ले भाई माता ओ ले थारो (मैं तो पाछो उलाग दियो तूं थारो बोबो में (पाछो ठाणै कर कीयो)। साडूमाता से दूध को जापतो व्हिया कोनी (म्हे)। कीयो लाल मैं समझ गी अब (हां मैं समझूं अब समझी कीयो)। थारी करामातवूं इता दिन ठा कोनी हो (हां ठा कोनी हो)। म्हारावूं दूध तो बोबो में कोनी गलै (हां कोनी गले)। कीयो नी गलै जरां माजी सा बीर हो जावो (चालो कीयो)। तो जी दिन दरबार उलटी कर दूध की तलाई बनाई नै (म्हे)। बा आज दिना कह दूधी तलाई बाजे बीनै (वाह वाह)।।

ए गाड़ां जूप गा तो जी ए ई बाळा देव का रे।
बा गाड़ां की ठाकरां जी खै असमाना जाय।
रात अर दिना को भगवान करिया बै खेड़बा।
दिन पेंतालीस सूं डेरा दीयाजी धार की गोरियां आज।
(भलां जी भलां) देव भलां

गाड़ां जूप गा नारायण देव का (म्हे)। बा गाड़ां की खै असमाना (अब जाय)। रात अर दिन को भगवान करियो खेड़बा (वाह वाह)। दिन पेंतालीस सूं डेरा दिया धार की गोरियां (आय)। पेंतालीस दिन लागा लेरै (वाह वाह)। ऊज्जनी धार पेंतालीस दिन में पूगिया (वाह वाह)। देव महाराज बूझणा (करी हैं)। कीयो रे भाई गाड़ा ही नारां की खाणिया ही जकी आज करवायज गी (म्हे)। हेंर गाय दूबली (हां थक गी)। तो ई जागां जळ भी अच्छो दीखै (म्हे)। खळ भी (हां अच्छो है कीयो)। तंबू ताण दियो अर गोरियां आपणी धार की (म्हे)। गायां नै खड़ में छोड़ो (वाह वाह)। देव महाराज का तंबू तो तण गा है (वाह)। गायां गुआल चरबा लाग (गिया जी कीयो)। तो ऊज्जनी धार का राजा का पूंवार के बाई ही (म्हे)। पगावूं पांगी ही आंखियांवूं आंधी ही डील में रिगचा (कोढ बहवां)। माथा पर सींगड़ो हो (वाह वाह)। देवी को मिण्दिर हो गांव के बाहरलै छेड़ै (म्हे)। चार जना पालकी नै उठाय (वाह वाह)। अधर की अधर बी देवी के मिण्दिर आय अर परिकरमा दिरावै (हां परिकरमा दिरार पाछी ले जावे)। बी मिण्दिर को बारणो (साव देव महाराज के सामै साम हो)। देव का तंबू को देवी का मिण्दिर को बारणो एक मिल गो (वाह वाह)। बी दिन पीपळदे राणी को तो पालकी आबो व्हियो (म्हे)। देव महाराज को जागबो (हां व्ही ग्यो)। तीन तिलोकी को भगवान अम्मी की नजर झांकी (म्हे)। तो पीपळदे राणी की तो काया कंचन की हो गी (वाह वाह)। हेंर सींगड़ा हींगड़ा मिट गा अर काया कचन की कोय (वाह वाह)। हेंर आंखियांवूं दीखबा लागो अर देव महाराज पग देयी (हां पगावूं चालीजबा लाग ग्या जी कीयो)। तो पीपळदे राणी की काया सुधारतां (म्हे)। आंखियां देंता (वाह वाह)। अर जलम दरबार का हुकमूं सुधारतां जय बोलो श्री देवनारायण भगवान की (जय)। दरबार का हुकमूं राणी नै पग दिया नै भगवान (म्हे)। जरां गाजा बाजा (व्हिया है)। शाही सम्मान (व्हिया की कीयो)। कीयो भाई इता दिन ताणी रही ही पीपळदे की पालकी जा जो है (म्हे)। इता दिना से आज देबी टूटी (आज देबी टूटी है कीयो)। तो पीपळदे राणी की काया जी की कंचन की हो गी (वाह वाह)।

पीपळदे राणी कीयो श्री महाराज पिता नै जार कीयो पिताजी जो म्हारी काया है नै थांकी देबी कोनी सुधारी (हां देबी कोनी सुधारी है)। जो बो मिण्दिर के सामनै तंबूवालो आयो है नै आदमी (म्हे)। बो आदमी म्हनै तो जीव दान (दिन्यो है)। तो म्हारो तो ओ कहनो है की आलागीला बांस कटार म्हनै तो बी के पल्लै लगा दियो ब्याव कर दियो शादी कर दियो (ईवूं परणा दियो म्हनै तो)। कीयो देख पीपळदे ओ रास्तो है माळवा को (वाह वाह)। तो मारवाड़ का लोग है नै (म्हे)। जका ई रास्तै बीहा करै रोज का ही (हां रोजीना ही बहवो करे)। घणा ही बहवै गायां का गुआल (वाह वाह)। तो म्हारी लड़की गायां का गुआल नै थोड़ी परणावूं (हां लाखां ही नैइ परणीजे)। कीयो पिताजी गुआल नी है ओ (हां भगवान है कीयो)। औतारी पुरुष म्हानै ई नै (म्हे)। कीयो औतारी म्हानै जहां म्हारै कोय जमाना में ई धार के दरवाजा के सरवधात का किंवाड़ा होतां (म्हे)। तो दांतां का गढ गाजना का देंत आया जको बै किंवाड़ उतार ले गा (हां उतार ले ग्या कीयो)। बे किंवाड़ा म्हारा पाछा अठै आजावै (आवे)। तो औतार जरूरी (मान जावूं)। धार को राजा लिख कागज (म्हे)। देव के बठै तंबू में भेज दियो (हां ओ लियो कीयो)। देव महाराज बांच कागज अर भाट नै बूझणा (करी है)। अरै बाबा भाट (म्हे)। म्हांकै नौकरी आयगी भाई (हां नौकरी आगी कीयो)। ए श्री महाराज आपके (हां क्येंकै नौकरी आवै कीयो)। सुण रे भाट ई की भूमी में आपां रिया (म्हे) तो आराम मिलियो (वाह वाह)। तो अतो कीयो तो भाई आपां ही करां (हां किंवाड़ तो लिया राळा ही तो उबड़ियां)। तो दांतां के गढ गाजनै चड़ाई कुण कुण कराई (म्हे)। भैरवानाथ अर देव महाराज ए दोई गिया (वाह वाह)। दांतां के गढ गाजनै पूगता (व्हिया है)। देंत सागळा ही आर भगवान के पगां (लाग ग्या जी कीयो)। देव महाराज बूझणा करी रे भाई बोलो थै आया हो मैं काम आया है थां कन्नै (जकी पहली सुणो)। कांई (कांई काम पधारिया महाराज)। कीयो ऊज्जनी धार का सरवधात का किंवाड़ व्हिया जका बा नै पूगता करो (हां पाछा पूगावो कीयो)। कीयो श्री महाराज लियाड़ी चीज मैं ईताणी (देवां आज कोनी कीयो)। लाखां कोनी देयां मैं (वाह वाह)। मैं पगां आपके यां पड़िया के म्हारै कन्नै चांवटी बाई है कुंवारी तेंहरां बरस की लड़की (म्हे)। छाती जान बाजार में तो म्हांकै कोई आगै हाथ नैइ आवै (हां) जै म्हांकै बर हाथ आजावै (म्हे)। तो मैं तो गेला में ही (हां खा जावां कीयो)। आप आयगा जको कुंवारपण उतर गो (हां बाई को कुंवारपण म्हांको उतारणो जरूरी है कीयो)। आपणै बै जो हथळेवा में आ जको किंवाड़ (हां आपणै बक्षीस कर देस्यां)। सकलप दे दियां बी को (वाह वाह)। ईंयां तो किंवाड़ दियां कोनी (इयां कोनी दियां)। देव महाराज कीयो भैरवानाथ के बांतां भाई कांई करणो है आपणै (हां कींयां करां)। कीयो आ जमां मूं कुण झगड़ो करी (हां झगड़ो कुण करी बी आपणै तो ब्याव जीरे)। आपणै ठीगार पोटार अर काम कढो (ब्याव क्युं कर लियो नै कीयो)। दांतां गढ गाजनी गिया जकै दिन चांवटी से दूजा ब्याब (देव महाराज करिया जी कीयो)। तो दरबार का हुकमूं जी टैम में हथळेवो जोड़ियो नै चांवटी राणी से (म्हे)। हथळेवो चड़ायो जी टैम में सरवधात का किंवाड़ देंत का जका सकलप (हां देव महाराज नै कर दिन्या)। ओ लियो श्री महाराज (आ लियो कीयो किंवाड़)। कीयो पूगार आओ भाई (चालो पूगार आवो)। देंतां के मेल माथै (म्हे)। हेंर धार की गोरियां ले जार (हां नका दिया)। पाछा आर पोढी (हां लगा दिनी)। दिन गे गिया किंवाड़ां नै देखिया लोग भाज्या (म्हे)। श्री महाराज बै किंवाड़ तो आयगा आपका (आपका आयगा पाछा कीयो)। धार को धणी देख किंवाड़

नै (म्हे) । कीयो भाई लिखबा में गलती है (हां आपणी गलती हो गैइ) । आपां आ कह दियां के कीवाड़ दरवाजा के चड़ना चाहीज्यै (चड़ना चाहीज्ये) । तो चड़ जाता (हां चड़ जाता) । पण अब बाई नै परणानी जरूरी (हां हो गी किंवाड़ ही चड़ै कोनी बाई नै परणानी हो गी) । भाट कन्नै पूगता व्हिया (वाह वाह) । कीयो भाट थारा धणी को ब्याव करां भाई (म्हे) । कीयो म्हारो धणी ब्याव दो कर लिया (अब कींयां का करै दो तो पहली कर ली ब्याव) । कीयो म्हांकै बाई सा हठ कर लियो भाई (म्हे) । कीयो श्री महाराज हठ ही कर लेयो नै तो देव महाराज पोढी लगा मेली सुता को ब्याव करो जरूर (कर देवो) । और ईंयां तो म्हारा धणी ब्याव कोनी (हां अब कोनी करावेला) । जो ब्याव को सामान है जको अठै लेयावो (वाह वाह) । तो बसी का लोग सागै आयगा (म्हे) । ऊज्जनी धार को राजा बाई को लेयायो सागे ब्याव को समान है जको सागै (लियाया) । भाट कीयो देखा सुणो भाई (म्हे) । के जी टैम में भगवान जागेला (वाह वाह) । मैं सैन करूं (से का से भाग जाईज्यो) । पीपळदे राणी नै कीयो तूं देख डोलिया के नीचै बड़ जाय (हां डोलिया के नीचलै छेड़ै बड़ जाईज्यो) । आ जळ की झारी है नै (म्हे) । जाग्यां पछै भगवान के मुण्डा के (सामनै कर दीज्यो) । निजर जळ के ऊपर (हां भगवान की पड़ी) । ठण्डी पड़ी (वाह वाह) । पिण्डत आपके चवरियां माण्ड दी सामान रच गो (वाह वाह) । और ब्याव की बिदी होबा लागी (म्हे) । मोहरां देव को नांव लेर भाट नै खूंजियां मूं घणी काढै (वाह वाह) । चवरियां नै भर दी मोहरांवूं (काटी भर दीनी) । तीन पाटियां बोल अर पीपळदे का फैरा को दस्तूर व्हियो (वाह वाह) । तीजा फैरा में भगवान के डील नै मरोड़ियो (हां पसवाड़ो फैरियो) । भाट कीयो सैन करी ए तो भैइ जागै भाजावो (हां भागो कीयो से का से) । बसी को लोग तो मतै मतै ही (भाज गिया है) । बिरामण मन में देखियो (म्हे) । अरै भाई ओ चीज उठालियां आ चीज घाललियां (हां मोहरां अठै की अठै रह जायली) । तीन तिलोकी को नाथ देव महाराज जागतां ही जहर की नजर (झांकिया है) । तो चारो बिरामण बी जागां ही पित्थर का ही (बन ग्या जी कीयो) । पीपळदे राणी डोलिया के नीचै (बड़ ग्या है) । देव महाराज बैठा और निंगै करी तो पीपळजी फट मुण्डा के खड़ी (हां झारी लिया ऊबा जी कीयो) । कीयो रे भाट (म्हे) । ओ काम अबकाळो कुण करियो (हां दो तो मैं करिया ओ कुण करियो औरूं तीजो) । कीयो श्री महाराज दो तूं करिया एक मैं ही कर दियो (हां एक ब्याव मैं करियो) ।।

ए सरगां में जी पीपळदे म्हाना झूंपड़ा रे ।
मैं तो राणी ये कुळ में आदू चार ।
घणी पिसतावै राणी ये पीपळदे पूंवार ।।
(भलां जी भलां) देव भलां

सरगां में राणी झूंपड़ा है म्हारै (म्हे) । मैं कुळ में आदू ही चार (चार) । अरै घणी पिसतावै राणी तूं म्हारै ही (घरवास) । राणी दुख पायो (दुख घणी पायी कीयो) । कीयो श्री महाराज (म्हे) । मैं तो आपकी चरणा में आणी चावूं (वाह वाह) । म्हारै घरवास की जरूरत कोनी (हां अतो ही चाहीज्ये) । मैं आपके चरणा में आयगी नै (म्हे) । मैं तो बस ओ इतो ही चावूं (और कोई कोनी चावूं) । और कांई नी चावूं तो दरबार का हुकमूं कह बतावै झूटी सांची के चार बै खूंटिया रोपी नै (म्हे) । बै तो चार भगवान दरखत पैदा कर दिया भाई (वाह वाह) । हेंर बिरामण है जका गोखै हाल पित्थर का हियोड़ा बैठा

बताया (हां चारूं का चारूं बियां ही बैठया है)। आज दिन मैजूद चवरियां में बतावै बठै देव महाराज बूझणा करी रे भाट (म्हे)। ई देश में शादी हो गैइ म्हारी (वाह वाह)। पाणी पीबा को धरम नी रियो (हां अठै पाणी नैइ पीवूं)। दरबार का हुकमूं गाय नै गुआल नै कह दियो भैइ की बिदा हो जायज्यूं (वाह वाह)। तो राणी नै दरबार का हुकमूं पहली जो पीपळदे को बाप हो न्यारी अलग दे दी (म्हे)। साडूमाता की बेल ही जकी भाइयां की घरूं लियाई (हां लियाड़ी सागै ही)। पदमावती दासी साडूमाता के कन्नै साथ में ही (म्हे)। एक दासी राणी पीपळदे नै दे दी बीको बाप (वाह वाह)। तो पीपळदे राणी को साडूमाता के सागै रथजूपी (गियो है)। गायां अर गुआल (म्हे)। और देव महाराज राजा माण्डल के तालाव पूगता हो गया (वाह वाह)। देव महाराज कीयो रे भाई ओ तळाव किसी भोमी में आयो बोलो (हां किसी भोमी में आयो कीयो)। कीयो श्री महाराज (म्हे) ओ तळाव आपका बड़कां को ही है (वाह वाह)। माण्डल राज व्हियो एक (म्हे)। बी को तो खुदायोड़ो है कीयो तळाव बड़ो आछो है (वाह वाह)। भाट कीयो अन्नदाता श्री महाराज तळाव तो बड़ो अच्छो है (म्हे)। ई में थोड़ी सी नुकस है (नुकस है कीयो)। कांई (कांई हो बाबा भाट)। कीयो माण्डलजी राजा चोखी तो पिसिया लगायां ईका (म्हे)। चोखो खुदायो (वाह वाह)। हेंर चोखी तरह ईको पाल गेट (हां करी ही)। पण नी समय ईंयां की आयी (म्हे)। माण्डल राजा घोड़ा असवार समेत डूब पीराण है जको तळाव में ई (ई में दे दिया)। कीयो बेसुध हो गो तळाव (हां जणा सुध में कोनी कीयो)। ई नै सुध में करिया बीनै मैं आगै नी कोनी जावां (म्हे)। तीन तिलोकी को नाथ होम बिदी करबा लागा बिरामणां नै पिण्डतां ने बुला लिया (वाह वाह)। हेंर होम बिदी होबा लागी (वाह वाह)। ओ तळाव सुध हुवेलो तो आगै चालां भाई (आगे नै चलां)। गाय अर गुआल ए आपका आगै (हां पूगता हो ग्या)। पिछोर को घाटो आयो (म्हे)। बी जागां शंकर महाराज चेला नै आडा राख दिया (वाह वाह)। कीयो आया गिया कन्नु डाण लेवो भाई (डाण लियो भांग गोटो अर मजा करो)। दरबार का हुकमूं जोगी बोलै (वाह वाह)। कांई जोगियां के गाड़ीवाना के बात (अब होवै देखां)।।

ए पिछोर के घाटा पर जी देव का गाड़ां जी हेटा उतरिया रे।
गाड़ा पर ठाकरां रे तणका माची ताण।
डाण दिया बिनै रे गाड़ीवान का।
गाड़ी हांकी तो रे शंकरनाथ की आण।
(भलां जी भलां) देव भलां

पिछोर के घाटा पर देव का गाड़ा आयगा भाई (म्हे)। गाड़ा पर तणका माच गी (ताण)। अरै डाण दिया बिनै गाड़ीवान का (म्हे)। गाड़ी आग्या नै हांकी तो शंकरनाथजी की है (तनै अब आण हे कीयो)। शंकर की आण है आगै गाड़ी पैड़ दियो तो (वाह वाह)। क्युं भाई बाबाजी को हुकम है म्हनै (हां हुकम है कीयो)। आयगियो कन्नु डाण लेवां भाई मैं तो (वाह वाह)। डाण तो दे दियो (पछ आगै नी जावो)। देव महाराज का गाड़ीवान बोलै (म्हे)। कांई जोगियां नै समचार कहवै देखां (कीआवूं जाणज्यो अब देखां कीआवूं जाणज्यो)। अबार कहवूं देखां देव का हुकमूं ले तूं (वाह वाह जी वाह वाह)।।

ए भूरी भूरी तो जी जो माथा पर बाबरियां रे।
राखूं भाई ये भगवां भेग का मान।
दे पुराणी का मदरा हेटा राळ द्यूं।
दर्शन बिनै नाथजी रे भूंडा लागै कान।।
(भलां जी भलां) देव भलां

भूरी भूरी जोगी बाबरी है थारै (वाह वाह)। दरबार का हुकमूं राखूं भगवां भेग को (मान)। दे पुराणी का मदरा हेटा राळ द्यूं (म्हे)। दर्शन बिनै नाथजी अबार भूंडा घणा लागी (थारा कान)। कोटी का सियाणा भूंडा लागी (भूंडा घणा लागेला कीयो)। किस्यो डाण लेवो थै अबार (वाह वाह)।।

ए भूरी भूरी तो जी ए ई माथा पर बाबरियां रे।
नाथजी ओड़ण पहरण का जी राखूं काचा सूत।
गाड़ा का मोहरा छोड़ एकानै हो जा कन फोड़ा मोडिया।
मारियो जासी भाई रे जोगेशर अबधूत।
(भलां जी भलां) देव भलां

भूरी भूरी जोगी माथा बाबरी है (म्हे)। ओड़ण पहरण का काचा (सूत)। गाड़ा का मोहरा छोड़ एकानै हो जा (म्हे)। मारियो जय जोगेशर (अबधूत)। एली साठ मारियो जाय (मारियो जायलो कीयो)।।

भूरी भूरी तो जी ए ई जोगी के बाबरियां रे।
आप तो नाथजी रे बी में भभूत रमाई रे।
गाड़ा का मोहरा छोड़ एकानै हो जा कन फोड़ा मोडिया।
पुराणी की मारी नाथजी की रे उडती फिरै सिधाई रे।।
(भलां जी भलां) देव भलां

भूरी भूरी तो माथा पै बाबरी है (वाह वाह)। दरबार का हुकमूं अंग में भभूत (रमाई)। गाड़ा का मोहरा छोड़ एकानै हो जा (म्हे)। अरै पुराणी की मारी नाथ की उडती फिरी (सिधाई)। आ सिधाई टणका है नै (हां ए उडती फिरेली बांटावूं)। एकानै हो जावो (वाह वाह)। डाण देतां ही (जावोला कीयो)। भूरी भूरी जोगी माथा पर बाबरी (वाह वाह)। ओड़ण पहरण का दिखिया काचा (सूत)। गाड़ा का मोहरा छोड़ एकानै हो जा (म्हे)। मारियो जाय जोगेशर (अबधूत)। अरै एली साठ मारियो जाय (वाह वाह)। अबकै कांई जोगी बोले (म्हे)। बाबजीआला गेला की बात हां (वाह वाह)। अर कांई देखां गुआलां नै कहवै देखां (कीआवूं जाणजयो कीआवूं जाणज्यो कींयां जाणज्यो)। अबार कहवूं भगवान देव का हुकमूं।।

ए डाण चुका द्यो जी जो गाड़ीवान का रे।
नी तो भाई रे माचेलो घाण मथाण।
भर भभूत की चिंवटी राळो रे गाड़ा के मांयनै

रथ अर बेलिया थारा जी दोन्यु कर द्यूं पाखाण।।
(भलां जी भलां) देव भलां

समचार कुण कीयो है जोगी कीयो (जोगी कीयो है)। कीयो डाण चुका द्यो गाड़ीवान का (म्हे)। अब माचीरै गाड़ा पर घाण (मथाण)। के भर भभूत की चिंवटी राळूं गाड़ा के मांयनै (म्हे)। अरै रथ अर बेलिया थारा दोन्यु कर द्यूं (पाखाण)। शंकर का चेला हां मैं (हां पाखाण का बनादेवूंला कीयो)। इती देख करामात है म्हां कन्नै (वाह वाह)। पित्थर का हो जावो (वाह वाह)। दरबार का हुकमूं इताक पहली मात खटाणी को रथ (हां लारूं आयग्यो)। बूझणा करी रे भाई कींयां ठामियां गाड़ा नै (हां गाड़ा नै ठामियां कींयां हो कीयो)। कीयो माता देख नागड़िया देख जोगी ऊबा आडा (हां डाण मांगै है कीयो)। साडूमाता बोलै (म्हे)। कांई समचार जोगियां नै कहवै देखां (कीआवूं जाणज्यो कीआवूं देखां)। अबार कहवूं धणी देव का हुकमूं देखां (वाह वाह जी वाह वाह)।।

ए सगळी धरती फिरयाई तो जी ए ई भोलानाथजी रे।
उगै राजा रे काछबजी को बाण।
मैं पीरूं आई साहरै जावूं रे भोलानाथजी।
अती दूर में नाथजी लाग्यो रे सुणियो कोनी डाण।।
(भलां भी भलां) देव भलां

सगळी धरती फिरयाई (म्हे)। उगै राजा काछबजी को (बाण)। अरै पीरूं आई साहरै जावूं भोलानाथजी (म्हे)। अती दूर में लाग्योड़ो सुणियो कोनी (मैं डाण)। नाथजी (म्हे)। नवों कठवूं लेयायां बोलो (हां ओ डाण कठूं पैदा करियो कीयो)। कीयो सुण ये माता (म्हे)। म्हानै शंकर का हुकम है (वाह वाह)। आया गिया कन्नु डाण तो (लेवां हां)। फैर भांग (घोटावां हां)। भगवान का हुकम है (म्हे)। दरबार का हुकमूं मात खटाणी बूझणा करी रे भाई (वाह वाह)। के नाथां का दियोड़ा टुकड़ा आपणी आंतड़िया उळझियोड़ा है (हां उळझियोड़ा है कीयो)। दरबार का हुकमूं तीन तिलोकी को नाथ राजा माण्डल के तळाव रियोड़ा है (म्हे)। बै आवेला (अर डाण चुकावेला)। तो आगा नै (चालांलां कीयो)। गाड़ा नै खोलो भाई (वाह वाह)। तीन तिलोकी का नाथ गाड़ा है जका पिछोर के परै खुल गा (वाह वाह)। दासियां नै हुकम (दिन्यो)। पीपळदे राणी को रथ है जको खुल गो (म्हे)। साडूमाता को ही (रथ खुल ग्या)। साडूमाता कहवै पदमावती दासी (म्हे)। अठै बावड़ी है बीवूं जळ ल्यावो (हां जळ की झारी भर ल्यावो)। नित नैम (कर लेवां)। एक दासी तो राणी पीपळदे के सागै जळ नै (हां ऊठ गी)। तो एक साडूमाता के (हां पदमावती दासी गैइ जी कीयो)। बावड़ी के ऊपर बड़ हो (म्हे)। बड़ के हेटै आधा के जोगी तो बैठां हा चौपड़ रमबा (वाह वाह)। आधा जोगी के घाटा पर (हां घाट पर हां)। बा जोगियां में (म्हे)। नेवाजी को कंवर भांगीजी सब मालक व्हियोड़ो बीचै बैठो (हां मालक व्हियोड़ा बीच में बैठिया जी कीयो)। दासियां देख जोगी की सुरत (म्हे)। बी जागां चकराई गी (वाह वाह)। क्युं तो झारी भरी की (कोनी भरी)। कांई दासी पाछी आवै (म्हे)। पदमावती कांई साडू नै समचार कहवै अब (हां आंवतां ही कींयां (कहवै देखां कीआवूं जाणज्यो भोपाजी . . .)। अबार कहवूं देव का हुकमूं कह द्यूं (वाह वाह)।।

ए बावड़ी बीचालै जी ए ई बांका बड़ थळ औवूं रे।
उतरी देखी ये जोगियां की जमात।
एक जोगी इसियो देखियो ये साडू सुलखना।
आपणा देवर है नेवा के उणियार।।
(भलां जी भलां) देव भलां

बावड़ी बीचालै बांका बड़ थळ (म्हे)। माजी उतरी देखी एक जोगियां की (जमात)। एक जोगी इसियो ई देखयाई (वाह वाह)। आपणा देवर नेवा के (उनियार)। नेवाजी को उणियारो (म्हे)। जोगी को उणियारो माजी एक मिल गो (हां एक को एक मिला जी कीयो)। तो दासी साडूवूं समचार कहतां (कहवतां)। देव महाराज का गाड़ा पिछोर का घाटा आतां (आंवता)। जय बोलो भाई श्री देवनारायण की (जय)।।

जीभ कटावूं जी जो हीड़ागर छोकरियां रे।
जीभ के लगा द्यूं ए जहरी कालर लूण।
झटका का मारिया बगड़ावतां ये बटका उपड़िया।
बावूं पदमावती ये जोगी व्है गा कोन।।
(भलां जी भलां) देव भलां

जीभ काटावूं थारी (म्हे)। जीभ के लगावूं पदमावती जहरी कालर (लूण)। जो झटका का मारिया बगड़ावत खारी पर बटका उपड़िया (वाह वाह)। बा मूं पदमावती अब जोगी व्हियो (अब कोन)। इसी कांई ठण्डी कोम ही बगड़ावतां की जो जोगियां में रळ गी (हां जोगियां में जा रळा हा कीयो)। पदमावती बोलै दासी (म्हे)। मात खटाणी ऊबी सुणै (कीआवूं जाणज्यो देखां कीआवूं)। अबार कहवूं धणी देव का ईका हुकमूं देखां (वाह वाह सा)।

ए क्यूंनै जीभ कटावो जी ए ई साडू सुलखना रे।
क्युं लगावै म्हारै जीभ के ये जहरी कालर लूण।
तेजा रावत को मदनो ये जोगियां में रळ ग्यो।
नीतर जोगी हो गो ये बारावत को भोण।।
(भलां जी भलां) देव भलां

क्युं जीभ कटावै म्हारी (म्हे)। क्युं के लगावै माजी जीभ के जहरी कालर (अब लूण)। के तो तेजा रावत को मदन सिंग जोगियां में रळ गो (म्हे)। नी जोगी हु गो बारावत को ही (भोण)। आ दोन्यां में लाखां कोय नी चकियो (हां लाखां ही टलिया नैइ कीयो)। पदमावती (म्हे)। किसी जागां चाल दिखाळ (हां म्हनै चाल बता कीयो)। तो पाछी साडूमाता अर पदमावती दासी (म्हे)। बी बावड़ी पर पूगती हुई (हां पाछी हुई है जी कीयो)। नेवाजी को सुतन सायबो दरबार का हुकमूं सब मालक व्हियोड़ो बीचै (बिराजमान हो रिया जी कीयो)। साडूमाता देख जोगी की (सूरत)। तो साडूमाता ही (चकराई जी कीयो)। हीड़ागर दासियां (म्हे)। आ तो बायदे बी घर की है (हां बी घर की है)। मात खटाणी बोलै (वाह वाह)। कांई समचार कहवै देखां (कीआवूं जाणज्यो देखां कीआवूं)।।

ए पांव पदम दीपै तो जी जोगी के हीड़ागर छोकरियां रे।
ई जोगी के पदमावती ये हीरो जबर लिलाड़।
मैं झूटी तूं सांची हो गयी ये हीड़ागर छोकरियां।
लाधी म्हाना ये मितवालां की आग।।
(भलां जी भलां) देव भलां

पांव पदम दीपै जोगी (वाह वाह)। हीरो तपै (लिलाड़)। मैं झूटी तूं सांची हो गी हीड़ागर छोकरियां (म्हे)। लाधी ये म्हारा मितवालां की (आग)। पदमावती (म्हे)। आ बायदे बी घर की है (हां है तो बी घर की)। पण भाइयां कांई ठी हे किस्या भूप को (हां आ ठा कोनी कीयो)। जोगी नै बूझां (हां बूझां जर पतो चाल जाय)। मतेई ठा पड़ जाय बात (वाह वाह)। मात खटाणी बोलै कांई कंवर भांगीजी ने बूझणा करै देखां (कीआवूं जाणज्यो देखां कीआवूं)। अबार कहवां धणी देव का ईका हुकमूं का ले (वाह वाह)।।

भूरी भूरी तो जी जो माथा पर बाबरियां रे।
थांकै नाथजी रे भूर भवंता केस।
माता गूजरी करै आपणै बूझणा।
आपको नाथजी रे किस्यो कीज्यै देश।।
(भलां जी भलां) देव भलां

भूरी भूरी तो माथा पर बाबरी है (म्हे) भूर भवंता (अब केस)। माता गूजरी करै बूझणा नाथजी आपको कुणसो कीज्यै (देश)। कुण देश को जोगी है भाई (हां कठूं आय अर बाबाजी का चेला मुण्डीज्या कीयो)। दरबार का हुकमूं भांगीजी बोलै (म्हे)। कांई समचार मात खटाणी नै कहवै देखां (कीआवूं जाणज्यो देखां भोपाजी महाराज अब कीआवूं)। अबार कहवूं देव का हुकमूं ले तूं (वाह वाह जी वाह वाह)।।

ए भूरी भूरी तो जी ए ई माथा पर बाबरियां रे।
म्हारै माजी ये भूर भवंता केस।
देश तो गूजरी ये देखियो कोय ने।
तनै खटाणी ये किस्यो बतावा देश।।
(भलां जी भलां) देव भलां

भूरी भूरी माथा पर बाबरी है (म्हे)। भूर भवंता (अब केस)। देश तो भाई माता गूजरी देखियो कोनी (म्हे)। तनै किस्यो बतावूं (अब मैं देश)। देश सार मैं समझूं ही कोनी (हां जाणु ही कोनी कांई देश होवे)। माजी मन में देखियो की देश की ठा कोनी ईनै (म्हे)। दूध की जरूर (हां ठा होली)। मात खटाणी बोलै कांई भांजीजी ने दूजा समचार कहवै (हां दूध का बूझै देखां)।।

ए भूरी भूरी तो जी जो माथा पर बाबरियां रे।
ओढ़ण पहरण का काचा सूत।
माता गूजरी करै आपणै बूझणा।
आपको नाथजी रे किस्यो कीज्यै दूध।।
(भलां जी भलां) देव भलां

भूरी भूरी तो बाबरी है (म्हे)। ओढ़ण पहरण का काचा (सूत)। आ गूजरी माता करै आपणै बूझणा (म्हे)। नाथजी आपको किस्यो कीज्यै (अब दूध)। कुण दूध को जोगी है ए बात तो कह दे म्हनै (हां आ बतावो किस्यो दूध है आपको)। भांगीजी बोलै कांई माजी नै समचार कहवै देखां (कीआवूं जाणज्यो देखां कीआवूं)। अबार कहवूं धणी देव का हुकमूं ले तूं (वाह वाह जी वाह वाह)।। तूं तो तूं ऊं ऊं . . .

भूरी भूरी तो जी जो माथा पर बाबरियां रे।
ओढ़ण पहरण का काचा सूत।
दूध तो गूजरी माता ये चाखियो कोय ने।
तनै गूजरी ये किस्यो बतावां दूध।।
(भलां जी भलां) देव भलां

भूरी भूरी माथा पर बाबरी है (म्हे)। ओढ़ण पहरण का काचा ही (म्हारै सूत)। दूध तो भाई माता गूजरी मैं चाख्यो कोनी (वाह वाह)। की को बतावूं (तनै अब दूध)। की के लागै है कीं (हां किस्या रूंख का दूध लागै है कीयो)। दरबार का हुकमूं मात खटाणी दासी नै कीयो दासी (म्हे)। देश को ही ठा कोनी दूध को ही (ईनै ठा कोनी)। नाथजी जरां मात पिता को नांव जाणो थें (हां मात पिता थांको नांव जाणो कीयो)। कीयो हां जरूर (जाणु कीयो)। कीयो बतावो जरां (वाह वाह)।।

ए भांग माता तो जी तप पिता ये माता गूजरिया रे।
माता म्हारी ये भांग तणू भोगी रे।
मात पिता को गूजरी ये ठा ही कोय ने।
डूंगर में तपतो देखियो ये रूपनाथ जोगी रे।।
(भलां जी भलां) देव भलां

भांग तो म्हारै देख माता है (म्हे)। अर तप पिता है (हां तप है जको म्हारो पिता है)। हेंर भांग तणा ही भोगी (म्हे)। मात पिता को गूजरी माता ठा कोनी (वाह वाह)। बो डूंगर में तपतो देखियो रूपनाथ ही (में जोगी)। ओ ई तो म्हारै मां है (अर ओ ई तो म्हारै बाप है कीयो)। ओ ले भाई (आ ले)। मात खटाणी कीयो भैइ पदमावती लाधियो कोनी (हां औरूं लाधियो तो नी है)। बायदे तो बी घर की है (म्हे)। कीयो नाथजी जोगियां के कोनी जलमियां थें (हां जोगियां के तो जलमियां ही कोनी)। कीयो माता (म्हे)। मैं तो भाई बाबाजी के जलमियो हूं (हां जोगी के जलमियो हूं)। दूसरा की म्हनै ठा कोनी (म्हनै ठा कोनी)। कीयो नाथजी के इता दिन व्हिया थें बाबाजी के मुण्डा के काम कर रिया हो (म्हे)। कोय दिना चोखो ही काम हो जावै (अर कोय दिन माड़ो ही काम हो जावे)। माड़ो काम होवै तो

लेरला नै याद (जरूरी करे)। ए चोखो होवै तो ही (लारला नै याद जरूर करै जी कीयो)। कोय बात की थानै निंगै है तो म्हनै कोय बात सुणाओ (हां बाबोजी कन्नै थानै कह अर बतलाया हां कीयो)। कीयो ले भाई माता एक दिन की बात याद आयगी म्हनै (हां याद आयगी)। जकी सुणा द्यूं तनै (हां बा तो म्हनै ठा है सुणा द्यूं तने)। सुणावो तो (वाह वाह कींयां सुणावै देखां)। अबार कहवां भगवान का देव का हुकमूं देखां ल्यो थै (वाह वाह सा)।

चेला ही चेला तो जी बाग लगायो ये माता गूजरिया रे।
बाग में रोपिया ये भांग तणा चेडा रे।
एक दिन राजी व्हियां बतलावै भोलेनाथजी।
साबास म्हाना रे नेवा का केड़ा।।
(भलां जी भलां) देव भलां

चेला ही चेला भाई माजी बाग लगायो (म्हे)। मैं भलां रोपिया बाग में भांग तणा (चेडा)। एक परसन हो राजी हो बोल्यो भोलोनाथजी (वाह वाह)। साबास म्हारा नेवा का (केड़ा)। नेवोजी भाई माजी हो तो कांई ठां कुण है (ई बात को म्हानै ठा कोनी)। बाबोजी नांव आतो लियो है (हां अतो ले अर बतलायो)। कीयो पदमावती दासी बो लाधियो (हां अब लाध गियो)। जकै दिन देवर नेवोजी बीर खेत में काम आयो नै (म्हे)। जकै दिन नेतूजी के पेट में छै महीनै की बूथ ही (हां छै महीना की आ बूथ पेट में ही)। पेट परनाळ (म्हे)। शंकर की धूणी पर (जांवती नाकदी)। आ बूथ है बा (हां छै महीना की बूथ है ईनै दूध को)। सांचो है ओ (देश को ठा ही कांई)। नी तो देश देखी (म्हे)। नी दूध चाख्यो (वाह वाह)। मात खटाणी बोलै (म्हे)। कांई भांगीजी नै समचार कहवै (हां कींयां कहवै देखां कीआवूं जाणज्यो भोपाजी महाराज)। अबार कह द्यूं भगवान का हुकमूं (वाह वाह जी)।।

ए नंगर नानेरो जी नान्या म्हाना जी नेकाड़ियो बिरावतो रे।
नान्या म्हाना जी पाट दड़ावट शहर।
भगवां भेग उतार देय रे कंवर भांगड़ा।
ले ले ये नान्याजी मितवालां का बेर।।
(भलां जी भलां) देव भलां

नंगर तो थारो नानेरो लाल (म्हे)। नेकाड़िया को बिरावत और पाट दड़ावट (शहर)। भगवां भेग नाथां नै दे दे (म्हे)। ले ले लाल मीठा मितवालां का ही (तूं बैर)। ओ समचार कुण कीयो है (साडूमाता कीयो है)। भांगीजी कीयो माजी साय (म्हे)। जोगी जलम का हो गा (वाह वाह)। डूंगा के राख (हां लगा लीनी)। म्हांकै बैर है (हां औरूं कींयां का बैर है कीयो)। लारला लाल लेरला जोगियां के एक के ही कोनी (हां एक के ही बैर कोनी)। थारो तो जरूरी (हां है कीयो)।।

ए नगर नानेरो जी थानो गूजरी ये देखिया कोय नै औवूं रे।
कोय नी देखियो पाट दड़ावट शहर।

मैं जलम को माजी ये जोगी बन ग्यो।
म्हां जोगियां के गूजरी ये क्यें को रह ग्या बैर।।
(भलां जी भलां) देव भलां

नंगर नानेरो मैं तो कोनी देखियो (म्हे)। कोनी देखियो थारो पाट दड़ावट (शहर)। जलम का भाई माता गूजरी जोगी बन गा (म्हे)। म्हां जोगियां के औरूं क्यें को रह गा (अब बैर)। डूं गा के राख ल गाई मैं (म्हे)। जलम का ही जोगी म्हांकै बैर थोड़ो ही है (हां म्हांकै कींयां का बैर है कीयो)। कीयो सुण रे लाल (म्हे)। ए लेरला जोगी एक के बैर कोनी पण थारै जरूर है (हां थारै जरूर ही है कीयो)। कठै है थारो बाबोजी (बता कीयो)। कीयो सामला डूंगर में (हां तापै है कीयो)। चाल जरां बाबाजी कन्नु चांलां (हां चाल कीयो)। कीयो थारै पीक है तूं जा (मैं तो कठै ई कोनी जावूं)। म्हांकै तो बाबाजी को हुकम है सुवा मण भांग को नशो तो एकदम करूं में (वाह वाह)। तो नशा तो देख आयगया कन्नु लेवूं डाण का भाइयां (हां डाण का ले लेवां)। रोटां है जको बाबोजी रसोईड़ा में (पका देवे)। सीधा ही आवै भाई (म्हे)। थारै पीक है तो बाबाजी कन्नु तूं जा मैं तो कोनी जावूं (मैं तो कोनी जावूं)। तो तीन तिलोकी को नाथ भगवान तो राजा माण्डल के तळाव पर (हां जुगविदी बंचा रिया)। हेंर मात खटाणी धूणी कानी बिदा (व्हिया जी कीयो)। लेरावूं जोगी अर गाड़ीवान दोन्यु सूना रह गा (हां हारेती नी म्हांकै काटी हो गी)। घणकरां तो जोगी काम आय गा (म्हे)। हेंर घणकरां गाड़ीवान (काम आयग्या बठै)। मात खटाणी जाती दीखी ईनै (म्हे)। बाबोजी देखियो मेणादे गूजरी आयो है ओळभो जरूर (देयि)। सारै गुफा ही गुफा में (आगलै छेड़ै बड़ ग्या)। बजरशिला (आड़ी सिरकादी)। मात खटाणी गी तो दरबार का हुकमूं धूणी तो जगती पड़ी (म्हे)। माता बोलै कांई देखां समचार नाथजी नै कहवै देखां (कीआवूं जाणज्यो देखां कीआवूं)। अबार कहवूं धणी देव का हुकमूं देखां (वाह वाह सा वाह वाह)।।

ऊंडी गुफा में जी जो बड़ बैठ गो रे भोलानाथजी रे।
नाथजी भोला रे बैठो पलक लगाये।
बगड़ावतां का जायां नै स्यामी कर दिया कन फोड़ा मोडिया।
बैठो रे नाथजी रे जुग में राख लगायै।।
(भलां जी भलां) देव भलां

ऊंडी गुफा में बड़ गो तूं (म्हे)। नाथजी भोला बैठो पलक (लगाये)। अरै बगड़ावतां का जायां नै तूं स्यामी करिया (म्हे)। नाथजी बैठो रे जुग में राख ही (अब लगाये)। बगड़ावत थारी बियां की सेवा करी देख (हां सांची ही)। पण नी तूं काम सांचो करियो (बांकै जायोड़ा नै जोगी करया कीयो)। बाबोजी मन में देखयो माजी नै दीघो दीखै (हां दीखां हां कीं हां आपां)। दरबार का हुकमूं मात खटाणी बोलै (वाह वाह)। कांई बाबाजी नै बतलावै देखां (कीआवूं जाणज्यो अब देखां अब कीआवूं)।।

पहली पेड़ी तो जी पग धरूं रे भोलानाथजी रे।
नाथजी भोला रे दूजी पांव घरां रे।

गुफावूं बाहरें नै आजा रे भोलानाथजी।
नीतर धूणी पर खंजर पहर मरा।।
(भलां जी भलां) देव भलां

साड़ूमाता समचार (कीया है)। कीयो पहली पेड़ी पग धरूं रे भोलानाथजी (वाह वाह)। ए दूजी पांव (धरां)। गुफा छोड़ा बाहरें नै आजा (म्हे)। नी जरां धूणी पर ताणी खंजर पहरी (अब मरूं)। नाथजी लोही को छांटो बिखरदेवूंलीं (वाह वाह)। बाबोजी मन में देखियो रे मेणादे गूजरी है तो (म्हे)। कांई कहली (हां आगती व्हियोड़ी सांचै ही नैइ कर ले ओ काम)। तो शिला के पटकारो नाथजी बाहरलै छेड़ै (आर खड़ा व्हिया)। मात खटाणी पगां पड़ी (वाह वाह)। आओ मेणादे आओ कीयो (आओ कीयो)। कीयो आयी नाथजी पण काम चोखो करियो (म्हे)। इसियो काम कोय नी करै (वाह वाह)।।

ए खेड़ै खेड़ै तो जी झूंझ गा रे ए बेटा बाग का रे।
झूंझ पड़िया साडू ये नंद खारी की तीर।
बारा दिना भोज का ये करियो कोय ने।
तनै तो साडू ये प्यारो लाग्यो पीर।।
(भलां जी भलां) देव भलां

दरबार का हुकमूं खेड़ै खेड़ै झूंझ गा बेटा बाग का (म्हे)। झूंझ पड़िया नंद खारी की (तीर)। बारा दिन तूं भोज का तूं करियो कोनी (म्हे)। तनै साडू प्यारो लाग्यो (पीर)। तूं बोलै जकी जाणु मैं (वाह वाह)। म्हनै कहवै ऊंडी गुफा में बड़ गो (हां) पण तूं साहूकार है जकी नै मैं जाणु (हां भोज का बारा दिन कोनी करिया पहली (भाज छूटी कीयो)। कीयो नाथजी कोय नी करिया (म्हे)। बाबोजी बोलै कांई समचार साड़ूमाता नै गूजरी ने कहवै देखां (कीआवूं जाणज्यो देखां कीआवूं)। अबार कहवूं देव का हुकमूं ले तूं (वाह वाह सा)। (तूं तो तूं म्हारा निरजन तूं के तो देव के निरजन तूं)।

डावो छोड़ गी जी ए ई खेड़ा चौसला रे।
माता म्हारी जी जीवणी छोड़ी राण।
भाज ऊठ गी माळागर की भोम में।
सवाई भोज का ये धुकता छोड़ मूसाण।।
(भलां जी भलां) देव भलां

डावो छोड़ गी खेड़ो चौसलो (वाह वाह)। जीवणी छोड़ी (राण)। ए भाज गी माळागर की भोम में (वाह वाह)। सवाई भोज को धुकतो छोड़ (मूसाण)। भोज को तो सेलो जुग रियो (अर तूं भाज अर ऊठ गी कीयो)। म्हनै ठा कोनी (हां से जाणु तनै जकै दिन)। साड़ूमाता का हेटै का जाड़ा तो हेटै रह ग्या ऊपर का ही (हां ऊपर रह ग्या)।

ए सोना रूपा तो जी ए ई दड़ावट में पहरता रे।
जिण दिन साडूजी मोतियां मरतां भार।

बीको पड़ियो अर बेमाता पालटी।
बीका में भाजी ए पाळी कोस पच्चास।।
(भलां जी भलां) देव भलां

सोना रूपा पहरती तनै ठा कोनी (म्हे)। माजी मोतियां ही मरतां (भार)। एक बीको पड़ियो अर बेमाता पालटी (म्हे)। बीका में भाजी पाळी कोस ही (तूं पच्चास)। रात नै छोड़ियो चौसला खेड़ नै (हां पच्चास कोस तांईं थारा पग ही कोनी (टीकिया कीयो)। म्हारै भगवान औतार लियो (हां जणा गैइ कीयो)। कीयो मानी बात (वाह वाह)। थारो दिन जकै नै दियोड़ो जोर को हो (हां औतार लेणो आया भगवान)। तूं पीर को टाबर ल्याई है कठवूं माळवाऊं (वाह वाह)। की ताणी राजगादी जाणी (हां राजगादी बैठाण)। देख नेवाजी को कंवर भांगीजी नै मैं पालियो है (म्हे)। छै महीना की कच्ची बूथ ही (हां ईनै पालियूं मैं कीयो)। राजगादी बैठाणै जरां ले जा भांगी नै (हां अटवूं ले जावो अर जावो)। नी जरां आया जका खोजां (पाछा बावड़ जावो)। कीयो नाथजी देखो भाइयां को टाबर तो कोनी है (हां भाइयां को टाबर कोनी ल्यावूं है तो भगवान)। साडू भगवान है (हां है सा)। दरबार का हुकमूं जरां कोय परच्यो तो दिखाळ (हां थारो भगवान को परच्यो दिखा म्हानै तो)। कीयो नाथजी कांई परच्यो ल्यो (हां कांई मांगो कीयो नाथजी थें)। कीयो नाथां कन्नै ईंयां का परच्या है (म्हे)। देखिज्यै आ धूणी तो जगै (हां गाड़ा घणकरां जूप रिया है)। लेरै लाठां पड़िया सूखा (हां सूखेड़ा लेरूं)। तो आगावूं बळै लेरूं सूखा पड़िया है (वाह वाह)। सूखा के सुवा सुवा हाथ की कूंपळियां चाली हरी (हरी चाल जावे)। तो औतार (जरूरी थारो मान जावूं)। नी जरां आई जका खोजां ही पाछी (हां माळवै नै बावड़ जाओ)। तो कांई मात खटाणी भगवान कन्नै परच्यो दिरावै देखां (कीआवूं जाणज्यो देखां कीआवूं भोपाजी महाराज अब)। अबार कहवूं धणी का ईका देवराला का हुकमूं कह दियां (वाह वाह सा)।।

कंवळाई फूल में जी ए ई आप उतरिया रे।
मिनखियो मिण्धारीजी पायो कोनी भेद।
धूणी पर परच्यो दीज्यो जी गोठालां राजवियां।
हेलो सुणज्यै रे साडूजी का ऊद।।
(भलां जी भलां) देव भलां

कंवळ का तो फूल में उतरियो हो (म्हे)। मिनखियो मिण्धारी पाया कोनी (थांका भेद)। धूणी पर परच्यो दियो गोठां का राजवी (म्हे)। हेलो सुणज्यो रे माजी का अलख निरजन (ऊद)। हे निराकार भगवान (म्हे)। तूं म्हारो हेलो (अब सुणोला)। जरां तो मैं भांगीजी कंवर नै मांग अर (लेयावूंली)। नी जरां ए आ धूणी में देखै मैं तो बळूं अब (अठै ही बळ अर मरूं कीयो मैं तो)। साडूमाता धूणी के सामनै (चाल्या है)। तीन तिलोकी को नाथ भगवान जुगविदी में बैठा हा (म्हे)। बक बक हेंसिया फैफ का फूल (झड़िया जी कीयो)। भैरवानाथ पेग मान लाग रिया बूझणा (कर लीनी)। भाट कीयो श्री महाराज क्युं आप क्युं हंसूं (कींयां व्हियो अता जोरूं कीयो)। अरै बाबा भाट (म्हे)। मात खटाणी देख रे नाथजी कन्नै परच्यो (हां धूणी पर मांगै कीयो)। कीयो श्री महाराज बूड़ा माईत को कीयो जरूरी (करणो चाहीज्यै)।

तीन तिलोकी को नाथ अम्मी की नजर (बैठिया झांकिया जी कीयो) । तो आगै लाठां जगां (म्हे) । जगतां लाठां की सुवा सुवा हाथ की री कूंपळियां भगवान नै चलाई (वाह वाह) । बाबाजी के निंगै (आयगी) । बाबोजी मन में देखियो रे औतार तो जरूर हु गो (हां आंपांवूं किस्यो छाना थोड़ा ई हा) । मेणादे गूजरी नै क्युं संतो (वाह वाह) । कीयो माता आजा उनै मान लियो मैं तो (हां मान गियो कीयो) । बाबोजी बोलै (म्हे) । मात खटाणी नै कांई समचार कहवै देखां (कीआवूं जाणज्यो देखां कीआवूं) ।।

लिखियो परवाणा तो जी ए ई बाबो जी मोकळिया रे ।
लिख दीना नान्याजी मोहरै छड़ियां का सुत ।
भगवां भेग नाथां नै देतो जायज्यै कंवर भांगड़ा ।
हो जायज्यै नान्याजी गोठां को रजपूत ।।
(भलां जी भलां) देव भलां

लिखिया परवाणा बाबोजी मोकळिया (म्हे) । मांय लिखिया मोहर छड़ियां का (सुत) । भगवां भेग तो म्हारा नाथां नै देतो जायज्यै (म्हे) । हो जायज्यै लाल गोठां को (रजपूत) । भांगी थारी गोठां है लाल (हां बठै जा अर) । दरबार का हुकमूं राजगादी को धणी हो जा (वाह वाह) । हेंर आ थारी आवै जकै मां ही मान लीज्यै (म्हे) । ले भाई मेणादे गूजरी (म्हे) । ओ लेयो ओ परवाणो म्हारै भांगीजी नै (ले जार दे देवो) । देतां जेज लागै पण थारै सागै होता जेज कोनी लागै (हां जेज कोनी लागै जी कीयो) । तो बाळो ठाकर तीन तिलोकी को नाथ धूणी पर परज्यो देतां (म्हे) । भांगीजी कंवर को बाबोजी हुकम देतां (देवतां) । जय बोलो श्री देवनारायण की (जय) । बोलो भैइ छोटा अर मोटा (स) । (दरबार का हुकमूं) कांई करियो के मात खटाणी तो धूणी पर ऊठ गी (म्हे) । तीन तिलोकी को नाथ हो जका राजा माण्डल के तळाव पर (हां रह अर गिया) । लेरावूं जोगियां के गाड़ीवान के भाई बिगड़ गैइ बात रे (वाह वाह) । मां बेटां दोन्यु जणा (सागै का सागै पूग ग्या) । दरबार बूझणा (कर लीनी) । अरै माजी साय (म्हे) । ओ बात कींयां कराया ईंयां (आ कींयां कराया ईंयां कीयो) । सूना सासतावूं चौसला खेड़ा की छड़ी रोपतां (म्हे) । पहल पोत भगवां पछेवड़िया नै (मरा दिया कीयो) । कीयो लाल मैं हीं कठै अठै (मैं अठै कोय नैइ) । सिधारूं गी तूं (कुनै गिया) । कीयो मैं तो थारै काका को बेटो भाई व्ही जोगियां में है भांगीजी नांव (हां आनै लियावण बाबाजी कन्नै ऊठ गी कीयो) । में मांगबा गी (म्हे) । लेरावूं लाल रे गाड़ीवान अर जोगीवान काम घणकरां (हां आयग्या कीयो) । तीन तिलोकी को नाथ अम्मी की नजर (झांकिया है) । गाड़ीवान देव देव कर बैठा (सगळा का सगळा हो ग्या है जी कीयो) । भांगीजी नै साडूमाता ले जार परवाणा (दे दिया) । भांगीजी कीयो माता (म्हे) । मान लियो (हां मान लिया) । तूं म्हारी मां है (वाह वाह) । बाबोजी लिख दी जटावूं (हां मां ही है) । देव महाराज बूझणा करी जरां दादा भांगीजी कीं की असवारी लेयो (हां असवारी ले लेयो अर चालो) । कीयो औतारी पुरुष (म्हे) । तूं थारा जका मरिया जका नै जिन्दा (पाछा बैठिया कर दिया) । हेंर म्हारै साथ रहबाळा आदमी ही नै (म्हे) । बै मरियोड़ा पड़िया है (हां ए मरियोड़ा अठै पड़ियोड़ा है कीयो) । आंकी में तथा जुगत करूं लेरवूं आवूं (हां पाछै आवूं लारूं कीयो) । कीयो दादा भांगीजी (हां कांई तथा जुगत करो कीयो) । कीयो आई तथा जुगत करूं (म्हे) । खाड़िया तो खोदूं (म्हे) । सगळा नै बोरूं (हां समाधी दिरावूं

सगळा नै कीयो) । कीयो जरां दिना घणा लागी (हां दिन तो आपणै घणा लाग जाई) । मैं तो ओळखा कोनी (म्हे) । तूं थारा नै (ओळखै सागै रियोड़ो है) । तूं जोड़ दे (म्हे) । बैठा तो मैं कर द्यूं भाई (हां बैठ म्हारा करणा आया कीयो) । भांगीजी बी टैम में सुवा मण को नशो सागै ही (करयोड़ा हा जी कीयो) । कुण को बांवल्यो तो कुण के (जोड़ दिन्यो) । हेंर कुण को माथो (की के चेप दियो) । कुण को पग (की के अड़ा दियो) । पछेवड़िया ओड़ा ओड़ा सगळा नै (हां सुवाण दिन्या) । ले भाई औतारी ओ ले (सुता अब तियार है बैठया कर) । तीन तिलोकी को नाथ भगवान के अम्मी की नजर (झांकिया है) । जोगी देव देव कर बैठा (सगळा का सगळा व्हिया जी कीयो) । ऊठता ही झगड़ो मचा दिया (वाह वाह) । कीयो म्हानो हाथ थारै कींयां चिप्यो भाई (हाथ कींया चिप्योड़ो कीयो) । अरै कीयो म्हारै पग थारै कींयां चिप्योड़ो (हां म्हानो पग है थारै कींयां चिप्यो) । भांगीजी कीयो औतारी पुरुष काम चोखो करियो (हां जिन्दा तो कर दिन्या) । पण राड़ घाल दी तूं (हां तूं राड़ घाल दी आंकै बीच में आपसरी में) । जकै दिन देव महाराज साण अर बा जोगियां नै बैठां करिया (म्हे) । बी दिन बा जोगियां का सिंधन रजपूत बनाया (वाह वाह जकै सिंधन है कीयो) । हां तो भांगीजी कंवर साथ होता (म्हे) । देव महाराज तीन तिलोकी को नाथ ए परच्या देतां (देवतां) । जय बोलो भैइ श्री देव नारायण भगवान की (जय) । मात खटाणी कांई करियो (म्हे) । माण्डलजी को मनारो हो जका के जार ऊपर बैठ ग्या (हां ऊंचा चड़ ग्या जी कीयो) । देव महाराज कीयो रे भैइ डोकरी कुनै गी (हां कुनै गिया माजी साय) । चौसला की छड़ी रोप दियां (वाह वाह) । तो सिरदारां कीयो श्री महाराज थांकी मां तो देखिज्यो बा मनारा पर बैठी ऊंची (हां ऊंचा बै बैठिया बठै कीयो) । दरबार जार बूझणा (करी है) । ए माजी साय (म्हे) । हेटा उतर जावो (हां चौसलै की छड़ी रोपां कीयो) । कीयो लाल म्हनै हेटी मत उतारै (म्हे) । साडू बोलै कांई भगवान सुणै देखां (कीआवूं जाणज्यो देखां कीआवूं) । अबार कहवां देव का हुकमूं ले तूं (वाह वाह सा) ।।

ए माण्डल के मनारै तो जी नान्या म्हारा जी मैं चड़ ग्या रे।
दीख गी पापणी जी खारी नंदी की तीर।
आ मोतियां की माळा रे खारी खाय गी।
खाय गी म्हाना रे भोजी नणद का बीर।।
(भलां जी भलां) देव भलां

माण्डल के मनारै ऊंची लाल मैं चड़ी (वाह वाह) । सामी दीखी देख पापणी खारी नंदी की (तीर) । अरै मोतियां की माळा खारी खाय गी (म्हे) । खाय गी म्हारा भोजी नणद का (बीर) । भगवान अब छाती समावै म्हारी (हां म्हारी छाती कीयो नैइ करै कीयो) । कीयो बिसरणो मत कर हेटी उतर जा कीयो (वाह वाह) । साडूमाता बोलै कांई समचार कहवै देखां (कीआवूं जाणज्यो देखां कीआवूं) ।।

ए माण्डल के मनारै तो जी नान्या म्हारा जी मैं चड़ ग्या रे।
दीख गा बगड़ावतां का आवूठाण।
भर भर बाथां रे बां नै निरती।

खाली पड़िया नान्याजी पखरेतां का ठाण।।
(भलां जी भलां) देव भलां

माण्डल के मनारै लाल ऊंची मैं चड़ी (वाह वाह)। दीख गा म्हनै बगड़ावतां का देख आवू ई (ठाण)। ए भर भर बाथां लाल मैं बां नै निरती (म्हे)। खाली पड़िया रे म्हारा पखरेतां का ही (ठाण)। देव महाराज कीयो माजी साय बिसरणा में कांई पड़ियो है (हां हेटा उतरियायो)। मात खटाणी बोलै अर कांई समचार कहवै देखां (कीआवूं जाणज्यो देखां भोपाजी महाराज अब कीआवूं)। अबार कहवूं भगवान का हुकमूं (वाह वाह जी)।।

ए माण्डल के मनारै तो जी नान्या ऊदलजी में चड़ ग्या रे।
दीख गा काटूं केरूंदाला केर।
ए सांथरां नान्या जी कदै खाटवे।
बगड़ावत खाटगा म्हारै जी पग पग ऊपर बैठ।।
(भलां जी भलां) देव भलां

माण्डल के मनारै ऊंची चड़ गी (वाह वाह)। दीख गा काटूं केरूंदाला (केर)। के सांथरां लाल कदै नी खाटवै (म्हे)। बै बगड़ावत खाटगा म्हारै पग पग ऊपरै (बैर)। ई भोमी में लाल म्हारो बैर हु गो (हां बैर म्हारो घणो है कीयो)। तो लाल ई जागावूं राण शहर नजीक है (म्हे)। कीयो माजी साय हेटी उतरिया (वाह वाह)। चौसला खेड़ा की छड़ी (जरूरी ही रोपां कीयो)।।

ए सींवली रो सियाणी तो जी थानो कदै नी हेटा उतरै ओवूं रे।
कोनी हेटै उतरै हींवरजी लीला को पिलाण।
हिया का उडरका म्हारां रे कदै नी भाजवे।
नेड़ी बसै पापणी जी बाळा खाणी राण।।
(भलां जी भलां) देव भलां

सिंवलियो को सियाणी लाल कदै हेटा नी उतरै (म्हे)। नी हेटो उतरै हिंवर लीला को (थानो पिलाण)। हिया का उडरका लाल म्हारै एक कोनी भाजै (म्हे)। नेड़ी बसै रे पापणी बाळा खाणी (राण जी कीयो)। राण शहर लाल अटवूं नजीक घणी है कीयो (हां नेड़ी बसै है कीयो)। साडूमाता बोलै (म्हे)। ओ समचार कुण कीयो है साडूमाता कीयो है (वाह वाह देव महाराज नै)। देव महाराज बोलै (वाह वाह)। कांई माता गूजरी नै समचार कहवै देखां (कीआवूं जाणज्यो अब देखां कीआवूं)।। तूं तो म्हारा निरजन तूं तूं तो देव के दाता तूं

ए सींवली रो सियाणी तो जी अब के माजी ये हेटा उतार लियां रे।
हेटो उतर लेवूं हिंवरजी लीला को पिलाण।
हिया का उडरका साबल बांध दियां।
गदां का हळ बूआ द्यूं ए बाळा खाणी राण।।
(भलां जी भलां) देव भलां

सींवली को सियाणी हेटो मैं उतारूं (म्हे)। उतारल्यूं हिंवर लीला को (पिलाण)। हिया का उडरका अब के साबत बांध देवूं (वाह वाह)। गदां का बूआ द्यूं बाळा खाणी (राण)।।

ए आछी निकरी तो जी नान्या म्हारा जी जम कर दालदियां रे।
बगड़ावतां की नान्या जी बदती काटा बेल।
भाड़ो देवूं रे जंवरा तनै गांठ को।
एकरसां बगड़ावतां नै मरत्यलोक में मेल।।
(भलां जी भलां) देव भलां

दरबार का हुकमूं साडूमाता समचार (कीया है)। कीयो आछी निकरी लाल जम के दालदियां ए बगड़ावतां की बदती काटी (बेल)। भाड़ो देवूं रे जंवरा तनै गांठ को (म्हे)। एकरसां पाछा बगड़ावतां नै मरत्यलोक में (मेल पाछा भेजो)। दरबार का हुकमूं ओ समचार साडूमाता (कीया है जी कीयो)। देव महाराज बोलै (म्हे)। कांई समचार (कहवै देखां कीआवूं जाणज्यो भोपाजी महाराज अब (कीआवूं)। अबार कहवूं धणी देव का हुकमूं देखां (वाह वाह सा)।।

ए आछी निकरी तो जी माता म्हारी रे जम के दालदियां रे।
बगड़ावतां की माजी ये बदती काटी बेल।
भाड़ो कोनी लेवै जंवरा गांठ को।
भाड़ो लेयावूं मरत्यलोक में ये मरण सकै नी कोय।।
(भलां जी भलां) देव भलां

आछी निकरी माता जम के दालदियां कीयो (म्हे)। बगड़ावतां की बदती काटी (बेल)। भाड़ो नी ले माता जंवरा गांठ को (म्हे)। ईंयां भाड़ो लेयावूं मरत्यलोक में मरण सकै नी (एक)। सरधा सारू अर पना सारू (भाड़ो स की स संसारी दे देवे)। भाड़ो लेवा लाग ग्या पछै दुनिया मरै कोनी (वाह वाह)। तीन तिलोकी को नाथ भगवान बोलै (म्हे)। कांई समचार आपकी मां नै कहवै देखां (कीआवूं जाणज्यो देखां कीआवूं)। अबार कहवूं भगवान का हुकमूं देखां (वाह वाह सा)।।

ए रोय रोय तो जी रुदन मत करै साडू सुलखना रे।
रोयावूं माजी ये होंसी हाण।
जुरियावूं बगड़ावत आवेला कोय नी।
जुर जुर भर ले माजी ये नंदियां का निवाण।।
(भलां जी भलां) देव भलां

जुरै मत तूं (म्हे)। माजी जुरियां होंसी (हाण)। जुरियावूं बगड़ावत पाछा कोनी आवेला (म्हे)। जुर जुर भर ले माजी नंदियां का (निवाण)। तूं आंसूआंवूं नंदी चला देय (म्हे)। तो ही बगड़ावत तो पाछा (आबा का कोनी कीयो)। माजी साय (म्हे)। रोय रोय तो अब नैन घमाना है (वाह वाह)। हेटी आयजा (म्हे)। चौसला की छड़ी रोप दियां (रोपां कीयो)। साडूमाता बोलै कांई देव नै समचार कहवै देखां (कीआवूं जाणज्यो कीआवूं देखां)। अबार कहवूं देव का हुकमूं (वाह वाह सा)।।

ए चौसलो मत बसावो जी जी बाळा देव जी रे।
चौसलो कैज्यै जी चौगांवां की रायां रे।
बसबा देयो खेड़ो तेजाजी को मनारियो।
मेल करां नै राज का रे पांचूं राज भायां रे।।
(भलां जी भलां) देव भलां

चौसलो मत बसावो थें (म्हे)। चौसलो कैज्यै चौगांवां की (रायां)। अरै बसालियो खेड़ा तेजा को मनारियो (वाह वाह)। मेल करज्यो राज का पांचूं ही (भाइयां कीयो)। पांचूं भाई भेळा हो जावो नै (हां जकै दिन चौसला की छड़ी रोप दीज्यो)। लाल हाल तूं एकलो है (म्हे)। एकला का थाक कठै कोनी लागै (वाह वाह)। कीयो माजी साय (म्हे)। छड़ी तो चौसला की रूपी (हां पहली छड़ी चौसलै खेड़ै की रूपी)।।

ए चौसलो मत बसावो जी ए ई बाळा देव जी रे।
चौसलो कीज्यै जी चौगांवां की सींव।
बसालियो खेड़ो तेजाजी को मनारियो।
बसालियो म्हारा जी अरजन छोटा भीम।।
(भलां जी भलां) देव भलां

चौसलो खेड़ो है नै (म्हे)। ओ मत बसावो कीयो (वाह वाह)। चौसलो कीज्यै चौगांवां की (सींव)। ए बसालियो खेड़ा तेजा को मनारियो (वाह वाह)। म्हारा अरजन बड़ा (भीम)। ए भीमजी महाराज चौसला की टाल करो (वाह वाह)। कीयो सुण ये मात (म्हे)। भोज की राजगादी है नै जकी चौसला की हुई पहली (हां अठै की छड़ी रूपी कीयो)। बूझणा करी रे लाल (म्हे)। चौसलो खेड़ो है नै ओ कळह को मूली है (हां ठेट को कळह को मूली है कीयो)। ई में कळह व्हिया बिनै लाखां ही (नैइ रहवै कीयो)। तो लाल तूं एकलो है हाल (म्हे)। जकै दिन पांचो भाई भेळा हो जावै पूंचै पाण हो जावै नै (वाह वाह)। जरां तो की कोनी (हां जका दिन छड़ी रोपो तो की बात कोनी है)। दरबार का हुकमूं तीन तिलोकी को नाथ भगवान कांई सुगण मनावै कांई सुगण मनावै (म्हे)। कांई चौसला की छेड़ी रोपतां सुगण करै देखां (कीआवूं जाणज्यो देखां कीआवूं)। अबार कहवूं देव भगवान काही का हुकमूं देखां (वाह वाह सा)।।

ए ऊंधो सरप तो जी जो बिल में बड़ै रे बैइ का भाट जी रे।
ऊंधो भाट जी रे खेजड़ा पर चड़ गो भेड़ बिलाव।
आ सुगणावूं दुश्मन राव नै आपां मार ल्यां।
कर दियां दुश्मन की रे तळ मुण्डी ऊपर पांव।।
(भलां जी भलां) देव भलां

ऊंधो सरप देख भाट बिल में बड़ै (वाह वाह)। ऊंधो चड़ गो खेड़जा पर बेड़ (बिलाव)। अरै सुगणावूं तो दुश्मन राव नै आपां मारां (म्हे)। कर दियां बैरी की तळ मुण्डी ऊपरै ही (पांव)। अरै बाबा भाट

(म्हे)। सूण किस्या व्हिया देख (हां सूण किस्या व्हिया जकी बता)। ए श्री महाराज मिनखा जूण नै (ए सूण कदै नी होवे)। औतारी पुरुष है नै तूं (म्हे) तनै ईंयां का सूण ये (व्हिया है कीयो)।।

ए चौसलो बसातां तो जी म्हाला देव नै जी हिरण मालयाड़ा होय।
चोर नैइ खेंचै आपकी गंवत्रियां।
आ सुगणावूं आप नै रे गंजै सकै नै कोय।।
(भलां जी भलां) देव भलां

चौसलो बसातां देव नै अब हिरण मालयाड़ा (हाये)। चोर नैइ खेंचै अन्नदाता आ सुगणावूं आपकी गंवत्रियां (वाह वाह)। अरै सुगणावूं (थानै गंज सकै नी कोय)। श्री महाराज (म्हे)। सूण ईंयां का व्हिया की गंजै जका नै (आप ही गंजो)। थानै गंजवालो (कोय नैइ मिलै कीयो)। दरबार भला ही बार घड़ी बार पूल (म्हे)। टैम अच्छी है जको चौसला की छड़ी नै (हां रोपो)।।

ए माही सातै तो जी ए ई छट भादवियां रे।
ए तो भाई जी आखा तीज समरथ बार।
इस्या जिमाज्यै खटाणी नारायण देव ने।
आपां नै खटाणी ये देव लंघावै पार।।
(भलां जी भलां) देव भलां

माही तो सातै (म्हे)। छट भादवी आखा तीज ईंयां का समरथ (बार)। इस्या जिमा खटाणी नारायण देव नै (म्हे)। आपां नै अब देव लंघावै (पार)। दरबार का हुकमूं बगड़ावतां की उजड़ भूमी पड़ी सात बरसावूं (वाह वाह)। आखा तीज के दिन आर भगवान चौसला की छड़ी रोप दी (हां पाछी छड़ी रोपी जी कीयो)। तो दरबार का हुकमूं तीन धोक भगवान बरोबर बता दी (वाह वाह)। के बडी तो माही तो सातै (वाह वाह)। अर भदवा की छट (म्हे)। अर आखा तीज फल तीन धोक है भगवान की तीना को फल एक है (हां बराबर ही फल है तीन्या को)। किसी नै मानो आखा तीज के दिना धूप करै मानै तो ही बो ई फल है माही सातै के दिन दरबार को मानै धूप ध्यान करै तो भी बो ई फल है भादवा के दिन छट में एक सौ ही फल है माही सातै तो आती धोक है क्यु के जी टैम में भगवान (औतार लियो)। छट के दिन रात को शनीवार छट हो जकै चार बजियां देव को जलम व्हियोड़ा है (वाह वाह)। मुण्डा के उगती साता आयगी धोक तो साता की ही लागै (हां सातियां की लागै छट की लागना को प्रशन नी ऊठे)। हां

ए चौसलै बिराज्या तो जी ए ई धरमराज देवजी रे।
बिराज गा अणियाला ऊंचै थान।
गादी बैठ गा मणवा रावत भोज की।।
लीना दरबार जी जुकता तोरण भाण।।
(भलां जी भलां) देव भलां

चौसलै बिराज्या भाई नारायण देवजी (वाह वाह)। बिराज गा अणियालै ऊंचै ही (थान)। अरै गादी बैठा मणवा रावत भोज की (वाह वाह)। लिया भगवान जुकता तोरण (भाण)।।

ए चौसलै बिराज्या तो जी जो बाळो देवजी रे।
बिराज गा अन्नदाताजी घूघरवाली खाट।
मेघनाथ बजावै मुण्डा के कींगरो।
भलो बिड़दावै देव नै छोछू नारद भाट।।
(भलां जी भलां) देव भलां

चौसलै बिराज गो नारायण देवजी (वाह वाह)। बिराज गो घूघरवाली (खाट)। मेघनाथ बजावै मुण्डो के कींगरो भलो बिड़दावा लाग गियो छोछू बंगाली (अब भाट)।।

ए चौसलै बिराजा तो जी ए ई पणमेसर देवजी रे।
बिराज गा अन्नदाता आपो ही आप।
कोढियां का कलंक झाड़ै नारायण देवजी।
काट दे खावण रे पुरब पाछला पाप।।
(भलां जी भलां) किषन भलां

देव का नांव लिया तो भैइ सदा ही (भलां जी कीयो)। फैर बूझणा (करी है)। कीयो चौसलै बिराज्यो भाई नारायण देवजी (म्हे)। बिराज गा आपो ही (आप)। कोढियां का कलंक झाड़ै नारायण देवजी झाड़ दे दाता म्हारो पुरब पाछला ही (पाप)। तीन तिलोकी को नाथ कोढियां का तो कलंक झाड़बा लागो (म्हे)। आंधा नै आंखियां देबा (लाग ग्या)। दरबार का हुकमूं रावजी साय को गांगो भाट हो (म्हे)। बो सुणियो भाई के भगवान आया है कोढियां का कलंक झाड़ै आपां ही चालां (हां आपणी देही बिगयोड़ी है कीयो)। रावजी को सरप कोढियो हो गांगो भाट हो जको (वाह वाह)। देव के चरणा आयो नै (म्हे)। दरबार का हुकमूं भगवान अम्मी की नजर झांकी काया कंचन की (कर दीनी)। अब गांगो भाट कहवै (म्हे)। कीयो गंगा ही अठै अर गोमती अठै (वाह वाह)। अरै अठसठ तीरथ है ई जागां अठै (अठै)। राव को गांगो भाट कह मैं देव का चरण छोड़ जावूंला ही (कठै कीयो)। मैं तो भगवान की चरणा मैं अठै ही (हां रहवूं कीयो)। तो सात बरसावूं उजड़ भूमी पड़ी ही नी बगड़ावतां की (म्हे)। चौसला खेड़ा की छड़ी भगवान रोपतां हेंर गांगा भाट की देही सुधारतां (सुधारतां)। जय बोलो भैइ श्री देवनारायण भगवान की (जय बोलो छोटा अर मोटा स)। दरबार का हुकमूं चौसला की छड़ी रोपी नै (म्हे)। तो सब जगा केयां नै थोड़ो थोड़ो ठा पड़ गो (वाह वाह)। क्युं के देवजी वाला गायां ही जकी मला के मांयनै जाती जणै पंद्रा बीस पंद्रा बीस गांवां का माल भेळिया बिनै लाखां ही (हां कोनी आवती)। पहल पोत अजमेर को धणी कांई परवाणा देवै (म्हे)। हेंर कांई दरबार का हुकमूं रावजी सा अर अजमेर को धणी सीत कर दे (वाह वाह)। हेंर कांई भगवान देव के परवाणा भेजै देखां (कीआवूं जाणज्यो देखां कीआवूं)।।

ए गायां चरे तो जी ए ई गोरम का भाखरां रे।
आंती जांती करियो जी घर माळागर में खोज।
बाबो राव नै खोज साल गो बैइ का भाटजी।
म्हनै सालियो रे सितमितवाला भोज।।
(भलां जी भलां) देव भलां

गायां तो चराई भाई गोरम का भाखरां (म्हे)। आंती जांती करियो दीखै रावजीवाला माला के मांयनै (खोज)। ए बै बाबा राव नै दरबार का हुकमूं खोज साल गो (म्हे)। म्हनै सालियो सितमितवालो (अब भोज)। भोज ईंयां का बैर है (हां जका मैं याद ही करिया कोनी कीयो)। दरबार का हुकमूं म्हांकाली गायां का खोज ही कोनी सुवाया लोगां नै (वाह वाह)। इताक पहली दीया का ओळबा का परवाणा (हां लेर का लेर औरूं आयग्या जी कीयो)। कांई भगवान परवाणा बांचै (म्हे)। कांई समचार कहवै देखां (कीआवूं जाणज्यो अब कीआवूं)।।

गायां ऊबी तो जी जो माळा के मांयनै औवूं रे।
आंती जाती खायी दीखे गहूं चन्ना की पूली रे।
दीयाजी नै पूली साल गी रे बैइ का भाट जी।
म्हनै साल गी भोज की रे साखत सुधी बंवळी रे।।
(भलां जी भलां) देव भलां

गायां तो ऊबी माळा के मांयनै (म्हे)। दीया की खाय गी दीखै आंती जांती गहूं चन्ना की (पूली)। दीयाजी नै आ पूली साल गी (म्हे)। म्हनै साली भोज की रे साखत सुधी (बंवळी)। बंवळी जियान को माल है दीया कन्नै (हां मैं तो बी घोड़ी नै याद ई करी कोनी कीयो)। अरे म्हांकाली कोय गायां की पूली बिखेर दी जकी दीया ने सवाई कोनी देख (हां सवाई कोनी ओळबा का परवाणा भेज दिन्या (है कीयो)। दरबार का हुकमूं लिख रावजी साथ परा कागद (म्हे)। अजमेर भेज दिया (वाह वाह)। कीयो बगड़ावत तनै भैइ खरणी भरतां ठेट का (म्हे)। देव महाराज माळवा में आयार गोठ खेड़ा बसा दिया तनै याद ही कोनी करियो (हां याद ही कोनी करिया थानै तो कीयो)। या तो खरणी मंगा लियो (म्हे)। या देव महाराज का चड़बाळा लीलागर घोड़ा हे जका बै (हां बै मंगा लियो खरणी के वास्ते)। हेंर बो ही नी देवै (म्हे)। शंकर की दियोड़ी गाय है सुरेमाता (बा मंगा लियो)। अर बी नै नी देवै (म्हे)। संपाड़ो करै भगवान कूण्डी बा मंगा लियो आपां (हां पाणी की कूण्डी है बा मंगा लियो)। तीन ही करामात है आंका देवजी कन्नै (हां चोथी करामात नैइ है कीयो)। अजमेर को धणी लिख परो कागद (म्हे)। देव कन्नै भेज दियो (वाह वाह)। देव बोलै (वाह वाह)। कांई समचार कहवै देखां (कीआवूं जाणज्यो देखां कीआवूं)।।

ए गायां ऊबी तो जी जो माळा के मांयनै औवूं रे।
आंती जांती खायो दीखै रे गहूं चन्ना को बूंठ।
दादाजी नै बूंठा चाल्या रे बैइ का भाट जी।

म्हनै साल गा रे मोहरां भरयोड़ा ऊंठ।।
(भलां जी भलां) देव भलां

गायां तो गी माळा के मांयनै (वाह वाह)। अरै आंती जांती खायो दीखै कोय गहूं चन्ना का (बूंठ)। दादाजी नै बूंठो ही साल गो (म्हे)। म्हनै साला दे मोहरां भरयोड़ा (हां ऊंठ)। ए कागदां में लिखयोड़ा पड़ियोड़ा भाई (म्हे)। महाभारत चलू व्हियो नै बगड़ावतां को (वाह वाह)। बी टैम में सितर ऊंठ मोहरां से भर अजमेर की कछेड़ी की बतावै काकोजी नेवोजी पूगाया (हां पूगार आया कीयो)। पण मैं तो हाल याद ही कोनी करिया (हां बती मोहरां नै याद ही कोनी करी)। हेंर दादाजी नै खरणी कींयां भायी इती बेगी (वाह वाह)। लेर को लेर औरूं खरणी को परवाणो आयगो (वाह वाह)। कीयो के तो खरणी जल्दी लियावो (म्हे)। नी जरां भाई आयो जका खोजां पाछो जा (हां बावड़ जावो थांका बठै (ही जावो कीयो माळागर की भोम में ही)। अरे बूझियो नी ताझियो मालक बन बैठ गा (वाह वाह)। तीन तिलोकी को नाथ भगवान बोलै (म्हे)। कांई भाट नै समचार कहवै देखां (कीआवूं जाणज्यो कीआवूं)। अबार कहवूं भगवान देव का इका हुकमूं कह दियां (वाह वाह सा)।

परवाणा बांचिया तो जी ए ई दादेजी के हाथ का रे।
म्हारै भाटजी रे मन में चाली हूक।
दादाजी नै खरणी भावै रे बैइ का भाटजी।
दादाजी के भाटजी रे क्यें की रह गी भूख।।
(भलां जी भलां) देव भलां

परवाणा बांचिया रे भाट मैं दादोजी का हाथ का (वाह वाह)। म्हारै अब मन में चाल गी (हूक)। दादाजी नै खरणी भावै बैइ का भाट दादाजी कींयां की रह गी (औरूं भूख)। म्हानी खरणी की खातर भूखा बैठा है कांई (हां ईंयां थोड़ा ही बैठया है कीयो)। कीयो श्री महाराज दोहरो मत मानो आप (म्हे)। खरणी बगड़ावत देतो (हां ठेट के ही लागै है कीयो)। बाबा भाट जरां खरणी देनी पड़ी (हां श्री महाराज)। डेढ ताकड़ी लागी महाराज (वाह वाह)। तो भाट जरां गांव तो हाल बसिया कोनी इन्यायी पहली आयगा (वाह वाह)। आपणो बसणो तो होवै कोनी अठै (हां बसणो दोहरो ही है)। क्युं के दीया का परवाणा आयगा उनू रावजी का परवाणा (आयग्या)। उनै अजमेर का धणी का (परवाणा आयग्या जी कीयो)। बाबा भाट खरणी भरवा नै जरां चालां पहली ओ ई जण (हां पहलो काम तो ओ ई करसिया कीयो)। हां श्री महाराज भरियावूं लार छुटै आगी (वाह वाह)। तीन तिलोकी को नाथ कांई भगवान पालासानी नै हुकम देवें (म्हे)। कांई लीलागर घोड़ा नै पिलाणै (वाह वाह)। कांई खरणी की चड़ाई होवै (कीआवूं जाणज्यो देखां अब भोपाजी महाराज कीआवूं)। अबार कहवूं देव का हुकमूं देखां (वाह वाह सा)।।

पाला ही फूंक पिलाणज्यो कर लीलागर बाहरें बेगो आण।
लीलो चाल्या धरती माता धरै हरै बासक डरै पियांळ।
लीलो अब करै गियो धरमराजा देवजी लीला के हला दी बाग।

अब के कर द्यो गोठां का राजवी औरूं पिला दूधां धायां काबरिया टार।
मकेरिया नै माथै मार दे पालासानी पड़ी चरण दे लांप।
पिलाण ले काळी जायो लीलड़ो बैरियो में घाला अंवळी संवळी जाप।
लीला पर ई नारायण को बैसणो जी पर देव बिराज्यो आय।
नौसर खरां पर पाखड़ पड़िया रे।
काळका देबी बड़योड़ी करै भैरूं नै बूझणा।
आसांगावूं लंका नै तोड़ी देव की रे नै कुनै हुई चड़ाया रे।।
(भलां जी भलां) देव भलां

पालासानी भाई फूंक पिलाणज्यो (वाह वाह)। कस लीलागर बाहरें बेगो (आण)। लीलो चाल्या धरती माता धर हरै (वाह वाह)। बासक डरै (पियांळ)। लीलो परणालिया गियो धरमराजा देव की लीलै हला दी (बाग)। हुकम कर द्यो गोठां का राजवी (म्हे)। औरूं पिलाणूं दूधां का धायां काबरिया (अब टार)। मकेरिया नै माथै मार पालासानी भाई पड़ी चरण दे (लांप)। अरै पिलाण काळी जाय लीलड़ो (म्हे)। अब बैरियां में घाल अंवळी संवळी (जांप)। लीला ऊपर नारायण को बैसणो जी पर देव बिराज्यो (आय)। नौसर खरां पर पाखर (पड़िया)। काळका देवी करै बड़योड़ी बूझणा (म्हे)। आसांगावूं तो लांका नै तोड़ी आज भगवान देव की जाणै कुण हुई (हां चड़ायां कीयो)। भैरवानाथ (हां कुनै चड़ायां हुई कीयो)। म्हांकाला खप्पर भरीज गी (हां कोनी भरीजेला)। क्युं कठा की चड़ाई है (खरणी भरणै जाय अजमेर देव महाराज)। तीन तिलोकी को नाथ पिलाण लीला घोड़ा नै (वाह वाह)। हेंर पागड़ा के मांय ही पाग (दिया जी कीयो)। तारा गढ की बींटली का तीन कांकरां टूट हेटा (मतै ही जार पड़िया)। अजमेर को धणी बूझणा (करी है)। अरै सिरदारां (म्हे)। ए कांकरां मतै कींयां टूटया भाई (हां आंधी न बायरो न मेह की छांट कोनी कीयो)। कीयो श्री महाराज म्हानै तो कांई ठी (म्हानै ए बात को ठा नी है)। पिण्डतां नै बुलावो (हां बा नै बूझो)। बुलार पिण्डतां नै बूझणा करी रे भाई बिरामणां (म्हे)। ए कांकरां मतै क्युं टूटिया (हां आ बतावो देख अर टीपणा में देखे)। पिण्डत बोल्या श्री महाराज काळ का दिना में थै परवाणा दिया है नै (म्हे)। खरणी का (वाह वाह)। बो धणी आप के घरां से बिदा होवै (खरणी भरबा नै पागड़ै में पांव दिन्यो है)। कीयो बिरामणा (म्हे)। पागड़ा में पग देतां ही कांकरां हेटा पड़ गा (वाह वाह)। अठै आयीं जरां (कांई होसी हो कीयो)। कीयो तेश मेश हुई भाई (वाह वाह ईंयां को जोग है कीयो)। कीयो जरां खरणी आपणै चावां कोनी (हां पाछो जावै जियान की बिदी आपणै कोय बनावो)। बिना बिरामणा (म्हे)। ओ सकस तो आपणै गांव में नी आवै (हां जिसी बिदी बनावो कीयो)। कीयो श्री महाराज भगवान की चड़ाई है (म्हे)। तो पाछी तो झटकेन की ईंयां की जावै कोनी (हा) सरणी भगवान की चड़ाई पाछी (क्यें की बावड़े)। एक बात है श्री महाराज (म्हे)। सांवरा भैंसां मंगावो (वाह वाह)। सिंदुरूं तेलूं गेडू (काटा कर देवो)। तो गोठां के गोरवें जको गेला पर बा नै गेर दियो (हां सामा गेर देवो)। औतारी पुरुष है बोसुण मान जायै (जरां तो पाछा बावड़ जावे)। निजर लाखां कोनी बावड़ै (वाह वाह)। इता ही थोक व्हिया (म्हे)। सांवरा भैंसां मंगा लिया (वाह वाह)। सिंदुरूं तेलूं गेडू कर गोठां के गोरवें गेर दिया (हां सामा गेर दिया जी कीयो)। भगवान

नै ए आतां (दीखियाया)। भाट नै बूझणा (करी है)। बाबा भाट (म्हे)। आगै नै आ भाई (हां ए कांई आवै अरै काळा काळा जिनावर कीयो)। कीयो श्री महाराज बगड़ावतां का मरिया पछै नजर कोय नी रही म्हारै (हां कीयो मन्दो ही दीखे म्हनै)। म्हनै ऐनाण-सैनाण पूरा बतावो (जणा तो मैं बता द्यूं आप नै)। कीयो बैइ का भाट काळा काळा जानवर लाग्या म्हनै (म्हे)। सिंदुरूं तेलूं गेडू करियोड़ा है भैइ (काटा गेडू अब करियोड़ा है कीयो)। अरे श्री महाराज म्हारो अर पालियो को काळ आयग्यो (हां काळ ही है कीयो)। थारै तो बिगड़ै कांई (हां थें तो औतारी पुरुष हो थांको बिगड़ै की कोनी)। बगड़ावतां की बी डाबोनी ही (जको म्हानै सागै ले अर आयो कीयो)। अरे भाट जा कांई व्हियो (हां की व्हियो कांई बात है)। श्री महाराज बोसुण है (हां बोसुण करिया है कीयो)। तो जरां अब (कींयां करां)। कींयां तो कांई करो भाई महाराज आप के जचै जियान करो (हां आप ही जाणो ई बात नै)। पाछा चालो श्री महाराज (वाह वाह)। तीन तिलोकी को नाथ भगवान बोलै (म्हे)। कांई भाट नै समचार कहवै देखां (कीआवूं जाणज्यो देखां कीआवूं)। अबार कहवूं देव कांई का हुकमूं देखां (वाह वाह सा)।

ए माथा नै खा जावै जी जो सिर की पागड़ियां रे।
बैइ का भाटजी रे गाय नार नै खाय।
मथरा की जागां बनै रहबा दुवारका।
जरां असवारी रे चड़ी पाछी जाय।।
(भलां जी भलां) देव भलां

माथा नै खावै रे भाट सिर की पागड़ी (वाह वाह)। गाय नार नै (खाय)। मथरा की जागां बनै भाट द्वारका (वाह वाह)। जरां चड़ियोड़ो असवारी भगवान की पाछी (म्हारी जाय कीयो)। ठा तो है तनै (हां अता काम व्हिया जणा म्हारी) (असवारी बावड़े कीयो)। पाछी लिया इकै बिरदवूं घणू (म्हे)। ओ बिरद तो भरिया है भाई (वाह वाह)। दरबार का हुकमूं श्री महाराज मैं तो बचां ही कोनी जरां (हां म्हांकी तो मौत ही है कीयो)। दरबार का हुकमूं रे बाबा भाट डर मत (हां बंचनवालो कोय नैइ बिदी बता कीयो)। दरबार का हुकमूं बांका सूण बा में झाड़ द्यूं जरां (जणा तो म्हारा धणी)। चाहीज्यै कांई कीयो (वाह वाह)। पण श्री महाराज ओ जानवर आवै जको जळ को अर खळ को (हां है कीयो) ईकी मनसिया पूरो होवै (वाह वाह)। जरां काम बैठै (जणा हुवै कीयो)। बाबा भाट मनसिया पूरण कींयां होवै कीयो (हां जकी बता कीयो)। कीयो श्री महाराज चोखो तो बिरखा व्हियोड़ी हुवै (म्हे)। हेंर गोड़ा गोड़ा सुध हरियो घास (हां व्हियो है ऊबो)। ए जानवर भूखा है अबार घास चरै (म्हे)। हेंर पछै जळ भरियोड़ो तलाई होवै (काटी)। बी के मांयनै पाणी पीर जळ में (म्हे)। लोटै (वाह वाह)। जरां ही बूड़ो जीव है जको खुशी (हां हुवै कीयो)। तीन तिलोकी को नाथ तो बी जागां ही लीलागर को पागड़ो छोड़ दियो (वाह वाह)। बोल इन्द को आधार (म्हे)। उतम पछेवड़ो ओड़ पोढी लगाली (हां सोय ग्या जी कीयो)।

बादल कर तो जी गरमियां कर दी रे गोठालां राजवियां रे।
पलक में अन्नदाताजी हरिया करिया घास।

भैंसां का अन्नदाता कंवळ उजाड़िया।
बांका ठाकरां जी रोड़ दियो आकाश।।
(भलां जी भलां) देव भलां

बादल कर गरमियां कर दी (म्हे)। दरबार का हुकमूं भगवान पलक में हरियो करियो (घास)। भैंसां का कंवळ उजाड़िया (म्हे)। आंका ठाकरां रोड़ ग्या (अब आकाश)। भगवान इन्द को आधार बोल्यो (म्हे)। पलक में तो मेह बरस गो (वाह वाह)। हेंर पलक में हरिया घास (हां हो ग्या जी कीयो)। अर पलकूड़ी तलाई हे नी बा (म्हे)। ऊसरी नांव तलाई को (वाह वाह)। बी ऊसरी तलाई के मांयनै भगवान ठाटूं भर दी बीनै जळवूं (वाह वाह)। के तो जानवर गैलै गैलै (बह रिया)। हेंर घास दीखियो नै (म्हे)। टपकेन का गेलावूं टल आपका घास चरबा लागी (गिया जी कीयो)। घास चर (वाह वाह)। निंगै करी जळ दीखियो तलाई में (हां तलाई भरेड़ी निंगै आयगी)। जार पाणी में (नाहवणो लाग ग्या)। अताक पहली दरबार दरबार का हुकमूं ऊठ अर खाण्डो भायो (म्हे)। दोन्यो ई भैसां का शीश पाछा अजमेर की कछेड़ी में जार (हां कछेड़ी में जांवता पड़िया जी कीयो)। अजमेर को धणी बिरामणा ने बूझणा (करी है)। बिरामणा (म्हे)। आं कांई बात हुई है (हां आं कांई बात व्हियो)। श्री महाराज थारा सूण थारा में ही (पाछा झाड़ दिन्या कीयो)। कीयो जरां अब (अब कांई व्हियै कीयो)। कीयो आयो भाई शुरू कर दे (हां अब तो आसी कीयो रुकै कोनी)। कीयो दरबार का हुकमूं भाई दरवाजा मंगल करय दियो (हां दरवाजा मंगल करा द्यो)। बारी खुली (रखा द्यो बारी मांय कर कोनी आवे)। औतारी पुरुष है जको कांई ठी ई जागावूं पाछो मुड़ जाय तो ई चोखो (हां चोखी बात है कीयो)। धोळा दोपारां अजमेर को धणी दरवाजा बन्द करा दिया (वाह वाह)। बारी खुली (रखा दीनी)। तीन तिलोकी को नाथ भाट दरवाजा कन्नै (पूगता व्हिया जी कीयो)। देव महाराज बूझणा करी रे बैइ का भाट (म्हे)। धोळा दोपारां दरवाजा (आज बन्द कींयां हो कीयो)। कीयो आपवूं डरता (करिया है कीयो)। श्री महाराज आ बारी है नै (म्हे)। घोड़ा असवार समेत चड़ियोड़ो असवार मावै ई में (हां चड़िया असवारी मावै कीयो (बारी मांय कर चाल जावो)। तो देव महाराज बोलै (म्हे)। कांई समचार बैइ का भाट नै कहवै देखां (कहवै देखां कीआवूं जाणज्यो अब कीआवूं)। अबार कहवूं भगवान देव का हुकमूं कह देवूं (वाह वाह सा)।

ए माथा नै खाजावै जी जो सिर की पागड़ियां रे।
बैइ का भाट जी रे बाड़ खेत ने खाय।
मंगरिया को पाणी पाछो चेला पर बैइ का भाटजी।
जरां असवारी बारी मांय व्है कर जाय।
(भलां जी भलां) देव भलां

माथा नै खावै भाट सिर की पागड़ी (वाह वाह)। बाड़ खेत नै (आ खाय)। अरै मंगरी को पाणी पाछो चेला चड़ै (म्हे)। जरां असवारी म्हारी बारी मांय करै (जाय)। डूंगर को पाणी उतरिया पछै पाछो चड़ै जरां म्हारी असवारी पाछी गिरै (हां नैइ तो कोय नी गिरै कीयो)। पालय ई के बिरद घणा (म्हे)।

अरै भूखा हां आजा अजमेर की कछेड़ी में चांलां सैन्धा-मैन्धा हां आपां तो (हां जांवतां ही आसका द्यां दोय थाळ अबार (पुरसीजै आजाई जरां देयी बाटकियां)। पालोसानी बैइ को भाट बगड़ावतां को (म्हे)। घोड़ा को खेंच खेंच बारी मांय कर (बड़ ग्या जी कीयो)। अजमेर की बात है (ओ ई अजमेर की)। तीन तिलोकी को नाथ घोड़ा की बाग नै के बी जागावूं पाछी अपूठी राळी (वाह वाह)। घोड़ो पाछ पगलिया पाछ पगलिया पाछ पगलिया तीन कोस पर जार ठमियो (वाह वाह)। बी जागां देव तीन तिलोकी को नाथ घोड़ा को ऊबटो (खेंचियो)। तो जकै दिन खरणी भरबा आया नै (म्हे)। जकै दिन देव महाराज के बतावै लीला को ऊबटो खेंचियो बी जागां (वाह वाह)। तो बो के हाल तक म्हारो तो कोय नी देखियोड़ो भाई पण दुनिया कहवै की देवरो हाल खड़ो है ऊबटो (वाह वाह तीन कोस दिखणादू)। दरबार का हुकमूं बनाय ऊबटा को बी जागां देवरो (म्हे)। के घोड़ा की बाग नै ऊंची सारी भगवान (हां ऊंची सारी जी कीयो)। भाट अर पालोसानी तो पुगिया कोनी (म्हे)। तीन तिलोकी को नाथ दरवाजा के ऊपरै आ करी कछेड़ी में (हां पूगता व्है ग्या)। तो जमीमाता से लीलागर घोड़ो सुवा हाथ ऊंचो चालै (वाह वाह)। घोड़ा से अधर सुवा हाथ पिलाणो ऊंचो रहवै (वाह वाह)। पिलाणो सुवा हाथ ही भगवान बिराजमान (हां ऊंचा व्है रिया जी कीयो)। शीश पर सुवा शेश मण को छत्थर (हां सुवा शेश मण को छत्थर बो ई सुवा हाथ (ऊंचो अधर तपे)। हेंर छत्थर के ऊपरै धज्जा धोवती भगवान के ऊपर तपै हो (वाह वाह)। इण के भांत से लीलागर घोड़ो कछेड़ी के मांयनै भगवान फैरै (हां आमु सामू फिरा रिया हा)। इताक पहली बगड़ावतां को भाट है जको कछेड़ी में पूगो (वाह वाह)। कीयो रे पालिया (म्हे)। देख देव लेरै छोड़ आया तमास निकर ग्या (हां आगेवूं आया आपणावूं तो)। ईंको पार कोनी पायो आपां (हां ईंको पार ही कोनी है कीयो)। बगड़ावतां को भाट औरूं आसका बी जागां अजमेर का धणी नै दीनी (वाह वाह)। आद राजा आद का जुगाद जुगाद का काछब काछब का रणधोळ (म्हे)। रणधोळ का कजली कजली का मण्डळी मण्डळी का हरीरामजी (म्हे)। हरीरामजी का के बाघ व्हिया अर बाघ का भोज (व्हिया जी कीयो)। भोज का देव (व्हिया है)। अगणकुण्ड का ऊपनिया अर कुली बड़ा हूं (चुहाण)। पगतळी पदम बिराजै खूंवा राजा (खैम)। मूका में है नागर (बैल)। अरै लीला की बाग से पताल में हेम जळ गाजियो जद डूंगरा व्हिया (व्यवार)। देव का औतार व्हिया जिण दिन धरती बिचै आबा बिचै व्हिया (उजास)।। भोज का उदल पड़ता आबा (झेळ)। अजमेर को धणी कीयो देख भैइ आसका (हां दीनी जोरां ही)। अरै बाबा भाट हां श्री महाराज (म्हे)। ओ धणी थारो (थारो है कांई कीयो)। कीयो सागै को सागै है जको म्हारो है कीयो (हां म्हारो है कीयो देव)। कीयो घोड़ा को फैरणो सांचो व्हिया (हां घोड़ा चोका फैरै है कीयो)। अरे बाबा भाट थारा धणी नै कहवै कि म्हांकै टारड़ो फैरा दे (हां म्हांकै एक घोड़ो है दरबार में जको फिरार (देखां तियारी कर देवे)। भाट बूझणा करी श्री महाराज दादाजी को हुकम है घोड़ो फिरावै (हां फैर देवो कांई आप)। कीयो रे बैइ का भाट दादाजी ने कह दे (म्हे)। खुला रमावो भैइ (बाहरें मांगा दियो फैर दियां कीयो)। कीयोड़ो तो करां ही (वाह वाह)। दरबार का हुकमूं बूझणा करी श्री महाराज जरां बुलावो (हां मांगा दियो कीयो)। कीयो खुलावा जरां तो भाट (हां मैं ही फैर)। मैं ही फैर लेवां (फैर लेवां कीयो)। खुलावा कोनी टारड़ो (वाह वाह)। दरबार बूझणा करी बाबा भाट बूझ किसी पायगा में जरां (हां बन्धयोड़ा की जगा है कीयो)। कीयो ओ सामू पायगा बन्धयो रंग को

कल्डयो है (वाह वाह)। देव महाराज कांई करियो के लीलागर ने बागडोर पर (छोड़ दिन्यो खुलो)। हेंर कल्डयो घोड़ा की पायगा पूगता (व्हिया जी कीयो)। जातां ही घोड़ा के के थापी (दीनी)। घोड़ो फट मण्ड गो (वाह वाह)। दरबार का हुकमूं बियां ऊबिणै घोड़ा पर कल्डया चड़ ऊबा रिया दरबार (वाह वाह)। ओ लीलो चालो है नी (म्हे)। बीवूं सवायो (हां चालबा लागगियो)। अजमेर को धणी कीयो वाह भैइ (हां घोड़ा को तो थारो धणी फैरणियो आछो है कीयो)। तीन तिलोकी को नाथ भगवान घड़ी दो घड़ी घोड़ा नै तो (हां उनै को उनै फैरियो)। तो के भगवान एड़ी को मसड़को (दिन्यो)। घोड़ा नै तेंहरवीं पिताल में (मेल दिया जी कीयो)। कीयो बैइ का भाट (म्हे)। दादाजी ने कह दे रे भैइ जमीमाता है नै आ (हां घोड़ै को भोग मांग लियो)। मैं तो धरती नै भोग घोड़ा को (दे दिया कीयो)। दरबार का हुकमूं अजमेर को धणी बोलै (म्हे)। कांई समचार देव नै कहवै (कीआवूं जाणज्यो देखां अब कीआवूं)। अबार कहवूं भगवान कांई का हुकमूं कह द्यां (वाह वाह सा)।

> भैंसां ही मारिया तो जी ए ई म्हाना सांवरा रे।
> भाट नारदी रे कर कल्डया की बानी रे।
> थाना देव नै आयो जियान पाछो ले जा बैइ का भाटजी।
> मैं तो भाटजी रे रेख चाकरी दोन्यु ही भर माणी।।
> (भलां जी भलां) देव भलां

भैंसां मार नाकिया म्हारा सांवरा (वाह वाह)। अरै कर कल्डया की (बानी)। के धायी दरबार का हुकमूं में रेख चाकरी (म्हे)। थारा धणी आयो जियान पाछो ले जा मैं रेख चाकरी दोन्यो ही (भर माणी)। अरै भाट मानली भैइ (हां ओ लियो कागद कीयो)। अजमेर को धणी लिख परा कागद (म्हे)। दिया आपकी मोर छाप (वाह वाह)। हेंर भाट नै (दे दीनी)। मैं रेख मांगा नैइ भाट अब चाकरी (हां कदै ई नी मांगा जावो परा थे)। म्हानै आ ठा कोनी पड़ियो पहली (वाह वाह)। लाखो रुपिया को तो भैंसां को उजाड़ कर दियो (म्हे)। हेंर सुवा लखीणो टार हो (ई नै खतम कर दिन्यो)। देव नै ले जार परवाणो के भगवान नै दिखायो (म्हे)। कीयो भाट बाबा दादाजी नै कह दियो कोय बात की कमी होवै तो औरूं (हां पूरती कर देवां कीयो)। कीयो नैइ श्री महाराज पधारो धाप गा मैं तो (व्हियोड़ी है म्हांकै तो कीयो)। दियोजी जोधको बठै अजमेर का धणी को भाणजो हो (म्हे)। बो देखियो माठो देव आयो जियान नी जातो रह (हां आपणै ईनै ठा पड़ेलो कोनी)। दीयो जोधको ईंयां का बाणावळी है ठा तो पटका (ठा पटका ई देव नै कीयो)। तो एक तेल को कढाव भरियो (म्हे)। बी में देख छायां (वाह वाह)। आकाश के घरां कांवली हुवै के तीर की दीनी (हां टेक कांवली नीची आंवती पड़ी जी कीयो)। पड़ती कांवली भगवान के मुण्डा कन्नै (निंगै आयगी)। अरै बाबा भाट (म्हे)। ओ जानवर कांई पड़ियो म्हनै दे उली कानी (हां उली कानी ल्यावो देखां)। तीन तिलोकी को नाथ ले कांवली नै के पांखां है जकी सारी बी की (कोस लीनी)। तो पांखां अम्मी का नजर झांकी जती पांख ही (म्हे)। जती कांवली पैदा (हां उडा दी)। दीया मार एक नै मार कांई सायो (हां अब मार कीयो देखाणी थारो ताकत देखूं (कतोक बाणावळी है कीयो)। दीयो बोलै (म्हे)। कांई समचार देव नै कहवै देखां (कीआवूं जाणज्यो देखां कीआवूं)। अबार कहवूं भगवान का हुकमूं देखां (वाह वाह सा)।

ए दड़ावट दौड़ो आवां तो जी ए ई गूजरी का डावड़ा रे।
नीतो म्हारी जी सावर दौड़ो आव।
अब कालै ओसर दे मारूं कोय ने।
राताकोट का महाभारत में रे करल्यूंला पीराण।।
(भलां जी भलां) देव भलां

दरबार का हुकमूं कुण समचार कीयो है (दीयोजी कीयो है)। दड़ावट दौड़ो आवूं भैइ गूजरी का डावड़ा (म्हे)। नीतर तूं म्हारी सावर दौड़ो (आय)। अरै ई ओसर में नी मारूंलां (म्हे)। राताकोट का महाभारत में (वाह वाह)। दरबार का हुकमूं ईंयां मार लेवूं कूंकड़ा नै जाणै गल गो बसली भेड़ी (बिलाव)। कूंकड़ा नै मारै नै भेड़ बिलाव (म्हे)। इती टैम कोनी लगावूंला (हां की टैम कोनी लगावूंला कीयो वाह भैइ दियाजी)। दरबार का हुकमूं तीन तिलोकी को नाथ भगवान बोलै अबकै (म्हे)। कांई दीया नै समचार कहवै (कीआवूं जाणज्यो देखां अब कीआवूं)। अबार कहवूं भगवान का हुकमूं वाह वाह सा)।

ए म्हनै बनायो तो जी दीया भाई रे तूं कूंकड़ो रे।
तूं तो दीयाजी रे बन गो असली भेड़ बिलाव।
फौजामूं फांटार फांटार मारूं रे माझी जोधका।
जकै दिन जाणज्यै रे तीन भवन को नाथ।
(भलां जी भलां) देव भलां

म्हनै बनायो दीयाजी तूं कूंकड़ो (म्हे)। तूं बन गो असली भेड़ (बिलाव)। अरै फौजामूं फांटार फांटा राताकोट का मोरचा में मारूंलां (म्हे)। जकै दिन देखजीयै असली तीन भवन को (ओ नाथ)। अबार कांई मारूं तनै (वाह वाह)। ई जागां दीयाजी थनै मारल्यूं मैं (म्हे)। तो राताकोट का महाभारत में थारा बिनै सामनो कुण करै म्हारूं (हां झेळणवालो कुण होसी)। अरै तूं थोड़ü सामनो तो करी (वाह वाह)। जकै दिन फोज मूं फंटार फंटार पीराण काड़ü थांका कीयो (वाह वाह)। कुण कीयो समचार (दियाजी को)। देव महाराज कीयो है (देव महाराज कीया है दीयोजी को)। अजमेर को धणी बोलै (म्हे)। कांई समचार कहवै देखां (कीआवूं जाणज्यो देखां कीआवूं)। अबार कहवां देव का हुकमूं देखां।।

ताणा धणी नै तो जी जो पाछो ले जा रे तलाई ऊसरियां रे।
दीया नै खिनावूं राजा रे अजयपाल के नळा रे।
दोन्यु अमराव कछेड़ी में आव ग्या।
जाणै भाटजी रे पाणी आग जलै ई रे।।
(भलां जी भलां) देव भलां

थारा देव नै तो पाछो ले जा भाट तलाई ऊसरी (म्हे)। अरै दीया नै खिनावूं राजा अजयपाल के (नळ)। ए दोन्यु भड़ देख कछेड़ी में आविया (म्हे)। जाणै पाणी आग ई (जले)। दोन्यु सगस है नै (म्हे)। भेळै खटवाला कोनी (हां अठै खटावै कोनी कीयो ले जावो)। थारा धणी नै भाट रे बेगो ले जा अब (वाह वाह)। देव महाराज नै भाट जार बूझणा (करी है)। श्री महाराज दादाजी को हुकम होवै (म्हे)।

जको आप तो ई जागां अब दादाजी को छाती सहन कोनी होवै (हां पधारो आप)। जितै दीखोलागै थै (म्हे)। जितै रे बाबा भाट धापिया बेगा कीयो (हां बेगा धापिया नै)। अजमेर को धणी मेदूजी कंवर भैरूंदा को ठाकर ले गो है नै बगड़ावतां का धरम भाई हो जरां (म्हे)। तो जी टैम में अजमेर का धणी नै ठा हुई के भैइ मेदू तो आपणो ही है (वाह वाह)। मेदूजी कंवर नै पड़ाई करा दी पाळ पोस कर दियो (म्हे)। हेंर सळाव सिरदारां के कंवर मेदू नै परणाय दियो अजमेर को धणी नै (वाह वाह)। बटूट थाणा की थाणादारी मेदू नै (दे दीनी)। बटूट रहबा लागो भैइ (वाह वाह)। तीन तिलोकी को नाथ भगवान खरणी भर (म्हे)। हेंर करां माफ अर परवाणा लेय (वाह वाह)। बिदा (पाछा बावड़िया)। मेदू की कंवरराणी महल में बैठी बोलै अर कांई देखां लालजी सा नै बतलावै देखां (हां कीआवूं जाणज्यो देखां कीआवूं)। अबार कहवूं देव का हुकमूं ले तूं (वाह वाह सा)।

ऊबा रीज्यो जी ए ई म्हाना लाल सा रे।
मैं आवूं लालजी रे रथ के बेलिया जोत।
आरी जावूं रे म्हारा लाल की ये।
फिर फिर भेळो करै जी मितवालां को गोत।।
(भलां जी भलां) किषन भलां
देमाली नाथ का नांव लेवां तो आप नै भोपा सदा ही (भलां जी कीयो)

मेदू की कंवरराणी को समचार कीयोड़ो है (म्हे)। कीयो दरबार का हुकमूं ऊबा रीज्यो म्हारा लाल सा (म्हे)। मैं आवूं रथ के ई बेलिया (जोत)। अरै आरी जावूं म्हारा लाल के (म्हे)। ओ फिर फिर भेळो करबा लागो मितवालां को (आज गोत)। सिरदारां (म्हे)। खरणी भरबा कोनी आयो है (हां ओ तो म्हानै लेवण नै आयो है कीयो)। ओ आप गोत नै भेळो करै अब (वाह वाह)। तो मेदू की कंवरराणी रथ नै जुताय (वाह वाह)। देव महाराज खरणी भरबा आया जी दिन आपके देव के साथ बिदा हो गी (हां दड़ावट आयगी)। खरणी भरतां (म्हे)। अजमेर का धणी नै परच्या (हां देवता)। मेदू की कंवरराणी सागै (आंवतां)। जय बोलो श्री देवनारायण भगवान की (अब जय)। बोलो दियो छोटा मोटा (स)।। अजमेर को धणी मन में देखियो रे मेदू की कंवरराणी जांती री नै (म्हे)। मेदू थारै कन्नै अब कींयां रही (हां रहणै का कोनी कीयो)। लिख परो कागद (म्हे)। हेंर दरबार का हुकमूं बटूट भेज दियो। (वाह वाह)। मेदू देव महाराज आया भैइ जको थारी पदमणी नै (सागै ले ग्या है)। हेंर गोठ खेड़ा मतेई (बसा लिया कीयो)। भोज को बेटो टीकायत तूं है (म्हे)। राजगादी की देव मांगै कांई (हां राजगादी को धणी तो तूं है कीयो)। मेदूजी कंवर देव का हुकमूं कांई दादेजी का हाथ का परवाणा (बांचै है)। कांई सिरदारां नै समचार कहवै देखां (कीआवूं जाणज्यो देखां अब कीआवूं)।।

ए परवाणा बांचिया तो जी ए ई दादेजी का हाथ का रे।
मैं तो सिरदारां रे दादाजी की बात पिछाणी रे।
पट्टा पोळी उतरिया पछै भूमी के मांयने।
मैं तो सिरदारां रे परतण पियां पाणी।।
(भलां जी भलां) देव भलां

परवाणा बांच लिया दादाजी का हाथ का (म्हे)। मैं आज दादाजी की बात (पिछाणी)। अरै पट्टा पोळी उतरिया पछै भोमी के मांयनै सिरदारां परतण पियां (पाणी)। पट्टा पोळी उतार लिया म्हारा (वाह वाह)। भोमी के मांयनै सिरदारां पाणी भर कोनी पियां भैइ (वाह वाह)। मेदूजी कंवर घमसाय घोड़ो (वाह वाह)। हेंर घोड़ा नै बिदा कर दियो (म्हे)। दरबार का हुकमूं अजमेर का धणी नै आर बूझणा (करी है)। कांई दादाजी ईंयां करी थै (हां आ कांई बात है कीयो)। कीयो भैइ मेदू कंवर मैं तो थारावाणी बात करी है (ए) तो (वाह वाह)। अरै राजगादी को धणी तूं है (म्हे)। तनै बूझियो नी तनै ताझियो नी मतेई राजगादी बन गो धणी (वाह वाह)। जा मेदू मैं तो भैइ थारै सिरी हां (म्हे)। एक दिन आयो जियान पाछो खिना द्यूं माळवै (पाछो खिना दे राजगदी को धणी बै ही (हो जाय कीयो)। मेदूजी कंवर काटो रीस के मांय आयगो (वाह वाह)। माठो आपणी रांड नै ले गो अटवूं (हां) राजगादी को धणी मतेई बन गो देवजी (वाह वाह)। काम तो जबरो करियो (हां आपणो तो की नांव ही कोय नी)। बिनै रामा शामा ही मेदू कंवर बिदा हु गो (वाह वाह)। आगै आयो तो कांई करियो माळा के मांय देव महाराज की गायां चरै (वाह वाह)। गुआल देव का छप्पनजी भैरूंजी की लूरियां तो बोल रिया (म्हे)। और मसका बजावै (वाह वाह)। दरबार का हुकमूं मेदू कंवर बोलै (म्हे)। कांई गुआलां नै बतलावै देखां (कीआवूं जाणज्यो देखां अब कीआवूं)। अबार कहवूं देव का हुकमूं ले तूं (वाह वाह सा)।।

ए कुण की कीज्यै तो जी ए ई माता गंवत्रियां रे।
थै तो भैइ रे कुण का कैज्यो गुआल।
बेटो रजपूत भूप को करै थानै बूझणा।
कुण का भुजावूं भेळ दिया रे बदशाहियां का माल।।
(भलां जी भलां) देव भलां

कुण की कीज्यै भैइ सिरदारां माता गंवत्रियां (म्हे)। कुण का कीज्यै (थै गुआल)। रजपूत भूप को बेटो करै थानै बूझणा (म्हे)। कुण का ई भुजावूं भेळ दिया बदशियां का ही (माल)। गुआलां (म्हे)। गहूं चन्ना की साख कींयां भेळी अठै (हां उनाळो साख कींयां भेळियो जकी बतावो कीयो)। तो साडूमाता को गुआल नै कीयोड़ो हो (म्हे)। कीयो सुण रे भैइ थै जावो माळा के मांयनै (वाह वाह)। थानै कोय बूझ लिया की गायां कुण की (हां कुण की बतावोला कीयो)। देवजी की मत बता दीज्यो भैइ (वाह वाह)। म्हारो मेदू अजमेर रहवै (वाह वाह)। गायां बीकी बता दियो (हां गायां बांकी बतायज्यो मेदूजी की)। तीन तिलोकी को नाथ बी नांव नी ली बी जागां (वाह वाह)। गुआल देव का बोलै (म्हे)। कांई समचार मेदू कंवर नै कहवै देखां (कीआवूं जाणज्यो कीआवूं देखां)। अबार कहवूं देव भगवान का हुकमूं देखां (वाह वाह सा)।।

ए मेदू की कीज्यै तो जी ए ई माता गंवत्रियां रे।
साडू का मेदूजी पीर का कीज्यै गुआल।
भुज की कां बतावां बेटा रजपूत भूप का।
म्हांका भुजावूं भेळ द्या रे बदशाहियां का माल।।
(भलां जी भलां) देव भलां

दरबार का हुकमूं ओ समचार कीयो है (म्हे)। कीयो मेदू की बाजै भैइ ये माता गंवत्रियां (वाह वाह)। साडूजी का पीर का बाजा (मै गुआल)। अरै भुज की कां होतां बेटा रजपूत भूप का (म्हे)। म्हांका ही भुजावूं भेळ दिया बदशियां का ही (माल)। भुज भैइ तो दुजाला म्हानै (काम ही कद आवै कीयो)। ई जागां राड़ दंगो हो जाय तो भुज तो म्हांकाला ही काम दे (वाह वाह)। हेंर गायां मेदूजी कंवर है बटूट के थाणेदारी में (हां बांकी है कीयो)। ए भैइ माळवा की भोम का साडू का पीर का गुआल हां मैं (वाह वाह)। मेदूजी कंवर के जो ऊफणता दूध के छांटो दिया नै पाणी को (म्हे)। जै डील के छांटो लगो (हां एकदम ठण्डा हो ग्या जी कीयो)। अरे गायां को नांव थारो (हां जणा राजगादी थारी है)। थारी है (कीयो)। दुनिया झूटी है सब सेंसारी (हां लड़ावन नै करे)। भायां भायां लडावै आपां नै (वाह वाह)। चरावो भैइ रे अब (हां चरावो मोकळी फैर फैर कीयो)। साडूमाता दरबार का हुकमूं आ मेदू की पदमणी गिया पछै अंवळी संवळी महलां में (ऊंचा फिरिया)। तो मेदू का घोड़ा को परतंग पड़ियो (म्हे)। साडूमाता बोलै (वाह वाह)। कांई समचार कहवै देखां (कीआवूं जाणज्यो भोपाजी महाराज कीआवूं)। अबार कहवां भगवान देव का हकमूं देखां (वाह वाह सा)।।

ए किलंगा तोरिया तो जी मेदू कंवर का मैं ओळखिया रे।
ओळख ली म्हारा जी मानक बछेरा के री चाल।
उणियारा तो दासी ये बांका भूलग्या।
आज आयगो म्हारो एकलड़ो असवार।
(भलां जी भलां) देव भलां।

किलंगा तोरा कंवर मेदू का मैं ओळखिया हूं (म्हे)। ओळख ली भैइ म्हारी मानक बछेरा के री (चाल)। उणियारा तो दासी मैं घणा दिनावूं तो भूल गी (म्हे)। आज आयगो म्हारो एकलड़ो (असवार)। मेदू आय रियो है भैइ (वाह वाह)। साडूमाता बोलै कांई समचार कहवै देखां (कीआवूं जाणज्यो कीआवूं देखां)। अबार कहवूं देव का हुकमूं देखां (वाह वाह सा)।।

केसर कटोरा जी घालो हीड़ागर छोकरियां रे।
भरल्यो दासी जी बीज मोतियां थाळ।
आयोड़ा मेदू को साज ल्यो हीड़ागर आरतियो।
आज आयगो म्हानी ये राइतन को रिचपाल।।
(भलां जी भलां) देव भलां

केसर कटोरा घालो (वाह वाह)। दासी भरल्यो बीज मोतियां (थाळ)। आया मेदू को साज ल्यो हीड़ागर आरतियो (म्हे)। आज आयगो म्हारो रैइत को (रिचपाल)। दासियां (म्हे)। राइत को धणी पूगो है (हां आज आया है कीयो)। साडूमाता बोलै बैइ को भाट आयगो सारै बी नै कांई बतलावै देखां (कीआवूं जाणज्यो कीआवूं देखां)। अबार कहवां देव का हुकमूं ले तूं (वाह वाह)।।

केसर कटोरा जी घालो रे बैइ का भाटजी रे।
आयोड़ा म्हाना रे मेदू नै आगो ल्यो रे।

ए राजगादी का टीका नारल रे बैइ का भाटजी।
ए राजगादी का टीका नारल रे बैइ का भाटजी।
म्हाना कंवर रे मेदूजी नै द्यो रे।।
(भलां जी भलां) देव भलां

केसर कटोरा घालो बैइ का भाटजी (म्हे)। म्हारा कंवर आयोड़ा है नै आगो (ल्यो)। अरै ई राजगादी का ए टीका नारल है नै (म्हे)। जका म्हारा कंवर मेदूजी नै ही (अब द्यो)। बाबा भाट (म्हे)। मेदूजी आयगो आज (हां राजगादी का तिलक मेदूजी के करो कीयो)। दरबार का हुकमूं इता दिन की बात कोनी देव महाराज बिराजमान हो मेलिया भैइ (म्हे)। म्हारो मेदू आयगो तो धणी राज को भैइ (हां बड़ा ए है कीयो)। टीकायत बेटा भोज का है नै (म्हे)। जको अब पूगियो है (हां मेदूजी है कीयो)। भाट बोलै (वाह वाह)। कांई समचार कहवै देखां (कीआवूं जाणज्यो देखां कीआवूं)। मेदूजी कंवर नेड़ो आयगो (वाह वाह)।।

ए उजला देख देख तो जी ईंयां राचै ये साडू सुलखना रे।
उजलो माजी ये बागां में फूल कण्डील।
उजलो देखज्यै नारायण देव ने।
बीकै साडू ये अकल घणी शरीर।।
(भलां जी भलां) देव भलां

उजळा देख देख मत राच (म्हे)। दरबार का हुकमूं उजला बगां में फूल (कण्डील)। उजला देखज्यै माजी नारायण देव नै (म्हे)। दरबार का हुकमूं बीका अकल घणी हो जायै (शरीर)। आज तो मेदूजी आयगो (म्हे)। राजगादी मेदूजी नै (हां तूं देबा लागी)। तड़कै तेजाजी को मदन सिंग आजायी (हां तड़कै कह देयी राजगादी आणै देयो)। क्यूं बो ही टीकायत को बेटो है (म्हे)। माजी साय कुण कुण नै दे (वाह वाह)। राजगादी को धणी तो भगवान ही रही अब (हां देव महाराज ही रहसी कीयो)। मेदू कंवर मन में देखियो रे माजी साय तो ठीक बोलै ई (हां थारेवाणी बोला हा)। पण ओ भाटड़ियो गाण गमा दियो (हां ओ गाण गमायो है)। दरबार का हुकमूं थोड़ो करड़ो बोल अबार (अबार राजगदी आपां नै देवै कोनी नारयल देखां)। मेदूजी कंवर बोलै कांई समचार कहवै देखां (कीआवूं जाणज्यो देखां कीआवूं)। अबार कह द्यां देव का हुकमूं भैइ (वाह वाह)।।

ए काका बाबा कानै तो जी माजी तूं तो ये मौसा जाणिया रे।
नी बूझी माजी ये काका बाबा कानै आण।
बरसतां मेवां गुदड़ा भेज द्यूं माळागर की भोम में।
जरां जाणज्यै ये मेदू म्हारो नांव।।
(भलां जी भलां) देव भलां

काका बाबा कानै तो मौसा जाणिया (म्हे)। नी बूझी भैइ काका बाबा कानै (आण)। बरसतां मेवां गुदड़ा फैंकूं पाछा माळागर की भोम में (वाह वाह)। जरां जाणज्यो मेदू म्हारो (अब नांव)। थै कोय नै बूझियो

नी (अर कोय नै ताझियो कोनी)। मतेई मालक बन गा (वाह वाह)। कांई मांगो थें ई जमीन के (म्हे)। दरबार का हुकमूं ओ समचार मेदूजी कंवर कीयो (वाह वाह)। साडूमाता बोलै (म्हे)। कांई मेदू नै समचार कहवै देखां (कीआवूं जाणज्यो देखां कीआवूं)। अबार कहवूं देव का हुकमूं ले तूं (वाह वाह जी वाह वाह)।।

गाड़ां के दिरावां जी मेदू भोज का रे पूठी रे पाचरा रे।
हंकती कर द्यूं पाछी जी माळागर में गाय।
बा भूमी नान्या थारी ताणा बाप की।
ईमै नान्या जी राई अर मेथी बाय।।
(भलां जी भलां) देव भलां

दरबार का हुकमूं समचार साडूमाता कीयो है (म्हे)। गाड़ां के दिरावां लाल मैं पूठी पाचरा (वाह वाह)। हंकती करूं माळागर में (पाछी म्हारी गाय)। आ भूमी लाल थारी ताणा बाप की (म्हे)। ईमै राई अर मेथी (मोकळी तूं बाय)। तनै मैं सुवाया कोनी (हां पाछा ऊठ जा माळागर की भोम में)। ओ समचार कीयो है (साडूमाता कीया है)। पीपळदे राणी देव महाराज की अस्त्री है नै आ (म्हे)। जकी ओ समचार सुण लियो (वाह वाह कीयो जको)। हां सा (वाह वाह)। पीपळदे राणी बोलै (म्हे)। कांई समचार पाछो कहवै देखां (कीआवूं जाणज्यो देखां कीआवूं)। अबार कहवूं भगवान का हुकमूं (वाह वाह)।।

कींयां दिराया जी जो गाड़ां के बूजी ये पूठी रे पाचरा रे।
कींयां हंकती कर दी ये पाछी माळागरै गाय।
आ भूमी सुसरा सुवाई भोज की।
जेठ मेदू कन्नु ये अंधी लीवूं रे बंटाय।।
(भलां जी भलां) देव भलां

कींयां दिराया बूजी गाड़ां का थै पूठी पाचरा (वाह वाह)। कींयां हंकती कर दी माळवा नै (पाछी गाय)। आ भूमी सुसरा सवाई भोज की (म्हे)। जेठ मेदू कन्नु आधी लेवूं (परबातै ई बंटाय)। आधी मूं तो सेल की बूड़ी टीकै (हां जती मेदू कंवरजी कन्नै जेठ सा) (कन्नै छोड़ूं कोनी कीयो)। मेदूजी मन में बिचार (करियो है)। अरै आध की धिराणी कुण बन गी (हां आ कुण है कीयो)। साडूमाता (म्हे)। आ कठवूं लेयाई है तूं (वाह वाह)। दरबार का हुकमूं बूझणा करी रे लाल (म्हे)। आ तो देव महाराज की अस्त्री है नै बा (हां पीपळदे जी)।

बड़बड़ बोलै जी बूजी पीपळदे म्हनै बोलड़ा रे।
पदमणी भायां ये नैना सुरमो सार।
पीपळदे नै करियो माजी पीर नै पूगता।
मेदू बोलै ये राळावूं जीव से मार।।
(भलां जी भलां) देव भलां

बड़बड़ बोल्या बू पीपळदे बोलड़ा (वाह वाह)। नैना सुरमो (सार)। पीपळदे नै कर दे माता तूं पीर नै पूगता (वाह वाह)। दरबार का हुकमूं मेदूजी कह मैं राळूं जीव से (अब मार)। म्हारै सहन कोनी होवै अबार (हां म्हरावूं कीयो सहन कोनी होवेली कीयो)। ओ समचार मेदू कंवर (कीया है)। देव महाराज की अस्त्री बोलै (वाह वाह)। कांई मेदू कंवर नै समचार कहवै देखां (कीआवूं जाणज्यो देखां कीआवूं)। अबार कहवां सा देव का हुकमूं देखां (वाह वाह सा)।।

ए मारबो तोड़बो तो जी जो जेठजी म्हारावूं कदवूं सीख गा रे।
कहतां आप नै जी आई कोनी लाज।
सवाई भोज नै दुशमन रावजी मार ग्यो।
जी दिना दुशमन राव नै रे क्युं घाली नै बाथ।।
(भलां जी भलां) देव भलां

मारबो तोड़बो जेठ सा कदूं सीखया बोलो (म्हे)। कहतां आई कोनी आप नै (लाज)। राठोड़ां का बीर खेत में (म्हे)। दुशमन रावजी भोज नै मारियो (वाह वाह)। जकै दिन बो दुशमन नै क्युं घाली नै (थे बाथ)। म्हनै तो मारबा नै सज गा है (म्हे)। बी रावजी नै तो कोनी मारियो (हां जकै दिन कढावन कठै कोय गांव भेज (दी कांई कीयो)। कठै हा आप कीयो (वाह वाह)। दरबार का हुकमूं मेदू कंवर पाछो बोलनी कोनी आयो (म्हे)। मेदूजी बोलै अब (वाह वाह)। कांई समचार कहवै देखां (कीआवूं जाणज्यो कीआवूं)। ओ अबार कहवां देव का हुकमूं (वाह वाह सा)।।

ए बड़बड़ बोल्या तो जी बू पीपळदे म्हनै बोलड़ा रे।
महल में पदमणी ये बैठी मुख नै मोड़।
बहता डोला नै परणायी ताणो बापलियो।
बैठी पीपळदे ये म्हां भाइयां की जोड़।।
(भलां जी भलां) देव भलां

बड़बड़ बोल्या बू पीपळदे म्हनै बोलड़ा (म्हे)। महल में बैठी मुख नै (मोड़ अर)। बहता डोला नै ताणो बाप लियो परणायी (म्हे)। देखियै पदमणी म्हां भाइयां की (जोड़)। म्हारी जियान का भाई है नै लेरै (हां जणा बहतै डोला नै (ताणो बाप परणायी कीयो)। आडो फिर परणायी (वाह वाह)। ओ समचार मेदूजी (कीया है)। पीपळदे राणी बोलै (म्हे)। कांई जवाब दे पाछो देखां (जेठ सा नै)।

ए बड़बड़ बोलूं तो जी जेठजी आप नै बोलड़ा रे।
महल में जेठजी रे बैठी मुख नै मोड़।
बिखा में गियो बाळक भाई माळागर की भोम में।
जी दिन कोनी जेठजी रे थां भायां की जोड़।।
(भलां जी भलां) देव भलां

बड़बड़ बोल्या मैं आप नै बोलड़ा (म्हे)। महल में बैठी मुख नै (मोड़ अर)। बिखा में गियो बाळक भैइ

ताणो माळागर की भोम में (म्हे)। जकै दिन जेठ सा नी थां भायां की (हां जोड़)। कठै है आप (हां कठै आप कीयो जकी बतावो)। भगवान एकला ही तो गिया अर एकला ही पाछा आया (वाह वाह)। जेठजी झूट बोल गा (म्हे)। दरबार का हुकमूं मन में देखियो ई जागां लुगाइयां को राज है (म्हे)। हेंर लुगाइयां से जपयावूं थारी बात हळकी (हां पड़ जावे)। कहतो ही भाटड़िया को लूण गायोड़ो पड़ै (म्हे)। जको ओयी तो राजगादी पहली नट गो (हां ओयी नट गियो)। उनै पीपळदे राणी जका ई जवाब कर रही है (हां नटै है)। अरै बगड़ावतां को गरू मैजूद बैठो है जका बी नै तो इतला करां (हां बै गरू सा के जियान बात हो जायी)।

ए लिखिया परवाणा तो जी मेदू कंवरजी नै मोकळिया रे।
बाबा नाथजी रे हाथूं हथ बंचाय।
म्हारै अर देव के टीका पर बीगड़ी।
उनै नाथजी रे टीका द्यो जिलवाय।।
(भलां जी भलां) देव भलां

दरबार का हुकमूं लिखया परवाणा कंवर मेदू मोकळिया (म्हे)। बाबा नाथजी लियो क्युं नै हाथ्यूं हाथ (बंचाय)। म्हारै अर देव के टीका पर बिगड़ गी (वाह वाह)। गरूजी आप टीका देयो (आर जिलाय)। थारा हाथूं तूं देवै जका नै सही है कबूल कर लियां मैं (वाह वाह)। कासींद (म्हे)। ए परवाणा ले जार शंकर की धूणी पर दे भैइ (हां रुपायली पूगता कर देवो)। कासींद ले परवाणो टारड़ो हांक दियो बी जगावूं (वाह वाह)। दरबार का हुकमूं रुपायली पूगता (व्हिया है)। बाबाजी नै परवाणा (ले जार दे दियो)। बाबोजी बूझणा करी ठहर भैइ (म्हे)। एक म्हारा हाथ को पाछो परवाणो (हां ले जावो कोय जोगी नै फोड़ा घालूं कीयो)। बाबोजी बोलै कांई परवाणा लिखै देखां (कीआवूं जाणज्यो देखां अब कीआवूं)।।

ए दोन्यु बेटा तो जी जो थें भोज का रे।
म्हारासूं मेदूजी कूड़ी न के नै जाय।
टीका तो जका नर पावै बेटा भोज का।
दुशमन दीया की सावर रे घोड़ी छुड़ाबा जाय।।
(भलां जी भलां) देव भलां

दोन्यो ही बेटा भोज का हो थै (म्हे)। मेदू म्हारावूं कूड़ी के नै (जाय)। अरै टीका तो जका ही नर पावै बेटा भोज का (म्हे)। दुशमन दीया की सावर घोड़ी छुड़ाबा नै (जाय)। दीया कन्नै घोड़ी है थांका बाप की (म्हे)। बा तो बन्ध में है दुख में है हाल (हां थानै राज गदियां चाहीज्यै कीयो)। बी घोड़ी की बन्ध कटार लेयावो राजगादी मैं देयूं (हां जका नै दे देयूं जकी सही है कीयो)। कासींद (म्हे)। ले ओलै भैइ (ओ परवाणो ले जाय अर मेदूजी नै दे द्यो कीयो)। कासींद ले परवाणो बी जागावूं टारड़ा नै (पाछो हांक दिन्यो)। दरबार का हुकमूं ल्यार परवाणो मेदू नै (दियो है)। मेदूजी कीयो बाबोजी कावळ उपेट दी बात नै (म्हे)। दरबार का हुकमूं अरै बैइ का भाट (म्हे)। सावर दौड़ो करां जरां तूं

चालै कोय नी चालै भैइ (हां म्हारा सागै चालै कोय नी चालै कीयो)। श्री महाराज दूजा के सागै तो मैं चालूं पगां पगां (हां थारै सागै मैं माथैवाणी चालज्यूं कीयो)। देव नै बूझियो नी साडू नै बूझियो नी (म्हे)। जरां ले भैइ बिदा हो गैइ (चालो कीयो)। बिनै बूझिया बिनै ही भाट बैइ को मेदू कंवरजी बिदा हो गा (वाह वाह)। दरबार का हुकमूं सोनेर की बरड़ आयगी (वाह वाह)। बी में पारबती सोमहादेव (ताप रिया)। तो पारबती देख अर शंकर नै बूझण (करी है)। अरै दरबार का हुकमूं बाबाजी निंगै कर (हां ए जी कुनै जाय असवार कीयो)। कीयो चण्डी ए तो भोज को लड़को है (म्हे)। हेंर सावर दौड़ो करियो है (वाह वाह)। कीताणी (क्यॆंताणी जाय कीयो)। ईका बाप की घोड़ी हे दीया कन्नै (हां जकी छुटार लियो कीयो)।। दरबार का हुकमूं उतम राय कंवर परणीजबा नै गियो अठी कावूं के तूं (म्हे)। कीयो म्हाना ई सिंग नै छोड़ऊं अबार (हां)। चीर बगा देय (दो झटका कर देय कीयो जांवतों ही)। दीयोजी कंठीबन्ध चेलो है म्हारो (वाह वाह)। दीया नै साथ द्यूं पूरो (म्हे)। दरबार का हुकमूं पारबती के सिंग के थापी की (हां दीनी)। ऊठ मद देखां कीयो (हां जाय ओगाज करिया कीयो)। थापी देतां ही जेज लागी नौ नार बांस फलां कूदबा लागो (वाह वाह)। मेदू कंवर नै आतो (हां दीखियाया)। कीयो रे बाबा भाट (म्हे)। एक जानवर आयग्यो रे कूदतो जको एक बांस बांस की फलांगा (हां मारै है कीयो)। कीयो श्री महाराज बगड़ावतां मरिया पछै म्हनै तो दीखै कोनी (हां दीखै कोनी मन्दो दीखै सपा ई)। सैनाण बता पूरा (जणा तो मैं नाको पा द्यूं)। मेदूजी कंवर बोलै (म्हे)। कांई सैनाण बतावै (कीआवूं जाणज्यो देखां कीआवूं)। अबार कहवां देव का हुकमूं देखां ले तूं (वाह वाह सा)।।

ए मिनकी का लाग्या तो जी ईकै भाटजी के लीकड़ा रे।
बाबा भाटजी रे माथो भूण की नाय।
सोनेर की बरड़ बैइ का भाटजी।
निंगै करज्यै भाटजी ये कांई जिनावर जाय।।
(भलां जी भलां) देव भलां

मिनकी का लाग्या भाटजी के लीकड़ा (म्हे)। अर माथो भूण की (नाय)। सोनेर की बरड़ में रह बैइ का भाट (म्हे)। ओ कांई जानवर (जाय कीयो)। निंगै कर देख (कांई जिनावर है कीयो)। अरै म्हारा धणी ओ तो आयगो बाघ (हां बाघ है कीयो)। कीयो म्हांकाला दादोजी आयगा (हां बाघ है) कीयो दादोजी कोनी (हां ओ जिनावर जंगल को है कीयो)। ओ तो मिनख हो थांको। दादो तो (म्हे)। एक माथो माथो ही नार नार को हो (वाह वाह)। ओ बन को बाघ है (म्हे)। कांई करै ओ (ओ कांई करियो कीयो)। कीयो नार डै तो टाबरियो है (बैर)। नार डै भाटड़ै (बैर कीयो)। हेंर नार डै टाल डै (बैर है कीयो)। ए तीनो चीजां आपां कन्नै (है कीयो)। आंतां ही तो काचो टाबर है तूं थारो ही गटको (हां करी)। पछै आ घोड़ा नै (हां आंको गटको करि)। हेंर म्हारा हाड़किया पछी चबेली (हां मैं बूड़ो आदमी) हूं (म्हारा हाड़किया पछी चबेली)। पण श्री महाराज मैं थारा सागै नी आवूं नै (म्हे)। रहवूं कठै (हां रहवूं कठै)। बगड़ावतां की डोली तो सागै लियो हे तूं (हां म्हनै आगै लियायो जको अठै डबो ई बैइ नी कीयो)। बाबा भाट जरां ओ (कांई करां कीयो)। श्री महाराज मैं तो कांई बतावूं (हां म्हनै ई बात को ठा ही कोनी)। कीयो पाछा भाग चालां (बाह म्हारा धणी)। बाह वाह भली बिचारी (वाह वाह)।

आगे करै तो घोड़ो मेदूजी को नीकल जाय (म्हे)। करै भाट को (आगै नीकल जावे)। दरबार का हुकमूं गोठां के गोरवें (पाछा पूगता व्हिया जी कीयो)। भाट बूझणा करी श्री महाराज अब मत भाजो (हां अब बी की हिद कोनी आगी नै बो नार कोनी आवै कीयो)। कीयो बाबा भाट (म्हे)। अरै बच तो ग्यां आपां (वाह वाह)। पण देव तीन तिलोकी को नाथ अबार जातां ही बूझ लेय तो जरां कांई जवाब देयां भैइ (हां के घोड़ी कठै है जरां कांई जवाब देयां कीयो)। कीयो श्री महाराज वाह भली सोच करी (हां आ बांतां को कांई सोच करो कीयो)। मैं खाटियायी आं बांतां कावूं (वाह वाह)। दरबार का हुकमूं इसियो काम करो (म्हे)। आंखियां का पाटी बांधो (हां आंखियां के पाटी बांध लेवो)। मैं कह द्यूं (म्हे)। आंखियां दूखणी आगी मेदू कंवर की जो की जागां ले जावूं (हां बठै लड़ाई होवै खाण्डै की जोत पड़ जाय कीयो)। आंखिया बिगड़ जाय (वाह वाह)। धोळा दोपारां मेदू के आंखियां की पाटी बन्धा दी भाट (वाह वाह)। तीन तिलोकी को नाथ भगवान देव बोलै (म्हे)। कांई समचार कहवै भाट नै देखां (कीआवूं जाणज्यो देखां भोपाजी महाराज अब कीआवूं)। अबार कहवां ई धणी का हुकमूं देखां (वाह वाह जी वाह वाह)।।

रात गिया तो जी दिन नै आया रे बैइ का भाट जी रे।
भाट नारदी रे चिनक वार लगायी।
सवाई भोज की रे घोड़ी चांवण्डा।
बाबा भाट जी रे कुण से ठाण बन्दाई रे।।
(भलां जी भलां) देव भलां

रात तो गिया दिन आयगा (म्हे)। चिनक वार (लगायी)। सवाई भोज की घोड़ी माता चांवण्डा (वाह वाह)। बाबा भाट कुण से ठाण (अब थै बन्दाई)। मैं दर्शन कर आवूं अरै बी का (हां दर्शन तो करां औतारण घोड़ी बतावै कीयो)। भाट बोलै कांई देव नै समचार पाछो कहवै देखां (कीआवूं जाणज्यो देखां अब कीआवूं)।।

ए रात गिया तो जी दिन नै आया रे गोठालां राजवियां रे।
मैं तो अन्नदाताजी चिनक वार लगाई रे।
सवाई भोज की घोड़ी माता चांवण्डा।
अन्नदाता कोय रे नर मूंछयांवाला ल्याई रे।।
(भलां जी भलां) देव भलां

रात गिया दिन नै आयगा मैं (म्हे)। चिनक वार (लगाई)। सवाई भोज की घोड़ी माता चांवण्डा (म्हे)। अन्नदाता मैं मूंछयांला (जका ल्याई)। देव बूझणा करी बाबा भाट (म्हे)। थारै अर मेदू दादा के मूंछियां कोनी (हां मूंछियां ही कोनी कांई कीयो)। कीयो नी श्री महाराज पूळा का पूळा ही ऊबा देखियो (हां पूळा का पूळा ऊबा है कीयो)। ऊबाऊं कांई होवै (म्हे)। घोड़ी कोनी आयी (वाह वाह)। देव बूझणा करी रे भाट बात अंवळै गैलै संवार दी थै (म्हे)। मेदू नै बूझो (वाह वाह)। राजगादी करै जरां घोड़ी की बन्ध बेगी कटावो (हां कटार ल्यावो)। हेंर नी घोड़ी आवै (म्हे)। जरां भैइ ए देख गुवाई चूंतरो

है (वाह वाह)। न्यायगादी को (म्हे) ओ ले लेयो (ओ ले लेयो)। मेदूजी कंवर कीयो रे बाबा भाट देव नै कह दे भैइ (म्हे)। आ राजगादी दोहरी घणी (म्हारै चाहीज्यै ही कोनी कीयो)। आपां तो ई चूंतरा की न्याय हे जकी ले लेयां (हां आ करबो करां कीयो)। आया गिया की न्याय आपां ही करां पछै (वाह वाह)। साडूमाता नै बूझणा करी माजी साय (म्हे)। न्याय चूंतरा को तिलक राजगादी को कर द्यो मैं तो (हां बेगा कर देयो कीयो)। मात खटाणी कंवर मेदू के जकै दिनवूं ओ आयो है नै बो (म्हे)। बटूटवूं (वाह वाह)। जकै दिन राजगादी को तिलक है जको चूंतरा को करियो (वाह वाह)। कीयो न्याय तो थारी (म्हे)। अर गांव है जको है भगवान देव को (देव को)। मेदू कंवर के चूंतरा को तिलक होतां हेंर दरबार के सामिल आतां (आंवता)। जय बोलो श्री देव नारायण भगवान की (जय)। देव महाराज बूझणा करी रे बैइ का भाट (म्हे)। राजगादी मैं ई कोनी बैठूं (हां अब राजगादी बैठां नैइ कीयो)। घोड़ी की बन्ध कटाई तो राजगादी (जरूर बैठां कीयो)। बाबा भाट चालां (हां चालो कीयो)। श्री महाराज मैं तो कठै जावूं मैं तो आप के कन्नै रहवूं (वाह वाह)। पालासानी घोड़ा नै पिलाण माण्ड लिया भैइ (वाह वाह)। तीन तिलोकी को नाथ बैइ को भाट (म्हे)। अर पालोसानी (हां तीनयो बीर व्हिया)। बंवळी घोड़ी की बन्ध कटावा नै बीर हो गा (वाह वाह)। दरबार का हुकमूं बी जागां गिया बण में (म्हे)। गेला दो ही (हां फंट गिया है)। देव महाराज बूझणा (करी है)। बाबा भाट (म्हे)। आगा नै आवो गेला दो कींयां के (सावर गेलो किस्यो जाय जकी बताय कीयो)। कीयो श्री महाराज दोन्यो सावर (हां जाय कीयो)। बाबा भाट अरै गांव एक गेला दो कींया बोल (हां कींयां है कीयो)। कीयो श्री महाराज एक गेलो तो है छै महीना को (हां लागै छै महीना कीयो)। एक है गेलो इसियो है (म्हे)। तीन दिनावूं ठाणै पूग जावां (आ लियो)। बाबा भाट छै दिनाला में कांई गुण है (म्हे)। तीन महीनाला में कांई (ओगुण है कीयो)। कीयो श्री महाराज ओ तीन दिनालो गेलो है नी ईमै नार बघेरा धाड़वी (मोकळा है कीयो)। पार लाखां कोनी होवै (वाह वाह)। छै महीनाला गेलो है नी (म्हे)। ईमै जिनस पड़ जावै आपणी (हां आपां ही आर उठावां दूसरो उठाणी नैइ लाधे)। कीयो सुण रे बैइ का भाट (वाह वाह)। अता वादा कोनी म्हारा (हां अता वादा ही म्हांका कोनी)। आपां तो तीन दिनाला गेलो है चालां (बेगा सा घोड़ी छुटार आजावां)। तो भगवान तीन तिलोकी को नाथ तीन दिनाला गैलै घोड़ा नाक दियो लीला नै (वाह वाह)। पारबती के ओ दरबार को घोड़ो निंगै (आयग्यो)। कांई ऊठै बोलै कांई शंकर नै बतलावै (कीआवूं जाणज्यो देखां कीआवूं)। अबार कह द्यूं देव का हुकमूं ले तूं (वाह वाह)।।

ए अधर धोवती धवती आवै तो जी ए ई भोला देवजी रे।
आय रियो भैइ रे इनख भांत असवार।
पलक खोल निंगै कर ले रे भोलानाथजी।
सोनेर की बरड़ में रे कांई ब्यान देव को जाय।।
(भलां जी भलां) देव भलां

अधर धोवती देख धवती आवै (म्हे)। आय रियो भोलानाथ एक इनख भांत (असवार)। सोनेर की बरड़ में पलक खोल (म्हे)। निंगै कर कांई ब्यान देव को (जाय)। अरै अधर ही चालै ओ (हां ओ कांई ब्यान

है देव को कीयो) । महादेव बूझणा करी चण्डी ओ तो देव है देव (वाह वाह) । कीयो किस्यो देव (ओ कीसियो देव व्हियो कीयो) । देव चार जारां मन में देखिया देव तो चार ही है (म्हे) । पांच्वो देव मैं तो जाणु कोनी भेइ (वाह वाह) । दरबार का हुकमूं चार देव जरां किस्या व्हिया कीयो अन्नदेव (म्हे) । जळदेव (वाह वाह) । पवनदेव (वाह वाह) । हेंर दरबार का हुकमूं कांई अगण नै बातायो पवन जळ अन्न ए देव है इस धरती पर चार ही मैं तो मानिया (हां चार ही दीखै है कीयो) । ओ पांच्वो देव तूं आज पेदा करियो है आज (हां कठूं ल्याया हो कीयो) । कीयो सुण चण्डी (म्हे) । जो भोज के पछेवै भगवान जोत में जेत फंटी है (वाह वाह) । तीन तिलोकी को नाथ भगवान आयो है (खुदा खुद ही आया कीयो) । कांई करी ओ (म्हे) । कीयो ऊठै जाय सावर ही (सावर जाय) । कीयो पहलकालो गियो है नै (हां इसियो ओ जाय) । कीयो बी के भरोसै मत रह जाय अबकै (म्हे) । कांई करी तूं (वाह वाह) । कीयो बोई में सिंग नै छोड़ü (वाह वाह) । और दो फांक कर भगा देय (म्हे) । कीयो पाली हो जायली चण्डी (हां बा बात कोय नी कीयो) । म्हाना नान्या पर मैं कोनी छोड़üला (हां झाटक्या सगळा लारूं (सुनथाला कर देवेली कीयो) । दरबार का हुकमूं पारबती ऊठ अर के सिंग के थापी (दीनी) । जा रे मरद ओगाज कर सामी (वाह वाह) । सिंग ऊठता जेज लागी देव की सिंग की एक नजर (हां मिली है) । तो सिंग तो पाछो ही जमीन के चिप गो (बठै को बठै चिप ग्यो जी कीयो) । पारबती फैर थापी की (दीनी) । नार तो नीचा नै नजर करै ऊंचो देखै कोनी (वाह वाह) । मन में देखियो जलम हो गा (म्हे) । शंकर नै बूझणा करी ओ भोला महादेव (म्हे) । कांई करियो ईंकै (हां एक झगड़ो कराय कीयो) । कीयो तूं कुण है तूं कहनी अबार (वाह वाह) । सिंग चीर भगा दी छोड़ देखां (हां छोड़ तो सरी थारै नै) । कीयो नी छोड़ै जरां थारै महारै गैला दो ही है ओ ले (हां म्हारै कोय नी जचै कीयो) । सोन चिड़ी को रूप धारण कर (म्हे) । डाळी पर आंतरै जार बैठ गी (वाह वाह) । शंकर कीयो आजा चेन मत कर कीयो (हां आजा कीयो) । कीयो नैइ सिंग के अर नारायण के झगड़ो करावै (जणा आवूं कीयो) । कीयो ओळमो मत देय देख पाली होवेली मन ठा नी है (हां म्हनै ई बात को ठा कोय नी है पाली (चालणो पड़ेलो) । कीयो भलां ही पालो चालो (वाह वाह) । झगड़ो करां देय (झगड़ो एक करावो) । दरबार का हुकमूं शंकर ऊठ के थापी की (नार के दीनी) । जा मरद एक हो गा तो कर (आजा कीयो) । तो कांई सिंग चालै (म्हे) । कांई भगवान आतां ही सिंग नै बतलावै देखां (कीआवूं जाणज्यो देखां कीआवूं) । अबार कहवूं देव का हुकमूं ले तूं (वाह वाह जी वाह वाह) ।।

मैं नारायण तो जी ए ई बण का सिंगनिया रे।
तूं नार है तूं ही पिछाड़ी गाय।
गती कर द्यूं रे बण का सिंगनिया।
काळियादे में गेरो माथ नाहाय।।
(भलां जी भलां) देव भलां

मैं तो नारायण हूं (म्हे) । तूं बण को गादड़ो तूं ही पिछाड़ी होली (गाय) । अरै गती कर द्यूं बण का सिंगळी (म्हे) । काळिया तळाव में गेरो माथो (नाहाय) । सिनान कर आवो (हां थारी गती आज कर देवूंला कीयो) । नार नै समचार सुणता जेज लाग्यो (वाह वाह) । बाईं पगां पाछो (बावड़ियो) । काळियोदे

भरियो (म्हे)। कूदर सिंग तो मांयनै (कूदर पड़ियो जी कीयो)। नौ नौ बांस गज (पाणी ऊंचो उछलियो)। भाट मन में देखियो थारी मां जाणु पाणी में करी जकी की जकी करिया आपां में (हां आपां में अब जकी की जकी करसी आंतां ही ओ)। सारै ही पच्चासो हो जाटां को (म्हे)। भाट तो पच्चासां के चारूंमेर फिरबा लागो (वाह वाह)। मन में देखियो ऊंचा चड़ जावां (हां बंच जावां ज्यूं)। पूळा को झूंडो पकड़ै भाट बगड़ावतां को (वाह वाह)। गलयोड़ो डोको टूट जाय भाट देखेणै हेटो (आवतो पड़े)। देड़ा बोलबा लागा (वाह वाह)। देव महाराज बूझणा (करी ही)। अरै बाबा भाट देड़ा कींयां बोलै (हां पड़ै ऊठै अरै पड़ै क्यां ताईं है कीयो)। कीयो श्री महाराज टारड़ा काळ का भूखा है (कोय नयो पूलो मैं तो हेरू हूं)। लाधै कोनी (बोदी खाध है)। कीयो पूळा है जको म्हनै ठा पड़ गो (हां अठै आ म्हारै कन्नै कीयो)। आवो नार झगड़ो करां (वाह वाह)। अरै श्री महाराज मैं किसी दिन झगड़ोवूं करियो (हां म्हन तो नार को झगड़ो डर लागै कीयो)। तो भाट नेड़ो आजा तूं (वाह वाह)। ईंयां दुख मत पा (म्हे)। थारो जापतो कर द्यूं (वाह वाह)। बै तो श्री महाराज कींयां करी जापतो (हां जकी बतावो)। बाबा भाट ई सिला पर ऊंचो बांध द्यो अबार (हां ऊपर बैठियो रह)। बाह वाह रे म्हारा धणी भली बिचारी (वाह वाह)। कीयो पालिया (म्हे)। भाट को जापतो करो ऊंचो (हां हाथ काटा सिलै के बांध अर आवो कीयो)। दरबार का हुकमूं डाळा के ऊपर छोड़ भाट नै (म्हे)। अंगूछो हो जको अंगूछा के डाळा के दे आंटो (वाह वाह)। अर गांठ (दे दीनी)। कीयो देव महाराज बतलायो बाबा भाट कांई सला भैइ (कांई सला कीयो)। बाह श्री महाराज सिलो पड़ै तो अब (बन्धो पड़ै कीयो)। अब कोनी छोडूं (वाह वाह)। बांध्या पहली तो श्री महाराज तूं अर नारडो झगड़ो करता नै (बीच में आर पड़तो)। क्युं के हाथ छूट जाता म्हारा (हां धूजतो ही)। देव महाराज बूझणा करी पालासानी (म्हे)। लीलागर नै बांध दे कीयो (वाह वाह)। झगड़ो हुई अब (वाह वाह)। पालोसानी ले जार घोड़ा नै बी सिला के (हां बी के ही बांध दिन्यो)। भाट कीयो रे पालया (म्हे)। जां सिला जां ही लीला (जां ही लीला कीयो)। थारा बाप नै अठै बांधवा ल्यायो दूजो कोनी हो कांई (हां दूसरै सिलै के बांधो म्हनै पटकी कीयो)। दूधां को दायोड़ो टार अबार फटकार दे सिलो उपड़ जाय थारो बाप (वाह वाह)। कीयो अब कहवै कुण पालोसानी (म्हे)। कांई भाट नै समचार कहवै देखां (कीआवूं जाणज्यो देखां कीआवूं कींयां कहवे)।।

ए पच्चासां हो हुंअर तो जी साठां हु गो रे बैइ का भाटजी रे।
हु गो भाटजी रे सितरां बरसां डेण।
ग्यारह बरस का बच्च्या नै नार के मुण्डै के बैइ का भाटजी।
अब भाटजी रे जीवेलो की काळ।।
(भलां जी भलां) देव भलां

दरबार का हुकमूं समचार कुण कीयो पालोसानी कीयो है (वाह वाह)। कीयो पच्चासा हो हुंअर साठा है तूं (म्हे)। अरै हु गो सितर बरस को (डेण)। ए ग्यारह बरस का बच्चा नै नार के मुण्डै दे दियो (म्हे)। अब भाटजी कतरा (काल)। ए बेटी का बाप शरम आवै कताक दिन (हां कताक दिन जिणो है थारै कीयो)। ई बच्च्या नै तो नार के मुण्डै दे दियो अर तूं जीबा नै करै (वाह वाह)। तो ओ समचार पालोसानी (हां बैइ के भाट नै कीयो)। भाट बोलै कांई पाला नै बतलावै (कीआवूं जाणज्यो कीआवूं)।।

तूं ही रणसी के जी दो ई भैइ रे पाला सायन्या रे।
मैं म्हारी माता ए देळूजी जी के एक।
तीरूं डूबो तीरूं डूबो मत करै कारू जात कुमहार की।
तूं तो पालियाजी किरिया देव का देख।।
(भलां जी भलां) देव भलां

दरबार का हुकमूं थै रणसी के दो भाई हो (म्हे)। मैं म्हारी माता देळूजी के (एक)। अरै तीरू-डूबू तीरू-डूबू मत कर कारू जात कुमहार की (म्हे)। ओ किरिया देव का (अब देख)। ओ देव जका कार करै जका देख ले (हां ए देखिया जा देव महाराज कांई करै देखां)। कांई करै देखां (वाह वाह)। कीयो कर लिया बेटी का बाप शरम कोनी तनै (म्हे)। कीयो शरम आयी पण देख थै दोय हो मर जाय तो एक रह जावै (म्हे)। मैं तो एक ही हूं म्हारी मां के (वाह वाह)। अरै भगवान ही माळवा में जोगणियां खाय गी जो जिन्दा दूसरा ही करियो एक की खातिर (वाह वाह)। दरबार का हुकमूं इताक पहली सिंग तो नाहाय (म्हे)। हेंर पाछो (आयग्यो)। कांई भगवान के सिंग के झगड़ो हो जावै देखां (कीआवूं जाणज्यो कीआवूं देखां)। अबार कहवूं देव का हुकमूं ले तूं (वाह वाह सा)।।

हकालियो नार तो जी जो पाछो बावड़ियो रे।
ओ तो ठाकरां रे नार आयग्यो नळां।
बण का बाघ नै दरबार झाटक्यो।
जरां सिंग नै करियो खळा-डळां रे।।
(भलां जी भलां) देव भलां

हकालियो नार पाछो बावड़ गो (म्हे)। नार आयगो (नळां)। बण का बाघ नै दरबार झाटक्यो (म्हे)। कर दियो खळा राज ही (डळां कीयो)। नार तो एकानै पड़ियो (म्हे)। माथो (एकानै जांवता पड़ियो)। बैइ को भाट ऊंचो डाळा पर हो (म्हे)। क्युं तो अंगूचो दांतांवूं (फाड़ियो)। क्युं दरबार का हुकमूं हाथावूं गांठ नै (खोली जी कीयो)। देखेण हेटा आर पड़ियो (कूद अर नीचै आंवतो पड़ियो)। कड़ियां में तांबा भरणी कटारी (म्हे)। भाट खेंच अर (काढ लीनी)। काढ कटारी पकड़ पूंछड़ो (म्हे)। ए के नार के देबा लाग गियो (हियो)। हियो हियो देव महाराज बूझणा (कर लीनी)। अरै भाट मूई माटी नै क्युं गमावै (हां गमावै क्युं ईने)। कोय जोगेसर के काम आवै (हां खालड़ो काम आवै कीयो बिछाण बैठे)। कीयो सुण रे देवजी (म्हे)। के पालयो सानी तनै सरायो (हां) तूं मतेई सरीज गो (सरीजगियो)। तनै नार मारबा को ठा ही कोनी (हां ठा कांई है तनै कीयो)। एक नस काटी तूं (म्हे)। नौ नाड़ियां अर बहतर कोटा को जीव देख (ए तांबा भरणी कटारीवूं म्हान्यू काढयूं हूं कीयो)। मैं मारियो नार नै (वाह वाह)। कीयो बैइ का भाट नार मार नाकै तूं (हां मार नाकूं कीयो)। कीयो बैठो अर देखो (टैम ही कोनी लगावूं)। दरबार का हुकमूं बगड़ावतां की गुआलां की रोटी लेर गोरम का भाखर पर (हां मैं जांवतो)। दो नार सामा (मिल जातां)। पकड़ गूदी (म्हे)। एक नै उनै भगा द्यूं (हां भिड़ार माथा ऊनै ऊनै फैंक अर नीकल जातो)। तीन तिलोकी को नाथ अम्मी की नजर (झांकिया)। तो एक तो धड़

को पाछो (बैठियो व्हियो)। एक शीश को (बैठियो व्है ग्यो जी कीयो)। ले रे भाट ओ ले दोन्यु ही तियार है कीयो (हां ए दो नार रिया अब मार कीयो)। भाट आगै नार दोन्यु लेरै (हां दोन्यु नार हो गिया)। बो ही पच्चासो (जाय लियो)। आंटा देवै अर नारडा लेरै फिरै (वाह वाह)। देव महाराज बूझणा करी बाबा भाट इयां कींयां (हां भागै कींया कीयो)। अरै श्री महाराज म्हारी तो रांड अचपळी ही है (हां आ अचपळी है कीयो)। मैं किस्यो नार देखिया अर किस्यो दिन (मारिया हा कीयो)। थारो गेलो तूं ही सांवट ओ (हां म्हारावूं तो कोनी पार पड़े)। बाबा भाट कोनी मरै नार (कोनी मरे)। अरै म्हारा धणी देखियोड़ा है कोनी (हां) तूं मारबा की कहवै तीन तिलोकी को नाथ सैन कर नारां नै कह बुलाया (म्हे)। कीयो जाओ भैइ एक तो पारबती के संग (पाछो ऊठ जावो)। एक बण में (हां रम जावो)। तो बण में नार नै छोड़ियो नै (म्हे)। जको कोय छै महीना पहली बाळद (नीकलयोड़ी ही)। सुगंद लेय (म्हे)। खोज ले अर बिदा (लारै हुगियो)। देव बूझणा करी रे भैइ ई जानवर नै पाछो बुलावो (हां पाछो बुलावो कीयो सुगंद आवे)। तो मिनखा जूण ईमै नै छोड़ेलो ही कोनी (वाह वाह)। बुला पाछो पकड़ गूदी (म्हे)। देव महाराज नै सिंग के नाक पर (मुक्की की दीनी)। आज रह अर जाय सुगंद मत आय तनै (हां सुगंद बिलकुल ही मत आयज्यो)। गुआल स्याळ सीटी देवै डूंगर भाखर (लांघ जायज्यो)। हेंर नंगारबंद सिरदार (आवै चड़ अर)। जका के ओगाज कर सामनू (हां आजाज्यो)। पारबती का नार नै कीयो जा तूं पारबती के संग में जा पाछो (वाह वाह)। दरबार तीन तिलोकी को नाथ कांई करियो के बिदा हो गा (वाह वाह)। तो भाटजी उजड़ चालै (म्हे)। हेंर देव महाराज गैलै गैलै (चाल रिया)। बाबा भाट (म्हे)। उजड़ कींयां चालै (हां गेला आजाय कीयो क्युं झाड़क में भाजे)। श्री महाराज आगै दीया को दरबार है (म्हे)। कोय जीव बचांवूं मैं तो (हां म्हारा जीव की जापतो करूं)। भाट कन्नै आंगोछो हो (म्हे)। दरबार का हुकमूं बण के मांयनै उडिया तीतर उडै (वाह वाह)। निंगै आजावै भाट जका के ऊपरै अंगोछो राळ दे (वाह वाह)। जींवतो पकड़ लिया (हां जींवतो जींवता तीतर नै पकड़ लेवे)। घास के मांयनै तीतर चालतो दीखियो ऊपरो अंगूछो राळ दे (वाह वाह)। जींवतो ही जींवतो ही (पकड़ लेवे)। पकड़ जींवता तीतर नै (म्हे)। कड़ियां के गिड़दो बांध दियो (वाह वाह)। देव महाराज बूझणा करी कांई करी (वाह वाह)। कीयो श्री महाराज दिया का दरबार के मांयनै झूट सांच को परच्यो है बठै (हां अधर चकर चाले) झूट बोल जावै (म्हे)। शीश मतेई परै जांवतो (पड़ै कीयो)। देबी को बरदान है (वाह वाह)। झूट बोल्या बिनै दीयोजी घोड़ी नै (ले अर आवै कोनी)। दरबार का हुकमूं पांच दस तीतर नै मार मार जींवता नै पकड़ (म्हे)। कड़ियां के बांध दिया (वाह वाह)। टीम के तळाव (हां आयग्या)। देव महाराज बूझणा करी रे बाबा भाट (म्हे)। सावर को गोरवूं आयगो अर सावर दीखबा ही लागी (वाह वाह)। मैं तो सावर जातां रांह सदे ही बैकुण्ठ नै (सगळी की सगळी सावर बैकुण्ठ जावै कीयो)। अती दूर तो मैं आयगो (म्हे)। अती दूर दुशमन नै घोड़ी पर चड़ाय (अर लियावो)। पछै मैं जाणै अर दीयोजी (जाणै कीयो)। कीयो श्री महाराज (वाह वाह)। के झूट बोल्या बिनै तो दीयोजी घोड़ी नै खोलै कोनी (म्हे)। झूट बोलूं तो म्हारो शीश तो मतेई बठै ही (हां जांवतो छेड़ै पड़ी)। कुण घोड़ी नै ल्याई (हां घोड़ी नै कोनी आवै अठै)। कीयो भाट जियान आटां में आपां लूण राळां नै (म्हे)। जा बतरी माफ है झूट बोल जाय (झूट बतो तो बोल जाय भलां ही (कीयो थारो की नी बिगड़बा द्यूं)। अरे श्री महाराज अती झूट तो कांई ठा कता ही काम कर द्यूं (हां उनै का पूरा

उनै बसा द्यूं उनै का पूरा) । उनै बसा द्यूं (वाह वाह) । बगड़ावतां को भाट तो दरबार का हुकमूं सावर नै बिदा हु गो (म्हे) । तीन तिलोकी को नाथ भगवान तळाव पर रह गा (बिराजमान हो ग्या है) । दरबार का हुकमूं ए दीया की पणियारियां ही जकी पाणी नै आयी (म्हे) । देख दरबार की सुरता (म्हे) । हेंर चकरा गी (वाह वाह) । कीयो ए पणियारियां तळाव के ऊपरै सुरजी दो उगा आज (हां दो ही सुरजी उगयोड़ा है) । जकै दिन भाट गियो नै सावर में (म्हे) । बी टैम दरबार का हुकमूं उतम राय कंवर की शादी हुई (दियाजी के) । दीयाजी के उतम राय कंवर हो जी दिन बी की शादी हुई तो गाजा बाजा शाही सनमान (व्है रिया हा) । गाजा बाजा में सिरदारां नै कोय आदमी की पिछाण कोनी (वाह वाह) । भाट बोलै (म्हे) । कांई जांतो ही एक दीया नै समचार कहवै देखां (कीआवूं जाणज्यो देखां अब कीआवूं) । अबार कहवूं धणी देव का हुकमूं ले तूं (वाह वाह सा) ।।

माथावूं दियाड़ो जी ढळ गो रे माझी जोधका रे ।
ढळ गी थाना रे भखम कोट की छांय ।
अती गपलत दीया का दरबार में ।
आयोड़ा मणियार नै रे पेटिया मिलिया की नाय ।।
(भलां जी भलां) देव भलां

दरबार का हुकमूं भाट जातो ही समचार (कीया है) । कीयो माथावूं दियाड़ो ढळ गो दीया जोधका (वाह वाह) । अरै ढळ गी थारा भखम कोट की (छांय) । अती गपलत दीया का राज में कींयां हुई (म्हे) । आयोड़ा मणियार नै पेटिया ही मिलिया (नाय) । है बेटी का बाप भूखा मरतो मर गो मैं तो (वाह वाह) । तो दरबार का हुकमूं ग्यान कुण करो बठै (हां कुण निंगै करे) । तो कांई भाट बोलै अर कांई तोड़ जोड़ दीया नै समचार कहवै देखां (कीआवूं जाणज्यो कीआवूं देखां) । अबार कहवां धणी देव का ई का हुकमूं कह देवां (वाह वाह जी वाह वाह) ।।

ए औरां री बेळियां तो जी दीया भाईजी सावण भादवो रे ।
म्हानी बेलिया गियो रे भर भादूड़ै खेंच ।
घर की खरची खाता रे माझी जोधका ।
ताणी सावर में रे महीना बीत गा पांच ।।
(भलां जी भलां) देव भलां

औरां की बेलिया दीयाजी सावण भादवो हु गो (म्हे) । म्हानी बेलिया गियो रे तूं भर भादूड़ै (खांच) । घर की खरची खाता माझी जोधका (म्हे) । सावर में ताणी में महीना बीत गा (म्हनै पांच) । ए बेटी का बाप खरची निवट गी सारी म्हारी (हां पांच महीना हो ग्या कीयो) । अरै पांच महीना धिका दी पण आखो की को धिकै बै तो कहवै (वाह वाह) । तूं तो कलवन्ता बुला रियो कंवर का ब्याव के मांय गेलो हु गो (वाह वाह) । दीयोजी बोलै (म्हे) । कांई मीर नै समचार कहवै देखां (कीआवूं जाणज्यो अब कीआवूं) । अबार कहवां भगवान का हुकमूं (वाह वाह जी) ।।

तासा रा बाजा तो जी मना करावो काळू मीरजी रे।
म्हनै करा द्यूं बांखियां बिरगू बैर।
कोय मणियार दरबार में भूखो रह ग्यो।
दीया नै भाई रे भावै टूटता बोल।।
(भलां जी भलां) देव भलां

दरबार का हुकमूं ए तासा का बाजा है नै मना करा द्यूं (वाह वाह)। मना करावो बांखा बिरगू बैर (बैर)। अरै कोय मणियार दरबार में देख भूको रह गो (वाह वाह)। अब दीया नै बहावै टूटतो (बोल)। ए बेटी का बापां कीयो (म्हे)। मणियार नै भूखो रख दियो (वाह वाह)। बन्द करावो बाजा (म्हे)। तो दरबार का हुकमूं बगड़ावतां को भाट कांई करियो (वाह वाह)। एक झूटो ही कागदो लिखी (म्हे)। हेंर आपको पलेन बना लियो (वाह वाह)। बो कागद ले जार दीया नै (दे दियो)। ले दीया कागद देख भैइ (हां ओ कागद लेयो)। कीयो रे भैइ कठा का है तूं (कठो आयो कीयो)। कीयो अजमेर को हूं मैं (वाह वाह)। नांव कांई है (जकी बता)। जगीशयो कहवै दुनिया (वाह वाह)। जगीशया (म्हे)। अजमेर तो किसी नवी बात कोनी आणो जाणो है म्हांको ठेट को ही (ठेट को ही आणो जाणो है तनै देखियो ही कोनी) (कीयो)। हां श्री महाराज सांचा हो थै कोनी देखियो (हां म्हनै कोनी देखियो)। क्युं कींयां देखो के अजमेर के भाटै खोड़लो कंवर जलम गियो है नै बो (म्हे)। खोड़ीला नकत्रा हो (हां होतां ई) बी नै ई जलमत्यां ही नानेरै पूगायो मैं साथ जातो रियो (हां म्हनै सागै भेज दियो)। श्री महाराज कठवूं देखूं बोलो (वाह वाह)। भाट बोलै कांई दीया नै समचार कहवै देखां (कीआवूं जाणज्यो देखां कीआवूं)।।

ए अजमेर री जाळियांसूं जी दीया भाई रे कोला सूर ऊठगिया रे।
ताणा तळाव में रे टीम के आर थिया।
थारै कन्नै सवाई भोज की घोड़ी माता चांवण्डा।
म्हानू कंवरजी तनै रे पांच गांव पट्टा का दीया रे।।
(भलां जी भलां) देव भलां

अजमेर की जाळियां से कोला सूर ऊठ गा (म्हे)। टीम के तळाव पर आर थिया (थिया जी कीयो)। काळी चिट्:टी का गांवड़ा (म्हे)। म्हानू कंवरजी लेरै दियाया पांच कीया (हां थारै नांव कीया)। ले ओ ले (ले ले समाल पांच गांव कीयो)। दरबार क: हुकमूं म्हारो कंवरजी सूररो के लेरै घोड़ा दबायो (म्हे)। हाथ बिसत के आंतरै हाथ बिसत के आंतरै सूर बह रियो (वाह वाह)। दरबार का हुकमूं कीयो रे भाट तनै कुण कीयो रे भैइ सुर नै ईंयां आंतरै जाय कोनी हाथ आवै (हां जकी बता)।।

गुआल पालती तो जो कांकड़ में दियाजी चाला चाल रिया रे।
ताणी पणियारियां रे म्हनै कीयो आतां रे।
सवाई भोज की घोड़ी रे माता चांवण्डा।
जींवता सूर नै पकड़ली रे भंवर राज दांतां रे।।
(भलां जी भलां) देव भलां

गुआल पालती कांकड़ में चाला चाल रिया (म्हे)। दीया ताणी पणियारी नै कह दियो (आतां)। सवाई भोज की घोड़ी बताई रे थारै कन्नै चांवण्डा (म्हे)। जींवता सूर नै पकड़ ले भंवर राज ही (दांतां)। दरबार का हुकमूं भोज की घोड़ी बताई थारै कन्नै (हां) दांतांवूं सूर नै जींवता नै अधर को अधर (उठा ले कीयो)। म्हारो कंवरजी तो बी जागां ठम गो (हां बठै ही घोड़ो को छोड़ पागड़ो अर उतर बैठ ग्या)। पणियारियां कीयो देख किनक भांत को असवार है (म्हे)। अरै रांड का हाथ बिसत का हाथ नै सूर जा जको हाथ कोनी आयै (हां हाथ ही कोनी आयो कीयो)। ई बेलिया में आपणो धणी होवै दीयोजी असवार (हां बंवळी घोड़ी पर चड़योड़ा होवे)। तो ई सूर नै जींवता नै पकड़ ले अबार (वाह वाह)। म्हारो कंवरजी तो कीयो भैइ भोजाली घोड़ी आवै बंवळी (म्हे)। सूर नै जींवता नै पकड़ देखां जर म्हारै जुगत बैठी (जणा जुगत बैठै कीयो)। पांच गांव तो लिख दिया (म्हे)। हेंर लेर रिया पांच मैं दिरा द्यूं औरूं दस देवूं (हां म्हारी तरफवूं कोशिस कर अर पांच थानै और (दिरा द्यूला)। कांई करी कीयो घोड़ी नै चड़ अर चाल सूर नै पकड़ा द्यूं (वाह वाह)। कीयो सुण रे भाट (म्हे)। ग्यारह बरस हो ग्या घोड़ी ल्याया नै (वाह वाह)। ग्यारहा बरसां मैं तो घोड़ी नै खोली कोय नी भैइ (हां खूंटा ठाण खोली कोनी)। तूं खोल अर लियावै (म्हे)। तो चड़ तो भैइ में (चाल जावां)। मीर कीया याद दीया दगो है (हां ई बात में दगो लागै कीयो)। तेरै को मालुम नी पड़िया (हां भाट हो बगड़ावतालो छोछू सागै है कीयो)। दियो बूझणा करी तूं बैइ को भाट बगड़ावतां को नी होवै दगो हु गो म्हांकै (हां म्हांकै ई बात में दगो है कीयो)। कीयो बगड़ावतां को भाट हूं तो ई जीव की सोगण (वाह वाह)। तीतरियो तो मर जावै (भाट खड़यो को खड़यो रह जावे)। दीयोजी बूझणा करी रे मीर (म्हे)। सोगण काट गो भैइ (वाह वाह सांचो है ओ झूटो नैइ है)। दरबार का हुकमूं झूट बोल जाय तो देबी को चकर मतेई चालतो अबार (हां अधर चकर देबी का चालै है भाट को शीश (परै जांवतो पड़तो कीयो)। जा रे भाट खोलिया (लिया)। बगड़ावतां को भाट दरबार का हुकमूं मद की बोतलां भराली (वाह वाह)। हिरदा में घाल ली अर आपको बिदा (व्है ग्यो है)। भाट बोलै (म्हे)। कांई समचार कहवै देखां (कीआवूं जाणज्यो कीआवूं देखां)।।

ढाको हेरै तो जी बंगालो हेरियायो ये घोड़ी चांवण्डा रे।
घोड़ी माता ये हीयै नै बेगा झोल।
सवाई भोज की ये घोड़ी चांवण्डा।
घोड़ी बंवळी ये बेहरै हुवै तो बोल।।
(भलां जी भलां) देव भलां

ओ भाट समचार कीयो है (म्हे)। दरबार का हुकमूं ढाको हेर बंगालो हेरियो घोड़ी माता चांवण्डा (म्हे)। हीयै नै बेगा (जोल)। सवाई भोज की घोड़ी माता चांवण्डा (म्हे)। तूं डूंगर में बेहरै तो (बोल)।

ढाको ही हेरै तो जी बंगालो हेरियो ये घोड़ी चांवण्डा रे।
हेरियायो मैं तो जी सावर की चारूं कूण्ट।
कांई दुशमन दीयो सौदागरां नै बेच दी।

कांई भोज नै ले चड़ी ये इन्द्रासन बैकुण्ठ।।
(भलां जी भलां) देव भलां

दरबार का हुकमूं ढाको हेर बंगालो हेरियो (म्हे)। हेरियायो सावर की चारूं (कूण्ट)। कांई दुशमन दियो तनै सौदागरां नै बेच दी (वाह वाह)। कांई भोज नै ले चड़ी भगवान की इन्द्रासन (बैकुण्ठ)। एक तो भोज नै ले अर बैकुण्ठ जाती रहीक (म्हे)। दुशमन दिया जको तनै सौदागरां नै (हां बेच दी कीयो)। ओ समचार बैइ को भाट (कीयो)। घोड़ी बोलै (म्हे)। कांई समचार कहवै देखां (कीआवूं जाणज्यो कीआवू)।

पहली बोल्यो जी भाट जी तूं चौकठै रे।
दूजा बोल्यो दुशमन रे दीया के दरबार।
मैं बोली ओळखी घर का भाट की।
जरां भाटजी रे कोको हेंसी ठाण।।
(भलां जी भलां) देव भलां

पहली बोल्यो भाट चौकठै ई (म्हे)। दूजा बोल गो दुशमन दीया के (दरबार)। मैं बोली ओळखी घर का भाट की (म्हे)। जरां भाट मैं कोको हेंसी (ठाण)। तूं पहली बोल्यो जरां ही ओळख लियो मैं तो (वाह वाह)। घोड़ी माता भाटवूं बोलतां (म्हे)। भाट भंवरै (हां जांवता)। जय बोलो श्री देवनारायण भगवान की (जय)। बोलोज्यो छोटा अर मोटा (अब भैइ स)।।

हां जी हिंदवा नै ऊदल मानणा तुरकां नै उद सिलार।
फैर दलां दोनियां में मानणो घोड़ा री रेंवत छतरधारी।
रेंवत लीलालो असवार वाह रे घणी खम्मा।
ए दळां दोन्यां में ठाकर मानणा जी।
हां जी घोड़ा रेंवत छतरधारी रेंवत लीलाड़ो ई असवार घणी खम्मा।
ए दळां दोन्यां में ठाकर मानणा जी।।
(भलां राज जी भलां) किषन भलां

देमाली नाथ का नांव लेवां नै (म्हे)। ए सदा ही (भलां जी कीयो)। कीयो हिंदवा नै ऊदोजी मानणा (वाह वाह)। तुरकां नै उद (सिलार)। दळां ही दोन्यु में मानणा (वाह वाह)। अरै घोड़ा लीला रेंवत का (असवार)। ई देव महाराज नै मानज्यो (वाह वाह)।

हांजी पहली भोज नै गावणो गोकल नै गोपी सार।
एक घड़ी के मवो गावणो रे मनवो लाखां छतरधारी।
लाखां लूमियालो ही दातार घणी खम्मा।
ए सदा सुरंगो बेटा बाघ का जी।
हांजी मनवो लाखां छतरधारी लाखां लूमियालो ही दातार घणी खम्मा।
ए सदा सुरंगा बेटा बाघ का जी।। (भलां राज जी भलां) किषन भलां

पहली भोज नै गावज्यो (म्हे)। लीज्यो हरी का (नांव)। पहली भोज नै गावज्यो अर गोकल नै गोपी (सार)। अरै घड़ी एक मीठा भोजाजी नै गावज्यो (वाह वाह)। भोज को घड़ी घड़ी को (दातार)। भोज बगड़ावत नै (पहली गावणा जी कीयो)। दरबार का हुकमूं बगड़ावतां को भाट तो घोड़ी के भंवरै गियो नै (म्हे)। तो घोड़ी बोलै (वाह वाह)। बैइ को भाट बगड़ावतालो ऊबो हो कांई भांतवूं (सुणै देखां कीआवूं जाणज्यो अब कीआवूं)। अबार कहवां देव का ई का हुकमूं काहं (वाह वाह जी)।।

ए सियाळै सियां मरू तो जी परदेशी पंछड़ा रे।
भाट नारदी रे ऊनाळै बळूं लूआं रे।
सवाई भोज तो सरग नै ऊठगा।
ए दुख तो भाटजी रे भूलूंली मुआं।।
(भलां जी भलां) देव भलां

सियाळा में भाट सियां मरूं (वाह वाह)। ऊनाहा बळ गी (लूआं)। सवाई भोज तो देख इन्द्रासन ऊठ गा (म्हे)। ए दुख भाट मैं भूलोली (मुआं)। सुण रे भाट (म्हे)। मरियावूं भूलूं (हां पहली भूलनी नी आवेला कीयो)। बगड़ावतां को भाट दरबार का हुकमूं घोड़ी नै बो मन में देखियो इता बरसां हुवै घोड़ी मितवाल करती जको फिकी बोलै आलै (म्हे)। गिरदो में दरबार का हुकमूं सराब दे गो (वाह वाह)। कटोरा में घाल दियो (वाह वाह)। घोड़ी माता दरबार का हुकमूं ले कटोरा के मांयनै दूध जी जागां दारू (म्हे)। हेंर हुई मितवाली (वाह वाह)। बोलै अर कांई भाट नै समचार (कहवै देखां)।।

खुरताला ही खाली पड़ गी तो जी बैइ का भाटजी रे।
लालै बद गा लांबा केश।
गोठां में औतार सुणियो रे बाळा देव को।
औरूं दिखावै म्हने रे बदनोरा को देश।।
(भलां जी भलां) देव भलां

खुरताला तो भाट देखा भाई खाली पड़ गी (वाह वाह)। लालै बद गा का लांबा (केश)। अरै गोठां में औतार धारयो बतावै भाट औरूं दिखावै के म्हनै बदनोरा को ही (देश)। देश दरबार का हुकमूं बदनोर को देश दिखाबालो है की भाट (हां कोय व्हियो पैदा कीयो)। कीयो थोड़ी धीरी रह जा (वाह वाह)।।

परनाळियां पाणी पीवूं तो जी बैइ का भाटजी रे।
दुशमन दीयो राळै रे भर भादूड़ै कांसी रे।
औतार सुणयो रे बाळा देव को।
लेवण नै आयो रे मथरा रो बासी रे।।
(भलां जी भलां) देव भलां

परनाळियां भाट देख पाणी पीवूं मैं (म्हे)। हेंर दुशमन दीयो राळै रे म्हनै भर भादूड़ै (कांसी)। औतार

सुणयो बाळा देव को (म्हे)। लेबा नै आगो दीखै म्हनै मथरालो ही (बासी)। भाट बो ही कांई (हां सागै आया है की दूसरो कोई)। कीयो सागै को सागै है (आया है कीयो)। पण माता थोड़ोसो नेठाव राख (वाह वाह)।।

ए परनाळियां तो जी पाणी पीवूं रे बैइ का भाटजी रे।
दुशमन दीयो म्हनै राळै रे भर भादूड़ै कांसी रे।
औतार सुणियो रे धरमराजा देव को।
औरूं दिखावै घोड़ा जी इन्द्र पगांली लास।।
(भलां जी भलां) देव भलां

दरबार का हुकमूं परनाळियां देख पाणी पीवूं मैं (म्हे)। दुशमन दीयोजी राळै म्हनै भर भादूड़ै (कांसी)। अरै औतार सुणयो धरमराजा देव को (म्हे)। दरबार का हुकमूं आयो बतावै मथरा को ही (बासी)। बूझणा करी ये घोड़ी (म्हे)। कीयो भाया थोड़ोसो धीरप ले ले (वाह वाह)। सागै को सागै बो मथरा को बासी बोलै नै (म्हे)। बो को बो आयो लेबा नै (म्हे सा)।।

ए ओळ नोळ तो जी थाना झाड़ द्यूं ए घोड़ी चांवण्डा रे।
झाड़ द्यूं घोड़ी जी कंठा की कंठ बेल।
बैइ को भाट करै तनै बूझणा।
घड़ेक दुशमन दीया को ये आसन फैरूं झेळ।।
(भलां जी भलां) किषन भलां

ओळ नोळ झाड़ूं थारा (म्हे)। घोड़ी माता काट देवूं कंठा की कंठ (बेल)। बैइ को भाट करै बूझणा (म्हे)। दुशमन दीया को माता घड़ेक आसन (अब झेळ)। सुण ये माता (वाह वाह)। दिया को आसन झेळणो पड़ी तनै (वाह वाह)। कीयो रे भाट (म्हे)। आ कहवै जकी तो म्हारै कम ही जचै भैइ (हां आ म्हारै नैइ जचै कीयो आसन झेळबा की)। के तो पीठ पर भोज चड़ियो (म्हे)। भोज बिनै मैं तो हाल तो रे भैइ भाट चड़ायो कोनी (हां जड़ावूं कोय नै कोनी कीयो)। कीयो माता (म्हे)। ईंयां दीयोजी दुशमन है जको थारै जीकै तनै ले अर जावै कोनी (वाह वाह)। ए भगवान नट गो भैइ (हां टीम के तळाव तांईं चालणो ही पड़ी)। अती दूर भगवान कोय नी आवेलो (वाह वाह)। सुण रे भैइ भाट म्हारो मन तो कोनी दुशमन नै देखिया ही म्हनै आंख मारी दरबार का हुकमूं बळै (म्हे)। पण कोय बात कोनी (हां चालां कीयो)।।

ए पगां की काटी तो जी घोड़ी की बै हथकड़ियां रे।
काट दी घोड़ी की जी कंठाली कंठ बेल।
घोड़ी की बन्ध काट दी बगड़ावतालो भाटजी।
छोड़ जाज्यै घोड़ी आ सावर गढ को गोरवों।
लेवण नै आयो ये किसन मुरारी देव।।
(भलां जी भलां) देव भलां

पगां की काट दी घोड़ी की हथकड़ियां (म्हे)। हेंर काट दी बगड़ावतालो भाट कंठा की कंठ (बेल)। छोड़ घोड़ी सावर गढ को गोरवूं (म्हे)। लेवण नै आग्यो ये किषन मुरारी (देव)। ओ भगवान बोलै है नै (म्हे)। जको का जको आयो है पण सावर गढ को गोरवो जाण (हां चाल) दुशमन नै भैइ आसन पर लेनो पड़ी (वाह वाह)। घोड़ी नै दीयोजी कांई करियो मीर बूझणा करी रे भाई दीया म्हारै तो विश्वास नैइ आयो (म्हे)। भाट बगड़ावतां का है बो (सागै है कीयो)। इस्यो काम करो (म्हे)। बगड़ावतां को भाट है जरां घोड़ी अर भाट बांतां (करै है कीयो)। थारा सेसूं खिना द्यै (हां लारेवूं सेसूं खिना द्यो जको बांतां सुणयावे)। चार दीयोजी सेसूं भेज दिया (हां लारेवूं)। सेसूं चोखी तरह बांतां (हां घोड़ी की अर भाट की सुणी है)। पाछा जार कीयो श्री महाराज (म्हे)। के घोड़ी अर बो मानवी बांतां मिनख करै जियान की जियान (हां आछी तरह दोन्यु करै है कीयो)। कीयो जरां दीया नी बोल्यो दीया यार दीया जोधका भाट बगड़ावतालो आयग्यो सागै को सागै (हां बो को बो है कीयो)। दीयोजी बूझणा करी (म्हे)। के दरबार का हुकमूं तूं तो भाट बगड़ावतां को है भैइ (वाह वाह)। भाट बूझणा करी श्री महाराज (म्हे)। बगड़ावतां को भाट हूं तो म्हारा ई जीव की सोगण (हां ई जीव की सोगण है कीयो)। तीतर तो मर जावै (भाट खड़ो को खड़ो रह जावे)। मीर कांई सला है भैइ (हां भाट बो तो कोनी कीयो)। कीयो नी म्हारै तो दगो भैइ मावै कोनी (वाह वाह)। दीयोजी कीयो सुण रे भाट (म्हे)। म्हारै सेसूं खिनाय मैं (वाह वाह)। जको तूं अर घोड़ी मिनख बांतां करै जियां बांतां करां रे भैइ कीयो (हां बोला आछी थारहवूं कीयो)। कीयो श्री महाराज बात सांची है कीयो (म्हे)। एक झूटा करै जर (हां ए झूटा कोनी)। घोड़ी म्हारा पर चालै ईमै घोड़ी नै दाकलो (हां बेहरो गूंजो)। ए देखियो की बांतां ही करै (बांतां करे)।।

> घोड़ा ई होता तो जी जो दीया भाई रहवै कागड़ा रे।
> घास नै खावै रे जमी माता से खूंद।
> घोड़ा मुण्डै नी बोलै रे माझी जोधका।
> आंका भगवान रे दीया मुखरा बून।।
> (भलां जी भलां) देव भलां

के घोड़ा तो होता कागड़ा (वाह वाह)। धरती माता सूं घास नै खावै सूं से (खूंद अर)। घोड़ा मुण्डै नी बोलै रे माझी जोधका (म्हे)। भगवान दिया मुखरा (आंका बून)। दरबार का हुकमूं थारा दरबार में घोड़ा ऊबा है (वाह वाह एक नै ही बतला तो सरी)। अरै सेंकड़ी घोड़ा है जको एक नै ही बुला तो सरी (वाह वाह)। बेटी का बाप साव ही झूटो बोलै (म्हे)। मीर बूझणा करी दीया दगो तो है भैइ (वाह वाह)। दरबार का हुकमूं ओ कहवै की मैं भाट बगड़ावतां को कोनी हूं (म्हे)। तो साखत घोड़ी की है नै (हां ई धणी कन्नु मांगाय कीयो)। कीयो भैइ भाट ईंयां कोय ऊबीणी पर थोड़ी चरा (वाह वाह)। जावो भंवरो में घोड़ी की साखत काड अर (लियावो)। भाट देखियो सांचो काम व्हियो (वाह वाह)। दरबार का हुकमूं भंवरो में भाट पूगतो (व्हियो है जी कीयो)। रोड़ां घोड़ां का जीण मोकळा पड़िया है (म्हे)। उतर उतर आंतरै (फैंकतो गियो)। सागै घोड़ी को पिलाण आयो (म्हे)। सेंस मुखियां का टोप भोज का घोड़ी के बी का जीण का ऊपर बांध्योड़ा पड़िया (वाह वाह)। ए डील को छकड़िया

बखतर हो नै (हां बो बी के ऊपर बोध्योड़ो हो)। काना का जगमोती बी जागां (हां पड़िया हा)। जो सात सिण्गार ससत्र पाती (वाह वाह)। भोज का हा जका सारा बी पिलाण के ऊपर बांध्योड़ा (हां हा जी कीयो)। भाट देखियो सांचो काम व्हियो (वाह वाह)। दीया झट काढ दरबार का हुकमूं घोड़ी के ऊपरै साखत कर दी (वाह वाह)। मीर कीयो कांई सला (बो को बो है कोनी भाट कीयो)। नीतो ईनै कांई ठा ही की ई घोड़ी के आ साखत है कीयो (हां आ साखत है कीयो)। दीयोजी कीयो रे भाट मैं कोनी चलूं (वाह वाह)। क्य (अब क्युं कोनी चालो कीयो)। क्युं भाट बगड़ावतां को है (हां बगड़ावतालो को है)। ए श्री महाराज (म्हे)। कांई पिछाण करी (आप कींयां पिछाण करियो)। कीयो सागै को सागै तो जीण ल्यायो (म्हे)। के तूं घोड़ी नै खोल (हां लियायो)। कीयो श्री महाराज ई घोड़ी को जीण म्हारावूं छानो है की (हां छानो थोड़ो ही है कीयो)। बगड़ावतां को अजमेर को शहर में आणो जाणो (हां सदा को ही हो)। तो ई घोड़ी पर दिन में तीन तीन बारी पिलाण म्हारो करियोड़ो है (हां म्हारो करियोड़ो है जी कीयो)। बठै साव ही संचो बोल गो भैइ (वाह वाह)। ईयूं थानै दगो है तो ई जीव की सोगण है म्हार की (वाह वाह)। तीतर खतम हो जावै भाट जिन्दो को जिन्दो ही (रह जावे)। दरबार का हुकमूं दीया नै ठिगाय पोटाय (हां घोड़ी असवार करियो)। तो दीया की पदमणी है नै (म्हे)। बूझणा करी है दासियां (वाह वाह)। आज को तो दिन भाई खोटो घणो (हां है कीयो)। श्याम नै बरजावो (हां बरज अर आवो म्हनै सपनो रात आयो जको खोटो (घणो आयो कीयो)। दासियां नै हुकम दियो जावो दासियां ये दरबार का हुकमूं कह दियो थांको अन्त्येवर बजै (हां बाहरें नी जाणो अब)। आज के दिन (वाह वाह)। दासियां आर कीयो श्री महाराज म्हारा बाईजी को हुकम कोय नी है आज (हां बाहरें मत पधारीज्यो)। भाट देखियो छोटो छोटा कांकरिया भेळा कर मेहल आपां (चुणियो)। रांडां की हेटलो कांकरो काढ लियो (वाह वाह)। दीयो बूझणा करी रे भाट मैं तो भैइ रे अब कोनी चांलां (हां अब कोनी चांलां कीयो)। म्हांका अन्त्येवर है नी मायला (हां घराला बरजै कीयो)। भाट देखियो करी तो जबरी (वाह वाह)।।

म्हारै भाटणियां तो जी जो दो है रे माझी जोधका रे।
दीया जोधका रे काळी कंकाळी दोय।
बांका सुगण रे बां मैं झाड़ दियां।
जरां आगै रे दूणी दुगाणी ओट।।
(भलां जी भलां) देव भलां

म्हारै तो घर में भाटणियां दो है (म्हे)। काळी कंकाळी (है दोय)। अरै बांका सुगण बां में झाडूं (म्हे)। आगै ए मत भैइ दीया म्हनै दूणी दुगाणी (होय)। लाख की आसा कर जावूं में (म्हे)। तो म्हनै आर कांई करै दोन्यु की दोन्यु म्हारी लुगाइयां जकी आर बरजै म्हनै (हां बाहरें मत जावो चड़ाई करो न कीयो)। तो दो दो चार चार जूत है जको बांकै ऊपर में (हां ठोक देवूं)। हजार की लाख की आसा पर जावूं नै (म्हे)। चार लाख मिलै (वाह वाह)। थोड़ा तूं ही सूण झाड़िया (हां सूण झाड़ द्यो म्हारा धणी कीयो)। दीयो जोधको कर रीस (म्हे)। हेंर रंग महला ऊंचो (चड़ियो)। जार दरबार का हुकमूं राणीजी के ताजणो (हां बाहयो जी कीयो)। राणीजी खंबा के सारै हो ग्या (वाह वाह)। खंबा के

लागी बटीड़ (म्हे)। बोल्यो (हां बरखत रामा एक)। एक ही लागी है बो ताजणो बोल्यो जीसै में दासियां ही जकी बी जागावूं पग छोड़ दिया (हां भाग छूटी)। भाट नाळ के मांयनै पेड़ियां आडो फिर गियो (वाह वाह)। आवै जकी दासी के दे थाप की टाम टूम में जकी आपकी (सगळी कोस लेवे)। दे थपेड़ा के हेटी डाल द्यै (हां जा कीयो)। दीयोजी राणी के तीन ताजणा की देय (म्हे)। पाछो (बावड़यो)। आगै नाळ में दासियां भरी पड़ी (हां पेड़ियां में भरयोड़ी ही)। कीयो रे भाट कांई करियो (ओ कांई करियो कीयो)। कीयो श्री महाराज रास तो तूं लाटली (बूंबळा मैं रळकाया हूं)। म्हारी गिरगराट हो मन में (म्हे)। राणीजी तो हुकम छोड़ आयी (पण मुण्डा के से मुण्डै ए दासियां आर बरज्यो कीयो)। जको म्हारै थोड़ो सूण झाड़यावूं मैं तो (हां आंका सूण आमै झाड़यावूं देयो)। दीयोजी देखियो मुंगतो है खोड़ीलो (वाह वाह)। दरबार का हुकमूं दीयो सवार व्हिया पाछो (हां वाह वाह)। तो राणीजी बोलै (म्हे)। कांई समचार कहवै देखां (कीआवूं जाणज्यो देखां कीआवूं)।।

ए डाई बोल गी तो जी ए ई श्याम नै कोसरियां रे।
बोली दासियां जी डूंगर की बाखाण रे।
देव का कूंकूं बरणा ई बै सेलड़ा।
श्याम के लागै है कूंकूं बरणी खांखां रे।।
(भलां जी भलां) देव भलां

डाई तो बोलै देख श्याम नै कोचरियां (वाह वाह)। दासियां बोल गी डूंगर की (बाखाण)। देव धणी का सेलड़ा (म्हे)। श्याम के लागेला एक कूंकूं बरणी (खांखां)। इस्या सुगण व्हिया भाई (वाह वाह)। भगवान का सेल है नी (म्हे)। म्हाना श्याम का जरूर लागी (हां आज लाग्या बिना नैइ रहवै कीयो)। दरबार का हुकमूं राणीजी बोलै (म्हे)। कांई सुगण बतावै (कीआवूं जाणज्यो कीआवूं)। अबार कहवूं धणी देव का ई का हुकमूं भगवान कावूं (वाह वाह जी वाह वाह)।।

ए काळा बळदां तो जी श्याम नै गाड़ो मिल गो ये हीड़ागर छोकरियां रे।
मिल गी आंतो ये बोड़ै गडै पाणी के पणियार।
काळ को खेंचियोड़ो जावै दीयो जोधको को।
चाल्यो दासी ये सावर गढ को राव।।
(भलां जी भलां) देव भलां

काला बळदां देखो श्याम नै गाड़ो मिल गो (वाह वाह)। मिल गी ये दासी सामी आ बोड़ै गडै पाणी की (पणियार)। काळ को खेंचियोड़ो जावै हीड़ागर छोकरियां (म्हे)। चाल्यो सावर गढ को (राव)। निंगै करो देख (हां काळ को खेंचियोड़ो आज जावै है कीयो)। देव महाराज का सेल की लागी (म्हे)। हेंर श्याम का चारूं दांत चोकाला टूटी (हां दांत तुड़ार आई कीयो)। दरबार का हुकमूं बे का बै सुगण दियाजी के सेमुण्डै आयग्या (वाह वाह)। काळा बळद नै गाड़ो मिल गो (म्हे)। हेंर बोड़ै गड पाणी की (पणियार मिल गी)। तो दीया नै दरबार का हुकमूं घोड़ी नाचै कुदे ही (म्हे)। नीम्बू मंत्रयोड़ो हो भाट कन्नै (वाह वाह)। घोड़ी के काना के बीचै (हां दीनी)। घोड़ी दरबार का हुकमूं फट बी नीम्बू

से राळिया से जपी (म्हे)। दीया नै कर सवार टोप अर बखतर पहराई (वाह वाह)। कीयो वाह वाह भैइ भोज जकै दिन चड़तां जरां ओपतो (म्हे)। आज दीयाजी घोड़ी पर तूं ओपियो (हां तूं ओपियो है कीयो)। घोड़ी बी जागावूं दड़ंगो दियो (वाह वाह)। दरवाजा के ऊपर आकर घोड़ी कूद अर पड़ गी (वाह वाह)। पड़तां ही फटकारो लाग्यो (म्हे)। दीया को माथा को टोप है जको फटकै हेटो पड़ गो (हां आगलै छेड़ै जांवतो पड़ियो जी कीयो)। दीयोजी घोड़ी परूं (हां उतरियो)। भाट कीयो लेरेवूं (वाह वाह)। ईंयां कींयां श्री महाराज हेटा कींयां उतरिया (हां पाछा कींयां उतरिया कीयो)। कीयो रे भाट कसूण हो गा भैइ (वाह वाह)। कांई (कांई कसूण व्हिया कीयो)। माथा को टोप हो म्हांको भैइ जको मतै पड़ गो (हां पड़ गियो कीयो)। स्यान ही जकी पड़ गी जर म्हारी हार ही होवै (हां हार होवै चड़ अर कोनी चांलां कीयो)। म्हारा धणी एक तो लेरां नै पड़ गो आगा नै बा बता (हां जकी बतावो आप)। कीयो आगा नै (पड़ियो तो आगा नै कीयो)। कीयो जरां आगलो नैइ तूं (हां तूं कोनी नीवै कीयो)। झटकाय टोप नै दीया के माथा पर (मेल दियो)। मेल कसी जकी काटी ई जागावूं झाड़ दी (हां झड़ दियो बटन)। घोड़ी पटकारो देयली तो आ नी है दुशमन औरूं ठम जावै (हां पड़ जावेलो तूं)। बूझणा करी श्री महाराज पधारो अब (हां अब चालो कीयो)। गेला के मांयनै पाणी की पणियार दिया नै (सामै मिल गी)। दीयोजी बोलै कांई पणियारां नै बूझै देखां (कीआवूं जाणज्यो ओ कीआवूं)। कीयो है दासियां पणियारियां (म्हे)। हां श्री महाराज (फरमावो)। कीयो टीमकया तळाव पर खोड़लो कंवर है (हां खोड़लो कंवर उतरियोड़ो है कांई कीयो)। कीयो श्री महाराज खोड़ला कंवर की तो म्हनै ठा कोनी (म्हे)। तळाव पर ही सुरजी दोय तपिया (हां दोय उगयोड़ा देखयां)। दीयोजी कीयो रे भाट म्हांकै दगो हो गो औरूं ही (वाह वाह)। कांई कहवै पणियारियां (हां दो सुरजी कींयां बतावै कीयो)। कींयो साव सांची बात है (ए सांची है)। सासू आगली बूबा है रोटी कोनी दिया (हां रोटी तो जीमयोड़ी कोनी)। पाणी नै आई है (म्हे)। एक सुरजी तो बाहरें दीखै ही है (अर एक पाणी के मांयना आनै दीखियायो)। तूं ही देख ले तनै दीखावूं (हां ए सांची है कीयो)। झूटी कोनी (वाह वाह)। दीया के रूम रूम जचा दी (म्हे)। दरबार का हुकमूं ठिगाय पोटार दीया नै कांई करियो टीमकया पर बाड़तो कर दियो (वाह वाह)। देव महाराज तीन तिलोकी को नाथ लीला पर चड़ा ऊबा हा (म्हे)। दीया की नजर अर देव की नजर एक मिली (हां एक मिली पाळ पर चड़तां ही)। दीयोजी बूझणा करी रे मुंगता (म्हे)। जाळ तो जबरो करियो नी करियो (वाह वाह)। अती कहर घोड़ी नै पाछी हांक दी (हां पाछी पुड़ै राळ दीनी)। घोड़ी को पोड़ बोल्यो (म्हे)। हेंर भाट बूझणा करी श्री महाराज दोहरो लायो (हां आयोड़ो पाछो जाय नी कीयो)। कीयो बाबा भाट (म्हे)। प्रण है म्हारै (हां भाग्योड़ा के लारै मैं नैइ भागां कीयो)। ओ तो भाग गो (म्हे)। भाट मन में देखियो देव तो नट गो देखां घोड़ा नै औरूं बतला देखां (हां घोड़ै नै तो की बतलावो)। लीला घोड़ा नै भाट बोलै कांई शबद कहवै देखां (कीआवूं जाणज्यो देखां कीआवूं)।।

ए नळी कटावूं तो जी घोड़ा थारी लीलड़ा रे।
कटाल्यूं भाई रे लाला बीचली लाल।
हाथ बीसत करै बां आंतरै।

दुशमन दीयो घोड़ी रे बंवळी डकाया जाय।।
(भलां जी भलां) देव भलां

नळी कटावूं थारी (म्हे)। घोड़ा लीलड़ा दरबार का हुकमूं कटावूं लाला बीचली (लाल)। अरै हाथ बीसत के आंतरै (म्हे)। दुशमन दीयो देख घोड़ी बंवळी लियां (जायै नी कीयो)। बेटी का बाप ऊबो है नै तूं कीयो (हां ऊबो देख आडो फिर भाग अर)। कीयो भाट बेहरो कींयां हु गो (म्हे)। घोड़ी कुण है आ (है कुण जकी तो बता कीयो)। म्हारी मासी है मासी के लेरै मैं कोनी भाजूं (हां मैं तो मासी के लारू भागूं कोनी पीट ताकूं)। भाट मन में देखियो देव ही तो नट गो (म्हे)। ए देखियो (ओ घोड़ी ही लार को लार लीलड़ो नट गो)। जरां देव नै कांई दोष है (वाह वाह)। भाट बोलै कांई समचार देव नै कहवै देखां (कीआवूं जाणज्यो देखां कीआवूं)।।

ए घोड़ा से तो जी घोड़ा मिलाया रे बाळा देवजी रे।
मिल गा भाई रे घोड़ा का लाला रे।
तीतर तो बण में उडा दिया गोठां रा राजवियां।
अब अन्नदाता जी छोछू है निरवाला रे।
(भलां जी भलां) देव भलां

घोड़ा से तो घोड़ा मिल गा (म्हे)। ठाकर से ठाकर मिलिया घोड़ा का मिल गा (लाला)। ए तीतर तो अन्नदाता बण में उडा (म्हे)। कांई मरियोड़ा नै (वाह वाह)। आ नै जिन्दा कर कीयो (वाह वाह)। तीतर तो बण में उडा दे गोठां का राजवी अब छोछू भाट है (निरवाला)। तूं जाणै अर थारा दीयोजी जाणै अर आ घोड़ी जोणै (वाह वाह)। म्हारो तो मिलानो हाथ हो (मिलां दिया)। मैं मिलां दिया कीयो (वाह वाह)। तीन तिलोकी को नाथ भगवान अम्मी की नजर झांकिया (म्हे)। तीतर तो उड अर आपका बण में (ऊड़ग्या)। घोड़ा की लीला की बाग नै नीचा नै दाबी (वाह वाह)। सावर गढ के गोरवें जार घोड़ो सामू (हां नीकलयो)। दीया को देखणो हु गो (वाह वाह)। तीन तिलोकी को नाथ सामू आयगा (वाह वाह)। मन में देखियो रे लेरै छोड़यो देख दुशमन नै (हां आगै नै आयो है कीयो)। दरबार का हुकमूं दीयोजी कांई बिद्या करी (म्हे)। के कबूतर जुवांर चुगा हा छोड़ घोड़ी को (आनो)। देही बदल दी (वाह वाह)। गाड़ां की गढार के मांयनै (बन कमेड़ी अर चुगबा लाग्यो जी कीयो)। दरबार देखियो बिद्या तो फैला तो ओ दीनी (वाह वाह)। तीन तिलोकी को नाथ छोड़ घोड़ा को (हानो)। ए सिकरा (बनया जी कीयो)। दरबार का हुकमूं कांई बोलै अर कांई समचार कहवै देखां (हां कीआवूं जाणज्यो अब कीआवूं)।

दीयो बन गा तो जी ए ई बै देगकड़ियां रे।
बालो देव बन ग्या बै भी चतर सुजान।
अब कालै ओसर दिया म्हारूं कोय ने।
राताकोट का भारत में रे हरलेवूंला पिराण।।
(भलां जी भलां) देव भलां

दीयोजी बन गो भैइ देगकड़ी (म्हे)। तीन तिलोकी को नाथ बन गा चतर (सुजान)। ई ओसर नी मारूं दीया कियो (वाह वाह)। राताकोट का महाभारत में अरे हरलेवूंला (थारा पिराण)। घोड़ा असवार हो जा मारूं कोनी डर मत कीयो (हां मारूं कोनी हाल कीयो)। तो दरबार का हुकमूं दीयो देखियो ओ ई देही बदल दी (म्हे)। तूं बदली तो (वाह वाह)। फैटा दीनी तीन चार मन में देखियो अठै छोड़ै तो कोनी (हां छोड़ै कोनी कीयो)। कमेड़ी का पांखड़ा कोस नाकिया (वाह वाह)। तीन तिलोकी को नाथ बूझणा करी दिया देही धार घोड़ै असवार हो जा (वाह वाह)। तो दीयोजी पाछो देही धार (म्हे)। घोड़ी ऊपरै (असवार व्हियो)। तीन तिलोकी को नाथ लीला पर (असवार व्हिया जी कीयो)। सामा आतां ही दीया के भगवान सेल की पूड़ी (हां सामै दांतां दीनी)। चोखाला चारूं दांत टूट देखेण का हेटा (आर पड़िया)। दीयोजी चकर खार घोड़ी बंवळी घोड़ीवूं हेटै पड़ गो (वाह वाह)। भाट के निंगै (हां कन्नै ही खड़ो आयग्या)। दरबार का हुकमूं दांत तो हेटावूं पड़िया है नै जका नै उठाय (म्हे)। अर दीया के हाथ में दिया दीया ले समाल भैइ (हां चार तनै गांवां को कीयो हो)। ए म्हार कन्नु देख मैं कीयो नै (हां ए चार गांव तो ले ले)। हेंर छकड़िया बखतर तोड़बा लागो काना का जगमोती है जका फाड़बा लागो भाट (वाह वाह)। देव महाराज कीयो अरै बाबा भाट कांई करै ईंयां (हां कांई करो हो कीयो)। कीयो श्री महाराज थारा तो कांई ठा बाप की घोड़ी हाथ आयी (वाह वाह)। म्हारै तो ए ई खटी (हां म्हारै तो ए ई हाथ आयी कीयो)। दरबार का हुकमूं देव महाराज बूझणा करी रे भाट (म्हे)। घोड़ी माता नै छोड़ दे भैइ (हां छोड़ दियो कीयो)। आपां तो भगवान की दियावूं घोड़ी की बन्ध कटाबा का सिरी हां (वाह वाह)। बन्ध घोड़ी की आपां कटा दी (हां कटा दीनी)। अब भोज के घरां सोरी रही तो दड़ावट जाओ (हां बठै ऊठ जावो)। दीयोजी घोड़ी नै सोरी राखी हुवे तो भलां ही दीया का दरबार में पाछी (हां सावर ऊठ जावो)। घोड़ी नै छोड़तां जेज (लागी)। सावराला गैलै घोड़ी दड़ंगो दे गी (वाह वाह)। तो निंगैवान थारा साथी अर म्हारा साथी मोकळा (हां दरबार में बैठिया दीयै के)। निंगै राखा कीयो ए बा घोड़ी देख असवार राळ दे देखो अब बो आवै (हां दीयोजी नै पटकर आवै कीयो)। घोड़ी तीन चार गढ के चकर लगायां (वाह वाह)। कीयो सिरदारां ईंयां कोनी बड़ै आ (हां ईंयां हाथ आवेली कोनी)। ईका जो सागै आयोड़ा है ने बै बछेरा (म्हे)। बा नै छोड़ो (सागै छोड़ अर पछै पकड़ लियो)। तो बी साथवूं घोड़ी बड़ती (हां हो जासी)। दरबार का हुकमूं घोड़ी के सागै लूट में बिछेरा गियोड़ा (म्हे)। तो बांकी सांकळा सब की झाड़ दी (वाह वाह)। घोड़ी के सागै हो गा बै (म्हे)। सब ही बछेरा खुलतां घोड़ी दड़ंगो दियो (म्हे)। कोय सिरदार के सारै कोनी री (वाह वाह)। दड़ावटालो गेलो (हां ले लियो)। दीया का चारूं दांत तोड़ता ग्यारहा बरसावूं बंवळी घोड़ी की बन्ध कटतां (कटतां)। जय बोलो भैइ श्री देव नारायण की (अब जय)।। भगवान बंवळी घोड़ी की बन्ध कटाय (म्हे)। हेंर सांखळी घाटी पर आयगा (वाह वाह)। उतम राय कंवर लेरावूं आयो (म्हे)। बाप नै देखियो ईंयां (हां दांत टूटयोड़ा)। कंवर नै रीस आयगी (वाह वाह)। दरबार का हुकमूं देव के घाटी पर आर आडो फिर गो (म्हे)। ले अब की जागां जाय भैइ कीयो (हां अब कोनी जाण द्यूं कीयो)। कीयो रे भैइ उतम राय कंवर (म्हे)। हाथां का कांकड़ डोरड़ा तूं खोलिया कोनी गांव का देवातण (हां पूगिया कोनी)। दरबार का हुकमूं आयो जियान पाछो जा (हां पाछो ऊठ जा कीयो)।

सुगण चाहवै तो (वाह वाह)। पण उतम राय के रीस बैठयोड़ी पाछो कीको जाय आडो फिर गो (हां आडो फिर ग्यो)। तो दरबार घोड़ा के मुण्डा के आयो (म्हे)। पागड़ा के दीनी जको शीश कंवर को परै जातो पड़ियो (हां परै जांवतां पड़िया जी कीयो)। पागड़ा की फटकार से (वाह वाह)। पड़ै का लेख है ए दरबार का हुकमूं पागड़ा के घोड़ा के लीला के सारै पटकार दियो जको पागड़ा से शीश टूट गो (वाह वाह)। दरबार का हुकमूं भाट बूझणा करी कंवराणी नै श्री महाराज धोला आडो दिया अबार ही देवातण धोकिया पहली (म्हे)। तीन तिलोकी को नाथ भगवान आय पाछा (वाह वाह)। हेंर राजगादी आंतां ही बैठां ले भाट अब तो बै जावां भैइ (हां अब गादी बैठां कीयो)। गादी पर बिराजमान हुवै (म्हे)। हुतां ही कांई देखां है बैइ का भाट नै सोचना देवै देखां (कीआवूं जाणज्यो देखां कीआवूं)।।

ए देव दुलीचै जी ए ई दरबार बिराज गा रे।
लियो बाईजी बैइ का भाट नै बुलाय।
रावजी अर बगड़ावत दोन्यु लड़ पड़िया।
कह कीनै भाट जी रे निरजन बूझै न्याव।।
(भलां जी भलां) देव भलां

अब देव दुलीचै बिराज्या (म्हे)। हेंर लियो भैइ रे बैइ का भाट नै (बुलाय)। के दरबार का हुकमूं तीन तिलोकी को नाथ करै बूझणा कह कीनै बाबा भाट तनै अब निरजन बूझबा लागा (न्याव)। बैइ का भाट न्याय कीज्यै अन्याय मत कीज्यै भैइ (वाह वाह सांची बोल अर कह द्यो कीयो)। जियां बात व्हियोड़ी है नै (म्हे)। जियान की जियान ही (हां म्हानै बताय कीयो)। भाट कोनी बोल्यो (वाह वाह चुप रहगियो)। तीन तिलोकी को नाथ भगवान बोलै (म्हे)। कांई भाट नै बतलावै देखां (कीआवूं जाणज्यो देखां कीआवूं)। अबार कहवूं देव का ईका हुकमूं (वाह वाह जी)।।

ए आगला जुगा को जी भाटजी तूं आदमी हां रे।
तनै भाटजी रे स बांतां का खोज।
झगड़ां में झूटो रे धणी राण को।
सांचो म्हानो जी पिता सवाई भोज।।
(भलां जी भलां) देव भलां

आगला जुगां को आदमी है तूं (म्हे)। बाबा भाट है जूनी बांतां का तनै (खोज)। झगड़ा में तो देख झूटो धणी राण को (म्हे)। सांचो हो म्हारो पिता सवाई (अब भोज)। सवाई भोज हरो नै (हां जका को साव ही सांचा हा)। रावजी सा झूटो (हो जी कीयो)। ओ समचार कुण कीयो (देव महाराज कीयो)। बैइ को भाट अब बोलै (वाह वाह)। कांई भगवान नै पाछो जवाब देवै देखां (कीआवूं जाणज्यो देखां अब कीआवूं)।।

ए आगला जुगां को जी ए ई मैं आदमी हां रे।
म्हनै अन्नदाताजी स बांतां का खोज।
झगड़ा में सांचो जी धणी राण को।

झूटों आपको जी पिता सवाई भोज।
(भलां जी भलां)। देव भलां

आगला जुगां का हूं मैं (म्हे)। म्हनै है सारी बांतां का (खोज)। झगड़ा में सांचो धणी राण को (वाह वाह)। झूटो आपको पिता सवाई (भोज)। सवाई भोज तो झूटा लड़िया (म्हे)। रावजी सा है जको (साव ही सांचो लड़ियो)। देव महाराज बूझणा करी रे बाबा भाट (म्हे)। जका का लूण पाणी खाया नै (हां बांकी तूं कटती करै कीयो)। कीयो श्री महाराज आप कांई फरमायो अबार (हां साव सांचो बोली कीयो)। कीयो देव को दुलीचो है भगवान को दरीखानो है ओ (म्हे)। अठै झूट मती बोली (वाह वाह)। श्री महाराज मैं तो सांच बात ही जका आपणै (हां कीवूं कीयो)। बाबा भाट (म्हे)। कींयां तो बगड़ावत झूटा व्हिया कींयां रावजी सा पाछो सांचो है जकी माण्ड अर बात कह म्हनै (हां सूल माण्ड अर बताओ कीयो)। दरबार का हुकमूं भाट बोलै (वाह वाह)। कांई समचार देव नै कहवै देखां (कीआवूं जाणज्यो देखां कीआवूं)। अबार कहवूं धणी देव का हुकमूं देखां (वाह वाह जी)।।

ए पागड़ी बदली तो जी ए ई बेटा बाघ का रे।
बदली बैठ छतरजी चौबारां की छांय।
रावजी पकड़ाई बगड़ावतां नै चिटली आंगलियां।
बगड़ावत निगला जी खुवां समेत ही बांय।।
(भलां जी भलां) देव भलां

पागड़ी बदली भैइ पड़ीहार बेटा बाघ का जी (वाह वाह)। बदली बैठ छतर चौबारां की (छांय)। रावजी सा पकड़ाई बगड़ावतां नै चिटली आंगली (म्हे)। बगड़ावत निगल गा भुजा समेत ही (बांय)। खुवां समेत निगल गा (वाह वाह)। कीयो भाट तूं कहवै मैं झूट कोनी बोलूं (हां साव ही झूट बोल ग्यो नी कीयो)। अरे आंगली तो मिनखा मुण्डा में जरूर मावै (म्हे)। आ बांय की बांय भुजा की भुजा कींयां मायी (हां कींयां मायी जकी बता)। दरबार का हुकमूं बात नै माण्ड के सावल म्हारै समझ में कोनी आयी आ (वाह वाह)। तो दरबार का हुकमूं बैइ को भाट बोलै (म्हे)। कांई भगवान देव नै समचार कहवै देखां (कीआवूं जाणज्यो देखां अब कीआवूं)।। तूं तो तूं म्हारा निरजन तूं तूं तो तूं म्हारा दाता तूं म्हारा दाता तूं म्हारा दाता तूं म्हारा दाता तूं।

एक एक प्यालै तो जी दारू पीतो जी बेटा रे बाघ का रे।
बगड़ावत कर नाकियो जी रंग के मांय कुरंग।
राणी ले चड़िया जी हिंदवा राव की।
रावजीआला महलां के बगड़ावजी लगा दी सुरंग।।
(भलां जी भलां) देव भलां

दरबार का हुकमूं एक एक प्यालै दारू पीतो बेटा बाघ का (म्हे)। बगड़ावत कर नाकियो रंग के मांय (कुरंग)। अरै राणी ले चड़िया हिन्दवा राव की (म्हे)। बगड़ावत रावजीआला महलां के लगा दी (सुरंग)। रावजी इस्यो धरम बिचारयो (म्हे)। बगड़ावत सातू गुण का भाणजा (हां जी कीयो)। जका नै न्यालै

अर प्यालै (करिया)। बरोबर का भाईसा (जाणया कीयो)। हेंर बगड़ावत ओ धरम बिचरयो (म्हे)। रावजी की राणी पर हाथ राळ दिया (हां बांकै सुरंग लगायी महल के)। श्री महाराज राणी नै ले आया जरां बगड़ावत मारियो गिया (वाह वाह)। बाबा भाट राणी एक तो रावजी की ही बगड़ावतां की हो बा के (बा बता कीयो)। कीयो श्री महाराज राणी तो पछै रावजी की हीक (म्हे)। कीयो रे भाट जरां सगद बडाबडी का भूंवाल से टीका नारल पहली कुण के आय अर कुण झेलिया (हां कुण झेलिया जकी बताओ)। कहूं रे श्री महाराज के टीका नारल तो बगड़ावतां के ही (आया कीयो)। कीयो जरां दरबार का हुकमूं कळस आरतियां भूंवाल में पहल पोत हीरादासी कुण नै मनाया (हां किन नै मनाया हा कीयो)। श्री महाराज भोज नै ही (मनाया कीयो)। तोरण कुण मारयो पहली (म्हे)। कीयो श्री महाराज बगड़ावत (भाण्यो)। हेंर खाण्डावूं फैरा एक तो रावजी के बाद खाया पहली (पहली खाया जकी बता)। कीयो श्री महाराज भुवानी राणी पेट दुखाय (म्हे)। खाण्डो पहली मंगा लियो (हां खाण्डावूं फैरा पहली लिया रावजीवूं कीयो)। लोग दिखावूं रावजी के जोड़ै बैठ फैरा (खाया जी कीयो)। जरां बाबा भाट कांई मांगै रावजी राणी के (हां राणी तो सवाई भोज की ही कीयो)। मतेई धणी बन गो राणी को (वाह वाह)। कीयो श्री महाराज लोग दिखावूं राणी रावजी की ही (हां रावजी की ही कीयो)। राणीजी की खातर अती बांतां हो गी (वाह वाह)। भाट राणी की खातर हुई (हां राणीजी की खातर हुई)। हां श्री महाराज (वाह वाह)। तीन तिलोकी को नाथ भगवान बोलै (म्हे)। कांई समचार पाछो कहवै देखां (कीआवूं जाणज्यो कीआवूं देखां)। अबार कहवूं धणी देव का ई का हुकमूं देखां (वाह वाह जी वाह वाह)।।

ए एक राणी की तो जी दोय राणी दे द्यूं रे बैइ भाटजी रे।
कर द्यूं भाटजी रे होंकारै एक हजार रे।
आपां मांगां राव कन्नु रे बेटा बाघ का।
मांगां बाबा भाटजी रे बै घोड़ा बै असवार।।
(भलां जी भलां) देव भलां

एक राणी की दोय राणी दे द्यूं (म्हे)। भाट बाबा कर द्यूं होंकारै एक ही (हजार)। ए आपां अब मांगां रावजी कन्नु पाछा बेटा बाघ का (म्हे)। मांगां बाबा भाट बै घोड़ा अर बै का बै ही (पाछा असवार)। रावजी की एक राणी ले गा नी बगड़ावत (म्हे)। एक की दोय देवै तो दे द्यूं (म्हे)। दोय की दो सौ लेवै तो (हां मैं दे द्यूं)। आपां तो पाछा बगड़ावत लेयां आपणा (हां सागै बै का बै मांगां कीयो दे द्यो)। दरबार का हुकमूं भाट बूझणा (करी है)। श्री महाराज तूं तो औतारी पुरुष है (म्हे)। लाख की तो दोय लाख कर द्यै दोय लाख की ही चार लाख ही (हां कांई ठा कर देवो)। पण रावजी सा मिनखियो मळधारी है (म्हे)। बगड़ावतां को एक घोड़ो (अर एक ही असवार बांवूं तो पछो बैठियो नी हुवे)। अरे बाबा भाट (म्हे)। रावजीवूं बगड़ावत बैठा कोनी हुवै (हां कोनी हुवै श्री महाराज)। कोनी हुवै श्री महाराज (वाह वाह)। कीयो जरां कोय कळह लगा जका बगड़ावतां को बैर काढूं कीयो (हां बैर काढा कीयो)। श्री महाराज ई बात का खाटिया खावूं (हां खाटियो ही खावूं थें कहवो जणै (कळह लगा द्यूं)। कह तो तीजी घड़ी कह तीजे दिन (म्हे)। उनै का डूंगर तो उनै मेल द्यूं उनै का पूरा हे

जका (उनै बसा द्यूं) । कीयो श्री महाराज इस्यो काम करो (म्हे) । आपणा कांकड़ सींव पर रावजी सा का कांकड़ सींव पर एक बावड़ी (हां खुदावो) । सोना रूपा के ऊपर कली (हां लगावो) । तो पणियारां तो रावजी की आय बूनु (म्हे) । उनू आपणी (पणियारियां जाय) । लुगाई की जात घाटा पर लड़िया बिनै (लाखां ही रहवै कोनी) । कोय इडूणी बदली कोय पगरखी (बदलेसी) । कोय नेज (हां बदल देवै जी कीयो) । रावजी की पणियारियां जार रावजी नै पुकार (हां घाली) । हेंर आपणी पणियारां जको (आपां नै आप पुकार सुणासी) । उनू तो चड़ रावजी आजायी (म्हे) । उनू चड़ आपां है जको (ऊठ चाला) । दे बड़छियां की राठा रमै (म्हे) । बावड़ी के ऊपरै बगड़ावतां का बैर है जका बठै (आच्छी तरहवूं काढ लेवां कीयो) । कीयो बाबा भाट (म्हे) । आ कळह तो म्हारै दाय (कोनी लागी) । क्युं (रांडी राड़ है कीयो) । रांडी राड़ में चौईस भाई बगड़ावत हा जका ही मारिया गिया (वाह वाह) । तो मैं तो पांच ही तूंतड़ा हां (हां आ कळह म्हारै तो दाय नैइ लागै कीयो) । देख भैइ हाल भेळा कठै व्हिया मैं (वाह वाह) । भेळा को नांव लियो अर दरबार की आंख खुली रे भूणोजी कोनी आपां कन्नै (वाह वाह) । दरबार का हुकमूं रे भाट आ कळह दाय तो कोनी लागै म्हारै (म्हे) । श्री महाराज दूजी लगावूं कीयो (हां दूसरी लगा द्यूं) । जेठ को महीनो है नै भगवान बरसात करै नै (म्हे) । जरां आपणा करसां रावजी का करसां कांई करै अगूणो आतूणो खेत में (बाय ज्यावे) । आपणा करसां नै हुकम दे द्यो (म्हे) । उतराद दिखणाद (हो बायावै कीयो) । रावजी का करसां जार रावजी नै पुकार (हां सुणावेला) । आपणा करसां (आपां नै आर पुकार सुणासी) । बूनु तो रावजी चड़ (आजावे) । हेंर उनू आपां ही (चड़ अर चालां कीयो) । दे बड़छियां की राठा रमै (म्हे) । कांकड़ की उपरै (बैर आछी तरहवूं बगड़ावतां का आपां काढ (लियां कीयो) । कीयो रे भाट (म्हे) । करसो बारह महीनै की रोटी की खातर हल जोतै बठै (वाह वाह) । आपां रोटी कोय नै देवां के भैइ कोय रे कीयो कोस (हां कोसणी म्हारावूं तो कोनी आवै भाट बाबाजी) । आपां देवाल हां (वाह वाह) । आ गलत दाय (म्हारै कोनी लागी) । श्री महाराज तीजी कळह लगावूं अब (हां तीजी लगा द्यूं कीयो) । हां ल गा (लगा कीयो बाबा भाट) । माळागर की भोम में आया हो (म्हे) । घर घरांवूं आपके चोखो (उछरे) । नौ लाख असी हजार गाय है (म्हे) । जासा का निरपाल नै हुकम कर द्यो (वाह वाह) । आ ऊनाळो रावजी साय की गहूं चन्ना की साख ऊबी देखो (हां ईनै भेळा द्यो कीयो) । तो धरम का तो धरम अर करम का (करम हो जाई) । दरबार का हुकमूं रावजी सा भेळियो म्हांको माल (माल) । अरै म्हेका आपां का घेरली म्हांकी (की गाय) । चोखी तरह बगड़ावतां का बैर है जका (आच्छी तरहवूं बठै काढ लेवां) । बी जागां भाट नै देव महाराज सरायो (वाह वाह) । बाह वाह रे भाट कळह को तो (मूली है कीयो) । तीनु तक देख अब के सागै मिल गी मतेई (हां म्हानै घर में आ अब के मिली है कीयो) । गहूं खावै जरां तो उनै धन बदे (म्हे) । उनै धीणो (बदे) । उनै बगड़ावतां का बैर है जका (काड़ लेवां) । दरबार का हुकमूं कीयो बाबा भाट (म्हे) । तो जरां दादा भूणो कठै है (हां जकी बतावो) । ईंयां कींया छोड़ां माळां में बा गायां नै (वाह वाह) । भैइ तो आ लोगां के बीखरयोड़ा पड़्या है (म्हे) । तीन तिलोकी को नाथ बोलै (वाह वाह) । कांई समचार भाट नै कहवै देखां (कीआवूं जाणज्यो कीआवूं) । दरबार का हुकमूं देव महाराज कीयो रे बाबा भाट (म्हे) । भूणा को हेरो तो थारै बिन तो होवै कोनी (हां हेरो कर लियावो कीयो) । तीन

तिलोकी को नाथ भगवान फरमाई नै (म्हे)। तो भाट कांई बोलै कांई समचार देव नै कहवै देखां (कीआवूं जाणज्यो कीआवूं देखां)।।

ए हेरो करेला तो जी ए ई मीणा बावरियां री रे।
कह करेला राज का रे उजलाईत राज मीणा रे।
मैं बैइ को भाट हूं रे गोठां का राजवियां।
कर द्यो म्हनै रे दान दुगाणी दूणा रे।।
(भलां जी भलां) देव भलां

हेरो तो करै अन्नदाता मीणा बावरी (म्हे)। कह करी राज का उजलाईत (मीणा)। मैं बैइ का भाट हां (म्हे)। म्हनै कर द्यो अब दान दुगाणी (थै दूणा)। श्री महाराज दान लेबालां हां (मैं तो दान दुगाणी दूणा देवो तो ले लियां)। ए हेराला धंधो मावूं कीवूं होवै (वाह वाह)। देव बोलै (म्हे)। कांई समचार भाट नै कहवै देखां (कीआवूं जाणज्यो अब देखां कीआवूं)।।

ए थै म्हासूं गिया तो जी बैइ का भाटजी रे।
भाट नारदी काम काजसूं जावो ई रे।
तिरतां पर बांध लेयो भाटजी थै झूंपड़ा।
आटो भाटजी रे मांग मांग खावो रे ।।
(भलां जी भलां) देव भलां

थै म्हासूं जातां रिया भाटजी कीयो (म्हे)। अर काम काज से जावो (जावो)। अरै तिरतां बांध ल्यो झूंपड़ी (म्हे)। पछै आटो मांग मांग अर ई (अब थै जावो खावो कीयो)। म्हांकै काम का कठै रिया (वाह वाह)। म्हांको काम तो करो कोनी जरां ही हो मावूं तो गियोड़ा हूं (वाह वाह)। अरै श्री महाराज ईंयां कींयां करो थै (हां ईंयां कींयां करो बांतां कीयो)। बगड़ावतां को घर को कुत्तो जावै राण शहर में (म्हे)। जका नै दुशमन (रावजी मरा देवै कीयो)। मैं मिनखा जूण जातो रहवूं म्हनै छोरो छोरो जाणै (हां सगळा राण शहर का जाणै कीयो)। श्री महाराज (म्हे)। बैइ तो डुबोनी हुवै तनै (हां तो मैं ऊठ जावूं कीयो)। दरबार का हुकमूं नी जरां म्हारावूं पार नी पड़ै कीयो (वाह वाह)। तीन तिलोकी को नाथ भगवान अम्मी की नजर झांकिया (म्हे)। तो भाट को खोळियो बदल दियो (वाह वाह)। देव बोलै (म्हे)। कांई भाट नै बतलावै (कीआवूं जाणज्यो कीआवूं)।।

साठा होर तो जी पच्चासा आयगो रे बैइ को भाट जी रे।
हु गो भाटजी रे जोधको जवान।
दरपण ले लियो रे थै हाथ में।
देख लीज्यै भाट रे राज तणो दिदार।।
(भलां जी भलां) देव भलां

साठ बरस को हो (म्हे)। पच्चासा आयो (वाह वाह)। हु गो भैई जोधको (जवान)। हु गो जोधतणो

जवान दरपण ले ले बीरा भाट तूं हाथ में (म्हे)। देख लियो राजतणो (अब दिदार)। भाट निंगै कर (हां थारो किस्योक उणियारो है कीयो)। दरबार कावूं दरपण की नै बोलतां है (कांच नै)। हां तीन तिलोकी को नाथ भाट नै कांच में मुण्डो दिखायो (वाह वाह)। तो आपको रूप हो जको भाट नै दे दियो (म्है पच्चीस बरस को जवान बना द्यो)। भगवान भूणा का हेरा की खातर भाट देही बदल दी (वाह वाह)। भाट की देही बदलता (म्हे)। भूणाजी की हेरा की बांतां चालतां (चालतां)। जय बोलो भैइ श्री देव नारायण भगवान की (जय)। दरबार बूझणा करी रे भाट (म्हे)। जा माजी साय कन्नै जा देळू कन्नै (वाह वाह)। थारी जलम की देवाल देळूजी ओळख ले (हां जणा तो राण शहर में ही तनै ओळख लेसी)। नी जरां भूणो को हेरा करणो पड़ी (वाह वाह)। तीन तिलोकी को नाथ भगवान हुकमूं दियो जाओ माजीवूं मिलो देळूवूं (वाह वाह)। आपको रूप भगवान दे दियो भाट नै (म्हे)। दरबार का हुकमूं भाट बगड़ावतां आपके घरां पूगतो (व्हियो जी कीयो)। तो भाट की मां बोलै (म्हे)। कांई समचार देखां भाट नै कहवै देखां (कीआवूं जाणज्यो देखां अब कीआवूं)। अबार कहवूं भगवान का हुकमूं देखां ले तूं (वाह वाह सा)।।

ए बगां दीखै तो जी ए ई आपण नै सोवणा रे।
अन्नदाता मांयनै रे सोना की कळियां रे।
अन्नदाता करै आप नै बूझणा।
कींयां पधारिया जी भाटां री गलियां रे।।
(भलां जी भलां) देव भलां

देळूमाता बूझणा करी (म्हे)। कीयो बगां सोहवै आप नै दरबार सोवणा (म्हे)। मांय है सोना की (कळियां)। देळू भाटणी करै श्री महाराज बूझणा (म्हे)। कींयां आयगा भाटां की (आज गलियां)। अरै अन्नदाता म्हांकाली गलिया कींयां आया (हां कींयां पधारिया हो कीयो)। भाटजी कीयो ओळखै तो कोनी (म्हे)। भाट बैइ को बगड़ावतां को बोलै (म्हें)। कांई आपकी मां नै समचार कहवै (कीआवूं जाणज्यो देखां अब कीआवूं)।।

ए बगां सोहवै तो जी देळूमाता ये म्हानै सोवणा रे।
मांयनै ये देळू ये सोना री कळियां रे।
दड़िया रमबा ये देळू भाटणियां।
भूल अर आयगा ये मैं तो भाटां की गलियां रे।।
(भलां जी भलां) देव भलां

बगां सोहवै सोवणा कीयो (म्हे)। मांय है सोना की (कळियां)। मैं दड़िया रमबा नीकलया (म्हे)। भूल अर आयगा ए देळू मैं भाटां की (गलियां)। भैइ मैं तो भूल गा (हां दड़िया रमता ई आयग्या कीयो)। भाट हेंसियो है नै जकी दांतां की बतीसी ही जकी भाट की बी भाट की लुगाई नै दीख गो (वाह वाह)। तो भाटणी बोलै भाट की लुगाई (म्हे)। कांई समचार कहवै देखां (कीआवूं जाणज्यो देखां कीआवूं)।।

ए पिण्डिया दीखै तो जी बूजी म्हारी हे परण्या श्याम री रे।
ई की माजी ये सुरत दीया की लोय।
भाटणी करै तनै बूझणा।
कींयां भूल गी माजी ये ताणा जायां की ओळ।।
(भलां जी भलां) देव भलां

परण्या की दीखै पिण्डिया बूजी ई की (म्हे)। ई की सुरत दीया सी (लोय)। भाट की लुगाई करै तनै बूझणा (म्हे)। कींयां भूली है माता थारा जायोड़ा की (ओळ)। थारो बेटो कोनी है ओ (हां ताणै बेटै की ओळ तूं भूल गी कीयो)। जी टैम में देळूमाता खीचड़ो कूटै ही (म्हे)। बो होवै नी दरबार का हुकमूं केवटणो बोलै कोय (हां कोय केवटणो बोलै तो कोई)। मुसळ ई कहवै (कोय मुसळ ई कहवै सा)। हाथ में ले मुसळ अर के भाट के लेरै (हां हुई)। दरबार का हुकमूं म्हारो बेटो बूड़ो हे जरां तूं म्हारी बेटा की बूह नै छलबा नै आयो कांई (हां छलबा नै आयग्यो कीयो)। झूटयाणी देव ने धणी दरबार का हुकमूं म्हारा बेटो बनावै (वाह वाह)। मुसळ लियै लेरै भाजी उनै भैइ आपकी बूह देकाली (वाह वाह)। भाट हेंसियो (म्हे)। कीयो माता ईंयां कींयां करै बेटो कोनी थारो सागै छोछू मैं (हां सागै को सागै हूं कीयो)। देळूमाता के कीयो थोड़ोसो हेंसियो नै बो (म्हे)। बतीसी निंगै आयगी कीयो बतीसी माठी कींयां फरक पड़ गो (हां बा की बा ही लागै कीयो)। देळूमाता बोलै कांई भाट नै समचार कहवै (कीआवूं जाणज्यो देखां कीआवूं)।।

ए कठा की तो जी नान्या म्हारा रे धुणी कसेरिया रे।
तूं तो छोछू रे की जागावूं धुण लगाई रे।
देळूमाता करै तनै बूझणा।
थारी छोछू रे कुणसै नर देह बदलाई रे।।
(भलां जी भलां) देव भलां

कठा की भैइ छोछू धुणी कसेरी तूं (वाह वाह)। की जागां धुण लगाई (लगाई)। ताणी माता करै बूझणा (म्हे)। अरै लाल कुणसै नर थारी देही (हां बदलाई)। आ देही कुण पलटी भैइ (हां कुण रूप दियो तनै कीयो)। भाट बोलै कांई समचार आपकी मां नै कहवै देखां (कीआवूं जाणज्यो कीआवूं देखा)।।

ए गोठां में जी देळूमाता ये धुणी कसेरिया रे।
मैं तो माजी ये दड़ावट धुण लागाई रे।
ओ भूणा को हेरो करावै धरमराजा देवजी।
ऊदोजी माजी ये बिण से देही बदलाई।।
(भलां जी भलां) देव भलां

दड़ावट में भोज की मैं धुणी नै (म्हे)। बी का धरम से बा धुणी कसेरी ही (वाह वाह)। अर गोठां धुण (लागाई)। ए भूणा को हेरो करावै अब धरमराजा देवजी (म्हारै ऊदोजी देह) (पलटायी)। ओ आपणो देवजी है नै (हां बै देही पलटी)। पण माजी भूणा को हेरो करावै बोल कांई कहवै तूं अब

(हां जकी बताय)। अरै लाल बोबा चूंगायां जकी कोनी ओळखो जको राण शहर को राजा तो कांई ओळख लेय तनै (हां ओळखी कांई ले तनै कीयो)। चोखी तरह जाओ कीयो (वाह वाह)। भाटजी बिदा हु गो नै (म्हे)। देव महाराज कीयो ईंयां कींया हुई (हां ईंयां कींयां हुई कीयो)। बाबा भाट परवाण ले जा कीयो (वाह वाह)।।

लिखिया परवाणा तो जी जो दरबार मोकळिया रे।
मांयनै लिखिया जी मोकळा घणा हरोळ।
बांचतै परवाणै भूणाजी बेगा पधारज्यो।
सूनी पड़ी आप की रे बाप तणी बागोर।।
(भलां देव भलां) देव भलां

लिखिया परवाणा भगवान मोकळिया (म्हे)। मांयनै घणा लिखिया (हरोळ)। बांचतै ही परवाणै भूणोजी बेगो आवज्यै (वाह वाह)। सूनी पड़ी रे बाप तणी (थारी बागोर)। बगड़ावतां का छिन्नवै खेड़ा बसा लिया मैं (म्हे)। थारा बाप को खेड़ो है नै बागोर को (हां जको सूनी ही पड़ियो है कीयो)। माजी बोली भाटजी ठहर जाओ (हां एक परवाणो म्हारै ही हाथ का लेता जाओ कीयो)। पांचिया पटेल बोल्या माठा आ नैइ हुवै भूणा नै रामा श्यामा कोनी देवै (म्हे)।।

लिखिया परवाणा तो जी ए ई साडू मोकळिया रे।
लिख दीना भाईजी परवण वालै पान।
बांच परवाणै भूणाजी बेगो आवज्यो।
थाना माजी रे हु गा पाका पान।।
(भलां जी भलां) देव भलां

लिखियार परवाणा माजी मोकळिया (म्हे)। लिखिया परवाणो वालै (पान)। बांचतै परवाणै भूणा बेगो पधारज्यै (वाह वाह)। थाना माजी हु गा पाका ही (पान)। मैं तो लाल खिरबाळा हो भैइ (हां जाणाला ही हां कीयो)। मावूं तो मिलणो है (बेगो आजावो)। राणी पीपळदे मन में देखियो तूं लेरै नी रहज्या (हां परवाणो जेठ सा नै तूं ही (सागै को सागै लिख दे)।।

लिखिया परवाणा जी जो पीपळदे मोकळिया रे।
लिख दीना पीपळदेजी दे घूंघट की ओट।
बांचतै परवाणै जेठजी बेगा पधारज्यो।
आंतां दियावो दुशमन का रे छाज्जा के ऊपर चोट।।
(भलां जी भलां) देव भलां

अब लिखिया परवाणा राणी पीपळदे मोकळिया (म्हे)। लीख दियो दे घूंघट की (ओट)। परवाणो बांच बेगा पधारज्यो म्हारा जेठजी (म्हे)। आतां दिया जो दुशमन का छाज्जा उपरै (चोट)। आ नी बिने सैनाणी आजावो (हां सैनाणी कर अर आयीज्यो कीयो)। भाटजी दरबार का हुकमू बिदा व्हियो जरां

आ देव महाराज की अस्त्री ही नी पीपळदे (म्हे)। कंवळ कंवळ खुल गो राजी हो गी (वाह वाह)। भलो काम व्हियो।।

लिखिया ई परवाणा जी जो पीपळदे दूजा मोकळिया रे।
लिख दीना भैइ जी पीपळ वालै पान।
बांचतै परवाणै जेठजी बेगा पधारीज्यो।
बाळक बूह का कुण राखै जी था बीनै बीनणी का मान।।
(भलां जी भलां) देव भलां

लिखिया दूजा परवाणा मोकळिया (म्हे)। लिख दिया परवाण वालै (पान)। बांच परवाणो जेठजी बेगा ही पधारो (म्हे)। अरै ए बाळक बूह का कुण राखेलो (मान)। थामै तो बाळक मैं ही हूं (हां मान थै आवोला जरां म्हारा घणा बडेला कीयो)। दरबार का हुकमूं भांगीजी बूझणा करी रे भाट (म्हे)। एक छोटो सोक परवाणयो म्हारा ही ले जा (हां म्हारो ही जांवता ले जावो कीयो)।

ए लिखिया परवाणा तो जी जो भंगेरियो मोकळिया रे।
लिख दीना भाईजी दे मूंछियां की आंट।
बांचतै परवाणै बेगो आजा रे कंवर महाबळी।
नी राळूंलां दुश्मना भेळो रे मिरचां शामल बांट।।
(भलां जी भलां) देव भलां

लिखिया परवाणा भांगीजी मोकळिया (म्हे)। ए दे मूंछियां की (आंट)। परवाणो बांच बेगो आजाय (म्हे)। नी जरां राळूंला दुशमना भेळो तनै ही (मिरचां भेळो बांट)। दुशमना के भेळै बट जायेलो (वाह वाह)। म्हनै ठा कोनी है (म्हे)। सुवा मण भांग को नशो करूं परभात की टैम में (वाह वाह)। आपका पराया म्हनै (ठा नी रिया करै पछे)। ले भाट ओ म्हानो काग द्यो दे दीज्यै (हां भूणाजी नै देयीज्यै कीयो)। दरबार का हुकमूं कांई भांगीजी दूजा परवाणा देवै औरूं देखां (हां कीआवूं जाणज्यो कीआवूं)। अबार कहवां देव का हुकमूं।।

लिखिया परवाणा जी कंवर भांगीजी मोकळिया रे।
खाजावूं भाईजी पोटां ऊपरै पोट।
तूं बांचतै परवाणै बेगो चड़ाज्यै कंवर महाबळी।
एक लाठ का टोरा में गुड़ा द्यूं ताणो नौ गज रातो कोट।।
(भलां जी भलां) देव भलां

लिखियार भांगीजी परवाणा मोकळिया (वाह वाह)। दरबार का हुकमूं लिख दी पोटां ऊपरै (पोट)। ये परवाणे बांच बेगो आजाय (म्हे)। एक लाठ का टोरा में गुड़ा द्यूं ताणा बाबाजी को नौ गज रातो ही (कोट)। हाथ में चटियो राखूं (म्हे)। एक चटिया की देवूं मैं (वाह वाह)। अतो पावर है कीयो (हां अतो ही पावर है कीयो थारा बाबोजी में बस)। पांचिया पटेल भाट नै कीयो रे भाट (म्हे)। भैइ म्हांका

हा ही हाथ को एक कागद (हां ले जाज्यो)। पांचिया पटेल परवाण मोकळिया लिखिया मांयनै घणा लिखिया हरोळ (हरोळ)। के बांचतै परवाणै बेगो आज्यै भाई कंवर महाबली (म्हे)। सूनी पड़ी बाप की (बागोर)। बागोर को खेड़ो भूणा देख सूनो है कीयो (वाह वाह)। दरबार का हुकमूं ले पधारो लेयो साई (हां जावो कीयो)। पावरावूं भर लियो कागजावूं सारो (म्हे)। और छेड़ा कोनी भगवान का ईका (वाह वाह)। आपां नै ठय ठय परवाणा लिखिया है भाट बगड़ावतां को पावरो तो कागजावूं भर दियो (म्हे)। हेंर दरबार का हुकमूं अब फूलरियो घोड़ा की देही बदल दे कोनी (वाह वाह)। कीयो रे श्री महाराज म्हारी तो खोळियो कर दियो (म्हे)। ओ टारड़ो कींयां पार हुई (हां बो को बो ही है सागै कीयो बूड़ो)। कीयो भाट याद म्हनै करज्यै (म्हे)। कर द्यां भैइ (हां तूं) दोहरी बेळियां थारा में ही पड़ जाय तो म्हनै याद करी (हां जचै जटै याद कर लेय कीयो)। थारै जाणै किनै बी जागां ई कन्नै ऊबो मैजूद (वाह वाह)। कीयो जरां बाह वाह धणी जरै तो डर ही कोनी (हां जणा भूणाजी नै ले ई आवूं)। तो दरबार का हुकमूं फूलरिया घोड़ा पर भाटजी असवार होय (म्हे)। बी जागां घोड़ा नै (हांक दीन्यो)। दरबार का हुकमूं कांकड़ के ऊपरै (म्हे)। शीरस हो जको बगड़ावत बी जागावूं कांई करतां के बूनु ही तो आतां शीरस के हेटै आराम करतां (वाह वाह)। जाजमा बिछाता फूल बिछाता ऊपर चौपड़ पासा (खेलता)। डाळी डाळी के ऊपर मन्द का होर दरबार हुकमूं मद का भातर टांग देता (वाह वाह)। बो बगड़ावत मरिया पछै शीरस कांई करियो (म्हे)। सूख अर आपके साळर (हुगियो)। देव औतार रियां के बाद में (म्हे)। कांई करियो जड़ है बी की हरी हो गी (हां पाछी हरी हो गी जी कीयो)। दरबार का हुकमूं भाट बोलै कांई तरह शीरस नै ओळबा देय देखां (कीआवूं जाणज्यो कीआवूं)।।

> ए ताणी जड़ां नै तो जी सेवळी क्युं खोदी नै बीरा शीरसड़ा रे।
> क्युं जकोली नै भाईजी उनाळा की बाळ।
> बै नर सरग नै गिया रे बण का शीरसड़ा।
> बा नै भूल गो हो गा रे गेरी हरिया डाळ।।
> (भलां जी भलां) देव भलां

थारी जड़ नै शीरसै सेवळियां कोनी खोदी भैइ (म्हे)। अरै दरबार का हुकमूं क्युं कोनी जकालियो तनै ऊनाळी का बाळ (बाळ)। अरै बा नरां नै कींयां भूल गो बैरी शीरसड़ा (म्हे)। आज कींयां हु गो हरियो (डाळ)। दरबार का हुकमूं बेटी का बाप बा नरां नै तो भूल गो (म्हे)। हेंर हरियो गेमड हु गो (वाह वाह)। कीयो भाट गेलो कींयां हु गो तूं (हां गेलो कींयां है कीयो)। सूखयोड़ी डाळियां है जकी पाछी हरी कींयां हुई तनै सोच तो है (हां तनै ठा है कांई कीयो)। क्युं खोदे जड़ म्हारी सेवळियां (म्हे)। क्युं म्हनै जिकोला ऊनाळो की (बाळ)। गोठां में औतार दे दियो बालो ठाकर देवजी (म्हे)। जरां भाट म्हारी जड़ गैइ (पियाल)। पताला बैठ गी पाछी (वाह वाह)। भगवान औतार लियो जी टैम में (हां जकै टैम पाछो हरियो व्हियो)। भाट देखियो थारी मां जाणु बण को पोध है जको ही भगवान नै ओळखै (वाह वाह)। अती कांई अब (म्हे)। तो शीरस से भाट बिदा होतां ओळभो देतां (म्हे)। हेंर भूणा को हेरो होतां भाट बिदा होतां जय बोलो श्री देवनारायण की (जय)। दरबार का

हुकमूं लेरै भगवान कीयो सुण भाट (म्हे)। म्हांका घणा वादा कोनी है जेज मत लगाज्यो (हां घणा टैम मत लगार आज्यो कीयो)। दरबार का हुकमूं बगड़ावतां को भाट आम्बासर की बावड़ी पूगतो (व्हियो जी कीयो)। भाट मन में देखियो के बावड़ी के पणियारियां के समचार व्हियां से तो टैम घणी लाग जाय (म्हे)। हेंर आ पणियारां नै देखां आपां ओळखा कोनी ओळखा देखां पणियारां आपां नै (हां ओळखै कोनी ओळखै देखां)। भाट नारदी पेड़ी पर बैठ चोखी तरह कुल्ला अर पाखळा (करबा लाग्यो)। तो पाणी ही नै (म्हे)। भाट बैठो बी टैम में बगड़ावत मरिया पछै बावड़ी को पाणी पताल में बड़ गो (वाह वाह)। तो भाट बूझणा करी ए बावड़ी (म्हे)। अती ऊंडी कींयां आगी भैइ जका समचार कहवो (हां कह कीयो)। कीयो भाट कांई बूझै बात नै तूं (म्हे)। के भाटां भेळा करिया बगड़ावत कीयो (वाह वाह)। दरबार का हुकमूं चिन्नार मूंगी कर गा एक कीरत बगड़ावतां की बोल नौ पेड़ी उबक से आय सामै पाणी (हां ऊंची आवूं कीयो)। दरबार का हुकमूं बांकी चिनायोड़ो हूं (म्हे)। एक कीरत कह दे भैइ (हां एक कीरत कहतां ही नौ पेड़ी तांईं उबक (जावूं कीयो)। कीयो भगवान को भेज्योड़ो आयो नै पछै दीखै कोनी तनै (वाह वाह)। ए कागद देख ले (म्हे)। दरबार का हुकमूं बगड़ावतां को नांव लेतां देव को नांव लेतां जळ आ पताल के मांयनू ऊंचो (हां)। नौ पेड़ी भाट के (हां ऊंचो आयो)। भाट कुल्ला पाखळा कर (म्हे)। हेंर बी जागावूं बिदा (व्हेग्यो)। लेणूदी कुमहारी के घरां (पूगतो व्हियो जी कीयो)। दिन तो आंत गो (वाह वाह खुवा पियो)। मन में देखियो (म्हे)। कलाळी की हेली आंतरै रह गी (आंतरै है)। रात रात अठै ही रहवां (लेणूदी के घरां) ही रहवां (जरां बात जुगत बैठ जावे)। भाट बगड़ावतां को कांई लेणूदी कुमहारी के घरां (जावे)। कांई कुमहारी जातो बतलावै देखां (कीआवूं जाणज्यो देखां अब कीआवूं)। अबार कहवूं भगवान देव का हुकमूं देखां (वाह वाह जी वाह वाह)।।

ए माथावूं दियाड़ो जी ढळ गो बेटी कुमहार की रे।
माच गी बाळा ये धूंदळ मांयनै खेव।
रात रात को बासो लेवूं ये बेटी कुमहार की।
परभातै बाळा ये आंधी गिणो नै मेव।।
(भलां जी भलां) देव भलां

माथावूं दियाड़ो ढळ गो (म्हे)। माची धूंदळ मांयनै (खेव)। रात रात को बासो लेवूं बेटी कुमहार की परभातै बाळा आंधी गिणो नै (कोय मेव)। परभात हो जायी नै (म्हे)। मैं म्हारो बेगो ही (बीर हो जावूं कीयो)। ओ समचार कुण कीयो (बैइ को भाट कीया जी कीयो)। लेणूदी कुमहारी बोलै (म्हे)। कांई भाट नै समचार कहवै देखां (कीआवूं जाणज्यो कीआवूं देखां)। अबार कहवूं भगवान देव का हुकमूं ले तूं (वाह वाह जी)।।

ए पोळ में तो जी पुन्या बड़ै रे परदेशी पंछड़ा रे।
गुआड़ै बैठै जी छालर भींडळ गाय।
डेरा कर दे अड़दू का बजार में।
भूखा रहवै तो पंछी राबड़ी पीज्यो आय।।
(भलां जी भलां) देव भलां

पोळ में भैइ पुन्या बड़ै (म्हे)। अरै गुआड़ा में बैठै छालर भींडळ (गाय)। तूं डेरा कर पंछी बजार में अड़दू का में (वाह वाह)। भूखो रहवै तो राबड़ी पीज्यै (आ अर)। घरां रहबाळो को बिचार कोनी भैइ (हां म्हारो बिचार कोनी जगां की कोनी अठै)। भूखो तिसियो होवै नै (म्हे)। तो म्हानै घरां (राबड़ी पी जावो अर बीर हो जावो)। भाट बोलै कांई लेणूदी कुमहारी नै समचार कहवै देखां (कीआवूं जाणज्यो कीआवूं देखां)।।

म्हाना घोड़ा को जी जो पत्थरणो बिछावूं ये बेटी कुमहार की रे।
जावूं बाळाजी ओटयाना में सोय।
बेळियां ऊठ रस्तै लाग जावूं बेटी कुमहार की।
पत्थरणा नै लेवूं ये नाड़ी खावड़ै धोय।।
(भलां जी भलां) देव भलां

म्हारा घोड़ा को है नै ओ (म्हे)। पत्थरणो (बिछा लेवूं कीयो)। जावूं थारा ओटयाणा में (सोय)। भेळिया ऊठ रस्तै लागू बेटी कुमहार की (म्हे)। पत्थरणो नै लेवूं नाड़ी खावड़ै (आगै धोय)। पत्थरणो खराब हुई और तो की कोनी होवै (वाह वाह)। आगै जार म्हारावूं धोलेवू (म्हे)। अर साबन भैइ सरफ लगा देवां और तो कांई करां (वाह वाह)। रात रात नै तो बाळा (हां बासो म्हनै अठै ही द्यो कीयो)। कीयो नी रे भाट (म्हे)। कोनी रहबा को बिचार कोनी (हां अठै बिचार कोनी)। दरबार का हुकमूं कांई करियो के मन में देखियो देव महाराज को कीयोड़ो है (म्हे)। देव को नांव लेय बगड़ावतां को भाट जेब में हाथ (घालियो)। तो पांच मोहर धोकड़ा का खिरा (नीकलयाया जी कीयो)। कीयो लेणूदी कुमहारी (म्हे)। ले भैइ बासो तो भला ही थारै खुशी पड़ै तो (हां दाय पड़ै तो देय)। ए पांच मोहर साडूमाता तनै कांचळी की (दीनी है)। दरबार का हुकमूं लेणूदी कुमहारी बूझणा करी रे भाट (म्हे)। तूं बगड़ावतां का नी होवै (हां बो ई तो कोनी है कीयो)। कीयो सागै को सागै (हां हूं कीयो)। कीयो भाट रे बगड़ावतां मरिया पछै कम दीखै भायां (म्हे)। तनै पछाड़ियो कोनी (हां पछाड़ियो कोनी कीयो)। कीयो अब (अब पछाड़ियो)। दरबार का हुकमूं कांई कुमहार नै लेणूदी कुमहारी नै हुकम देवै (म्हे)। कांई भाट नै बासो दे देवै देखां (देखां कीआवूं जाणज्यो कीआवूं जाणज्यो)।।

ए पोळमूं पुन्या तगड़ द्यो जी जो बेटा कुमहार का रे।
गूआड़ा सूं घेर दे रे छालर भींडळ गाय।
घणा दिनावूं आयगो परदेशी पांवणा।
हुवै म्हारै रे बांतां का बिचार।।
(भलां जी भलां) देव भलां

पोळमूं तो पुन्या नै घेर दे (म्हे)। गुआड़ा से घेर भैइ छालर भींडळ (अब गाय)। ओ घणा दिनवूं आय रे भैइ परदेशी पांवणो (म्हे)। म्हारै हुई बै बांतां का (बिचार)। दुख सुख की बात करां भैइ (हां बगड़ावतां की घर की दुख सुख की मैं (बांतां करां कीयो)। कुमहार भाट ताणी दो माचा ल्यावो (वाह वाह)। कुमहार भाज्यो जको भाटजी ताणी दो माचा (लियार ढाल दिन्या)। एक माचा पर तो भाटजी कमर

खोल दी (म्हे)। एक माचा पर (बिराजमान हो ग्या जी कीयो)। कुमहारी तातो पाणी कर भाट की पग चम्पी (लागी)। सेर पांच एक चन्ना मोठ दळ (म्हे)। घोड़ा के पावरो (हां चड़ा दियो)। चोखी तरह गहूंवां का फैंपड़ा पोय (अर भाट राजा नै जीमाया जी कीयो)। बगड़ावतां का घर की दुख की सुख की रात दोन्यु जणा (हां बांतां करी)। तो परभात को टैम (व्ही ग्यो)। फूलरिया घोड़ा पर आपको पाछो जीण (हां माण्ड लियो)। जीण माण्ड मन में बिचार (करियो है)। के रात तो भगवान तनै मोहरां दे दी (म्हे)। जरां बासो (दे दियो)। आपां आया भूणाजी के (म्हे)। कांई ठी तो छै महीना लागी कांई ठी बारह महीना (हां लाग जावे)। आज शाम का मोहरां में देवै अर कोय (देवै नी कीयो)। अरै मोहरां दे देर (बासा किताक दिन रहसियां कीयो)। ए मोहरां तो पाछी लेवां जरां तो जुगत ही (बैठ जावै कीयो)। बीर व्है ग्यो लेणूदी कुमहारी (म्हे)। हां बीरा भाट बोल (हां रात म्हारा हाथवूं अन्याय मोटी हो गी कीयो)। कांई (जकी बता)। कीयो मैं नागौर रियो (म्हे)। नागौर के मांयनै देख गरम नरम म्हारै कन्नै मोहरां (मोकळी बापरियोड़ी ही)। साडूमाता मोहर दी जकी ई जेब में (रह गी)। रात बाळां ये बै खोटोड़ी मोहरां है जकी तनै (हां देयजगी कीयो)। ओ काम हु गो ऊंधो (हां ओ ऊंधो काम हु गो मां कीयो)। कीयो रे भाटजी (म्हे)। कह बहन बेटी नै कांचळी नी देनी (म्हे)। जै देवै (तो चोखी देवणी ही)। बाहरें महीना तो गमोड़ अर (पहर लेवे)। फाटै राळी जरै राळी गुदड़ा में (हां घाल अर बाहरें महीना (बियां ओड़ै कीयो)। कीयो बीसी की बीसी देवूं सागै के सागै लेयां (बै पाछै दे) म्हनै पाछै दे (वाह वाह)। तो लेणूदी कुमहारी कन्नु ले मोहरां राताली पाछी (म्हे)। जेब में (हाथ घालियो)। दरबार का हुकमूं टकां की कोथळी (हां काढ लीनी)। ले भैइ रेणूड़ी कुमहारी (म्हे)। ओ टका तो रात बास उतरिया जका को (ले लेवो)। हेंर ओ टको घोड़ा नै दाणो दियो नै (हां बीको ले ले)। ओ टको दो बाटियां दिया म्हनै (हां बै ले ले कीयो)। रांड टका तीन व्हिया कसम की कमाई मेलली मोहरां बाप की थोड़ी थारी (हां पंचतोली मोहरां पांच ले ली कीयो)। अतरी कह फूलरिया घोड़ा नै हांक दियो (वाह वाह चालो)। कुमहारी मन में देखियो राम मारियो सांची करी (म्हे)। बासो ही तो ले गो (वाह वाह)। हेंर मोहरां पाछी (ले ग्यो कीयो)। पण इस्यो काम कर (म्हे)। रावजी का अमरावां के मांय चौगीनो तूं करज्या आगो (हां जांवता ही ईनै घाणी) (में घाल अर पहल देज्यू)। तो रेणूड़ी कुमहारी ऊंची रंग महलां चड़ गी (म्हे)। कांई रावजी का अमरावां नै हेला मारै देखां (कीआवूं जाणज्यो भोपाजी महाराज (अब कीआवूं देखां)। अबार कहवूं देव का हुकमूं ले तूं (वाह वाह जी वाह वाह)।।

हेलो सुणज्यो जी ए ई राजा नीमदे औवूं रे।
हेलो सुणज्यै रे दीयाजी अपळी बाण।
राण में अग्यो रे बगड़ावतालो भाटड़ो।
परभातै ले जावै रे भूणो अपळी बाण।।
(भलां जी भलां) देव भलां

हेलो सुणज्यै राजा नीमदे (म्हे)। अरै सुणज्यै दीयाजी अबळी (तूं बाण)। ओ राण शहर में आयगो आज बगड़ावतां को भाट (वाह वाह)। परभातै ले जायै कोय भूणाजी अबळी (बाण)। थां कन्नै भूणोजी है (म्हे)। ई को लेवाळ आयगो भैइ (हां लेवाळ आयग्यो है कीयो)। भाट कीयो रांड मरै म्हनै तो

(हां चौगीनो करै है नै कीयो)। कीयो करूं तो कींयां कोनी तूं चोखी कर गो नै (वाह वाह)। कीयो ठहर जा (ठहर कीयो अठै ही रही)। घोड़ा नै ठाम दियो बगड़ावतां को भाट (वाह वाह)। ठाम घोड़ा नै बोलै अर कांई समचार कहवै भाट ही देखां (कीआवूं जाणज्यो भोपाजी महाराज अब कीआवूं देखां)। अबार कहवूं धणी का हुकमूं कांह भैइ (वाह वाह सा)।।

अबकाळै हेलो सुणज्यो जी जो दीयाजी जोधका रे।
सुणलीज्यै भैइ रे नीमा राज कुंवार।
बगड़ावतां को घर को अटूट पोरसो।
ओ तो निमा रे लेणूदी के पास।।
(भलां जी भलां) देव भलां

अबकाळ हेलो सुण भैइ दीयाजी जोधका (वाह वाह)। हेलो सुणज्यो नीमाजी राज (कुंवार)। अरै बगड़ावतां को घर को बो अटूट पोरसो (म्हे)। है ई लेणूदी के (पास)। बगड़ावतां की सारी धन मांया है नै (हां ई लेणूदी कुमहारी कन्नै है कीयो)। कुमहारी कीया राम मारिया टाबरियो मंगल होवै (हां बड़ो करी की म्हारो कीयो)। कीयो करै कठै हाल (अब करस्यूं ठहर)। हाल तो बड़यों हूं राण शहर में (वाह वाह)। कीयो में नांव कोनी लेवूं (हां भागजा कीयो तूं)। तूं आगै जा थारो (वाह वाह)। बजार के मांयनै कर बगड़ावत भाट बहरियो (म्हे)। रावजी साय को गांगो भाट नै सामा (मिल ग्या जी कीयो)। चोखी तरह (बाही पसार)। मिल गा (वाह वाह)। बगड़ावतालां भाट की मां ही नागौर की ही (म्हे)। हेंर गांगा भाट की मां ही (नागौर की ही जी कीयो)। ए मासिया भाई लागता (वाह वाह)। बूझणा करी रे भाट रात कठै हो भैइ (हां रात कठा हा भैइ कीयो)। कीयो लेणूदी कुमहारी के घरां (हा कीयो)। कीयो आज जरां (आज तो थांकाळै घरां चांलां कीयो)। ओ ले (वाह वाह)।।

घोड़ा ही छूट गा जी जो मकेरै परा आग्या रे मासी आया बीरजी ई रे।
घरां टाबरां नै रे माता केरो खेरूं भाव।
डेरा कर द्यो अड़दू का बजार में।
भूखो रहवै तो भाटजी रे राबड़ी पीज्यो आय।।
(भलां जी भलां) देव भलां

घोड़ा छूट गा भैइ (म्हे)। मकेरै परा आग्या घरां देख टाबरां नै है माता को (भाव)। तूं डेरा कर देय पंछी बजार में (वाह वाह)। भूखो रहवै तो राबड़ी पीज्यै म्हारै घरां (आय)। रहबा को बिचार कोनी (हां अठै रहणो को बिचार कोय नी कीयो टाबरां नै) (माता को भाव है)। थारै कन्नै टारड़ो है (हां छोत पड़ जाय तो माता बिगड़ जावे)। ओ समचार कुण कीयो (गांगा भाट कीयो जी कीयो)। बगड़ावतां को भाट बोलै कांई गांगो नै फैर बतलावै देखां (कीआवूं जाणज्यो भोपाजी महाराज अब कीआवूं)। अबार कहवां धणी देव का हुकमूं कह द्यां भाई (वाह वाह जी वाह वाह)।।

ए तूं रे ताणा बाबोजी तो जी आगला के घरां दो दो माचां
पर कमरियां खोलता रे।

भाट गांगला रे बांतां तणा लबाळ।
आयोड़ा भाटां नै नी दिया कदै बैसणा।
भाट गांगलिया रे ठेट का लोड़ी टाल।।
(भलां जी भलां) किषन भलां

देमाली नाथ को नांव लेवां (म्हे)। सदा ही (भलां जी कीयो)। दरबार का हुकमूं छोछू भाट समचार कीयो है (म्हे)। कीयो तूं ताणो अर बाबोजी आगला घरां दो दो ही माचां कमरियां खोली (वाह वाह)। थै हो ठेट का बांतां तणा (लबाळ)। अरै आयोड़ा भाटां नै कदै नी दिया बैसणा (म्हे)। भाट गांगला ठेट का लोड़ी (टाल)। ओ घर है नै ठेट को लोड़ी टाल है (हां का ही टाळवा हो थे)। न्याती का बेटा ने राबड़ी पायोड़ी याद कोनी आवै भैइ (वाह वाह)। घरां डोरी पड़ै जरां ईंयां ही होवै (हां ईंयां होवै कीयो)। कीयो रे भाट रावजी का अमरावां नै ठा हो जावै (म्हे)। के गांगा भाट के घरां बगड़ावतां को भाट (हां आयग्यो)। अरै तनै तो मारै जको मारै (हां सागै म्हनै औरूं मारै कीयो)। आ मौत क्युं खरीदे रे भैइ (वाह वाह)। बूझणा करी कोय बिचार कोनी डरी मत तूं (वाह वाह)। मोआ घरां जावूं (म्हे)। थानै जियान का घरां में की ना आवै गेलो (हां रहवूं कोनी कीयो)। बजार में मुण्डा के परमा मोदी की दुकान आयगी (वाह वाह)। जो बगड़ावत आतां नै राण शहर में (म्हे)। जी दिन परमा मोदी को सामान दुकान से जांवतो (सगळो को सगळो बटवूं जांवता जी कीयो)। दरबार का हुकमूं बगड़ावतां को भाट बोलै (म्हे)। कांई परमा मोदी नै बतलावै जांतो ही (कीआवूं जाणज्यो देखां अब कीआवूं)। अबार कहवां सा देव का हुकमूं देखां (वाह वाह जी वाह वाह)।।

ए हाट उघाड़ो जी जो परमा मोदी का रे डावड़ा रे।
हुवै डावड़ा जी घड़ी घड़ी ऊंवार।
इन्द्रासन नू पाछा दारू पीबा नै आयग्या रे बेटा बाघ का।
बांका डेरा रे व्हिया नोलकै बाग।।
(भलां जी भलां) देव भलां

हाट उघाड़ दे (म्हे)। परमा मोदी का डावड़ा होवै घड़ी घड़ी (म्हनै ऊंवार)। अरै इन्द्रासन नू पाछा आया बेटा बाघ का (वाह वाह)। बांका डेरा हो गा सीरै नोलकै (बाग)। इन्द्रासन सूं बगड़ावत आयगा (वाह वाह)। जो दुकान को थारो सामान पहली जातो नै (हां बो सगळो)। रसोई पाणी को (हां बो सगळो को सगळो जाय तियारी कर पूगाय कीयो)। दरबार का हुकमूं परमो मोदी बोलै (म्हे)। कांई भाट नै बतलावै देखां (कीआवूं जाणज्यो अब कीआवूं देखां)।

ए गेलो ऊबो तो जी भाटजी तूं बावळो रे।
हो गो दीखै जी बनखण्ड मांयलो मोर।
कठूं दीखिया बेटा रे बाघ का।
देखयायो भाटजी रे गैलै ही बहता और।।
(भलां जी भलां) किषन भलां

देमाली नाथ का नांव लेवां (म्हे)। सदा ही (भलां जी कीयो)। कीयो गेलो हो गो दीखै भाट बावळो (वाह वाह)। हु गो बनखण्ड मांयलो (मोर)। अरै कठवूं ल्यायो बेटा बाघ का (म्हे)। देखियै भाट गैलै जातां (तूं और)। कात्तिक को महीनो है आज (वाह वाह)। गैलै गैले पुष्कर के मेलै जातरी (हां जा रिया है कीयो)। नंगारबंदी सिरदार घणा ही जावै (म्हे)। राजावो को मेलो को बो पहली (वाह वाह)। किस्यो (पुष्कर को)। घोड़ा घोड़ी आतां जरूर (वाह वाह)। दरबार का हुकमूं तूं आयो कीनै जका समचार कह रिया है (हां सूल कह कीयो)। परमा मोदी की नजर चकाय (म्हे)। जेब में हाथ देव को नांव घाल पांच मोहर नीकली धोकड़ा खिरा दुकान के मांयलै छेड़ै भगा दी (हां छानै से भगा दी जी कीयो)। कीयो परमा सामान कोनी दे (हां कोनी द्यूं कीयो)। अरै गेलो हो गो किस्या सामान है कद मरिया बगड़ावत तनै ठा है (वाह वाह)। रोळा कत्तो करिया (म्हे)। मिठाई की छाबड़ी भाट उठार बिदा (हां व्है ग्यो)। परमो मोदी कीयो ठहर जा घणा दिन व्हिया तनै (हां चोर है कीयो)। खोल जूता (म्हे)। परमो मोदी लेरावूं नावड़ गो (वाह वाह)। शहर का महाजन भेळा हो गा (म्हे)। कीयो लाखीणो तो आदमी है लाख का कपड़ा है ई कन्नै (हां पहरण नै)। लाखीणी जोड़ी पगरखी (है नी ई के)। तूं दरबार का हुकमूं ई की शान कींयां गुमावै रे भैइ (हां परमा मोदी ईंयां कींयां करे कीयो)। भाट बूझणा करी सेठ साहूकारां (म्हे)। ई की दुकान के मांयनै समालो लियो भैइ कांई कत्तो माल मूल है (हां कतेक माल को धणी है कीयो)। कीयो सौ दोय सौ तो मोकळा है ई के (वाह वाह)। मोहरां कीयो मोहरां ई का बाप दादा ही कोनी देखी (हां ई कन्नै है ही कठूं कीयो)। कीयो मोहरां दुकान में लाध जावै जरां तो चोर है परमु (हां)। नी जरां भैइ मैं चोर (हूं ही कीयो)। निंगैवान गिया तो धोकड़ा खिरा पांच मोहर (दुकान के मांयलै छेड़ै मिली जी कीयो)। कीयो परमा मोदी (म्हे)। मोहरां तो ले ली लेख को हिसाब हाल करियो कोनी (हां करियो ई कोनी)। हेंर इजत गुमावै आदमी (वाह वाह)। भाट खोल जूता तीन चार माथा में जूता की (हां परमा मोदी की मेली जी कीयो)। कीयो रे भाट इयां कींया करै (हां ईंयां क्युं करै है कीयो)। तूं आयो की ताणो बै समचार कह (सूल के)। कीयो मैं आयो तो और ही कामवूं (म्हे)। पण तूं तो बासो देवै कोनी तूं रहबा दे कोनी (वाह वाह)। कलाळी के हेली जावो जको गेलो भूल गो (हां कलाळी की हेली को म्हनै गेलो म्हनै बता द्यो कीयो)। तो परमो मोदी बोलै (वाह वाह)। कांई कलाळी का हेली का गेला बतावै देखां (कीआवूं जाणज्यो भोपाजी महाराज कीआवूं देखां)। अबार कहवूं भगवान का हुकमूं ले तूं (वाह वाह सा)।।

बिदा हो जावो जी ए ई परदेशी पंछड़ा रे।
तूं तो भाई रे मती लागावो बार।
बा सामी दीखै रंग पातर की कोटड़ियां।
बठै भाटजी रे चुगै परेवो दाल।।
(भलां जी भलां) देव भलां

भाट बिदा हुई जा कीयो (म्हे)। मती लागावो (बार)। सामी दीखै रंग पातर की कोटड़ियां (वाह वाह)। बठै चुगै परेवां (दाल)। परेवो जानवर है नै (म्हे)। कलाळी की हेली मिलै और कोनी मिलै (हां और जगा नैइ मिलेलो कीयो)। दरबार का हुकमूं परमो मोदी बोलै (म्हे)। कांई भाट नै पूरी कड़ी बतावै

(कीआवूं जाणज्यों कीआवूं देखां)। अबार कहवां देव का हुकमूं देखां।।

सीधो जाज्यो जी ए ई बिदा बीरा जी रे।
भाट नारदी मत जाज्यो और गलियां ई रे।
चिन्नार मूंगी कर गा रे बेटा बाघ का।
लगाय गा भाटजी रे सोना की कळियां रे।।
(भलां जी भलां) किषन भलां

देव को नांव ल्या सदा ही (भलां ही जी कीयो)। दरबार का हुकमूं तूं बिदा ही हो जा कीयो (वाह वाह)। भाट नारदी मत जाज्यै और (गलियां)। अरै चिन्नार मूंगी कर गा बेटा बाघ का लगाय गा सोना की (कळियां)। सोना की कळी (हां बी हेली की है कीयो)। और गांव में शहर में कोय मकान के कोनी (वाह वाह)।

ए बिदा हो जावो जी जो परदेशी पंछड़ा रे।
तूं तो भाटजी रे मती लागावो बार।
सामी दीखै रंग पातर की कोटड़ियां रे।
बठै मुण्डा के रे केळ जबूकै बार।।
(भलां जी भलां) देव भलां

अब बिदा हो जाय कीयो (म्हे)। भाट नारदी मती लगावो (बार)। सामी दीखै रंग पातर की कोटड़ियां (वाह वाह)। बठै केळ जबूकै बार (बार)। भाट (म्हे)। केळ को रूंख देख बी जागां एक ही जागां है (हां दूसरी जगा नैइ है कीयो)। बगड़ावतां को भाट हो जको फूलरिया घोड़ा नै बटवूं (हांक दिन्यो)। तो दरबार का हुकमं कलाळी के हेली पूगतो (हां भाट व्हियो है)। तो पोळ तो दरबार का हुकमूं जड़योड़ी पड़ी ही (म्हे)। बारी खुली (पड़ी कीयो)। पोळियो अनण्दरामजी आंधो व्हियोड़ो जको मुण्डा के सुतो पड़ियो (वाह वाह)। भाट बोलै कांई समचार जाता ही पोळिया आनण्दरामजी नै कहवै देखां (कीआवूं जाणज्यो कीआवूं देखां)। अबार कहवां सा देव का हुकमूं ले (वाह वाह जी वाह वाह)।

ए पोळ उघाड़ द्यो जी ए ई पोळिया आनण्दरामजी रे।
होवै म्हनै जी घड़ी घड़ी ऊंवार।
इन्द्रासन नू दारू पीबा नै आयग्या रे बेटा बाघ का।
बांका डेरा रे हु गा नोलकै बाग।।
(भलां जी भलां) देव भलां

पोळ खोल भैइ (म्हे)। पोळिया आनण्दरामजी रे हुवै घड़ी घड़ी (म्हनै ऊंवार)। इन्द्रासन नू दारू पीबा पाछा आयगा बेटा बाघ का (म्हे)। बांका डेरा हो गा नोलकै (बाग)। पोळियो अनण्दरामजी (पोळ खोलो कीयो)। पोळियो अनण्दरामजी बोलै (म्हे)। बूझणा करी रे भाट (वाह वाह)। ग्यारह बरस हो गा भैइ (दरवाजा बन्द करियो नै कीयो)। बारी खुली पड़ी है नै (हां आजावो कीयो मांयने)।।

ए ग्यारह ग्यारह बरस हु गा तो जी दरवाजो झड़िया नै रे बैइ का भाटजी रे।
भाट नारदी ताला के जम गी लील।
कूंचियां को झूमको ले रंग पातर चड़ गी महलां के गोखड़ां।
बगड़ावत मरिया पछै रे सारा होम दियां शरीर।।
(भलां जी भलां) देव भलां

ग्यारह बरस हो गिया नै दरवाजा झड़िया नै (म्हे)। भाटजी ताला के जम गी अब (लील)। अरै कूंचियां को झूमको ले रंग पातर चड़ गी महलां की गोखड़ै (म्हे)। बगड़ावत मरिया पछै सारा होम दियां (शरीर)। कूंचियां म्हार कन्न कोनी (हां म्हारै हाथ मैं कूंचियां रही कोनी कीयो)। दरवाजो तो खुलावै (म्हे)। कलाळी के महलां के हेटै जा (हां तळेटियां जावो कीयो)। बारी खुली पड़ी है (आवै जरां बारी मांय कर आजावो)। घोड़ा समेत असवार चड़ियोड़ो मावै (वाह वाह)। कीयो रे पोळिया अनण्दराम (म्हे)। बारी म्हांकै तो कांई जावां रे है (हां कांई जावां कीयो)। कलाळी के महलां के तळेटै जाय (वाह वाह)। हेंर सुरबीण को बाजो जको भाट (बजाबा लाग्यो जी कीयो)। गोड़ी मलागिरी की राग (हां काढण लाग्यो)। कलाळी नै रंग महलां (ऊंची सुणीजी)। हीड़ागर दासियां (म्हे)। बगड़ावतां का भाट की जियान की बीण की आवाज आयी महल में (हां बीण की की बाजै निंगै करो ए कीयो)। तो सहलियां घाल घाल झरोका में (मुण्डो)। हेंर निंगै करी (वाह वाह)। भाट ऊपरां निंगै करी तो दासियां दीखी (वाह वाह)। भाट बोलै (म्हे)। कांई दासियां नै बतलावै देखां (कीआवूं जाणज्यो अब देखां कीआवूं)। अबार कहवूं देव का हुकमूं ले तूं (वाह वाह जी)।।

ए सातूं बहना तो जी ए ई दीखो दीखो सारसियां रे।
ओड़बा नै बाळां ये झीणी झीणी लोय।
परदेशी पंछी करै थानै बूझणा।
थामाली बाळां ये पातू कुणसी होय।।
(भलां जी भलां) देव भलां

सातूं सहलियां दीखी म्हनै सारसी (वाह वाह)। ओड़बा नै झीणी झीणी (थांकै लोय)। परदेशी पंछी करै बूझणा (म्हे)। थामाली बीरा पातू कुणसी (अब होय)। आ पातू कलाळी बाजै कुण हो थामाली (जकी बातावो बाळां कीयो)। तो सहलियां बोलै (म्हे)। कांई समचार बैइ का भाट बगड़ावतालां नै पाछो कहवै (कीआवूं जाणज्यो देखां कीआवूं)। अबार कहवां भगवान का हुकमूं ल्यो (वाह वाह जी वाह वाह)।। तूं तो तूं म्हारा निरजन तूं तूं तो देव के दाता तूं

ए सातूं बहना तो जी ए ई दीखां सारसियां औवूं रे।
ओड़बा नै म्हांकै जी झीणी झीणी लोय।
मैं तो बाजा जी पातू की छोकरियां।
पातू नै पंछी रे रंग महलां में जोय।।
(भलां जी भलां) देव भलां

दरबार का हुकमूं सातूं बहना सारसी हां (म्हे)। ओड़बा नै झीणी झीणी (म्हांकै लोय)।। मैं तो बाजा रे पंछी पातू की छोकरियां (वाह वाह)। ई पातू नै रंग महलां में (तूं जोय)। मैं तो कलाळी की दासियां हां (हां अठै कोनी नी है बाईजी कीयो)। कीयो जरां बाळां थावूं बात ही कांई करां अब (वाह वाह)। दासियां कांई कलाळी के पाछी महल में (पाछी जावे)। एक जाती देखां समचार कलाळी ने (कांई कहवै देखां कीआवूं (जाणज्यो भोपाजी महाराज अब कीआवूं)। अबार कहवूं देव का हुकमूं ले तूं (वाह वाह जी)।।

पगां लखीणी जी बाईजी म्हारा रे पंछी के मोजड़िया औवूं रे।
बाई म्हारी जी कैळू चटियो हाथ।
गांव नांव तो ये पंछी का भूल ग्या।
एकरसां आंतोजी मितवालां के साथ।।
(भलां जी भलां) देव भलां

पगां लखीणी बाई पंछी के मोजड़ी है (वाह वाह)। कैळू चटियो (अब हाथ)। गांव नांव तो बाईजी ए पंछी का मैं भूल गी (म्हे)। पण एकरसां आतो मीठा मितवालां की (साथ)। बगड़ावतां के साथ आतो नै (जियां को भाट म्हानै लागै है कीयो)। पण नी क्युं फरक तो है (हां क्युं ही तो फरक है)। बगड़ावतां के सागा तो बी दिन साठ बरसां को (डेण हो कीयो)। बाईजी आज तो पच्चीस बरस को जुवान (हां है कीयो)। और ऐनाण-सैनाण बै का बै (सागै है)। बै ई तो गला में तूंबा है (म्हे)। हेंर बो ही फूलरियो (सागै घोड़ो है कीयो)। कलाळी बूझणा (करी है)। दासियां (म्हे)। थानै ई बात को ठा कोनी कीयो (वाह वाह)। भूणा कंवर का हेरा है (म्हे)। बगड़ावतां को भाट सागै है भाट की देही पलटी है भगवान (हां देव महाराज देही पलट अर भेज्यो (है कीयो)। लेयो कूंचियां को झूमको ओ ल्यो (हां जांवो पोळिया अनण्दरामजी नै दे द्यो)। दरवाजो खोल देयलै छेड़ै (म्हे)। भाट मांयनै (आजावै कीयो)। जिका धणी आंटीला (बांका मुंगता आंटीला है कीयो)। बारी मांय कर कींयां आवै भाट (वाह वाह)। दरबार का हुकमूं पोळिया अनण्दरामजी ने ले जार दासियां कूंचियां को झूमको (दे दियो)। पोळियो अनण्दराम बी कूंचियो लगाबा लाग्या ग्यारह बरसां का ताला कीकां खोलै (हां काटवूं काटा भरिया जी कीयो)। भाट कीयो रे पोळिया अनण्दराम (म्हे)। कांई करै (टैम बोहळो लागियो ताला खुलिया कोनी कांई कीयो)। कीयो रे भाट कूंचियां कोनी लागै भैइ कीयो (वाह वाह)। कीयो बगा दे एकानै (हां कूंचियां नै एकानै फैंक द्यो)। देव को नांव ले ताला पर हाथ मेल (हां देव देव करतां जावो अर ताला पर हाथ (मेलता जावो)। देव को नांव लेतो गियो ताला पर हाथ मेलतो गियो (वाह वाह)। भुजागळा परै जांवती जी (पड़ी जी कीयो)। दरवाजा खुलिया अर भाट मांयलै चड़ (बड़तो व्हियो)। दरबार का हुकमूं पोळियो अनण्दरामजी बूझणा (कर लीनी)। भाट (म्हे)। बगड़ावत सुरजी के उगतै दरवाजो म्हार कन्नु (खुलाता)। ए सोना को टको (देतां जी कीयो)। अरै बेटी का बाप एक तांबा को टको दे (वाह वाह)। खाली हाथां दरवाजो खुला लियो म्हारै कन्नु (म्हे)। देव को नांव ले अर भाट जेब में हाथ (घालियो)। बै ई पांच मोहर धोकड़ा खीरा (नीकलया जी कीयो)। ले रे भैइ ओ पोळियो अनण्दराम ओ ले मोहरां जाण भला ही टको जाण पिसियो जाण (हां ए लेयो)। देव

का घर की भाट ने भाट मोहरां देतां पोळिया अनण्दरामजी के (म्हे)। आंधो हो ग्यारह बरसावूं (वाह वाह)। झटकेन आंखियां (खुलतां)। तो भाट दरवाजा में बड़तां हेंर मोहरां हाथ में देतां (देंवतां)। देव महाराज का नांव लेतां आंखियां पोळीरामजी की खुलतां (खुलतां जी कीयो)। जय बोलो श्री देव नारायण की (जय)। बोलो भैइ रे छोटा अर मोटा ही (स)। बगड़ावतां को भाट कलाळी के महल पूगतो (व्हियो जी कीयो)। कलाळी मून की माळा फैरै (वाह वाह)। भगवान का जाप (जपै है)। भाट बोलै (म्हे)। कांई कलाळी नै जांतो बतलावै देखां (कीआवूं जाणज्यो देखां अब कीआवूं)। अबर कह द्यूं भगवान का हुकमूं ले तूं (वाह वाह जी वाह वाह)।।

डूंगर के खिड़का पर जी ए ई ताणी कोटड़ियां रे।
लाग रिया कलाळी ये अजब झरोका बार।
कलाळ बैठो है ताणू जींवतो।
कींयां तज गी ये सोळा सौ सिण्गार।।
(भलां जी भलां) देव भलां

डूंगर के खिड़का पर कलाळी थारी कोटड़ियां है (म्हे)। बाळां लाग रिया अजब झरोका (बार)। ओ कलाळ तो बैठो ये कलाळी ताणो जींवतो (म्हे)। कींयां तज गी सोळा सौ (अब सिण्गार)। सोळा सौ सिण्गार बतीसूं आभण कर दी तूं (हां आगा कींयां तज अर बैठी है कीयो)। धोला कींयां लिया (वाह वाह)। कलाळी बोलै कांई समचार भाट नै कहवै देखां (कीआवूं जाणज्यो देखां कीआवूं)।।

चार बात का जी जो खण लियोड़ा बीरा भाटजी रे।
भाट नारदी अन्न बिन रियो नी जाय।
सोळा सौ सिण्गार बतीसूं आभण जरां करूं बीरा भाटजी।
बगड़ावत बिराजे रे सोहन कटोरै आय।।
(भलां जी भलां) किषन भलां

दरबार का हुकमूं चार बात का भाट म्हारै खण ले लिया बगड़ावत नै व्हिया जरां (म्हे)। हेंर अन्न बिन रियो नी (जाय)। सोळा सौ सिण्गार बतीसूं आभण जरां करूंला (म्हे)। अरै बगड़ावत बिराजै सोहन कटोरै (अब आर)। चौईस भाई आवै बगड़ावत बैठ सोहन कटोरो पर दारू पीयै (वाह वाह)। जरां सोळा सौ सिण्गार बतीसूं आभण (हा करूं कीयो)। कीयो भाट (म्हे)। अरै बगड़ावतां मरिया पछै बेकीयोड़ो फिरै (हां बेकीज्योड़ो फिरै तूं तो)। गेलो हु गो को भाटजी बावलो (वाह वाह)। हु गो दीखै बनखण्ड मांयलो ही (तूं मोर)। कठूं ल्यायो बेटा बाघ का (वाह वाह)। देख तूं गैलै जातां ही (ओर)। गैलै जातां और देखियायो भाई (वाह वाह)। तो भाट बैइ को बोलै (म्हे)। कलाळी बोलै अर भाटजी सुणै (कीआवूं जाणज्यो भोपाजी महाराज अब कीआवूं देखां)। अबार कहवूं धणी का हुकमूं (वाह वाह जी वाह वाह)।।

ए बगड़ावतां रा खेतरां पर तो जी जो खेजड़ा बद ग्या रे।
बद गी भाटजी रे गांठियावाली धोब।

कठवूं ल्यायो बेटा तूं बाघ का।
बांका सहला ऊपरै घास चरै है ढोर।।
(भलां जी भलां) देव भलां

बगड़ावतां का सहला पर भाट खेजड़ा बद गा भैइ (वाह वाह)। दरबार का हुकमूं अब बद गी गांठियावाली (अब धोब)। तूं कठवूं ल्यायो बेटा बाघ का (म्हे)। बांका सहला पर भाट घास चरै (ढोर)। दिन ढोर चरै बठै (वाह वाह)। बगड़ावतां नै कठवूं ल्यायो तूं (हां कठवूं ल्यायो पाछा कीयो)।।

ए बगड़ावतां रा सहला पर तो जी जो खेजड़ा बद ग्या रे।
भाट नारदी धोळा धन व्हिया ई रे।
कठवूं ल्यायो बेटा तूं बाघ का।
हत्यारी पापणी रे हाथां होम दिया रे।।
(भलां जी भलां) देव भलां

बगड़ावतां का खेतरां पर भाट खेजड़ा ही बद गा (म्हे)। दरबार का हुकमूं धोळा धन (ऊपर फिरिया)। कठवूं ल्यायो बेटा बाघ का हत्यारी पापणी हाथां ही होम ही (दिया जी कीयो)। हाथावूं होमिया बा नै (वाह वाह)। भाट जिन्दा कर कठवूं ल्यायो (हां पाछा कठवूं ल्यायो कीयो)। कीयो कलाळी (म्हे)। बगड़ावत दारू पीबा नै आयगा (हां आयग्या तूं ठांयचै कर पूरी)। थारी जो मितवाल होती नी बगड़ावतां की पहली बा (म्हे)। ग्यारह बरसावूं आज पूरी मितवाल हुई पाछी (हां होयली कीयो)।

ए गांव गियोड़ा होवै तो जी आजावै बीरा भाट जी रे।
आजावै भाटजी रे देशां परदेशां गिया रे।
कठवूं ल्यायो तूं बै बेटा बाघ का।
बगड़ावत भाटजी रे कुण से पंत गिया रे।।
(भलां जी भलां) देव भलां

गांव गियोड़ा होवै तो भाट आजावै (वाह वाह)। हेंर आजावै भैइ देशां परदेशां (गिया)। तूं कठवूं ल्यायो बेटा बाघ का (म्हे)। बगड़ावत भाट किस्यै पंत (गिया कीयो)। तनै ठा तो है बगड़ावत आबालै गैलै गिया है बिना आबाले गैलै (हां गैलै गिया है जकी तनै ठा कोनी कांई कीयो)। भाट आबलै गैलै बगड़ावत कोनी गिया (वाह वाह)। बिना आबाळा गैलै जातां रिया (वाह वाह)। पाछा कोनी आवै (म्हे)। तूं आयो की नै जका समचार कह कीयो (हां सूल माण्ड अर बात कहवे)। कीयो कलाळी मैं तो आयो तो भाई जो दरबार का हुकमूं बगड़ावतां का आवूठाण देखाबा आयो मैं (म्हे)। कीयो जरां अठै क्युं बैठो (हां आ म्हारै सागै मैं दिखावूं)। बगडावतां का आवूठाण और सोहन कटोरा अलूप निराप (?) (हां दिखावूं कीयो)। पकड़ बांवल्यो अर भाट सोहन कटोरा पर ले जार भाट नै छोड़ दियो (वाह वाह)। तो बगड़ावतां की नोपत ही दारू पीबा की बजातां नी डाको देता जर (म्हे)। कलाळी की हेली रहती (वाह वाह)। भाट के निंगै (हां आयगी)। कीयो कलाळी कलाळी (हां आ कांई है बाळां कीयो)। कीयो नोपत है नै (हां नोपत है कीयो)। थारै नोपत कांई करै तूं (हां काम ही कांई है कीयो)। कीयो

बगड़ावत एक लाख की म्हारी हेली पर दारू (पींवता हा)। एक डंको नौपत पर (देवतां जी कीयो)। दोय लाख की दारू (पींवता)। दो डंका (देता कीयो)। तीन लाख की दारू उपड़ जाती (म्हे)। तीन डंका (हां देवतां)। राण खुमाण (सारी की सारी धूजती जी कीयो)। रावजी के डेरै ठा हो जातो की तीन लाख की दारू आज उपड़ गी (हां बगड़ावतां का डेरा में उपड़ी है जी कीयो)। बगड़ावतां को भाट तो ढाल गोड़ी कचूस अर बाद बी नै बैठी कर दी (हां सुंई करी है)। दरबार का हुकमूं डाका पड़िया सरै (म्हे)। गिणती कोनी राखी (हां पांच चार डाका ठोकिया ही गियो)। तो दरबार हुकमूं कीयो रे भाट (म्हे)। टापरो मंगल कर दियो (हां म्हारो टापरो तूं मंगल कर दिन्यो)। उनै आव कीयो औरूं तनै बगड़ावतां का आवूठाण दिखावूं (हां ए दिखाया कोनी आगला दिखावूं चाल कीयो)। आगै सात भंवरा में ऊंडो बाड़ भाट के आडा ताला लगा दिया (ताला ठोक दिन्या)। राम मारिया थारो डोळ ईंयां को है अठै चमचेड़िया खाबा दियो (हां अठै पड़ियो रे चमचेड़ा खावो तनै)। रावजी के कछेड़ी में ठा हु गो (म्हे)। दीया मीर कलाळी के हेली ग्यारह बरसावूं नोपत पछी बाजी आज (आज कींयां बाजी कीयो)। तो के तो तीन लाख की दारु पीबालो सिरदार आज (हां आयो हे जकै नै म्हारै सामनै ल्यावो)। नितर बगड़ावतां का बीजक कलाळी को ई दाब मेलिया जका आज (परगट करियो है कीयो)। बी नै भी सामनै ल्यावो (वाह वाह)। जावो (बेगा चड़ाई करो)। काळू मीर दीयोजी पांच पांच से घोड़ा अर पांच पांच से असवार लेर (हां चड़ाई करी है)। घोड़ा नै हांक दिया (वाह वाह)। दरबार का हुकमूं कलाळी के हली पूगता (व्हिया जी कीयो)। कलाळी कांई करियो (म्हे)। ले लोहै को झूमरो (वाह वाह)। रंग महलां ऊपर (हां ऊंची चड़ी)। तोड़ा छाज्जा (अर नोपत के ऊपर राळ दिया जी कीयो)। मून की माळा फैरबा लागी अर भगवान का जाप (जपबा लागी)। मीर नै बूझणा करी रे मीर निंगै करो भैइ (हां) कलाळी नै बतला (हां बतलावो कीयो)। मीर आर कीयो ए कलाळी कलाळी (हां कहवो भैइ कहवो)। कीयो के तो तीन लाख की दारू पीबालो सिरदार जको म्हानै सामनै (हां सामनै कर कीयो)। नीतर बगड़ावतां का बीजक दाब मेलिया है तूं (आज परगट करियो थै बी नै सामनै ल्या कीयो)। ए श्री महाराज (म्हे)। कठै तो धरतीमाता पर तीन लाख की दारू पीबाळा सिरदार है (हां रिया कोनी)। हेंर कठै म्हारै कन्नै (बगड़ावतां का बीजक दाव नै हा कीयो)। बगड़ावतां थकां (म्हे)। पिसियो मोकळियो म्हारै कन्नै (बापरियो)। केई दूर में भींतड़ा जका (हां खड़िया करवा दिया जी कीयो)। बगड़ावतां मरिया पछै म्हारै कन्नै तो पिसियो तो एक ही (बापरै कोनी)। शहर का टाबर रह गा राम मारियो (कीं अचपळा)। भींतां के लेव कोनी लाग्यो (हां लेव लाग्यो कोनी रातयूं छाज्जा पर कूदे)। छाज्जा टूटै करमा की मतेई नोपत ही (बाजै कीयो)। मीर ही ऊबो दीयोजी बूझणा करी रे मीर (हां निंगै पाड़ देखां)। दरबार का हुकमूं मीर गियो जरां तीन चार पत्थर पड़िया (हां नोपत के ऊपर ही पड़िया जी कीयो)। कीयो यार दीया (म्हे)। बिचारी नै कोय बात का दोष (हां कोनी कलाळी नै)। छाज्जा टूटै करमा की आ तो (नोपत मतेई बाजै कीयो)। चालबा दियो असवारी पाछी (चालो)। चड़ी असवारी पाछी बिदा (हां दीयै अर काळू मीर की ऊठ गी जी कीयो)। बगड़ावतालां भाट नै असवारी गिया पछै खोल ताला अर बाहरें (काड़ियो)। भाट धोळा दोपारां टापरो मंगल कर दियो बेटी का बाप (हां बाहरा क्यें थै आयो जकी बात बता (सूल माण्ड अर)। कीयो सुण ये कलाळी (म्हे)। मैं धाणी म्हारा भूणाजी के हेरै आयो हूं (हां भूणोजी के हेरै आयो हूं कीयो)। भूणा नै मिलां (वाह वाह)। कीयो

भाट दरबार का हुकमूं कलाळी बोलै अब (म्हे)। कांई समचार भाट नै कहवै देखां (कीआवूं जाणज्यो देखां कीआवूं)। अबार कहवां देव का हुकमूं देखां (वाह वाह जी वाह वाह)।।

सौ साण्डिया तो जी जो भूणा के लद भरी बीरा भाटजी रे।
भाट नारदी रे सौवूं ए लदोर।
भूणोजी अठै कोनी रे बीरा भाटजी।
रावजी घोड़ा खरीदबा नै भेज्या रे बांकी गढ लाहोर।।
(भलां जी भलां) देव भलां

सौ साण्डिया तो भूणा के भाट लद भरी (म्हे)। सौवूं ए (लदोर)। भूणोजी राण में कोनी बीरा भाट (म्हे)। रावजी घोड़ा खरीदबा नै भेज दियो बांकी गढ (लाहोर)। लाहोर में घोड़ा आछा होवै (हां बठै खरीदन नै घोड़ा ल्यान नै गिया कीयो)। अठै कोनी भूणोजी (वाह वाह)। कीयो कलाळी (म्हे)। म्हारो धणी आज भूणोजी राण शहर में कोनी (कोनी)। म्हारो बीरा ई रहबा को धरम कोनी (हां अठै पाणी पीण को ई म्हारो धरम ही कोनी कीयो)। लाहोर को गेलो बता (बेगो जावूं कीयो)। कलाळी बोलै कांई गेलो बतावै देखां (कीआवूं जाणज्यो कीआवूं देखां)।।

बण बांका तो जी जींटा घणा रे परदेशी पंछड़ा रे।
गेला में नंदियां रे बहवै असंगा नौ नौ धार।
ताणो टारड़ो बूड़ो लाग्यो परदेशी पंछड़ा।
कोनी उतरै रे नंदियां पैलै पार।।
(भलां जी भलां) देव भलां

बण बांका भाई जींटा घणा है (म्हे)। गेला में देख नंदियां बहवै असंगा नौ नौ (धार)।। ताणो टारड़ो बूड़ो लाग्यो म्हनै (म्हे)। भाट नी उतरेलो नंदियां के पैलै (ओ पार)। थारी तो भगवान देव महाराज देही पलट दी (म्हे)। दरबार का हुकमूं थारो घोड़ो है नै (बो को बो है बूड़ोलो को बूड़ो कीयो)। नंदियां कींयां पार हुवी (मांयनै ले अर नंदी में डूबेलो कीयो)। दरबार का हुकमूं भाट बोलै (म्हे)। कांई समचार कलाळी नै कहवै (कीआवूं जाणज्यो देखां कीआवूं)। अबार कहवां देव का हुकमूं ले (वाह वाह जी वाह वाह)।।

ए भलां बण बांका जींटा हो तो जी ए ई रंग पातरा रे।
गेला में नंदियां असंगा बेगो ये नौ नौ धार।
गोठां में औतारियो धरमराजा देवजी।
म्हनै कलाळी बो उतारै ये नंदियां के गैलै पार।।
(भलां जी भलां) देव भलां

भलां ही बण बांका जींटा हो (म्हे)। गेला में बहवै नंदियां असंगा नौ नौ (धार)। देख गोठां में औतार ले लियो धरमराजा देवजी (वाह वाह)। कलाळी बो उतार देय नंदियां के पैलै ही (म्हनै पार)। नंदियां पार करबालो धणी दूजो है म्हारै (म्हारै लारै है कीयो)। सुण कलाळी (म्हे)। लाहोर को गेलो जल्दीवूं

जल्दी बता दे (वाह वाह)। कीयो रे भाट (म्हे)। म्हारो तो रांड को सभाव है अठै ही है भूणोजी (हां भूणोजी अठै है कीयो बो लाहोर कोनी गियोड़ा है)। कीयो अठै कठै है (हां जकी बता)। करां तो कहवै लाहोर अर करां कहवै अठै (वाह वाह)। कीयो गोरम के भाखर भूणोजी सूरां की शिकार खेलबा नै (गिया है कीयो)। घड़ी सात नै (पाछा आबाळा ई है कीयो)। दरबार का हुकमूं आराम कर ले थोड़ोसो (वाह वाह)। मैं मिला द्यूं अबार (म्हे)। तो भाट तो घोड़ा नै बांध आराम करबा लाग गो (वाह वाह)। कलाळी कांई करियो मूंग मोती घाल थाळ में (वाह वाह)। ऊंची रंग महल के गोखड़ै जार (बैठ गी)। कीयो बाबा भाट (म्हे)। भूणाजी को पाछी गिरती फौज को नंगारो (बाजी)। मूंग अर मोती मतै एक जागां (हां भेळा हो जाय कीयो)। जरां आपां नै ठा हो जाया की भूणाजी को नंगारो (हां बाजै पाछी बावड़ गी असवारी)। दरबार का हुकमूं कलाळी मूंग अर मोती घाल अर रंग महल ऊंची चड़ गी (वाह वाह)। भूणाजी की फौज पाछी गोरम का भाखर से (हां बावड़ी)। तो फौज को नंगारो (बाजियो है)। दरबार का हुकमूं मूंग अर मोती हा जका मतेई भेळा (व्हिया जी कीयो)। कांई कलाळी रंग महलां में हेटी (आ जावे)। कांई समचार भाट नै (कहवै देखां जाणज्यो कीआवूं)। अबार कहवां देव का हुकमूं ले तूं (वाह वाह वाह वाह)।।

सुतां सुतां तो जी दिन बीत गो रे परदेशी पंछड़ा रे।
आंतबा ऊठ गो राजाजी काछबजी को बाण।
ताणा धणी नै ओळख ले बीरा भाटजी।
ओळख ले भाटजी रे दोन्यु दळां के मांय ये।।
(भलां जी भलां) देव भलां

सुतां ई सुतां देख दिन बीत गो अठै (म्हे)। दरबार का हुकमूं आंतबा ऊठ गो राजा काछबजी को (बाण)। थारा धणी नै ओळख अब (म्हे)। भाट दोन्यु दळां के (माई)। दोन्यु दळ कुण का (म्हनै तो कांई ठा है)। एक फौज पलटन तो भूणाजी की ही (म्हे)। एकै फौज राजा नीमदे के सागै (हां बताई)। ए दोन्यो दळ बता दिया (वाह वाह)। भाट नारदी ऊठ (म्हे)। फूलरिया घोड़ा नै पिलाण (करियो है)। भाट बिदा होबा लाग्यो कलाळी बूझणा करी भाट बिदा कींयां हुवै (हां तूं किस्यो भूणोजी नै जाणै थोड़ो ही है कीयो)। ओळखै (वाह वाह)। कीयो मैं भूणाजी की खीर किस्या दिन खाई हाथ की (म्हे)। जरां ठहर थोड़ोसो (हां भूणाजी का तनै ऐनाण-सैनाण है जका बता द्यूं)। कलाळी बोलै (म्हे)। कंवर भूणा का कांई ऐनाण-सैनाण भाट नै बतावै देखां (कीआवूं जणीज्यो भोपाजी महाराज कीआवूं)। अबार कहवां ई भगवान का हुकमूं ले तूं (वाह वाह जी वाह वाह)।।

ए डावै बळ तो जी बांधै कंवर भूणोजी पागड़िया औवूं रे।
जीवणी भाई रे राखै मूठ कटार।
ताणा धणी नै ओळख लीज्यै रे बीरा भाटजी।
भूणो चालै बाबा रे बावाजी की चाल।।
(भलां जी भलां) देव भलां

डावै बळ बांधै देख भूणोजी पागड़ी (वाह वाह)। जीवणी राखै मूठ (कटार)। तूं जातो ओळखी भूणो चालै बाबा बावाजी की (बै चाल)। बावोजी बगड़ावत चालतो नै (जियां का जियान भूणोजी चालै कीयो)। दूजा की फौज में चाल ही कोनी मिलै (वाह वाह)। भाटजी बिदा होबा लागो (म्हे)। ठहर जा बिदा मत होय (हां बिदा मत होणा ठहर) (पूरा ऐनाण-सैनाण बता द्यूं)।।

ए भूणा री फौज में तो जी ए ई सुसरा पालकीया औवूं रे।
पालकी के भाई रे हीरा को बरणाट।
जातो ही ओळखी बीरा भाटजी।
भूणो बाजै घोड़ी रे बोर को असवार।।
(भलां जी भलां) देव भलां

दरबार का हुकमूं भूणा की फौज में भाट सुसरा पालकी है (म्हे)। पालकी के हीरा को (बरणाट)। तूं जातां ही ओळखी भूणो कीज्यै घोड़ो बोर को (असवार)। सुसरो की नै बोलै जो घोड़ा घोड़ी के आगला आंठू में होवै (म्हे)। तो कीयो सुसरा दूजो के कोनी बोर के ही है (वाह वाह)।।

ए भूणा री फौज में तो जी ए ई सुसरा पालकियां औवूं रे।
कीज्यै भाईजी हीरा सोवै एक हजार।
जातो ही ओळखी बीरा भाटजी।
भूणो चालै रे मितवालां की चाल।।
(भलां जी भलां) देव भलां

भूणा की फौज में है नै (म्हे)। सुसरा पालकी है (वाह वाह)। पालकी के दरबार का हुकमूं हीरा सोवेला ही एक (हजार)। तूं जातो ही ओळखी भूणो चालै मीठा मितवालां की (चाल)। बगड़ावत चालतां नै (जियां का जियान भूणोजी चालै है कियो)। थोड़ो ठहर (और बता द्यूं भूणोजी की बैठ गा है जकी बतावूं)।

सुतन सोवै तो जी ए ई भूणा के सोहरटा रे।
भाट नारदी रे नाड़ो लाल गुलाल।
जातो ओळख लीज्यै बीरा भाटजी।
भूणो चालै काका रे नेवाजी की चाल।।
(भलां जी भलां) देव भलां

सुतन सोवै रे भाट भूणा नै सोहरटो (म्हे)। नाड़ो लाल (गुलाल)। तूं जातां ही ओळख ले भूणो चालै काका नेवाजी की (चाल)। नेवाजी की चाल अर भूणा की चाल (एक ही है कीयो)। ओ समचार कुण कीयो (कलाळी कीयो है)। अब के भाट बगड़ावतां को बोलै (म्हे)। कांई समचार कलाळी नै (कहवै देखो)।।

ए आंख मीच तो जी ओळख ल्यूं ए रंग पातरा रे।

ओळखल्यूं कलाळीजी कर जामा की तोड़।
खोद खोद मत बतायै रंग पातरा।
कांई छानी म्हारावूं ये म्हारा धणियां की ओळ।।
(भलां जी भलां) देव भलां

आंख मीच ओळखल्यूं (म्हे)। कलाळी कर जामा की (तोड़ अर)। खोद खोद कांई बतावै रंग पातरा (वाह वाह)। कांई छानी है म्हारावूं म्हाना धणियां की (अब ओळ)। म्हारा धणी म्हारावूं छाना थोड़ा ही है (हां छाना थोड़ा ही है) जको म्हन तूं (अता बतावै ऐनाण-सैनाण)। रांड करां काळा झीकबा लागी (वाह वाह)। कलाळी बूझणा (करी है)। ले रे भाट (म्हे)। तनै पूरा ऐनाण-सैनाण बताया रे काला झकीया भैइ (हां काला ही झकीया अती बार कीयो)।।

छौड़ै हेरज्यै जी जो भूणा नै तूं चौखठै औवूं रे।
हेरज्यै हीरा रे घानी वारी हाट।
कलाळां के लाधै भूणोजी दारू पींवतो।
नीतर लाधै रे दुर्जनसाल की पाट।।
(भलां जी भलां) देव भलां

छौड़ै हेरज्यो भूणा नै चौखठै (वाह वाह)। के हेरी हीरा घानी की (हाट)। के लाधै भूणोजी कलाळां के दारू पींवतो (वाह वाह)। नी लाधज्या दुरजनसाल की (पाट)। ओ ले भैइ ई जागां अती जागां चिकै कोनी (हां अती जागां भूणोजी की बैठक है कीयो)। हीरा का घानी भूणाजी के धरमेलो है (म्हे)। जरूर दो बात करियो बिने रह कोनी (हां मिलिया बिनै कोनी जावे)। चौखठा पर है जको जरूर भूणोजी (जांवता ही तनै के मिल जावे)। कलाळी की हेली जरूर आजावै (वाह वाह)। अती जागावूं चिकै (म्हे)। रावजी के डायी भुजा के सारै बिराजमान व्हियोड़ा जरूरी (हां भूणोजी लाधै कीयो)। कलाळी बोलै (म्हे)। कांई समचार भूणा नै कहवै (कीआवूं जाणज्यो कीआवूं देखां)।।

ए ऊठती नै सालियो तो जी म्हनै हेली को गोखड़ो रे।
सालियो बोर रे बंवळी घोड़ी को ठाण।
तीन साल बगड़ावत छाती पर छोड़ग्या।
चोथो छोड़ गा राण में रे भूणोजी बळी1वाण।।
(भलां जी भलां) देव भलां

देव का नांव लियां सदा ही (भलां जी कीयो)। कीयो ऊठती नै सालै रे भाट हेली को गोखड़ो (म्हे)। दूजा सालै बोर बंवळी घोड़ी को (म्हनै ठाण)। ए तीन साल तो देख बगड़ावत म्हारै छाती पर ई छोड़ गा (म्है ऊठता ही सामै दीखे)। चोथो छोड़ गा राण में भूणो बळी1 (वाण)। आनै बिसावरो (म्हे)। भूणोजी बगड़ावतां को डावड़ो है (हां) राण बसै भैइ (हां राण में बसै ओ फिरतो निंगै आजावै (म्हारी छाती समाव नैइ करै कीयो)। भाट रे सोल है (वाह वाह)। साल छोड़ गा बगड़ावत म्हार कन्न (वाह वाह)।।

बिदा हो जावो जी ए ई बीरा भाटजी रे।
तनै भाटजी रे सकरा हुज्यो सूण।
अड़दू का बजार में रे बीर भाटजी।
सामू मिलज्यो रे बारावत का भूण।।
(भलां जी भलां) देव भलां

अब तूं बिदा हो जाय कीयो (म्हे)। भाटजी थानै सकरा घणा हुज्यो (सूण)। अरै अड़दू का बजार में (वाह वाह)। सामू मिल जाय तनै बारावत को ही (जांवतां ही भूण)। देव को हुकम होवै (म्हे)। भाट रे भूणोजी सामू मिलज्यो (वाह वाह)। बिदा हो जावै (म्हे)। कलाळी दरबार का हुकमूं भाट नै सीख दे दी (म्हे)। कलाळी के भाट के बात होतां (म्हे)। भाट बगड़ावतां को बिदा (होंवतां)। जय बोलो श्री देवनारायण भगवान की (जय)। बोलो भैइ छोटा अर मोटा (स)।। दरबार का हुकमूं बगड़ावतां को भाट बजार में पूगतो (व्हिया है)। तो फूटयोड़ी दुकान निंगै (आयगी जी कीयो)। फूलरिया घोड़ा नै मांयलै छेड़ै (बाड़ दिन्यो)। सुरबीण नै (खूंटी पर टांक दीनी)। गुड़गुड़ी कन्नै ही (वाह वाह)। खूंटी पर (टांक दी जी कीयो)। के दूर को बजार में कर धूलो भेळो (वाह वाह)। बगड़ावतां को भाट तो बी जागां धूल ऊफणबा लाग गो (हां ढाल में घाल अर रेत ऊफणबा लाग्यो)। दरबार का हुकमूं नीमदे की असवारी आगै ही (म्हे)। मुण्डा आगला सिरदार बूझणा (करी है)। अरै भाई धूलिया (म्हे)। एकानै हो जा कंवर खाण्डेराव की असवारी (हां राजा नीमदेजी की असवारी आवै है कीयो)। कीयो रे सिरदारां (म्हे)। के नीमा ही बसै अर भैइ पीमा ही (हां राण शहर में बसै है कीयो)। नीमा के पीमा के कीयोड़ी जिनस पड़ गी म्हारी बजार में (हां छोड़ अर ऊठ जावूं थोड़ो ही कीयो)। धूल में भर ढाल नै (म्हे)। घोड़ा असवार के चारूंमेर घणको (हां दे देवै काटा कपड़ा रेतवूं बूर देवे)। आगै ही जार झटकाय रेत आदमी ओ लियो बळबा द्यो आगो (हां जाण द्यो कीयो)। राजा नीमदे हां नीमदे की तंब असवारी (आयगी)। तो नीमदे बोलै कांई भाट नै अब बतलावै देखां (कीआवूं जाणज्यो देखां कीआवूं)।।

पगां लखीणी जी ए ई थारै मोजड़िया रे।
धूलिया भाई जी कपड़ा धोळा सेत।
नीमदे करै तनै बूझणा।
क्युं ऊफणै ढालां ढालां जी बाजारां की रेत।।
(भलां जी भलां) देव भलां

पगां लखीणी धूलिया भाई मोजड़ी है (म्हे)। कपड़ा धोळा (थारै सेत)। राजा नीमदे करै तनै बूझणा (म्हे)। क्युं ऊफणै रे म्हाना बाजारां की ढालां ढालां (अब तूं रेत)। लाखीणो आदमी लाग्यो भैइ (म्हे)। लाख का थारा कन्नै (कपड़ा पहरण नै है)। अरै धूलवूं बाथियां क्युं पड़ै (जकी बताय कीयो)। ओ समचार कुण कीयो (राजा नीमदेजी आंवतां की कीयो)। दरबार का हुकमूं भाट मन में देखियो (म्हे)। देखां नीमा नै अटकल ले सुरग्याणी है के बेसुरग्याणी देखां (हां फूटियो ढोल ही अग्याण है कांई

देखां) । भाट बोलै कांई समचार नीमजी नै कहवै देखां (कीआवूं जाणीज्यो भोपाजी महाराज कीआवूं देखां) ।।

पगां लखीणी जी जो राजाजी म्हारै मोजड़िया औवूं रे।
नीमा म्हारै जी कपड़ा धोळा सेत।
चौईस लाल गमा दी ताणा बजार में।
मैं तो नीमाजी हीरो गमायो एक।।
(भलां जी भलां) देव भलां

पगां लखीणी मोजड़ी है (म्हे)। कपड़ा धोळा (म्हारै सेत)। चौईस तो लाल पड़ गी भैइ ताणा बजार में (म्हे)। नीमा (हीरो गम गियो एक)। चौईस तो लाल पड़ गी (म्हे)। एक हीरो (हां गमा दियो)। बा नै ढूंडू हूं भैइ (हां बा नै ढूंडू मैं तो कीयो)। राजा नीमदे सुरग्याणी थोड़ो है जको (हां बात में समझो हो)। बगड़ावतां को भाट तो रती भरियो झूट तो कोनी बोल्यो (वाह वाह)। लाला तो बगड़ावतां नै बनाई (म्हे)। हेंर हीरो हो जको (भूणोजी नै बना दियो)। राजा नीमदे के समझ कोनी बैठी (वाह वाह)। नीमदे बोलै (म्हे)। कांई समचार भाट नै कहवै देखां (कीआवूं जाणज्यो देखां अब कीआवूं) ।।

पगां लखीणी जी परदेशी भाई रे थारै मोजड़िया औवूं रे।
परदेशी भाई रे मोतियां सूं जड़िया रे।
नीमदे करै रे तनै बूझणा।
म्हाना बजार में रे कांई रकम पड़िया रे।।
(भलां जी भलां) देव भलां

हीरा रतन की जाळी दीखी म्हनै (म्हे)। अरै डावड़ा थारै मोतियां सूं जड़िया (जड़िया)। दरबार का हुकमूं राजा नीमदे करै बूझणा (म्हे)। म्हाना बजार में कांई रकम (थारा पड़िया)। अती बडी कांई रकम पड़ गी रे भैइ (वाह वाह)। धूलवूं बाथियां पड़ै (म्हे)। दरबार का हुकमूं भाट मन में देखियो बैरी समझयो कोनी (हां है तो फूटियो डोळ अग्याणी)। इसी जागां राळ दे रे (म्हे)। सोचूं ही (फिरबो करे)।।

हीरो ई रतन की जाळी जी ए ई राजा नीमदे ई रे।
म्हारै नीमाजी मोतियां सूं जड़िया रे।
अमल पाणिया को म्हारै बगत व्है ग्यो।
बगड़ावतां की बारां की रे मोहरां लाध्यावै पड़ी रे।।
(भलां जी भलां) देव भलां

हीरा रतन की जाळी है (म्हे)। नीमाजी मोतियां सूं (म्हारै जड़ी)। अमल पाणिया को बगत हु गो (म्हे)। बगड़ावतां की बारां की म्हनै मोहर लाध्यावै (आज कोय पड़ी)। अरै अमलदार आदमी हूं (म्हे)। मैं सुणयोड़ी बात है भैइ नीमा रे (हां देखियोड़ी कोनी कीयो)। के कोय जमाना में बगड़ावत व्हिया (म्हे)। पंचतोली मोहरां काचा तारां में पोय पोय (अर अटीकर घोड़ा के गलै (में राळ राळ दपटाया बतावै

है कीयो)। कह बतावै बै मोहरां भेइ रे टूट टूट अर (हां पड़ी बजार में)। मैं देखूं (म्हे)। एक ही म्हनै मोहर (आज लाध जावे)। आज आज को अमल पाणी (म्हारै हो जावै कीयो)। मैं देखूं भगवान खरचो दे म्हनै (वाह वाह)। नीमदे कीयो रे मुंगता (म्हे)। कुण देश को है बोल (कुणसो देश को आयो तूं कीयो)। कीयो सात समंदरा पार को हूं (हां सात समंदरा पार का हूं)। कुण लोग है (जकी बता)। कीयो राजावों को बेइ को भाट हूं (वाह वाह)। नांव सेंसारी दुनिया जगीशयो कह अर बतलावै (हां जगीशयो कह अर बतलाया करै कीयो)। जगीशया (म्हे)। सुवा सुवा हाथ जमीमाता रोज का म्हारी घोड़ा की खुरतालावूं आकाश जाय (हां जमीन ऊठै है कीयो)। कित्ता बरस व्हिया तनै ठा तो है (जकी ठा कोनी कांई कीयो)। अरै मोहरां कठै ही अठै गेला (अठै मोहरां कठै लाधै हो कीयो आज)। तो भाट मन में देखियो के माहरां तो लाधै (म्हे)। देव देवै अर बैरी नै ओजा को नाका जर ही पार (हां पड़ै कीयो ईयां चम्पो मानै कोनी राजा)। कांई भगवान देव नै याद करै (वाह वाह)। कांई देव कन्नु मोहरां मांगै (देखां कीआवूं जाणीज्यो देखां कीआवूं)।।

ए माथावूं दियोड़ो जी ढळ गा रे बाळा देवजी रे।
माच गी अन्नदाता रे धूंदळ मांयनै खेंव।
कर जोड़ियां करूं आपणै बीनत्यां।
पांच मोहर अन्नदाता रे ढाल में मांगी द्यो रे।।
(भलां जी भलां) देव भलां

दरबार का हुकमूं माथावूं देखो दियोड़ो डळ गो (म्हे)। मांची धूंदळ मांयनै (खेंव)। कर जोड़ियां बेइ को भाट करै आपणै बीनती (म्हे)। अन्नदाता पांच मोहर ढाल मैं मांगी (अब द्यो)। थै मांगियोड़ी मोहरां देवोलां (म्हे)। बैरी नै (हां) दिखावूंला (वाह वाह)। हेंर म्हारी बात रह जावै भूणाजी ने लेयावूंला (वाह वाह)। देव को नांव लेय (म्हे)। भाट बगड़ावतां को ढाल नै रेतुल में (हां ऊबी करी जी कीयो)। तीन तिलोकी को नाथ भगवान चौसलै खेड़ै बिराजमान (हु रिया हा)। बक बक हेंसिया (म्हे)। फैफ रा फूल (झड़िया)। भैरवानाथ बूझणा (कर लीनी)। कीयो श्री महाराजा हंसणो (आपको कींयां व्हियो जी कीयो)। कीयो देख रे भाट नै रेतुल के मांयनै मोहरां भावै (हां अड़दू के बजार में मोहरां चाहीज्यै कीयो)। कीयो श्री महाराज बूड़ा माईत को कीयो जरूरी (हां करणो आपणे)। देव को नांव लेय अर धूल में भर ढाल नै (म्हे)। के ऊबी (करी है)। तो पहल तो बगड़ावतां की बारां की पंचतोली (मोहरां)। ए ई कांचोड़ा (तार में पोयोड़ी)। ठै कह नी हेटी (आर पड़ी जी कीयो)। भाट कोय नीचो (म्हे)। पकड़ डोरो के ऊंची कर (हां मोहरां नै ऊंची उठाई)। नीमा (म्हे)। निंगै कर (थारै बारै की है)। मोहरां बगड़ावतां की बारां की है बोल (हां ए बता कीयो)। नीमदे मुण्डा में आंगली घाली सिरदारां (म्हे)। अरै बगड़ावतां जियान का आगै तो व्हिया कोनी अब होबा का ही (दातार नैइ है)। अरै आयोड़ा मुंगता की आसा पूरण (औरूं ही करै कीयो)। राजा नीमा के कोय बात समझ कोनी बैठी (वाह वाह)। राजा नीमदे कह सिरदारां (हा) असवारी चालां (हां चालण द्यो कीयो)। तो सुरबीण ही जकी नीमदे की निंगै (आयगी)। कीयो धूलिया (म्हे)। हां श्री महाराज (फरमावो)। सुरबीण को बाजो कुण कन्नै (थारै कन्नै है कांई कीयो)। कीयो हां श्री महाराज म्हारै कन्नै ही है (हां म्हारै कन्नै है कीयो)। कीयो भेइ घणा दिन व्हिया

सुणिया ईनै (म्हे)। बगड़ावतां को भाट बगड़ावतां थका सागै आतो (वाह वाह)। जकै दिन बाजो (हां ओ सुणता कीयो)। थोड़ो सुणा दे भैइ (हां सुणा जणा कींयां बजावे)। हां श्री महाराज ए ही काम है पछै काम कांई है अठै (वाह वाह)।।

बीण बजावै जी ए ई परदेशी पंछड़ा रे।
थारै भाई रे कान्धै बीण ऊसास।
नीमदे करै रे तनै बूझणा।
थारो धूलिया जी किस्यो दिशावर बास।।
(भलां जी भलां) देव भलां

दरबार का हुकमूं तूं बीण घणी फूटरी बजावै (म्हे)। बीरा कान्धै बीण (थारै ऊसास)। राजा नीमो करै तनै बूझणा (म्हे)। धूलिया थारो किस्यो दिशावर (बास)। म्हारै समझ कोनी बैठी (हां कठै को है तूं)। बगड़ावतां को भाट मन में बिचार करियो (म्हे)। ओ फूटियो डोळ है समझै तो आत कोनी (हां जचै जियान ही बता देवो)।।

चार कूंट में जी ए ई बांधोयोड़ा झूंपड़ा रे।
म्हारै नीमाजी कान्धै बीण ऊसास।
हरचन्द राजा को बैइ को भाट हूं रे राजा नीमदे।
म्हारो नीमाजी मथराजी में बास।।
(भलां जी भलां)। देव भलां

दरबार का हुकमूं चार कूंट में बांध्योड़ा झूंपड़ा है (म्हे)। दरबार का हुकमूं कान्धै राखूं बीण (ऊसास)। मैं हरचन्द राजा को तो बैइ को भाट हूं (म्हे)। नीमा म्हारो मथराजी में (बास है कीयो)। मथराजी रहबाळा आदमी हूं (वाह वाह)। बगड़ावतां को भाट रती भरियो ही (झूट नी बोल्यो)। हरचन्द राजा कुण नै बनायो (सवाई भोज महाराज नै बना दिया)। मथरा को बैसणो (ठाकर देव महाराज को बनायो जी कीयो)। राजा नीमदे सुरग्याणी कोनी जको समझ जावै (हां बात में समझो)। बूझणा करी सिरदारां (म्हे)। ओ हरचन्द राजा कठै व्हियो भैइ (हां जकी बतावो कीयो)। कीयो श्री महाराज लांबो छोड़ा देश है (हां घणी ही जगा है कठै हो जाय कीयो)। खुणु खचूणी के हो जाय घणी (वाह वाह)। कुण अठै निंगै राखै नीमदे बूझणा करी सिरदारां (म्हे)। जरां असवारी चालबा द्यो (चालण द्यो कीयो)। भाट मन देखियो रे दुशमन आयोड़ो जाय नै (हां कीं लचकाणो कोनी पड़ियो कीयो)। आती असवारी आसका कोनी दीनी जांती नै आसका दे देय (हां आसका तो दे देयो देखां)। बगड़ावतां को भाट कांई आसका बनावै (म्हे)। नीमदे राजा नै आसका देवै अब देखां (कीआवूं जाणज्यो देखां कीआवूं)। अबार कहवूं भैइ।।

ए नीमा री फौज में तो जी जो देश देश का राजवी रे।
मोकळा ठाकरां रे मुंगल घणा पठाण।
जगीशया भाट की आसका मानज्यो।

मानज्यो सिरदारां रे सभी सेत कल्याण।।
(भलां जी भलां) देव भलां

कंवर राजाजी की फौज में देश देश का राजवी है (म्हे)। मुंगल मोकळा (घणा पठाण)। जगीशया भाट की आसका मान लीज्यो (म्हे)। सभी सेत (कल्याण)। घोड़ा नै (म्हे)। असवार नै सागै आसका (दीनी)। निंगैवान सिरदार चोखी तरहवूं (निंगै करी जी कीयो)। कीयो आसका तो आज ताणी (हां आज दिन को सुणी कोनी) हेंर आब सुणबा की (आगै कोनी है)। निंगैवान सिरदारां कीयो श्री महाराज (म्हे)। आसका तो बडी चोखी (हां मुण्डावूं बहुत फूटरी दीनी)। पण डावा हाथावूं (आसका थानै दे दीनी)। तो राजा नीमदे रळकाय बती दरबार का हुकमूं भाट नै दकाळियो (वाह वाह)। कीयो मुंगता (म्हे)। डावा हाथावूं म्हानै आसका कींयां दी बोल (हां कींयां दियो कीयो)। मैं किस्यो दातार कोनी (हां दातार कोनी कांई कीयो)। कीयो श्री महाराज गुणो माफ होवै (हां माफ चाहवूं कीयो)। ओ जीवणो हाथ है (म्हे)। घर को कोनी (म्हानै घरां को कोय है नी)। कुण को है (बता कीयो)। लोगां के गहणां को रखियोड़ो है (हां अडाणै रखियोड़ो है मोदीखानै)। मोदीखानै (वाह वाह)। धूलिया हाथ का हाथ गहणांवूं रख दिया (म्हे)। कांई लेवै (कांई खावै है ओ कीयो)। कीयो श्री महाराज अमल खावूं नै पछै (हां अमल खावूं कीयो)। पाव खाण्ड (खावै है कांई कीयो)। कीयो ऊंचो (खावूं)। सेर दो सेर (कीयो ऊंचो ही खावूं)। किस्यो पांच दस सेर (कीं ऊंचो)। दरबार का हुकमूं जगीशया (म्हे)। थारो मावो जरां म्हनै बता भैइ (हां बता कीयो)। कीयो श्री महाराज के तो कोय म्हारो मावो (बूझै कोनी)। जै मावो बूझै (म्हे)। बी नै पूरो मावो करिया बिनै आगा नी जाबा द्यूं (हां बी सिरदार नै अटेवूं हलन कोनी देवूंला कीयो)। मावो पूरो करावो जरां बतावूं (हां नैइ तो कींयां के बूझो थांकै गेलो लागो कीयो)। कीयो धूलिया (म्हे)। राजा नीमदे हूं (हां छोटीसी बात कहूं कीयो)। रावजी को छोटो भैइ हूं मैं (वाह वाह)। दरबार का हुकमूं मावो थारो पूरो करा द्यूं (हां पूरो करा द्यूं बतावो कीयो)। दरबार का हुकमूं कीयो रे भाट (म्हे)। तो ईंयां मण दो मण खावै थोड़ो ही (वाह वाह)। कीयो श्री महाराज मैं तो ऊंचो ही (हां खावूं कीयो)। कीयो जरां भैइ मावा तो बता दे अब भैइ (हां बतायावूं ठा पड़ै जगीशया कीयो)। बगड़ावतां को भाट बोलै (म्हे)। नीमदे नै कांई भांत को आपको मावो बतावै (कीआवूं जाणीज्यो देखां कीआवूं)। अबार कहवां देव का हुकमूं ले तूं (वाह वाह जी वाह वाह)।।

ए सुवा मण मावो तो जी परभातै करूं रे राजा नीमदे औवूं रे।
पाछली टैम का रे खाजावूं ताकड़ी सात।
अतरो तो मावो थितियो करूं रे राजा नीमदे।
पछै नीमा रे जी डळियां को अन्त न पार।।
(भलां जी भलां) देव भलां

सुवा मण मावो तो परभातै ही करूं (म्हे)। नीमा पाछली टैम को ताकड़ी (मांग लेवूं सात)। अतरो मावो तो थितियो करूं (म्हे)। पछै डळियां को अन्त न (पार)। सुवा मण मावो तो घरांवूं ऊठतो ही करूं (वाह वाह)। पछै राजावां का बेटा कन्नै (ऊठ जावूं)। बै दरबार का हुकमूं डळिया की डळियां

म्हानै कन्नै (फैंकबो करे)। बै सुना घर में भाटां राळै नी (हां जियान राळबो करूं कीयो)। बा गिणती कोनी (हां बो तोल में कोय है नी)। कीयो रे सिरदारां (म्हे)। अमलदार मोटो मिल गो (हां अमलदार तो मोटो ही मिलियो कीयो)। जगीशया (म्हे)। हां श्री महाराज (वाह वाह)। अतरो मावो करै जठैवूं क्युं ठूंगार औरूं करै बो सागै मांगा द्यूं (हां ऊपर ठूंगार करै कोनी करै कीयो)। कीयो करूं महाराज (करूं कीयो)। कीयो दो बारी फोड़ा पड़ी भैइ (हां सागै ही बता कीयो)।।

ए ढाई मण तो चाबा जी नीमाजी मैं भूंगड़ा।
सुवा मण खावूं लटियांवाली भांग।
फैरूं नी उगै राजा नीमदे।
जहरी बिष का ढाई रे टांका ल्यूं ल्यूं मांग।।
(भलां जी भलां) देव भलां

दरबार का हुकमूं ढाई मण का तो भूंगड़ा चाबू (वाह वाह)। सुवा मण खावूं लटियांवाली (औरूं भांग)। औरूं नी उगै (म्हे)। जहरी विष का ढाई टांका औरूं लेवूलो (मांग)। ए कांई (जहरी विष कांई होवै कीयो)। आकड़ा नीमड़ा धतूरा घोल घोल पीवूं (हां जरां म्हारै की थाकड़ो लागै कीयो)। नीमदे कीयो सिरदारां अमलदार तो मोटो मिल गो भैइ (वाह वाह)। पण नी अब तो मावो तो ई नै (करावां जरां ही जुगत बैठै है कीयो)। नीमदे राजा के हुकम में काम हो (म्हे)। कहतां जेज (लागी)। दरबार का हुकमूं सुवा मण मावो आतां जेज (नैइ लागी)। ढाई मण भूंगड़ा (आयग्या है)। सुवा मण लटियांवाली भांग (औरूं आयगी जी कीयो)। दरबार का हुकमूं काळोजी गोरोजी महाराज दरबार का हुकमूं दूजा अमराव है नै (म्हे)। आकड़ा नीमड़ा घोल घोल दो तबला (हां जहरी बिष का ल्यार भर मेल दिया जी कीयो)। ले भैइ ओ ले (घूलिया)। मावो तियार है कीयो (कर कीयो)। कीयो नीमा (म्हे)। दातार तो बड़ो जोर को मिल गो (हां बजार में दातार तो बड़ो जोर को मिलियो)। पण अकल को बीज कोनी (हां फूटियो डोळ सपा ही अग्याण है कीयो)। कीयो तनै मावो करायै जरां (हां फूटियो डोळ अग्याण बाजियो कांई कीयो)। नैइ नैइ नैइ नैइ (इयां कोनी बाजियो)। बजरखाणो लियार मेल दियो म्हाना मुण्डा में कींयां मावै (हां बडी बडी डलियां पड़ी है (मुण्डै में कींयां खावूं कीयो)। नुकरा करा देय (वाह वाह)। रजपूतां का बेटा चकूड़ा कन्नै हां कहतां जेज (लागी कीयो)। नुकरा होता जेज (नैइ लागी)। जगीशया (वाह वाह)। ओ ले भैइ मावो तियार है (तियार है अब कर कीयो)। कीयो नीमा अकल को बीज कोनी थारा में (हां अकल को तो बीज ही कोनी कीयो)। कीयो अब के कांई कसर है (अब के कांई कसर रह गी कीयो)। कीयो सिरदार कता ऊबा है आपणो चारूंमेर (म्हे)। आंकै सामनै मावो खाजावूं नी तो (वाह वाह)। तो फाट अर मर जावूं मैं (हां कोय सिरदार की नीजर लागै चन्ना की कोटी (फाटै जियान फाट अर मर जावूं कीयो)। कनात तणा मांयनै बैठो बैठो मावो करूं (आच्छी तरहवूं मावो करूं मांयनै कनात में (बैठियो बैठियो)। राजावां का काम है (म्हे)। कहतां जेज (लागी कीयो)। कनात तणता जेज ही (नैइ लागी है जी कीयो)। ले भैइ धुलिया ओ ले (अब कर कीयो)। धीकाय देय भाट नै मांयनै छेड़ै कनात में (बाड़ दीन्यो)। कीयो मावो थारो पूरो हो जावै नै (जणा हेलो पाड़ लेयी जको तनै बाहरें (काड़ लेयाज्यूं)। मुण्डा आगला सिरदार कीयो श्री महाराज

पाड़ लिया हेला (हां ओ तो हेलो पाड़योड़ो है कत्तो खायावूं मरजायी)। दरबार का हुकमूं बगड़ावतां को भाट मनवार को ही लियोड़ो कदै कोनी हो (हां मनवार को कदै ही लियो कोनी हो)। हेंर जरां बोल गो (झूट)। मन में देखियो खाय जरां तो पाव खाण्ड जहर खजी थारावूं (हां मांयनै अठै मरजायसी)। हेंर नी खायी (जणा राजा नीमदे बाहरें नीकलता ही मारसी कीयो)। आ मौत बाजै जकी तो आ आयगी (हां हेलो पाड़ अर बुला लियो)। आंतरै खिरकी पड़ी (म्हे)। बगड़ावतां को भाट देखां मन में देखियो चाखां तो सरी (हां खारो है की मीठो)। उठाय (म्हे)। जीभ पर (मेली)। खारो लागियो तूं म्हारै राम मारिया रे खारो रे खारो खारो खारो खारो (वाह वाह) पाछो थूक दियो (म्हे)। भाट मन में बिचार करियो भगवान भेज्यो हे नै तनै (म्हे)। जरां आ बात की (दोहरी बेळियां पड़ै जरां म्हानै याद कर लेयी कीयो) आ बात ईयूं दोहरी कांई आयी (हां ईयूं दोहरी तो कोय आणै की कोनी)। कांई भगवान नै हेलो मारै (म्हे)। कांई समचार अड़दू का बजार में कहवै देखां (कीआवूं जाणज्यो देखां कीआवूं)। अबार कहवूं भैइ देव का हुकमूं (वाह वाह)।

ए असमाना रा घरां सूं सुतो जी ताणा भाटजी रे अब लड़ टूटगिया रे।
भाट में मांगियो जी हींडावालो खेल।
काया के घेरो लागो जी गोठालां राजवियां।
हेलो सुणज्यै रे अलख निरजन देव।।
(भलां जी भलां) देव भलां

दरबार का हुकमूं भाट कीयो है समचार (म्हे)। कीयो असमाना का घरांवूं ताणा भाट की अब लड़ टूट गी है भैइ (वाह वाह)। भाट बै माच गो हींडावालो (खेल)। ओ काया के घेरो लागो गोठां का राजवी (वाह वाह)। तूं हेलो सुणज्यै अलख निरजन (देव)। ले म्हारा धणी ओ ले भैइ (हां हेलो सुणोला)। तो भूणाजी को हेरो होवेलो (और नी जरां ओ खार अठै ही मरू कीयो)। आ बगड़ावतां की बैइ देखां अठै खतम होवै अब (वाह वाह)। देव महाराज बक बक हेंसिया (म्हे)। भैरवानाथ बूझणा (कर लीनी)। श्री महाराज (आपको हंसणो)। कींयां व्हियो (वाह वाह)। कीयो भैरवानाथ निंगै करो (म्हे)। बजार में बाबो भाट हेला मारै (हां हेलो पाड़ै है कीयो)। कीयो श्री महाराज बूड़ा माईत का कीयो कोनी करो पछै (हां कीयो तो करसियों ही आप कहवां (नी कर द्यां कीयो के)। कीयो भैरवानाथ (म्हे)। थां बिना ईयां कीयो कोनी होवै (वाह वाह)। जावो दरबार का हुकमूं भोग होवै जको थै ले लीज्यो (हां थांको है)। फतै भाट की (हां हो जावै कीयो)। मूठी का देवातण हां (म्हे)। बावन तो भैरूं चौसट जोगणियां (म्हे)। अठतर खेतरपाल (हां लेय)। हेंर कनात के मांयलै छेड़ै भाट नै बतला लियो (हां बोलो भाटजी म्हानै याद कींयां करियो कीयो)। कीयो दोहरी बेळियां पड़ी जरां (जण करया हूं)। कांई दोहरी पड़ गी (जकी बतावो)। कीयो बजरखाणो पड़ियो ईनै सांवट दियो थांकै थान मकान मतै मतै (हां जातां रहियो)। कीयो भाटजी (म्हे)। रंग लगावो (वाह वाह)। बगड़ावतां को भाट हाथ में ले अमल (म्हे)। कीयो रंग है जी काळागोरा भैरवानाथ मितवाला जी नै (मितवाला रंग है कीयो)। तो बावन तो भैरूं चौसट जोगणियां किरकाड़ पड़िया (वाह वाह)। बी के अमल की किरची हाथ लागी ताणी नाथ निंदा में ईंयां ई (हां रह ग्या)। कोय के भांग की लटी हाथ आयी (अर कोय के कोनी

आयी)। कोय लप भूंगड़ा आया अर कोय के (कोनी आया जी कीयो)। गोरो जी महाराज कचूस (म्हे)। जहर नै (हां पी ग्या कीयो)। कीयो भाट कांई सला (वाह वाह)। बाह वाह रे म्हारा धणी कीयो (हां अब जावो कीयो अब मैं आनै समाल लेवूं)। दरबार का हुकमूं मूठी का देवातण हां दूजा नै कोनी ठा पड़ियो (वाह वाह)। ए मतै में थान मकान (हां ऊठ ग्या)। घड़ी सात तो भाट कनात के मांयलै छेड़ै (बैठियो रहियो)! हेंर ले ऊबासी (म्हे)। अधबीचमूं कनात नै फाड़ी (हां बीचमूं फाड़ी जी कीयो)। नीकल बाहरें अर ऊबासी (लीनी)। ए नीमा बेटी का बाप कोरो रे रे ल्यार मेलियो (हां कठवूं ओ भेळो कर ल्यार मेलियो आगलो हो जको (म्हारो पूरो उतार दियो)। उतार दियो म्हारा आगलो ही नशो दर में कोनी आयो म्हनै (म्हे)। नीमदे कीयो सिरदारां (वाह वाह)। सात गांवां का हासल तो डाकी (सागै खायगियो)। औरूं कहवै म्हारो नशो ही (हां उगियो कोनी)। कोय बात कोनी गढ में चांलां नी बठै (म्हे)। औरूं मावो बठै ही करां (हां बठै ही करां चालो सागै ही चालूं)। नीमदे कीयो सिरदारां सात गांवां को हासल डाकी (अठै खायगियो)। औरूं कहवै की गढ में पूरो मावो करां (वाह वाह)। दो तीन दिन आपां के गांव के मायंनै ओ (घरां रह जावे)। तो गांवड़िया सगळा ही घणावूं (मिलार जावेला कीयो)। लाख आगै दान कोनी (म्हे)। ई नै लाख को दान तो कर द्यो (अठवूं मुंगता नै सीख दे देवो)। म्हांकै तो तूं बस्ती में मत पड़ै भाज जा (हां कांकड़ ही छोड़ जा कीयो)। दरबार का हुकमूं निंगैवान सिरदार की बूझणा करी निंगै तो करो देखो मांयलै (हां निंगै तो करो अमल खायो की ईंयां कहवै कीयो)। कनात के मांयनै बड़ सिरदार कीयो श्री महाराज (म्हे)। बठा की जो रेत रियोड़ी है नै आ (हां सुवा सुवा हाथ बा ई ऊंडी बैठ गी कीयो)। कांकरी कोनी अठै (वाह वाह)। बाळो ठाकर देव महाराज तीन तिलोकी को नाथ भाट को हेलो सुणता (म्हे)। हेंर बगड़ावतालो भाट को पूरो मावो (हुंवता)। जय बोलो श्री देव नारायण भगवान की (जय)। लाख टका को नांव लियो नी नीमदे (म्हे)। बगड़ावतां को भाट बोलै (वाह वाह)। कांई समचार नीमा नै कहवै (कीआवूं जाणज्यो देखां अब कीआवूं)। अबार कहवूं देव का हुकमूं देखां (वाह वाह जी वाह वाह)।।

अतरा दिन ताणी तो जी सोळवा सोना पड़ता रे राण के मांयनै औवूं रे।
राजा नीमाजी तांबे गोद भरै ईं रे।
सिंगां करै नीमा को साथ रे।
ऊबो नीमाजी स्याळयो खेल करै।।
(भलां जी भलां) देव भलां

अता दिन तो भैइ नीमा ई राण में सोळवा सोना मिलता (म्हे)। आज तूं तांबै गोद (भरे)। अरै सिंगां करै साथ रे नीमा राज कोय स्याळयो खेल (ऊबो करै कीयो)। नीमदे बूझणा (करी है)। अरै मुंगता (म्हे)। छोड़ दे लेरली बात नै (हां बता कीयो स्याळ तो कुण)। कुण व्हिया सिंग कुण व्हिया बोल (जकी बता)। बतावूं महाराज (वाह वाह)।।

ए बावो अर नेवो तो जी दोन्यु भाई रे सिंगांज्युं गूंजता रे।
बै तो भाई रे सिंग पींजरै ल्यार धरै ईं रे।

बा सिंगा के नीमाजी तूं साथ रे।
ऊबो रे नीमा रे स्याळयो खेल करै।।
(भलां जी भलां) देव भलां

दरबार का हुकमूं बावोजी नेवो दोन्यु भाई सिंगांज्युं गूंजिया भैइ (म्हे)। बै सिंग पींजरै ल्यार (धरे)। अरै बा सिंगां के साथ रे (म्हे)। नीमा तूं ऊबो स्याळयो खेल (करै कीयो)। सिंग तो व्हिया बगड़ावत (बै व्हिया कीयो)। स्याळ तूं व्हियो (स्याळ तूं है कीयो)। दरबार का हुकमूं राजा नीमदे का सिरदार बूझणा (करी है)। श्री महाराज देखो (म्हे)। साहब नै स्याळ बनाया कीयो (वाह वाह)। कीयो मुंगता की नाड़ियां को आवळ कावळ (हां बहबा लागी कीयो)। आपणै असवारी चालो कोनी आगै (हां घड़ी सात नै ओ मरणालो है)। दरबार का हुकमूं बड़ा घरां का मुंगतो है ओ (म्हे)। कोय सिरदार आपां नै (ओळमो मोटो देवेला कीयो)। राजा नीमदे की असवारी बिदा हो गी (वाह वाह)। भाट मन में देखियो रे बैरी आयोड़ो जाय (हां की लचकाणो पटका औरूं कीयो)। भाट बगड़ावतां को बोलै (वाह वाह)। कांई नीमदे नै बतलावै औरूं (कीआवूं जाणीज्यो कीआवूं देखां)। अबार कहवां धणी देव का हुकमूं कह द्यां (वाह वाह जी वाह वाह)।।

ए कुंवारी किन्या तो जी नीमा रे माथै रिण घणा औवूं रे।
म्हारै नीमाजी रिप्या चाहीज्यै लाख।
लाखां की दातारी कर पधारै राजा नीमदे।
नीतर भूणा महाबळी को रे डेरो द्यूं बताय।।
(भलां जी भलां) देव भलां

कुंवारी तो किन्या है (म्हे)। माथै रिण घणो (वाह वाह)। म्हनै रिप्या चाहीज्यै (लाख)। लाखां की दातारी कर बा आगा नै जाज्यै (म्हे)। नी भूणा महाबळी को डेरो दे (म्हनै बताय कीयो)। सुण रे नीमा (म्हे)। चार छोकरियां घरां भैइ (वाह वाह)। कन्ने तो पिसियो लगाबा नै एक ही (म्हारै कन्ने है कोनी)। हेंर आगला को खरचणो चाहवूं कोनी (हां सामलै भाट को खरचावूं चाहवूं कोनी)। मैं देखूं (म्हे)। सिरदार कोय लाख को दान करबालो (मिलजावे)। तो डावड़ियां नै टिबी लंघती आपकी (हां पीला हाथ कर धोरै चड़ा द्यूं)। दरबार का हुकमूं लाल मैं तो नीमा थारै जणा आयो भैइ (हां ई वास्तै आयोड़ा हूं)। नीमदे बोलै (वाह वाह)। कांई समचार भाट नै कहवै देखां (कीआवूं जाणज्यो कीआवूं देखां)। अबार कहवूं देव का हुकमूं ले तूं (वाह वाह जी वाह वाह)।।

ए भूणोजी घोड़ा तो जी म्हाना पर चड़ियो रे बैइ का भाट जी ई रे।
ओ तो डावड़ा रे धनपत म्हारो खायो रे।
ई राण में बड़तां रे बीरा भाटजी।
तनै भाटजी रे भूणो कुण बतायो रे।।
(भलां जी भलां) देव भलां

भूणोजी घोड़ा ही म्हारा चड़ियो (म्हे)। धनपत म्हारो (खायो)। ई राण शहर में बड़तां बीरा भाट (म्हे)।

तनै भूणो नांव कुण बतायो (हां जकी बता कीयो)। भूणोजी कह अर बोल्यो आ कह म्हनै (वाह वाह)। भूणोजी कह दे नै जका नै घाणी में पिलार तेल नीकालूं (वाह वाह)। कंवर खाण्डेराव बाजै कोनी (हां तनै ठा कोनी नांव को कीयो)। भाट मन में देखियो कावळ जागावूं पकड़ियो है डोकरै नै (हां अबकाळै की फस ग्या बात में)। भाट बोलै कांई समचार देखां नीमदे नै कहदे देखां (हां कींयां समंद खोज राळ देवां देखां)।।

ए कांकड़ में तो जी गुआल पालती राजाजी चाला चालरिया रे।
दीनी भाई रे पाणी पर पणियारियां आग लागाय।
आंतो टळियो ढळ पीलोदा की कोटड़ियां।
पीलोदाला कुमहारड़ा दियो रे भूणो नांव बताय।।
(भलां जी भलां) देव भलां

दरबार का हुकमूं कांकड़ में भाई गुआल पालती चाला चाल्या (वाह वाह)। दीनी म्हनै पाणी पर आग लगाय (पणियारियां आग लागाय)। अरै आतो टळियो मैं पीलोदाली कोटड़ियां में (वाह वाह)। बै पीलोदाला कुमहारड़ा दियो भूणो नांव म्हनै (बताय)। मैं लाख की दान की खतर गियो पिलोदे (म्हे)। मैं देखियो सिरदार ए ही क्युं बांका है नी (हां ए कांई लाख को दान कर देवे)। बै कीयो भैइ मावूं तो लाख को दान कोनी सज आवै (हां सज में आवै कोनी)। लाख को दान बगड़ावतां को डावड़ो है भूणो नांव (हां बै रोजीना दातण फाड़ै) (जरां लाख रिप्या को दान कर पछी दातण करै कीयो)। इयां दातण कोनी फाड़ै बो (वाह वाह)। सुरजी के होदे लाख रिप्या बांटै (वाह वाह)। जणा कांई दोरा है भैइ (हां कीं दोरा कोनी बा में तो)। श्री महाराज म्हनै धारापती सिरदार कीयो ओ ले (हां बै नांव बतायो है)। तो ऊनै तो किस्या मोयला का गुआल नै (जार अर बूझे)। ऊनै बरोबरियावूं भिड़ा दिया (हां बांको नांव ही कुण लेवै जी कीयो)। हिरण बांका होवै (वाह वाह)। नीमदे कीयो बळबा दियो आगो मुंगता नै (जाण दियो कीयो अमल में)। ईंयां ही लेहरां देवै ओ (म्हे)। दरबार का हुकमूं बगड़ावतां को भाट कांई करियो (म्हे)। बठै ही जार धूलो भेळो (पाछो करबा लाग गियो जी कीयो)। नीमदे ठाणै हु गो (वाह वाह)। कंवर खाण्डेराव की असवारी (आयगी है)। मुण्ड अगला सिरदार कीयो रे भैइ धूलिया (म्हे)। क्युं के घूल को धंधो करो धूला ही कपड़ा हे धोळा (वाह वाह)। कीयो धूलिया एकानै हो जा भैइ कंवर खाण्डेराव की असवारी अब के आरी है (हां कंवर खाण्डेरावजी पधार रिया है कीयो)। कीयो सिरदारां (म्हे)। राण शहर बारा बारा चौईस कोस में (हां बसै है कीयो)। खाण्डा के बूचा के कीयोड़ी म्हारी जिनस छूट गी जकी छोड़जावूं (हां ऊठ जावूं कांई कीयो)। दरबार का हुकमूं ढाल में घाल रेतुल घोड़ा असवार के चारूंमेर घणको देजावै (वाह वाह)। कपड़ा आंतरै जार झटकावै (हां ऊबा ही कोनी रहवे)। दरबार का हुकमूं भूणा की असवार तनू आयगी (वाह वाह)। भूणोजी फट बोर घोड़ी नै रोकी (म्हे)। देखियो बिचार भूणोजी बोलै (म्हे)। कांई समचार अब भाट नै कहवै (कीआवूं जाणज्यो देखां कीआवूं)। अबार कहवूं देव का हुकमूं देखां (वाह वाह)।।

पगां लखीणी जी धूलिया भाई रे थारै मोजड़िया औवूं रे।
थारै धूलियाजी कपड़ा न धोळा सेत।

कंवर खाण्डेराव करै तनै बूझणा।
क्युं ऊफणै ढालां डाळां रे बाजारां की रेत।।
(भलां जी भलां) देव भलां

पगां लखीणी भैइ मोजड़ी है (म्हे)। कपड़ा धोळा (थारै सेत)। कंवर खाण्डेराव करै बूझणा (वाह वाह)। धूलिया क्युं ऊफणै बाजारां की (ढालां ढालां रेत)। लाखीणो आदमी दीखियो बेटी का बाप (म्हे)। लाखां थारै कन्नै (कपड़ पहरण नै है)। धूलवूं बाथियां कींयां पड़ै आ कह (हां जकी बताय कीयो)। भाट मन में देखियो (म्हे)। थारा धणी नै बो ही समचार कह (हां राजा नीमदे नै कीयो जको को जको ही (कह द्यो)। सुरग्याणी है (जरां तो समझ जायी)। फूटो डोळ है जरां तो बो गियो जियान ओ ही अबार (हां जायी आपां भाइयां भेळो ले चालर) (करसियां ही कांई कीयो)।।

पगां लखीणी जी कंवरजी म्हारै मोजड़िया औवूं रे।
कंवरजी म्हारै रे कपड़ा न धोळा सेत।
चौईस लाल पड़ गी ताणा बजार में।
म्हारो कंवरजी रे हीरो गम गो एक।।
(भलां जी भलां) देव भलां

पगां लखीणी मोजड़ी है (म्हे)। कपड़ा धोळा (म्हारै सेत)। अरै चौईस तो लाल पड़ गी थारा बजार में (वाह वाह)। नीमा म्हारो हीरो ही गम गो कंवरजी (एक)। सुणो कंवर साय चौईस तो लाल (गमादी)। एक हीरो (पड़गियो)। दरबार का हुकमूं भूणोजी बूझणा (करी है)। कुण देश को आदमी है तूं (जकी बताय कीयो)। कीयो श्री महाराज सात समंदरा पार का हूं (हां हूं कीयो)। कुण लोग है (म्हे)। कीयो राजावो का बैइ को भाट (हां हूं कीयो)। नांव (कांई है कीयो)। श्री महाराज सेंसारी दुनिया जगीशया कह अर (बतलावै कीयो)। अरै जगीशया (म्हे)। लाला भैइ पड़ गी जठावूं खोई गी घरै (हां हर है कीयो)। श्री महाराज लाला तो खोई गी (हां खोईज गी कीयो)। हीरो (हां हीरै की अब आस है कीयो)। दरबार का हुकमूं भूणोजी सिरदारां नै बूझणा (करी है)। अरै सिरदारां (म्हे)। ईका धणी को कोय टाबर गम गो (वाह वाह)। बी नै ढूंढतो (फिरै कीयो)। गेला बना दिया दुनिया नै (म्हे)। भूणोजी ओ समचार कीयो भाट मन में देखियो थारा धणी नै सुरग्याणी सुणयो (पण सुरग्याणी जरूर ही है कीयो)। सुरग्याणी है बेग्याणी तो कोनी (वाह वाह)। भूणोजी बूझणा करी जगीशया (म्हे)। बावन गढां का दफ्तरखानै हाथ में (हां म्हारै हाथवूं चूकै है)। बावन गढां में थारा हीरा को नांव (आ जावे)। तो लेख को हिसाब रोकड़ को कर लेवूं (म्हे)। नामवूं काट थारा हीरा नै थारै मुण्डा के (हां कर देवूं ले जाय कीयो)। श्री महाराज (म्हे)। तूं हीरा नै सोधेलो (जरूरी म्हारो हीरो लाधेलो)। भूणोजी बोलै (वाह वाह)। कांई समचार भाट नै कहवै देखां (कीआवूं जाणज्यो कीआवूं)। अबार कहवूं देव का हुकमूं ले तूं।।

ए ताणा हीरा पर तो जी जो बिरखा घणी हो गी परदेशी पंछड़ा रे।
हीरो ऊठ गो दीखै जी नंदी नरबदा पार।

धूल में हीरा रे लाधेला कोय ने।
राजकुलियां में रे चतुराई सूं नाळ।।
(भलां जी भलां) देव भलां

ताणी हीरा पर भाई (बिरखा घणी हु गी कीयो)। हीरो ऊठ गो दीखै ताणो नंदी नरबदा के (पार)। धूल में हीरा कोनी लाधै (म्हे)। राजकुलियां में चतुराई से (नाळ)। बेटी का बाप सगळा नै गेला बनाया (हां धूल में कोय हीरा थोड़ा ही है कीयो)। सिरदारां टाबर सोधतो ई फिरै (वाह वाह)। ठीक तो है कीयो (म्हे)। भिनाय के नोरो आजायी (वाह वाह)। दरबार का हुकमूं भूणोजी अती कह अर (हां घोड़ी की एड़ी की मसकायी)। मन में देखियो के आती असवारी नै ता आसका (आपां दीनी ही कोनी)। एक जाती नै तो आसका तो (जरूरी देवां कीयो)। भाट बगड़ावतां को बोलै (वाह वाह)। कांई आसका बनावै (अर कांई भूणोजी नै आसका देवै देखां)। अबार कहवूं भगवान का हुकमूं देखां (कीआवूं जाणज्यो भोपाजी महाराज कीआवूं)।।

ए कंवर की फौज में तो जी देश देश का राजवियां औवूं रे।
मोकळा भाईजी मुंगल घणा पठाण।
जगीशया भाट की आसका मानज्यो।
मानज्यो भाई रे सांमर धणी चुहाण।।
(भलां जी भलां) देव भलां

दरबार का हुकमूं (म्हे)। कंवर की फौज में देश देश का राजवी है (वाह वाह)। हेंर मोकळा घणा मुंगल (पठाण)। जगीशया भाट की आसका मान लीज्यो (म्हे)। दरबार का हुकमूं सांमर राय (चुहाण)। सांमर को नांव लेय चुहाणां के नांव से (आसका भूणोजी नै दीनी ही)। साडा सात बीसी चुहाण सिरदार (नौकरी करता)। ओ तो गियो है भैइ भाट (म्हारो)। ओ कीयो (भाट है म्हारो)। भाट मन में देखियो आसका दीनी तूं (म्हे)। पण ताणा धणी नै तो (पूगण कोनी दी बीच की बीचै ही बोच लीनी)। दूजी आसका बनावै (अर) कांई भूणोजी नै आसका देवै (कीआवूं जाणज्यो भोपाजी महाराज अब कीआवूं)। अबार कहवूं धनी देव का ई का हुकमूं ले तूं (वाह वाह जी वाह वाह)।।

ए रावालां बागां में तो जी आज अजमेरी केवड़ा रे।
ए तो भाई जी स ही फूल भिड़ा रे।
सिरै फूल नै देवूं करां को आसका।
कदै तपतो रे गोठां राज चुहाणां रे।।
(भलां जी भलां) देव भलां

दरबार का हुकमूं रावजी का बागां में अजमेरी केवड़ा है (म्हे)। स ही फूल (भिड़ा)। अरै सिरै फूल नै देवूं करां को आसका (म्हे)। कदै तपता गोठां राज (चुहाणां)। गोठां को नांव ले अर (हां आसका भूणोजी नै दीनी ही)। सिरदार सारा ही नट गा (वाह वाह)। गोठां म्हालो आपांलो तो भैइ (एक ही कोनी कीयो चुहाण दूजा गांवां का हा आपां तो (वाह वाह)। भूणोजी कीयो रे सिरदारां (म्हे)। थै

रोळो क्युं करो बीच में (हां बीच में लड़ो कींयां है कीयो)। आगलो आसका दे अर कांई नांव लियो अबार (हां सिरै फूल नै आसका दीनी है ओ)। थानै सिरै फूल आज के दिन (मैं हूं कीयो)। आसका देवै तो म्हनै (दी है कीयो)। भूणोजी रळकाय घोड़ी की बड़छी (अर के पाछो बावड़ियो)। ए मुंगता (म्हे)। चुहाणां के नांव से म्हनै आसका कींयां दीनी बोल (हां कींयां दी कीयो आज)। म्हाना बाप दादा को नांव जाणै कोनी (हां तूं जाणै कोय नी कांई कीयो)। कीयो ताणा बाप दादा की खीर खाबा कद आयो मैं (हां म्हनै किस्या दिन खीर फलका जिमाया कीयो)। दरबार का हुकमूं भूणोजी बूझणा करी सुण रे भाट (म्हे)। के मैं छाना कोनी रिया मण्डोवरा पड़ीहार (वाह वाह)। पड़ीहार को नांव लियो जरां भाट के एड़ी की चोटी जाळ लागी जी जाळा (हां लागी कीयो)। दरबार का हुकमूं भाट बगड़ावतां को बोलै (म्हे)। कांई समचार कंवर भूणा नै कहवै देखां (कीआवूं जाणज्यो देखां कीआवूं)। अबार कहवूं देव का हुकमूं ले तूं (वाह वाह जी वाह वाह)।।

जात पलट गो जी ए ई कंवर महाबळी रे।
जियान भाई रे काशी नै पलटी ठठियारां।
अतरा दिन तो गोठां में रे चुहाण बाजता।
रळ बेठा दीयाजी दीया और पड़ीहारां रे।।
(भलां जी भलां) देव भलां

जात पलट गो रायजादा महाबळी (म्हे)। जियान भैइ काशी नै पळटी (ठठियारां)। अता दिन तो गोठां में चुहाण बाजिया (म्हे)। आज रळ बेठा दिया और ही (पड़ीहारां)। भलो काम व्हियो (हां जात पलट गियो कीयो)। दरबार का हुकमूं भूणा के और ई के संबन्ध खोज (पड़ ग्या है)। आ कांई बात हुई (म्हे)। तो बै चुहाण सिरदार हां (म्हे)। सब नट गा (वाह वाह)। कीयो गोठांमालो चुहाण एक ही कोनी (म्हां में तो नैइ है)। दरबार का हुकमूं भूणोजी बोलै (वाह वाह)। कांई समचार कहवै देखां (कीआवूं जाणज्यो अब भोपाजी महाराज कीआवूं)।।

ए दौड़ो देवा नै गिया तो जी ए ई बाबो दियो रावजी रे।
गिया बतावै रे सात समंदरा पार।
छै महीना का पकड़योड़ा आया नौथेरी राण में।
जठा पछै बाजा रे मण्डोवरा पड़ीहार।।
(भलां जी भलां) देव भलां

दरबार का हुकमूं कीयो बाबो रावजी दौड़ो देवा गिया बतावै देश में (म्हे)। गिया बतावै भैइ सात समंदरा (पार)। अरे छै महीना का पकड़योड़ा आया मैं नौथेरी राण में (म्हे)। जकै दिन पछै बाजा मण्डोवरा (आज पड़ीहार)। म्हनै लोग कहवै भैइ (म्हे)। के भूणा (वाह वाह)। तनै सात समंदरा पारूं पकड़ा ल्याया बै (वाह वाह)। भूणाजी के आंटो आयोड़ो (म्हे)। दरबार का हुकमूं के भाट नारदी बूझणा करी (म्हे)। कीयो भैइ अता दिन तो चुहाण ही बाजता (वाह वाह)। पण आज जात पलट गो तूं कीयो (वाह वाह)। तो दरबार का हुकमूं भूणोजी बोलै कांई समचार कहवै देखां (कीआवूं जाणज्यो कीआवूं देखां)। अबार कहवां भैइ भगवान का हुकमूं देखां।।

ए दौड़ो देबा नै गिया तो जी ए ई बाबो रावजी ई रे।
गिया बतावै भाटजी रे सात समंदरा पार।
छै महीना का पकड़योड़ा आया नौथेरी राण में।
जठूं बाजा रे मण्डोवरा पड़ीहार।।
(भलां जी भलां) देव भलां

एक दौड़ो देबा गिया बाबो रावजी बिण देश में (म्हे)। गिया बतावै भाट सात समंदरा (पार)। अरै छै महीना का पकड़योड़ा आया भैइ नौथेरी राण में (वाह वाह)। जठा पछै भाट बाजा मण्डोवरा (मैं पड़ीहार)। जठा पछै भैइ रे पड़ीहार बाजा मैं (म्हे)। कीयो जरां भैइ तूं कह नै मैं रावजी के दरबार का हुकमूं के म्हानै ईंयां आसका कींयां दीनी तूं रावजी को जलमयोड़ो तो है कोनी (वाह वाह)। तूं कहवै के सात समंदरा पार पकड़ (ल्याया है कीयो)। ईंयांका की आसका है कोनी म्हारै कन्नै (हां दौड़ दसिया की म्हारै कन्नै आसका ही कोनी)। दौड़ दसियो (हां सा)। दरबार का हुकमूं भूणोजी मन में सोचार बिचार करियो (म्हे)। ई भाट नै बजार में मुंगता नै छेड़ियो नै (वाह वाह)। जर दौड़ दसियो और बाज गो (वाह वाह)। असवारी चालबा दियो (हां चालण दियो)। भूणोजी दरबार का हुकमूं बोर घोड़ी नै (हांक दीनी)। भाट मन में देखियो (वाह वाह)। की आयोड़ो धणी जाय (आगै कुण मिलबा देय आपां नै कीयो)। ओ तो तनै ओळखै तो कोनी (वाह वाह)। आ टारड़ी ओळखती हुली (हां ई नै बतलावो)। तो भाट बोलै (वाह वाह)। कांई घोड़ीमाता नै समचार कहवै देखां (कीआवूं जाणज्यो कीआवूं देखां)। अबार कहवां भैइ देव का हुकमूं देखां (वाह वाह जी)।।

ए लाला कटावूं तो जी घोड़ीमाता ये ताणा ऊबटा रे।
कटाल्यूं घोड़ी ये लाला बीचली लाल।
अठवूं आगै नै सिरकी तो ही घोड़ी चांवण्डा।
तेईसां भाइयां की थै तामै तीन तलाक।।
(भलां जी भलां) देव भलां

लाला कटावूं घोड़ीमाता थारा ऊबटा (वाह वाह)। मैं कटावूं लाला ही बीचली (अब लाल)। अठवूं आगा नै सिरकी तो घोड़ी चांवण्डा (म्हे)। तेईस भायां की तामै तीन (तनै तलाक है कीयो)। घोड़ी (हां आगेनी मत सिरक)। बगड़ावतां की आण है भायां (वाह वाह)। जियान खंबा रोपे नै (म्हे)। जियान घोड़ी सूमा नै (रोप दिन्या)। भूणोजी घोड़ी के एड़ी की दे घोड़ी तो लेरै नै लड़ंगो (देवै जी कीयो)। आगै नै पैंड ही (नैइ भरे)। भूणोजी मन में देखियो की अबार कहवै नी की मुंगतो सात समंदरा पार को रहबाळो (हां हूं कीयो)। टारड़ी नै कामण कर दिया (हां जादू कर दीन्या)। कीयो मुंगता घोड़ी नै कामण कींयां करिया भैइ (वाह वाह)। तो भाट बोल्यो कोनी (वाह वाह)। भूणोजी कीयो देखा सांग आवै (हां आण द्यो कीयो)। आबा देय भैइ देव का घर की बजरशिला माथा पर आडी है (आडी है कीयो)। पहली सांग भूणा की भाट का माथा के ऊपर (चाली)। ज्यूं कढाव के मांय घोड़ो खड़कै नै (म्हे)। जी भांत से (सांग खड़की जी कीयो)। कीयो भाट कांई सला (हां जगा ही खड़ियो)। कीयो

रूंगतो तो कोनी कटियो हाल (वाह वाह)। मन में देखियो कांई बात हुई माथा नै कामणावूं बांध ल्यो (हां माथा नै काटो बांध लियो कीयो जादूवूं)। दरबार का हुकमूं पसवाड़ै पर देय (जको आर की पार जान नीकल जावे)। कीयो जरां मुंगता अब के आवै भैइ (हां सामू कीयो)। आण दे (म्हे)। देव का घर की बजरशिला म्हारै (आडी है कीयो)। दूजी सांग भाट का पसवाड़ा पर भूणाजी की (चाली)। बी भांतवूं ही सांग दरबार का हुकमूं फिसल गी (वाह वाह)। भूणोजी मन में देखियो (म्हे)। पसवाड़ा नै मुंगतो काटो बांध ल्यो (वाह वाह)। मौरा में देय जका काळजा मांय कर काढ दे (आर की पार काढ देवां कीयो)। अंजस कर भूणोजी कीयो अब के आवै (हां आण द्यो कीयो)। देव का घर की बजरशिला म्हारै तो (आडी है कीयो)। तीजी सांग भाट का मौरा के ऊपर भूणोजी बाही (वाह वाह)। जार कढावा के मांय घोलो खड़कै भी भांत से सांग खड़की (हां खड़क अर नीचै जांवती पड़ी)। अरै भाट कांई सला (हां जगा ही खड़ियो हूं मैं तो)। भूणोजी मन में देखियो (म्हे)। के ई पर बाह करयावूं आपणी तो (हां हल्की होवै कीयो)। दरबार का हुकमूं कोय रावजी का अमराव देखलेयी (म्हे)। आ के की भूणोजी आपां में ही दाकलां (करै कीयो)। अरै कुण देश को एक मुंगतो मिलियो (हां जको की कोनी बीगड़यो भूणोजीवूं तीन सांग (बाही कीयो)। अब आपणै बाही करियावूं हार होवै (वाह वाह)। दरबार का हुकमूं काळू मीर दीयोजी इयां का तमाशा (हां देख रिया जी कीयो)। मीर बूझणा करी दीया (म्हे)। तनै ठा व्हियो कोनी व्हियो (हां तनै ठा पड़ियो कोनी पड़ियो)। कुण है ओ (जकी बताय)। दरबार का हुकमूं बगड़ावतां का छोछू भाट भूणावूं मिल गो (हां सागै को सागै बो ही है कीयो)। कीयो रे मीर (म्हे)। तूं कहवै नी मुसलमान की जात में झूट (बोलां कोनी कीयो)। बेटी का बाप बगड़ावतां थका ही साठ बरस को डेण (हां हो कीयो)। अरै ओ तो पच्चीस बरस को जवान है (हां आज दिन है कीयो)। कीयो तेरै को पता नी इस बात का (म्हे)। भूणा का तो है हेरा (म्हे)। हेंर दरबार तीन तिलोकी को नाथ इसका खोळिया पलट दिया (हां खोळिया पलट अर भेज्या है कीयो)। बूझणा करी जरां बतला (हां बतलावो कीयो देखां)। कीयो लियो अबार जेज कांई अब (वाह वाह)।।

कुण दाबै जी जो काळा की पूंछड़ियां रे।
कुण देवै भाई रे जातां सिंग नै साई रे।
आज दिन भूणावूं भिड़ जावै रे बीरा भाटजी।
नर मर जावै भाटजी रे बिन टूटी बिन आयी रे।।
(भलां जी भलां) देव भलां

दरबार का हुकमूं समचार कीयो है (वाह वाह)। कुण दाबै भाटजी काळा की पूंछड़ी (वाह वाह)। अरै कुण देवै जातां सिंग नै (अब साई)। आज दिन भूणावूं भिड़ जावै (म्हे)। जको नर तो मर जावै बिन टूटी बिन (आयी कीयो)। ताणा धणीवूं आज दिन भिड़वालो कोनी (वाह वाह)। मीर बोलै (वाह वाह)। कांई समचार कांई भाट नै कहवै देखां (भाट नै कहवै देखां कीआवूं जाणज्यो कीआवूं)। अबार कहवूं भगवान का हुकमूं ले तूं (वाह वाह जी)।।

मुख मीठो जी हाथ कतरणी रे बीरा भाटजी रे।
भाट नारदी ये सांचो सांचो बोलै औवूं रे।
लरड़दियां के रे इयाड़ै भाट नारदी।
जांतोड़ा सिंग की रे सांकळ मत खोलै रे।।
(भलां जी भलां) देव भलां

मुख तो थारो मीठो है (म्हे)। ए करां को भाटजी सांचो ही सांचो (तूं बोले)। कीयो लरड़ियां के इयाड़ै भाट नारदी (म्हे)। अरै जांतोड़ा सिंग की सांकळ मत (अब खोले)। मैं ईकै मुण्डा के लरड़ियां हां (म्हे)। म्हानै तो भैइ रे इयाड़ा में (जार बड़बा दियो कीयो)। पछै थारा धणी नै (जाण करायी कीयो)। म्हानै ठाणै होबा दे (वाह वाह)। बगड़ावतां को भाट हाथ को फटकारो (हां दीयो जांतां रियो कीयो)। नी अब मरा द्यूंला (वाह वाह)। कीयो दीया कांई सला भैइ (हां कोनी भाट सागै कीयो)। कीयो सागै को सागै है भैइ (वाह वाह)। तो ए अमराव दोन्यु जणा बिदा (व्है ग्या है)। भूणोजी मन में देखियो (म्हे)। अरै रावजी का सारा अमराव है जका (उठ ग्या कीयो)। तूं एकलो ऊबो अठै भूंडो लागी (म्हे)। आपां ही चालणो अच्छियो अबार (हां चालां कीयो)। दरबार का हुकमूं भूणोजी घोड़ी नै पाछी हांक दी (म्हे)। तो भाट मन में देखियो के ई नै ठा तो हाल पड़ियो कोनी (वाह वाह)। हेंर धणी आयोड़ो जाय पछै मिलबा दे कोनी दे बैरी (हां मिलण तो देवेला ई नैइ कीयो)। दरबार का हुकमूं तो घोड़ी नै ई बतलायी आपां (म्हे)। जको आ ई ठम गी (वाह वाह)। तो दरबार का हुकमूं आंका पातू कलाळी रंग महल में तमाशा (देख रिया हा)। देख तमाशा (अर कह गोखड़ै पर आयी ऊंची)। पातू कलाळी बोलै (वाह वाह)। कांई समचार कहवै देखां (कीआवूं जाणज्यो कीआवूं देखां)। अबार कहवूं भैइ देव का हुकमूं देखां (वाह वाह)।।

क्युं बाहवै तो जी जो बोर नै ताजणा रे।
नान्या भूणा रे क्युं एड़ी सूं मसकावो रे।
भाट तो भूणाजी थारो अर ताणा बाप को।
तनै देखिया से रे करड़ा जबान बाहवै।।
(भलां जी भलां) देव भलां

क्युं बाहवै भूणा बोर घोड़ी नै ताजणो (म्हे)। हेंर क्युं एड़ी सूं (मसकावो)। अरै दरबार का हुकमूं भाट तो भूणा थारो अर तणा बाप को (है कीयो)। तनै देखिया से करड़ा जबान (अब बाहवे)। तनै देख देख करड़ो बोलै ओ (वाह वाह)। भूणोजी के ऊपरा नै निंगै (करी है)। दरबार का हुकमूं पातू कलाळी कांई कह रही है भैइ (हां आ कांई कहवै है कीयो)। भूणोजी पातू कलाळी ने कहवै तो भुवाजी (म्हे)। पण आ ठा कोनी की किस्या साख (हां भुवाजी लागै है कीयो)। लेरलावूं लागै (ईयूं लागै कीयो)। कलाळी बोलै (म्हे)। कांई समचार कंवर भूणा नै (औरूं कहवां देखां लगतो ही)।

ए आकड़ा नीमड़ा तो जी क्यें नै जुरै रे कंवर महाबळी रे।
मत बहवै घर को ओ चारण भाट।

मारलै दुर्जनसाल पड़ीहार ने।
खाया बैठो ताणो रे भोज नै सरिसो बाप।।
(भलां जी भलां) देव भलां

आकड़ा नीमड़ा क्युं जुरै कीयो (म्हे)। भूणाजी क्युं मारै घर का चारण (अब भाट)। अरै मारलै दुर्जनसाल पड़ीहार नै (वाह वाह)। खाया बैठो रे थारा भोज सरीसा (बाप)। ई नै मारयावूं कांई हुई भैइ (वाह वाह)। रावजी नै मारलै (म्हे)। जको बैर तो नीकलै एक (वाह वाह)। दरबार का हुकमूं भूणोजी मन में बिचार (करियो है)। अरै भुवा पातर ईयां की बोल बोलै जरां जठांवूं हेरो थारो हु गो (हां हेरो थारो ही है दूसरै को कोनी कीयो)। बूझणा करी रे भाट (म्हे)। एक तो आगा नै कठै जायी के म्हारै कन्नै (हां म्हारै ही कन्नै आयो है तू)। कीयो श्री महाराज आगा नै म्हारै कोय निवतो तो (घालनो कोनी)। मैं तो थारै कन्नै ही (आयो हूं कीयो)। कीयो जरां म्हारा भायां का कागद पतर ल्याय (हां ल्यायूं हूं कीयो)। कीयो नोकळा सारा है (वाह वाह)। दरबार का हुकमूं कागदांवूं पावरो भरियो हो (म्हे)। तो भूणाजी कन्न आगै (भाट कर दीन्यो)। कांई देव का हाथ का पहली परवाणा बंचै देखां (वाह वाह)।।

ए पहली परवाणा बांचिया तो जी ए ई देव के हाथ का रे।
देवजी मांयनै रे घणा लिखिया हरोळ।
बांचतै परवाणै भूणाजी बेगा पधारज्यो।
सूनी पड़ी आप की रे बाप तणी बागोर।।
(भलां जी भलां) देव भलां

पहली परवाणा बंचिया भैइ देव के हाथ का (वाह वाह)। देव महाराज घणा ही लिखिया (हरोळ)। बांचतै परवाणा बेगो आजै कंवर महाबळी (वाह वाह)। सूनी पड़ी बाप तणी (थारी बागोर)। और सब खेड़ा है जका बगड़ावतां का बसीवान हो गा भैइ (म्हे)। थारा बाप को खेड़ो है नै (हां जको उजड़ी पड़ियो है कीयो)।।

परवाणा बांचिया जी भाई भंगेरिया का हाथ का रे।
लिखदीना भाईजी दे मूंछियां की आंट।
बांचतै परवाणै बेगो पधारज्यो कंवर महाबळी।
नी जरां राळूं रे दुशमना सागै बांट।।
(भलां जी भलां)। देव भलां

परवाणा बांचिया भैइ भाई भंगेरिया का हाथ का (म्हे)। भांगीजी लिखिया दे मूंछ की (आंट)। हां परवाण बांच बेगा पधारज्यो (म्हे)। नीजर राळूंलां दशमना भेळो मिरच्यां सामिल (बांट)। दरबार का हुकमूं दुशमना के भेळै थारो ही मरजायलो मन ठा कोनी है (वाह वाह)। भूणोजी बूझणा करी बाबा भाट ओ भाई है कांई (हां भाई है सा कीयो)। श्री महाराज भाई है आपको (वाह वाह)।।

ए परवाणा बांचिया तो जी ए ई पीपळदे का हाथ का रे।
लिखदीना पीपळदे रे परवणवालै पान।

बांचतै परवाणै जेठजी ओ बेगा पधारज्यो।
बाळक बूह का थां बिनै जी कुण राखेलो मान।।
(भलां जी भलां) देव भलां

परवाणा बांचिया भैइ पीपळदे का हाथ का (वाह वाह)। पीपळदे राणी लिखिया परवणवालै (पान)। परवाणो बांच बेगा पधारज्यो (वाह वाह)। बाळक बीनणी का कुण राखी थां बिनै ही (मान)। जेठ साय आप आयो तो म्हारा ही मान भी (हां बेसी रहवै कीयो)।।

ए परवाणा बांचिया तो जी जो साडू के हाथ का रे।
माता लिखिया जी परवण वालै पान।
बांचतै परवाणै बेगो आजाज्यो कंवर महाबळी।
ताणा मांजी रे हुगा पाका पान।।
(भलां जी भलां) देव भलां

दरबार का हुकमूं परवाणा बांचिया माजी का हाथ का (वाह वाह)। माता लिखिया भैइ परवणवालै (पान)। बांचतै परवाणै बेगो आजै रे कंवर (महाबळी)। थारा मांजी लाल हु गा पाका ही (पान)। मैं तो खिरबाळा हां तड़की खिरजां लाल (हां आजावै तो मेला आपणा हो जाय कीयो)। दरबार का हुकमूं भूणोजी बूझणा करी रे बाबा भाट (म्हे)। आ म्हारी मां है कीं (हां) बडी मां है श्री महाराज कीयो (बडी मां है कीयो)।।

ए परवाणा बांचिया तो जी जो राणी पीपळदे का हाथ का रे।
लिखदीन्या पीपळदेजी दे घूंघट की ओट।
बांचतै परवाणै बेगा आज्यो म्हाना जेठ सा।
आंतां दियाजो दुशमन का रे छाज्जां ऊपर चोट।।
(भलां जी भलां) देव भलां

दूजा परवाण बंचिया राणी पीपळदे का हाथ का (म्हे)। पीपळदे राणी लिखिया दे घूंघट की (ओट)। परवाणो बांच बेगा चड़ायज्यो म्हारा जेठ सा (वाह वाह)। आंतां दियाजो दुशमन का छाज्जां ऊपरै (चोट)। बैरी के सैनाणी कर (हां आयज्यो कीयो)। परवाणो बांचिया भैइ दरबार का हुकमूं तेजाजी का मदना का हाथ का (म्हे)। मदन सिंग लिखिया मोकळा मुजरां (मान)। परवाणो बांच बेगो आज्यै (म्हे)। गोठां में भाई बेठा बीन बिसूणी (जान)। जानी घणा ही हा (हां बीन बनबाळा कोनी कीयो)। दादा भूणा बेगो आज्यो भैइ (वाह वाह)।।

भाट छोड़यायो जी जो घोड़ा फूलरिया को पागड़ो रे।
बावड़ आयो रे बळवन्तकारी भूण।
धणी गुसाईं बजार में हद मिलिया।
आंका ठाकरां जी कौतक देखै कुण।।
(भलां जी भलां) देव भलां

भाट तो छोड़ियो घोड़ा फूलरिया को पागड़ो (वाह वाह)। बावड़ आयो बळवन्तकारी (अब भूण)। अरै धणी गुसाईं दोन्यु ई बजार में हद मिलिया (वाह वाह)। आंका कौतक देखै (कुण)। शहर का महाजन बूझणा (करी है)। सिरदारां (म्हे)। अती दार तो देखो ए लड़ां (दोन्यु जणा लड़ा)। हेंर अब घड़ी घड़ी में सैण व्हिया है (म्हे)। बाथां तो घालै अर दोन्यु जणा बजारां में (मिलै है कीयो)। आंको पार कोनी पायो (वाह वाह)। तो दरबार का हुकमूं बगड़ावतां को भाट भूणा से मिलतां (म्हे)। ए देव का हाथ का परवाणा (बंचता)। भूणा नै भाट के जाण होतां (म्हे)। जय बोलो भैइ श्री देवनारायण भगवान की (जय)। ग्यारहा बरसावूं दरबार का हुकमूं भूणोजी पाछो भाट से मिलियो (वाह वाह)। रावजी का अमराव काळू मीर दीयोजी ए दोन्यो सगस कछेड़ी में पूगता (हां पहली हो ग्या जी कीयो)। जांतां ही रावजी के फिराद (हां सुणायी है)। कीयो मीर (म्हे)। आ फिराद (क्वें की ल्यायो कीयो)। कीयो श्री महाराज जों बगड़ावतां को भाट हो नै ओ (म्हे)। जको कंवर भूणा से (आज मिल गियो है कीयो)। तो रावजी का अमराव तो रावजी की कछेड़ी में (हां पूग ग्या है)। तो कंवर भूणोजी अर भाट (म्हे)। भिनाय के नौरै (पूगता व्हिया जी कीयो)। मीर बूझणा करी हमारा कीयो करो (म्हे)। कांई मीर (हां जकी बताओ)। कीयो कात्तिक को महीनो है पुष्कर राज को मेलो है (म्हे)। कंवर भूणा नै तूं एक महीना की खातिर मेला की रूखाली भेज दियो (हां रूखाली बठै भेज द्यो एक महीना (तो कांई बेसीज जावां ज्यूं)। रावजी साय लिख परो कागद (म्हे)। हेंर कंवर भूणा के डेरै (हां पूगतो करियो है)। भूणोजी बांच परवाणो (म्हे)। कांई भाट नै बतलावै देखां (कीआवूं जाणज्यो कीआवूं देखां)। अबार कहवूं धणी देव का हुकमूं ले तूं (वाह वाह जी वाह वाह)।।

ए हलकारो फैरो नै जी जो बैइ का भाटजी रे।
भाटजी सांवता ई खबरै बेग मंगावो ई रे।
भूखी भगवन्ती भोग मांगै बैइ का भाटजी।
आपां भाटजी रे पोखरजी नै ध्यावो।।
(भलां जी भलां) देव भलां

हलकारो फैर बाबा भाटजी (वाह वाह)। सांवता की खबर बेगी (मंगावो)। अरै भूखी भगवन्ती भोग मांगै बैइ का भाट (म्हे)। पोखरजी नै (अब ध्यावो)। बाबा भाट पुष्कर चांलां (हां चालो कीयो)। बाह वाह रे म्हारा धणी भली बिचारी (म्हे)। दरबार का हुकमूं आ तो जबरी बिचारी (हां मैं ही बठै सिनान करियावूं कीयो)। बुढापा में म्हारै हाड़किया खुली (वाह वाह)। अठारां हजार की सायबी भूणाजी की भिनाय के नौरावूं बिदा (हुई है जी कीयो)। मीर दिया नै बूझणा (करी है)। अरै यार दीया (म्हे)। हमारा कीया (करो कीयो)। कांई (कांई करणो है कीयो मीर)। कीयो भूणा की फौज है जकी बजार में अबार (हां आरी है)। आपणा मंगाना हाथी है नै (म्हे)। इसनै मद पाय (भूणाजी के सामा छोड़ द्यो कीयो)। बैरी का एक झटका दो बटका बार (हां हाथी जातां ही कर देय कीयो)। रावजी नै तो बूझियो कोनी (म्हे)। बिनै बूझिया बी नै भूणा के सामनै हाथी नै (छोड़ दिन्यो)। ओ हाथी है जको भाट नै आतो (दीखियायो)। मन में देखियो दुश्मना को छोड़ोयोड़ो हाथी (आवै है कीयो)। तनै डर ही कांई है (म्हे)। धणी कन्नै ऊबो है नै (हां भूणोजी सागै है तनै डर (की बात को है कीयो)।

ए हाथी के तो जी दोय दांतली रे कंवर महाबळी रे।
थारै भूणाजी मुख में दांत बतीस।
मारलै जंगजीत हाथी नै कंवर महाबळी।
काटलै भूणाजी ऐरापत को शीश।।
(भलां जी भलां) देव भलां

हाथी के दोय दांतली है (म्हे)। भूणा थारै मुख में दांत (बतीस)। अरै मार जंगजीत हाथी नै रायजादा महाबळी (म्हे)। काटलै ऐरापत को ई (अब शीश)। एक झटको दो बटका कर राळ (वाह वाह)। भूणोजी मन में देखियो रे ओ कठवूं आयो कुबदीकारो (वाह वाह)। भाट नै दरबार का हुकमूं कानावूं सुणयो (म्हे)। आंखियां देख लियो (हां है तो कुबदीकारो ही कीयो)। दरबार का हुकमूं भाट तो बोलै कांई भूणा नै बतलावै देखां (कीआवूं जाणज्यो कीआवूं)।।

ए बैरियां का गणकड़ा मारया सूं जी कंवर भूणा रे दोका मानवै औवूं रे।
थारा पर भूणाजी लाख को गजराइत हींडतो आयो रे।
मार जंगजीत हाथी नै कंवर महाबळी।
बैरियां में बनजावै रे तोल मोल सुवायो रे।
(भलां जी भलां) देव भलां

बैरियां को तो भूणा गणकड़ो मारिया दोको मानै (म्हे)। हेंर थारा पर लाख को गजराइत हींडतो (आवे)। आयो मार जंगजीत हाथी नै रायजादा महाबळी (म्हे)। बैरियां म्हनै तोल मोल ही (सुवायो)। भूणा (म्हे)। बैरियां को कुत्तो मरियोड़ो चोखो कीयो (वाह वाह)। भूणोजी मन में देखियो रे लाख रिप्या का उजाड़ बाबाजी के दिन सहजायीं (हां कीयां होवै कीयो)। भूणोजी तो बोल्या कोनी (वाह वाह)। भाट मन में देखियो भाव ई धोळी आंखियां को है ओ तो (हां ईमै तो रीस तो कोनी कीयो)। ई नै भायां के भेळो ले जार तूं (करी कांई कीयो)। भाट बोलै (वाह वाह)। दरबार का हुकमूं कांई समचार कंवर भूणा नै कहवै देखां (कीआवूं जाणज्यो कीआवूं देखां)। अबार कहवूं देव का हुकमूं ले तूं (वाह वाह जी)।।

ए बारावत के बाई जलमियो की नै जी ए ई कंवर महाबळी रे।
ठिकाणो थारो जी करतां चोखो देख।
जांतां भाट देती नै बाईजी बैसणा।
जांतां भाट नै मिलती रे लांबी भुजा पसार।।
(भलां जी भलां) देव भलां

बारावत जी के भूणा बाई क्युं जलमी नै तूं (म्हे)। हेंर ठिकाणो करतां चोखो (देख अर)। जांतां भाट नै बाईजी देती बैसणा (म्हे)। जांतां मणियारवूं मिलती लांबी भुजा (पसार)। धोळी आंखियां का बगड़ावतां को जलम कांई लियो तूं (हां क्यें नै जलम लियो कीयो)। बाई जलमियो होवेक (हां ठिकाणू चोखी तरह करतां कीयो)। आगै म्हारै रोटियां हाथ आती (वाह वाह)। भूणोजी मन में देखियो (म्हे)। अरै

बाबा भाट नै कानावूं सुणयो (पण आंखियांवूं आज देखियो कीयो)। है तो कळह को मूली भैइ (वाह वाह)।।

ए एक समा में जलमिया तो जी ए ई दड़ावट की कोटड़ियां रे।
नान्या भूणा बाजियो ओ सोहन थाळ।
तूं जलमियो जकी रात तेल बळियो जको घर में बावड़ियो कोय ने।
ताणा बाबोजी रे मंगल खरच्या चार।।
(भलां जी भलां) देव भलां

एक समा में जलमियो रे भूणा दड़ावट की कोटड़ियां में (वाह वाह)। जकै दिन बाजिया सोहन (थाळ)। तूं जलमियो जकी रात तेल बळियो जको म्हांका तो घर में हाल (कोनी बावड़ियो)। ताणा बाबाजी भैइ कबसरियां नै मंगल बांटियां (चार कीयो)। चार तो हाथी दिया (म्हे)। हेंर अरै हाथी तो आगड़ा ही गिया (वाह वाह)। तेल बळियो तूं जलमियो जी टैम नै (म्हे)। अरै बो ही म्हांकै तो आज गुण कोनी आयो (हां बो ही गुण कोनी लागियो तेल ही हालतां ही (हाथी तो आगा गिया)। दरबार का हुकमूं भूणोजी मन में देखियो (म्हे)। है तो कळह का मूली भाट (वाह वाह)। बगड़ावतां को भाट बोलै (वाह वाह)। कांई कंवर भूणा नै बतलावै देखां (कीआवूं जाणज्यो कीआवूं देखां)। अबर कहवूं धणी का हुकमूं ले तूं (वाह वाह जी वाह वाह)।।

ए राठोड़ां में तो जी रूंजट हो गा रे कंवर महाबळी।
बठै बीती तरवारियां की जाळ।
अबार की बेळियां में कोनी रह नेवाजी को कंवर भांगड़ो।
हाथीड़ो कांई रे जूजळो भाग्यो जाय।।
(भलां जी भलां) देव भलां

राठोड़ै भूणा रूंजट घणो ही हो (म्हे)। बठै बीती तरवारियां की (जाळ)। अरै अबार की बेळियां में कोनी रह नेवा को कंवर भांगड़ो (म्हे)। बो हाथीड़ो कांई जूजळो सो भाग्यो ई (जाय)। धोळी आंखियां का (म्हे)। तनै बतलायो मैं तो (वाह वाह)। म्हारा भांगीजी नै बतला द्यूं ई तो (म्हे)। जियान जूजळो नै मारै जती टैम ही कोनी लगावै हाथी नै मारतां (ई हाथी नै मारतां कीयो)। भूणोजी मन में देखियो (म्हे)। कीयो बाबो भाट आयो जरां कोय कंवर भांगीजी को ही नांव (हां घणो लेवै है)। हेंर रावजी की कछेड़ी में आपां नांव सुणा (हां भूणोजी कीयो)। कीयो देव की दड़ावट है बांकी (म्हे)। बठै ताबै नेवा को जोधखान भांगड़ी खान अरे नौटान बिसन करै (म्हे)। किलै गढ अर (कोट)। गढ कोट किला गिळबालो थारै लेरै भाई है (म्हे)। तनै डर ही (की बात को है कीयो)। दरबार का हुकमूं कांई हाथी पर कंवर भूणोजी (चाले)। कांई हाथी के भूणा बाजार में भूणा के झगड़ो हुवै देखां (वाह वाह)।।

ए मिसरी सूंती तो जी कंवर भूणोजी बाहर मियान से औवूं रे।
पूग गो भूणा नै जी हनुमत कासा पाण।
हाथी नै मारियो कंवर महाबळी रे।

बजार में भूणा नै रे कटका चड़ गियो पाण।।
(भलां जी भलां) देव भलां

मिसरी सूंती कंवर मियान से (म्हे)। पूग गो हनुमत कासा (पाण)। मारियो जंगजीत हाथी नै कंवर महाबळी (वाह वाह)। बजार में भूणा नै ठाकरां कटका चड़ गो (पाण)। तो हाथीड़ो नै तो एकानै जार (पड़ियो)। सूंड (एकानै जांती पड़ी)। मावत एकानै (पड़ियो जी कीयो)। मीर दरबार का हुकमूं दिया नै बूझणा (करी है)। कीयो दीया (म्हे)। तोबा तोबा तोबा तोबा तोबा तोबा तोबा (हां इन्याय कर दिया कीयो)। अरै रावजी नै बूझियो कोनी (म्हे)। ए हाथी नै आपां परबारो (हां छोड़ दीन्यो)। रावजी साय बडो औलमो देय (आपां नै देय कीयो)। रावजी नै जार मीर जांच करी (वाह वाह)। कीयो मीर (कांई है बात है कीयो)। कीयो श्री महाराज मंगाना हाथी होतो नी दरबार में (म्हे)। कीयो व्हिया (हां कीयो)। बी नै भूणोजी आज की तारीख में मार गेरिया (वाह वाह)। कीयो दरबार का हुकमूं खूंटै ऊबा नै ही (खूंटै ऊबै नै भूणोजी कींयां मारियो कीयो)। कीयो नैइ नैइ (कीयो खूंटै ऊबै नै कोनी मारियो)। तो भाई भूणा के सामनै हाथी नै कुण छोड़यो रे मीर (म्हे)। श्री महाराज हाथी नै तो मैं छोड़दियो (वाह वाह)। मैं देखियो (म्हे)। के हाथी भूणा नै अबार बजार में (हां मार देयी)। आप नै सुविधा ईका सौदा (हुई जावै कीयो)। रावजी बूझणा करी रे मीर (म्हे)। तूं भूणा पर एक हाथी नै (छोड़यो कीयो)। भूणा के ग्यारह हाथियां को बळ है भूणा में (वाह वाह)। ग्यारह हाथी भूणा के पग के अंगूठा के (बांध देवे)। तो ठरड़ अर भिनाय के नौरै (ले जाय कीयो)। एक हाथी नै क्युं मरिया रे भैइ (हां कींयां मरायो क्यें तूं)। दरबार का हुकमूं पुष्करराज के मेलै (हां) बीर हु गा (वाह वाह)। रावजी साय का परवाणा लिखयोड़ा के भूणा मेला में भैइ हाका दड़बड़ मत होबा दीज्यो (वाह वाह)। जापता पूरा (रखायज्यो)। एक महीना की मेला की रूखवाली आपणी है भैइ कीयो (म्हे)। बगड़ावतां को भाट दरबार का हुकमूं अधबीच जार थोगो मार लियो (हां काटा पग रोप लियो कीया मैं तो नी चालूं)। भाट (म्हे)। तनै चिर आवै कांई (हां चिर आवै कीयो ओ बाबा भाट)। कीयो बगड़ावतां थका ठेट की आवै कोय सारा की थोड़ी है आ (म्हे)। कीयो क्युं ऊबो कींयां रियो (हां मेलै चालै कोनी कीयो)। श्री महाराज मैं तो पाछो ही जावूं (हां मैं मेलै कोनी चालूं)। क्युं (क्युं कोनी चालै भैइ)। कीयो म्हारो सिनान दोहरो घणो (हां है कीयो)। के सोरो अन्नदाता (वाह वाह)। दोय भांत को कींया हो भाट कीयो श्री महाराज बगड़ावतां का महाभारत व्हिया (म्हे)। जकै टैम में बगड़ावतां को धन हो जको रावजी के बावन गढ है (म्हे)। बावन गढां में थोड़ो घणो (हां लूट में गियो कीयो)। ई जागां सिरदार आया बिनै (हां मेलै में रहवै कोनी)। ओ बगड़ावतां को घर को धन लियावै नै (म्हे)। मैं आंख सूं (देख लेवूं)। तो सिनान म्हारै दोहरो (हां हो जावे)। इस्यो कोय बगड़ावतां का पछै में जलमयोड़ो होवै (म्हे)। आगला कन्नु कोस म्हनै (म्हारै मुण्डा के कर देवे)। मैं ले जार देव की दड़ावट में (छोड़देवूं)। बो सिनान है म्हारो (सोरो कीयो)। भूणोजी बूझणा (करी है)। सुण रे भाट बगड़ावतां के मैं जलमिया बंस में (म्हे)। बै कह तूं बतायी मत (वाह वाह)। सागै बता देय (ओ छूटाय थारै मुण्डा के कर द्यूं कीयो)। चाल (चाल मेलै कीयो)। सिनान थारो मैं करावूं (वाह वाह)। वाह रे म्हारा धणी भरोसो है कीयो (हां ए तो थारा भरोसा ही पड़ै भूणाजी कीयो)। मेला की चड़ाई होतां (म्हे)। भूणोजी अर भाट मेलै बिदा

होंवतां (होंवतां) । जय बोलो श्री देवनारायण की (जय) । बोलो भैइ छोटा अर मोटा (स) । तो दरबार का हुकमूं पुष्कर के मेला कन्नै हां चड़ाई हु गी भूणाजी की (वाह वाह) । कंवर भूणा की दरबार का हुकमूं सुधै बाई डेरा व्हिया (वाह वाह) । बगड़ावतां को भाट तो म्हानी नाय तूंबा तो गला में (घाल लीन्या) । हेंर मेला में फिरबा लागो (वाह वाह) । बगड़ावतां को कोय धन (हां धक्कै आयो कोनी) । तो बगड़ावतां को भाट जका दो बाटियां खायां नै बी को तो रंगत नैइ बैठी (दो बाटियां खायां जी कीयो) । बी के गली कोनी (कळह कोनी हुई जी कीयो) । तो सगळा मेला में फिरतो फिरयो धारापतियां का चार भाई बारहठ भाट नै (सामा मिलिया जी कीयो) । तो सैन्धा-मैन्धा हा (म्हे) । चोखी तरह बाय घाल अर मिलिया (वाह वाह) । बगड़ावतां को भाट बोलै (म्हे) । कांई धारापतियां का बारहठां ने समचार कहवै (कीआवूं जाणज्यो देखां अब कीआवूं) ।।

ए पोखर की परबी तो जी जो हद भरीजै बीरा बारहठ जी रे।
दूर दूर की मेला में मेदनी आर धसी रे।
ताणा धणी मेला में आया कोय ने।
सारा पहली आंतां रे रावळजी रणसी ।।
(भलां जी भलां) देव भलां

बारहठां नै बगडावतां को भाट समचार (कीयो है) । पोखर की परबी हद भरी बीरा बारहठ जी (म्हे) । दूर दूर की मेदनी आर मेला में (धसी) । अरै ताणा धणी मेला में कींयां कोनी आया (म्हे) । सारा पहली आतां रे भाई रावळजी (रणसी) । रावळजी रण सिंग दोन्यो भाई सारा तो पहली (आंवतां) । सारा पछै ही (मेलै में जांवतां कीयो) । मेला को जापतो धारापतियां को हो (हां ठेट को ही कीयो) । ओ समचार कुण कीयो (भाट जी कीयो) । बाहरठ मन में देखियो (म्हे) । थारा धणियां को सैन्धो-मैन्धो (हां है कीयो) । कोय दुख सुख का समचार (हां कर बूझेलो) ।।

ए हळबळ माचिया ई जी जो पीलोदा री कोटड़ियां रे।
डेरा में भाटजी रे फिरै घणा नकीब।
म्हाना धणी मेला में दोन्यु भाई आवतियां।
कस्ता छोड़यायो में तो जी ऐरापतयां पर जीण ।।
(भलां जी भलां) देव भलां

हळबळ माची भाट धर पीलोदाली कोटड़ियां (म्हे) । डेरा में घणा फिर गा (नकीब) । म्हाना धणी मेला में आयी (म्हे) । कस्ता छोड़यायूं मैं ऐरापतयां पर (जीण) । दरबार का हुकमूं निशनियां लाग री हाथीड़ा के (म्हे) । अंबाबाड़ियां (हां मिल रही कीयो) । घड़ी सात में (मेलै में आबाळा ही है जी कीयो) । ओ समचार कुण कीयो (बारहठ जी कीयो धारापतियां का) । दरबार का हुकमूं बगड़ावतां को भाट बोलै (म्हे) । कांई बारहठां नै समचार कहवै देखां (कीआवूं जाणज्यो कीआवूं देखां) ।।

ए ताणा धणी तो जी बासक की माथा की दारू पी रे बीरा बारहठजी रे।
रहवै भाई रे रजपूतां बड दानियां रे।

ताणा धणी मेला में कीं का आवै रे सुदाना बारहठजी।
भौ तो धणी रे भूणा का मानिया रे।।
(भलां जी भलां) देव भलां

ताणा धणी बासक की माथा की दारू पी है (म्हे)। रहवै रजपूतां बड (दानियां)। थारा धणी मेला में कीं को आवै बीरा बारहठ (म्हे)। भौ तो म्हारा धणी कंवर भूणा का (मानिया)। तनै ठा कोनी (हां भूणोजी का अठै डेरा सुधै बाई (पहलीवूं लागयोड़ी है कीयो)। आज के दिन (म्हे)। ताणा धणी आबो तो घणी चाहीज्यै (वाह वाह)। मेला कानै दरबार का हुकमूं पगातिया कन्न कोनी सोवै (वाह वाह)। ओ समचार दरबार का हुकमूं बगड़ावतां को भाट कीयो (वाह वाह)। धारापतियां का बारहठ बोलै (म्हे)। कांई समचार कहवै देखां (हां कीआवूं जाणज्यो देखां कीआवूं)।।

ए असमाना रा घरां सूं तो जी जो कुण हेटा उतरै औवूं रे।
कुण तो भाटजी भालै आसन करै रे।
तूं भौमानबा की बात के रे बीरा भाटजी।
ताणो धणी म्हाना धणियां के जोड़ै रे दो ही बात नी करै औवूं रे।।
(भलां जी भलां) देव भलां

दरबार का हुकमूं असमाना का घरावूं भाई कुण हेटो उतरै (म्हे)। कुण भालां पर आसन (करे)। तूं तो भौमानबा की बात कहवै (म्हे)। ताणो धणी भूणोजी म्हारा धणी को जोड़ै बैठ दो बात ही (हां कांई करै कंईं कीयो)। दो बात कोनी करणी आवै (वाह वाह)। भौ तो घणी चीज है (म्है बारहठां के पूण्चै पाण हो)। दरबार का हुकमूं बगड़ावतां को भाट बोलै (म्हे)। कांई बारहठां नै जवाब पाछो दे (कीआवूं जाणज्यो कीआवूं)। अबार कहवूं धणी का हुकमूं देखां (वाह वाह जी वाह वाह)।।

ए असमाना रा घरांसूं तो जी जो इन्दरपग हेटा उतरै औवूं रे।
बाजीगर पेट की खातर रे भालै आसन करै औवूं रे।
पांचो भाई गौज धार चड़ै राताकोट की राड़ में।
सिंग सादूड़िया भाई रे माथा फोड़ मरै रे।।
(भलां जी भलां) देव भलां

असमाना का घरांवूं इन्दरपग हेटो उतरी जावै (म्हे)। ए पेट की खातर बाजीगर भालां पर आसन (करै है)। दरबार का हुकमूं म्हाना धणी गौज धार चड़ै राताकोट की राड़ में (वाह वाह)। सिंग सादूड़िया मतेई माथा फोड़ ही (मरे)। थारा धणियां की छै महीनै की आरबळ है (हां क्यें के बोज्यां मरो कीयो)। मतेई मरज्याय बै (वाह वाह)। गेलो है कित्ता दिन जी (म्हे)। बारहठ मन में देखियो (म्हे)। बगड़ावतां का भाट पूण्चै पाण है (हां आकरो घणो बोलै कीयो)। धणियां नै ठा करां (जणा जुगत बैठे)। चार भाई बारहठ मेला में (आयेड़ा हा कीयो)। दोय तो मेला में (रह ग्या)। दो गढ पीलोदा सामा घोड़ा पाछा हांक दिया (वाह वाह)। दरबार का हुकमूं गांव के गोरवें गिया बिचार (करियो है)। इस्यो काम करो भाई (हां जांवतां ही पहली बाह)। आपणी सुणाई होवै जिस्यो काम करावो (हां सुण लेवै कीयो)।

कांई करां (कींयां करां कीयो)। घोड़ा का मुण्डा तो आगा नै असवारां का लेरां नै कर द्यो (हां लारां नै असवारां का मुण्डा करो)। ऊंधा चड़ दरबार में बड़जावो मतेई बूझ लेयी अबार (हां ईंयां कींयां आया हो)। धारापतियां का भाट ऊंधा घोड़ा पर चड़ दरबार में बड़ गा (वाह वाह)। आंकी लार सिरदारां हां (म्हे)। बूझणा (करी है)। अरै ऊंधा चड़ कींयां आयगा (जकी बतावो कीयो)। आला बासड़ावूं कूटबा लागा बारहठां नै (वाह वाह)। धारापती कीयो रे भाई सिरदारां (म्हे)। बारहठ नै कूटो मत (बूझो कांई बात है)। कींयां आया ईंयां (म्हे)। कीयो बारहठां बात कांई है जका समचार को (हां सूल माण्ड अर कहवो ईंयां कींयां ऊंधा चड़ अर) (आया जकी बतावो)। धारापतियां का भाट बोलै (म्हे)। कांई समचार कहवै (कीआवूं जाणज्यो कीआवूं)।।

ए भाला री कोरावूं जी जो जाजम कठै रे धणी चितौड़ का रे।
भलो भरियो ताणा रे भायां को दरबार।
मेला में चड़ चाल रे धणी चितौड़ का।
मेलो में बाजियो घोड़ी रे खोखर को असवार।।
(भलां जी भलां) देव भलां

दरबार का हुकमूं भाला की कोरां से देख जाजम कठै है (म्हे)। भलो भरियो थारो भायां को (दरबार)। मेला में चड़ चाल धणी चितौड़ का (म्हे)। मेला में बाजियो रे घोड़ी खोखर को (असवार)। मेला को लोग हल्को बोलै (म्हे)। पण म्हारावूं कोनी कहनी आवै (कहनी कोनी आवै कीयो)। मेला का लोग ईंयां कहवै (म्हे)। के दरबार का हुकमूं धारापती कुमहारड़ा बै गढियां पर चड़बाळा कोनी आया (हां बै कींयां कोनी पूगिया कीयो)। राख पादणियां दुनिया आ कहवै (वाह वाह)। पण म्हारावूं तो कहनी कोनी आवै श्री महाराज (हां और कांई कहवूं और)। धारापती सिरदार बोलै (वाह वाह)। कींयां समचार कहवै देखां (कीआवूं जाणज्यो कीआवूं देखां)। अबार कहवूं धणी देव का हुकमूं ले तूं (वाह वाह जी वाह वाह)।।

ए कुण का डेरा में तो जी बारहठजी भाई रे चाला चाल्या रे।
कुण का डेरा में चाली म्हारी चाल।
जको आ दोकी म्हनै बता दे सुदाना बारहठजी।
काट माथा दोकी के दिरावूं रे नाळा छोड़ गी धार।।
(भलां जी भलां) देव भलां

कुण का डेरा में भाई चाला चाल्या म्हारा (म्हे)। कुण का रजपूतां में चाली म्हारी (चाल)। जको दोकी म्हनै बता सुदाना बारहठजी (म्हे)। देख काट माथो (म्हे)। दोकी के दिरावूं अब नाळा छोड़ गी (धार)। दरबार का हुकमूं माथो तो काट द्यां (म्हे)। हेंर छोरांवूं मूतियां करा द्यां (वाह वाह)। म्हारो नांव लेवै जका के (म्हे)। तो दरबार का हुकमूं बारहठ बोलै कांई समचार कहवै देखां (कीआवूं जाणज्यो कीआवूं देखां)। अबार कह द्यां देव का हुकमूं ले तूं (वाह वाह जी वाह वाह)।।

ए कंवर भूणा का डेरा में तो जी आपांका राजाजी चाला चालिया रे।
बगड़ावतांलो को भाट मेला में चलायी थांकी चाल।
मेला में चड़ चालो धणी चितौड़ का।
मेला में बाजियो घोड़ी रे गदियां को असवार।।
(भलां जी भलां) देव भलां

भूणा का डेरा में आपका चाला चाल्या (म्हे)। हेंर बगड़ावतां को भाट मेला में फिर फिर चलायी थांकी (चाल)। मेलै चड़ चाल धणी चितौड़ का (म्हे)। मेला में बाजियो घोड़ी गदी को (असवार)। ओ मेला को लोग तो हल्को बोलै म्हारावूं तो कहनी कोनी आवै (हां श्री महाराजा म्हारावूं कीज्यै कोनी कीयो)। धारापती सिरदार बूझणा (करी है)। मोकळ सिंग कंवर (म्हे)। रावजीवालो पालयोड़ो है नै ओ भूणोजी (हां) अबीड़ो चालै आलै (कीं अबीड़ो चाले)। तो रतन सिंग ईंयां करो मोकळ सिंग भाई (म्हे)। मेला की चड़ाई करावो (वाह वाह)। दरबार का हुकमूं बी का बाप को आपां कन्नै (हाथी है कीयो)। हाथी नै ले जावो (म्हे)। भूणा नै दिखार (हां ल्यावो कीयो)। थारा बाप को है भैइ हाथी (देख ले ओ रियो म्हार कन्नै है कीयो)।

ए धारापती आया तो जी हाथी जयमंगला की पायगा रे।
ऊबा दोन्यु भाई रे हाथ जोड़ हजूर।
बळ भेंट मांग ले गुणेश ई देवता।
मेलै चालज्यै रे म्हारा रे कजळीबन गजराज।।
(भलां जी भलां) देव भलां

धारापती सिरदार गिया हाथी जयमंगला की पायगा (वाह वाह)। ऊबा दोन्यु भाई हाथ जोड़ (हजूर)। बळ भेंट मांग गुणेश देवता (म्हे)। मेलै चालै म्हारा नै कजळीबन (गजराज)। गुणेश देवता (मेलै पधारो)। मेलै चालो (वाह वाह)। मोकळ सिंग कंवर हाथी नै लेयो भैइ कीयो (वाह वाह)। मोकळ सिंग कंवर बूझणा (करी है)। श्री महाराज (म्हे)। आपणै दरबार के मांयनै एक सूणी रहवै (हां सूणी रहवै कीयो)। सूणा का तो रोजगार (हां देवां हां)। हेंर सूणा का पेटिया (लेवां कीयो)। आपणै अतरा दिन सूणा को (काम पड़ियो कोनी)। आज मेलै जाबा को काम पड़ियो (म्हे)। सूण तो बूझो (हां सूण बूझां सूणी नै कीयो)। दरबार का हुकमूं कांई सूणी नै धारापती बुलावै (म्हे)। कांई मेला का सूण बूझै देखां (कीआवूं जाणज्यो कीआवूं देखां)। अबार कहवां देव का हुकमूं देखां (वाह वाह)।।

ए सूण बिचारोजी जो पीलोदाला सूणियार रे।
कह दे थारा रे सुगणावाली बात।
जयमंगला नै खोला रे पीलोदाली कोटड़ियां।
पाछो बन्धै कोनी बन्धै रे पीलोदाली पाट।।
(भलां जी भलां) देव भलां

सुगण बिचार भैइ गढ पीलोदा का सूणिया (म्हे)। के भाई थारा सुगणा के (बात)। जयमंगला नै

खोला पीलोदाली कोटड़ियावूं (म्हे)। पाछो आवै कोनी आवै रे पीलोदा की (पाट)। सूणी (म्हे)। ए सूण देख (हां सूण देख अर चोखी तरहवूं अर बता कीयो)। कीयो श्री महाराज (म्हे)। म्हारा सुगणा नै झूटां कोनी राळूं (हां दीखेली जिसी कहवूंला कीयो)। कीयो जा सुगणी सात ही गुणा माफ है (वाह वाह)। तनै दीखै जिसी बात कह भाई (म्हे)। तो सुगणी कांई धारापतियां को सुगण (मनावे)। हां बिचारै कांई धारापतियां नै सुगणा का समचार कहवै देखां (कीआवूं जाणज्यो कीआवूं देखां)। अबार कहवां भगवान का हुकमूं देखां (वाह वाह जी)।।

ए उडरमेरी बोलयाई जी ए ई मान समंदरा रे।
भुवानी बोल गी रे डावा बड़ की कुण।
मैं आपणै हारयोड़ा देखिया पीलोदा रा राजवियां।
मेला में जीतियो रे बारावत को भूण।।
(भलां जी भलां) देव भलां

दरबार का हुकमूं उडरमेरी बोली राजाजी मान ही समंदरा (म्हे)। भुवानी बोल गी डावा बड़ की (कुण)। मैं आपणै तो हारयोड़ा देखिया गढ पीलोदा का राजवियां (म्हे)। मेलो में जीत गो भैइ बळवन्तकारी (भूण)। भूणाजी नै जीतयोड़ो (देखियो)। हेर आपणै (हारयोड़ा देखिया हूं)। भलां ही मेला की चड़ाई करावो (अर भलां ही मत करावो)। कीयो सूणी (म्हे)। बात नै गल्त कह दी (हां माण्ड अर सूल देख सुगण ले के)।

देवूं मेदू से जी मिलियोड़ो बोल्यो रे सूणी रावळा रे।
तूं तो रे सुगणी कर गो मिलावूं बात।
राठोड़ां का बीर खेत में भोज नै हाथावूं झाटक्यो।
जरां म्हारै रे भूणो कती की बात।।
(भलां जी भलां) देव भलां

दरबार का हुकमूं कीयो सुगणी (म्हे)। देव अर मेदू मिलियोड़ो बोल ग्यो तूं (वाह वाह)। हेंर कर गो मिलावूं (तूं बात)। सवाई भोज नै बीर खेत में मैं हाथावूं झाटक्यो (म्हे)। जरां भूणो डावड़ो म्हारै कतै की (अब बात है कीयो)। भूणोजी है तो बा का जलमयोड़ो ही (वाह वाह)। ई बड़ो बाप हो नै भूणाजी कन्नै (म्हे)। जका नै मैं झाटक्यो (हां बीर खेत में म्हारा हाथावूं मारियावूं कीयो)। ओ समचार कुण कीयो धारापती सिरदार (कीयो है)। सुगणी मन में देखियो रे रहणो तो थारो अब होवै कोनी अठै (हां रहणो तो अठै है ही कोनी)। जिसी देखियोड़ी बात है (जिसी की जिसी कह देवै हो ओ)।।

ए कंकाळी देबी ल्याया जी ए ई बेटा बाघ का रे।
बै जातां रिया राजाजी आदी सगत की गेल।
राठोड़ां का रे बीर खेत में।
कुण बाहयां भोज नै थामालो रे खूंटियांवालो सेल।।
(भलां जी भलां) देव भलां

दरबार का हुकमूं कंकाळी देबी ल्याय बेटा बाघ का जी (म्हे)। बै नर गिया आद सगत की (गेल)। अरै राठोड़ां का बीर खेत में (म्हे)। कुण बाहयां भोज नै थामालो भाई खूंटियावाला (सेल)। मैं हाजर हां बठै (हां कुण मारियो थामूं जकी बतावो)। बै तो सगत बड़ाबड़ी ल्याया (म्हे)। अरै बी का अधर चकर चाल्या मतेई मरया गिया (वाह वाह)। धारापती सिरदार बूझणा (करी है)। अरै सुगणी (म्हे)। तूं एक तो मावूं भेद मांगियो हैक (सुगणा की बात बतावै कीयो)। श्री महाराज दीखै जकी बात कहूं नै (हां दीखै जिसी कहूं)। कीयो सुगणी सुण भाई (म्हे)। बा पुल तो एक दूजी अब काळी पुल है (दूसरी)। घड़ी पुल को फरक पड़ जाय (म्हे)। सुगण दूजा बिचार (हां अब दूसरा बिचार बता देखां)। कीयो श्री महाराज सुगणा नै झूटां तो कोनी राळूं मैं (वाह वाह)। म्हनै दीखेक जियान का जियान (सूण बतावूंला कीयो)। कीयो सात ही गुणा माफ है कीयो (बताय कीयो)। दीखै जियान की बता दे (वाह वाह)। सुगणी कांई सुगणी (मनावे)। दरबार का हुकमूं कांई सूणा का समचार कहवै (कीआवूं जाणज्यो भोपाजी महाराज कीआवूं)। दरबार का हुकमूं जरा।।

ए नार छाली तो जी बड़तलै राजाजी भेळै ही बोल गा रे।
मैं तो भाईजी बै ई बिचारया सूण।
काशमेरी तंबू जयमंगलो हाथी जांतां ही कोसलियो।
मेला में जीतियो रे बारावत को भूण।।
(भलां जी भलां) देव भलां

नार छाली बड़तलै राजाजी अब के भेळै बोल गा (म्हे)। मैं बै ई बिचारिया (सूण)। मैं आप नै तो हारयोड़ा देखिया (म्हे)। काशमेरी तंबू जयमंगलो हाथी मेला में जातां ही कोस लियो बारावत को ही (भूण)। ओ लियो सा चड़ाई भलां ही करावो (अर चाहै मत करावो कीयो)। भूणाजी नै तो जीतयोड़ा (देखया हूं)। आप नै (हारयोड़ा देखया हूं कीयो)।।

झूटो झूटो जी ए ई सूणी डावड़ा रे।
झूटो सुगणीजी करै झूट की बात।
मेलै जार पाछा आबा दे सूणी सिरकार का।
पाछो आंतां कटा द्यूं रे हाथर ताणा नाक।।
(भलां जी भलां) देव भलां

दरबार का हुकमूं झूटो झूटो रे सूणी सिरकार का (म्हे)। कर गो दरबार का हुकमूं करां को झूट की (तूं बात)। म्हनै मेलै जार पाछा आबा द्यै सूणी सिरकार का (म्हे)। पाछो आंतां ही कटावूं थारा हाथ अर दोन्यु ही (नाक)। चौरंगियो कर छोड़ देवूं मैं (वाह वाह)। सूणी मन में देखियो (म्हे)। दुशमन मेलै गियोड़ो तो पाछो लाखां ही (आबा को कोनी)। हेंर ई जागां अबार ई को बोल नीकल जावै की हाथ नाक काटो (म्हे)। घर बैठा उजाड़ हो जावै (हां घर बैठा उजाड़ हो जाय कीयो)। मेलै तो गियोड़ो पाछा लाखां ही (आवेलो ही कोनी कीयो)। दरबार का हुकमूं राजोजी बूझणा करी रे सूणी (म्हे)। छोड़दे लेरली बात नै (वाह वाह)। नार छाली एक जागा भेळै कीयां व्हिया (जकी बताय कीयो)।

श्री महाराज एवड़ को गुआल एवड़ नै लेर डूंगर में (गियो हो)। थाकियोड़ी बकरी है जको खोह में (हां रह गी)। रात पड़ गी (म्हे)। दरबार का हुकमूं रात का गुफा में सिंग रहवो (वाह वाह)। कर ओगाज (म्हे)। दुर के बाहरें (नीकलयो)। गोन पोपाड़ करियो डरती (म्हे)। सिंग मन में देखियो (वाह वाह)। अता दिन ताणी ई भोमी में अर ई डूंगर में सामनो करबालो जानवर (हां हो ही कोनी)। आज थारावूं सामनो करै ओ (हां ओ जिनावर थारावूं सामनो करबालो है कीयो)। जको आज मोटो है (वाह वाह)। कह तो ओगाज कर दुर के बाहरें (नीकलयो)। घाल गाण्ड में पूंछड़ो (म्हे)। पाछो दुर में ही (बड़ गियो जी कीयो)। गोठां सामी तो ई छाली (म्हे)। गढ पीलोदा सामू हो (नार)। नार नै तो हारयोड़ो देखियो छाली नै (जीतयोड़ी देखी मैं तो कीयो)। थै तो नार हो (म्हे)। भूणोजी थांकै मुण्डा के (हां छाली है कीयो)। श्री महाराज मैं छाली नै जीतयोड़ी देखी (वाह वाह)। चड़ाई भलां ही करावो अर भलां ही (मती करावो)। कीयो सूणी सगळी बात मिलावूं कर गो (वाह वाह)। दरबार का हुकमूं हाथ नाक नैइ काटूं जतै कांई व्हियो हाल (वाह वाह)। सूणी मन में देखियो घर बैठा उजाड़ नी हो जावै (हां अबार ई का हुकम छूटता ही टैम लागे)। तो धारापतियां को सुगणी तो थूक मूठियां आ भाज ऊबो रियो (वाह वाह)। सिरदार बूझणा (करी है)। श्री महाराज सूणी भाज गो (भाजन द्यो कीयो)। जाबा द्यो (वाह वाह)। मोकळ सिंग कंवर मेला की अब चड़ाई (कारावो कीयो)।।

ए पशूनी घालो तो जी हाथी के मोकळा पाट का रे।
होबा दे हावड़ा रे सोहन कटोरै खळळाट।
बळ भेंट मांगै रे गुणेश देवता।
मेला में चालै म्हारो रे कजळीबन गजराज।।
(भलां जी भलां) देव भलां

पशूनी घालो कंवर मोकळा हाथी के पाट की भैइ (म्हे)। होबा द्यो सोहन कटोरै (खळळाट)। अरै बळ भेंट मांगी गुणेश देवता (म्हे)। मेला में चाली म्हारो कजळीबन (गजराज)। गुणेश देवता मेलै पधारो (वाह वाह)। मोकळ सिंग भाई मेला की चड़ाई होवै (वाह वाह)।।

धाटां बांधो सिरदारां धेट का करो अमल असराळ।
सांमरी पेटी कसो नर भादरो अर कस लियो असल गैण्डा की ढाल।
आपणा दरबार मूं काढ दियो जूनी पाग सिरपाव।
जाटां बांधो धेट का करो अमल असराळ।
आपणा दरबार मूं काढ दियो जूनी पाग सिरपाव।
घोड़ा पीलानो ताजी आरबी धाटी घोड़ा बोर।
रातेड़ मुंआरै ठाकरां धोळां घणा सफेद।
बजर मूंछियां ठाकरां कुमहार चड़ ग्या बरसतो आयो काळ।
चड़ दरवाजा बाहरें धारापती नीकलया।
धारापतियां नै घोड़ो रे साडी पांच हजार।।
(भलां जी भलां) देव भलां

धाटां बांधो ठाकरां धेट का (म्हे)। करल्यो अमल असराळ (असराळ)। सांमरी पेटी कसो नर भादरो (वाह वाह)। कस लियो भाई असल गैण्डा की (ढाल)। अरै आपणा दरबार मूं काड़ लियो जूनी पाग सिरपाव (पाव)। घोड़ा पिलाणो ताजी आरबी (म्हे)। धाटी घोड़ा (बोर)। रातेड़ मुंआरै ठाकरां धोळा घणा (सफेद)। बजर मूंछियां कुमहार चड़ गा (म्हे)। बा के भालै बरसतो आयो (काल)। चड़ दरवाजा बाहरें धारापती सिरदार नीकलया (म्हे)। घोड़ो साडी पांच ई (हजार)। साडी पांच हजार घोड़ो लेय (म्हे)। मेला की चड़ाई करा दी (वाह वाह)। दरबार का हुकमूं गांव की बारहलै छेड़ै (नीकलया जी कीयो)। दोन्यु भाई मचको खाय गा (हां ऊबा रह ग्या)। मोकळ सिंग कंवर (म्हे)। मेला की तो भाई रे चड़ाई दोन्यु भाई थै करो (हां थै ई जावो कीयो)। क्युं (म्हे)। कीयो मैं दोन्यु भाई मेला में जावां म्हांकां डाकियां को सौ नांव है (वाह वाह)। दरबार का हुकमूं आज काळ का दिना में भूणोजी को अबीड़ो (चालै है कीयो)। देबी को सत्ता हो जावै (म्हे)। लोह की लाग जावै अर भूणोजी (मारयो जावे)। रावजी साय बड़ो (ओळमो म्हानै देवै कीयो)। हेंर कांई ठी भूणोजी पगपीटियो करै अर म्हांका ही पग टूट जावै (म्हे)। तो ही रावजी साय (ओळमो देय कीयो)। मैं तो मेलै गिया कोनी अर म्हांको डावड़ो गियो (म्हे)। धारापती सिरदारां नै पगपीटो करो जको भज छूटिया (वाह वाह)। तो ही म्हांकी तो बात में हल्की (हो जाय कीयो)। थै दोन्यु भाई जावो (म्हे)। थानै भजाण देय तो बाद में मैं (परोट लेस्यां)। मैं तो गिया कोनी श्री महाराज (म्हे)। म्हारा छोरा गिया (वाह वाह)। थांकाळो भूणोजी म्हांकालो टाबरां नै भजाण दिया (वाह वाह)। हेंर थै मारियावो तो ही बात नै (मैं परोट लेस्यां)। के थांको भूणोजी म्हांका टाबरां नै छेड़िया क्युं हां (हां छेड़िया क्यें न कीयो)। लोह की लागी मारिया गिया (वाह वाह)। अब कांई होवै (म्हे)। बाद में मैं सगळी बात नै केवटल्यां (वाह वाह)। तो दरबार का हुकमूं पांच घोड़ावूं धारापती सिरदार पाछो गढ पीलोदा साजियो (वाह वाह)। मोकळ सिंग कंवर भाई दोन्यु भाई मेलै जावो (हां थै ही जावो कीयो)। मेलै में बिदा हो गा दोन्यु सिरदार (वाह वाह)। दरबार का हुकमूं ए पुष्करराज पूगता (व्हिया जी कीयो)। सुधै बाई में डेरा तो कंवर भूणाजी का हा ही (म्हे)। हेंर बूढै पोखर (हां धारापतियां का)। धारापती सिरदार डेरा दे दी (वाह वाह)। रजपूतां का बेटा तंबूड़ा ताण दिया (म्हे)। हेंर भालां के तो बाड़ दिराबा लागा भालां के अणी कढाबा लाग तरवारियां के (बाड़ दिराबा लाग ग्य)। रसोई पाणी की जुगत (हां होवण लागी जी कीयो)। बगड़ावतां को भाट तो मेला में डोलतो ही फिरै (हां कातो कातो फिररियो हो)। दरबार का हुकमूं हाथी ऊबो निंगै आयो (वाह वाह)। तो धारापतियां का डेरा पर फैर पूगतो (हुई ग्या जी कीयो)। जाजम बिछायोड़ी (म्हे)। जाजम के ऊपर जार (हां बिराजमान भाटजी हो ग्या)। भाट बोलै (म्हे)। कांई समचार धारापतियां का कंवरां नै कहवै देखां (कीआवूं जाणज्यो देखां कीआवूं)। अबार कहवूं धणी का हुकमूं ले तूं (वाह वाह जी वाह वाह)।।

हाथी ल्यातां तो जी जो भूंडी घणी करी कंवर मोकळा रे।
तूं तो मोकळा रे भूंडी बिचारी बात।
हाथी नै भूणा के डेरै पूगतो कर दे कंवर मोकळा।
भूणा का कानड़ा भरै रे छोछू नारद भाट।।
(भलां जी भलां) देव भलां

हाथी लेयातां भूंडी घणी करी (म्हे)। कंवरजी भूंडी बिचारी (बात)। ई हाथी नै भूणा के डेरै पूगतो कर द्यो (म्हे)। भूणा का कानड़ा भरै छोछू बंगाली (अब भाट)। बो बगड़ावतां को भाट है नै (म्हे)। थारा हाथी हाथी की बांतां चालै (हां हाथी हाथी की बठै बात चालै कीयो)। दरबार का हुकमूं कंवरजी बूझणा (करी है)। अरै कुण देश को है तूं (जकी बता कीयो)। कीयो सात समंदरा पार का हूं (म्हे)। नांव सेंसारी दुनिया जगीशयो कह अर बतलावै (वाह वाह)। जगीशया हाथियां का लेवाळ नै लिया (अर तूं सागै आजा कीयो)। अरै श्री महाराज मैं तो आपको होर बात की है (हां आपको होर मैं तो की हूं)। म्हारा पर दोहरो मान गा आप (म्हे)।।

हाथी मांगयोड़ो जी नैइ ल्याया परदेशी पंछड़ा रे।
कोनी ल्यायो रे हाटियां बिकतो मोल।
मैं हाथी ल्यायो राठोड़ां का बीर खेत में।
ल्यायो भोज कर रे तंग तरवारियां तोड़।।
(भलां जी भलां) देव भलां

दरबार का हुकमूं हाथी मांगयोड़ो कोनी ल्यावूं मैं (म्हे)। नी ल्यायो हाटियां बिकतो (मोल)। हाथी ल्यायो राठोड़ां का बीर खेत मूं (म्हे)। भोज की तंग तरवारियां (तोड़ अर)। भोज का फींपरा फोड़ियां (म्हे)। जरां हाथी हाथ लाग्यो (वाह वाह)। सेजायीं हाथी नै कीयो मांगयोड़ा थोड़ा है जो बना द्यूं (हां बनाद्या कीयो)। कीयो श्री महाराज मैं तो आपको होर बात की है (म्हे)। ए चीजां है नै मेला में ऊबा रहबा की नी है (हां टहलानै की होवै कीयो)। सेंसार दुनिया मेला में टहलावै जको दर्शन तो करै (वाह वाह)। दर्शनी चीज है (म्हे)। गुणेश के रूप में है नी (वाह वाह)। धारापतियां के सिरदारां के रूम रूम में जच गी अबकाळी आ बात ठीक है श्री महाराज आपकी शोभा हुई (वाह वाह)। के हाथी कुण को (म्हे)। कीयो धारापतियां को है (हां धारापतियां को है कीयो)। दरबार का हुकमूं धारापतियां को डेरा मूं बगड़ावतां का घर का हाथी जयमंगला नै भाट खुला दियो (वाह वाह)। मेला में टहलाबा लागा (म्हे)। भाट बगड़ावतां को जाय भूणाजी के डेरै बूझणा (करी है)। अरै सिरदारां भूणोजी कठै है बोलो (हां कठै है कीयो)। कीयो बै तो पुष्कर में गिया (वाह वाह)। सिनान करै पीड़ी पर (म्हे)। कीयो पेड़ी पर सिनान करै जको चोखो (वाह वाह)। अरै धारापतियां को हाथी मेला में टहलै (म्हे)। ई आपणा हाथी नै छोड़ो जको आपणो मेला में (हां टेहलार ल्यावो कीयो)। जयमंगलो हाथी हो जको बगड़ावतां को घर को (हां हो)। भूणा की फौज में गजमंगलो हाथी हो जको ई बगड़ावतां को घर को (हो जी कीयो)। बिवूं भूणाजी का डेरावूं हाथी नै खुला दियो (वाह वाह)। दरबार का हुकमूं मावत नै कीयो रे मेला में टहलाल्या भाई (वाह वाह)। हाथी हाथी से ओळ पिछाण (म्हे)। नासक में हाथी दोन्यु (मिल ग्या जी कीयो)। दे सूंड को आंटो (म्हे)। हाथी पछै दोन्यु मिल ग्या (वाह वाह)।। गजमंगलो हाथी दरबार का हुकमूं बगड़ावतां का घर को भूणा कन्नै हो नै (म्हे)। जको धणी कन्नै हो तो दुख कांई हो (वाह वाह)। लूट में रावजी सा ल्यायो (म्हे)। दरबार का हुकमूं जयमंगलो हाथी हो जको ओ बन्ध में हो भैइ (वाह वाह)। जयमंगला हाथी के दरबार का हुकमूं हाथी दोन्यु जरां मिलिया नै (म्हे)। बी टैम में आंख में आंसू आयगा (वाह वाह)। बगड़ावतां को भाट बोलै कांई हाथी नै समचार

कहवै (कीआवूं जाणज्यो कीआवूं)। अबार कहवूं देव का हुकमूं ले तूं (वाह वाह जी वाह वाह)।।

धीरो धीरो तो जी ए ई गुणेश देवता रे।
आंखियां का आंसू ताणा परा मोल।
आज बन्धियो रे बैरियां के बारणे।
तड़कै बन्धावूं रे दड़ावट आगली पोळ।।
(भलां जी भलां) देव भलां

धीरो धीरो गुणेश देवता (म्हे)। आंखियां का आंसू परा (मोल)। अरै आज तो बन्धियो भाई बैरियां के बारणै (म्हे)। तड़कै बन्धावूं दड़ावट आगली (तनै पोळ)। तड़कै बन्धा द्यूं (वाह वाह)। ओ समचार कुण कीयो (बैइ को . . .) बगड़ावतां को भाट कीयो (वाह वाह)। हाथी बोलै (म्हे)। कांई भाट नै समचार कहवै देखां (कीआवूं जाणज्यो कीआवूं देखां)।।

पीलोदे ताजी फिरै तो जी ए ई परदेशी पंछड़ा रे।
बां सिरदारां की भाई रे करड़ी घणीं कबाण।
सेजा कींयां बन्धायो रे दड़ावट की कोटड़ियां।
पीलोदो कीज्यै रे चौरासी गढावूं दूसरी राण।।
(भलां जी भलां) देव भलां

दरबार का हुकमूं ओ हाथी समचार कीयो है (म्हे)। पीलोदे भाई ताजी मोकळा फिरै कीयो (वाह वाह)। बां सिरदारां की करड़ी घनी (कबाण)। तूं सेजा कींयां बन्धाय रे भाई दड़ावट की कोटड़ियां (म्हे)। पीलोदो कैज्यै चौरासी गढावूं दूजी (राण)। ईंयां की माड़ी बात जाणै तूं (हां हळकी सी बात कोय नी कीयो)। पीलोदो रावजी सा धड़को मानै (वाह वाह)। चौरासी गढावूं दूजी राण शहर कोनी मानै ई नै (म्हे)। मुंगताजी तूं उनै का उनै करो कीयो (वाह वाह)। मैं अबकै ठाणै कोनी (वाह वाह)। मोटा घरां हूं मैं (म्हे)। दरबार का हुकमूं ग्यारह बरसावूं हाथियां का मिलाप करां दिया भाट तो (वाह वाह)। कीयो भाई रे म्हारो तो मिलाप करबो हो आज तो जको थानै (हां करां दियो)। दरबार का हुकमूं धारापतियां का भाट नै हां मावत नै बूझणा करी तूं थारा ने ले जा भैइ (म्हे)। हेंर भूणाजी का डेरा हाथी नै कीयो तूं थारै डेरै (ले जावो)। बगड़ावतां को भाट पुष्करराज के पेड़ी पूगतो (व्हियो जी कीयो)। जी टैम में भूणोजी पेड़ी के ऊपरै सिनान नाहबा नै (बैठिया हा)। जी टैम में भाट (पूगगियो)। भाट बोलै कांई धणी नै बतलावै देखां (कीआवूं जाणज्यो कीआवूं देखां)।।

ए सूरत के नाळै तो जी मत नाहवै रे कंवर महाबळी रे।
नान्या भूणाजी नीर बहवै ज्यूं तेल।
जयमंगलो ऊबो रे बैरियां के बारणे।
बैरियां का सेलड़ा रे देही ऊपर झेळ।।
(भलां जी भलां) देव भलां

दरबार का हुकमूं सूरत के नाळै कांई नाहवै तूं (म्हे)। भूणा नीर बहवै ज्यूं (तेल)। अरै जयमंगलो ऊबो

देख बैरियां के बारणै (म्हे)। बैरियां का सेलड़ा रे भूणा देही ऊपरै (तूं झेळ)। बेटी का बाप हाथी तो ऊबै बैरियां में (म्हे)। अर तूं सिनान करै (वाह वाह)। तनै सिनान सुझियो कांई अबार की टैम में (म्हे)। भूणोजी कीयो आवो बाबा भाट आवो (आवो कीयो)। तनै कानावूं सुणयो मैं (पण आंखियांवूं देख लियो)।।

ए देव के भाई तो जी ए ई औरूं मोकळा रे।
तनै भूणाजी कद कद करसियां चीत।
हाथी थारावूं लियो जावै कोय ने।
मेला में राम को ले तूंबा रे बनजा नै अतीत।।
(भलां जी भलां) देव भलां

दरबार का हुकमूं देव के तो भाई माकळा है भैइ (म्हे)। भूणा मैं अब तनै कद कद करां (अब चीत)। अरै हाथी थारावूं कोनी लियो जावै (वाह वाह)। मेला में ले तूंबा राम को बनजा (अतीत)। सेठ साहूकार लाडू जिमावै आज (हां लाडू मत गमा कीयो)। तूं ही जीमलै (वाह वाह)। थारावूं हाथी तो लियो जावै कोनी (म्हे)। दरबार का हुकमूं बूझणा करी बाबा भाट कळह को मूली है तूं (वाह वाह)। बगड़ावतां नै ईंयां की कळह कर कर म्हनै तूं ही खपाया दीखै (म्हे)।।

ए जयमंगलो ऊबा तो जी जो मेला के मांयनै औवूं रे।
हीरा सोवै एक हजार।
बगड़ावत तो साळगराम की सेवा चालता।
बी हाथी पर भूणा रे चड़ियोड़ा फिरै पीलोदे लाल कुंवार।।
(भलां जी भलां) देव भलां

हाथी ऊबो मेला में धूंदळो (म्हे)। हीरा सोवै एक ही (हजार)। बगड़ावत तो भाई साळगराम की सेवा मेलतो (म्हे)। बी हाथी पर भूणा चड़ियोड़ा फिरै पीलोदे लाल (कुंवार)। धोळी आंखियां का चड़ियोड़ा फिरै नै कठै जाय लेरै बगड़ावतां के पछै थारै जियान का जलमिया (वाह वाह)। भूणोजी देखियो ए भाट तो कळह को मूली है (वाह वाह)। तो भूणा के भाट के बांतां होतां पेड़ियां पर (म्हे)। जय बोलो श्री देवनारायण भगवान की (जय)। दरबार का हुकमूं भूणोजी बूझणा करी रे भाट (म्हे)। निंगै कर तोला तो मैं तुलो हूं (वाह वाह)। हेंर बिरामणा नै सोनो (बांटूं हूं)। एकांलो सोनो तूं ही उठालै (हां एकांलो एकांलो तूं ही ले ले कीयो वाह भैइ)। दरबार का हुकमूं भाट नारदी बोलै (म्हे)। कांई समचार देखां कंवर भूणा नै कहवै पाछो देखां (कीआवूं जाणीज्यो देखां कीआवूं कींयां सोना देवे)।।

ए एक लाख देवै तो जी दोय लाख दे दे रे कंवर महाबळी रे।
जाणु थारी रे धूल बरोबर लाख।
मन मानियोड़ा सिरदार के दुगाणी देवां कोय ने।
जै ले लेवूं तो म्हनै रे तांबै तीन तलाक।।
(भलां जी भलां) देव भलां

एक लाख देय अर भलां ही दोय लाख देय (म्हे)। जाणु रे थारी मैं धूल बरोबर (लाख)। मन मानियोड़ा सिरदार की दुगाणी कोनी लेवूं (म्हे)। जै ले ल्यूं तो तांबै तीन (म्हनै तलाक है कीयो)। मन मानिया सिरदार की दुगाणी कोनी ल्यूं (हां थारी दुगाणी मैं तो आज कोनी लेवूं कीयो)। भूणोजी कीयो बाबा भाट (म्हे)। मन मानयोड़ा कुण है (कुण है कीयो)। कीयो तूं ही है (तूं है म्हारा धणी और तो कुण है)। तूं रावजी को जलमियोड़ो थोड़ो है कीयो (म्हे)। जकै दिन भायां के समील जाय नै देव के भेळै (हां जकै दिन म्हनै सुवा हाथ को अंगूछो (देदेज्ये)। तो लाख परसाव कर मानल्यूं (वाह वाह)। जरां दरबार का हुकमूं भूणाजी तूं बगड़ावतां के जलम फायदो कांई करियो रे भैइ कीयो (म्हे)। कीयो रे बाबा भाट (म्हे)। ए बाबू दुनिया मेला में भेळी क्युं हुई (हां क्यें के वास्तै हुई है कीयो)। श्री महाराज सिनान करबा नै हुई है (हां और तो क्यें नै हुई है)। हेंर धरम पुण करबा नै (हां हुई है कीयो)। कीयो बाबा भाट (म्हे)। अरै सेंसारी दुनिया तो धरम करै (वाह वाह)। अर आपां करम फोड़ां (हां करम करां कीयो)। कीयो श्री महाराज जो धरम होवै जको तनै हो जाय (म्हे)। अर पाप हुई जको (ओ म्हनै है कीयो हाथी छुड़ावो)। पुष्करराज भख को ठेट को ही भूखा है (म्हे)। तूं तो पुष्कर नै भोग दे द्यै (वाह वाह)। बड़ो राजी हुई थारा पर पुष्करराज (हां राजी हुई पुष्करराज तो)। दरबार का हुकमूं जरां बाबा भाट (म्हे)। ए पांच दिन पंचतीरथियां का है नै (हां ए तो टलबा द्यो)। हेंर एकम के दिन तूं के जका काम पछै करां (हां पछ करां अब)। आज तो दरबार का हुकमूं ग्यारस हुई है भैइ (म्हे)। ग्यारस के दिन ओ काम नैइ करां (वाह वाह)। ग्यारस टल गी अर बारस (टल गी)। बगड़ावतां को भाट कीयो रे म्हारा धणी (म्हे)। पांच दिन बता दिया पांच बरस बरोबर नीकलजायी (हां म्हारै तो दिन घणा लागी म्हनै तो)। मेला में नीकल गियो लेय तूंबा अर मानी नाय (वाह वाह)। ग्यारस मेला में फिर गो अर बारस मेला में फिर गो अर तेरस मेला में (फिरयो)। चौदस के दिन मेला में ही (हां फिरियो जी कीयो)। पूनयोआला दिन कर सिनान (म्हे)। सूरजी महाराज उगतै ही भूणा के डेरै पूगतो (हु गियो)। बी टैम में भूणोजी दरबार का हुकमूं सिरदारांवूं तमाशा आरिया (वाह वाह)। रसोई पाणी की जुगत हो रही (हां रसोई जिमा रिया हा)। कोय का सिरदार के थाळ में तो साग पूरसा (म्हे)। कोय सिरदारां के फैंफड़ा (पूरसा हा)। भाट तो आंतरै ऊबो रह गो (वाह वाह)। भाट बोलै (म्हे)। कांई भूणा नै बतलावै देखां (कीआवूं जाणज्यो देखां कीआवूं)। अबार कहवूं धणी का हुकमूं ले तूं (वाह वाह जी वाह वाह)।।

ए छतीस भोजन होतां तो जी ए ई मनवा भोज के औवूं रे।
होतां छतीसूं भोजना का अधकार ई रे।
एक तमाशो मेला में रे बतो देखियो।
नाई की जागां रे भलां जिमाया सिरदार।।
(भलां जी भलां) देव भलां

दरबार का हुकमूं छतीस भोजन होतां मनवा भोज के (म्हे)। भूणा होतां छतीसूं भोजना का अधकार (अधकार)। एक तमाशो आज मेला में बतो देखियो (म्हे)। नाई की जागां भलां जिमाया (सिरदार)। बगड़ावतां का बस में नाई कोनी रियो भैइ (हां तूं नाई व्हियो चोखो काम भूणाजी करियो कीयो)।

ओ समचार कुण कीयो के बगड़ावतां को बैइ को भाट भूणा ने (जांवतां ही कीयो)। भूणोजी बोलै (म्हे)। कांई समचार भाट नै कहवै देखां (कीआवूं जाणज्यो देखां कीआवूं)। अबार कहवूं देव का हुकमूं देखां (वाह वाह)।।

अबै पूजाला जी भाटजी देबी सांमरा रे।
भरूंला भाटजी नौसर चन्दा भोग।
आपां चालां रे जलम भोम का देश में।
लेरेवूं कांई चितारै परगै केरा लोग।।
(भलां जी भलां) देव भलां

अब पूजा भाट देबी माता सांमरा (म्हे)। भरां नौसर चन्दा (भोग)। अरै चालां जलम भोम का देश में (म्हे)। लेरावूं कांई चितारै भाई परगै केरा (लोग)। सुण रे भाट आ चेतावनी करां (हां चेतावनी है कीयो)। भाट कीयो श्री महाराज (म्हे)। थारी चेतावनी कोनी है आ (आ कोय नै कीयो)। आ तो नायां की है (म्हे)। थार कन्नै शस्तरपाती है तो कोय सिरदार नै (चोका देदेवो)। हेंर के चोखो को टटू होता है तो (हां सिरदार नै देदेवो)। तो बा थारी चेतावनी है (हां थांकी चेतावनी कंवर साय बा है कीयो)। आ चेतावनी नायां की है (हां नायां की है कीयो)। आ कहवै की भूणाजी के डेरा में गिया चोखो भोजन जिमियो भैइ नाई अच्छो हो (हां चोखी तरहवूं जिमावतो)। श्री महाराज आपको काम थोड़ो है ओ कीयो (म्हे)। भूणोजी बोलै कांई भाट नै बतलावै देखां (कीआवूं जाणज्यो देखां कीआवूं)। अबार कहवूं धणी देव का हुकमूं ले तूं (वाह वाह जी वाह वाह)।।

ए चड़बारो घोड़ो तो जी ए ई थारै कन्नै फूलरियो।
ओड़ण नै पाटू चन्दवा खोल।
म्हनै धारापतियां में भिड़ावै बीरा भाटजी।
ताणा देव कन्नै कती छोड़ी रे फौजांवाली ओड़।।
(भलां जी भलां) देव भलां

चड़बा को घोड़ो फूलरियो है (म्हे)। ओड़ण नै पाटू चन्दवा (खोल)। तूं म्हानै आज धारापतियां को भिड़ावै (म्हे)। अरै ताणा धणी देव कन्नै कती छोड़ी फौज की लेरें (ओड़)। जोर कत्तो है थारा धणी देव कन्नै (हां फौजां कती है जकी बता कीयो)। मुंगता (म्हे)। आयो जद को भिड़ाव भिड़ाव करै (वाह वाह)। भाट बोलै कांई समचार (देव नै कहवै पाछो देव नै कांई) भूणा नै कहवै (कीआवूं जाणज्यो कीआवूं)। अबार कहवूं देव का हुकमूं ले तूं (वाह वाह)।।

ए चड़बालो घोड़ो तो जी जो म्हार कन्नै फूलरियो रे।
ओड़ण नै अन्नदाताजी पाटू चन्दवा खोल।
सीता के संदेसै गियो धरमराजा देवजी।
बी दिन कतीक ले गो रे फौजांवाली ओड़।।
(भलां जी भलां) देव भलां

चड़बा को घोड़ो फूलरियो बगड़ावतां का दियोड़ा है (म्हे)। ओढ़ण नै पाटन चन्दवा (खोल)। दरबार का हुकमूं सीता के संदेसै गियो धरमराजा देवजी (म्हे)। जकै दिन भूणा कतीक ले गो फौज की (ओ ओढ़)। सीताजी के संदेसै गियो जकै दिन फौज कती ले गो (हां भगवान कन्नै कतीक ही जकी बतायो कीयो)। भूणोजी बूझणा (करी है)। अरे मुंगता (म्हे)। जो सीता के संदेसै गियो है नै (म्हे)। जको धणी ताणो है कांई (हां थारो है कांई कीयो)। कीयो सागै को सागै है (बो को बो है कीयो)। कीयो मुंगता किताक दिन व्हिया तनै (वाह वाह)। पकड़ बांवल्यो अर पुष्कर की पेड़ी पर ले गो (हां आगलै छेड़ै लेगियो)। ठहर जा भाट कीयो (हां अब ठहर कीयो)। सीता के संदेसै गियो थारो धणी (हां जणा अब ठा पाड़लियां कीयो)। अबार ठा पाड़ूं (वाह वाह)। भूणाजी को दूधां को धायोड़ो खाण्डो हो पेड़ी पर (मेलदीन्यो)। तीर कबाण ही जकी (पेड़ियां पर मेल दी जी कीयो)। सुण रे भाट (म्हे)। बो ही धणी है नी ताणो (वाह वाह)। खाण्डो मतै तो दळ बाहरें (होजावे)। हेंर तीर कबाण मतै चिलै (चड़ जावे)। जणा तो सीता के संदेसै गियो जको धणी थारो (हां है कीयो)। नी जरां अब मुंगता पाणी में के तनै बोवा द्यूं काट माथो (हां तनै पुष्कर में थारो) (बाबा भाट भोग देवूं कीयो)। बगड़ावतां को भाट थूक मूठियां में (म्हे)। जूतियां कोनी खोली जूतियां समेत ही पुष्कर के मांयत (दे के ई कूद गियो जी कीयो)। चिम्की मार गो (वाह वाह)। ऊंचो आवै कांई भगवान देव नै हेला मारै देखां (कीआवूं जाणज्यो देखां कीआवूं)।

कंवळराई फूल में जी ए ई आप उतरिया रे।
मिनखियो मळधारी जी पायो कोनी भेद।
ई भूणा नै परच्यो दीज्यो पेड़ी के ऊपरे।
हेलो सुणज्यै रे जी साडूजी का ऊद।।
(भलां जी भलां) देव भलां

दरबार का हुकमूं ओ समचार कीयो (वाह वाह)। कंवळ का फूल में आप औतार लियो कीयो (वाह वाह)। मिनखियो मळधारी पाया कोनी आपका (भेद)। धूणी पर परच्यो दीज्यो गोठां का राजवी (म्हे)। हेलो सुणज्यै रे साडूजी का (ऊद पुष्कर की पेड़ियां पर हेलो सुणो)। श्री महाराज (म्हे)। तूं म्हारो हेलो सुणी नी ई जागां (वाह वाह)। जरां तो मैं ई जींवतो आवूंला अर भूणा नै (सागै ल्यावूंला)। नी जरां ए आ देख बी डूबै बगड़ावतां की (हां) दूजा चिम्की मार गो (चिम्की मार गो जी कीयो)। पाणी में रहवूं अबें (हां अठै ही मरूं कीयो)। देव महाराज म्हारो धणी चौसलै खेड़ै बिराजमान (होरिया जी कीयो)। काळो अर गोरो भैरवानाथ पेग (लाग रिया हा)। देव महाराज बक बक हेंसिया (वाह वाह)। फैफ का फूल (झड़िया है)। भैरवानाथ कीयो श्री महाराज आपको हंसणो (हां कींयां व्हियो आज)। अरै कीयो बाबो भाट है नै (म्हे)। जको पेड़ियां पर परच्या मांगै अब (हां डूब अर मरै है कीयो)। कीयो श्री महाराज बूड़ा माईत को कीयो जरूर करणो (वाह वाह)। भैरवानाथ (म्हे)। भाट नै बाहरें बेगो काढो रे बगड़ावतां की बैइ डूब जाय भैइ (वाह वाह)। बेगा जावो (म्हे)। मूठी का देवातण हा (वाह वाह)। पवनवूं बांतां करतां ए (वाह वाह)। दरबार का हुकमूं भैरवानाथ आर बांवल्यो पकड़ भाट को के ऊंचो (हां खेंचियो)। पाणी में क्यें ताणी डूबै (हां डूब अर कींयां मरै है कीयो)। कीयो दोहरी

बेळियां पड़ गी न पछै (हां जणा)। कीयो कांई दोहरी है तूं कहवै (म्हे)। कीयो सब मेला नै ही ऊंधो कर द्यां (हां तहस महस उडा द्यां कीयो)। कीयो नैइ नैइ नैइ नैइ (ओ काम नै)। दरबार का हुकमूं आ तीर कबाण चिलै छोड़ो (हां आ मतै चिलै चड़ जावे)। हेंर ओ खाण्डो है नी (ओ दळ बाहरें हो जावे)। ए चीज तो दोय तो ए करो (हां बस अती करजावो)। थोड़ासा भूणा के डाई भुजा पर बिराजमान (हां हो जावो)। अतो काम करो (वाह वाह)। मूठी का देवातण हा (म्हे)। गोरोजी महाराज कचूस (म्हे)। बाण नै चिलै पर छोड़ दी (वाह वाह)। दरबार का हुकमूं काळोजी महाराज दे मूठ के सारो (म्हे)। खाण्डा नै दळ के बाहरें (हां कर मेल दियो)। भूणा के निंगै (आयग्यो)। भूणोजी कीयो बाबा भाट (म्हे)। पुष्कर के बाहरें पाणीवूं नीकल (हां म्हारा बढेरां की बैइ डूब जायली कीयो (बेगो बाहर आव कीयो)। अरै कोय गोयल्या जिनावर खाई (वाह वाह)। बाहरें आजा मान लियो मैं (म्हे)। थारो धणी जको सीता नै ल्यायो है नै (बो को बो ही है कीयो)। मान लियो भैइ (वाह वाह)। अब तूं मेला मैं कह जकी थोक अब कर देयां (हां अब करूं कीयो)। दरबार का हुकमूं भूणोजी बूझणा (करी है)। बाबा भाट देरी मत कर अब (हां बेगी चड़ाई करावो कीयो)। तीन तिलोकी को नाथ भगवान देव भूणा नै परच्यो देतां (म्हे)। भैरवानाथ भूणा के भुजा पर बिराजमान (होंवतां)। जय बोलो भैइ श्री देवनारायण की (जय बोलो भैइ छोटा अर मोटा स)।।

अब सजजा बीका भाटजी हो ज्यां फूलरिया घोड़ै पर असवार।
नौसरा घाटी रोकलै बाबा भाटजी रोको सुधाबाई।
मेला में बीरजको रायजादो महाबळी कुमहार का ड़ावड़ा कदै नी जींवतां जाय।
अत कहतां भाटजी ऊठ ठाकरां फूलरिया घोड़ा पर असवार।
बणिया तेरी हाट उठाल्यूं उठाल्यूं हाट नाळ बजार।
मेदनी चड़ो भाई डूंगरा मण्डी मीठा मितवालां किसी राळ।
मेला में काळू मीर दीया को ठाकरां में लोग पड़ियो संजोग।
एकरसां हाथी नै रहबाद्य कंवर महाबळी।
दीया कन्नु बंवळी घोड़ी ले ले रे सुवाई भोज का बैर।।
(भलां जी भलां) देव भलां

अब सजै नै बाबा भाट (म्हे)। हो जा फूलरिया घोड़ा पर (असवार)। नौसरा घाटी रोक लियो (म्हे)। रोकलै सुधा (बाई)। अरै मेला में बीरज गो रायजादो महाबळी (म्हे)। कुमहार का डावड़ा भाट अब कदै नी जीवतां जाय (जाय पाछा जीवतां कोनी जाय)। के अतीक कहतां सजियो भाट बाबो भाटजी (म्हे)। हु गो भैइ फूलरिया घोड़ा पर (असवार)। अरै बणिया तेरी हाट उठा लियो (म्हे)। भाई उठावो हाट नाळ (बाजार)। मेदनी चड़ जावो भाई डूंगरा (म्है ऊंची चड़जावो)। मण्डी मीठा मितवालां किसी (अब राड़)। बगड़ावतां को भारत व्हियो नै (हां जियान को अठै भारत होय थै सगळा (ऊंचा चड़जावो)। एली सारड़ मर जावोला (वाह वाह)। काळू मीर दीया का मेला में भाई भला पड़ गा (संजोग)। एकरसां हाथी नै रहबा द्यो (म्हे)। दीया कन्नु बंवळी घोड़ी ले ल्यो सवाई भोज का (बैर)। बंवळी घोड़ी है ई कन्नै (हां बा पहली ले ल्यो क्युं आयग्यो सामै कीयो)। क्युं हाथी तो पछै छुड़ाल्यां (वाह वाह)।

दरबार का हुकमूं मीर दीयो जोधको डोला सिण्गार (म्हे)। ए सिनान करबा नै मेला में (आयग्या)। मीर कीयो तोबा तोबा तोबा तोबा दीया (म्हे)। ओ ले भाई रोजा बिगड़ी अब (अब रोजा बिगड़ी कीयो)। अरै कंवर भूणा नै हाथवूं सीख दीनी (हां आपां नै याद कोनी आयी बात)। ओ देख आयगो ऊबो (वाह वाह)। भूणोजी बोलै (म्हे)। कांई दीया नै बतलावै पहली तो (कीआवूं जाणज्यो देखां कीआवूं)। अबार कहवां देव का हुकमूं ल्यो थै (वाह वाह जी वाह वाह)।।

सावर गढ का तो जी ए ई ससकराम सिंगजी रे।
थै तो भाई रे जात का बाजो दीया रे।
राठोड़ां का जी बीर खेत में।
सवाई भोज का थामालो रे जस कुण लिया रे।।
(भलां जी भलां) देव भलां

दरबार का हुकमूं ओ समचार कंवर भूणोजी दीया ने कीयो है (वाह वाह)। सावर गढ का बाजो भाई थै सकराम सिंगजी (म्हे)। जात का हो दीया (दिया दीयोजी का नांव सकराम सिंगजी हो)। के राठोड़ां का बीर खेत में थामालो दीया भोज का जस कुण लिया (हां जस कुण लियो जकी बतावो कीयो)। जस कांई होवै की रावजी नै ईंयां जार कुण कीयो के भोज नै मैं मारयो (हां मैं मारयो जको जस होवे)। कीयो तोबा तोबा तोबा तोबा तोबा मीर बोल्यो (म्हे)। बडी जुगत से बोल्यो (वाह वाह)। मीर बूझणा करी यार दीया (म्हे)। बडी जुगत से बोली (हां सूल बोली नै मौत आयगी है कीयो)। दीयोजी बोलै (म्हे)। कांई कंवर भूणा नै समचार कहवै पाछै (कीआवूं जाणज्यो देखां कीआवूं)। अबार कहवां देव का हुकमूं ले (वाह वाह जी वाह वाह)।।

सावर गढ का जी बाजा कंवरजी रे सकराम सिंग जी।
कंवरजी मैं तो रे जात का हा दीया रे।
जस की कंवरजी रे ठाई कोय ने।
हुई भंगी जी मैं तो जी खापन खेंच लिया रे।।
(भलां जी भलां) देव भलां

सावर गढ का तो सकराम सिंगजी हा (म्हे)। जात का बाजा (दिया)। सवाई भोज की जस की भाई ठा कंवर कोनी (म्हे)। हुई भंगी खापन खेंच (लिया)। खेत पड़िया सिरदार को कुण लेवै (भंगी लेवे)। मरियोड़ा को गाबो भंगी लेय श्री महाराज (म्हे)। मैं फौज मुसायब आदमी हो जकै दिन रावजी को फौजां का समालै लेवो मैं खारी का डाव पर गियो नी बी टैम में (म्हे)। सवाई भोज की लोथ ही जमी पर पड़ी (हां नीचै धड़ पेड़ी)। हेंर घोड़ी कन्नै ऊबी (वाह वाह)। काना का जगमोतियां बठै ही पड़िया (म्हे)। सकड़िया बगतर हो जको डील में पहरयोड़ो हो भोज के (हां पहरयोड़ो हो कीयो)। मैं कन्नै जार बी नै खोल लियो (वाह वाह)। टोप हो जको मैं ले लियो (हां ले लियो)। हेंर काना का जगमोती हां जका मैं (ले लिया कीयो)। लगाम घोड़ी की हाथ में भोज के ही (म्हे)। मैं दे फटकारो अर लगाम छुड़ाया घोड़ी नै ल्यावो (वाह वाह)। तो खेत पड़िया रजपूत को ल्यायो मैं तो (हां आ

म्हनै ठा कोनी भोज नै मारियो कुण हो)। मारबा की म्हनै ठा कोनी (वाह वाह)। घोड़ी म्हारै कन्नै है (तूं कहवै तो थारै कन्नै पूगती कर द्यूं (वाह वाह)। अर तूं कहवै नै (हां तो देव महाराज कन्नै दड़ावट पूगती कर द्यूं)। वाह भैइ दीया कोय बात नी आयगी कीयो (आजायी)। मीर कीयो तोबा तोबा भलो फूटरो बोल्यो (हां फूटरो बोल्यो जान बचाई कीयो)। भूणोजी बोलै कांई मीर नै बतलालै (हां कीआवूं जाणज्यो देखां कीआवूं)।।

भैंसयां की ऊठी जी ए ई मनवा भोज के औवूं रे।
बैठी पूठावूं पूठो जोड़।
भैंसयां नै ले गो रे काळू मीरजी।
सागै भाई रे बिरजा बिरमो गोड़।।
(भलां जी भलां) देव भलां

भैंसयां होती मनवा भोज के (म्हे)। बैठती पूठावूं पूठो (जोड़ अर)। भैंसयां नै ले गो रे काळू मीर सागै हो बिरजा ई बिरमा (गोड़)। बै भैंसयां कठै छोड़ी (जकी बतावो)। मीर बूझणा करी कंवर साय (म्हे)। पांच से ले गो भैइ (वाह वाह)। आज दिन हजार ऊबी है (हां जार ऊबी है म्हारै कन्नै)। मैं तो कंवरजी रे रळायी है बामै (हां धटाई को हूं नै)। तूं कहवै तो थार कन्नै पूगती करूं (म्हे)। तूं कह द्यै थारा देव कन्नै (पूगती कर देवूं)। मैं कांई घटायो भाई बामै (मैं तो कीं कोनी खायो दूध खायो जको तो खायो)। कोय बात कोनी भैइ (म्हे)। मीर आजाय कोय बिचार कोनी (वाह वाह)। मीर बूझणा करी रे कंवरजी तनै मेला की जापता की खातर भेज्यो मैं (म्हे)। ओ कांई धंधो करियो (चड़ाई कींयां कराई हो)। मेला तो लोग तो सभी हलबळो माच गियो (म्हे)। कीयो मीर ओ भाट है बैइ को है म्हारो (म्हे)। धारापती सिरदारां कन्नै भैइ म्हारा बाप को हाथी बतावै (हां जको छुटार ल्यावूं कीयो)। ए श्री महाराज इयां रोळा बेधा कर हाथी की नै छुड़ावो (हां अबार मैं अर दीयोजी जावां)। बिसटाळो करल्यावां (वाह वाह)। अर हाथी नै जार ल्यावां (वाह वाह)। भूणोजी कीयो मीर जरां झगड़ो मैं करणो चावां कोनी (हां म्हान तो हाथी ही चाहीज्ये)। म्हांकै हाथी की जरूरत है भैइ (वाह वाह)। तो श्री महाराज आप जणा ईयां ही खड़्या रहो (हां अठै ही ठहरो मैं जावां कीयो)। काळू मीर दीयोजी (म्हे)। धारापतियां के डेरै पूगता हो गा (वाह वाह)। दरबार का हुकमूं कांई बिसटळा की बांतां होवै (म्हे)। कंवरजी के मीर के अर दीया के बांतां हो जावै अब (कीआवूं जाणज्यो देखां कीआवूं)। अबार कहवां भगवान का हुकमूं (वाह वाह)।।

ए हाथी ल्यातां तो जी भूंडी करी रे कंवर मोकळा औवूं रे।
थै तो डावड़ा जी भूंडी बिचारी बात।
हाथी नै म्हानै सूंप रे कंवर मोकळा।
मेला में कानड़ा भर भूणा का रे छोछू नारद भाट।।
(भलां जी भलां) देव भलां

हाथी ल्यातां बात भूंडी घणी कर ली (म्हे)। मोकळ सिंग थै भूंडी बिचारी (बात)। अब हाथी नै म्हानै

सूंपो (म्हे)। मेला में भूणा का कानड़ा भरबा लागो छोछू बंगाली (भाट)। थानै हाथी नै मेला में नी ल्यानो (हां ल्यानो नैइ हो)। दरबार का हुकमूं मेला में आज ई हाथी हाथी की बात दुनिया चलावै (वाह वाह)। हाथी नै म्हानै दे (हां जको भूणोजी के डेरै पूगतो कर देवां)। मेला के लोग के दुख दाई कोनी होवै थांकै दुख दाई (हां कोनी होवे) जींवतां का जींवतां थांकै (घरां पूगजावो)। बूझणा करी दरबार का हुकमूं दिया (म्हे)। हाथियां का लेवाळ नै सागै क्युं को नी ल्यायो भैइ (हां सागै कोनी ल्यायो कोनी कीयो)। मोकळ सिंग कंवर बोलै (वाह वाह)। कांई दीया नै समचार कहवै (कीआवूं जाणज्यो देखां भोपाजी महाराज अब कीआवूं)। अबार कहवूं देव का हुकमूं ले तूं (वाह वाह जी वाह वाह)।।

हाथी मांगियोड़ो जी जो कोनी ल्यायो रे माझी जोधका रे।
कोनी ल्यायो जी हाथियां बिकतो मोल।
हाथी ल्यायो राठोड़ां का बीर खेत में।
सुवाई भोज की रे तंग तरवारियां तोड़।।
(भलां जी भलां) देव भलां

हाथी कांई मांगियोड़ो थोड़ो ही ल्यायो हूं (म्हे) नी ल्यायो हाथियांवूं बिकतो (मोल)। अरै हाथी ल्यायूं राठोड़ां का बीर खेत मूं (वाह वाह)। सवाई भोज की तंग तरवारियां (तोड़ अर)। सवाई भोज का फींपरो फोड़ियो मैं (हां जणा म्हांकै हाथी हाथ लाग्यो कीयो)। हाल तो हाथां का बूकियां का बळ ही कोनी नीकलया बेटी का बाप (म्हे)। ईंयां हाथी कोनी देवां (वाह वाह)। दीयोजी बूझणा करी रे कंवर मोकळा (म्हे)। काळर जात कुमहार की अबार काळर हो थै (हां काळर जावो कीयो)। जाणु मैं थानै (वाह वाह)। भूणोजी थांको बाप मेला में भीचयोड़ो ऊबो है आज दिन (म्हे)। जाणै है तूं बी नै (वाह वाह)। दीया के कंवर के बांतां होतां (म्हे)। भूणोजी मेला में बिरचतां जय बोलो श्री देवनारायण भगवान की (जय)। दरबार का हुकमूं दीयोजी बूझणा करी रे कंवर मोकळ सिंग भाई (म्हे)। तूं काळर जात कुमहार की है अबार काळर जायी (वाह वाह)। मोकळ सिंग कंवर बोलै कांई दीया ने समचार कहद्यें देखां (कीआवूं जाणज्यो कीआवूं देखां)। अबार कहवां देव का हुकमूं ले तूं (वाह वाह जी)।।

ए पागड़ा सूं घास गी तो जी ए ई पग की मोजड़िया रे।
घास गी भाई रे खांधा सूं तरवार।
हाथी राखबो कदूं सीख गा कंवर मोकळा।
अन्त तो घोड़ी रे खोखर को असवार।।
(भलां जी भलां) देव भलां

पगवूं घास गी भाई दीयाजी मोजड़ी (म्हे)। हेंर खांधा सूं घास गी (तरवार)। अरै हाथी राखबो दरबार का हुकमूं कदूं सीख गा (म्हे)। अन्त तो घोड़ी खोखर का (असवार)। थांकी जात लेरली कुण है (हां जकी ठा कोनी कांई कीयो)।।

ए उकलड़िया पर तो जी रतनिया जी ताणो सांथरो रे।

राखै भाई रे खाडा सूं ब्यहवार।
हाथी राखबो रे कदवूं सीखगा।
अन्त तो घोड़ियां रे खोखरवाला असवार।।
(भलां जी भलां) देव भलां

दरबार का हुकमूं दीयोजी समचार (कीया है)। अरै उकलड़िया पर रतनियाजी भैइ थारा सांथरां है (म्हे)। राखै खाडा सूं (ब्यहवार)। अरै हाथी राखबो कदूं सीख ग्या (म्हे)। अन्त तो घोड़ी खोखर को (के असवार)। पछेबो बो है थांको (वाह वाह)। कंवरजी बोलै कांई समचार दीया नै कहवै देखां (कीआवूं जाणज्यो कीआवूं देखां)। अबार कहवां देव का हुकमूं देखां (वाह वाह)।।

ए पागड़ासूं घास गी जी दीया भाई रे म्हानी मोजड़िया रे।
घास गी म्हारी रे खाधा सूं तरवार।
मैं पोता बाजा रे चकवै बीन का।
म्हाना दाता के रे दाय कुमहारी लाग।।
(भलां जी भलां) देव भलां

सुण भाई दीया (म्हे)। पागड़ा से घास गी म्हारी मोजड़ी (वाह वाह)। घास गी खाधा सूं (तरवार)। पोता बाजा रे भाई चकवै बीन का (म्हे)। म्हानै दादाजी के दाय कुमहारी (लाग)। दादाजी के कुमहारी दाय (लागी ही)। जणा कुमहार को नांव लेर थै (बतलावो कीयो)। नी जरां कुमहार को नांव लेवै जको को फूलडोळ फोड़ नाका मैं (वाह वाह)। कीयो दीया सुण भाई मोकळ सिंग कंवरजी कीयो (म्हे)। मैं तो भाई रे सही बात कहबा नै आया थै मानो जरां तो (म्हे)। काळर जात कुमहार की हो पछेबो थांको लेरलो माड़ो घणो (है कीयो)। अबार भूणा के मुण्डा के अबार काळर होवै (वाह वाह)। कीयो जा दरबार का हुकमूं भूणा ने सागै ल्यार तूं ही साथ आजायी (हां सागै औरूं आजाज्यो कीयो हाथी दिरा द्यूं)।।

ए तूं बिसटाळै आयो तो जी ए ई माझी जोधका रे।
म्हारावूं करां को करै बात अंवळी रे।
म्हार कन्नु हाथी दिरावै जोधका।
तूं देय किनै सागद सुधी बंवळी।।
(भलां जी भलां) देव भलां

दरबार का हुकमूं ओ समचार कुण कीयो है मोकळ सिंग कंवर (कीयो है)। कीयो तूं बिसटाळै आयो रे माझी जोधका (म्हे)। करां को म्हारावूं करै बात अंवळी (अंवळी)। तूं म्हार कन्नु तो हाथी दिराबा लागो (म्हे)। तूं दे भोज की सागद सुधी (अब बंवळी)। बेटी का बाप म्हारा नांव दूणो माल लिया बैठो है (हां थारै कन्नै दूणो माल है कीयो)। कीयो थारा बापूं पहली बोथ अर आया हूं (हां देणो बोथ अर आयो हूं कीयो)। कीयो तूं बोथेलो होवै भैइ मैं तो बोथां कोनी (वाह वाह)। मैं तो फींपरा फोड़ तो हाथी ल्याया (म्हे)। हेंर भालां का भचड़ के हाथी कोय लेबालो हो तो दे द्यां (देयां कीयो)।।

मैं बिसटाळै आया तो जी ए ई कंवर मोकळा रे।
थै दोन्यो भाई रे कानी कानी ताणो रे।
मैं दोन्यो घरां नै जावां रे कंवर मोकळा।
मेला मैं तूं अर थारी रे भूणोजी जाणो रे।।
(भलां जी भलां) देव भलां

मैं तो दोन्यो अमराव बिसटाळै आया भैइ (म्हे)। अरै थै दोन्यो भाई मतै मतै कानी कानी (ताणो)। मैं दोन्यो अमराव घरां नै जावां अब (म्हे)। मेला में तूं अर थारी भूणोजी (जाणो)। दोन्यो थै ही जाणोला भैइ (वाह वाह)। कीयो जा खिना देय बी हाथी का लेवाळ नै (वाह वाह)। के तूं ही घरां नै क्युं जावै भला ही साथ ही आजा (म्हे)। दरबार का हुकमूं बिसटाळा मानया कोनी (वाह वाह)। दीयोजी हेंर मीर पाछा भूणा कन्नै पूगता (व्हिया जी कीयो)। अरै कंवरजी कंवरजी (म्हे)। म्हांकां तो बिसटाळा मानया कोनी (हां मानया कोनी कीयो)। कीयो मैं करां कीयो रे भैइ (वाह वाह)। मतेई मान ही अबार (वाह वाह)। कीयो कंवरजी म्हांको दोन्यो अमरावां को डाकियां को नांव है (हां नांव बड़ो है कीयो)। आपको हुकम हो जावै तो मैं म्हांका घरां नै (हां ऊठ चाला)। थारै सामिल हो जावां (म्हे)। तो ही म्हानै ओळमा (मिल जावे)। हेंर में बांकै सामिल होवां नै (म्हे)। तो रावजी सा ओळमो देवै तूं ही बेराजी हो जावै (हां हो जावै कीयो)। कीयो कोय बात कोनी जावो भैइ (जावो कीयो)। धारापती सिरदार सामा राड़ का नंगारा बजा दिया (वाह वाह)। कीयो आजा भैइ झगड़ो कर हाथी ले जाणो हुवै तो (वाह वाह)। भूणा की डेरा के मांयनै राड़ का नंगारा (बाज ग्यो है)। आया कीयो तो दरबार का हुकमूं कांई धारापती सिरदारां के भूणा के बात होवै देखां (वाह वाह)। धारापती सिरदार परवाणो भूणा नै देवै (म्हे)।।

ए चन्दन बिनास्या जी म्हाना बाबोजी रे बीर खेत में औवूं रे।
बिनास्यूं भूणा रे चन्दन को कातो रे।
सवाई भोज नै हाथावूं मारियो।
थामालो भूणा रे कुण मांगै पाछो रे।।
(भलां जी भलां) देव भलां

चन्दन बिनास्यूं म्हाना बाबोजी बीर खेत में (म्हे)। अर बिनास्यूं चन्दन को ही (कातो)। सवाई भोज नै तो बीर खेत में देख मैं हाथावूं झाटक्यो (म्हे)। पण थामालो भूणा कुण मांगबा लागो (अब पाछो)। सवाई भोज को बैर कोय लेबालो है (हां बतावो कीयो)।।

ए चन्दन बिनास्या जी ताणो बाबोजी रे बीर खेत में औवूं रे।
बिनास्या मोकळा रे चन्दन का काता रे।
भोज की गादी रे भगवान उतरिया।
कदै ले लेला रे पाना फुला सुधा पाछा रे।।
(भलां जी भलां) किषन भलां

दरबार का नांव लेवां तो सद ही (भलां जी कीयो)। कीयो चन्दन बिनास्यो ताणो बाबोजी बीर खेत में (म्हे)। हेंर बिनास दियो चन्दन को ही (काता)। दरबार का हुकमूं भोज की गादी भैइ भगवान उतरिया (म्हे)। ले लेय कदै पाना फूला सुधा (पाछा जी कीयो)। सुणो भैइ (म्हे)। जो पाछा लेबाळा बगड़ावतां का बैर आगो कीयो (वाह वाह)। कोय बिचार कोय है नी कीयो (म्हे)। मोकळ सिंग सजजा भैइ (वाह वाह)। दरबार का हुकमूं धारापतियां के डेरै पाछो भूणोजी परवाणा (दीन्यो है)। भूणोजी कांई भाट नै बोलै (म्हे)। कांई पहली झगड़ो दरबार का हुकमूं देखां धारापतियांवूं करै देखां भूणोजी (कीआवूं जाणज्यो देखां कीआवूं)।।

चरक भवानी चोड़ द्यूं ठाकरां तोपां मेलो बाट।
जो बावड़ो म्हाना देशो तो थै दियो मूठ पर हाथ।
उतरी कहतां जोधा बावड़िया ठाकरां दिया मूठ पर हाथ।
तरवारियां ताली उडबा लागी भालां की बरसबा लागी बाल।
सुरां ठाकरां सांचां लड़िया कायर मतेई तज गा पिराण।
जो मेला में थै बजा द्यो कंवर महाबळी ठाकर अब करियो उजास।
कुमहारां का डावड़ा नै भूणोजी झाटक्या ठाकरां कर कर पूण्चा पाण।
सरको बाजियो सारको रे।
मेला में जीतियो रे कंवर महाबळी।
कुमहारां नै सूंपियो जी चाक राज थापो।।
(भलां जी भलां) देव भलां

चरक भवानी चोड़ भाट (म्हे)। तोपां मेलो (भाट)। बावड़ो म्हारा देशो तो द्यूं मूठ पर (अब हाथ)। हकाळिया पाछा बावड़िया (म्हे)। सब दिया मूठ पर (हाथ)। अरै तरवारियां ताली उडी (वाह वाह)। भालां की बरसबा लाग गी (बाल)। सुरां तो अब सांचां लड़िया (म्हे)। अर कायर मतेई तज गा (पीराण)। फौज में बै नाळ गोला बै दुजबान (म्हे)। कड़ी खड़कै ठाकरां उडै उजाळो (सार)। भूणोजी तेग उजाटियो (म्हे)। मेला में आभै करियो (उजास)। कुमहारां का डावड़ा नै भूणोजी झाटक लिया करकर पूण्चा ही (पाण)। सरको बाज गो सारको (म्हे)। मेला के मांयनै जीतियो रायजादा महाबळी कुमहारां नै सूंपियो चाक राज ही (थापो)। बासन घड़ो (अर मजा करो)। दरबार का हुकमूं हाथी तो भूणाजी आपका बाप को हो जको कुमहारां कन्नु (छुड़ाल्यो)। हेंर कीयो ल्यो भाई कंवरजी थांको ओ काम नी है (म्हे)। बासन घड़बा को काम (है कीयो)। तो धारापतियां सिरदारां की हार होतां (म्हे)। मेला में कंवर भूणाजी की जीत होतां हाथी लेतां (वाह वाह)। जय बोलो श्री देवनारायण भगवान की (जय)। भूणोजी बूझणा करी बाबा भाट अब (म्हे)। बाह वाह रे म्हारा धणी कीयो (वाह वाह)। कीयो ओ हाथी श्री महाराज म्हनै दे द्यो (म्हे)। मैं देव के दुलीचै ले जार बांध देवूं (वाह वाह)। आप कींयां आवो जकी समचार को (हां जकी बता द्यो)। कीयो रे बाबा भाट थारा धणी देव नै कह देय (म्हे)। ईंयां कोनी आंवूंला मैं (हां ईंयां नैइ आंवूंला)। गढ पीलोदो भेळेलो आ ताणो धणी देवजी (म्हे)। जरां मैं पाछो आंवूंला (हां नैइ तो जदे नैइ आंवूंला)। परच्यो दियो बिनै मैं कोनी आंवूंला कीयो (वाह वाह)। दरबार का हुकमूं

भूणोजी तो मेला से सिनान ध्यान कर पून्योवाला दिन (म्हे)। हेंर हाथी देर तो बाबा भाट नै बिदा कर दियो (वाह वाह)। हेंर आप है जको राण शहर के मांयनै (हां बिदा व्हिया कीयो)। बगड़ावतां को भाट कांई दड़ावट के मांयनै आजावै (म्हे)। कांई हाथी को गुणेश को भगवान आरतियो करै देखां (कीआवूं जाणज्यो कीआवूं)। अबार कहवूं देव का हुकमूं ले तूं (वाह वाह जी वाह वाह)।।

ए गुणेशजी आया तो जी हीड़ागर सूण ऊलाळतो रे।
ई का हीड़ागर ये पाछा पड़ै नी खोज।
तूं एकलो कींयां आयो रे गुणेश देवता।
सागै क्युं ल्यायो नै तूं तो रे सतमितवालो भोज।।
(भलां जी भलां) देव भलां

हाथी आयो भैइ हीड़ागर छोकरियां सूण ऊलाळतो कीयो (म्हे)। ई का पाछा पड़ै है (खोज)। एकलो कींयां आयो भैइ रे गुणेश देवता (म्हे)। अरै सागै क्युं लेयायो नै सतमितवाला (भोज)। थारा धणी नै कोनी ल्यायो भैइ (हां सागै ले अर कोनी आयो कीयो)। भाट कीयो सुण ये मांजी सा बिसूणा नी करणा ईंयां का (वाह वाह)। बठै गियोड़ा पाछा देखिजै अब आयग्या कीयो (हां आनै का नैइ है)। भगवान आयो एकरां जको बी को आरतियो करो (वाह वाह)।।

केसर कटोरा जी घाल लियो हीड़ागर छोकरियां रे।
भरल्यो हीड़ागर ये बीज मोतियां थाळ।
आया भाट रे हाथी को साज ल्यो हीड़ागर आरतियो।
आयो म्हानो जी एकलड़ो असवार।।
(भलां जी भलां) देव भलां

केसर कटोरा घालो कीयो (म्हे)। दासी भरो बीज मोतियां (थाळ)। ए आयोड़ा हाथी को भाट जी को साज ल्यो आरतियो (म्हे)। आज आयो म्हारो एकलड़ो (असवार)। हाथी एकलो आयो भैइ असवार ऊपर कोनी (म्हे)। पण नी गुणेश देवता को आरतियो कर ल्यो (वाह वाह)। भर बीज मोतियां का थाळ (म्हे)। हेंर गुणेश देवता को आरतियो करियो (वाह वाह)। तो ग्यारह बरसावूं बगड़ावतां के घरां पाछो हाथी आतां (आंवतां)। भाट की जीत होतां (म्हे)। साडू माता आरतियां साजतां जय बोलो श्री देव भगवान की (जय)। देव नै बूझणा करी बाबा भाट (म्हे)। दादो भूणो तो कोनी आयो (वाह वाह)। कीयो श्री महाराज पीलोदो भेळबा को कीयो है (वाह वाह)। थै पीलोदा भेळोला तो भूणोजी भायां के सामिल (आवेलो)। पीलोदा की दरबार कहतां जेज लागी (म्हे)। पालासानी घोड़ा नै पिलाण भैइ बेगो (वाह वाह)। घोड़ा नै पिलाण पीलोदा की चड़ाई कुण कुण कराई ए पांचू भाई भाई दरबार का हुकमूं भेळा तो हा कोनी (म्हे)। हेंर मेदूजी देव महाराज हेंर दरबार का हुकमूं कंवर भांगीजी (वाह वाह)। गढ पीलोदा की चड़ाई कराली (वाह वाह)। गोरवें गिया देव महाराज बूझणा (करी ही)। अरै दरबार का हुकमूं दादा भांगी (म्हे)। मैं तो भैइ गांव में तो कोनी बड़ा (हां चड़ी असवारी गांव में तो नैइ बड़ा)। मैं गांव में बड़ जावूं नै अबार की घड़ी (म्हे)। पीलोदो गढ है जको सेंदेही बैकुण्ठ जातो

रहै (हां सगळो को सगळो बैकुण्ठ जाय)। भांगीजी कंवर कीयो दादा भाई आप तो अठै रह जावो पीलोदा मैं ही सांठो (हां घणो एकलो ही)। दरबार का हुकमूं देव महाराज तो पीलोदा गढ के गोरवै तंबू ताण दिया (म्हे)। रसोई पाणी की जुगत (होबा लागी)। भांगीजी काळवी घोड़ी लेय (म्हे)। एकलो गढ में पूगतो (व्हियो है)। जी टैम में सिरदार धारापती जाजम पर बिराजमान (हुरिया हा)। ले जार दरबार का हुकमं सुवा मण भांग को नशो तो सागै करियोड़ो हो (म्हे)। लाठ नै ले जार बीचै जाजम पर राळ दी (वाह वाह)। कीयो ल्यो भैइ सिरदारां (म्हे)। एक हाथवूं म्हारी लाठ नै चक्कर कठावो कीयो (वाह वाह)। सिरदार तो सब हाथर लाग ग्या लाठ तो (भूणोजी) की भांगीजीवाली हली कोनी (म्हे)। भांगीजी कीयो सुणो सिरदारां (म्हे)। मैं फैरूं अब (म्हे)। फूल ढोल फूट गा मर गा तो म्हनै ठा कोनी हा भैइ (हां अब म्हनै ठा कोय नी है चेतो जावै तियारी)। कंवर भांगीजी लाठ नै फैरी नै (वाह वाह)। कुमहारां का दरबार हा जका सारा ही भरिया भाज गा (वाह वाह)। भांगीजी कंवर तो लाठ नै फैरी तीन तिलोकी को नाथ भगवान जहर की नजर (हां) जहर की नजर झांकी पीलोदा सागै जूप गो (सारो को सारो जूप ग्यो जी कीयो)। तो रावजी साय ऊंचा बैठां हा (म्हे)। बूझणा (भूणाजी नै करी है)। अरै भूणा (म्हे)। गढ पीलोदा सामू धुंआड़ो कींयां लागै रे आज (हां धुंआड़ो क्यें को नीकलै ओ कीयो)। भूणोजी बोलै (वाह वाह)। कांई रावजी नै समचार अब कहवै देखां (कीआवूं जाणज्यो देखां कीआवूं)। अबार कहवां भैइ भगवान का हुकमूं देखां (वाह वाह जी वाह वाह)।।

हल हीसोड़िया जी धारापतियां का रहगिया रे गेलिया रावजी औवूं रे।
आंकां भाई रे रह गा भातड़ै बीज।
बाळो ठाकर दौड़ो दौड़ ग्यो।
दौड़ियो दीखै रावजी रे पहलै सावण की तीज।।
(भलां जी भलां) देव भलां

हल हीसोड़िया धारापतियां का रह गा (म्हे)। खोजै रह गा (बीज)। दरबार दौड़ो दौड़ दियो दीखै पहल सावण की (तीज)। अरै रावजी (म्हे)। भगवान दौड़ो दे दियो (वाह वाह)। अरै भूणा तो धूंआड़ो कींयां लाग्यो अतो (हां धूंआड़ो कींयां नीकलै है कीयो)। भूणोजी बोलै कांई समचार कहवै रावजी नै देखां (कीआवूं जाणज्यो देखां कीआवूं)।।

कुंवारी किन्या जी धारापतियां के गेलिया रावजी रे।
आज रावजी रे घर घर मण्ड ग्यो व्याह।
बासना में कुमहार पूज आया कोय ने।
जरां कुमहार हाथां पचावै न्याव।।
(भलां जी भलां) किषन भलां

देमाली नाथ को नांव लेवां नै (म्हे)। ई सदा ही (भलां जी कीयो)। कुंवारी किन्या धारापतियां के मोकळी है (म्हे)। आज घर घर मण्ड गो दीखै (ब्याव)। अरे बासना में पूज कोनी आया (म्हे)। जरां धारापती सिरदार हाथां ही पचाया (न्याव)। छोरियां घणी है (हां ब्याव मण्ड ग्या सागै का सागे)।

कुमहार तो बासन दिया कोनी (म्हे)। ए रावजी साय रे धारापती सिरदार ताणा हाथां ही न्यावड़ा पचावै (वाह वाह)। रावजी सा मन में देखियो रे आज भूणा ईंयां कींया बोल्यो (म्हे)। कीयो भूणा बात है जिसी कह भैइ कीयो श्री महाराज तीन तिलोकी को नाथ भगवान दौड़ो दे दियो (वाह वाह)। हाथी तो मैं ल्यावो (म्हे)। हेंर पीलोदा नै भगवान भेळ दियो आज कीयो (वाह वाह)। रावजी कीयो रे सिरदारां भूणा के अब पूण्चो पाण हो गियो भैइ कीयो (वाह वाह)। थांको कोनी रिया भूणोजी अब (हां अब आपणो कोय है नी कीयो)। भिनाय के नौरै भूणोजी पूगतो हू गो (वाह वाह)। दरबार का हुकमूं भिनाय के नौरै गियो ने (म्हे)। जरां कांई करियो के भूणो जी देश नै आपका बिदा होबा लाग्या नै (वाह वाह)। जरां मन में देखियो रे भैइ रावजीवूं बाईवूं सगळावूं चोखी तरह मिल अर आंवां भैइ (हां मिल अर पछी चालां कीयो)। रावजी मन में देखियो के थारावूं तो कांई ठी भूणो मिलै के कोनी मिलै ठा कोनी (म्हे)। पण देश नै जाय जरां बाईवूं तो जरूर ही (मिली)। कीयो सिरदारां इस्यो काम करो के भूणोजी दरबार में जरूर आय भैइ (म्हे)। मीर बूझणा करी की म्हारा कीया करो हम नै अकल उपजी एक (हां जको बतावो जकी काम करो)। कांई रे मीर (म्हे)। दरबार के मांयनै सार का चिना (बखेर द्यो)। भूणोजी दरबार में बड़ी नै (म्हे)। जरां बैरी नै ई जागां ही तिसलता ईयूं दाब देवां (वाह वाह)। ई जागां को जागां ही पापो ही (काट देवां कीयो)। रावजी कीयो बाह वाह रे मीर अकल को ऊजीर है कीयो (हां अकल तो धणी थारै में)। सार का चिना बिखेर दिया (म्हे)। हेंर दरवाजो मंगल करा द्यो (वाह वाह)। बारी के दरबार का हुकमूं दोन्यां उमराव आड़ा बैठ गा ले ल्यै छूरियां तरवारियां (हां काठा दोन्यु बैठया दीयो काळू मीर)। भूणोजी बारी में मुण्डो घालै नै (म्हे)। बी टैम ही नाड़ पर ठोको जको राख लियां (अठै को अठै ही राख द्यां)। दरबार का हुकमूं बाई मन में देखियो रे बैरी दगो तो सांचो रोपियो (वाह वाह)। भूणोजी दरबार का हुकमूं दरवाजा के सांकला आयगा (म्हे)। बाई मन में देखियो रे भूणोजी आरियो है हेंर अब दादा भूणा की तो मौत (आयगी)। तो दरवाजा के सांकलो भूणोजी आवै (म्हे)। कांई समचार कहवै देखां (कीआवूं जाणज्यो कीआवूं)।।

ए कड़ियां कटारो जी ए ई भूणा के बांकड़ो रे।
ऊपर भाई रे सोना की खोळियां रे।
ठोकर बाही रे कंवर महाबळी।
काळू मीर दीयोजी दोन्यु रे कूद गा डोली।।
(भलां जी भलां) देव भलां

कड़ियां कटारो भूणा के बांकड़ो (म्हे)। ऊपर सोना की है खोळी (खोळी)। ठोकर बाह खेंखारो करियो रायजादो महाबळी (म्हे)। काळू मीर दीयो दोन्यु अमराव कूद गा (डोली)। दरबार का हुकमूं बारी में मारबा नै बैठां हा (म्हे)। बो कींवाड़ा को भचीड़ बोल्यो नै (वाह वाह)। मीर बोल्यो यार दीया थारो बाप आयगो भाजै नै आगो (हां भागो कीयो)। दीयो तो कूद गो अर मीर आखड़ दरबार का आखड़ दरबार का हुकमूं भूणा का पगां में ही (जाय पड़ियो)। पड़तां मीर के भूणोजी छाती पर पग दे दियो (वाह वाह)। ए कंवर साय ईंयां कींयां करै काळी ढोरी कोनी थारी (हां काळी गाय हूं कीयो)। बाईजी ऊंची गोखड़ै (बैठी ही)। दरबार का हुकमूं बाई बोलै (म्हे)। कांई भूणा नै समचार कहवै (कीआवूं जाणज्यो अब कीआवूं)।।

ए छाती परूं तो जी पांव मत उतारै कंवर महाबळी रे।
दुशमन मीर की रे गैण दिशा में जाय।
काळती गाय को झेरणो खूटियां में टांक द्यो।
आपणै तो भूणा रे धीणा बिनाई सार।।
(भलां जी भलां) देव भलां

छाती परूं पांव ऊंचो मत करज्यो (म्हे)। अरै भूणा ई दुशमन को गैण दिशा नै (जाय)। काळती गाय को झेरणो खूंटी पर ऊंचो टांक (म्हे)। आपणै धीणा बिनै (अब सार)। भूणा ई धीणा में की सार कोनी (वाह वाह)। मोको आयगो जको बैरी नै आगो मार (म्हे)। कीयो भैइ हिन्दु को धरम कोनी (वाह वाह)। ए गौ बन गो (म्हे)। हिन्दु धरम थोड़ो है जो गाय नै मारूं (हां गाय नै मैं तो कोनी मारूं)। फट भूणोजी के पग नै खेंच ल्यो (वाह वाह)। बाई कीयो भूणा थारै बिरद घणो भाई (म्हे)। ए दुशमन जको तनै जीबा दे कोनी अब (हां आंकै दोकी घणा है कीयो)। बाईजी बोलै कांई समचार भूणा नै कहवै देखां (कीआवूं जाणज्यो कीआवूं देखां)। अबार कह द्यां भैइ भगवान का हुकमूं देखां (वाह वाह)।।

ए कूड़ा कूड़ा तो जी दादा भूणा रे बाबो रावजी रे।
नान्या भूणा रे बिखेरिया सार चिना।
दरबार में आणो जाणो रे परो छोड़ द्यो।
थारै दरबार में रे दोकी लोग घणा रे।।
(भलां जी भलां) देव भलां

कूड़ो कूड़ो बाबो रावजी है भूणा (म्हे)। कूड़ी है देख महलां बैठी (मांय)। कूड़ो बाबो रावजी भूणो थारा तणी देख बिखेरिया सार (चिना)। अब दरवाजो हो कर दरबार में आणो जाणो परो छोड़ (वाह वाह)। दादा भूणा थारा पर दोकी लोगी ही (घणा कीयो)। बी रावजी का अमराव है नै (म्हे)। थार पर सब दोकी है (हां से का से दोकी है थारा)। ईंयां ही आवै तो भैइ म्हारा आबा जाबा की बारी है जको अठी कर (आबो कर कीयो)।

माथ नै खावै जी बहनड़ी म्हानी ये सिर की पागड़िया रे।
जणा बाईजी बाड़ खेत नै खाय।
मथरा की जागां ये बनै द्वारका।
जरां भूणो ये बारी हो कर जाय।।
(भलां जी भलां) देव भलां

दरबार का हुकमूं भूणोजी समचार (कीयो है)। माथा नै खावै बाईजी सिर की पागड़ी (म्हे)। बाड़ खेत नै (आ खाय)। मथरा की जागां बनै द्वारका (म्हे)। जणा म्हानी असवारी बारी मायं कर (आजाय)। गैली कींयां हो गी ईंयां (हां बारी मांय कर थोड़ो ही आणालो हूं)। कीयो भूणा थारै बिरद घणा (म्हे)। दरबार में दोकी लोग ही (थारै घणा है कीयो)।

कूड़ा ई कूड़ो जी दादा भूणा रे हिन्दवा रावजी रे।
कूड़ी आपणी रे महलां बैठी मांय।
कछेड़ी में आणो जाणो रे आजवूं छोड़ द्यो।
आवै तो भूणा रे बारी हो कर आव।।
(भलां जी भलां) देव भलां

कूड़ो घणो बाबो रावजी (म्हे)। भूणा कूड़ी आपणी महलां ई बैठी (अब मांय)। अरै कछेड़ी में भूणा आणो जाणो परो छोड़ (वाह वाह)। जै आणो होवै तो म्हारी बारी मांय कर (आवे)। मिलणो तो म्हारावूं ही हैक तनै (वाह वाह)। कछेड़ीवूं कांई लेय जार (हां काम ही कांई है)। कीयो बाई साय (म्हे)। सुंवा दरबाजा आवां कीयो (वाह वाह)। लुक लुक मैं तो (कदै कोनी आवां)। दरबार का हुकमूं भूणोजी दरबार में बड़ियो नै (म्हे)। सार का चिना बिखेरयोड़ा हा (वाह वाह)। भूणोजी तो दरबार का हुकमूं बीर व्हियो जरां चिना नै जियान जमी मातावूं बड़े नै मांयनै जियान नै (म्हे)। जियान चिन सारा ही फूट गा (वाह वाह)। भूणाजी नै एल ही कोनी आयो (म्हे)। दरबार का हुकमूं और तो भूणाजी कंवर से डरता सारा सिरदार भाज गा (म्हे)। रावजी सा एकला गादी पर (बिराजमान हुरिया है)। रावजी कांई करै करै तो ऊंचा ऊठै अर पाछा (पड़ जावे)। फैर ऊंचा ऊठै अर बी जागां (पड़ जाय कीयो)। भूणोजी बूझणा (करी है)। बाबा रावजी ईंयां कींयां करो (हां ईंयां कींयां कर रिया कीयो)। अरै भूणा बेटा करूं कांई (म्हे)। के जकै दिन म्हारी बन्ध कटाई नै तूं (वाह वाह)। जतै तो तूं म्हारावूं राम राम (करतो)। हेंर खनार में बन्ध कटाया बाद में (म्हे)। भाई रे थारावूं राम राम ई पहली में करूं (हां मैं करूं कीयो)। मैं देखूं के भूणा से मिलां (म्हे)। ऊठनी कोनी आवै लाल (वाह वाह)। कीयो बाबा रावजी म्हनै ठा पड़ गो आपको कीयो (म्हे)। भूणोजी कांई करियो बन्दी कमरियां (हां बीवूं ऊठ ग्या)। कछेड़ी में ऊठ गा (वाह वाह)। रावजी सा बूझणा (करी ही)। भूणा थारा ई तो कायदा बांध्योड़ा हा तूं ही कींयां तोड़ियो भैइ (हां कायदा नै तोड़दिया कीयो)। थारा बांध्योड़ा हे कायदा (म्हे)। के सस्तरबाण कछेड़ी में नैइ आणो (वाह वाह)। भूणोजी बोलै कांई समचार कहवै देखां (कीआवूं जाणज्यो देखां कीआवूं)।।

सगळी धरती फिरयायो जी ए ई गेलिया रावजी रे।
ल्यायो मैं तो रे बाड़ियांली झीकोल।
कड़ियां की कटारी कड़ियां में भूखी रह ग्या।
मांगबा लागी रे बाबा राव का भोग।।
(भलां जी भलां) देव भलां

सगळी धरती में मैं फिरयायो (म्हे)। ल्यायो म्हारी बाड़ियांली नै (झीकोल अर)। आ कड़ियां की कटारी रावजी कड़ियां में भूखी रह गी (म्हे)। आज मांगै रे बाबा राव को (भोग)। ताणी धूंध है नै ई में बड़बा नै करै म्हारी कटारी (वाह वाह)। रावजी दरबार का हुकमूं धक्क धक्क धूजबा लागो (म्हे)। मन में देखियो रे भूणा के फरक आयोड़ा है (वाह वाह)। ओ सजियोड़ो है अब (हा) ओ बैर अठै ही काढी (वाह वाह)।

बाई बोलै कांई समचार कंवर भूणा नै कहवै देखां (कीआवूं जाणज्यो कीआवूं देखां)। अबार कहवूं देव का हुकमूं देखां (वाह वाह)।।

आप पाटघात तो जी मत करज्यै रे कंवर महाबळी रे।
तूं तो मत मारै नै रे तूं ही बाबो राव।
पाटघात मत घालज्यै कंवर महाबळी।
थारै रावजी रे बाजियो धरम को बाप।।
(भलां जी भलां) देव भलां

भूणा पाटघात मत घालज्यै (म्हे)। दरबार का हुकमूं मत मारै नै बाबो (राव)। अरै दरबार का हुकमूं पाटघात घालिया से थारै रावजी हो धरम को (बाप)। थारै अर म्हारै तो भाई रे धरम को बाप है कीयो (वाह वाह)। भूणा डोकळडा नै मार मत नाकी (म्हे)। बाई कहवै जी टैम में तो दरबार का हुकमूं भूणोजी बाई को कहनो मानणो ही पड़ै (वाह वाह)। माई सांखली दरबार का हुकमूं दो कांसा बना दिया (म्हे)। रावजी ताणै तो अमरत को (बनायो)। हेंर भूणा ताणी जहर को (बना दियो)। मन में देखियो दुशमन आयो है (म्हे)। जहर कर दियो जको ई जागां ही पाप कट जायी (हां मर जायज्यूं)। कांसो जी टैम में सांखली राणी खिनायो नै (म्हे)। भूणोजी ले जळ की झारी (वाह वाह)। दातण कुल्ला (करबा लाग्यो)। बाई महल में बैठी बोलै (म्हे)। कांई भूणा नै समझावै देखां (कीआवूं जाणज्यो कीआवूं देखां)। अबार कह द्यां देव का हुकमूं ले तूं (वाह वाह जी वाह वाह)।।

ए नंदियां बहवै तो जी नान्या भूणाजी बहवै उतावलियां रे।
बूगलो भूणा रे घणी करै उछाळ।
समझायोड़ो समझा रे कंवर महाबळी।
आयगो भूण रे अनचीतयोड़ो काळ।।
(भलां जी भलां) किषन भलां

देव को नांव ल्यां तो भाई रे सदा ही (भलां जी कीयो)। दरबार का हुकमूं समचार बाई कीयो है (म्हे)। नंदियां बहवै भूणाजी उतावली (म्हे)। बूगलो मांयनै धणी करै (उछाळ)। अरै म्हारो समझायोड़ो समझाज्यै (म्हे)। आयगो थारो अनचीतयोड़ो (काल)। तो दरबार का हुकमूं कंवर भूणाजी नै राणीजी जहर को कांसो बनायो है नै (म्हे)। तो दरबार का हुकमूं भूणोजी तोड़ फलको अर एक कुत्ती ऊबी जकी नै (राळियो)। राळतां जेज (लागी)। क्युं बो बाईजी समचार कीयो है नै (म्हे)। भूणोजी मन में देखियो कीयो सुरग्याणी हो भूणोजी (वाह वाह)। मन में देखियो ए बाईजी समचार कीयो जठेवूं पाणीवूं तूं अबार उछाल तूं करै (हां तनै ही समचार कीयो है)। समझनो चोखो है (वाह वाह)। दरबार का हुकमूं कुत्ती नै टुकड़ो राळियो कुत्ती भुंवाळी खार तरणेटी खार हेटी पड़ गी (वाह वाह)। भूणोजी कड़ियां के मांयनू काढ कटारी (म्हे)। हेंर थाळ के मांयनै (रोप दीनी)। रावजी साय बूझणा (करी हैं)। भूणा (म्हे)। ईंयां कींयां करी तूं (हां ईंयां कींयां करी आज)। अरै सोना का थळ में (म्हे)। चान्दी की मेख (कींयां लागाई है कीयो)।

सगळी धरती खूंदयायो जी ए ई बाबा रावजी रे।
ल्यायो म्हारी रे बाड़ियांली झीकोल।
आ कड़ियां की कटारी कड़ियां में भूखी रह ग्या।
अब मांगै रावजी रे ताणी धूंध का भोग।।
(भलां जी भलां) देव भलां

सगळी धरती मैं फिरयायो (म्हे)। दरबार का हुकमूं ल्यायो म्हारी बाड़ियांली (झीकोल अर)। आ कड़ियां की कटारी कड़ियां में भूखी रह गी (म्हे)। रावजी मांगै रे थारी धूंध का (भोग)। ताणी धूंध में बड़ी अब लाखां कोनी रहा (वाह वाह)। रावजी साय धक्क धक्क धूजबा लागा (म्हे)। बाईजी आर कीयो दादा भूणा इयां मत कर भाई कीयो (वाह वाह)। डोकळडो को जीव नीकल जायलो डरता को (म्हे)। बाई कहवै जरां तो भूणाजी की दरबार का घर में ऊफणता दूध के छांटो देवां नै आपां (म्हे)। जियान शरीर के छांटां (लाग जावे)। भूणोजी बूझणा करी बाई साय (म्हे)। ये मैं तो मिलबा की खातिर आया हूं थारावूं (वाह वाह)। मैं देश नै जांवूं अब (म्हे)। तो दरबार का हुकमूं भूणाजी के अर बाई तारादे के कांई बांतां होवै (कीआवूं जाणीज्यो देखां)। अबार कहवां देव का हुकमूं ले तूं।।

तूं ही जावै जी दादा भूणा रे ताणा देश में औवूं रे।
अठै कोनी रह जामन जायो बीर।
कुण आसी रे बाई का ब्याव में।
कुण ओड़ावे म्हनै जी भोम दिखण का चीर।
(भलां जी भला) देव भलां

तूं चाल्यो लाल भूणा थारा देश में (म्हे)। म्हारै लेरै कोनी भाई म्हांको जायो (बीर)। तूं जावै ताणा देश में सांज का ब्याव में कुण ओड़ायै म्हनै दिखण भोम को (चीर)। आ थारै भाणजी है सांजा बाई (म्हे)। ई का ब्याव में कुण आयै भैइ (जकी बताय)। भूणोजी बोलै कांई समचार बाई नै कहवै देखां (कीआवूं जाणज्यो कीआवूं देखां)। अबार कहवूं देव का हुकमूं देखां।।

ए मैं जावूं तो जी बहनड़ी म्हारी ये म्हाना देश में औवूं रे।
ल्यावूं मेदू मदनो बीर।
मैं आवां ये सांज का ब्याव में।
ल्यांवां बाई ये भोम दिखण का चीर।।
(भलां जी भलां) देव भलां

मैं जावूं बाईजी म्हारा देश में कीयो (म्हे)। अब के आतो ल्यावूं सागै मेदू अर मदनो (बीर)। मैं आवां बाई सांज का भात (म्हे)। मेदू ओड़ायी तनै भोम दिखण का ही (चीर)। ए समचार कंवर भूणोजी (कीयो है)। बाई कीयो रे अब दादा भूणा (म्हे)। थांकै ब्यहवार ज्यादा है कांई (वाह वाह)। लेरली बात पिछाण तूं (म्हे)। तूं दड़ावट में भायां के समिल जातो रह नै (वाह वाह)। जर आ बात तनै खतम हो जाय थारी (हां आ बात कोनी रहवेली कीयो)। पछै बात बा चाली के रावजी नै मारा अब दुशमन

नै (वाह वाह)। दुशमनी चारो है नी भूणा थांकै कीयो दरबार का हुकमूं म्हारै तो मांयरो करणो होवै (म्हे)। अबार की घड़ी करै (हां अब ही कर जावो)। भायां के भेळो कीयोड़ो दादा भूणो पाछो कोनी आवेलो (वाह वाह)।।

ए दौड़ो देवूं तो जी ए बहनड़ी म्हारी ये बिन देश में औवूं रे।
ल्यावूं गायां भैंसयां रा टोळा घेर।
चोखी गायां दीज्यै ए बाई के डयजे।
बाकी की म्हारी ये पाछी दीज्यो घेर।।
(भलां जी भलां) देव भलां

मैं जावूं बाईजी म्हाना देश में कीयो (म्हे)। ल्यावूं गायां भैंसयां का टोळो ही (घेर)। चोखी गायां दीज्यै बाई के डायजै (म्हे)। बाकी की म्हारी बाई ये पाछी दीज्यो (घेर)। चोखी लागै नै जकी जकी बाई के डायजै (देज्यो)। तारादे बाई बोलै कंवर भूणा नै समचार कांई भातूं कहवै देखां (कीआवूं जाणीज्यो कीआवूं देखां)। अबार कहवूं देव का हुकमूं ले तूं।।

गाय भैंस का जी जो डायजा रे जाट गूजरां रे।
दादा भूणा बै दियावूं रे मेर हुवै राजी।
बाई नै परणीजबा आवै भाटी जेसलमेर का।
हथळेवा में मांगै रे आंटीलो हाथी रे।।
(भलां जी भलां) देव भलां

गाय भैंस को डायजो जाट अर गूजरां बै दीया सूं मेर हो जावै राजी। बाई नै परणीजबा आवै भाटी जेसलमेर को हथळेवा में मांगै आंटीलो हाथी। के जाट गूजरां बै ई राजी होवे। बाई को हथळेवो कोनी छोड़ी। तो भूणोजी कहवै अर कांई बाई बाई सा सुणै (कीआवूं जाणज्यो सा कीआवूं)।।

एक दौड़ो देवां जी जो कजळीबन के मांयनै औवूं रे।
लियावूं बहनड़ी ए हाथियां रा टोळा घेर।
भूरिया हाथी दीज्यै बाई के डायजे।
कोनी मावै ये भाटियां की जेसलमेर।।
(भलां जी भलां) देव भलां

दरबार का हुकमूं एक दौड़ो देवूं कजळीबन के मांयनै (म्हे)। बाई ल्यावूं हाथियां का टोळा ई (घेर अर)। चोका हाथी दीज्यै बाई के डायजै (म्हे)। कोनी मावै भाटियां की (जैसलमेर)। सगळी कोनी भर द्यूं जेसलमेर नै कीयो (वाह वाह)। भलो सोच करियो गेली वाह (वाह वाह)। दरबार का हुकमूं कीयो दादा भूणा (म्हे)। अरै भाइयां के भेळो गियोड़ो पछै मांयरो कोनी भरीजै (वाह वाह)। भूणोजी मन में देखियो रे रावजी साय के आपांणा के आपणै समपरक तो कोनी भैइ (म्हे)। बैरीवाड़ा को ही है (वाह वाह)।।

ए बाजारां गियो तो जी ए ई कंवर महाबळी रे।
मुलाया भूणो रे भोम दिखण का चीर।
ओढ़ै नै तारादे बहनड़ियां।
तनै बाई ये ओढ़ावै भूणो बीर।।
(भलां जी भलां) देव भलां

बाजारां गियो भैइ कंवर महाबळी (वाह वाह)। मुलाया भोम दिखण का (चीर)। ओढ़ै नै तारादे बहनड़ी अब ओढ़ाबा लागो भूणो ही (तनै बीर)। बाई सा ओढ़ ले भैइ जरां और कांई (वाह वाह)। हाथ कांचळी सज आवै नै (म्हे)। जिसी ले ल्यो आगी (वाह वाह)। पछै कांई ठी बाई साय भायां के भेळै गिया पछै कांई ठी म्हारावूं आणी आवै कोनी (हां आवै कीयो)।।

ए बाजारां गियो तो जी ए ई मितवालां का डावड़ो रे।
ओ तो ठाकरां रे चिनकवार ही वार।
सितर हजार मेल दिया थाळ के मांयने।
घड़ेक रथ नै ठामयो राजा काछबजी का बाण।।
(भलां जी भलां) देव भलां

बाजारां गियो रायजादो महाबळी (म्हे)। लगाई चिनक (वाह)। अरै सितर हजार बाई का थाळ में घालिया भूणोजी रोकड़ी (म्हे)। रथ नै ठामयो राजा काछबजी को (बाण)। सुरजी महाराज कह बतावै घड़ी खाण्ड ठम अर भूणाजी को मायरो (देखियो हो)। तो तारादे बाई को सांज को भातवूं भात भरतां (म्हे)। हेंर भूणोजी मायरो राण शहर में भरतां (भरतां)। जय बोलो भैइ श्री देवनारायण भगवान की (जय)।।

सदा सिंवरूं तो जी भाग भवानी है देवी शारदा रे।
धुंधाळा देव के जी गणपत लागू पाय।
गजानन्द देव नै सिंवरियावूं सुख सांपते।
शारदा नै सिंवरिया जी हिरदै बिराजै आय।।
(भलां जी भलां) देव भलां

सदा ही सिंवरूं भवानी शारदा (म्हे)। धूंधाळा देव के गणपत लागू (पाय)। गजानन्द देव नै सिंवरियावूं भाई भोपा सुख सांपतै शारदा नै सिंवरियावूं हिरदै बिराजै (आय)।।

भैरूं नै भजबो कर जी ए ई भोला मानवियां रे।
दोन्यु भायां की बोली प्यार घणी सुत्यार।
चोमका नै थरपियो रे पांचू पाण्डवा।
दुसासन भैरूं नै रे ई आप श्री किरतार।।
(भलां जी भलां) देव भलां

भैरूं नै भजबो कर भोला मानवी (म्हे)। अरै दोन्यु भैरूं की बोली प्यार घणी (सुत्यार)। चोमका नै तो थरपियो रे भाई पांचू पाण्डवा (म्हे)। दुसासन भैरूं नै आप श्री (किरतार)। दुसासन भैरूं भगवान को थरपियोड़ो है (वाह वाह)। चोमको भैरूं पाण्डवां की बार की मांयनै (थरपीज्योड़ा है कीयो)।।

भैरूंजी कटोड़ै जायोजी कठै ऊपनियो।
काळूड़ा कटोड़ै जायो रे कठै ऊपनियो।
हर नै कुण जी लडायो हर नै लाड बड़ली का भैरूं लाडलो।
सियां म्हारी काशी में जायो रे गोठां ऊपनियो।
सिरगा काशी में जायो सियां गोठां ऊपनियो।
म्हानै नापोजी लडायो हर नै लाड बड़ली का भैरूं लाडलो।
भैरूंजी घाटियां में सुणी जरै हर का घूघरा।
भैरूंजी घाटियां में सुणीज्येला हरवला घूघरा।
हर सागै ठमकिया जाणै लीलागर का पोड़ बड़ली का भैरूं लाडलो।
भैरूंजी कटोड़ै घड़ा द्यूं जी हर का घूघरा।
जामीड़ा कटोड़ै घड़ा द्यूं जी हरवला घूघरा।
हां मैं तो कटोड़ै घड़ा द्यूं रिमजोल बड़ली का भैरूं लाडलो।
सियां म्हारी घटिया में घड़ीज्यै म्हाना घूघरा।
हां सियां घाटियां में घड़ीज्यूंला हरवाला घूघरा।
हां म्हारी पाली में घड़ीज्यै रिमझोळ बड़ली का भैरूं लाडलो।
भैरूंजी का में पेवा द्यूं हर का जी घूघरा।
हां जामीड़ा का में पेवा द्यूंला हरवाला घूघरा।
हां मैं तो का में जी पेवा द्यूं रिमझोळ बड़ली का भैरूं लाडलो।
सियां म्हारी केसा में पूयीज्यै हर ना घूघरा।
सियां केसा में पूयीज्यला हरवाला घूघरा।
हां आतो रेशम में पवीज्यै रिमझोळ बड़ली का भैरूं लाडलो।
भैरूंजी की जागां बन्धा द्यूं जी हर का घूघरा।
भैरूंजी की जागां बन्धा द्यूं हरवल घूघरा।
मैं तो की जागां बन्धा द्यूं रिम झोल बड़ती का भैरूं लाडलो।
सियां म्हारी कड़ियां रे पहनीज्यै म्हाना घूघरा।
सियां कड़िया के पहनीज्येला हरवल घूघरा।
हां म्हाना पगलियां के पहनीज्यै रिमझोळ बड़ली का भैरूं लाडलो।
भैरूंजी देवर जेठाणीजी मोसा बोलिया।
जामीड़ा देवर जेठाणीजी मोसा बोलिया।
हां म्हारा परणयोड़ो ल्यावै रे लोड़ी सोक बड़ली का भैरूं लाडलो।

भैरूंजी सासू के लगा द्यूं जी चौसट जोगण्यिां।
जामीड़ा सासू के लगा द्यूं रे चौसट जोगणियां।
म्हारी नणदन के लगा द्यूं बावन बीर बड़ली का भैरूं लाडलो।
भैरूंजी एकर बाळूड़ो म्हानै देवज्यो।
जामीड़ा एकर बाळूड़ो म्हानै देवेज्यो।
म्हारी बांझड़ी को नांव हटाय बड़ली का भैरूं लाडलो।
भैरूंजी पीवर का गेला में जी हर को देवरो।
ओ जामीड़ा पीवर का गेला में हरवालो देवरो।
तो मैं तो आती रे जातोड़ी देवूं जात बड़ाली का भैरूं लाडलो।
भैरूंजी म्हाना रे बाळूड़ा नै सोरो राखज्यो।
जामीड़ा म्हाना रे भाण्या नै सोरो राखज्यो।
ओ म्हारा परण्या पर राखीज्यो दोन्यु हाथ बड़ली का भैरूं लाडलो।

जय बोलो भैइ भैरूंनाथ महाराज की (जय)। कांई भैरूंनाथ की आठ पोहर की चोखी होवै जकी को नांव जरूर लेनो है।। तो दरबार का हुकमूं बाई को तारादे को सांज को भर मायरो भूणोजी (म्हे)। कांई बिदा होबा लाग (गिया जी कीयो)। रावजी का अमराव बोल्या (म्हे)। मीर बोल्यो हमारा कीया करो अकल उपजी (हां अकल उपजायी कीयो)। मीर कीयो बतावूं (हां बतावो कीयो)। कीयो श्री महाराज ई के बाप की बावड़ी है भूणाजी का बाप की खुदायोड़ी (म्हे)। बठै गिया बिन भूणाजी लाखां ही (रहवै कोनी)। मैं अर दीयोजी जांवां (म्हे)। बावड़ी के ऊपरै ओ बावड़ी में बड़ी जरां बैरी नै बी जागां ही दुशमन नै मारल्यां (हां बावड़ी में ही राखल्यां कीयो)। रावजी सा बूझणा करी बाह मीर अकल को (ऊजीर ही है कीयो)। पांच पांच से घोड़ा अर पांच पांच से असवार (म्हे)। ले सिरदार बावड़ी के ऊपरै तंबूड़ा ताण रिया (वाह वाह)। भूणोजी आवे जर ग्यान राखो भैइ बैरी ने ई जागां ही मारणो है कीयो (हां अठै ही मारणो है कीयो)। तो कुण कुण आया दीयोजी जोधको आग्यो अर काळू मीर की फौज (आयगी)। टोडा के सोलंकी रावजी साय के जंवाई हो (हां बांकी फौज आयगी)। बाई नै निंगै हुई तारादे ने (म्हे)। तारादे अर भूणोजी है नै (म्हे)। जी दिन रावजी साय पकड़ ले गा नै भूणा नै महाभारत में (म्हे)। जकै नै छै महीना को हो भूणोजी (हां हा कीयो)। तो बाई तारादे रावजी साय की लड़की ही (वाह वाह)। तो बा चूंगै बोबा तो बो के जोड़ै ही दरबार का हुकमूं भूणा नै कीयो राणी नै कीयो ई नै ही चूंगावो (हां ई नै ही बोबा चूंगाबो करे)। एक बोबो बाई नै देवो (म्हे)। एक भूणाजी नै (हां देवो कीयो)। तो दोन्यु बहन भाई जोड़ै चूंगयोड़ा जको ओ दूध को मुलायजो राखता (वाह वाह)। बाई मन में देखियो रे ताणा भाई ने तो दुशमन देख थारो ही परणियोड़ो है जको दगो करबा नै है (हां हूं सम ग्यो)। बाई तारादे बोलै कांई कंवर भूणा नै समचार कहवै देखां (कीआवूं जाणज्यो देखां अब कीआवूं)। अबार कहवूं भगवान का हुकमूं भैइ।।

आगै मेलूं जी नान्या भूणा नै मैं चरख ल्यो रे।
नान्या भूणाजी लेरे ल्यो पछीत।

आपका बैरी नै रे भूणाजी मारतां।
मत करज्यो भाई रे तारादे नै चीत।।
(भलां जी भलां) देव भलां

आगै लेवूं भूणा मैं चरख ल्यो (म्हे)। हेंर लेरै लेवूंली (पछीत)। अरै आपका बैरी नै भूणा मारतां (म्हे)। मत कर देयी भाई थारी तारादे नै (चीत)। तूं देखेलो बाई के लांबी कांचळी अब पहरी जाय (म्हे)। बो सोच मत करी (वाह वाह)। मैं तो सेर को सूत कात अर पेट भरलेवूं (वाह वाह)। पण दुशमन देख थारा पर ही दगो गियो है थारो बहनोई (हां निंगै राखी कीयो)। भूणोजी बीर होबा लाग गियो नै (म्हे)। बाईजी बोलै (वाह वाह)। कांई समचार आपका भाई नै कहवै (कीआवूं जाणज्यो देखां कीआवूं)। अबार कहवूं भगवान का हुकमूं देखां।।

एकर पाळणै जी नान्या भूणा रे आपां पोड़ता रे।
नान्या भूणाजी भेळै चूंगिया थान।
जात भांत की दादाजी ठा पड़ी कोय ने।
आज निंगै हु गी नान्या रे तूं गूजर मैं रजपूत।।
(भलां जी भलां) देव भलां

एकर पाळणै आपां हींडता (म्हे)। नान्या भूणा मैं भेळै चूंगिया आपां (थान)। अरै जात भांत की अता दिन ठा कोनी पड़ी (म्हे)। आज ठा पड़ गी (वाह वाह)। तूं गूजर मैं हूं (रजपूत)। भूणा तूं तो गूजर है (म्हे)। मैं रजपूत हां भैइ (वाह वाह)। पण अता दिन भेळै ही तो चूंगिया अर भेळै ही हींडिया (म्हे)। जांच कोनी पड़ी (हां निंगै कोई नै)। दरबार का हुकमूं भूणोजी बीर होबा लागो (वाह वाह)। बाईजी बोलै कांई समचार कहवै देखां (कीआवूं जाणज्यो देखां कीआवूं)। अबार कहवूं भगवान का हुकमूं ले तूं (वाह वाह जी)।।

तूं ही जावै जी नान्या भूणाजी ताणा देश में औवूं रे।
घोड़ी की कर दी राण दिशा नै पूठ।
थोड़ी डोड़ी हो जो ये भिनाय की डूंगरियां।
जातां बीरा की ये निरखण दीज्यो पूट।।
(भलां जी भलां) देव भलां

भैइ भूणोजी जावै भैइ आपका देश में (म्हे)। अरै घोड़ी की कर दीर राण दिशा नै (पूठ)। जो थोड़ी के डोड़ी हो जायज्यो राण भिनाय की डूंगरिया (म्हे)। जातां दादा की निरखण दीज्यो (म्हनै पूट)। डूंगरिया नै कीयो समचार कीयो बतावै (वाह वाह)। राण भिनाय की डूंगरिया ई (म्हे)। बाई का कहना से थोड़ीसी डोड़ी हो गी (वाह वाह)। भूणोजी कंवर दरबार का हुकमूं बावड़ी में पूगता (व्हिया जी कीयो)। पूगता ही भूणाजी बा सिरदारां नै देखिया (म्हे)। मन में देखियो हां आय तो ग्या दुशमन (हां आया तो है ही)। दरबार का हुकमूं बनू बारहठ सागै ही हो (म्हे)। बूझणा करी रे बना बाबा (म्हे)। बावड़ी कुण की है आ (हां कुण की खुदायोड़ी है ओ कीयो)। कीयो बगड़ावतां की श्री महाराज (हां

बगड़ावतां की खुदायोड़ी है)। कीयो जरां इस्यो काम करो (म्हे)। राव का अमराव है जका का पाणी बन्द करो स का (हां स नै पाणी बन्द कर द्यो कीयो)। पखाला कोय नै बाल्टी कोय नै भर ले जाणो मनी करो (वाह वाह)। पखाल बन्द करा दी (म्हे)। बाल्टी लोटो बन्द (करां दियो)। ऊनयाळा की टैम ही (हां ऊनाळा की मौसम ही)। घड़ी खाण्ड दो घड़ी काटा मीठा व्हिया (म्हे)। मीर दीयोजी बिचार करियो रे भैइ कंवरजी ने जार कहवां तो सरी (हां तिसा मरतां मरां कीयो)। देखियो आंतो आंतो कंवरजी किस्यान की बात करी है (वाह वाह)। धणी बन गो ओ तो (म्हे)। दोन्यु अमराव भूणा के डेरा आर बूझणा (करी ही)। कंवर साहब मुजरां (हां मुजरां है कीयो)। आवो मीर (आ जावो)। कीयो ईंयां कींयां करी थै आतां ही (म्हे)। फौज पलटन तिसा कोनी मरै म्हारी (हां तिसा मरतां मरां हा नै कीयो)। कीयो रे मीर बावड़ी म्हारा बाप की है भैइ (वाह वाह)। पाणी पीणो है बावड़ी में आर अठै ई पील्यो (हां बावड़ी के मांय बड़ बड़ पी पी (नीकलजावो)। पाणी ले जाबा कोनी (वाह वाह)। तो भैइ यार दीया जाण तो जीवती रही (हां पाणी पियो तो सरी)। तंबूड़ा नेड़ा ताणो भैइ (वाह वाह)। और तो कांई करूं मीर हुकमूं दियो के कंवर साय का हुकम है आजावो पाणी पीणो होवै तो (वाह वाह)। पलटन फौज सारी बावड़ी के मांयनै (हां पाणी पीवण नै बड़ी ही)। भूणोजी पेड़ी पर ऊंचो ऊबो रियो (हां आर ऊपर ऊबा रहगिया)। जो सिरदार पाणी पी अर पाछो जावै (म्हे)। भूणोजी एकांली मूंछ काटली अर एकानै थोड़ोसो कानेड़ा (काट लेवे)। मीर आयो दरबार का हुकमूं एक मूंछ अर कानड़ो काटियो (वाह वाह)। मीर कीयो कोय बिचार कोनी आजावो सिरदारां (हां डराली बात कोय नी)। जीव नै जाकीयो कोनी (वाह वाह)। यह तो मूंछ है सावण का घास है कल पाछी जागी (हां पाछी आजासी)। कानड़ा है जको पगड़ी के हेटै दबल्यां (दाबल्यां कीयो)। कोय भूंडो बिचार कोय नी (म्हे)। राव का अमराव सार ही पाणी पी नीकलया तो भूणोजी सब के सैनाणियां कर दी (वाह वाह)। टोडा को सोलंकी के भूणाजी निंगै आयो (हां आयग्यो)। दे थपेड़ की आंतरै (हां फैंकदीन्यो)। एकानी जा आगो (वाह वाह)। मीर बूझणा करी तोबा तोबा तोबा तोबा तोबा रे एकलो तोड़ा को सोलंकी कींयां रियो (हां ओ बंच गियो नी कियो)। दीयोजी बूझणा (करी है)। मीर तनै हाल ई बात को ठा कोनी पड़ी (हां ठा कोनी कीयो)। भूणोजी मुलायजा राखिया बहनोई का (हां बहनोई का मुलायजा राख ई का मूंछ अर (कान कोनी काटियो कीयो)। भूणोजी कीयो रे सिरदारां (म्हे)। एक तो बियां जावो के एक सावल ही थांकै माजनावूं (हां ऊठ जावो पाछा)। कीयो कंवरजी तिसा मरतां मतेई जावा मैं तो (वाह वाह)। बाई कीयो दादा भूणा (म्हे)। अरै दुशमन तनै मार लेयी तो म्हनै कांई ठा पड़ी (हां ठा कींयां पड़ी कीयो)। कीयो बाई सा ताणा अमराव गिया है नै बै (म्हे)। तो सुवा नंगारा आजाय बाजता ढोला (वाह वाह)। जरां जाणज्यै दादा भूणा नै मारिया है (हां मारयाया)। हेंर ऊंधा नंगारो आवै (म्हे)। जरां देखलेय की दादो भूणा खुशी खुशी आपका देश में (हां पूग गियो भायां के समिल है)। मीर बोल्यो यार दीया (म्हे)। बाजता नंगारा पर कोनी चालां भैइ हार हो गी आपणी तो (वाह वाह)। क्युं एक एक कान कट गो (म्हे)। एक एक मूंछ कट गी तो ऊंधा नंगारा नाक कर ए तो राण शहर में पाछा ही बड़तां (हो ग्या जी कीयो)। बाई निंगै राखी मन में देखियो रे (म्हे)। भूणो पूगतो गियो (वाह वाह)। भूणोजी दरबार का हुकमूं बटवूं बिदा (व्हिया है)। दरबार का हुकमूं बगड़ावतां का बीर खेत में पूगतो हु गो (म्हे)। खारी नंदी बहवै ही (वाह वाह)। हेंर नंदी के डावा के ऊपरै देवळी

से देवळी अड़ मेली (हां देवळियां रूप री ही)। बूझणा करी बना बाबा (म्हे)। ओ कांई हिसाबदारो है भैइ (हां अता पत्थर कींयां रूपयोड़ा हो कीयो)। कीयो श्री महाराज आपका बड़कां को बीर खेत (आयग्यो)। कीयो अठै (हां देवळियां है कीयो)। देवळियां श्री महाराज (वाह वाह)। कीयो जरां भैइ बीर खेत है तो म्हारा बाप की अर म्हारा मां की देवळी जरूर है (हां है कांई अठै)। कीयो है सा (है कीयो)। आपकी मां को नांव सलूण हो (म्हे)। सलूण के नांव से देवळी है जकी आपकी मां की है (वाह वाह)। भूणोजी बीर खेत में सगळै फिरयो (म्हे)। सलूण के नांव की देवळी आयी जठै ही भूणोजी घोड़ी को आनो छोड़ियो (वाह वाह)। भूणोजी हेटो उतरै कांई देवळी नै निवण करै कांई समचार देवळी अर भूणा के होवै बीर खेत में (कीआवूं जाणज्यो देखां कीआवूं)। अबार कहवूं भगवान का हुकमूं कहवूं (वाह वाह जी)।।

> खड़ काटै तो जी गंवळी भरै कंवर महाबळी रे।
> दुपट्टावूं झाड़ै जी मांत सतियां की बींट।
> ग्यारह बरस का देवळियां ये आपां बीछड़िया।
> आपां नै देवळी ये देव मिलाया नीठ।।
> (भलां जी भलां) देव भलां

खड़ काटै गंवळी पर (म्हे)। खड़ को नांव कांई की घास पूस देवळी कन्नै हो नै (हां जको काटे)। हेंर दरबार का हुकमूं गंवळी भरै कंवर महाबळी दुपट्टां से झाड़ै मात सतियां की बींट (बींट)। ग्यारह बरस का देवळी माता ये आपां बीछड़िया (म्हे)। आपां नै अब देव मिलाया (नीठ)। देव को औतार व्हियो भगवान को (हां जणा आपणा मां बेटां का मेला व्हिया कीयो)। नी जरां देवळीमाता कठै पड़िया मेला (वाह वाह)। भूणोजी बोलै कांई पत्थर नै बतलावै (कीआवूं जाणज्यो कीआवूं)। अबार कहवां देव का हुकमूं भैइ (वाह वाह सा)।।

> खड़ काटै तो जी गंवळी पर कंवर महाबळी रे।
> दुपट्टावूं झाड़ै रे मांत सतियां की खेंव।
> ग्यारह बरस का ये देवळियां आपां बीछड़िय।
> मांवूं देवळी ये मुख बोलो नै थै।।
> (भलां जी भलां) देव भलां

खड़ काटै गंवळी पर ए भैइ बगड़ावतां को डावड़ो (वाह वाह)। दुपट्टावूं झाड़ै मात सतियां की खेंव (खेंव)। ग्यारह बरस का ये देवळीमाता आपां बीछड़िया (वाह वाह)। म्हां से मुख बोलो नै (थे)। ले भैइ तूं म्हारी मां की देवळी है नै सलूण की (म्हे)। देही धार म्हारावूं मुण्डै बोल (हां दर्शन म्हानै द्यो कीयो)। जरां जाणू (म्हे)। म्हारी मां की देवळी है (वाह वाह)। दरबार का हुकमूं कांई पत्थर में परकाश बनै (म्हे)। कांई मां बेटां के ग्यारह बरसावूं पाछी बांतां हो जावै (कीआवूं जाणज्यो देखां कीआवूं)। सतूकार हो जरां होवै (है सतूकार)।।

भूणोजी ऊबो तो जी ए ई बीर खेत में औवूं रे।
ऊबो भाईजी रजधारी रजपूत।
चूड़ सूधो हाथ काढ देवळी भूणा के माथा पर मेलियो।
जरां देवळी मूं रे धक धक चाल्या दूध।।
(भलां जी भलां) देव भलां

भूणोजी आयो बीर खेत में (म्हे)। आयगो रजधारी (रजपूत)। चूड़ सूधो देवळी मूं हाथ काढ (म्हे)। हेंर भूणो के माथा पर मेलियो (वाह वाह)। जी दिन देवळी मूं धक धक चाल गो (दूध)। पत्थर मूं दरबार का हुकमूं दूध की धार चाल गी (वाह वाह)। भूणा के मूछारां में जाती (हां पड़ी है)। भूणोजी कीयो रे बना बाबा (म्हे)। ग्यारह बरसावूं सलूण का दूध आज पाछो चाख लियो (हां चाख्यो कीयो)। देवळी बोलै कांई भूणा नै बतलावै देखां (कीआवूं जाणज्यो कीआवूं देखां)। अबार कहवां भैइ देव का हुकमूं देखां (वाह वाह जी)।।

ए राण शहर सूं जी नान्या भूणाजी बिदा व्है गया रे।
कर दी बोर की रे राण दिशा नै पूट।
जरां म्हनै खबर लाग गी।
लागी भगवान की री इन्द्रासन बैकुण्ठ।।
(भलां जी भलां) देव भलां

राण शहर भूणा भाई तूं बिदा हु गो (म्हे)। अरै बोर की कर दी राण दिशा नै (पूट)। जरां म्हनै खबर लागी रे भूणा भगवान की इन्द्रासन (बैकुण्ठ)। बैकुण्ठ में भगवान का बैराट मण्डया (म्हे)। सब देवता भेळा व्हिया (वाह वाह)। तो बी जागां बांतां चाली अब (म्हे)। कीयो भैइ ग्यारह बरसावूं बगड़ावतां को डावड़ो है आज भायां के सामिल आवै (वाह वाह)। मैं देखियो (म्हे)। भूणोजी बीर खेत में आया बिनै तो (हां रहवै कोनी)। हेंर अबार पत्थरां में ओळमा (काड़ी)। तो लाल रे तूं तो है मरतयुलोक में रहबाळो (मानवी)। मैं हूं स्वरगलोक में (रहबाळा मानवी कीयो)। तूं जाणेलो रोजीना ही माजी सा बीर खेत में लाधी कोनी (हां पत्थरां में कोनी लाधेलां कीयो)। मैं तो लाल रे जी की खातर परकाश धारयो पत्थर में (वाह वाह)। दरबार का हुकमूं देवळीमाता बोलै (वाह वाह)। कांई आपका बच्चा नै देखां बूझणा करै देखां (कीआवूं जाणज्यो कीआवूं)।।

कुण तो ही आपणै जी नान्या भूणा रे हालरिया हुलरावतो रे।
नान्या भूणा रे कुण चूंगायो थान।
देवळी माता करै रे तनै बूझणा।
राण शहर में थारा रे कुण राखियो बै मान।।
(भलां जी भलां) देव भलां

कुण तो लाल भूणा तनै भाई हालरियो हुलरायो (वाह वाह)। अर कुण चूंगायो (थान)। अरै देवळी करै अब तनै बूझणा (म्हे)। राण में भूणा कुण राखियो थारो (मान)। एक तो लाल दोहरो रियो भैइ

(सोरो रियो कीयो)। बै समचार (हां माण्ड अर बतावो)। तो ग्यारह बरसावूं भूणोजी पाछो मावूं बोलै (म्हे)। कांई मां बेटां के बांतां हो जावै देखां (कीआवूं जाणज्यो कीआवूं देखां)। अबार कहवू धणी देव का हुकमूं ले तूं (वाह वाह सा)।।

ए काको नीमो तो जी देवळीमाता ये हालरिया हुलरावतो रे।
राव की राणी ये सांखली चूंगायो थान।
पोळिया में बैठो रहतो ये बाबो रावजी।
देवळीमाता ये घणा बधाया मान।।
(भलां जी भलां) देव भलां

काको नीमो तो देवळीमाता म्हनै हालरियो हुलरायो (वाह वाह)। राव की राणी सांखली कंवळावती चूंगायो (म्हनै थान)। पोळिया में बैठो रहतो बाबो रावजी (म्हे)। देवळीमाता ये म्हारा घणा बधाया (बै मान)। सोरो घणो राखियो म्हनै (हां सोरो तो घणा ही राखिया कीयो)। सोरा को नांव (लियो)। देवळीमाता बोलै (म्हे)। कांई समचार दरबार का हुकमूं भूणा नै कहवै देखां (कीआवूं जाणज्यो कीआवूं देखां)। अबार कहवां भगवान का हुकमूं ले तूं (वाह वाह सा वाह वाह)।।

चन्दा ज्यूं कुण्डल करै तो जी ताणी घोड़ी रे कंवर महाबळी रे।
नान्या भूणाजी डकळ भरै ज्यूं डाण।
देवळी करै रे तनै बूझणा।
जो कींयां तागण कर छोड़ज्यायो रे बाळा खानी राण।।
(भलां जी भलां) देव भलां

ताणी घोड़ी चन्दा ज्यूं कुण्डल करै (म्हे)। डकळ भरै ज्यूं (डाण)। देवळीमाता करै बूझणा (म्हे)। कींयां थागण कर छोड़ी रे भूणा (आ राण)। अतो सोरो रियो नै (हां जर राण शहर छोड़ अर कींयां आया कीयो)। मां बेटां के बांतां होतां इन्द्रासनवूं देवळीवूं परकाश होतां (म्हे)। जय बोलो भैइ श्री देवनारायण भगवान की (जय)। दरबार का हुकमूं देवळी बूझणा करी रे लाल भूणा (म्हे)। अतो सुख पायो जरां भैइ राण शहर नै कींयां छोड़ी (हां कींयां छोड़र आयग्या कीयो)। बा बात बता भैइ (वाह वाह)। दरबार का हुकमूं भूणोजी बोलै (म्हे)। कांई समचार देवळीमां नै कहवै देखां (कीआवूं जाणज्यो कीआवूं देखां)। अबार कहवूं भगवान का हुकमूं ले तूं (वाह वाह सा)।।

म्हानी घोड़ी तो जी चन्दा ज्यूं कुण्डल करै ये माता देवळियां रे।
देवळीमाता ये डकळ भरी ज्यूं डाण।
बगड़ावतां का बैर म्हनै याद आया।
मतेई छूट गी म्हारी ये बाळा खानी राण।।
(भलां जी भलां) देव भलां

दरबार का हुकमूं (म्हे)। म्हानी घोड़ी चन्दा ज्यूं कुण्डल करै (वाह वाह)। डकळ भरै ज्यूं (डाण)। बगड़ावतां

का देवळीमाता म्हनै बैर याद आया (म्हे)। आ मतेई छूट गी म्हारी बाळा खानी (अब राण)। छुटाई कोय कोनी (हां छुटान नै कोय को हो नै)। बगड़ावतां का बैर म्हनै याद आयो नै (म्हे)। जरां राण शहर खारी हो गी (वाह वाह)। दरबार का हुकमूं जरां लाल कोय थारा पर दगो पाणी तो नैइ करियो (हां दगो तो कोय नी करियो कीयो)। कीयो ले भैइ देवळीमाता दगो दीयोजी करियो जकी बात तनै सुणाय द्यूं (हां बा तो बता द्यूं)। भूणोजी बोलै कांई देवहीमाता और सुणै (कीआवूं जाणज्यो देखां कीआवूं)। अबार कहवां देव का हुकमूं ले तूं।।

ए मण्दपार हाथी तो जी देवळीमाता ये दीयोजी छोड़ियो रे।
हाथीड़ो गियो ये मावतड़ा नै पेल।
ओ सुमत बिचारी है गुणेश देवता।
अधर को अधर लीनो म्हनै ए अंबाबाड़ी में मेल।।
(भलां जी भलां) देव भलां

मण्दपार हाथी दीयोजी म्हारा पर छोड़ियो (म्हे)। हाथीड़ो गियो मावतड़ा नै (पेल)। सुमत बिचारी देवळीमाता गुणेश देवता (म्हे)। अधर को अधर लियो म्हनै अंबाबाड़ी में (मेल)। दीयोजी मन में देखियो (म्हे)। बैरी नै मार नाकी हाथी (वाह वाह)। मण्दपार (हां छोड़ियो कीयो)। देख दरबार का हुकमूं भाला की आंकसा की हाथी के (म्हे)। म्हारा के ऊपर छोड़ दियो (वाह वाह)। हाथी कांई करियो (म्हे)। दे सूंड को आंटो (अर ऊंचो अधर को अधर अंबाबाड़ी (पर बैठा दीयोजी कीयो)। म्हनै तो देवळीमाता ये एल ही कोनी आयो (वाह वाह)। भूणोजी बोलै कांई देवळी नै बतलावै (कीआवूं जाणज्यो कीआवूं)। अबार कहवूं धणी देव का हुकमूं ले तूं (वाह वाह जी)।।

कांई गौ मारी जी देवळीमाता ये दीनानाथ का रे।
कांई लूटी जी धोळा दियाड़ा राण।
भूणोजी करै तनै बूझणा।
कींयां हो गा ये मिनखा का पाखाण।।
(भलां जी भलां) देव भलां

कांई थै गौ मारी माता दीनानाथ की (म्हे)। अर कांई लूटी धोळा दियाड़ा (राण)। कंवर भूणोजी करै तनै बूझणा (म्हे)। देवळीमां थें कींयां हो ग्या थै मिनखा का (अब पाखाण)। कोय जमाना मिनख हा थै (म्हे)। पत्थर का क्युं बन्या (वाह वाह)। देवळी बोलै कांई समचार कहवै देखां (कीआवूं जाणज्यो कीआवूं)। अबार कहवूं देव का हुकमूं ले तूं (वाह वाह)।।

गौउ नी मारी तो जी नान्या भूणा रे दीनानाथ का रे।
कोनी लूटी जी धोळा दियाड़ा राण।
बळ जळ भसम की ढेरियां व्है ग्या।
बळ गी नान्या भूणा रे कुळ थाना की लार।।
(भलां जी भलां) देव भलां

कुळ थारा की (लार)। भूणाजी (म्हे)। मैं तो भैइ रे थारा कुळ के लेरै (हां बळ गी कीयो)। देवळीमाता बोलै (म्हे)। कांई कंवर भूणा नै समचार (कहवै देखां)।।

ए हस्तीदान्त का चूड़ा तो जी नान्या भूणा रे खूंटिया पर टांक लिया रे।
अगणमाता रा नान्या जी चूड़ा पहरिया हाथ।
दुनिया में भूणाजी चुगरै चालबे।
साडूवूं मिलबा नै रे चालूं थारी साथ।।
(भलां जी भलां) देव भलां

हस्तीदान्त का चूड़ा भूणा मैं खूंटिया मोलयायी (वाह वाह)। अरै भैइ अगणमाता का चूड़ा ही पहरिया (हाथ)। दुनिया में भूणा चुगरै चालबै (म्हे)। साडूमातावूं रे मिलबा नै चालूं थारी (अब मैं साथ)। पण लाल सेंसारी दुनिया में चुगरै चाल जावै (वाह वाह)।।

ए हस्तीदान्त का चूड़ा तो जी जो खूंटिया मोलिया रे।
अगणमाता रा रे चूड़ा पहरिया लाल।
बळ जळ भसम की ढेरियां व्है रियां।
बळ गी नान्या भूणा रे कुळ थारा की लार।।
(भलां जी भलां) देव भलां

हस्तीदान्त का चूड़ा लाल खूंटिया मोलयायी (वाह वाह)। अगणमाता का चूड़ा ही पहरिया (लाल)। दरबार का हुकमूं बळ जळ भसम की ढेरी हो गी रे भूणा कुळ थारा की (लार)। मैं तो थारा कुळ के लेरै बळ गी भैइ (वाह वाह)। अताक पहली दड़ावट में ठाकर देव की चार बजियां की सेवा होबा लागी (वाह वाह)। सेवा का नंगारा (हां बाजिया है)। भूणोजी बूझणा करी बना बाबा (हां ओ नंगारो क्यें को बाजियो कीयो)। कीयो श्री महाराज देव की सेवा होवै दड़ावट में (हां चार बजै की सेवा दड़ावट में हो रिया है (भगवान की)। भूणोजी सेवा में ध्यान देदिया (वाह वाह)। तो मां बेटां के बांतां होतां (म्हे)। भूणोजी सेवा में बैठतां (म्हे)। जय बोलो श्री देवनारायण भगवान की (जय)।

(ठुमरी) भंवर बना का डेरा जी बाग ब में (कांई मिस चांलां जी)।
ए अध रातियालां का (डेरा तो बाग बागां में कांई मिस चांलां जी)।
ए बधक भरालियां सरो तो सोहवणी भंवर कलाळी (बन चांलां जी)।
जो बतक भराल्यां (सबक सोहवणी भंवर कलाळी बन चांलां जी)।
ए भर भर प्याला (पावूं ए भोजाजी नै पीली पीली मोहरां ल्यांवां जी।
ए भर भर प्याला पावूं ये भोजाजी नै पीली पीली (मोहरां ल्यांवां जी)।
ए पीली पीली मोहरां (लियावां म्हारा रायबर जांझरियां गड़ावां जी)।
पीली पीली मोहरां (ल्यावूं म्हारा रायबर जांझरियां रे घड़ावां जी)।
ए जांझरियालै (रमकै जमकै सुतो शेर जगावां जी)।

सुण बागल और बिलावूं हुरड़ियां कोयलियाड़ा (उड़ चालां जी)।
ए बागल और बिलावूं रे हुरड़ियां (कोयलियाड़ा उड चालां जी)।
पण ईड़ दे की आण भारत में बनड़ा गावस्यां जी। मितवालां रा डेरां तूं बाग
बागां में (कांई मिस चालां जी)।
ए मितवालां रा (डेरा तो बाग बागां में कांई मिस चालां जी)।
ए सूई कतरणी ले ल्यां तूं बगल में दरजण के (मिस चालां जी)।
जो सूई कतरणी (ले ल्यां बगल में दरजण के मिस चालां जी)।
ए बा गो बिनता भंवर केसरिया कंवरां नै (निरखयावां जी)।
ए बा गो बिनता (भंवर केसरिया पण कंवरां नै निरखयावां जी)।
ए मितवालां रा डेरा जी बाग (बागां में कांई मिस चालां जी)।
ए कपड़ा छांटां (साबन से पण धोबन के मिस चालूं जी)।
मैं कपड़ा छांटूं (साबन से पण धोबन के मिस चालां जी)।
ए बिड़लो मोहर पच्चास को पण तमोलण बड़ (चालां जी)।
ए मितवालां रा डेरा तो बाग (बागां में कांई मिस चालां जी)।
ए मितवालां का (डेरा तो बाग बगां में कांई मिस चालां जी)।
ए फूलड़ा में भरल्यां छावड़ां पण मालन के (मिस चालां जी)।
जो फूलड़ावूं में भरल्यां (छावड़ां पण मालन के मिस चालां जी)।
ए भंवर बना रे खूंटा सेंवरा बंवळी के (फूलमाळा जी)।
ए भंवर भोज के (गूंटां के सेंवरा पण घोड़ी रे फूलमाळा जी)।
मैं बागल और मिलावूं रे हुरड़ियां (कोयलियाड़ा उड चालूं जी)।
ए बागल और मिलावूं रे हुरड़ियां (कोयलियाड़ा उड चालां जी)।
म्हन ईड़ दे की आण मूंडया की माळा फैरीस्यां जी।।

तो सुवा पहर भगवान की सेवा हुई (म्हे)। जितै भूणोजी सेवा में ध्यान राखया (वाह वाह)। तो देवळीमाता ई नै (हां अन्तरधान हो ग्या जी कीयो)। पाछो बी भूणोजी निंगै करियो बना बाबा जलम की बात हो गी भैइ (वाह वाह)। ई देवळीमांवूं बात पूरी कोनी हुई (म्हे)। इन्द्रासन गियोड़ा बाबा भाट पाछा कोनी आवै अब (वाह वाह)। सवाई भोज की देवळी बता द्यो अब (हां बाबाजीवूं मिल लेवां कीयो)। कीयो श्री महाराज बी देवळ को म्हनै ही ठा कोनी (हां म्हनै ही ठा कोनी)। चाम्पानेहरी नांव गांव बतावै अठै (म्हे)। तो चाम्पानेहरी से एक सूजो पटेल है (म्हे)। जिनै बुला ल्यो हेंर आप निंगै करा ल्यो (हां बै बता सकै है)। भूणोजी ऊंठ को ओठी भेज्यो (वाह वाह)। चाम्पानेहरी में सूजा पटेलजी नै बुलार (लियाया)। भूणोजी बोलै (म्हे)। कांई सूजा पटेल नै समचार कहवै देखां (कीआवूं जाणज्यो कीआवूं देखां)। अबार कहवां देव का हुकमूं ले

हाथी दे द्यूं जी ए ई तनै रीझ को रे।
दे द्यो तनै काळसेवाली कुवाय।

सवाई भोज को रे म्हनै देवळियांई।
सूजा बाबा रे आप द्यो बताय।।
(भलां जी भलां) देव भलां

हाथी देवूं रीझ को (म्हे)। दे द्यूं तनै काळसेवाली (कुवाय)। ए सवाई भोज की देवळी सुजा बाबा थै म्हानै दियो (बताय)। सूजा बाबा (म्हे)। बड़ा बाप की देवळी की जागां है बता बा (बतावो कीयो)। सूजो पटेल बोलै (म्हे)। कांई समचार भूणा नै कहवै (कीआवूं जाणज्यो देखां कीआवूं)। अबार कहवां धणी देव का हुकमूं लियो थै (वाह वाह सा)।।

ऊंचा चंवरां जी जो चार खण रे कंवर महाबळी रे।
सामी दीखै अब पापणी खारी नंदी की तीर।
सवाई भोज को देवळ बठै नळज्यो।
मेदू की माता रे पोसवाळ होमिया शरीर।।
(भलां जी भलां) देव भलां

ऊंचा चंवरां लाल चार खण है (म्हे)। सामी दीखे रे बा पापणी खारी नंदी की (तीर)। सवाई भोज का देवळ बी जागां देखज्यै (म्हे)। मेदू की माता पोसवाळ गूजरी होमियो (शरीर)। मेदू की मां है नै पोसवाळ (म्हे)। जकी भोज के लेरै सतीवाड़ै गी (वाह वाह)। साडूमाता तो पछै क्युं के बचन हो भगवान को जको मालासर की डूंगरी में जार सेवा करबा लाग गी भगवान की (वाह वाह)। हेंर मेदू की मां ही नै (म्हे)। जकी भोज के लेरै सतीवाड़े हो गी (वाह वाह)। दरबार का हुकमूं भूणोजी खारी का डावा पूगतो (व्हिया है)। सवाई भोज को देवळ निंगै आयगो (म्हे)। भूणोजी बोलै कांई देवळ नै बतलावै देखां (कीआवूं जाणज्यो कीआवूं देखां)। अबार कहवूं देव का हुकमूं ले तूं (वाह वाह सा)।।

रातयूं गायां तो जी रातयूं बजाया रे कंवर महाबळी रे।
दे दे भाई रे कांसिया ऊपर धाय रे।
म्हारा पहरा बाबाजी पूरा व्है ग्या।
जागर दर्शन द्यो की नी रे तेईसूं थै ऊबा बीर।।
(भलां जी भलां) देव भलां

रातयूं गायां भूणोजी रातयूं बजाया (म्हे)। दे देय कांसिया ऊपर (धाय)। ए म्हारा पहरा तो बाबाजी पूरा हो चुकिया (म्हे)। अरै जाग अर दर्शन द्यो की नै अब तेईसूं (थै भाई)। तेईस बगड़ावत हा थै (म्हे)। तेईसूं म्हारावूं मिलो जरां दरबार का हुकमूं जाणु में (वाह वाह)। कांई सवाई भोज का देवळी मूं परकाश बन जावै (म्हे)। कांई दोन्यां के देखां बात बनै देखां (कीआवूं जाणज्यो कीआवूं जाणज्यो देखां)। अबार कहवां सा देव का हुकमूं ले तूं (वाह वाह सा)।।

साडू जियान की तो जी नान्या भूणा रे सतियां व्है ग्या रे।
सती व्है गी जी छोटकी बहन सलूण।
सवाई भोज को देवळ मुण्डावूं बोल गो।
नेड़ो आजा म्हारा रे बारावत का भूण।।
(भलां जी भलां) देव भलां

साडू जियान की भूणा सतवंती हो गी (म्हे)। सती हो गी लाल छोटकी बहन (सलूण)। सवाई भोज को देवळो मुण्डावूं बोल्यो (वाह वाह)। आगो आजा रे म्हारा बारावत का (अब भूण)। बेटा नेड़ो आजा कीयो (वाह वाह)। इन्द्रासन गियोड़ा के ग्यारह बरसावूं बांतां होवै (वाह वाह)।।

घणी भटियां की जी दारू मंगावो रे नर भादरो रे।
मंगा ल्यो भूणा ताणी जी बाकरियां हळवान।
ताजा कर दीज्यो कंवरजी का जापता।
बिसुर जावै भूणा रे बाळा खानी राण।।
(भलां जी भलां) देव भलां

घणी भटियां की दारू मंगावो (म्हे)। मंगा ल्यो भूणा ताणी बाकरियां (हळवान)। ताजा करो भैइ भूणीमल का जापता (वाह वाह)। बिसर जावै रे सिरदारां बाळा खानी (अब राण)। चोखी तरह मनावो भैइ (वाह वाह)। दरबार का हुकमूं बाप बेटा के बांतां हुवी (म्हे)। परभात की सेवा है नै जकी भगवान की औरूं होबा लागी (वाह वाह)। बा सेवा तो चार बजियां की ही रात की (म्हे)। हेंर आ सेवा पो बेळियां की (हां होबा लागी)। भूणोजी बूझणा करी बना बाबा (म्हे)। अबकाळो नंगरो (क्यें को बाजियो औरूं कीयो)। कीयो श्री महाराज पो बेळियां की सेवा है नै भगवान की (हां पो बेळियां की हो रही है सेवा कीयो)। तो दरबार का हुकमूं भूणोजी औरूं सेवा में ध्यान (दे द्यो)। देवळियां के मांय परकाश हो नै (म्हे)। जको अन्तरधान व्हियो (वाह वाह)। भूणोजी पाछो फिर निंगै करी कीयो रे भैइ पूरी बात तो ईवूं कोनी हुई (वाह वाह)। बीर खेत में घोड़ावूं तो घोड़ो अड़ मेलियो (म्हे)। असवारूं (असवार अड़ मेलिया)। दरबार का हुकमूं भूणा की असवारी बीर खेत में तंबूड़ा ताण मेलिया (म्हे)। मात खटाणी देव की धरम की धाय रंग महलां अंवळी संवळी (ऊंचा फिर रिया हा)। देख भैइ भूणा की फौजां (म्हे)। आंवती (म्हे)। कांई भाट नै बतलावै देखां (कीआवूं जाणज्यो कीआवूं)। अबार कहवां भैइ देव भगवान का हुकमूं देखां (वाह वाह सा)।।

ए झाड़तो आवेलो जी ए ई सिरदार देवळियां रे।
भाट बीर का रे लेतो आवै सूण।
राठोड़ां का रे बीर खेत में।
के कीनै भाटजी रे ओ चौरासियो कुण।।
(भलां जी भलां) देव भलां

झाड़तो आवै रे भाट ओ देवळियां (म्हे)। लेतो आवै (सूण)। राठोड़ां का बीर खेत में के कीनै बाबा

भाट (म्हे) । अबकाळो चौरास्यो (कुण) । अरै बाबा भाट ओ कुण है अबकाळो (वाह वाह) । भाट बोल्यो कोनी (वाह वाह) । साडूमाता बोलै (म्हे) । कांई समचार भाट नै कहवै देखां (कीआवूं जाणज्यो देखां कीआवूं) । अबार कहवां भैइ भगवान का हुकमूं देखां ।।

गूडर लाग्या जी ए ई सिरदार का उजला रे।
दीखी भाटजी रे रेशम नेजाधारी रे।
बीर खेत में कुण चौरासियो उतरियो।
ईवूं म्हानी रे दड़ावट धूजी सारी ।।
(भलां जी भलां) देव भलां

गूडर दीखिया सिरदार का भाटजी उजला (म्हे) । दीखी रेशम नेजा (धारी) । अरै बीर खेत में कुण चौरासियो उतरियो (म्हे) । भाट दड़ावट धूजै सारी (वाह वाह) । म्हारी दड़ावट है नै (हां धूजै सगळी कीयो) । अतो बळवान कुण आयो (वाह वाह) । अब भाट बोलै (वाह वाह) । कांई समचार साडू नै कहवै देखां (कीआवूं जाणज्यो कीआवूं देखां) । अबार कहवां भैइ देव का हुकमूं देखां ।।

गूडर लाग्या जी जो सिरदार का उजला रे।
दीखी माजी ये रेशम नेजाधारी रे।
बागोठ को ठाकर भूणोजी आयगो थारै पांवणा।
दड़ावट फूल गी है केसर की क्यारी ।।
(भलां जी भलां) देव भलां

गूडर दीखियो भैइ सिरदार का उजला (वाह वाह) । दीखी रेशम नेजा (धारी) । के बागोठ को ठाकर भूणोजी आयगो थारै पांवणो (म्हे) । दड़ावट फूली है माजी केसर की (क्यारी) । दड़ावट धूजै कोनी (हां फूलै है कीयो) । फूलीज गो ज्यूं शहर है जको हल्लै (वाह वाह) । कीयो भाट (म्हे) । कुण आयगो रे भूणोजी आयगो (हां भूणाजी आयग्या कीयो) । कीयो श्री महाराज आययो (वाह वाह) । सुणो ओ भाटजी (म्हे) । पारस पीपळी हेटै जाजमा ढालो अब (वाह वाह) । हेंर भायां का मिलाप करा द्यो (वाह वाह) । तो बगड़ावतां को भाट कांई भायां का कन्नै जावै (म्हे) । अर कांई साडूमाता दासी नै हुकम देवै आरतियां का देखां (कीआवूं जाणज्यो देखां कीआवूं) । अबार कहवां देव का हुकमूं ।।

ए केसर कटोरा घालो नै जी ए ई हीड़ागर छोकरियां रे।
भर ल्यो दासी ये बीज मोतियां थाळ।
आया भूणीमल को साज दे आरतियो।
आज आयगो म्हानी रे राईतन को रिचपाल ।।
(भलां जी भलां) देव भलां

केसर कटोरा घालो (म्हे) । हीड़ागर दासी भरियो बीज मोतियां (थाळ) । आया भूणीमल को साज दे हिड़ागर आरती (वाह वाह) । आज आयगो म्हारा राइत को ही (रिचपाल) । जो राइत को धणी

(हां आज आयग्या कीयो)। आरतियां करो (वाह वाह)। भाट देव के दुलीचै पूगतो (व्हिया है)। जार बूझणा (करी ही)। कीयो श्री महाराज (म्हे)। आपको भाई भूणाजी राण शहरूं आयगो ग्यारह बरसावूं आज (म्हे)। चालो मिलबा के खातर पारस पीपळी के हेटै चालो (हां चालो मिल लियो कीयो)। भाई भाई मिलो (वाह वाह)। कहतां जेज लागी (म्हे)। सवाई भोज को मेदूजी पहल पोत ऊठियो (वाह वाह)। तेजाजी को मदन सिंगजी बी जागावूं (हां ऊठ ग्या)। नेवाजी को कंवर भांगीजी बठै हो जको बो ही (हां ऊठ ग्या जी कीयो)। ऊठ लकड़ा मूसळा ले अर आपको सुवा मण भांग घोटी (म्हे)। तो सुवा मण भांग को नशो कर सागै (वाह वाह)। औरूं मिलबा की (हां पारस पीपळी हेटै आयग्या जी कीयो)। देव नै बूझणा करी श्री महाराज (आप भी पधारो कीयो)। कीयो बाबा भाट (म्हे)। मैं तो कोय भाईवूं आज ताणी मिलिया कोनी (वाह वाह)। हां मिल जाणा कोनी (हां मिल जाणा कोनी कीयां मिलै कीयो)। मावूं मिली नै (म्हे)। अठ्है आर मिली (हां दुलीचै ही आजायी)। कांई सवाई भोज को मेदूजी पहल पोत कंवर भूणा से मिलै देखां (वाह वाह)।।

मेदू अर भूणो तो जी ए ई बै हद मिलिया रे।
मिल गा भाई रे धरती हाथ ल गाय।
बैरियां मूं आतां भली घणी करी रे कंवर महाबळी।
घोड़ा खरड़स्यां रे बोर घोड़ी के लार।।
(भलां जी भलां) देव भलां

सवाई भोज को मेदूजी भूणा से पहली हद मिलियो (म्म्हे)। मिल गो धरती हाथ (लगा अर)। तूं बैरियां मूं आतां आज भली घणी करी (म्हे)। मैं घोड़ा खड़ा भाई थारी बोर घोड़ी की (लार)। आगै घोड़ी थारी राखां मैं अब (वाह वाह)।।

ए तेजा रो मदनो तो जी कंवर भूणा से बै हद मिलिया रे।
राखियो कंवर रे भूणाजी को मान।
बैरियां मूं आतां रे कंवर महाबळी।
गोठां में भाई बेटा रे बींद बीसुनी जान।।
(भलां जी भलां) देव भलां

तेजाजी को मदनो ही हद मिल गो (म्हे)। राखियो कंवर भूणाजी का (मान)। तूं बैरियां मूं आतां आज भली घणी करी (वाह वाह)। गोठां में भाई बैठा रे मैं बींद बीसुनी (जान)। जानी मोकळा हा मैं (वाह वाह)। बींद बनबालो (हां एक ही म्हां में कोनी हो)। तूं आयगो (म्हे)। सिरायत बींद तनै ही राखां (वाह वाह)। नेवाजी को सुतन सायबो लकड़ा अर मुसळ लिया आंतरै (हां ऊबा हा कीयो)। भूणोजी बना भाट नै बोलै (म्हे)। कांई समचार कहवै देखां (कीआवूं जाणज्यो देखां कीआवूं)।।

ए नार भरणा तो जी नेतर लाग्या रे बीरा भाटजी रे।
दीखिया आवध पालियां में दूणा दूण।
देव का दळां में रे बीरा बारहठजी।

के कीनै बारहठजी रे ओ चौरासियो कुण।।
(भलां जी भलां) देव भलां

नार भरणा नेतर है (म्हे)। दीखियो आवध पातियां नै दूणा (दूण)। देव का दळां में बीरा भाट के कीनै ओ चौरासियो (अब कुण)। देव का दुलीचा में जम को कांई काम है (वाह वाह)। ओ जम कठवूं ल्याया थै (म्हे)। कंवर भांगीजी बोलै (वाह वाह)। दरबार का हुकमूं कांई भायां का समचार होवै देखां (कीआवूं जाणज्यो कीआवूं देखां)।।

ए नार भरणा तो जी नेतर लाग्या रे कंवर महाबळी रे।
दीखा आवध पातिया में दूणा दूण।
ओ है नेवा को रे कंवर भांगड़ो।
तूं कीज्यै नान्या जी बारावत का भूण।।
(भलां जी भलां) देव भलां

नार भरणा नेतर है (म्हे)। दीखियो आवध पातिया में दूणा (दूण)। ओ तो है नेवाजी को कंवर भांगड़ो तूं कीज्यै लाल बारावत को (अब भूण)। तूं तो बारावतजी को है (म्हे)। ओ नेवाजी को है (हां है कीयो)। भूणोजी मन में देखियो (म्हे)। ईंयां का भाई नार जियान का है (वाह वाह)। बैरियां में झूटां ही चून खाया इता दिन (वाह वाह)। भाईवूं मिलां (म्हे)। दरबार का हुकमूं भूणोजी मिलबा की खातर आगो सरकयो (वाह वाह)। भूणोजी देखियो बाथ घाली जिता नै भांगीजी पूण्चो पकड़ लियो (म्हे)। मन में देखियो रे माठो भाई जाळ नी हो जाय जम नी है (हां पूण्चो कींयां पकड़ियो कीयो)। पगां में नी राळ ले खेंच अर (वाह वाह)। भूणाजी के मांयनै ग्यारह हाथियां को बळ हो (वाह वाह)। ग्यारह हाथी भूणा के पग का अंगूठा के बांध देता (म्हे)। भिनाय के नौरा ताणी सात कोस ठरड़ अर ले जातो (वाह वाह)। भूणोजी मन में देखियो ए जम नै आपां कान्नै खेंचल्या अबार (म्हे)। जितो आंजस करणो जितो भूणोजी (कर लियो)। भांगीजी एक तिल जतो ही (हालियो कोनी बठवूं)। भांगीजी चिन्योसो फटकारो दियो भूणा के (म्हे)। ई जागां ऊबो हो जका नै ई जागां उनै राळ दियो (हां उनै ले जार खड़यो कर दिया जी कीयो)। ग्यारह हाथियां को बळ भूणा का बी जागां सब टूट गो (वाह वाह)। भूणोजी कीयो रे ओ जमै (म्हे)। पूण्चो छोड़ लाल हु गो (हां लाल हो गियो म्हारो कीयो)। दरबार का हुकमूं जम को नांव लियो नै (म्हे)। जरां भांगीजी कंवर बूझणा करी (वाह वाह)। कीयो धूंध धक्कै गोला तपै राताकोट जकै दिन अगर देखज्यै म्हनै (वाह वाह)। देख लीज्यै भूणा आवध पातियां में दूणा (दूण)। मैं हूं नेवा को कंवर भांगड़ो तूं रैज्यै बारावत को ही (भूण)। आज मत देख म्हनै (वाह वाह)। बैर पर चालां नी अबें (हां बठै देखिज्यै राताकोट की राड़ में कीयो)। बी जागां पाण बतावूं तनै (वाह वाह)। आज कांई बतावूं (म्हे)। कीयो मान लियो भाई (म्हे)। कीयो थारै तो काका को बेटो भाई लागूं मैं (म्हे)। कीयो मैं मान लियो तनै अब (वाह वाह)। पूण्चो छोड़ देय (म्हे)। तो बारहठ कन्नै ऊबो हो (म्हे)। बी नै बूझणा (करी ही)। बारहठ बाबा बगड़ावत भाई कता व्हिया (हां कता भाई हा हो कीयो)। कीयो श्री महाराज भाई तो बगड़ावत तेईस का (म्हे)। एक बहन ही सागै (बा चौईसा में गणीजता कीयो)। भोजी बहनड़ी हो (वाह वाह)। कीयो बारहठ बाबा तेईस बगड़ावत इन्द्रासन

गिया नै (म्हे)। जी टैम तेईसां की करामात (ई भंगेरिया भाई नै देयर ऊठगिया कीयो)। म्हानै तो एक तिल जती पाती कोनी आयी (वाह वाह)। कीयो श्री महाराज बगड़ावतां की होड़ थै नी करो (हां बांका डावा पग की होड़ अंगूठै की नैइ करो)। अता जोर का हा बगड़ावत (हां अता जोर का हा सा)। जर लेरली कोय बात सुणा म्हनै बाखाण बगड़ावतां की (वाह वाह)। दरबार का हुकमूं बारहठ बोलै (म्हे)। कांई लेरली बांतां सुणावै देखां (कीआवूं जाणज्यो देखां कीआवूं)।।

ए बावो अर नेवो तो जी दोन्यु भाई रे सिंगां ज्यूं गूंजता रे।
भौ मान गा अवूं रे बड़ा बड़ा भोपाल।
माथो दिया पछै बाघजी को सूरवूं।
बाय गो लेवै रे असी पहर तरवार।।
(भलां जी भलां) देव भलां

बावो अर नेवो दोन्यु भाई सिंगां ज्यूं गूंजिया (म्हे)। दरबार का हुकमूं भौ मान गा का भैइ बड़ा बड़ा (भोपाल)। दरबार का हुकमूं जकै दिन बासक हरियो (पियांळ)। नेवोजी बाघ को सूरवूं (म्हे)। माथो दिया पछै भारत में बाय गो भाई बिनै माथै असी पहर (तरवार)। असी पहर तरवार ई का बाप की चाली (वाह वाह)। कांई आपां नै बूझी बोल (वाह वाह)। माथो तो भुवानी नै दियो (म्हे)। असी पहर दरबार महाभारत कर लियो (वाह वाह असी पहर का कासा दिन होवे)।।

ए बावो अर नेवो तो जी दड़ावट में रे सिंगां ज्यूं गूंजता रे।
भौ मान गा भाई रे बड़ा बड़ा भोपाल।
नेवाजीवूं इन्द को आसन डगम ग्यो।
बावाजीवूं धड़कियो रे आप श्री किरतार।।
(भलां जी भलां) देव भलां

बावो नेवो तो दोन्यु भाई सिंगां ज्यूं गूंजिया (म्हे)। दरबार का हुकमूं भौ मान गा बड़ा बड़ा (भोपाल)।

नेवो अर बावो तो जी दोन्यु भाई रे सिंगां ज्यूं गूंजता रे।
भौ मान गा भाईजी बड़ा बड़ा भोपाल।
नेवावूं इन्द को आसन डगमगियो।
बावाजीवूं धड़कियो रे आप श्री किरतार।।
(भलां जी भलां) देव भलां

बावो अर नेवो दोन्यु भाई (म्हे)। दड़ावट में सिंगां ज्यूं गूंजिया (वाह वाह)। भौ मान गा बड़ा बड़ा (भोपाल)। अरै नेवाजीवूं इन्द को आसन डगम गो (म्हे)। बावाजीवूं धड़कियो आप श्री (किरतार)। भगवान महाराज चंपणो मानियो आवूं (म्हे)। ठा तो है तनै।।

जोगीसया जी ए ई बेटा बाघ का रे।
नारदी आनै रे माया दीनी ओपरी।

कदै भोज की दड़ावट बाजती।
कींयां हो गी रे सोजीआली सौपूरी रे।।
(भलां जी भलां) देव भलां

जोगीसया बेटा बाघ का (म्हे)। जरां बाबोजी माया दे दी (ओपरी)। कदै तो भोज की दड़ावट बाजी (म्हे)। आज कींयां हो गी सोजीआली (सौपूरी)। गांवां का नांव कींयां फैरिया (हां जकी बतावो कीयो)।।

ए बगड़ावत भगत भारी तो जी ए ई दीनानाथ का रे।
कींयां माच गो रे न्यारो न्यारो शोर।
इस्यो कांई भगती में छांटो पड़गियो।
बांका जायां कींयां हो गा रे घर घर का कठोर।।
(भलां जी भलां) देव भलां

बगड़ावत भगत तो भारी हा दीनानाथ का (म्हे)। मन में माचियो न्यारो न्यारो (शोर)। अरै इस्यो कांई भगती में छांटो पड़ गो (म्हे)। बांका जायां कींयां हो गा घर घर का (कठोर)। दरबार का हुकमूं अता ही भगती है ने बगड़ावत (म्हे)। तो बांका जायोड़ा मैं घर घर क्यु रुळिया भैइ (वाह वाह)। दरबार का हुकमूं बारहठ बूझणा (करी है)। बगड़ावत भगत भारी दीनानाथ का माचियो मन में न्यारो न्यारो (शोर)। बगड़ावतां के हथेली में दारू को छांटो पड़ियो (म्हे)। बी कारण नै हो गा लाल घर घर का (थै कठोर)। बगड़ावत शंकर का चेला का भगवान हा पहली जलम का रुषि हा (म्हे)। तो कलाळी के हेली जाय (वाह वाह)। एक दारू को बीड़ो भर आयो (हां जकावूं)। दरबार का हुकमूं पी नी बगड़ावत दारू (वाह वाह)। बीड़ो ही भर आयो (म्हे)। बी कारण भूणा बो दाग लागो बी कारण थै घर घर रुळ कीयो (वाह वाह)।।

गहूं बाया तो जी बगड़ावत रे कुळ रे खेतरां रे।
नान्या भूणाजी उगै हरिया व्हिया रे।
बगड़ावतां को की नी मरियो रे कंवर महाबळी।
धरती पर जोधा रे थारा सरीसा रिया रे।।
(भलां जी भलां) देव भलां

गहूं बाया बगड़ावत कुळ खेत में (म्हे)। नान्या भूणाजी उगर हरिया (व्हिया)। बगड़ावतां को की नी मरियो (म्हे)। जोधा धरती पर थारै जियान का (व्हिया)। थारै जियान का जोधा रह गा तब बगड़ावत अमर है (वाह वाह)। ई समचार पर भूणा को आंजस गियोड़ो हो नै (म्हे)। जको पाछो आयगो (हां पाछो बावड़ियो)। दरबार का हुकमूं आंजस आयो नै (म्हे)। तो कांई भूणा में आंजस आजावै कांई समचार कहवै देखां (कीआवूं जाणज्यो देखां कीआवूं)। अबार कहवां भगवान का हुकमूं ले तूं।।

अती कहतां तो जी केसरिया जामा की कसा रे मचड़कै टूट गा रे।
भूणा नै आयो रे हनुमत कासो पाण।

धिन धिन कुळदेवी तूं आसावरियां।
भलां राखिया धरती पर ये बड बांका बगड़ावत।।
(भलां जी भलां) देव भलां

अती कहतां केसरिया जामा की कसा भूणा की मचड़कै टूट गी (वाह वाह)। भूणा में आयो पाछो हनुमत कासा (पाण)। धिन धिन कुळदेवी आसावरी (म्हे)। भला राखिया धरती पर बड बांका (बगड़ावत)। बाह वाह ये कुळदेवी कीयो (वाह वाह)। बीज उबार तो म्हांका राख तो दिया तूं (म्हे)। पांच भाई रह गा अब सारा ई कोनी (वाह वाह)। बना बाबा कता भाई मिलिया अब (हां जकी बताओ)। कीयो श्री महाराज चार भाई मिलिया अबार तो (म्हे)। तो बो औतारी बोलै जको (बै कोनी मिलिया कीयो)। श्री महाराज नी मिलिया (वाह वाह)। तो बी भाईवूं कींयां मिलां (हां जकी जुगत बताओ कीयो)। कीयो श्री महाराज घोड़ावूं कोतल खेंचाव ले लियो हेटै उतरो (म्हे)। हेंर शस्तरपाती खोलो (वाह वाह)। हाथ जोड़ (म्हे)। भगवान के दुलीचै जार खड़ा हो जावो (हां सामनै खड़ा हो जावो)। मतेई मिल जायै आपो आप (हां आपो आप ही मिलजायी)। कीयो मुंगता (म्हे)। तूं तो जियान थै मुंगता मिलो नै बापू बापू (हां जकी बिदी बता दीनी)। बरोबरियो भाई है बाथ घाल जुगत मिलां (हां आछी तरहवूं मिलूं कीयो)। कीयो जरां श्री महाराज आप के जियान मनसिया होवै जियान मिलो (हां जियान मिललियो)। तो चड़ी असवारी भूणाजी की दुलीचै में बड़ती हुई (वाह वाह)। तीन तिलोकी को नाथ होंकारो करियो (म्हे)। होंकारा की समचै भूणा की फौज का मुण्डा हा जका अपूठा हो ग्या (हां पाछा सगळा का सगळा अपूठा फिर ग्या जी कीयो)। भूणोजी मन में देखियो आं कांई बात हुई (हां ईंयां कींयां हुई)। फैर देव मिलबा की खातर भूणोजी औरूं देव कानी मुण्डा करिया (म्हे)। देव महाराज होंकारो करियो पाछा सिरदारां का मुण्डा जका (हां) अपूठा फिर ग्या (पाछा फिर ग्या जी कीयो)। तीन बारी भूणोजी देवूं मिलबा की खातर देव कानी मुण्डो करियो (म्हे)। तीन बारी भगवान अपूठा फैर दिया (वाह वाह)। भूणोजी मन में देखियो भाई तो बहुत करड़ो है (हां ओ भाई घणो करड़ो है कीयो)। अरै तीन बारी आपां हाथ जोड़ियां तो ही ओ तो मिलै कोनी (हां मिलै कोनी अपूठो फिर बै जावै कीयो)। रीस कर (म्हे)। भूणोजी पाछो बिदा हो गो (वाह वाह)। आपणै रहणो कोनी अता भाई कन्नै (हां ई करड़ै भाई कन्नै रहणो कोनी कीयो)। पाछी गिरियो जी टैम में बगड़ावतां को बैइ को भाट मिल गो (हां सामै ही मिल गो)। कीयो श्री महाराज चड़ी असवारी कींयां बिदा हुई पाछी (हां पाछी बिद्या कींयां व्हियो कीयो)। तो दरबार का हुकमूं भूणोजी बोलै (म्हे)। कांई भाट नै दाकलै अब देखां (कीआवूं जाणज्यो देखां कीआवूं)। अबार कहवूं धणी देव का हुकमूं ले तूं (वाह वाह सा)।।

ए बठै माथा पर हाथ तो जी म्हारै रे हिन्दवा राव को रे।
रावजी देवो रे रूखां सेती राण।
आगै रूस गो रे बनद्राबन को राजवी।
बिनै पेड़ा देव को रे फिर बैठयो बियाण।।
(भलां जी भलां) देव भलां

बठै माथा पर हाथ तो बाबा भाट पड़ीहार को हो (म्हे)। रावजी देवो म्हनै रूखां सेती (राण)। आगै रूस गो देख बनद्राबन को राजवी (म्हे)। बिनै पेड़ा ताण देव को फिर बैठो (बियाण)। ई बियाण के पेड़ा कोनी (हां ईंयां ही मतेई फिरै कीयो)। अरै ईंयां को भाई करड़ो है जरां म्हनै भाट ठौड़ नी छुड़ानी म्हारी (वाह वाह)। सगळो ही ओळमो थारा में है (म्हे)। तूं गियो म्हनै जांच करां जरां मैं आयो भैइ (वाह वाह)। भूणोजी गुस्सो मार गा (म्हे)। भूणोजी बोलै कांई समचार कहवै देखां (कीआवूं जाणज्यो देखां कीआवूं)। अबार कहवूं भगवान का हुकमूं ले तूं (वाह वाह जी वाह वाह)।।

बठै माथै हाथ तो जी जो हिन्दवा राव को रे।
मैं आयगो भाटजी रे समंदरिया से तोड़।
आगै रूसयोड़ो बैठो बनद्राबन को राजवी।
ताणो देवजी रे बैठो पीठ मरोड़।।
(भलां जी भलां) देव भलां

बठै हाथ तो माथा पर हिन्दवा राव को (म्हे)। मैं आयगो रे भाट आज समंदरिया से (तोड़)। समंदरवूं तोड़यायो मैं (म्हे)। आगै रूस गो बनद्राबन को राजवी (वाह वाह)। ताणो देवजी महाराज से बैठो पीठ (मरोड़ अर)। दरबार का हुकमूं मैं तो आयो मिलबा की खातर (म्हे)। ताणो देवजी पीठ फैर गो भाई (वाह वाह)। कीयो श्री महाराज (म्हे)। भाट कहवै (वाह वाह)। थै आप थोड़ा से अठै रुको (म्हे)। मैं देव के दुलीचै जावूं (म्हे)। भायां का मिलाप थांका अबार मैं कारावूं (हां कर द्यूं कीयो)। ले भैइ भाट तूं जा कोय बिचार कोनी (जा कीयो)। तो भूणोजी तो असवारी चड़ी असवारी ऊबी है (म्हे)। हेंर बगड़ावतां को भाट देव के दुलीचै जावै है (वाह वाह)। कांई समचार जातो ही भगवान नै कहवै (कीआवूं जाणज्यो देखां कीआवूं)।।

ए भाईड़ा भला लागो जी जो गोठालां राजवियां रे।
भाई तो अन्नदाता रे बसै भाई के ओलै औवूं रे।
राठोड़ां का बीर खेत में खाण्डो बाजते।
भाई हुवै तो अन्नदाता रे बलू आपकी बोलै रे।।
(भलां जी भलां) देव भलां

भायां से भलां लागो (म्हे)। भाई तो बसै भाई के (ओले)। राठोड़ां का बीर खेत में खाण्डो बाजै नै (म्हे)। बी जागां भाई होवै तो बलू आपकी (बोले)। श्री महाराज भाई बतो है (वाह वाह)। दरबार का हुकमूं बेराजी व्हियोड़ो व्ही (म्हे)। जी टैम में बैरी मारी बी टैम में तो उछळ बाथियां पड़ी (हां बीकै सामलै की ही बाथियां पड़ी कीयो)। भूणाजी जियान का भाई है आ जका नै रीसार पाछो भेजो आप (हां रीसा दिया कीयो)। देव महाराज कोनी बोल्या (वाह वाह)। बैइ को भाट बोलै कांई भगवान नै देव नै ओळमा देवै देखां (कीआवूं जाणज्यो कीआवूं देखां)। अबार कहवूं देव का हुकमूं ले तूं।।

ए भायांसूं भलां लागो जी गोठालां राजवियां रे।
दुशमन दोखी रे मानै आप की काण।

टींटोड़ी अन्नदाता रे समंदर ऊंचियो।
ऊंचियो दरबार रे परिवारां के पाण।।
(भलां जी भलां) देव भलां

भायां सूं भलां लागो (म्हे)। दुशमन दोखी मानै आपकी (काण)। टींटोड़ी श्री महाराज समंदर ऊंचियो (म्हे)। ऊंचिया बो परिवारां के ही (पाण)। टींटोड़ी जानवर है नै (म्हे)। जकी समंदर नै जीत गी परिवार हो जरां (वाह वाह)। देव महाराज बूझणा करी रे भाट (म्हे)। लेरली बात नै छोड़ दे तूं (वाह वाह)। आ टींटोड़ी जानवर समंदर ने कींयां ऊंचियो भैइ (जकी बता)। कीयो श्री महाराज टींटोड़ी जानवर ही जकी समंदर के एकानलै इंडा देदिया (वाह वाह)। दिन तीन इंडा के ऊपर बैठी री (हां ऊपर ही बैठी रही)। टींटोड़ा आयो बूझणा करी टींटोड़ी भूखा क्युं मरै जा चूगो पाणी करिया (हां चूगो पाणी करिया कीयो)। कीयो भैइ इंडा की कुण निंगै राखै (हां इंडा नै रूखालै कुण)। मैं रूखालूं (वाह वाह)। तो टींटोड़ी बण में चूगो पाणी करबा नै (उड़ गी)। टींटोड़ो जानवर है जको कांई करियो इंडा के ऊपर ऊंधो सोय गो (वाह वाह)। समंदर बोह सारो कर बूझणा (करी ही)। जानवर दुख क्युं पावै भैइ सावल सोयजा (हां सावल बैठै नी कीयो)। कीयो तूं मत बोल (हां बोल मना कीयो म्हारू)। क्युं (म्हे)। कीयो इंडा पर जापतो करियो मैं (हां म्हारा इंडा रूखालूं कीयो)। कांई जापतो है (हां जापतो कांई करियो तूं कीयो)। कीयो आकाश पड़ जावै ऊपरावूं (म्हे)। दो पगां पर झेलूं (हां पगां पर राखल्यूं ऊंचो को ऊंचो ही)। हेंर तूं छोल देवै (म्हे)। तनै पांखां में झेळल्यूं (हां पांखां में उळझाल्यूं कीयो)। समंदर देखियो थारी मां जाणु छोटो सो एक जानवर है (हां तनै आसंग लियो)। अताक पहली कर ओगाज के छोल (दीनी समंदर)। टींटोड़ो तो अठवूं टौ टौ आकाश के घरां (उड़ ग्यो)। हेंर इंडा नै जको समंदर बोहवार (मांयनै लेगियो)। टींटोड़ी आयी कीयो टींटोड़ा इंडा कठै (हां ऊपर कींयां उडै हो कीयो)। कीयो थारो बाप समंदर काळ ले गो (हां बो तो काळ ही ले गो कीयो)। कीयो जलम कर दिया भैइ (म्हे)। अरै मैं तो दिन तीन हुई म्हारो नांव कोनी लियो समंदर (हां समंदर नांव ही कोनी लियो कीयो)। तूं समंदरवूं कूबद घमाई है (हां की न की कूबद करी है तूं)। कीयो ले भैइ टींटोड़ी इयां बूझियो म्हनै (म्हे)। एक ईंयां को समचार कीयो (वाह वाह)। हो तो घणो कीयो (घणो कीयो)। पण समंदर ले झगड़ो करां (वाह वाह)। कींयां करां अब (हां कींयां करां कीयो)। कीयो आपणी जाती न्याती में चालां (म्हे)। जको बा नै पुकार घाला (वाह वाह)। तो जतो इंडा से पैदा व्हियोड़ो नै जानवर (वाह वाह)। सब कन्नै गिया भैइ (वाह वाह)। कीयो समंदर इंडा ले गो म्हांका जको चालो भैइ म्हानै दिरावो (हां झगड़ो करां कीयो)। पंखेरो जानवर जितां हां (म्हे)। बी पर सारा समंदर के एकानलै भेळा हु गा (वाह वाह)। कीयो भेळा तो हो गा पण समंदरवूं झगड़ो कींयां करां (जकी बिदी बतावो)। एक पुटियो जानवर होवै अतोक बो कीयो भैइ सब में मालक राजा द्यो नै म्हानै थरपो नै (म्हे)। बिदी मैं बतावूं (हां थानै बिदी तो मैं बता द्यूं)। पण राजा मानणो पड़ै म्हनै (वाह वाह)। कीयो राजाजी मैं तो तनै ही माना (हां राजाजी माननलियां म्हांकै कांई)। धूल की ढिगली बनाय (म्हे)। पुटिया जानवर नै राजगादी सूंपी (हां गिदी पर बैठा द्यो)। लियो राजा साब फरमावो (अब बताओ कीयो)। कीयो फरमावां कांई भैइ सब जानवर है जका डाक अर पाणी में बड़

जावो (म्हे)। क्युं तो पाणी पेट में पीवो अर क्युं तो पांखां के लगावो अर क्युं (चांचां में ले ल्यो)। ए गोरी गोरी टिबड़ियां रेत की है (म्हे)। आ में जार (लोटो)। पाछा आंतां क्युं तो धूल पांखां का आंटा में (ल्यावो)। हेंर क्युं चांचां में (ल्यावो)। दो तीन हिलोळा द्यो जको अबार मतै (हां जगा छोड़ देयी कीयो)। कहतां जेज लागी (म्हे)। दरबार का हुकमूं दो तीन हिलोळा दिया जितां नै समंदर नै छोड़ दी जागां (हां जगा ज गा टीबा बांध दिया पाणी में)। समंदर कीयो रे जानवरां म्हनै ठौड़ क्युं छुड़ावो (हां कांई बात है कीयो)। कीयो इंडा ले गो जी की खातर झगड़ो करां थारावूं (हां इंडा ई टींटोड़ी का पाछा दियो कीयो)। नी जरां आ ठौड़ थारी रहबा दियो कोनी मैं तो (वाह वाह)। कीयो जरां भैइ बूरो मत (म्हे)। थांका इंडा है जका देदेवां (पाछा देदेस्यूं)। समंदर कर छोल (म्हे)। इंडा नै ले जार पाछा तीर पर मेल दिया (हां आ ल्यो समालो कीयो)। लेरै परिवार हो नै (म्हे)। जरां झगड़ो परिवार जीतियो कीयो (वाह वाह)। श्री महाराज भूणा जियान का भाई आया (जका नै थै रीसार कींयां भेजो कीयो)। तो भाट टींटोड़ी की बिदी बनाता भूणोजी दुलीचै आंवतां (आंवतां)। जय बोलो श्री देवनारायण भगवान की (जय)। दरबार का हुकमूं तो समचार देव महाराज नै कीयो है नै (म्हे)। कीयो श्री महाराज भूणा जियान का भैइ बळवान आबा का कोनी (वाह वाह)। जसा नै आप रीसार पाछो (हां खिना द्यां कीयो)। देव महाराज बोलै कांई समचार कहवै देखां (कीआवूं जाणज्यो कीआवूं देखां)। अबार कहवां भैइ देव का हुकमूं ले तूं (वाह वाह सा)।।

> ए राण मै परवाणो दियो तो जी भूणा नै बैइ का भाटजी रे।
> लिख दीनी कागदां काळी कोर।
> भूण नै सीख दिरावो नौथेरी राण में।
> खाळसै बन्धालेयो घोड़ी ये बारावत की बोर।।
> (भलां जी भलां) देव भलां

भूणा नै मैं परवाणो राण में दे दियो (म्हे)। लिख दीनी कागदां काळी (कोर)। दादा भूणा नै सीख दिरावो पाछो नौथेरी राण में (वाह वाह)। घोड़ी बन्धा ल्यो खाळसै बारावत की (अब बोर)। सुण रे भाट (म्हे)। ई बोर नै तो लीला के जोड़ै ल्यार बांधो (वाह वाह)। दादा भूणा नै कह द्यो (म्हे)। बा राण शहर पड़ी पधार (जाओ कीयो)। बो समचार भूणा नै सुणीज्य गो (म्हे)। भूणोजी देखियो रे भाई तो मिलबा की खातर कोनी बुलायो (हां ई घोड़ी के खातर बुलाल्यो)। पण ई भाई नै घोड़ी दियां कोनी (म्हे)। भूणोजी बोलै कांई समचार देव नै कहवै देखां (कीआवूं जाणज्यो कीआवूं)। अबार कहवां देव का हुकमूं

> ए घोड़ी मांगियोड़ी जी कोनी ल्यायो रे गोठालां राजवियां रे।
> कोनी ल्यायो रे हाटयां बिकती मोल।
> बैरियो आडो बळो भिलमाल को।
> घोड़ी ल्यायो दान्त भील का तोड़।।
> (भलां जी भलां) देव भलां

घोड़ी मांगियोड़ी थोड़ी ल्यायूं (म्हे)। कोनी ल्याया हाटयां बिकती (मैं मोल)। बैरियो आडो बळो भिलमाल को (वाह वाह)। घोड़ी ल्यायो अन्नदाता दान्त भील का (अब तोड़र)। भील का दान्त तोड़िया नै (म्हे)। जरां टरड़ी हाथ लागी म्हारी (वाह वाह)। ईंयां घोड़ी कींयां देवूं आपणै (हां मांगियोड़ी थोड़ी ल्यायूं कीयो)। म्हारै आसन घोड़ी है बोरड़ी अर आपके आसन घोड़ो (लीला)। भेरियो आडो बळो भिलमाल को मारियो दानो ही (भील)। दानो भील नै मारियो (म्हे)। जर टारड़ी हाथ (लागी कीयो)। भूणोजी दरबार का हुकमूं ए समचार कीया हे नै (म्हे)। देव महाराज भाट नै बतलायो (वाह वाह)। बाबा भाट (म्हे)। भाई तो बड़ो बीर खान लाग्यो म्हानै (हां बड़ो बीर खान है कीयो)। देव बोलै (वाह वाह)। कांई समचार कंवर भूणा नै कहवै देखां (कीआवूं जाणज्यो देखां कीआवूं)। अबार कहवां भैइ देव का हुकमूं ले तूं (वाह वाह सा)।।

बैरियां में पलियायो जी ए ई कंवर महाबळी रे।
चूगी भूणा परेवांवाली दाल।
कांई गोठ खेड़ा रे बगड़ावतां का नागलियां।
बगड़ावतां नै भूणा रे गोत दिराई गाल अर।।
(भलां जी भलां) देव भलां

तूं बैरियां में पलियायो (म्हे)। भूणा चूगी परेरावाली (दाल)। कांई बगड़ावतां का तूं गोठ खेड़ा नागलियां (म्हे)। अरै बगड़ावतां नै गोत दिराई (तूं गाल अर)। बगड़ावतां नै याद करिया गालियां कड़ाई तूं (वाह वाह)। ओ समचार देव महाराज (हां भूणाजी नै कीयो)। भूणोजी बोलै (म्हे)। कांई पाछो जवाब करै देखां (कीआवूं जाणज्यो भोपाजी महाराज कीआवूं)। अबार कहवूं भैइ भगवान का हुकमूं ले तूं (वाह वाह सा)।।

बैरियां में पलियायो जी जो गोठालां राजवियां रे।
चूगी अन्नदाता रे परेवांवाली दाल।
ताणी नांव हांती खानी को रे बाजियो कोय ने।
तूं पलियायो अन्नदाता रे मामा की हांती खाय।।
(भलां जी भलां) देव भलां

मैं बैरियां में पलियायो (म्हे)। चूगी परेवांसंधी (दाल)। ताणी नांव हांती खानी तो मैं कोनी बाजियो (म्हे)। तूं पलियायो थारो मामा की हांती (खाय)। तूं नानेरा में गियो बामणां की रोटी चड़ाई (वाह वाह)। पहली ताणी मांमियां बिरामणा नै एक रोटी (हां देंवती)। तूं गियो पछै कीयो रे आपणै बाईजीआलो भाण्यो आयो है नै (म्हे)। बामणां नै बन्द कर दियो ई भाणोजी नै देबो करो (हां भाणोजी नै देबो करो कीयो)। मैं बामणां की रोटियां कठै की कोनी छुड़ाई (वाह वाह)। बैरियां की छाती के ऊपर मूंग दलिया मैं (म्हे)। देव महाराज म्हारो धणी बक बक हेंसिया (वाह वाह)। वाह रे भाट वाह कीयो भाई तो बड़ो बीर खान ल्यायो (वाह वाह)। भूणोजी मन में देखियो किस्या मिलाप करणा है भायांवूं (हां चालो कीयो)। दरबार का हुकमूं घोड़ी कांई ठी थारेवाणी हे एकानी देववाणी (हां है कीयो)।

ई घोड़ी नै बतलावां (म्हे)। भूणोजी बोलै (वाह वाह)। कांई घोड़ी नै बतलावै देखां (कीआवूं जाणज्यो देखां कीआवूं)। अबर कहवूं देव का हुकमूं ले तूं।।

ए छांट बलू का डाग्रा राळूं जी ए ई घोड़ी चांवण्डा रे।
ए तूं भाई रे बिस करमोयी दाल।
महाभारत में घोड़ी ये कूड़ी बेगिया।
म्हाना पिता नै राळियो रे असंग दळां के मांय।।
(भलां जी भलां) देव भलां

छांट बलू का डाग्रा राळूं तनै (म्हे)। घोड़ीमाता क्युं बिस करमोयी (तनै दाल)। महाभारत में घोड़ी कूड़ी बेगी तूं (म्हे)। म्हारा पिता नै राळ दियो असंग दळां (तूं मांय)। म्हारा बाप में करी जकी म्हाना में करी नै (म्हे)। जरां ई जागां कह दी (हां पहलीवूं कह देय कीयो)। घोड़ी बोलै (म्हे)। कांई भूणा नै समचार कहवै देखां (कीआवूं जाणज्यो देखां कीआवूं)। अबार कहवूं रे भाई भगवान का हुकमूं देखां (वाह वाह सा)।।

ए छांट बलू का डाग्रा तो जी क्युं राळै रे कंवर महाबळी रे।
क्युं देवै जी म्हनै बिस करमोयी दाल।
थै हरकियां का कंवर दोन्यु भाई हरकियां लड़ मरिया।
म्हारी भूणाजी बाग अपूठी राळ।।
(भलां जी भलां) देव भलां

छांट बलू का डाग्रा म्हनै क्युं रालै (म्हे)। क्युं दे भूणा बिस करमोयी (दाल)। अरै हरकियां का कंवर दोन्यु भाई थै हरकियां लड़ मरिया (म्हे)। म्हारी भूणाजी बाग अपूठी (राळ अर)। दरबार का हुकमूं तूं कहवै नै इन्द्रासन ले जावूं तनै (म्हे)। ओ लेरलो ओळमो म्हनै मत दे (वाह वाह)। थारो पिता म्हारी पीठ पर झगड़ो कोनी करियो (हां म्हनै कोतल खिंचावो लारै ही कीयो)। मुण्डा के झगड़ै व्हियो (म्हे)। देबी का चकर चाल्या (वाह वाह)। शीश भवानी नै दिया बगड़ावत (म्हे)। म्हारै कांई हाथ में बात ही भेइ (वाह वाह)। घोड़ी बोलै (वाह वाह)। कांई भूणा नै समचार कहवै (कीआवूं जाणज्यो देखां कीआवूं)। अबार कहवूं भगवान का हुकमूं ले तूं (वाह वाह सा)।।

ए चड़जा चड़जा तो जी ए ई कंवर महाबळी रे।
नान्या भूणा चिपजा म्हारी पीठ।
हुकम कोनी दे नारायण देवजी।
ले अर चड़जावूं भगवान की रे इन्द्रासन बैकुण्ठ।।
(भलां जी भलां) देव भलां

चड़ भूणा महाबळी कीयो (म्हे)। अरे चिपजाज्यै म्हानी (पीठ)। हुकम कोनी नारायण देव को (म्हे)। नी ले चड़यूं भगवान की इन्द्रासन (बैकुण्ठ)। बैकुण्ठ दिखाळ द्यूं (वाह वाह)। पण भगवान को हुकम

कोनी (हां देव को हुकम कोनी कीयो) । भूणोजी मन में देखियो घोड़ी तो है तो थारावाणी (वाह वाह)। अब कोनी मिलां भायावूं (म्हे) । चालबा दियो अब (वाह वाह) । भूणोजी बोर घोड़ी नै दरबार का हुकमूं पाछी राण शहर का मार गा घाल दी (म्हे) । घोड़ी को पोड़ बोल्यो नै (वाह वाह) । पीपळदे राणी ऊंची गोखड़ै आयी (म्हे) । दरबार का हुकमूं कांई साडूमाता के रावळै (जावे) । कांई जाती ए पीपळदे राणी साडू नै समचार कहवै देखां (कीआवूं जाणज्यो देखां कीआवूं) । अबार कहवूं रे भैइ देव का हुकमूं ले तूं (वाह वाह सा) ।।

जेठजी री असवारी तो जी हद बन गी है साडू सुलखना रे।
सोवै जेठजी नै ये सिरै सोहवणी मोड़ी रे।
जातां जेठ नै बूजी ये मनार लावज्यो।
बीछड़ी जावै ये राम लिच्छमन की जोड़ी रे।।
(भलां जी भलां) देव भलां

दरबार का हुकमूं राणी समचार पीपळदे कीयो है ओ (म्हे) । कीयो देख जेठजी की असवारी बूजी हद बन गी (वाह वाह) । सोवै जेठजी नै सिरै सोहवणी मोड़ी (मोड़ी) । तूं जातां जेठ नै मनाल्यां (म्हे) । बीछड़ी जावै राम लिच्छमन की (जोड़ी) । राम लिच्छमन दोन्यु एक जागां भेळा व्हिया (म्हे) । जको दुशमना नै सुहाया कोनी कीयो (हां कुण बीछेड़्या आनै कीयो) । राणी पीपळदे बोलै (म्हे) । कांई समचार बूजी नै कहवै देखां (कीआवूं जाणजयो देखां कीआवूं) । अबार कह द्यूं देव का हुकमूं ले तूं ।।

ए जेठजी की घोड़ी हेंसी तो जी जो जांती बा चौखठै औवूं रे।
लीलागर हंस कर फोड़ियो ये गज गेरी को ठाण।
जांतां जेठ नै बूजी ये मनार ल्याज्यो।
नीतर टूटेली ये जेठ बूआं की काण।।
(भलां जी भलां) देव भलां

जेठजी की घोड़ी हेंसी बूजी जाती चौखठै (वाह वाह) । देव को लीलागर हंस कर फोड़ नाकियो लेरावूं गज गेरी को (ठाण) । जांतां जेठ नै मनाल्यां (म्हे) । नी जरां टूट जायली आज जेठ बूआं की (काण) । के तो जेठजी नै तूं मना अर (ल्यावो) । नी जरां बूजी (जेठजी नै मनाणनै मैं जावूं कीयो) । पण नी दुनिया की काण टूट जायी (वाह वाह) । मात खटाणी दरबार का हुकमूं कांई देव के दुलीचा आवै (वाह वाह) । कांई आतां ही भगवान नै समचार देव नै कहवै देखां (कीआवूं जाणज्यो देखां कीआवूं) । अबार कहवूं देव का हुकमूं ले तूं (वाह वाह सा) ।।

ए जीभ कटावूं जी ए ई देव का चौरासियां रे।
लगा द्यूं जीभ के रे जहरी कालर लूण।
पीला पोतड़ा को दाजियोड़ो।
कुण रीसायो थामालो रे ई बळवन्तकारी भूण।।
(भलां जी भलां) देव भलां

जीभ कटावूं भाई देव का चौरासियां (म्हे)। जीभ के लगावूं जहरी कालर (लूण)। अरै पीला पोतड़ा का दाजियोड़ा नै (म्हे)। थामालो कुण रीसायो रे म्हारो बळवन्तकारी (भूण)। भूणाजी नै रीसाय अर पछो कुण खिनायो भैइ थामालो (हां जकी बताओ कीयो)। देव महाराज कीयो कोय मत बोलज्यो भैइ (वाह वाह)। माजी साय आवै (म्हे)। मैं जवाब मतेई कर लेवूं म्हारो (वाह वाह)। दरबार का हुकमूं भांगीजी कंवर हो नै (म्हे)। लकड़ा अर मुसळा ले ऊबो (हां खड़ियो हो ग्यो)। भांगीजी कंवर बोलै कांई समचार माजी साय नै कहवै देखां (कीआवूं जाणज्यो देखां कीआवूं)।।

ए बागोठ को ठाकर तो जी देव से हद मिलो ये साडू सुलखना रे।
मिलो मांजी ये दोन्यु ही कर जोड़।
ताण टाबरियां में कुबाण भूंडी पड़गिया।
दादा भूणा से ये बैठो पीठ मरोड़।।
(भलां जी भलां) देव भलां

दरबार का हुकमूं ओ समचार कंवर भांगीजी कीयो है (कीयो है)। कीयो बागोठ को ठाकर तो माजी देववूं को हद मिलो (म्हे)। हेंर मिलो दोन्यो ही कर (जोड़ अर)। ई ताणा टाबरिया में कुबाण भूंडी पड़ गी (म्हे)। दादा भूणा से माजी बैठो पीठ (मरोड़ अर)। दूजा नै दोष एक नै कोनी (म्हे)। सगळो ही दोष थारा देवजी में है (हां ई में है कीयो)। आज तो ई भाई नै (हां रिसार खिना द्यो)। तड़कै म्हानै ई ओ तो (हां रिसार खिना देसी कीयो)। जी जागां भूणोजी जाय (म्हे)। जठै मैं जां भेळा (आ लेयो कीयो समालो थांकी गादी)। भांगीजी तो लकड़ा अर मुसळा ले अर भूणा के लेरै बिदा हु गो (वाह वाह)। देव महाराज मन में बिचार (करियो है)। भाई बिखर गा (म्हे)। दरबार का हुकमूं देव महाराज बोलै कांई समचार कहवै देखां (कीआवूं जाणज्यो कीआवूं देखां)। अबार कहवां ले तूं भगवान का हुकमूं देखां।।

क्यें नै जीभ कटावो जी ए ई साडू सुलखना रे।
क्युं लगावै म्हारै ये जहरी कालर लूण।
कांकड़ लोप ये जाबा द्यूं कोय ने।
कोय नै जाबा द्यूं ये बारावत का भूण।।
(भलां जी भलां) देव भलां

क्युं जीभ कटावै महारी (म्हे)। क्युं जीभ के लगावै जहरी कालर (अब लूण)। मैं कांकड़ लोप नी जाबा द्यूं माता थारा बळवन्तकारी (भूण)। मांजी साय (म्हे)। थोड़ो भूणा नै रोको (हां ठामो थोड़ो कीयो)। कांकड़ के बाहरें कोनी नीकलबा द्यो (वाह वाह)। माजी साय काळवी घोड़ी दरबार में ऊबी (म्हे)। ऊबीणी ई चड़ पड़ी परी घोड़ी पर (वाह वाह)। भूणाजी के लेरै घोड़ी नै दड़बा नाक दी (वाह वाह)। दरबार का हुकमूं भूणाजी के सांकड़ै पूगती हो गी (म्हे)। साडूमाता बोलै (वाह वाह)। कांई भूणाजी नै बतलावै लेरावूं देखां (कीआवूं जाणज्यो कीआवूं)। अबार कहवां भगवान का हुकमूं ले भैइ जरां।।

ए ताणी असवारी तो जी हद बनी रे कंवर महाबळी रे।

सोवै तनै रे सिरै सोहवणो सेलो रे।
थोड़ी बाग नै रोक ले रे कंवर महाबळी।
ताणी माता लेरेवूं देती आवै हेलो रे।।
(भलां जी भलां) देव भलां

ताणी असवारी हद बन गी (म्हे)। सोवै सिरै सोहवणो सेलो (सेलो)। थोड़ी बोर की बाग नै रोक (म्हे)। ताणी माता लेरावूं देती आवै (हेलो)। भूणा थोड़ी बोर नै रोकी भैइ (वाह वाह)। भूणोजी बूझणा करी रे सिरदारां (म्हे)। आ कुण है भैइ (हां कुण है ओ कीयो)। श्री महाराज आपकी बडी मां है नै आ (वाह वाह)। अरै डोकरीवूं मिलिया कोनी भैइ थोड़ा ठहर जावो (ठहरो कीयो)। तो भूणोजी असवारी नै रोकली (वाह वाह)। मात खटाणी भूणा नै बूझणा (करी ही)। भूणाजी चड़ी असवारी पाछी कींयां गिरी बोल (हां पाछी कींयां मोड़ियो कीयो)। नी तो म्हारावूं मिलियो अर नी देवूं मिलियो (म्हे)। मिलिया बिनै ही पाछो कींयां गिरियो बोल (हां जकी बताय कीयो)। कीयो मांजी साय थारावूं तो मैं कोनी मिलियो (हां मिलियो कोनी)। हेंर ताणो देवजी है नै (म्हे)। बीवूं चोखी तरहवूं मिल अर (आच्छी तरह मिल अर आणो हूं कीयो)। कीयो नी लाल देवजी तो है कोनी अठै (हां बठै हा ही कोनी दुलीचै मैं कीयो)। कठै ग्या (जकी बताओ)। कीयो देव के सुरेमाता को लाड घणो (हां घणो है कीयो)। सुवा पहर दिन चड़ै जितै नै गायां नै लेरें उछेरबा जाय (हां सुबह ही उछेरनै ऊठ जावे)। हेंर लेरली टैम चार बजियां (हां सुरेमाता के सामै पाछा ऊठजाय कीयो)। देवजी तो गायां नै उछेरबा गियोड़ा है (वाह वाह)। अठै है ही कोनी (है ही कोनी)। भूणोजी बोलै (म्हे)। कांई मां नै आपके समचार कहवै देखां (कीआवूं जाणज्यो देखां कीआवूं)। अबार कहवूं देव का हुकमूं ले तूं। (वाह वाह सा)।।

ए लीला के बन्ध्यो तो जी ए ई ताणो दरबार में औवूं रे।
बीछू स्यापां की लाग रही घड़ मोर।
कंवर भूणा करै तनै बूझण।
किस्या देव नै खिनायो ये गायां की गुआल।।
(भलां जी भलां) देव भलां

लीलागर घोड़ो दरबार में बन्धियो (म्हे)। बीछू स्यापां की लाग रही घड़ (मोर)। भूणोजी करै तनै बूझणा (म्हे)। किस्या देव नै खिनाया गायां की (गुआल)। देवजी दो तीन है जरां तो भायां को कोनी हो बो (म्हे)। एक ही देवजी हो नै (वाह वाह)। बी देवजी नै देख अर आयो मैं (अच्छी तरहवूं देख आयो कीयो)। मात खटाणी बूझणा करी रे सुण रे लाल (म्हे)। बै स्याप गोयरा की कहवै नै तूं (वाह वाह)। बसी का जाटां के सैन्धा व्हियोड़ा है राम मारिया (हां सगळो के सैन्धा है कीयो)। देवजी तो गायां उछेरबा जावै (म्हे)। जरां गोदियां में खिलाबा लाग जावै (हा) सगळा गोदियां (में खिलावै स्यापां नै अर बै बयां बीछूयां नै)। देव को उणियारो अर लोगां को घणो ही जाट को उणियारो एक को मिलै भैइ (वाह वाह)। अती बात है (म्हे)। भूणोजी मन में देखियो डोकळडी तनै झोलावै सांचो है (हां झूट बोलै है कीयो डोकरी)। भूणोजी बोलै कांई समचार मां नै कहवै देखां (कीआवूं जाणज्यो कीआवूं देखां)। अबार कहवां देव का हुकमूं ले तूं (वाह वाह जी वाह वाह)।।

ए दिल्ली जावूं जी माता म्हारी ये मैं आगरै औवूं रे।
जावूंला मांजी ये भाटियां की जेसलमेर।
बगड़ावतां का बैर पर चड़ै बगड़ावतां का डावड़ा।
जी दिन मांजी ये उरखो दीज्यो फेर।।
(भलां जी भलां) देव भलां

दिल्ली जावूं आगरै मैं (म्हे)। जावूं भाटियां की जेसल (मेर)। बगड़ावतां का बैर पर चड़ै बगड़ावतां का ड़ावड़ा (वाह वाह)। जी दिन साडू म्हनै उरखो दीज्यै (फेर)। भाई माजी ए कागदियो म्हनै ही दे दीज्यो (म्हे)। मैं म्हारा बाप को बैर काढूं ज्यूं (वाह वाह)। और पाछो कोनी चालूं (हां पाछो तो अब कोनी चलूं थारै देवजी कन्नै)। हेंर देवजी कन्नै कोनी जावूं तो राण शहर जाबा जिस्या कोनी रहयो (वाह वाह)। तोड़ियायो मैं तो (म्हे)। तीन तिलोकी को नाथ भगवान लीला नै सिण्गार (म्हे)। हेंर लीला की बागडोर नै कांई कीयो दुलीचावूं जमी में निची राळी (वाह वाह)। लीलागर घोड़ो जमीमाता के मांय बड़ गो (म्हे)। तीन कोस पर आगा नै जार (नीकलया)। घोड़ा नै पाछो दड़ावट के गैलै घाल दियो (वाह वाह)। सुवा हाथ घोड़ो जमीमातावूं अधर चालै (म्हे)। हेंर सुवा हाथ पिलाण ऊंचो अधर मेलियो (रह मेलियो)। सुवा हाथ ही भगवान पिलाण ऊंचा अधर बिराजमान हो मेलिया (वाह वाह)। सुवा सेस मण को छतर है जको भगवान के शीश के ऊपरै (तप रियो)। एक धज्जा धोवती अधर औरूं (चालै उडती)। साडूमाता के पहल पोत नजर देव पर गी (म्हे)। भूणाजी बतलायो (वाह वाह)। अरै लाल भूणा (म्हे)। तूं कहवो देवजी नै देखर आयो (वाह वाह)। आ देख म्हानो देवजी देख बो आवै निंगै कर अब (हां कांकड़ मूं आवै कीयो)। भूणोजी गेला कानै निंगै (करी है)। तो लीलागर आतो दीखियो (म्हे)। मन में देखियो रे ओ को ओ तो घोड़ो अर ओ ई टाबरियो (हां सागै ओ ई का ए ही हा)। पण उनू कांई आयगो (हां ओ तो सामू आवै कीयो)। देव महाराज आतां ही साडू नै बतलायी (म्हे)। ई माजी साय (वाह वाह)। थै कांकड़ में कींयां आया (हां आज कांकड़ में कींयां आया हो कीयो)। कुण की तो असवारी है अर कींयां थै आया जका समचार कह (हां बातावो कीयो)। कीयो लाल ओ भाई भूणोजी है थारो (वाह वाह)। कोय ताणा दरबार में ईयूं मजाक कर ली (म्हे)। तो रीस खार आर भूणो तो पाछो जावै (हां पाछो जावा हा)। जका ने मनावा की खतर मैं (हां कांकड़ में आयी कीयो)। कीयो माजी सा दादो भूणो है (हां सागै ई)। कीयो सागै को सागै ओ है (वाह वाह)। तो दादो भूणो आयो जरां किस्या म्हारावूं बात करिया बिन मिलिया बिन जावो कांई (हां मिलिया बिनै कींयां जावां कीयो)। भूणोजी मन में देखियो माठो बो टाबरियो दूजो हो कांई (हां बो दूसरो ही ओ कोय अड़बड़ ख्याल ओ दूजो है)। ओ स्याणो बोल्यो (वाह वाह)। तीन तिलोकी को नाथ भूणा के मुण्डा के पागड़ो छोड़ दियो घोड़ा को (वाह वाह)। कांई कांकड़ में भाई भाई (मिल जावे)। कांई वारता बनै देखां (कीआवूं जाणज्यो कीआवूं देखां)। अबार कहवां से देव का हुकमूं ले तूं (वाह वाह सा)।।

देव अर भूणो तो जी ए ई कांकड़ में हद मिलिया रे।
सहलियां भाई रे गायां मंगलागीत।

सुवा पहर शादी की तोपां चाल गी।
निंगै करज्यै भूणा रे राजांवाली रीत।।
(भलां जी भलां) देव भलां

भूणोजी अर देव महाराज कांकड़ में हद मिल गा (म्हे)। सहलियां भाई रे गायां मंगलागीत (गीत)। सुवा पहर शादी की तोपां चाली (म्हे)। निंगै कर भूणा राजांवाली (रीत)। देव महाराज जी टैम भूणाजीवूं मिलिया है नै (म्हे)। जी टैम अम्मी की नजर (झांकिया)। ठौड़ ठौड़ सहलियां का झूमका आनण्द ऊचाव मंगलाचार गाबा लागी (वाह वाह)। रूंख राय है जका गीत गाबा (लाग ग्या कीयो)। जागां जागां गाजा बाजा साही सनमान (हां व्हिया है)। भूणोजी चारा कानी निंगै (करी)। अरै थारी मां जाणु ईंयां का औतारी भाई हा (हां आपां मिलिया बिनै ऊठ जाता कीयो)। इयां का भाई फैर मिलबा का ही (कोनी हा कीयो)। महाराज बूझणा करी दादा भूणा (म्हे)। राण शहर में रिया तो कंवर खाण्डेरावजी क्युं बाजिया (हां कींयां बाजता कीयो)। कीयो श्री महाराज चान्दारूण का सांखला सिरदार हा जको म्हारी चिटली आंगली (काटी कीयो)। रावजी का साळा हा बै (वाह वाह)। कीयो म्हांको भाणजो करां नै (म्हे)। की सैनाण करां (हां सैनाण कर दूसरो नांव राखां हां)। जकै दिन ओ भूणो नांव तो हटा दियो (म्हे)। कंवर खाण्डेरावजी नांव (राखियो)। कीयो दादा भूणा म्हनै खाण्डा बूचा लाग ग्या कोनी भैइ (हां खाण्डा बूचिया कठूं दीखिया कोनी कीयो)। देव तीन तिलोकी को नाथ भूणा की भातवूं आंगली बतावै देखां (कीआवूं जाणज्यो कीआवूं देवां)।।

ए बैरियवूं आंतां तो जी जो भली घणी करी रे कंवर महाबळी रे।
तूं तो भूणा रे पिरजा पाळी पांगली।
बालो ठाकर भूणाजी कानै नाहलतां।
भूणा के ठाकरां रे धग धग बद गी आंगली रे।।
(भलां जी भलां) देव भलां

तूं बैरियवूं आतां आज भली घणी करी (म्हे)। नान्या भूणा तूं पिरजा पाळी (पांगली)। बालो ठाकर भूणा का नाहलतां (म्हे)। भूणा की धग धग बद गी (आंगली)। बरोबर हो गी (वाह वाह)। भूणोजी जीवणै हाथ कानै निंगै करी (म्हे)। आंगली बरोबर लागी (वाह वाह)। भूणोजी मन में देखियो भूल हो गैइ (हां डाव लियो हाथ नै होवै कीयो)। डावा कानै निंगै (करी है)। आंगली बरोबर (लागी)। भूणोजी मन में देखियो अरै भगवान है ओ (हां ईयूं कांई बांतां छानी है कीयो)। दरबार का हुकमूं भूणोजी समचार कीयो (म्हे)। कीयो तूं ही तो घड़ै अर तूं ही तो भानै (म्हे)। तूं ही तीन लोक ऊपरलो (लोग)। अरै कर जोड़ियां चाकर तपै (म्हे)। अखण्ड पुरुष नै धोक ही धोक (धोक)। आ भोपा नै जकी धोक करै नै दूजा (म्हे)। जका देव महाराज नै भूणोजी करी आ (वाह वाह)। जी दिनवूं आ धोक चाली है (म्हे)। जरां देव का पुजारी नै और भोपो है जका नै आवै जको के भोपाजी धोक (म्हे)। देव नै भैइ (हां देव नै धोक है)। अबार कोय भोपा नै नी कहवै तो भूणोजी भायां के सामिल आतां भूणो अर देव महाराज चोखी तरह कांकड़ में मिलतां (मिलतां)। जय बोलो श्री देवनारायण भगवान की

(जय)। बोलो भैइ छोटा अर मोटा (स)। तो देव अर भगवान भूणोजी मिलिया नै (म्हे)। भाई भाई भेळा हो गा जरां बिचार (करिया है)। कीयो रे भैइ भाई भाई भेळा हो गा देव महाराज कीयो भैइ म्हारा तो वादा कोनी अब (वाह वाह)। ग्यारह बरस का वादा है (म्हे)। सात बरस तो माळागर में ब्यतीत हो गा (वाह वाह)। हेंर अठै आया पछी टैम लागी (हां कासा दिन हो गिया कीयो)। जो बगड़ावतां का बैर काढा जकी बिदी बनावो (वाह वाह)। कीयो श्री महाराज अरे घर घरांवूं आपके चोखो है (म्हे)। जासा का निरपाल नै हुकम कर दियो (वाह वाह)। ऊनाळो गहूं चन्ना की साग के मांय गायां नै छोड़ो अब (हां भेळ दियो कीयो)।।

सेल सुथानै जी मेल दे रे मामा का डावड़ा रे।
तूं तो गुआलिया रे सिन्धन ल्यूं निरपाल।
आज हुकम देवै नारायण देवजी।
परभातै भेळ दे रे बदशहियां का माल।।
(भलां जी भलां) देव भलां

दरबार कीयो सेल सुथानै मेल मामा का डावड़ा (वाह वाह)। सिन्धन ल्यो (निरपाल)। अरै आज हुकम द्यां नारायण देवजी (म्हे)। परभातै भेळ दे बदशाहियां का (माल)। दरबार का हुकमूं गुआल घणा दिना का कोडायो कहतां ही जेज लागी (वाह वाह)। माळां के माईयै गायां नै छोड़तां टैम कोनी लागी (हां भचोभच छोड़ दी जी कीयो)। डरतो करतो डरतो करतो (म्हे)। पंद्रा बीस गांवां का माळां नै (हां भेळ अर स्याम का आयग्यो)। देव के गौ को लाड घणो हो (म्हे)। परभात की टैम तो सागै जातां लेरलां टैम ओ सामा (उठ जातां जी कीयो)। गाय के भगवान सामा गिया (म्हे)। सुरेमाता नै दरबार भाक (लगा दीनी)। तो सुरेमाता बाड़ में मुण्डो घाल दी दोबड़ी में (हां देव महाराज के निंगै आयी जी कीयो)। देव बोलै कांई गुआल नै ओळमा दे देखां (कीआवूं जाणज्यो देखां कीआवूं)। अबार कहवूं देव का हुकमूं देखां (वाह वाह जी)।।

कियां लागी जी गुआल सुरेमाता रे आमणदूमणया रे।
क्युं लाग रिया म्हारी रे कामधीण का भाक।
क्युं मरबा को डर लागो रे गुआल गाय का।
आ गायां नै परभातै रे दूजा मेलूं गुआल।।
(भलां जी भलां) देव भलां

दरबार का हुकमूं देव महाराज समचार (कीया जी कीयो)। कींयां लागी गुआल भाई सुरेमाता आमणदूमणी (म्हे)। क्युं लाग रिया म्हारी कामधेण का (अब भाक)। तनै क्युं मरबा को डर लागो (म्हे)। आ गायां मैं परभातै दूजा उछेर द्यूं (लारै गुआल कीयो)। तनै जीव प्यारो लागो (वाह वाह)। गायां प्यारी कोनी लागी (म्हे)। गुआल कीयो श्री महाराज आ गुआली दोहरी है (हां म्हारावूं चराज्यै ए गुआली कोनी कीयो)। घर बैठा आपकी नौकरी बजादेवूं (वाह वाह)। बीर की गेडी जकै देव के मुण्डा के (ठेकै ही राळ दीनी जी कीयो)। गुआल ईंयां कींयां करी भैइ (म्हे)। कीयो श्री महाराज आ गुआली दोहरी म्हारावूं

होवै कोनी (हां म्हारावूं कोनी होवै कीयो)। आ गायां नै गुआल दूजा जाय अब (वाह वाह)। कीयो सुण रे गुआल थारा जिस्यो लेरला नै हक कोनी भैइ (हां कोय गुआलां नै चराबा को हक नैइ है)। दरबार का हुकमूं तनै ठेट को ही ई बात को हक है (म्हे)। गायां में तनै जाणो पड़ी (वाह वाह)। गुआल बोलै (म्हे)। कांई समचार देव नै कहवै देखां (कीआवूं जाणज्यो कीआवूं देखां)। अबार कहवूं भगवान का हुकमं लियो थै (वाह वाह जी वाह वाह)।।

ए हाथां में राखां तो जी ए ई धो धामण की कामड़ियां रे।
चरावा अन्नदाता रे पारब्रिम की गाय।
पहल काला गुआल भाला राखता बीजळसार का।
लाग जाती अन्नदाता रे बांठ बांठ में लाय।।
(भलां जी भलां) देव भलां

मैं राखां अन्नदाता हाथ में धो धामण की कामड़ी (वाह वाह)। चरावा पारब्रिम की (गाय)। पहल काला गुआल भाला राखता बीजळसार का लाग जाती बो दरबार बांठ बांठ में (लाय)। श्री महाराज (म्हे)। ई का कामड़ीवूं माल अब मिलेगी म्हारावूं (हां आज मिलै कोय काळ मिलै कीयो)। गुआल का साज सिण्गार है जका तो गुआलां नै देवो (म्हे)। हेंर गाय का गहणा है जका गाय नै पहरावो (वाह वाह)। तो दरबार का हुकमूं आपको कीयो करो गायां के लेरै पाछो मैं जावूं (हां माल भेळ द्यूं कीयो)। कीयो गुआल (म्हे)। मैं जाणै कोय नी भैइ (वाह वाह)। कांई तो गुआलां का साज सिण्गार होवै अर कांई गाय को गहणो (हां होवै कीयो)। बतायावूं ठा पड़ै (हां ईंयां कांई ठा पड़ै कीयो)। कीयो सोना का बीर गढ सोना का (ईर गढ है)। हेंर सोना की कढावट मोड़ी (मोड़ी)। अता बकस धरमराजा देव की परभात की टैम धापड़ियो धीणतळाव की धोळी (धोळी न मोड़ी जी कीयो)। ओ तो गाय को गहणो (हां बकसो)। बगां भैरूं छींटां का देदिया काळोरी (काबाण)। अता दे रे बाळा देवजी परभातै भेळ बदशाहियां का (माल)। कीयो गुआल (म्हे)। तूं माल भेळबा की बांतां नी करै (हां ए म्हारूं माल भेळबा की बात को ही नी कीयो)। तूं तो मजाक कर ली (वाह वाह)। के तो मैं तो गायां को गहणो घड़ावूं (म्हे)। नौ लाख असी हजार गाय हा आपां कन्नै (वाह वाह)। हेंर कद गुआलां का (हां साज सिण्गार करावूं कीयो)। म्हांकी टैम कोनी अती भैइ (हां अती रुकना का ही वादा कोनी)। कीयो श्री महाराज घड़ावो क्युं (म्हे)। गुआल हा बगड़ावतां थकां ठेट का ही है (हां गहणां गांठा सब घड़ियोड़ा तियार पड़ियोड़ा (है कीयो मूं)। साडू कन्नै जावो (मांग अर ल्यावो)। तीन तिलोकी को नाथ भगवान सात बरसावूं पाछा बाळक बन गा मां की गोदियां में जार लोटबा लागा (वाह वाह)। साडूमाता मन में देखियो आ कांई बात हुई (हां आ बात ईंयां इयां कींयां हुई आज)। अरे सात बरसावूं भगवान बच्च्या कींयां बन गा पाछा (वाह वाह)। देव बोलै कांई समचार मां नै कहवै देखां (कीआवूं जाणज्यो कीआवूं देखां)। अबार कहवूं देव का हुकमूं ले तूं (वाह वाह सा)।।

खुलावो खुलावो जी माता म्हारी ये साळ ऊबरा रे।
तूं तो माजी ये कुंचियांयी ले लियो हाथ।

ए बगां है भैरूं काळा की छींट का।
परभातै दीज्यै ये सलै गुआलां बांट।।
(भलां जी भलां) देव भलां

खुलावो खुलावो माजी बाई साळ ऊबरा (वाह वाह)। कूंची ले लियो (हाथ)। बगां है भैरूं काळा की छींट का (म्हे)। दीज्यो भाई माजी सलै गुआलां नै परभातै (अब थै बांट)। गाय को गहणो तो गाय नै बांट द्यो पहरा द्यो (म्हे)। गुआलां का साज सिण्गार है जका (गुआलां नै दे द्यो कीयो)। साडूमाता मन में देखियो बळो बजराक आ बाह देय कुण बिखेर दी (म्हे)। बगड़ावतां का बारां का तीन मानवी है (वाह वाह)। एक काम तो बांका ही है (हां बांका ही है चोथो आदमी ही कोनी कीयो)। के तो सुरेमाता नै आगली आयी बाह देय बिखेरी है (म्हे)। हेंर के बगड़ावतां को बो भाटड़ियो (हां छोछू बखेरी है)। एक बो गुआल है नी गाय को (म्हे)। ओ ही कळह को मूली है (मूली है जी कीयो)। बूझणा करी श्री महाराज बगड़ावतां थकां गहणो हो (म्हे)। महाभारत होबा लाग्यो नै (वाह वाह)। जी दिन खुलाय गहणां नै आ भींतड़ा के मांयनै अठै ऊंडो दियो (हां कठै अठै गाडियोड़ो है जकै (की म्हनै ठा नैइ कीयो)। कांई ठी तो गहणो रावजी साय लूट में (ले ग्या)। तो ई ठा कोनी (वाह वाह)। अर कांई ठी लाल ई जागां रह गो तो म्हनै (हां म्हनै तो ग्यान कोनी कीयो)। म्हनै तो ध्यान तो रियो कोनी (वाह वाह)। देव महाराज कीयो माजी साय गहणां किस्या छाना थोड़ा ही है (हां म्हारावूं छाना कोनी)। तीन तिलोकी को नाथ बोलै (म्हे)। कांई मां नै समचार कहवै देखां (कीआवूं जाणज्यो देखां अब भोपाजी महाराज कीआवूं)। अबार कहवूं भगवान का हुकमूं (वाह वाह जी)।।

ए गहणां म्हारावूं जी ए ई छाना कोय नै औवूं रे।
गहणो पड़ियो जी भैंस ऊबरै ठेट।
तूं पोती राजा रणधीर की।
मैं तो थारो ए हाथ करूं नै मेट।।
(भलां जी भलां) देव भलां

गहणो तो माजी म्हारावूं तो छाना तो कोनी (म्हे)। हेंर गहणां पड़िया भैंस ऊबरै (ठेट)। तूं पोती राजा रणधीर की (म्हे)। मैं थारा हाथ करूं नै (मेट)। सुण ये माजी (म्हे)। मैं थारा हाथूं लियो चावूं (हां मतै लेनो चावूं कोनी कीयो)। दरबार का हुकमूं गहणो म्हारावूं छाना कोनी (वाह वाह)। मात खटाणी मन में देखियो (म्हे)। के ई कळा को तो तनै ठा तो है कोनी (हां कांई पार है कीयो)। माळागर की भोम में दूध मांगियो तूं (म्हे)। जिस्यो चूंगियो को जिस्यो को जिस्यो तनै दूध दे द्यो (हां पाछो दे दियो)। गहणां ईयूं किस्या छाना थोड़ा ही है (हां किस्या छाना थोड़ा है आवूं)। कूंचियां का झूमका देव नै साडूमाता (हां दे दिया)। खोल ल्यो लाल ल्यो पधारो कीयो (हां देख लियो क्वें में है)। तीन तिलोकी को नाथ भैंस ऊबरै पूगता हो गा (वाह वाह)। पताला के मांयनै शीशो गलियोड़ो हो ऊबरै गहणां के (वाह वाह)। ठोकर बाही शीशो परै जांवतो (पड़ियो)। मेल हमालां के (माथे)। गहणां नै गायां के गंवळियां के पूगतो (करियो है जी कीयो)। कांई भगवान चिरागां का चाण्दना (करे)। कांई

आपकी गायमाता नै अब सिण्गारै देखां (कीआवूं जाणज्यो देखां अब कीआवूं)। अबार कहवां देव का हुकमूं ले तूं (वाह वाह जी)।।

ए चिरागां के चाण्दनै तो जी दरबार सिण्गारै रे पारब्रिम की गाय।
सोहवण मुरकी है रतन जड़ाव की।
पहरा दे म्हाना रे काबर केरड़ के कान।
(भलां जी भलां) देव भलां

चिरागां के चाण्दनै भगवान सिण्गार ली पारब्रिम की (गाय)। सोहवण मुरकी है रतन जड़ाव की (म्हे)। पहरा दे रे म्हारै काबर केरड़ै (अब कान)। ए मोटोड़ी मुरकियां है नै (म्हे)। ए दरबार का हुकमूं आपणा केरड़ा के घालो (वाह वाह)। नागौर तहसील में तो बोलै सांड (वाह वाह)। हेंर दरबार का हुकमूं अजमार जिला के मांयनै केरड़ो बोलै सांड नै (वाह वाह)।।

कोइयां री गलावो जी छड़ा दियाली रे गुआल गाय का रे।
कोयां के गुआलिया रे नकावो घूघर मोल।
ओ नौ कीरोड़ को सांकड़ो रे गुआल ई गाय का।
नेवाजी रावत की रे नागली के गला में राळ।।
(भलां जी भलां) देव भलां

कोयां के नका गुआल भाई छड़ा दियाली (म्हे)। कोइयां के नकावो घूघर (मोल)। ओ नौ कीरोड़ को सांकळो गुआल गाय का (वाह वाह)। नेवाजी की नागली के गला में ही (हां राळ कीयो)। काका नेवाजी की नागली गाय है नै (हां बी नै पहराणो है कीयो)। बड़ोड़ो सांकळो नौ कीरोड़वालो (वाह वाह)।।

बागा बक्सियां जी जो काळै भैरूं काळ की छींट का रे।
नापा नै दियो जी शेश मुखियां का टोप।
बांको थानो गुआल बदनोर को।
मार ले भाई रे चड़तां पहली चोट।।
(भलां जी भलां) देव भलां

बागा दिया भैरूं काळा की छींट का (वाह वाह)। नापा नै भगवान दियो भैइ शेश मुखियांला (टोप)। बांको थानो रे गुआल बदनोर को (म्हे)। मार चड़तां पहली (अब चोट)।।

बागा बक्सियां तो जी जो भैरूं काळा की छींट का रे।
नापा नै दे द्यूं औरूं ही सुखपाल।
सिकराणी गुआलिया रे झण्डा रोप द्यो।
रोप दीयो दुशमन राव के छाती ऊपर साल।।
(भलां जी भलां) देव भलां

बगा दिया भैरूं की काळा छींट का (म्हे)। नापा नै भगवान दे दी सुख (पाल)। सिकराणी रे गुआल अब झण्डा रोप (म्हे)। रोप द्यो दुश्मन राव के छाती ऊपरै (साल)। बैरी के छाती पर औरूं साल राखियो (वाह वाह)। गुआल (म्हे)। गायां नै उछेरो भैइ (वाह वाह)।

सुरेमाता नै जी जो सुंवारै उछेर देय मामा का डावड़ा रे।
तूं तो गुआलिया उछेरतो नाक परी खेराट।
माल फूलिया का केकड़ी का भेळ दे गुआल गाय का।
भेळ दे राव को रे टोडो नागर चाल।।
(भलां जी भलां) देव भलां

दरबार का हुकमूं सुरेमाता नै गुआल भैइ सुंवारै उछेर दी (वाह वाह)। उछेरतो नाक परी (खेराट)। माल तो फूलिया केकड़ी का भेळ दे (म्हे)। भेळ दे रावजी को टोडो नागर (चाल)। टोडा को सोलंकी है नै सिरदार (म्हे)। बीकाला महलां के सारो गायां नै नीकलबा द्यो (हां जाण द्यो कीयो)। तीन तिलोकी को नाथ भगवान हुकम देदेयो गायां को (वाह वाह)। देव बोलै (वाह वाह)। औरूं गुआल नै समचार कहवै देखां (कीआवूं जाणज्यो भोपाजी महाराज कीआवूं)। अबार कहवूं भगवान का हुकमूं ले तूं (वाह वाह जी वाह वाह)।।

सुरेमाता नै जी जो परभातै उछेरी रे गुआल गाय का रे।
तूं तो भाई रे गुदलै पाणी पाय।
ओ गुदलिया को पाणी लागै रे तनै गादलो।
राजा नीमा के रे बान्दरवाड़ै पाव।।
(भलां जी भलां) देव भलां

सुरेमाता नै गुआल सुंवारै उछेर दी (म्हे)। हेंर गुदलै पाणी (पाय)। अरै गुदलिया को पाणी लागै तनै गादलो (वाह वाह)। राजा नीमा के बान्दरवाड़ै जातै (हां पाव जी कीयो)। सुण रे गुआल (वाह वाह)। गाय में सिण्गार बा में कमी होवै तो म्हनै ओळमा (हां देयीज्ये)। अब गाय भूखी तिसी रह गी (ओळमो है कीयो तने)। सावल देखलेय अबकाळै (वाह वाह)। गुआल मन में बिचार (करियो है)। अरै देव तो तनै सीख दे दी (म्हे)। देव की तो धरम की है धाय आपणी भुवाजी (हां)। ए घर की मलकनी है (बी नै आपां बूझियो कोनी)। ई नै बूझां तो सरी गायां उछेरां कोनी उछेरां देखां (हां बाड़ां में जाण द्यां कोनी जाण द्यां कीयो)। गुआल देव को कांई भुवाजी के रावळै जावै (म्हे)। जातो ही समचार कहवै देखां ल्यो अबार कहवां का हुकमूं ल्यो तो।।

गुदलियो तळाव तो जी जो राण के सांकड़ो रे।
राव का अमराव बांधै काचा सूत।
ओ गायां नै पाणी पुआवै धरमराजा देवजी।
मीठो लागेलो भुवाजी ये कामधीण को दूध।।
(भलां जी भलां) देव भलां

ओ गुदलियो तळाव तो भुवाजी राण के सांकड़ो आयगो (वाह वाह)। रावजी का अमराव बांधै नै काचा (सूत)। गायां नै पाणी पावै धरमराजा देवजी (म्हे)। परभातै मीठो लागी भुवाजी तनै कामधीण को (अब दूध)। परभात की टैम दूध मीठो लागेलो (हां गायां रावजी के माळां में जाय है कीयो)। दूध तो मीठो लागै (गायां के आडी फिर जावो)। अबार फिरजा (वाह वाह)। पछै म्हनै ओळमो देयली तूं (म्है पछै देय)।।

ए बगड़ावतां थकां तो जी जो सिकराणी भतीजा रे खांगा बैठतां रे।
काटता राजियाला बागां डाल रे।
पण गायां रूक जायली राताकोट में।
कुण नै मेलूं रे कामधीण की बार।।
(भलां जी भलां) देव भलां

ओ समचार साडूमाता (हां भतीजै नै कीयो है जी कीयो)। सिकराणी भतीजा बगड़ावतां थकां खांगा बैठतां (वाह वाह)। काटता रे थै नोलका बाग की (डाळ)। गायां रूकी भतीजा राताकोट में (म्हे)। कुण नै मेलूं लेरेवूं कामधेण की (बार)। भतीजा (हां बारूं किनै छोडूं हो कीयो)। दरबार का हुकमूं कांई सोची मन में तूं (हां आ कींयां सोची हो)। कीयो मैं कोनी सोची (म्हे)। तीन तिलोकी को नाथ भगवान सोची है (हां बै सोची है कीयो)। साडूमाता बोलै गुआल नै समचार कहवै देखां (कीआवूं जाणज्यो देखां अब कीआवूं)।।

ए सिकराणी पर तो जी ए ई खांगा बैठतां रे।
काटता नोलका बाग की लूम।
गायां रूक जायली भतीजा राताकोट में।
गोठां में भुवा भतीजो रे देतां फिरालां बूम।।
(भलां जी भलां) देव भलां

सिकराणी भतीजा खांगा घणा बैठतां कीयो (वाह वाह)। काटता नोलका बाग की लूम (लूम)। अरै गायां रूकी भतीजा राताकोट में (वाह वाह)। गोठां में भुवा भतीजा आपां देता फिरां (बूम)। आप नै तो बोबा को पांती आयी (हां और की पांती कोनी आवेलो कीयो)। गुआल (म्हे)। दरबार का हुकमूं कांई मन में सोची तूं (हां आ कींयां सोची है कीयो)। कीयो मैं करां सोची है (हां)। देव तीन तिलोकी को नाथ सोची है आ (वाह वाह)।

ए बगड़ावतां थकां तो जी जो सिकराणी खांगा बैठतां रे।
काटता नोलका बाग की डाळ।
ओ रावजी तो बो रे गुआल गाय का।
आपांणाला भतीजा रे सिला पछाड़िया बाळ।।
(भलां जी भलां) देव भलां

बगड़ावतां थकां खांगा घणा बैठतां (म्हे)। काटता नोलका बाग की डाळ (डाळ)। अरै रावजी तो बो ही है (म्हे)। आपां नै सिला पछाड़िया (बाळ)। लेरली बात क्युं भूलियो थै (हां आप नै सितर बाळकां नै राव सा सिला पर (पछाड़ पछाड़ अर मारिया कीयो)। बा लेरली बात भूल गो तूं (सफाई भूल गो बेटी का बाप)। दरबार का हुकमूं रे तीन तूंतड़ा है (म्हे)। हाल तो (वाह वाह)। पांच भाई है जका में दो तो भोला है लाई (हां दो भोला है भोला में (तो देव महाराज ही है कीयो)। तूं कीं आसं ग्यो (म्हे)। कीयो मैं करां आसं ग्यो है (ए देव महाराज तीन (तिलोकी का नाथ आसं ग्यो है जी कीयो)। गायां तो माळां में जाय भुवाजी की की कहवै भला ई (वाह वाह)।।

ए आप नै लिच्छमी तो जी भतीजा दे मोकळिया रे।
उछरी नै मावै सांकड़ै सेर।
देव को कीयोड़ो मत करै नै गुआल गाय का।
आपां नी गायां नै रे आप नै ही कांकड़ फैर।।
(भलां जी भलां) देव भलां

आप नै भातीजा लिच्छमी मोकळी है (म्हे)। उछरी कोनी मावै सांकड़ै (सेर)। देव को कीयोड़ो मत करै नै (वाह वाह)। आप नी गायां नै भाई आप नै कांकड़ (फैर)। अरै भूखियां का धणी आपां हो ज्यां (हां भूखियां का धणी तो आपां हां)। हेंर धायोड़ा का लोग ही (हां धणी होवेलां भतीजा कीयो)। कीयो भुवाजी गायां के आडी फिरै नै (हां अबार ही फिर जावो कीयो)। म्हनै भगवान को हुकम है (म्हे)। गहूं चन्ना की साख ऊनाळो मैं तो भेळूं भैइ (हां अब म्हारावूं तो गायां चरायां बिना कोनी (रहणी आवे)।

थारै अर देव के तो जी जो अब काल गुआल रंग राच गो रे।
जियान भाई रे कपड़ै राची आल।
देव को कीयोड़ो मत कर गुआल गाय का।
आपांणाला भतीजा रे देखै दियाड़ा चाल।।
(भलां जी भलां) देव भलां

दरबार का हुकमूं ओ समचार साडूजी कीयो (म्हे)। थारै देव के गुआल रंग राच गो (वाह वाह)। जियान कपड़ै राची (आल)। अरै देव को कीयोड़ो मत कर नै (म्हे)। आप ना लेरला देख दियाड़ा का दिन (चाल)। लेरलां दिन देखां चाल भाई (हां अब कींयां भूल ग्यो कीयो)। कीयो भुवाजी म्हानै भगवान का हुकम है (म्हे)। गायां तो माळां में जायी (वाह वाह)।।

मनै बरजै तो जी मानल्यूं रे गुआल गाय का रे।
मनै करा द्यूं बांकी गढ जावलियां ई रे।
तीन मूली म्हाना दरबार में मरिया कोय ने।
जासा को निरपाल सूरै रे छोछू भाट उतावली रे।।
(भलां जी भलां) देव भलां

मनै बरजै तो भतीजा मानू भैइ (म्हे)। मनै ही करा द्यूं बांकी गढ (जावलियां)। अरै तीन मूली म्हारा दरबार में मरिया कोनी (म्हे)। छोछू तो भाट जासा को निरपाल सुरेमाता (उतावलिया)। बगड़ावतां का बारां का तीनो मानवी (हां रहगिया कीयो)। ए तीनो बगड़ावतां के सागै मर गा है नै (हां तो आज म्हारै घर में सुख शांती रंहवती)। कीयो माजी कताक के गायां माळां में जाय (वाह वाह)। भगवान को देव को हुकम व्हियोड़ो है अब (म्हे)। तो दरबार का हुकमूं देव महाराज बूझणा हां हुकम दियो है नै (म्हे)। तो साडूजी कीयो भैइ जरां देव के थारै जची जियान ही (हां हूसी कीयो)। तो देव महाराज को गुआल कांई गायां नै जावै उछेरै (म्हे)। कांई वारता बन जावै देखां (कीआवूं जाणज्यो भोपाजी महाराज कीआवूं देखां)। अबार कहवां भगवान का हुकमूं ल्यो (वाह वाह सा वाह वाह)।।

जासोरा से गुआल देव को बिदा हु गो ठाकरां जाय उछेरी गाय।
जो उछेरतां गायां खेवान माच गो ठाकरां हुऐ नेवरियां झणकार।
सिरै सोना की खोली ठाकरां नीकल चाली पार।
नेजो बांध्यो निरपाल खटाणू घाल दियो गाय को सींवली थाना।
गांगो अर गोरसी भादलो भड़ाणो चारूं ऊबा करै बिचार।
मेल द्यो बदशाहियां का माल।
गायां उछेर गी ठाकर देव की उछेरी से लुवार।
सिकराणी पर गुआलिया झण्डा रोपगिया।
रोपिया दुशमन राव के रे छाती ऊपर साल।
(भलां जी भलां) देव भलां

जासोरा से देव को गुआल बिदा हु गो (म्हे)। ठाकरां जाय उछेरी (गाय)। अरै उदेरतां गायां खेवान माचियो (वाह वाह)। हु गा नेवरियां (झणकार)। सिरै सोना की खोली रे ठाकरां नीकल चाली (पार)। नेजो बांध्यो निरपाल खटाणो घाल दियो गाय को सींवली (थानो)। गांगो तो गोरसी अर भादलो भड़ाणो अर पदमू पोसवाळ चारूं ऊबा करै (बिचार)। भेळ दियो बदशाही का ही (माल)। अरै गायां उछेरी ठाकर देव की (वाह वाह)। उछेर गी से (लुआर)। लुआरियां लेरै कर दिया कांई ठी सता है (म्हे)। गायां नै रावजी का अमराव ले जावै तो बच्च्या भूखा रह जावै (हां मावां का दूध चूंगिया बिनै रह जाय कीयो)। सिकराणी पर गुआल झण्डा रोपिया (वाह वाह)। दुशमन राव के छती पर (साल)। सात कोस पर ही सिकराणी (वाह वाह)। दरबार का हुकमूं नौलाख अस्सीहजार देव की गायां माळां के मांयनै उछेर गी (वाह वाह)। तो भगवान तो हुकम देतां अर गायां नै माळां में छोड़तां (म्हे)। जय बोलो श्री देवनारायण भगवान की (जय)। सिकराणी पर एक सैन बना दी (म्हे)। नंगारबंद सिरदार राख दियो बी जागां कीयो भैइ गुआलां भिड़ पड़ जाय नै (हां ई जागावूं नंगारो बजावो)। दड़ावट में सात कोस पर सुणीज जावै (वाह वाह)। तो भांगीजी देव महाराज चड़ाई कर गुआलां के सामिल आजावै (वाह वाह)। हेंर उनै जको राण शहर का सिरदारां नै सुणीज जावै (हां गायां पर अट्टैक अब करी है)। दरबार का हुकमूं गायां पांच दस पंद्रा बीस गांवां का माल जरूर भेळद्या (वाह वाह)। पांचिया पटेल बस्ती का हुई भेळा (म्हे)। बिचार (करियो है)। देवजी वाली गायां गहूं

चन्ना की साख में खाय भैइ (हां आ नै ठोकर रातो कोट दिखा द्यो)। फाटक में बाड़ां आगी (वाह वाह)। गांवां का हुई पटेल भेळा (म्हे)। गायां नै पकड़बा नै आयगा (वाह वाह)। बैरीबाज गुआल नौ गज बांसड़ो राखतो (हां लंबो)। थोथो भाटा पर के फटकियो (वाह वाह)। मन में देखियो आपणी तो पकड़्योड़ी गायां तो नी जावै (म्हे)। अर नी गुआल (आपणा पकड़्योड़ा जावै कीयो)। अरै सैन्टो है जको ही (धणी है आपणो तो)। आपां रावजी की कछेड़ी में चांलां (म्हे)। गायां की गुआलां की पुकार सुणावां (वाह वाह)। दरबार का हुकमूं पुकार सुणी जरां तो रावजी के देश में (आपां बसां)। नी जरां मीठै देश मेवाड़ में देव कन्नै (हां बठै बस ज्यां कीयो देवमहाराज के पास में)। पटेल पांचिया हुई भेळा (वाह वाह)। गोरम का भाखर से राण शहर को गेलो ले लियो (म्हे)। जाण की जाण बहवै (वाह वाह)। कीयो बहवां तो हां पण सुणाई कीयां हुई (हां जकी पहली सोचो कीयो)। कीयो कामबळां का मुण्डासा मार ल्यो अर तगारियां में तेल घाल घाल चिरोगां जूवो (हां दिन में चिरोगां जो ल्यो कीयो)। हेंर माथा पर मेलो (वाह वाह)। मतेई बूझी (हां जांवतां ही बूझ लेयी)। तो बताई थोक बनावै (म्हे)। पटेल पांचिया कांई रावजी की कछेड़ी पूगता हुवै (कीआवूं जाणज्यो कीआवूं देखां)। ए अबार कहवां भगवान का हुकमूं ले तूं (वाह वाह सा)।।

दिनै चिरागां जोली जी ए ई धणी राण का रे।
आय पुकारिया मैं तो रे पड़ीहारां की पोळ।
एक नापो बस में नी व्हियो धणी राण का।
नापोजी घालियो रे बावन पड़गणै रोळ।।
(भलां जी भलां) देव भलां

दरबार का हुकमूं में दिनै चिरागां जोली (वाह वाह)। आय पुकारिया पड़ीहारां की (पोळ)। ओ एक नापो बस में नी व्हियो धणी राण का (वाह वाह)। अरै नापलै घाल दी बावन पड़गणै में ही (रोळ अर)। बावन गढ है थारा (हां जकां में सगळा ई गायां नै चरावै कीयो)। एक नापो ही बस में कोनी होवै (वाह वाह)। ओ समचार कुण कीयो (हां बसी का लोग कीयो जी कीयो)। काळू मीर दीयोजी बिचार करियो मीर कीयो तोबा तोबा तोबा तोबा तोबा तोबा ओ ले भैइ (हां) आ मौत आयगी (हां आपणा ही मौत है आ तो)। कीयो म्हारा कीया करो (म्हे)। कांई कीयो पटेल पांचिया जी टैम में समचार रावजी नै पुकार घालै नै (हां बी समचै आपणै सागै के सागै रोळो कर देवो)। रोळा के मांयनै सुणजै कोनी मतै पाछा जाय अबार (हां ऊठ जाय कीयो काळा जकर)। पटेल समचार ओ कीयो जी टैम में काळू मीर दीयोजी रोळो कर दियो माठा (वाह वाह)। रावजी के तो काना भणकारो ही (नैइ पड़ियो)। पटेल मन में देखियो एक समचार कीयो तो और कह द्यां (हां लार को लार एक और कहवो देखां सुणीज्यै तूं)।।

ए छिन्नवै खेड़ा तो जी सुभस बस गा गेलिया रावजी रे।
बस गा आळा रावत की आसीन।
ओ काळो सिरप सिराणो झोला खावै धणी राण का।

सुता नै रावजी रे कींयां आवै नींद।।
(भलां जी भलां) देव भलां

छिन्नवै खेड़ा बगड़ावतां का देवजी सुभस बसा लिया (वाह वाह)। बस गी आळा रावत की (आसीन)। काळो सिरप सिराणा झोला खावै ओ (म्हे)। सूता नै किण बदावै (तनै नींद)। रावजी सुतो नींद में कींयां सुतो (हां सुतिया कींयां हो इयां)। मौत घेरा घाल अर मेलिया है नी (वाह वाह)। ओ समचार पटेल कीयो बी टैम में दीयोजी कालू मीर रोळो कर दियो (दोन्यो का दोन्यो सागै रोळो मचा दियो)। तो रावजी के तो (काना भणकारो पड़ियो कोनी)। पटेल मन में देखियो भैइ दोई समचार कीया एक औरूं कहवो जै दीया (हां लार को लार एक औरूं कीयो जे सुणी लेवै डोकरो तो)। पटेल बोलै कांई समचार कहवै देखां (कीआवूं जाणज्यो कीआवूं देखां)।।

ए माळागरूं आया तो जी ए ई धरमराजा देवजी रे।
गायां लियायो घणी राज कटक अचाळ।
एक नापलो बस में नी व्हियो रे धणी राण का।
नापलै घालियो रे बरसतां मेवां काळ।।
(भलां जी भलां) देव भलां

मालागरूं आयो है धरमराजा देवजी (म्हे)। गायां लियायो घणी कटक (अचाळ)। ओ एक नापो ई थारावूं बस में नी व्हियो (म्हे)। नापलै घाल दियो रावजी रे बरसतां ही मेवां (काळ)। मेह तो घणा ही बरस्यो (म्हे)। पण ओ नापलियो काळ घाल दियो (हां गायां चर जाय जकै को भगवान कांई करै कीयो)। दरबार का हुकमूं ए समचार पटेल (कीया है)। जी टैम में दरबार का हुकमूं कालू मीर दीयोजी रोळो कर दियो (वाह वाह)। रोळा में तो समचार सुणियो कोनी पटेल आलो तो एलो ही गियो (हां ईंयां को ईंयां ही गियो)। दरबार का हुकमूं पटेल बोलै औरूं (म्हे)। कांई रावजी नै औरूं समचार कहवै देखां (हां औरूं देखां कींयां कहवै कीआवूं जाणज्यो कीआवूं)। अबार कहवूं देव का हुकमूं ले तूं (वाह वाह जी वाह वाह)।।

ए महतांली गायां तो जी जो मंगरा पर चरै रे धणी राण का रे।
ए तो डावड़ा रे खातियांली खड़ खाय।
थारो देव को की कोय नी बीगड़ियो रे धणी राण का।
मैं मर गा भाई रे आंधियां का देवाळ।।
(भलां जी भलां) देव भलां

महतांली गायां तो मंगरै चरै (म्हे)। अर खातियांली खड़ (खाय)। थारो अर देव को की कोनी बीगड़ियो (म्हे)। मैं मर गा भाई आधा का (देवाळ)। आधो देर खावां मैं तो (म्हे)। थांको कांई बीगड़िया भाई दोन्यो को ही (वाह वाह)। बी टैम में औरूं ही रोळो (हां कर दिन्यो)। रोळा का मांय रावजी नै तो समचार (हां सुणीज्यो ही कोनी)। दरबार का हुकमूं फैर बोलै पटेल नै कांई समचार कहवै देखां (हां लार को लार ही औरूं ही कह दे देखां)।

ए भैंसां भैंसां तो जी रावजी अब के आवड़िया रे।
करणा क्युं बांटा को खोगाळ रे।
थारो अर देव को नी बीगड़ियो रे धणी राण का।
मैं मर गा भाई रे आधा का देवाळ।।
(भलां जी भलां) देव भलां

भैंसां ही भैंसां अब के आवड़िया (वाह वाह)। करणा कीयो रावजी बांटा को (खोगाळ)। थारो अर देव को दोन्यो को कांई बीगड़ियो (म्हे)। मैं मर गा आधा का (देवाळ)। आधो देर खावां जका नै मुशकल है भैइ (म्हानै है मुशकल तो है तो कीयो)। पटेल बोलै कांई समचार औरूं कहवै देखां (कीआवूं जाणज्यो कीआवूं देखां)।।

ए महतांली गायां तो जी जो मंगरा पर ऊबी रे धणी राण का रे।
ए तो रावजी रे खातियांली खड़ खाय।
बगड़ावतांली गायां गहूं चन्ना चरै रे धणी राण का।
ए तो रावजी रे रळक मण्डोवर जाय।।
(भलां जी भलां) देव भलां

महतांली की जाटांलीं गायां तो मंगरा पर चरै (म्हे)। खातियांली खड़ (खाय)। अरै बगड़ावतांली गायां देख गहूं चन्ना चरै (वाह वाह)। रावजी रळक मण्डोवर ताणी (जाय कीयो)। कीयो मण्डोवर गांव है नै (म्हे)। जको रावजी के सा नाई को ही कीयो (हां नाभ को हो कीयो)। मण्डोवर को नांव लियो रावजी के क्युं काना के सारै भणकारो (पड़ियो है)। रावजी सा बूझणा करी रे भैइ नीमा (म्हे)। ए पटेल पांचिया भेळा हो अर की ताणा आया (हां मण्डोवर मण्डोवर कींयां करै ओ कीयो)। ए मण्डोवर को नांव कींयां लिया बोलो (वाह वाह)। पटेल दरबार का हुकमूं कीयो भैइ कोय सैन समनदरी है जकी करै कोनी (हां एनै समझावो कीयो)। दरबार का हुकमूं राजा नीमदे कान के सारै जार चेपो करियो (वाह वाह)। कीयो श्री महाराज ए तो पांचिया पटेल देवजीआली गायां की पुकार लेर (आया है कीयो)। दरबार का हुकमूं माळागर के मांय छोड़ दी बतावै गायां नै (म्हे)। कीयो नीमा (वाह वाह)। पटेलां नै कह दियो (हां क्युं ही पेट मोटो करो कीयो)। अरे बगड़ावतां थकां ही कांकड़ सारला माल तो भिड़ा देता बै (हां पांच दस गांवां का माल भेळ देतां कीयो)। हेंर सात बरसावूं बगड़ावतां का डावड़ा पाछा गोठ खेड़ा बसाया हेंर माळावूं (हां पाछा आया है कीयो)। आवूं लगती बात हाल करां ही कोनी (हां करां ही कोनी कीयो टाबर आ की का है कीयो)। क्युं बच्च्या है हाल (वाह वाह)। कह द्यो पटेलां नै पेट मोटो कर ल्यो (म्हे)। हेंर एस एस को हांसल है जको माफ कर द्यो (आ ल्यो)। ओ ल्यो भैइ (शाबाश)। कीयो माफ की को करी कांई लेयी (हां लेसी कांई कीयो)। जती दूर में थारी साही ढुलै नै (हां जती दूर में तो गायां सगळै फैरली कीयो)। कीयो जरां भाई (म्हे)। बगड़ावतां के डावड़ा के पूण्चै पाण हू गो (हां लड़ाई ....)। ए बगड़ावतां का बैर काढी अब (हां अब समो कीयो)। सामान को धणी सदाई बतो (हां रहवै कीयो)। सामान के निंगै करो भैइ (हां आपणै दरबार में सामान

देखो कांई है अर कांई की (कमी पड़ै है कीयो)। मतै मतै निंगैवान हा जका आप आपका सामान समालिया (वाह वाह)। कीयो रातो कोट सामानू सारो अळड़ाट करै (हां अळड़ाट करै दरबार कीयो)। घोड़ा ताणी कांसा कोरड़ कोनी आयी (हां आ थोरी कम है)। आ मांगावो (वाह वाह)। कुनूवूं मांगावा की बीजा महता नै हुकम देयो (हां ए ई लियासी जार कीयो)। बीजो महतो को मतबल कांई की जाट हो चौधरी महतो जाट (महता जात को)। कीयो बीजा महता (म्हे)। भैइ घोड़ा का कोरड़ ल्यायो रे कीयो (हां कोरड़ ल्यायो)। कीयो श्री महाराज ई जागां तो थारा एरिया में तो कोरड़ लाधै कोनी (हां अठै तो है कोनी)। कीयो आंतरावूं जायो भैइ जको बेगार में गाड़ी जूपै (म्हे)। जका गांववूं तो जूपा लीज्यो (बेगार में जूपा लियो)। नी जूपै (म्हे)। जका गांव के जार पंद्रा सौ रिप्या डण्ड का कर दीज्यो (हां थारै जचै जियान डण्ड कर कर देय कीयो)। बे ताणा टाबरां नै पूगता (घरां कर देय जको टाबर खरचै अर खावै कीयो)। पटेल देखियो भैइ घर आंपालो बन जाय भैइ (वाह वाह)। दरबार का हुकमूं रावजी साय कन्नु मोहर छड़ियां का कागज तो ले लिया (म्हे)। हेंर बठवूं नीकल गो (वाह वाह)। बेगार में गाड़ा जूप ग्या तो जूपा लिया नी जर बो तो डण्ड का रिप्या करिया (हां डण्ड का बेसी ठोकिया)। दरबार का हुकमूं टाबरा नै घरां पूगतां कर दिया (वाह वाह)। ईंयां कर पाली सोजत के (हां पड़गणै)। पाणी को तासो हो (म्हे)। बी जागां कोरड़ मीली (हां बठै गायां पूगेड़ी कोय नै)। बठै देवजीवाली गायां क्युं पाणी बिनै पूगी कोनी (हां पाणी को ही तासो बता दियो नै थे)। साडा सात बीसी गाड़ा कोय तो किळड़का बोलै (म्हे)। आपां शबद में बोलां मोठां की कोरड़ (कोरड़)। समझया नी देश देश की भाषा है घोड़ां को चारो बो ही है दरबार का हुकमूं कोरड़ का भर गाड़ा (म्हे)। हेंर बिदा कर दिया (वाह वाह)। गेला में डूंगर भाखर मोकळो (म्हे)। दरबार का हुकमूं नेवाजी का गढ के सारो कर गेलो नीकलयो (वाह वाह)। देव महाराज की गायां गोरम के भाखर के हेटै चरी है (वाह वाह)। तो गाड़ा की खै है नै (वाह वाह)। असमान के घरां चड़ गी (हां ऊंची चड़ गी जी कीयो)। गुआलिया दरबार का हुकमूं छप्पनजी की तो भैरूंजी की लूरियां बोला हा (म्हे)। चौपड़ पासा (हां खेल रिया हा)। आ खै दीखी कीयो रे भैइ आ खै कींयां आयी रही है (हां अती खै कींयां चड़ी है कीयो)। तीन बातावूं खै चड़ै (किसी किसी बातवूं)। तो कह तो साहूकार की महाजन की जान बहती होवै (म्हे)। तो सुरजी महाराज धूंधळो हो जावै (हां खै चड़ जाय बेसी हुवै जरां कीयो)। हेंर के लख्खी बिणजारा की बाळद बहती होवै तो खै (हां ऊंची चड़ै कीयो)। कह रावजी का बावन गढ चड़ै (म्हे)। तो जरूर सुरजी धूंधळो (हां दीखे)। तीन बात हुई एक बातवूं जरूर है (हां जल्दी करो कीयो)। कीयो जरां निंगै करो भैइ गायां नै पकड़ नी ले जावै रावजी की बाईसी चड़ आजावै तो (वाह वाह)। दरबार का हुकमूं पदमा नै हुकम दियो जाओ पदमा (हां थै निंगै करो क्यें बात की आसमान पर (खै चड़ी है कीयो)। कीयो भैइ निंगै तो मैं जरूर (कर लेवूं)। पण म्हारा में बी जागां दोहरी बेळियां पड़ जाय जर तूं आडो कठै आवै (थै आडा आवो कोनी आवो कीयो)। कीयो आपणी सैन कर दीज्यै (म्हे)। मैं जाणै थारै कन्नै ऊबा (सैन के समचै ही थारै सागै आजा कीयो)। कांई सैन ही म्हांकै (म्हानै तो कांई ठा भोपाजी)। के एक फर ही (म्हे)। जको तीर में पोय आकाश के घरां छोड़ देतां (ऊंची छोड़ देतां)। जतै फर को जोर रहतो जरां आकाश में जाती (हां) तीर को जोर रहतो तो जितै आकाश में (चड़ जाती)। पछै मतै आ भूंवती बा (वाह वाह)। तो बा म्हानै दीख जाय जरां

में देखां की पदमा भाई में तो भिड़ पड़ गी (हां भिड़ जरूरी पड़ गी)। थारै जाणै कन्नै ही (हां ऊबां हां कीयो)। ओ ले भैइ आ सैन कर दीज्यो (वाह वाह)। एकला घोड़ा को असवार पदमो पोसवाळ गोरम का भाखर से घोड़ो हांक दियो (वाह वाह)। दरबार का हुकमूं गाड़ कन्नै पूगतो हु गो (म्हे)। आगै देखियो रे ओ तो रावजी को बीजो महतो पटेल आयग्यो (हां पटेल है)। पण घोड़ा नै फोड़ा पड़िया (वाह वाह)। आपां पटेलजी कन्नै आयगा ईयूं राम राम तो आपां करतां ही चांलां (हां राम राम करियां बिनै तो कींयां चांलां कीयो)। अरे दरबार का हुकमूं राजावां को आदमी है (म्हे)। राम राम करां तो बड़ी जुगत से (हां खाली हाथ करां ही कोनी)। देव को नांव ले अर जेब में (हाथ घालियो है)। तो पांच मोहर दोकड़ा केरियां (नीकलया)। हथेली में ले मोहरां (म्हे)। रेकळा के सारै जाय हेंर गुआल छानै से कीयो पटेलजी राम राम साय (हां राम राम साय कीयो)। मन में देखियो बूड़ो आदमी हे ऊंचो सुणै (हां बोल्यो कोनी)। पटेलजी राम राम (हां राम राम)। कोनी सुणीजो (वाह वाह)। मन में देखियो ऊंचो ही सुणै (हां औरूं ऊंचो सुणतो होलो)। कान के सारै जाय अर चेपो कर देयो (जोरवूं)। पटेलजी राम राम साय (आ हेय हां अब तो सुणज्योलो अब)। के पटेलां आंख काढी (ए है)। अरै गूजरां का छोरा (म्हे)। आज कांई राम राम करै महारावूं (हां आज राम राम थारावूं कोनी करूं कीयो)। तड़कै पूटियां मसकियां बांध अर राताकोट में बुलालूं (हां जकै दिन बठै म्हारावूं राम राम करज्यो)। तीन बारी करज्यै दिन में (वाह वाह)। आज गेला है कांई राम राम करै (हां केंवूं राम राम करै कीयो चाल कीयो आल्यो)। गुआल मन में देखियो तूं जाणै जकी बात कोनी जोरां भरियो बोल्यो (हां नशै में होतो बो पूरो)। दरबार का हुकमूं पाछो गिर बोही बात करी (म्हे)। व्हियो तो ढाल गोडी (वाह वाह)। कचूस अर भाल नै तीर छोड़ दी (हां असमाना घरां छोड़ी जी कीयो)। तीर को जोर व्हियो तो फर नै आकाश ले गो (म्हे)। तीर को जोर हट गो तो के फर है जकी (हां घूमी है)। गुआल लेरलां निंगै राखां (वाह वाह)। के पदमा में देखज्यै बा भिड़ पड़ गी बा भूवै (हां फर घूमै कीयो बेगा चड़ो कीयो)। तूंबा को गाड़ो उलरै नै (वाह वाह)। गोरम के भाखर चौदाह सौ चम्मालीस गुआल सागै उलळ गा (वाह वाह)। दरबार का हुकमूं गाड़ा के सांकड़ा (हां जापता पूगगिया है)। सींवली को नंगारची नंगारा ने बजावां लागो (वाह वाह)। सींवली को नंगारो गोठां में देवजी नै सुणीज्या (हां जण)। भांगीजी कीयो रे गुआलां भिड़ पड़ गी (म्हे)। दरबार का हुकमूं भांगीजी आपका चड़ घोड़ पर (वाह वाह)। हेंर बिदा (हां गुआलां के सामिल व्हिया है)। तो गुआल अर भांगीजी सागै पूगता हो गा (वाह वाह)। भांगीजी आतां दीखिया कीयो रे दादो भांगीजी आयगो (वाह वाह)। भांगीजी भांगीजी करियो नै (म्हे)। दरबार का हुकमूं पटेलजी बूझणा करी रे भांगीजी किस्यो है (हां किस्यो है कीयो)। कीयो देवजीवालो भाई भंगेरियो नी होवै (हां बो तो कोनी है कीयो)। कीयो सागै को (बो ई है कीयो)। कीयो जरां भैइ थानै डर कोनी म्हानै डर है (हां म्हनै डर है ओ तो कीयो)। गाड़ा तो खोल द्यो (म्हे)। हेंर बैलियां रेकळा के जूतयोड़ा है जका नै ही (हां खोल देयो)। म्हनै माच के हेटै बाड़ द्यो ऊपर घास का करपा राळ द्यो (हां ऊपर म्हारै घास घणो सारो राळ देयो (देख नी ले कीयो)। म्हारो जापतो करो (वाह वाह)। दरबार का हुकमूं पटेलजी का पूरा जापता कर दिया (वाह वाह)। तो भांगीजी आतां ही बूझणा करी रे पदमा भाई के बांतां (हां के बांतां कीयो)। कीयो नी कोय बांतां दुख तो है कोनी (म्हे)। पटेलजीवूं राम राम करबा आयो मैं (वाह वाह)। म्हारो राम

राम कोनी करियो (म्हे)। कठै है पटेलजी (कठै है कीयो)। कीयो सा अबार बी रेकळिया में बैठो हो (हां बी रेकळा में हो कीयो)। कीयो भाज गो डरतोड़ो (वाह वाह)। आप नै इस्यो काम करो (म्हे)। ए गाड़ां तो कोरड़ भरिया जका गायां नै राळो (हां गायां नै खुवावो)। हेंर नारां की काढ नाथां (गायां के सामिल रळा लियो)। हेंसियां का हेंसबाळा हा अती टैम लगाई (वाह वाह)। काट काट नारां की नाथां (म्हे)। गायां के भेळै घेरद्या (वाह वाह चरो कीयो)। चरो भैइ थै तो (वाह वाह)। कोरड़ का गाड़ा जका खाली गायां नै राळबा लाग (ग्या है)। भांगीजी कीयो टैम घणी लागो भैइ (म्हे)। बी टैम भांगीजी सुवा मण भांग को नशो करयोड़ा हा (वाह वाह)। दरबार का हुकमूं दोन्यु हाथावूं सुगण पकड़िया गाड़ा का (हां दोन्यूं)। आपसरी में लड़ावै (म्हे)। दो गाड़ा सागै खाली (हां कोरड़ का हो जावे)। दरबार का हुकमूं कर गाड़ा ने खाली (म्ळे)। गायां नै राळ दिया (वाह वाह)। गाड़ा नै एक जागां भेळा (करिया है)। दे घास चारूंमेर गाड़ा के अर कीयो भांगीजी ने कीयो बूझणा करी सुणो भैइ (हां आनै जला दियो कीयो)। होळी मंगालो (म्हे)। आ गाड़ा में लोह लकड़ है (वाह वाह)। घोड़ां के अगाड़ियां पछाड़ियां बना (हां घड़ां द्यां कीयो)। हेंसिया का हेंसबाळा हा (गुआल)। ख्यालां का खेलबाळा (म्हे)। दरबार का हुकमूं बैरीबाज गुआल बायदे अर होळी मंगाळ दी (वाह वाह)। कीयो होळी होळी (हां होळी रे होळी है)। भांगीजी कंवर बूझणा करी रे गुआलां (म्हे)। ओ पटेलालो रेकळियो पड़ियो बी में ही लोह होलो थोड़ो घणो (हां बी नै ही मांय सागै राळो कीयो)। पटेल मन में देखियो थारा बाप दाग करी भेळै ही (हां अब गिरै ही अब बेगो नीकल)। अब कांई अब कांई करां (म्हे)। रेकळा ई नै राळी नै जर दाग तो होय मतेई (हां सागै बळां कीयो)। अब और नै कोय नै जाणै कोनी (म्हे)। कीयो पदमाजी भाई राम राम हां पदमाजी भाई राम राम (वाह वाह)। कीयो म्हारा हाथ में राम राम अब तो कोनी (हां अब म्हारै बस को रोग कोनी कीयो)। दादो भांगीजी करी नै (जियां ही चौधरियां हुई कीयो)। भांगीजी ओरियो पटेल तो रेकळा के माच के नीचै (वाह वाह)। भांगीजी हुई आगा (म्हे)। खोल घोड़ा को रस्सो (वाह वाह)। पटेल नै बांध्यो घोड़ा के आनै बांध्यो (वाह वाह)। आजावो सिरदारां कीयो (आ जावो कीयो)। रेकळिया नै दरबार का हुकमूं ठरड़ बी के मांयनै होळी में राळ दियो (म्हे)। भांगीजी कंवर दरबार का हुकमूं देव के दुलीचै पूगता (पाछा व्हिया जी कीयो)। लीला के पायगा के मायंनै ले जार चौधरी नै बांध्यो (बीजै महतै नै ले जार घोड़ै के पगां में बांध्यो)। दूधां को धायोड़ो टार को लीला के (म्हे)। पटेल के टापां की ठोकी (सारी रात ठोकी)। पटेलजी त्राहि (घाली है)। तो गुआलां की जीत होतां (म्हे)। पटेलजी नै घोड़ा हां पायगा बांधता (बांधता)। जय बोलो भैइ श्री देवनारायण भगवान की (जय बोलो छोटा अर मोटा स)। दरबार का हुकमूं बीजा महता नै ले जार बांध्यो नै (म्हे)। लीला के पायगा में (वाह वाह)। दरबार का हुकमूं रात्यूं त्राहि घाली (म्हे)। परभात को टैम व्हियो देव को दुलीचो लाग्यो (हां लाग्यो)। देव महाराज दरबार का हुकमूं भाट बैइ को आयो (म्हे)। हेंर आसका दीनी (वाह वाह)। आद राजा आद का जुगाज जुगाज का काछब काछब का रणधोळ रणधोळ का कजली कजली का हरीरामजी (हरीरामजी)। हरीरामजी का बाघ व्हिया बाघ का भोज व्हिया (म्हे)। भोज के देव (व्हिया जी कीयो)। अगणकुण्ड का ऊपनिया अर कुली बड़ा (चुहाण)। अरै पगतळी पदम बिराजै खुंवा थांकै खेम मुख में नागर (बेल)। लीला की हेम से (म्हे)। पताल में हेम जळ गाजियो (गाज ग्यो)। डूंगर पर व्हिया ब्यहवार (ब्यवहार)। देव को औतार

व्हियो जकै दिन धरती बीचै आबा बीचै बन गो (उजास)। भोज का उदेळ पड़ता का झेळ (झेळ)। कीयो आवो भाटजी (आवो कीयो)। पण रात आपकी नगरी में दुखी कुण हो (हां सारी रात त्राहि घालो कीयो)। कीयो श्री महाराज कोय भाई की आंखियां दूखती होली (हां जको त्राहि घालतो होलो)। कीयो रे भाट म्हारी नगरी में आंखियां दूखै औरूं (हां म्हारी नगरी में आंखियां कोय के (नैइ दूख सकै कीयो)। सावल के बात की (हां सूल बता)। कीयो श्री महाराज काल के दिन भांगीजी गुआलां के सामिल ग्या (म्हे)। कांकड़ में रावजीआला बीजा महतोजी निंगै आयगो (वाह वाह)। बी नै पकड़ घोड़ा की पायगा में बांध्यो (हां लीलागर की पायगा में ल्यार बांध दियो)। थांकाळो लीलागर दूधां को धायोड़ो टार हो (म्हे)। पटेलजी के रात्यूं टापां बाही (वाह वाह)। पटेल त्रय (घालो)। देव महाराज बूझणा (करी)। अरै बैइ का भाट (म्हे)। बाड़ में मूतियावूं बैर कोनी नीकलै (वाह वाह)। बैर तो है रावजी के अर आपणै है (हां करसावूं बैर थोड़ो ही है कीयो)। पटेल नै खुलावो बापड़ा नै (वाह वाह)। पटेल सुणज्यो मन में देखियो रे टाबरियो छोटोसो गादी बैठो पण अकल बहुत है (हां है तो स्याणो कीयो)। बेड़ी कठ जायी आपणी (म्हे)। तो पटेल नै खुलाय हेंर देव के दुलीचा ल्यार छोड़ दियो (वाह वाह)। देव महाराज नाई नै बुलायो (म्हे)। सुंवार खिजमत कराई (वाह वाह)। तातो पाणी कर पटेलजी नै नुहायो (हां नुहा दिया)। धज्जा तो धोवती नुई दीनी (वाह वाह)। हेंर पचरंग पाग दीनी (म्हे)। काना का जगमोती देदिया (वाह वाह)। पांच पच्चीस मोहर निजरानै पटेल की कर दी (हां पच्चीस मोहरां और दीनी)। पटेलजी पांच दिन रहवो तो घर थांको है (हां दस दिन रहवो तो घर है थांको)। गुआलिया काल थानै की दोहरो राखिया तो कोय ब्याकानी मत जाज्यो म्हार कानै देखिज्यो (हां म्हार कानै देखिज्यो)। पटेल मन में देखियो रे ओ टाबरियो तो बहुत अकलवान है सोरो राखियो तनै (वाह वाह)। पटेलजी कीयो भोजन ओजन (हां करो करसियों कांई कीयो)। कीयो काल का ही भूखा ही हां करियो कठवूं (हां भोजन तो करां दरबार कीयो)। साडूमाता नै ठा व्हियो दासी नै खिनायी जाओ दासी पटेलजी नै बुला ल्यो (हां रसोवड़ा में बुला लेवो जको जीम लेवे)। दासियां आर खड़ी हो गी (म्हे)। दासियां कींयां आयी (कींयां आयो कीयो)। कीयो पटेलजी नै म्हांका बाईजी रावळै (हां जीमनै के वास्तै बुलावै कीयो)। ओ लियो सा पटेलजी थांकै जीमन को नीवतो आयग्यो (हां जावो कीयो)। हां सा जावां (म्हे)। साडूमाता देखियो ई आदमी को आप नै रोजीना किस्यो (हां घरां आनै को काम क्यां नै पड़ै कीयो)। चोखी तो गायां की दूध की खीर बनाई (म्हे)। खाण्ड घाली (हां ऊपर से खाण्ड अर घी दोन्यु घालिया)। गहूंवां का फैंफड़ा बना लिया (वाह वाह)। हेंर चोखी तरह साग फैंफड़ा कर पटेलजी के थाळ तियारी कर दी (म्हे)। बाजोट पर थाळ नै रख दियो (हां पुरस रख दियो)। पटेलजी जाण आज की टैम ही नै ऊनाळो हो (म्हे)। ऊनाळो साख बोहळा नी (हां ऊनाळो)। तो गरमी का दिन हा जको बीजनो ले अर साडूमाता ऊठ खड़ी हो गी (हां हुवा घालबा नै पटेलजी नै)। दरबार का हुकमूं पच्चीस मोहर थाळ के हेटै मेल दी (वाह वाह)। ओ कद आया आपां ने घरां (हां कद आसीला ई नै मोहरां तो द्यो घणी)। पटेलजी कांई करियो के थाळ तक देखियो मन में देखियो रे ए दोन्यु मां बेटो थारावूं डर गा (हां) देवजी डर ग्यो (हां देवजी डर गो तो आ साडूमात आ ही डरै आपांवूं)। आ डरती इतो काम करियो नी करै करती (हां करती ही कोनी कीयो)। अब साडूमाता

बोलै (म्हे)। कांई पटेलजी नै समचार कहवै देखां (कीआवूं जाणज्यो देखां कीआवूं)। अबार कह द्यूं भैइ देव का हुकमूं ले तूं (वाह वाह सा)।।

ओछी नाड़ी जी ए ई पटेलजी उदलै औवूं रे।
समंदर को पटेलजी कदै नी आवै छे।
बै आज जंगल का गुआलिया।
किनी काळ कह दियो तो पटेलजी रे बूरो मती मानो थै व्है।।
(भलां जी भलां) देव भलां

ओछी नाड़ी पटेलजी ऊदलै (वाह वाह)। समंदर को नी आवै कदै (छे)। बै हा जंगल का गुआलिया (म्हे)। काळकी कह दियो तो पटेलजी बूरो मत मानो (थे)। बूरो मत मानज्यो (हां बूरो मत मानीज्यो टाबरां को कीयोड़ो)। म्हार कानै अर म्हाना देव कानै (देखिज्या)। पटेलजी मन में देखियो डर गी नै (हां डरै आतो)। थोड़ीसी धमकी दे देय (म्हे)। पच्चीस तो मोहर मेलियोड़ी है पच्चीस और ल्यायी आ (हां अबार औरूं मेल देय)। तो पटेल बोलै कांई साडू नै समचार कहवै देखां (कीआवूं जाणज्यो कीआवूं देखां)। अबार कहवां सा भगवान का हुकमूं ले तूं (वाह वाह सा)।।

ए ताणा गुआलिया तो जी म्हारा में हाजरी घणी करी साडू सुलखना रे।
म्हारावूं माजी ये मोटी हो गी धीज।
गायां जायली तड़कै मंगरा के ऊपरे।
आंतरा तड़कै ये आबा द्यूं नै एक।।
(भलां जी भलां) देव भलां

दरबार का हुकमूं म्हारा में ताणा गुआलिया काल हाजरी घणी करी (वाह वाह)। म्हारावूं मोटी माण्डी (धीज)। गायां जाय तड़कै म्हाना मंगरा पर ऊपरै (म्हे)। तड़कै आपां द्यूं नै (हां स्याम का एक)। गायां को दूध खावै तो आज ही खा लेयी (तड़कै कोनी है कीयो)। तड़कै उडीकेली गायां ऊबी (वाह वाह)। दरबार का हुकमूं भांगीजी कंवर ने औरूं सुणीज गो (हा) दुलीचा में (दुलीचा में ओ समचार सुणीज्यो)। कीयो रे भाट माजीआलै रसोड़े म्हांकाली गायां नै कुण टोळबा लागो (हां कुण ले जाय रसोड़े मूं वूं कीयो)। पटेलजी बी जागावूं भांगीजी कंवर भाज छुट्यो (वाह वाह)। भांगीजी का पग बोल्या माजी मन में देखियो रे भंगेरियो आवै (हां चौधरी नै मार ही लाय नै बीजी महता नै)। तो आंतो दीखियो तो साडूमाता बरज्यो तो घणो ही भांगीजी के (म्हे)। पण लुगाइयां को बांध्योड़ो भांगीजी किं को रहवै (हां कींयां रहवां हा)। दरबार का हुकमूं ठोकर बाही (म्हे)। जीकी पटेल के लागी कोनी बाजोट के लागी (वाह वाह)। तीन गुळेछ खाय गो बठै (म्हे)। घणा दिन व्हिया तनै म्हांकाली गायां घेरता नै (हां बोहळा दिन व्हिया ठहर कीयो)। बै मोहरां ही जकी बिखर गी (म्हे)। थाळ हो जको ढुल गो (वाह वाह)। पड़तां पटेल को बांवल्यो पकड़ भांगीजी तो आपको बिदा (हां ठरड़ अर बीर लियाया जी कीयो)। माजी सा दीखियो ओ लियो (आ लेयो)। रात की गसत की भैरूंजी की चोखी ही (म्हे)। सारी रात चारूंमेर फिरता बस्ती (चौफैर)। दरबार का हुकमूं भैरूंजी के ले जार हवालै कर दियो

(हां आ ल्यो कीयो)। ओ ल्यो भैरवानाथ रात रात नै थांकै हवालै है ओ (हां छोड़ मत देयज्यो ईनै)। ओ चारूंमेर बांठका में लिया फिरिया भैरूंजी (वाह वाह)। कठै तो धज्जा धोवती रह गी (म्हे)। कठै ही पचरंग (पाग रह गी)। काना का जगमोती कांटां में उळझ उळझ कठै ही फाट गा (हां टूटर पड़ ग्या जी कीयो)। परभात को टैम व्हिया (म्हे)। देव को दुलीचो जड़ियो अर भैरवानाथ ले जार देव का मुण्डा के खड़ो (हां बीजा महता नै कर दिन्या)। देव महाराज बूझणा करी भैरवानाथ (म्हे)। ई पटेल नै थानै कुण सोपियो (हां थानै कुण सोपियो कीयो)। कीयो कंवर भांगीजी (सोपिया म्हानै तो)। भांगीजी कीयो खुलायो कुण हो (म्हे)। कीयो देव महाराज (हां देव महाराज खुलायो)। कीयो भैइ देव का खुलायोड़ा पाछा कोनी बन्धै रे पटेल नै तूं बांध (हां अब औरूं बांधूं पाछो कीयो)। पण भगवान को खोलियोड़ो है बांधूं कोनी (हां बांधूं कोनी के मुलायजो राखूं)। देव महाराज बूझणा करी भैरवानाथ (म्हे)। ई नै भंगेरियो छोड़ै कोनी अठै (वाह वाह)। पटेल नै तो ईका धणी कन्नै पूगाय द्यो भैइ (हां राण शहर पूगतो कर देवो)। कीयो पटेलजी (म्हे)। पाछा जावो कांई (हां के अठै ही रहसियो)। कीयो नी श्री महाराज जाणू तो पड़ी (वाह वाह)। टाबरां नै समालूं (हां टाबरां नै समालूं कीयो)। तो दरबार हुकमूं भैरवानाथ बूझणा (करतां)। कीयो पटेलजी देव का घर की मोहताज लियो कांई (हां ले जाज्यो जांतां)। हां सा लेवूं (लेवूं कीयो)। तीन तिलोकी को नाथ के मुखारबिन्द फाड़ियो (म्हे)। पटेल देख (मुण्डै में कांई कांई है जकी रचना देख (थारा धणी नै देखै जिसी की जिसी बता देय कीयो)। तो दरबार का मुखारबिन्द में निंगै करी (म्हे)। तीन तिलोकी सारी दीखी (वाह वाह)। मन में देखियो रे ताणो धणी कींयां जीती ई नै (हां) ई नै कींयां जीती तीन तिलोकी मुण्डै में लियां (बैठियो है कीयो)। कोनी जीतै (वाह वाह)। भगवान तीन तिलोकी दिखाळतां मुखारबिन्द में (म्हे)। हेंर पटेलजी कामबळो मोहताज ताणै बिछातां (बिछांवतां)। जय बोलो भैइ श्री देवनारायण भगवान (की जय बोलो छोटा अर मोटा स)। तो दरबार का हुकमूं पटेलजी मन में देखियो (म्हे)। देवातण ख्याल है की मोहताज दे देय तो अमर तक निवड़ै कोनी (वाह वाह)। कामबळो बिछा ल्यो (म्हे)। गोरोजी महाराज मणेक धूळो घाल बांध चामट फोट माथो पर मेल दी (हां लेयो आ लेयो कीयो महताजी ए ले जाओ)। पटेलजी राजा मानियो आदमी बोज कोलाय के काम पड़योड़ो लायो कोनी के हो (हां कदै पड़ियोड़ो कोनी हो)। आवड़ी खाण्ड चाल्यो दे हेटी पोट नै पटकी (हां पटक दीनी)। गोरोजी महाराज मन में देखियो धापियो कोनी (हां मोहताजूं धापियो कोनी थोड़ी और बांधो)। खोल गांठ मण तो ही दो मण (कर दीनी)। माथा पर मेल दी (वाह वाह)। पटेलजी नै बोज लाग्यो दे हेटी पटक दी कीयो कोनी धापियो (म्हे)। तो दरबार का हुकमूं दो मण तो ही (वाह वाह)। चार मण दूणी कर दी (चार मण कर दीनी जी कीयो)। पटेल मन में देखियो अब के थारी मारांड नै हेटी पटकी नै (हां जा सीधी आठ मण हुई कीयो (ई के नीचै ही दबर मरेलो)। दोहरी सोरी ई नै पार करणो अच्छी है (हां कींयां ही आगी करां जण ही ठीक रहवे)। आवड़ी खाण्ड पटेलजी चाल्यो पसीनो होय अर जूतियां भरीज गी पसीना से (हां पग रोपगिया)। हेंर भैरवानाथ देखियो आपां देवातण ख्याल हां मिनखा जूण मरजाय नी (हां मर जायलो)। तो बुरजां ही (म्हे)। पोट के दोन्यां का नै बुरज का सहारा ले लिया (हां चालो कीयो पटेलजी अब)। उळा उळा चालो (वाह वाह)। तो राण शहर के गोरवा आतां पटेलजी नै पूगतो कर दियो भैरवानाथ (वाह वाह)। बुरज का सहारा से (म्हे)। दरवाजा के मांयनै बड़बा लाग्यो नै (म्हे)।

बी टैम में कीयो पटेल के की सैनाण तो कर दियां (हां सैनाण तो करां ईंयां कींयां ठा पड़ी कीयो)। दे बुरज को सहारो (म्हे)। गोरोजी महाराज ऊपरलो होट काट लियो (हां चौधरी को ऊपरो होट काट लियो)। कालू मीर दीयोजी ऊंचा बैठां निंगै करिया राखां (म्हे)। मीर बूझणा (करी है)। अरै दीया (वाह वाह)। देव का घर से पटेल आ रियो है (हां हेंसतो आवै ई नै कांई मोहताज जोरां ही (दी है भगवान)। बड़ी मिल गी मोहताज हेंसतो राजी हु गो ओ तो (म्हे)। राजी की को हो दान्त पूरा ही मतै ही दीखै पछै होट कट गो जरां पटेलजी कांई करियो सिरदार आपांणी नांव बिराजमान हुआ जकै के ले जा आर पोट नै बीचै राळ दियो (हां खेटकै राळी जी कीयो)। राळ पोट नै खोल गांठ (म्हे)। के धूल नै उछाळबा लाग्यो (चारुंमेर उछाळबा लाग्यो)। आगोळिया पाछोलिया पाछो होर रेत नै उछाळबा लाग्यो की देव का घर की गुलाल है (हां मोकळी लियो कीयो)। बांट बांट लीज्यो (म्हे)। कोय के भाई हाथ नी आवै तो फोड़ा तो म्हारा में पड़ी (जार और लावूंला कीयो)। दूजा जावूंला ल्यावूंला (वाह वाह)। बांटो भैइ (म्हे)। गुलाल है आ मीर कांई करियो की ठोकर बाही (म्हे)। धूल में सिरदारां कपड़ा करै कीयो (हां दीखै कोनी तनै कीयो)। तीन गुळेछै खाय गो पटेल (वाह वाह)। कीयो जरां ले भैइ रावजी को तो आजवूं बास छोड़यां (म्हे)। देव के मीठै देश मेवाड़ में जां (बस जां कीयो)। म्हारी साडी सात बीसी घर है (म्हे)। अबार जूपा द्यूं गाड़ा (हां स का स म्हारै कीयै में चालै कीयो)। रावजी साय कीयो नीमा (म्हे)। पटेलजी नै भजणियो कींयां (हां पाछो बुलावो कीयो)। टोडा का सोलंकी नै हुकम करियो जावो जुवाईंजी थै बुलार ल्यायो (हां पाछो ल्यायो चौधरी नै)। सोलंकी जार हेलो मारियो (म्हे)। अजी पटेलजी पटेलजी थानै रावजी सा याद कर रिया (हां आप जाओ कुनै हो कीयो)। कीयो ले भैइ सोलंकीयां का डावड़ा जातो तो कोनी (म्हे)। पण रावजी को है जुवाईं आयगो (हां थारै सागै पाछो चालूं)। म्हारो ही जुवाईं है पछै रावजी को है जांर (वाह वाह)। पाछो चालणो पड़ी भैइ (म्हे)। पटेल नै ले जार बैठाण दियो (म्हे)। रावजी सा बूझणा (करी है)। पटेलजी भाजो कींयां (हां ईंयां भागो कींयां कीयो)। देव महाराज तनै दोहरो राखियो सोरो राखियो के जकी बांतां कह (हां सूल माण्ड अर कह कीयो)। कीयो तूं कांई करै (तूं कांई करी कीयो)। तूं कह जियान ही (हां कर देवूं)। पटेल बोलै अर कांई रावजी नै समचार कहवै देखां (कीआवूं जाणज्यो कीआवूं देखां)। अबार कहवां देव का हुकमूं देखां (वाह वाह जी)।।

कालू मीर का जी जो भाला तुड़ा नाक रे धणी राण का रे।
नका दे बैरी के रे खाना मांयनै खाख।
दे तूंबा देश के बाहरें काढ दे धणी राण का।
ई मीर के रावजी रे रगड़ूं मुण्डा के राख।।
(भलां जी भलां) देव भलां

मीर का तो भाला तोड़ नाक (वाह वाह)। नका दे दुशमन के खाना मांयनै (खाख)। दे तूंबा देश के बाहरें काढ (म्हे)। मीर के रगड़ मुण्डा के (राख)। म्हारो कहनो करै नै (जणा ए काम पहली मीर में करो कीयो)। दरबार का हुकमूं मीर नै रीस आयी जको और ठोकर की दे पाड़ी (वाह वाह)। पटेलजी भाज बिदा हु गो ओ जावूं साय कीयो (कोनी बसूं थांकै गाम में ही)। दिया नै कीयो दियो (म्हे)।

पटेलजी नै कींयां खिनावो रिसार रिसार (पाछा ल्यावो कीयो)। पाछा ल्या (वाह वाह)। दीयोजी बोल्यो पटेलजी पटेलजी रावजी सा याद करिया थानै (हां पाछो आयो भागो मतना इयां)। कीयो दीया भैइ जातो कोनी तूं आयगो चालूं (हां चाल जावूं कीयो)। दीयोजी ले जार जाजम पर बैठाण दी (वाह वाह)। रावजी साय कीयो अरै पटेलजी भाजो मत (हां सूल बतावो कीयो)। थानै देवजी सोरा राखिया के दोरा राखिया जकी बांतां को (वाह वाह)। कीयो तूं कांई करै (म्हे)। कीयो तूं के जियान कर द्यूं (तूं के जियान करूं कीयो)। पटेलजी बोलै अर कांई समचार कहवै देखां (कीआवूं जाणज्यो कीआवूं देखो)।।

ए नीमा नै चूड़ा पहरावो जी ए गैंवर दान्त का रे।
करां दे रावजी रे मही बून्दी का बेस।
माथो चोटी गूंथ सीख दे देय रे धणी राण का।
दे द्यै भाई रे नर नापा की पेश।।
(भलां जी भलां) देव भलां

दरबार का हुकमूं पटेल समचार (कीयो है)। ताणा भाई नै चूड़ो पहरा दे गैंवर दान्त को (वाह वाह)। ई नीमदे के कर दे मही बून्दी को (बेस)। माथो चोटी गूंथ (म्हे)। सीख दे देय नर नापा जी की (पेश)। देवजीआलो गुआलियो है नी नापलियो (म्हे)। बी की लुगाई बनार खिनाय ई नै (वाह वाह)। म्हारो कीयो करै तो जरां अता थोक ई थाना भाई में कर (पहली कर कीयो)। नीमदे नै औरूं रीस आयगी (वाह वाह)। ठोकर बाही तीन गुळेछ खाय गो पटेल (वाह वाह)। ए जावां सा देव के बास बसां मैं तो (बसां ही कोनी अठै)। कीयो दीया पटेलजी नै सारो दिन भजाणो मती (हां ईंयां भगाणो मतना कीयो)। पाछो ल्यार पटेलजी नै जाजम पर (बैठाणो)। भाज्या सिरदार कीयो रावजी याद करै (वाह वाह)। ले भैइ चालतो तो कोनी पण गांव का पटेल पांचिया बोलै जर जावां (हां जां रहसियां ई कठै नैइ कीयो तो)। पाछो जाजम पर जार बैठ गो (वाह वाह)। रावजी कीयो भाजो कींयां (हां सूल बात करो नै कीयो)। कीयो तूं कांई करै (म्हे)। कीयो तूं कह जका थोक कर द्यूं (हां जका ही बनावूं कीयो)। तो कांई पटेल बोलै (म्हे)। कांई रावजी नै औरूं समचार कहवै देखां (हां कीआवूं जाणज्यो देखां कीआवूं)।।

ए तूं मत बांधै नै जी रावजी माथा पर पगड़ियां रे।
क्युं राखै हाथां में रे खूंटियावाला सेल।
पहलकाली राणी ले गारा बेटा बाघ का।
अबकाळी राणी जावै रे किस्यां बड़ां की गैल।।
(भलां जी भलां) देव भलां

दरबार का हुकमूं तूं मत बांधै माथा पर पागड़ी (वाह वाह)। तूं राखै हाथां में खूंटियावाला (सेल)। अरै पहलकाली राणी ले गा बेटा बाघ का (म्हे)। अबकाली राणी ले जाय किसी बड़ां की (गैल कह नै भैइ)। अब के राणीजी नै कुण के भेजी ताणी ने (हां जकी बताय)। रावजी कीयो अंवळो संवळो

बोलो (म्हे)। पटेलजी थूक मूठियां अर भाज छूटिया (वाह वाह)। दरबार का हुकमूं (म्हे)। सिरदारां बगड़ावतां के डावड़ा के पूण्चै पाण घणो है (वाह वाह)। दीयोजी आंतरो बैठो हो (म्हे)। रावजी बोलै कांई दीया नै समचार कहवै देखां (कीआवूं जाणज्यो कीआवूं देखां)।।

केर कट गा जी दीया भाई।
कट ग्या रे रात्यूं कटक बिया रे।
रूशण की बेलिया रे दीयाजी कोय ने।
राव बुलावै भाई रे आगो आ दीया रे।।
(भलां जी भलां) देव भलां

केर कट गा कुण्डल व्हिया (म्हे)। रात्यूं कटक (बिय)। रूशण की बेलिया कोनी आज (म्हे)। राव बुलावो आगो आ भाई (दिया रूशण मत बैठना कीयो)। हेंर देवजीआला गुआल देखलै खेतां को नाश कर दियो (वाह वाह)। गहूं चिन्ना की ऊनाळो साख खुवा दी बेटी का बाप (म्हे)। मीर नै बतलावै देखां (कीआवूं जाणज्यो कीआवूं देखां)। अबार कहवां देव का हुकमूं।।

ए आखा खावै जी मीरजी तूं सांवता रे।
खा जावै तूं भैंसां का अधवाड़ा रे।
गाय अर गुआल में बीड़ो झेळ ले काळू मीरजी।
नीतर छोड़ दे म्हारी बांकी गढ सरवाड़।।
(भलां जी भलां) देव भलां

दरबार का हुकमूं आखा खावै मीरजी सांवता (वाह वाह)। खा जावै तूं भैंसां का (अधवाड़ा)। अब गाय गुआलां बीड़ो झेळ (म्हे)। नी छोड़ दे म्हारी बांकी गढ (सरवाड़ा)। सरवाड़ को पट्टो जब्त है (आजूं कीयो)। मीर कीयो तोबा तोबा तोबा तोबा तोबा सरवाड़ को पट्टो जब्त व्हियावूं आपां कांई खां (हां आप नै कांई हासल पैदा होसी कीयो)। दरबार का हुकमूं की दीया सांठी समावो (वाह वाह)। हेंर गाय नै गुआल नै पकड़ ल्यावां तड़कै चांलां (हां तड़कै चांलां कीयो)। पट्टो जब्त व्हिया पार पड़ै कोनी (म्हे)।।

आवर सावर तो जी दीया भाई रे दोन्यूं भोगवै औवूं रे।
भोगवै पारा से गुड़ गांव ई व्हे।
गाय अर गुआलां पर बीड़ो झेळ ले दीयाजी जोधका।
नीतर छोड़ दे रे गढा समसा गांव।।
(भलां जी भलां) देव भलां

दरबार का हुकमूं आवर सावर दोन्यु भोगै (म्हे)। दीयो भोगवै पारा से गुड़ (गांव)। गाय अर गुआलां पर अब के बीड़ो झेळ (म्हे)। छोड़ दे म्हारा नी तो गढा समसा (गांव)। गढां समसा गांव दे मेलिया तनै (हां जकी को पट्टो आजवूं दीयाजी थारो ही जब्त है कीयो)। आवर ही भोगै सावर ही भोगै (म्हे)।

पट्ट जब्त है (वाह वाह)। मीर कीयो कांई सला दीया (हां अब देख कीयो मजा)। मीर बोलै (वाह वाह)। कांई समचार कहवै देखां (कीआवूं जाणज्यो देखां कीआवूं)।।

ए कांकड़ में जाबा द्यो जी जो धणी राण का रे।
बाजू मैं तो जी मीरां में मीर सुवायो रे।
गाय अर गुआल नै पकड़ ल्यावां राताकोट में।
जरां जाणज्यै ये रे मीर मल्लां को जायो रे।।
(भलां जी भलां) देव भलां

दरबार का हुकमूं कांकड़ में जावूं मैं (म्हे)। बाजू मीरां में मीर (सुवायो)। गाय अर गुआल नै तड़कै ल्यावां पकड़ राताकोट में (वाह वाह)। जरां जाणज्यै रे रावजी मीर मल्लां को (जायो)। गाय नै गुआल नै तड़कै ल्यावूंला ओ ले (आ ल्यो)। बाह वाह रे मीर मीर मीर थारो भरोसो ही पड़ै अब (हां ए तो थारा भरोसा ही हां कीयो)। पांच पांच से घोड़ो अर पांच पांच से अमराव (म्हे)। दरबार का हुकमूं दोन्यु राव लेय (वाह वाह)। हेंर गाय नै अर गुआल नै पकड़बा नीकल गा (वाह वाह)। उनै भगवान की गायां ही जकी गुदलिया आती (म्हे)। दरबार का हुकमूं ए गुदलिया तलाब पर जाय (वाह वाह)। ए देखियो गायां पाणी पीबा आयी नी अठै (अटवूं ही पकड़ लियो कीयो)। भेळी की भेळी आपणै हाथ लाग जायी (वाह वाह)। रजपूतां का बेटा जका जा तंबूड़ा (ताण दिन्या)। भांलां के अणी कड़ाबा लागा तरवारियां के (बाड़ दिराबा लाग्या कीयो)। रसोई पाणी की जुगत (हां होबा लागी)। तो ए दरबार का हुकमूं तंबू ताणता (म्हे)। हेंर गाय गुआल नै पकड़ सज जाबा ताण (सजातां)। जय बोलो भाई श्री देवनारायण भगवान की (जय)। बोलो छोटा अर मोटा (स)। तो दरबार का हुकमूं देव महाराज की गायां पहल पोत गुदलिया डूकती (वाह वाह)। तो सिरायत गुआल हो नै जको तो दरबार का हुकमूं भाखर पर रियोड़ो हो (म्हे)। हेंर आगली मोरी में गुआल दरबार का हुकमूं का नै जका गायां के लारै पूग (गिया)। दरबार का हुकमूं दीयोजी बोलै (म्हे)। पाल पर आवै अर कांई गुआल नै बतलावै देखां (कीआवूं जाणज्यो कीआवूं देखां)।।

बागां ही दीखिया जी गुआल भाई रे भैरूं छींट का रे।
दीखिया थै तो रे सारीसां गुआल।
दीयोजी करै था नै बूझणा।
कठै रह गो थारो रे जासावत निरपाल।।
(भलां जी भलां) देव भलां

बगां दीखिया गुआल भाई भैरूं छींट का (वाह वाह)। अरै दीखिया म्हनै सब सारीसां (गुआल)। दीयोजी करै थानै बूझणा (म्हे)। कठै रह गो बड जासावत (निरपाल)। जासा को निरपाल बोलै नै (म्हे)। बो किस्यो है रे भैइ था में (बो किस्यो है था में)। सिरायत गुआल कुण है (वाह वाह)। देव को गुआल बोलै (म्हे)। कांई दरबार का हुकमूं दीयो नै बतलावै देखां (कीआवूं जाणज्यो देखां कीआवूं)। अबार कहवूं देव का हुकमूं देखां (वाह वाह सा)।।

गुआल रह गो जी ए ई दड़ावट की कोटड़ियां रे।
रह गो भाई पाखर में भरपूर।
तूं रोळो दंगो करै तो म्हारावूं करज्यै माझी जोधका।
गुआलियो आया रे भागियाली भख भूर।।
(भलां जी भलां) देव भलां

गुआल तो रह गा दीया दड़ावट की कोटड़ियां (म्हे)। अरै रह गो पाखर में (भरपूर)। तूं रोळो दंगो करै तो म्हारावूं कर ले (म्हे)। गुआल आया भागेली भख (भूर भागतां नै मारग कोनी लाधेलो कीयो)। बिरामण भूराला पीसा ले अर (हां भागै है के)। जियान को जियान तनै मारग (हां लाधेलो नी भागतै नै)। मीर बूझणा (करी है)। यार दीया जोधका निंगै कर देख क्या बात करी गुआल स्याळ (म्हे)। दरबार का हुकमूं गुआल स्याळ देख चाबी चाबी बात कर गो (म्हे)। दे टाट में लाग को जाग ही (रह जाय)। कीयो रे मीर ईंयां कींयां करै (वाह वाह)। गुआल देवको बोलै (वाह वाह)। कांई समचार दिया के अर गुआल के बांतां होवै देखां (कीआवूं जाणज्यो देखां कीआवूं)। अबार कहवां भगवान का हुकमूं ले तूं।।

ए स्याम का खायायो जी जो गुआल भाई खाटी राबड़ियां औवूं रे।
परभातै पियायो रे ठण्डी सेरी छाछ।
गायां का मुहरां छोड़ एकानै हो जा रे गुआल गाय का।
गायां से गुआलिया रे हो जा एकन पास।।
(भलां जी भलां) देव भलां

कीयो सांजा रा खायायो गुआल खाटी राबड़ी (म्हे)। परभातै पियायो दीखै ठण्डी सेरी (छाछ)। गायां का मुंहरां दौड़ एकान हो जा (म्हे)। गुआल हो जा गायां से एकानै (पास)। ताणी गायां है नै (म्हे)। ए म्हांकी लियोड़ी ही समझ ले तूं (वाह वाह लियोड़ी ऊबी है कीयो)। दरबार का हुकमूं ओ समचार कुण कीयो के दीयोजी कीयो है (वाह वाह)। गुआल देव को बोलै (म्हे)। कांई समचार दीया नै पाछो कहवै देखां (कीआवूं जाणीज्यो देखां)।।

ए स्याम का पियायो जी दीया भाई रे सुरै का दूदड़ा रे।
परभातै भाई रे दही खायो मन चाख।
गायां का मुंहरां जरां छोड़ूं रे माझी जोधका।
थारै जियान का अमराव रे खेत पड़ेला लाख।
(भलां जी भलां) देव भलां

स्याम का तो दीया सुरेमाता का दूध पिया मैं (म्हे)। परभातै दही खायो मन (चाख अर)। के गायां का मुंहरां जरां छोड़ूं (म्हे)। थारै जियान का अमराव खेत पड़ेला (लाख)। एक हाथूं (लाख थारै जियान का मार द्यूं जणा जाणीज्यै गायां का (मुंहरो गुआल छोड़ द्यो)। अब के छोड़ियो है (वाह वाह)। ईंयां सहजां ही दरबार का हुकमूं गायां का मुंहरां छुड़ावै कोय (हां छोड़ां है कांई कीयो)। मीर बोल्यो

देखां यार दीया जोधका गुआल क्या बात कर गो (हां) दे टाट में जाग को जाग रहवै (रह जाय कीयो)। दीयोजी बोलै (म्हे)। कांई समचार गुआल नै कहवै देखां (कीआवूं जाणज्यो देखां कीआवूं)।।

ए म्हारै जियान का तो जी जो गुआलिया रे थोड़ा मारिया रे।
डिगै बड़ा बड़ा रे भोपालां का घात।
छतरपती नेजाधारी नै दाकल मारल्यां।
कोनी घाला रे हिरण गुआल स्याळ नै हाथ।।
(भलां जी भलां) देव भलां

दरबार का हुकमूं दीयोजी बूझणा (करी है)। कीयो गुआल स्याळ नै हाथावूं थोड़ो मारां (म्हे)। दरबार का हुकमूं जाणु भाई बिरामण समान (गुआल)। छतरपती नेजाधारी नै हाथावूं मारां (वाह वाह)। अरै कोनी घाला गुआल स्याळ नै (अब में हाथ)। सुण रे गुआल (म्हे)। गाय का गुआल नै मारो अर जंगल का स्याळ नै (मारो भलां ही)। बरोबर पाप (लागै है कीयो)। दरबार का हुकमूं स्याळ बनायो नै ओ (म्हे)। गुआल नै (वाह वाह)। गुआल बोलै (म्हे)। दरबार का हुकमूं और कांई समचार कहवै देखां (कीआवूं जाणज्यो कीआ कहवै दीयाजी नै)।।

ए म्हां जिस्या गुआल तो जी दीया धरती पर थोड़ा मारिया रे।
डिगै बड़ा बड़ा भोपालां का घात।
छतरपती नेजाधारी होवै तो मैं ही दाकल मारल्यां।।
कोनी घाला रे हिरण पुरख नै हाथ।।
(भलां जी भलां) देव भलां

म्हां जिस्या गुआल थोड़ा मारिया तूं धरती पर (म्हे)। म्हां जिस्या मारियावूं डिगै बड़ा बड़ा भोपालां का (घात)। अरै छतरपती नेजाधारी ने मैं ही दाकल मारल्यूं (म्हे)। नी घालयूं रे मैं दीया मैं हिरण पुरख नै (हाथ)। तनै मारो (म्हे)। भला हिरण नै (मारो कीयो)। अर तनै मारो भलां ही लुगाई नै (मारो कीयो)। दरबार का हुकमूं ए समचार (हां गुआल कीया जी कीयो)। मीर बोल्यो तोबा तोबा तोबा तोबा तोबा देखां तमकू दीया औरत बना दी गुआल (हां औरत बना दी कीयो)। अरे दे जाग को जाग टाट में जको ई जागां रह जाय (हां जाग को जाग रह जाय कीयो)। दरबार का हुकमूं ए समचार दीयोजी बूझणा करी म्हानै म्हनै कहवै तूं कोनी आवै आगो (हां आगो आर तूं दे ठा पाड़लै कीयो)। गुआल बूझणा करी रे गुआल गुआल सारो दिन मत कह (म्हे)। म्हानै भगवान देवरा को धणी दरबार हे नै देव महाराज (म्हे)। बो पद्दी दे राखी है (बी पद्दीवूं बतला कीयो)। कांई पद्दी है (हां म्हानै कांई ठा पड़े)। कीयो नापा बाजा (वाह वाह)। मीर कीयो यार दीया जोधका तमहारा बाप का क्या लिया नापलिया कह अर बतला दे (हां नापलिया कहबो करो)। के घोड़ां को असवार को सागै पापो काट घूंला। अबकै तो कह द्यो अबकै मत कै। मीर कीयो इस गुआलां की आगै देवमहाराज पद्दी दे राखी है। नापलियो कहर बतला दे। दरबार का हुकमूं गुआल बोलै कांई समचार कहवै पाछो देखां (कीआवूं जाणज्यो देखां भोपाजी महाराज कीआवूं)। अबार कहवां देव का हुकमूं (वाह वाह सा)।।

गुआल मत कहवै नै जी जो दीया जोधका रे।
कोनी म्हारी रे गुआलां केरी चाल।
इसी झाटकूं रे सिंवरिया सेल की।
उडा द्यूं दीया रे घोड़ा सेत असवार।।
(भलां जी भलां) देव भलां

गुआल मत कह। कोय नी गुआल जैसी चाल। अरै इसी झाटकूंला सिंवरिया सेल की। उडा द्यूं घोड़ा सेत असवार। औरूं मीर कीयो देख तेरै को जवाब करे। गुआल मत कह कीयो (म्हे)। गुआल कींयां से ऊठी म्हारै मन में मोटी (रीस)। घोड़ा का अनावूं परो फैंक द्यूं (म्हे)। दरबार का हुकमूं फैंक द्यूं पूरा ही पैण्ड (पच्चीस)। पच्चीस पावण्डा पर आंतरो जातो पड़ेलो (वाह वाह)। ओ समचार गुआल कीयो (वाह वाह)। गुआल बोलै कांई समचार कहवै देखां (कीआवूं जाणज्यो कीआवूं देखां)।।

ए गुआल मत कहवै नै जी जो माझी जोधका रे।
गुआल कींयां ऊठै मन में मोटी रीस।
घोड़ा का अनावूं रे परा ही फैंक द्यां।
फैंक द्यूं दीया रे पूरा पैण्ड पच्चीस।।
(भलां जी भलां) देव भलां

गुआल मत कह भैइ (म्हे)। अरै गुआल कींयां से ऊठी मन में मोटी (म्हनै रीस)। घोड़ा का अनावूं परो फैंक द्यूं (वाह वाह)। फैंक द्यूं पूरा ही पैण्ड ही (पच्चीस)। अब के गुआल कह अर बोल्यो है (हां अब के मत बोलीना कीयो)। अब के गुआल कह दियो तो कन्नो ई को बैठो उठावै बड़ा नो (हां कढाई मूं जियान को जियान अधर को अधर उठावूंला (कीयो)। मीर बोल्यो तोबा तोबा तोबा नापलो कह अर बतला भैइ (वाह वाह)। दरबार का हुकमूं गुआल बूझणा करी अरै थै आया जको थानै गायां देयां मैं (म्हे)। लेरली बात भूल गा थै (वाह वाह)।।

गायां ही चराबा जी दीया भाई रे गोरम का भाखरां रे।
जी दिन म्हारी रे सायब राखी टेक।
तूं अर मैं लड़िया रे गोरम का भाखरां।
जी दिन भाई रे गायां दीनी एक।।
(भलां जी भलां) देव भलां

मैं गायां म्हारी चराई गोरम का भाखरां (म्हे)। जकै दिन भाई दीया म्हारी सायब राखी (देक)। अरै तूं अर मैं लड़िया नै गोरम का भाखरां (वाह वाह)। जकै दिन दीयाजी मैं तनै गाय दीनी (एक)। अर बिना धणियां का हा बी दिन तो (हां जकै दिन ही कोनी दी जको आज तो म्हांकै लारै धणी है (तनै गाय द्यां ही कींयां की द्यां ही कीयो)। तनै ठा है तीन तिलोकी को नाथ भगवान औतार लियो है (वाह वाह)। अब कांई देवां गेला (म्हे)।।

ए छड़ छोटी तो जी जो भालो मोटो रे माझी जोधका रे।
सोवै भाई रे सेंस मुखियांलां टोप।
तूं दादो भाई लड़िया गोरम का भाखरां।
जी दिन दीयाजी दूरा नेजा रोप।।
(भलां जी भलां) देव भलां

छड़ तो छोटी (म्हे)। भालो मोटो रे माझी जोधका सोवै सेंस मुखियांलां (तनै टोप)। तूं दादो भाई लाड़िया गोरम का भाखरां (म्हे)। जकै दिन दीया दूरा नेजा (रोपर)। गायां तो जकै दिन मैं दीनी कोनी (म्हे)। हेंर थांकै बखां में (आया कोनी)। गायां के मत कर एसा दीज्यो ओ (वाह वाह)। गायां कोनी देयालां (म्हे)। दरबार का हुकमूं मीर बूझणा (करी है)। अरे यार दीया जोधका चौदाह से चम्मालीस गुआल बतावै (म्हे)। सगळा किस्या सा एका (सारीसां को होवै नी कीयो)। इस पदमा को तो धक्का जमकासा (हां है कीयो)। लेरली मुरी में जावूं (म्हे)। गायां नै अबार टोळ रातोकोट में (हां पूगती कर देवूं ई गुआल की तूं निंगै राखी कीयो)। दीयो बूझणा करी बाह वाह रे मीर अकल को ऊजीर रह गी (वाह वाह)। ई के निंगै मैं राखल्यूं (म्हे)। एकला घोड़ा को असवार मीर दरबार का हुकमूं गायां की लेरली मुरी टाल नाक दिया (वाह वाह)। लेरली मुरीवूं गुआल कुण कुण रहतो (वाह वाह)। लापड़ो तो झांपड़ो बैरीबाज बगूल सिंगजी (म्हे)। आपकी की कह कोनी चरूं पहला की (सुणै कोनी)। दरबार का हुकमूं बैरीबाज गुआल बोलै (म्हे)। कांई समचार गुआल नै दीया मीर नै कहवै देखां (कीआवूं जाणज्यो भोपाजी महाराज अब कीआवूं)। अबार कहवूं देव का हुकमूं ले तूं (वाह वाह जी)।।

ए ऊबी गाय नै जी जो घोड़ो मत घालै काळू मीरजी रे।
मान जा घोड़ी रे मशकी का असवार।
मीरजी गायां सुणी हुवै जका की घेरज्यो।
गायां के लेरै ऊबा रे नर मूंछयांलां गुआल।।
(भलां जी भलां) देव भलां

ऊबी गाय में घोड़ो मत घाल (म्हे)। मान जा घोड़ी मशकी का (अब असवार)। गायां तो मीर सुणी हुवै जका की घेरज्यो (म्हे)। गायां के लेरै ऊबा नर मूंछयांलां (गुआल)। आगा आव कींयां आवै (हां सुणी कोय नी गायां कीयो)। तो मीर की को मानै (वाह वाह)। दरबार का हुकमूं गुआल देव को बोलै (म्हे)। कांई मीर नै औरूं दाकलै देखां (कीआवूं जाणज्यो देखां कीआवूं)।।

ए ऊबी गाय में जी जो घोड़ो मत डकावै काळू मीरजी रे।
मान जा घोड़ी रे काळी का असवार।
ताणी डाढ में भाला रोप द्यां।
जियान खाती को बेटो रे हळ में जचावै हाल।।
(भलां जी भलां) देव भलां

दरबार का हुकमूं ऊबी गाय में घोड़ो मत घाल (वाह वाह)। मान जा घोड़ी काळी का (असवार)।

है ताणी डाढ में भालो रोप द्यूं (म्हे)। खाती को बेटो जागै हळ में जचावै (अब हाल)। कारीगर को बेटो हळ में हाल जचावै नै (हां जी भातवूं में डाढर भालो जचा द्यूंला कीयो)। के दरबार का हुकमूं गुआल देव महाराज को बैरीबाज कांई तो तीर कमठा नै हाथ (हां घालियो)। तीर समायो मीर देखियो मारिया (हां ओ बावूं होसियार है)। हेंर देख कीयो ईंयां को कीयो के हल के मांयनै आज हाल जचावै खाती (म्हे)। ईंयां डाढ के मांय भालो रोप द्यूंला (वाह वाह)। आगै नै आयगो तो (म्हे)। दरबार का हुकमूं मीर तो बाही पगां (पाछो बावड़ियो)। दीया नै आर बूझणा (करी है)। दीया तोबा तोबा तोबा तोबा तोबा मैं देख कीयो अरे लेरली मुरी के मांयनै गुआल क्युं (हलका है कीयो)। पण नी पदमा से ही (कीं तेज है कीयो)। ओ फूलडोल तो कोनी फोड़ै के (म्हे)। बैरीबाज गुआल दरबार का हुकमूं मन में सोचियो (वाह वाह)। रावजी की बाईसी चड़ अर आयगी (म्हे)। गायां नै पकड़ ले जाय (हां गायां नै पकड़ ले जाय अर गुआल अठै है कोनी)। सिरायत गुआल बोलै जको कोनी (वाह वाह)। तो बो कह म्हनै ठा ही कोनी पड़ियो कीयो (हां ठा कोनी कींयां करियो थै कीयो)। गोरम का भाखर रियोड़ो हे (म्हे)। अरै दादा भाई नै ठा करां (वाह वाह)। एकला घोड़ा को असवार (हां घोड़ै नै पाछो हांक दीन्यो)। दरबार का हुकमूं गोरम के भाखर लेरला गुआल बैठा हां (म्हे)। तो गोरम के भाखर बैठा बैरीबाज छप्पनजी भैरूंजी की लूरियां (गारिया हा)। देव महाराज को गुआल बोलै (म्हे)। बैरीबाज (वाह वाह)। कांई सिरायत नै जातो ही समचार कहवै देखां (कीआवूं जाणज्यो देखां कीआवूं)। अबार कहवूं देव का हुकमूं ले तूं (वाह वाह जी वाह वाह)।।

आप बैठा तो जी ए ई गोरम भाखरां रे।
आप की भली बैठ गी धाय।
पदमू भाई रे धारा जील पड़ियो।
हंकती हु गी रे आप की राताकोट नै गाय।।
(भलां जी भलां) देव भलां

आप बैठा दादा भाई गोरम का भाखरां (वाह वाह)। अर आप को भली बैठ गी (धाय)। के पदमू भाई तो गुदलिया का खाळ में धारा जील पड़ियो (म्हे)। हंकती हो गी आपकी राताकोट नै (गाय)। थै तो बैठा हो अठै (म्हे)। पदमू भाई तो गुदलिया का खाळ में धारा जील पड़ियो (वाह वाह)। हेंर गायां नै रावजीवाला अमराव (हां टोळ अर ले ग्या कीयो)। ओ समचार (हां जांवतां ही बैरीबाज गुआल कीया जी कीयो)। सिरायत बूझणा करी ईंयां कींयां बोल्यो (हां ईंयां कींयां बोलै भाई कीयो)। सिरायत गुआल बोलै (वाह वाह)। कांई बैरीबाज नै समचार पाछो कहवै देखां (कीआवूं जाणज्यो देखां अब कीआवूं)। अबार कहवां भगवान देव का हुकमूं ले तूं (वाह वाह जी)।।

धोळा अर धुंआ को जी जो भाज्योड़ो लाग्यो रे गुआल गाय का रे।
मुण्डा से डावड़ा रे चलती कर ग्यो बात।
कींयां हंकती हुई गायां नारायण देव की।
कींयां पड़ गो भाई जी पदमा ऊपर हाथ।।
(भलां जी भलां) देव भलां

दरबार का हुकमूं बहकीयोड़ो कींयां बोल्यो ईंयां (म्हे)। दरबार का हुकमूं धोळा धुंआ को भाज्योड़ो आयो तूं (म्हे)। दरबार का हुकमूं मुण्डा से चलती काढै (तूं बात)। अरै कींयां गायां हंकती हो गी नारायण देव की (कींयां पड़ ग्यो भाई पदमा ऊपर हाथ)। ईंयां बहकीयोड़ो कींयां बोल्यो (हां सूल माण्ड अर बात कह कीयो)। ईंयां झटकेन की तो गायां राताकोट में बाड़ दी रे भाई पदमू धारा जील पड़ियो (हां बात जची कोनी गुआल कीयो)। बैरीबाज तो एकर बोल्यो (हां दूसरा बोल्यो ही नैइ)। दरबार का हुकमूं सिरायत गुआल औरूं कहवै (म्हे)। कांई बैरीबाज नै बतलावै देखां (कीआवूं जाणज्यो कीआवूं)। अबार कहवूं धणी देव का हुकमूं ले तूं (वाह वाह सा)।।

ए खेड़ नी सुणी तो जी गुआलिया भाई रे खड़बड़ ना सुणिया रे।
कोनी सुणी मैं तो रे तोपांली उवाज।
कींयां गायां रूकी रे नारायण देव की।
कींयां बन्द हो गा देव का रे मद पीता गजराज।।
(भलां जी भलां) देव भलां

गुआल खड़बड़ नी सुणी खेड़ ई कोनी सुणी (म्हे)। अरै कोनी सुणी तोपां की (उवाज)। कींयां गायां बन्ध हो गी भैइ नारायण देव की (म्हे)। कींयां बन्ध हो गो मद पीता गजराज (हाथ)। सार दिन ही बहकीयोड़ो बोलै (वाह वाह)। देख हाथी फौज में हां (म्हे)। कींयां तो सहजां ही तो हाथियां की बन्ध (हां हु गी कीयो)। अर कींयां पदमो मारियो ग्यो जका समचार माण्ड कह (हां सूल बता कीयो)। बो तो एकर ही बोल्यो (वाह वाह)। बैरीबाज गुआल दूजा बोल्यो कोनी (म्हे)। दरबार का हुकमूं दूजो गुआल बोलै (वाह वाह)। कांई सिरायत नै समचार (कहवै देखां कीआवूं जाणज्यो कीआवूं)।।

गुआल आयो जी भैइ बैरीबाज गोरम का भाखरां।
ई की आपां मन में मानी रोळ।
चड़ चालज्यो दादा भाई गुदलिया का खाळ पर।
भरोसावूं घड़ा नै रे राळै ठीकरी फोड़।।
(भलां जी भलां) देव भलां

ओ समचार गुआल कीयो है। कीयो गुआलियो आयो भैइ गोरम का भाखरां। ई की आपां मन में मानी रोळ। चड़ चालो गुदलिया का खाळ में (म्हे)। अर भली बैठ गी (थांकै दाय)। चड़ चालो गुदलिया का खाळ में (म्हे)। दादा भाई भरोसावूं राळै घड़ा नै ठीकरी (फोड़)। थै तो भरोसावूं (बैठै रह जावां)। हेंर दुशमन जको गायां नै (हां ले जाय राताकोट कीयो)। बैरीबाज तो एकर बोल्यो आपको घोड़ा नै पाछो हांक दियो (वाह वाह)। दरबार का हुकमूं सिरायत गुआल कीयो भैइ दगो तो हो तो जाय (हां . . .)

ए चड़तो गुआल आयो तो जी ए ई शंकर के चूंतरै औवूं रे।
लाग्यो भाई रे सौ शंकर के पाय।
म्हां पर चड़ आयगो जी सावर गढ को सुलखना।

शंकर नाथजी आप लगावो पार।।
(भलां जी भलां) देव भलां

चड़तो सिरायत गुआल आयो शिवजी के चूंतरै (म्हे)। लाग्यो भाई सौ शंकर से (पाय)। अरै म्हां पर चड़ आयो आज सावर गढ को सुलखनो (म्हे)। शंकर करज्यो सांकड़ै (साय)। साय करज्यो (वाह वाह)। दरबार का हुकमूं कांई भैरूंजी के चूंतरै (हां गुआल जावे)। कांई भैरूंनाथ की करामात लेवै (वाह वाह)। अबार कहवां देव का हुकमूं ले तूं।।

ए चड़तो गुआल तो जी जो आयो भैरूं के चूंतरै औवूं रे।
लाग्यो भैरूंनाथ के पाय।
आज चड़ आयगो जी सावर गढालो सुलखनो।
भैरूंनाथ रे करज्यो सांकड़ै साय।।
(भलां जी भलां) देव भलां

चड़तो गुआल आयो भैइ भैरूं के चूंतरै (वाह वाह)। लाग्यो भैरूंनाथ के (पाय)। म्हां पर चड़ आयगो सावर गढ को सुलखनो (म्हे)। भैरवानाथ करो सांकड़ै (साय)। साय करज्यो श्री महाराज (वाह वाह)। अर आप पार लगाज्यो (म्हे)। दरबार का हुकमूं चड़तां गुआल की बैठ नंगारै गाई (हां पड़ी है)। तो नंगारो दरबार का हुकमूं रावजी का अमरावां नै (सुणीजगो)। दरबार का हुकमूं मीरजी को काळजो जागां (छोड़ ग्यो)। छोटो भाई नीमदे राजा को भाई हो (म्हे)। जका को काळजो (हां जगा छोड़ ग्या जी कीयो)। ओ तो दरबार का हुकमूं बिदा होबा लागो (म्हे)। दीयो बूझणा करी रे ईंयां कींयां भैइ (हां ईंयां कींयां करी रे गुआल कीयो)। दरबार का हुकमूं मैं तो थारी सीटी में (समझा कोनी)। तूं सीटी देय (म्हे)। ताणा धणी देवजी नै (बुला लिया)। दरबार का हुकमूं उनै जको राजा नीमदे पग छोड़ दिया (वाह वाह)। दीयोजी आडो फिरै कांई दाकलै देखां (कीआवूं जाणज्यो कीआवूं)। अबार कहवूं देव का हुकमूं ले तूं (वाह वाह)।।

भाजै मती ना जी ए ई राजा नीमदे औवूं रे।
भाज्यावूं घटै रे रजपूतां की पाण।
आगै हेंसेलो राण शहर को राजवी।
हेंसेली नीमा रे रूखां सेती राण।।
(भलां जी भलां) देव भलां

नीमा भाजै मत (म्हे)। अरै भाज्यावूं घटै तो रजपूती की (पाण)। आगे तो हेंसै राण शहर को राजवी (म्हे)। हेंसै रे नीमा रूखां सेती (तनै राण)। राण शहर सारी हेंसी (हां भाग अर आयग्या कीयो गायां पकड़ नै गिया हा)। कीयो दिया (म्हे)। हेंसी जको म्हनै (हेंसी कीयो)। मैं तो भाग जावां भाई (वाह वाह)। मरबा नै कोनी आया अठै (म्हे)। तो दरबार का हुकमूं रावजी को छोटो भाई हो नै (हां नीमदेजी)। जको भाज छुट्यो (वाह वाह)। मीर बूझणा करी ये यार दीया (म्हे)। रावजी का छोटा भाई भाग ग्या (हां आपां ही भाग चालो बीगल बजावो फौजां में कीयो)। भगी की बीगल बजावो तो भाजवा

दे (वाह वाह)। ईंयां कींयां भाजां (म्हे)। आया जका की सार तो लेवां देखां (हां ईंयां कींयां भाग जावा)। सेजा ही बेटी का बाप (हां भाग चालां कीयो)। दरबार का हुकमूं दीयो बूझणा करी रे गुआल स्याळ (म्हे)। बात और कींयां ही कर गो तूं म्हारावूं (वाह वाह)। दगो कर गो भैइ (दगो कर गो)। दरबार का हुकमूं दीयोजी बूझणा करी गुआल (म्हे)। ताणी सैन नै मैं तो कोनी समझा भैइ (हां समझा कोनी भाई कीयो)। तूं गुआल सैन कर (वाह वाह)। अर ताणा देव नै बुला ल्यायो कीयो (वाह वाह)। दरबार का हुकमूं जता नै मीर बोलै (म्हे)। कांई दीया नै औरूं बतलावै देखां (कीआवूं जाणज्यो कीआवूं देखा)।।

हाथियां रा मूंहरां तो जी दीया भाई रे पाछा फैर देयो रे।
कर द्यो आपणा रे राण दिशा नै खोज।
चड़ अर आयगो रे बाळो देवजी।
आयगो दीया रे सैइ उगावण भोज।।
(भलां जी भलां) देव भलां

हाथियां का मूंहरां दीयाजी पाछा फैर द्यो (म्हे)। अरै आपणा कर द्यो राण दिशा में (खोज)। दरबार का हुकमूं चड़ अर आयगो दीखै बाळो देवजी (म्हे)। आयगो रे भाई दीया उगावण (भोज)। ओ भोज को बैर लेवै (हां जका आयग्या है कीयो)। दरबार का हुकमूं कीयो मीर दीयोजी कीयो भाज मत (भाज मत ठहर तो सरी)। मैं बात करी है (म्हे)। दरबार का हुकमूं देवजी कोनी (म्हे)। गुआल कीयो रे भैइ देवजी कठै है (हां देवजी कोय नी थै आतां ही बूझियो हो)। कीयो सिरायत गुआल कठै है (जको अब आवै कीयो)। सिरायत गुआल आरियो है (वाह वाह)। कीयो दीया ईंयां सिरायत गुआल होता है की (वाह वाह)। दोवड़ा तो हाथी घमूता आवै (म्हे)। हेंर भांलां का भळका (पड़तां आवै कीयो)। दीयोजी बूझणा (करी है)। सुण रे मीर (म्हे)। ईंयां का गुआल नी होता नै (हां तो रावजी की ऊनाळो साख कदै कोनी भेळता कीयो)। गुआल ईंयां का जरां भाई ऊनाळो साख गांवां कानै (हां छोड़ी कीयो)। गुआल बोलै कांई समचार दीया नै कहवै देखां (कीआवूं जाणज्यो कीआवूं देखां)।।

ए पगां लखीणी जी जो गुआल के बै मोजड़िया रे।
दीया भाई रे गलै सोहवणी माल।
किलंगी दीपती आवै रे मोहर पच्चास की।
अबकाळै आयगो रे जासा को निरपाल।।
(भलां जी भलां) देव भलां

दरबार का हुकमूं पगां लखीणी भाई के मोजड़ी है (म्हे)। दरबार का हुकमूं गलै सोहवणी (माल)। किलंगी दीपती आवै रे दीया देख मोहर पच्चास की (वाह वाह)। अबकाळा आयगो बड जासा को (निरपाल)। तूं आतां ही है नै (हां जको गुआल अब पूगै है कीयो)। बो सिरायत मालक है जको म्हां में ओ है (वाह वाह)। वाह भाई मीर सुण रे भाई ईंयां का गुआल हा देव का (वाह वाह)। गुआल दरबार का हुकमूं दीयोजी बांतां करां (वाह वाह)। अताक पहली सिरायत गुआल आर बूझणा (करी

है)। पदमा के बांतां है (के बांतां कीयो के बात है कीयो)। कीयो कांई के बांतां (हां देख ही लेयो)। आ रावजी कानै निंगै करो अमराव आयोड़ो ऊबा दुशमन गायां के घेरो ले लियो (वाह वाह)। कीयो गायां के घेरो तो दियो जको तो चोखो रे पदमा (म्हे)। गायां नै पाणी पायो नी पायो बा कह (हां बै समचार कहवो)। कीयो दादा भाई थानै पाणी पीबा को बिचार लाग्यो कांई (हां पाणी मैं तो कोनी पायो कीयो)। ए जीकारा बोलया तो मैं ही पाछा (जीकारावूं बोलग्या)। ए रेकारा बोल्यो तो मैं ही रेकारा (हां पाछो बोल ग्या कीयो)। म्हांकै तो हारै तूं रे (हां हु रही है)। आप नै उडीका हा (हां लोहा ही मिलणै की देरी है कीयो)। कीयो नैइ नैइ नैइ (इयां मत करो)। बैरी का पेट में बड़ जावो (म्हे)। गायां नै आपांणाली नै पाणी पाय ल्यायो (हां पहली पाणी पाय ल्यायो कीयो)। कीयो सिरायत भाई मैं तो पेट में मावा ही कोनी बटीनै (हां थारावूं बड़नी आवै तो तूं बड़ कीयो)। मैं तो कोनी बड़ां (वाह वाह)। सिरायत गुआल घोड़ा को आणो छोड़ पालो हु गो (वाह वाह)। दरबार का हुकमूं कांई पाळ पर जावै दीया कन्नै (म्हे)। जांतो ही कांई समचार कहवै देखां (हां कीआवूं जाणज्यो देखां भोपाजी महाराज अब कीआवूं)। अबार कहवूं देव का हुकमूं देखां (वाह वाह जी वाह वाह)।।

ए ग्यारस करतो जी बारस करै रे माझी जोधका रे।
कोलड़ियां में बांटै रे धरम नैम की मिठाई रे।
तूं गायां तिसाई लिया ऊबो रे नारायण देव की।
जरां दीया रे हिन्दु धरम घटाई रे।।
(भलां जी भलां) देव भलां

दरबार का हुकमूं समचार आंतो ही गुआल (कीयो है)। तूं ग्यारस कर बारस कर माझी जोधका (वाह वाह)। अरै कोलड़ियां बांटै धरम नैम की (मिठाई)। है गायां तिसाई देख लिया ऊबो पाळ के ऊपरै (म्हे)। दीयाजी हिन्दुई धरम (घटाई)। ए बेटी का बाप तूं हिन्दु है (हां गायां तिसी ऊबी है कीयो)। हिन्दु का धरम नी है (वाह वाह)। दीयोजी बोल्यो कोनी (म्हे)। गुआल सिरायत बोलै कांई दीया नै बतलावै देखां (कीआवूं जाणज्यो कीआवूं देखां)।।

ए ग्यारस करतो जी तूं बारस करै रे माझी जोधका रे।
कोलड़ियां में बांटै रे धरम नैम का मोक।
ए गायां तिसाई ऊबी नारायण देव की।
जरां हिन्दु नै रे मोटो लागै दोख।।
(भलां जी भलां) देव भलां

ग्यारस करै तूं बारस करै (वाह वाह)। कोलड़ियां बांटै रे भैइ धरम नैम का (मोक)। ए गायां तिसाई लिया ऊबो नारायण देव की (म्हे)। जरां दीया हिन्दु नै मोटो लागै (अब दोख)। ए बेटी का बाप (हां पापां को भारी क्युं हुवै हो)। सगळी गायां तिसी ऊबी बेटी का बाप (म्हे)। मीर बोल्यो यार दीया ओ तो गुआल बहुत स्याणो बोल्यो (हां बहुत स्याणो है कीयो)। अरै पदमू गुआल है (म्हे)। ई का गम का टका (हां है कीयो)।

गंवत्री लेती रही मरण तण जीवन तया आधार।
बोथरनी नंदी लांघता हिन्दु नै गौ लंघावै पार।
गौ जींवता नै त्यारै मरिया पछै त्यारै पूंछड़ी पकड़।
(भलां जी भलां) देव भलां

गुआल कीयो है। गंवत्री दीया हिन्दु नै लेती रही। मरण तण जीवन तण आधार बोथरनी नंदी लांघता हिन्दु नै लगावै पार। दीया हिन्दु गौ लगाय पार। दीयोजी बूझणा करी तनै ठा कोनी मीर (म्हे)। जो मालक है नै (वाह वाह)। जको तो निरबल बोली (म्हे)। दरबार का हुकमूं दीयोजी बोलै (म्हे)। कांई सिरायत गुआल नै समचार (कहवै देखां कहवै जाणीज्यो कीआवूं)। अबार कहवूं देव का हुकमूं ले तूं (वाह वाह जी)।।

ए आ गायां नै जी तूं पाणी पालै रे गुआल गाय का रे।
मैं करां पीली पांबड़ियां की छांय।
गायां पाणी पीयै रे नारायण देव की।
जतै लोह करूं तो म्हनै रे जोध दीया की आण।।
(भलां जी भलां) देव भलां

आ गायां नै गुआल भाई पाणी पा दे (म्हे)। अरै मैं करसियां गायां के पीली पांबड़ियां (छांय)। ए गायां पाणी पी नारायण देव की (म्हे)। जतै भाई रे लोह करूं तो जोध दीया की (म्हनै आण है कीयो)। अरै गुआल (म्हे)। गायां नै पाणी पा दे (पाणी पा कीयो)। मैं हिन्दु ही हा किस्या भैइ मैं दूजा थोड़ा ही है (वाह वाह)। दरबार का हुकमूं सिरायत गुआल बूझणा (करी है)। पदमा (म्हे)। बैरी को हुकम छूट गो (हां गायां नै पाणी पालियो कीयो)। तो दरबार का हुकमूं देव महाराज की गायां नै गुआल सीटी देवै (म्हे)। कांई पाणी पावै देखां (कीआवूं जाणज्यो कीआवूं देखां)। अबार कहवूं देव का हुकमूं देखां (वाह वाह जी वाह वाह)।।

ए पगांला खोलिया तो जी बैरीबाजवै मोचड़ा रे।
मेल दी भाई रे जमदद खानै ढाल।
ढूक अर पी लीज्यो ऊदाजी की नागलियां।
पाणी पावै ये जासा को निरपाल।।
(भलां जी भलां) देव भलां

पगां का खोल दिया गुआल मोचड़ा (म्हे)। कांधा उपरूं मेल दी जमदद खानै (ढाल)। ढूक अर पीज्यो ऊदाजी की नागलियां (वाह वाह)। थानै पावै बैरीबाज (गुआल)। बैरीबाज गुआल हूं (म्हे)। जको आज थानै पाणी पावै (पाणी पी लियो कीयो धापर)। तो कहतां जेज (लागी)। नौ लाख असी हजार गाय देव की सागै पाणी पर (हां ढूक गी)। दरबार का हुकमूं दीयोजी काळू मीर (म्हे)। पाळ के ऊपर ऊबा (वाह वाह)। चार ढोर हा जका तो आंतरै ऊबा रह गा (हां पाणी के सांकड़ा ही नैइ आया)। गायां देव की पी पाणी (म्हे)। पाछी (पाळ पर चड़ी)। गुआल घोड़ै असवार (पाछा हो ग्या)। दरबार

का हुकमूं दीयोजी बूझणा करी गुआल भाई (म्हे)। पाणी पालियो (हां पालियो कीयो)। पालियो दीया (वाह वाह)। कीयो रे भैइ सौ पायी एक तिसाई कर दी (हां ईंयां कींयां करी कीयो)। कींयां (म्हे)। कीयो मैं निंगै राखो ए चार ढोर तो बेटी का बाप पाणी के नजीक आया नैइ (हां चारूं जानवर पाणी के नेड़ा ई कोनी आया कीयो)। कीयो दिया (म्हे)। आ नै भाई पाणी पाबा को आज दिन को (हां बिचार कोनी कीयो)। क्युं (म्हे)। के ए गायां ईंयां पाणी कोनी पीवै (हां ईंयां पीवै कोनी कीयो)। खटक करम बिदी बनावूं ए जरां गायां पाणी (हां जार पीवै कीयो)। दीयो बूझणा करी रे गुआल (म्हे)। तूं आज बिदी खटक करम करलै जका में देख लेवां (हां मैं बठै रातै कोट ले जांवां जरां मैं ही पाणी पाय (देयां नी तिसा मरती गायां मर जायै कीयो)। सूख जायलै महनै ठा कोनी है (वाह वाह)। पाणी पा (म्हे)। कीयो ईंयां कोनी पीजै पाणी (हां ईंयां कोनी पावूं कीयो)। दरबार का हुकमूं पाणी पालै रे गुआल (वाह वाह)। कीयो नैइ तूं औदर लियो ऊबा रे गाड़ीआलो (वाह वाह)। ई को डर लागै कीयो (हां ई को म्हानै डर लागै जाणै बाळा ज्यूं)। गुआल बोलै (वाह वाह)। कांई दीया नै समचार कहवै देखां (कीआवूं जाणज्यो कीआवूं)। अबार कहवूं भगवान का हुकमूं ले तूं।।

ए हिन्दु की तो जी खाख नी डिगै रे दीयाजी जोधका रे।
कोनी डिगै रे हणुमान की हाक।
आ गायां नै पाणी पुआवो रे माझी जोधका।
ताणा भांलां का रे टांचा हेटा राळ।।
(भलां जी भलां) देव भलां

हिन्दु की तो दीया खाख कदै नी डिगै (म्हे)। कोनी डिगै हणुमान की (हाक)। तूं आं गायां नै पाणी पुआवै थारा भाला का रे टांचा निचा (अब नाक)। ओ गाड़ी को औदर लिया ऊबो है नी (म्हे)। जतै गायां नै पाणी कोनी पावूं (हां भाला तोड़)। हेटा नाकै जरां पावूं (जणा पावूं कीयो)। दरबार का हुकमूं दीयोजी कीयो रे मीर (म्हे)। भाला का टांचा तोड़ना पड़ी भैइ (वाह वाह)। कीयो यार दीया जोधका सस्तर मत तोड़ (म्हे)। नापलो है नै (भूंडै हवाला मारलो कीयो)। कीयो हिन्दु को धरम है भैइ (हां तोड़ो पाणी पास्यां गायां नै)। न (?) दरबार का हुकमूं मीर नै बूझणा करी रे मीर (म्हे)। तूं ही भालो हेटो नाक (हां तोड़ अर नाक कीयो)। कीयो मत तुड़ा सस्तर मान जा कीयो (हां बूरी तरहवूं मारेला कीयो)। दरबार का हुकमूं गुआल (पाणी पा गायां नै कीयो)। चोखी तरह पा ले रोजीना पावै जियां पा ले (वाह वाह)। गुआल देव महाराज को कांई करियो सिनान ध्यान करियो पहली तो (वाह वाह)। पीतांबर धोवती (पहरी)। दरबार का हुकमूं जागता बनाया (वाह वाह)। कड़ियां कड़ियां सुधा पाणी में बड़तो (व्हिया जी कीयो)। बठै जाय (म्हे)। ई तजबीज को पछेवड़ो हो जको पाणी के ऊपर बिछा दियो (बिछा दियो)। चांरो पल्ला पर चार धूपेड़ा मेल दिया (वाह वाह)। दरबार का हुकमूं बंसरी गुआल के हाथ में ले ली (म्हे)। तो बंसरी घाल मुण्डा में (म्हे)। के गुआल बंसरी की टेर करी (वाह वाह)। बंसरी की उवाज से बै चारूं ढोर है जका पाळ के ऊपरूं चाल्या (वाह वाह)। पाणी पर ढूकै (म्हे)। कांई समचार गुआल कहवै देखां (कीआवूं जाणज्यो देखां कीआवूं)। अबार कहवूं देव का हुकमूं ले तूं।।

ए बंसरी बजावूं जी समझावूं ये छालर ढोर ने औवूं रे।
समझाज्यै म्हारी मनां सुहानी माय।
गाजरिया तो गहूं सरपटिया चिन्ना नितका जीमता ई।
जांकां नागली ये धणी पूग गा आज।।
(भलां जी भलां) देव भलां

बंसरी बजावूं समझावूं छालर ढोर नै (म्हे)। तूं समझै की नै म्हारी मनां सुहानी (माय)। दरबार का हुकमूं गाजरिया गहूं सरपटिया चिन्ना नितका खांवती (म्हे)। दरबार का हुकमूं पाणी पी अर नागली दड़ावट पाछी (अब चाल)। आज माळा मत जाज्यै (हां आज म्हारा धणी आंका आयगा है कीयो)। दरबार का हुकमूं गुआल की सीटीवूं बंसरी की टेरवूं चारूं सांसर चाल्या बटवूं (म्हे)। दरबार का हुकमूं दे दे पछेवड़ा पर मुण्डो (वाह वाह)। हेंर गायां पाणी पीबा लागी (हां छान छान अर पाणी पीवण लागी जी कीयो)। गुआल देव को बोलै (म्हे)। सुरेमाता नै कांई देखां पाणी पिती नै समचार कहवै देखां (हां औरूं कह देवे)। कींयां जाणीज्यै।।

ए गटल का घूंटा तो जी पाणी पीबो नागली ये परो छोड़ द्यो औवूं रे।
नागलीमाता ये मही घूंट से पींव।
नीर खळकै ये ताणा शरीर में।
घोड़ा आगै थारो ये दुख पावेलो जीव।।
(भलां जी भलां) देव भलां

गटल का घूंटा माता पाणी पीबो छोड़ देय (म्हे)। अर मही घूंट से (अब पी)। के नीर खळकै नागली थारा शरीर में (म्हे)। ओ घोड़ा आगै देख थारावूं दुख पावेलो (अब जीव)। थोड़ो पाणी (हां पी कीयो)। आ देख दुशमन का घोड़ा ऊबा है कीयो (वाह वाह)। देव को नापो बोलै अर कांई सुरेमाता नै समझावै देखां (कीआवूं जाणीज्यो देखां कीआवूं)।।

ए डकळ का घूंटा तो जी पाणी पीबो ये परो छोड़ द्यो रे।
बनजायली भायां ये पेट में पाणी वाली पोट।
दूरी रहवै ये दड़ावट की कोटड़ियां।
दूरो रह जावै नागली ये नौ गज रातो कोट।।
(भलां जी भलां) देव भलां

गटल का घूंटा ये नागली पाणी पीबो छोड़ दियो (म्हे)। दरबार का हुकमूं बन जावै पेट में पाणी की (पोट)। दूरी रहवै भायां दड़ावट की कोटड़ियां (म्हे)। दूरो रह दुशमन को ये नौगज रातो (कोट)। रातै कोट जावोली तो ही आंतरै (हां घणो है)। दड़ावट की कोटड़ियां अटवूं (हां आगी रहवै कीयो)। नागलीमाता क्युं थोड़ोसो (पी कीयो)।।

बंसरी बजावो जी ए ई छालर ढोर नै औवूं रे।
आज समझै नै म्हारी ये मनां सुहानी माय।

घोड़ो पाछै मत हो जाज्यै ऊदाजी की नागलियां।
तूं तो माता ये दड़ावट पाछी चाल।।
(भलां जी भलां) देव भलां

बंसरी बजावूं समझावूं छालर ढोर नै (म्हे)। समझाज्यै आज म्हारी मनां ई सुहानी (माय)। आ राव का घोड़ा के मुण्डा के मत हो जाज्यै (म्हे)। जर पाणी पी अर माजी ये तूं दड़ावट पाछी (अब चाल)। आ नी होवै घोड़ा के दुशमना के मुण्डा के (हां जायेली तू)। दरबार का हुकमूं गुआल देव महाराज को गायां नै चोखी तरह पाणी पाबा लागो (म्हे)। मीर बूझणा (करी है)। अरै दीया (वाह वाह)। देख नापलो ढाण्ढी नै कुबद सिखावै (हां कुबद सिखावै है कीयो)। दीयो बूझणा करी मीर बोल मत (हां बोल मत ना गाय नै पाणी पीवण दे पहली)। म्हांको हिन्दु को धरम है (म्हे)। कीयो धरम तो है पण अबार ठा पड़ी थारी धरम की (हां आगी ठा पड़ी कीयो)।।

पगां में पहरिया तो जी पाछा गुआलजी खड़ावूं बै मोचड़ा रे।
पाछी समाली रे जमदत खानै ढाल।
चोखी तरहवूं पी लीज्यो ऊदाजी की नागलियां।
तूं तो नागली ये दड़ावट पाछी चाल।।
(भलां जी भलां) देव भलां

गुआल पाछा पहर लिया पगां में खड़ावूं मोचड़ा (वाह वाह)। समाली जमदत खानै (ढाल)। चोखी तरह पाणी पी अर माता (म्हे)। दड़ावट पाछी (अब चाल)। दड़ावट चालज्यो (वाह वाह)। नौलाख अस्सीहजार गायां देव की पाणी चोखी तरह पी लियो (वाह वाह)। सुरेमाता पाणी पीतां (म्हे)। गुआल देव महाराज को गायां नै पाणी (पांवतां)। जय बोलो श्री देवनारायण भगवान की (जय)। बोलो रे भैइ छोटा मोटा (स)। चार ढोर तो है नै (म्हे)। गायां की डार के मांयनै जार (रळ गिया)। हेंर सुरेमाता ही नै बा औतारण (म्हे)। जकी सारै खाळो पड़ो हो (वाह वाह)। जाय खाळा में ए देखेण की कादा के मांयनै पग रोप पड़ गी (हां पड़ गी हो बूड़ीसी गाय)। रूप दूजो कर लियो (वाह वाह)। तो गाय कांई करै कादा में ऊठै अर पाछी (पड़ जावे)। उनावूं ऊठै उनावूं पाछी (पड़ जाय जी कीयो)। आ गाय निंगै कुण के आयी के मीर के (हां पड़ती निंगै आयगी)। मीर बूझणा करी रे यार दीया (म्हे)। दूजी गायां तो हाथ कोनी आवै (हां पकड़योड़ी आपणू चालै कोनी)। ताणा घोड़ा को रस्सो दे म्हनै (म्हे)। अरै कादा में पड़ी जकी ढाण्ढी कर घाल लियां (हां ई नै ले चांलां कीयो)। दरबार का हुकमूं देख भगवान ई जात नै माया दीनी नी बगड़ावतां नै (वाह वाह)। जरां देख इसी जागां ढाण्ढियां के सोनो घालियो (वाह वाह)। अरै ईंयां का जेवर सोना का कठै पड़िया है भैइ (हां कठे हा कीयो)। दरबार का हुकमूं आ गाय ई जागां तो पड़ गी (जणा तो गहणो आपणै हाथ लाग जासी)। पगां में नेवरियां हे नै (हां)। ए तो देयूं तनै (ए तूं ले लेय कीयो)। हेंर गला में सांकळो है नै बड़ोड़ो (वाह वाह)। ओ हमारी बीबी के नूवो बयाव करियो एस जकी के घालगां (हां क्युं कोनी घालेलो)। सींगां में खोळियां है सोना की (म्हे)। राजा नीमदे नै दे देतां (पण बो तो ऊठ ग्यो)। आपां दोन्यो अमराव

एक का एक पांती (बांट लियां कीयो)। पांती को नांव (हां लियो)। गुआल मन में देखियो रे बैरी पांती की की कर ली (हां पांती क्यें की करै कीयो)। तो घोड़े असवार हो पाळ के ऊपरै (पाछो आयो)। पाछो आयो तो सुरेमाता तो रूप धार मेलियो अर आप की कादा में लोटै (हां कदै उने पड़ै अर कदै उनै पड़े)। मन में देखियो बनी टैम में देखी माता नागली उत्तर दियो (हां उत्तर दे दियो कीयो माता तो)। गुआल सांकड़ो गाय के आवै (म्हे)। कांई समचार सुरेमाता नै कहवै देखां (कीआवूं जाणीज्यो भोपाजी महाराज अब कीआवूं)। अबार कहवूं देव का हुकमूं ले तूं (वाह वाह जी)।।

ए पोखराला गुरां नै देतो जी ए ई माता नागलियां रे।
नितर दे देतो चामळ का चोरां रे।
म्हारी भली हेंसी करा दी ऊदाजी की नागलियां।
राव का नागली ये ऊबो व्है असवारां।।
(भलां जी भलां) देव भलां

तनै पोखरजी का गुरां नै देतो (म्हे)। ए दे देतो मैं चामळ का (चोरां)। भली हेंसी करायी ऊदाजी की नागली (म्हे)। रावजी का ऊबोड़ां (असवारां)। देख रावजी का असवार तो ऊबा (म्हे)। ए म्हारी हेंसी करा दी (तूं हेंसी करायी कीयो)। दरबार का हुकमूं गुआल बोलै (म्हे)। कांई सुरेमाता नै समचार कहवै देखां (हां औरूं कहवै देखां कीआवूं जाणज्यो कीआवूं)। अबार कहवूं देव का हुकमूं ले तूं (वाह वाह सा)।।

पोखराला गुरां ने देतो जी ए ई ऊदाजी की नागलियां रे।
छोड़तो तनै ये ब्रिमा के मिण्दिरां रे।
भली हेंसी करायी ऊदाजी की नागलियां।
राव का भाई रे कादेला कंवरां रे।।
(भलां जी भलां) देव भलां

पोखराला गुरां नै देतो कीयो (म्हे)। हेंर के दौड़तो ब्रिमा के मिण्दिर में सकलप घाल (खुरा)। ए भली हेंसी करायी ऊदाजी की नागली (म्हे)। रावजी का दरबार का हुकमूं काछेला (कंवरां)। एक कंवर भंवर तो (ऊबा है)। जका में म्हारी तूं (हेंसी करां दीनी)। सुरेमाता बोलै कांई समचार गुआल नै कहवै देखां (कीआवूं जाणज्यो देखां अब कीआवूं)। अबार कहवां देव का हुकमूं देखां (वाह वाह)। गुआल कांई करियो गाय नै कीयो नै बठै (म्हे)। कीयो भैइ इस्या जाण जाण कोनी तो नै मैं तो देख राखी बांधबा आया नै बै बिरामण (वाह वाह)। पुष्कराला (हां बा नै दे देतो)। राखी में देतो (वाह वाह)। ए के ब्रिमाजी का मिण्दिर में (हां तनै चड़ा देतो)। के जको चोरां नै ले जाबो द्यो तीनो काम कर देतो थारा (वाह वाह पहली ठा ईंयां व्हियावूं ईंयां ही करतो)।

ए ई सींग संडासां जी म्हाना गुआल देबै मोड़िया रे।
म्हारी गुआलिया रे कढ जांपी किरतार।
आ बांतां को रे तनै ठा ही कोय ने।

मैं पावण आयी ताणा रे ऊदकरण नै दूध।।
(भलां जी भलां) देव भलां

सींग संडासां मोड़िया म्हारा (म्हे)। गुआल कढ जांपी (किरतार)। आ बांतां को तनै ठा कोनी पड़ियो हाल (म्हे)। मैं पावण आयी रे थारा ऊदकरण (दूध)। म्हारो देव को जोड़ो है (हां ठेट को ही जोड़ो है कीयो)। मैं तो भगवान नै दूध पाबा नै (आयी हूं कीयो)। दरबार का हुकमूं गाय बोलै (म्हे)। कांई समचार गुआल नै (कहवै देखां कीआवूं जाणज्यो अब कीआवूं)।।

मैं ई ऊबी तो जी ए ई गुदलिया का खाळ में औवूं रे।
म्हारा गुआलिया जी ढीला राळिया जाणया काण।
मैं ही मथरा में रह चौसट जोगणियां।
जी दिन ताणो देवजी रे गोपियां बिचलो कान।।
(भलां जी भलां) देव भलां

अबार तो ऊबी रे गुआल देख गुदलिया का खाळ में (म्हे)। म्हारा ढीला राळिया में (काण)। ताणो देव हां मथराजी में चौसट जोगणी (म्हे)। जकै दिन थारो देवजी हो गोपियां बिचलो (कान)। म्हारो अर देव को जोड़ो है (ठेट को ही है कीयो)। दरबार का हुकमूं जकै दिन मैं ही साथ ही ताणा देव के (वाह वाह)। कीयो माताजी नखरा निवारो (अर दड़ावट पधारो)। दरबार का हुकमूं गाय बोलै (म्हे)। कांई समचार कहवै देखां (कीआवूं जाणज्यो देखां कीआवूं)।।

आं ईं घोड़ां की जी मैं कंवळी
कर खाजावूं गुआल गाय का रे।
मार लेवूंला गुआलिया आठूं सूं असवार।
हुकम कोनी रे नारायाण देव को।
कन्नै ऊबो बरजै घोड़ा रे लीला रो असवार।।
(भलां जी भलां) देव भलां

दरबार का हुकमूं सुरेमाता समचार कीयो है (म्हे)। कीयो आ घोड़ां की असवारां की कंवळी कर खाजावूं मैं (म्हे)। मारल्यूं रे गुआलिया आठूं सूं (असवार)। अरै हुकम कोनी नारायाण देव को (म्हे)। दरबार का हुकमूं आ बांतां को तनै ठा कोनी पड़ियो कन्नै बो ऊबो घोड़ो लीला को (असवार)। दरबार का हुकमूं कन्नै ऊबो बरजै (हां देव महाराज बरजै नी सगळा काम (मैं एकेली कर द्यूं कीयो)। तनै लागताला घोड़ा असवार घणा (वाह वाह)। गुआल देखियो आ कांई बात है (हां आपां नै तो देव महाराज दीखै ही कोनी कठै ऊबा (है)। कीयो सुरेमाता झूट बोल गी भैइ (म्हे)। तनै तो देवजी दीखै म्हनै दीखै कोनी (हां आ कांई बात है कीयो)। सुरेमाता बोलै (म्हे)। कांई गुआल नै समचार कहवै देखां (कीआवूं जाणज्यो देखां कीआवूं)। अबार कहवां देव का हुकमूं।।

थारो जलम तो जी ए ई दड़ावट की कोटड़ियां रे।

तूं तो माथा पर बांधै कांचा सूत।
आ बांतां को गुआलिया रे ठा पड़ियो कोय ने।
मैं पावण आयी रे ऊदकरण नै दूध।।
(भलां जी भलां) देव भलां

थारो जलम है नै (म्हे)। जको दड़ावट की कोटड़ियां है देखी (वाह वाह)। तूं गुआल बांधै माथा पर काचा (सूत)। आ बांतां को तनै ठा कोनी पड़ियो हाल (म्हे)। मैं पावण आयी ऊदकरण नै (दूध)। दरबार का हुकमूं भगवान नै दूध पाबा नै आयी हूं (वाह वाह)। कीयो माजी सा नखरा निवारो (म्हे)। दड़ावट (चालो)। सुरेमाता कांई करियो बी जागां गुआल नै पांचमुखारबिन्द घोर दर्शन दिया (वाह वाह)। एक तो घोड़ी को धारयो (म्हे)। एक उडनमेरी को (धारयो)। एक सुरेमाता गाय को हो ही (म्हे)। एक सकत को (हां धारयो)। दरबार का हुकमूं सकताला मुण्डा में निंगै करी गुआल देख कांई रचना है (हां देख कीयो तूं)। तो बठै तो कांई सकत का मुण्डा में अधर चक्कर चालै (वाह वाह)। गाय का मुखारबिन्द में निंगै (करी ही)। सेंसार दुनिया रचबा को गेलो (हां सगळा दीखायो)। तीन तिलोकी सारी गौ का मुण्डा में (दिखा दी)। घोड़ा अर असवार सगळा ही बठै फिरै देव महाराज कन्ने गाय के उब जाणै (वाह वाह)। गुआल तो हाथ जोड़ (म्हे)। मुण्डा के खड़ो हु गो माता म्हनै ठा कोय नी पड़ियो (हां अता दिन थारो म्हनै आ ठा कोनी के तूं ईंयां है (म्हनै ठा ही गायां मांयली गाय है)। ए देव महाराज जरां रोज का ही थारा दर्शन करबा आवै (हां जणा पकड़ै सामै आवे)। अती करामात है थारा मैं (वाह वाह)। कीयो गुआल मैं की गायां मूं गाया थोड़ी हूं मैं तो भगवान नै दूध पाबा नै आयी हूं (वाह वाह)। कीयो माजी सा नखरा निवारो जरां अब कीयो (हां अब पधारो अब जाणज्यो)। सुरेमाता बोलै (म्हे)। कांई समचार गुआल नै कहवै देखां (कीआवूं जाणज्यो कीआवूं देखां)। अबार कहवूं देव का हुकमूं।।

चड़ चड़ चूंटूं जी ए ई कांकड़ में दोबड़ियां रे।
गुआल देव का रे चालूं पूंछ हलाय।
छोड़ दे सिकराणी का रे चौड़ा छापरां।
राव का घोड़ा बदे के देखां रे पारनमूनी गाय।।
(भलां जी भलां) देव भलां

चड़ चड़ चूंटूं गुआल कांकड़ में दोबड़ी (म्हे)। मैं चालूं पूंछ (हलार)। छोड़ सिकराणी का चौड़ा छापरा (म्हे)। देखां गाय बेजां रावजीआला घोड़ा पर बदे के देखां पारब्रिम की (गाय)। बरोबर छोड़ म्हनै (हां आगै देखाणी घोड़ा जावै गायां जाय कीयो)। कीयो गुआल तूं जाणै जकी बात कोनी कीयो (वाह वाह)। देखेन की पांच बरस की ढोरी होर कूद एकानै हुई (हां कूदर ऊबी रिनी)। गुआल आर कीयो माजी सा घोड़ा का उनै मत करज्यो मुण्डो (वाह वाह)। दड़ावट चाली आ तो (म्हे)। नापो देव महाराज को गाय के बांतां हो रही है (म्हे)। हेंर मीर देखो तमाशा जार दीया नै समचार (कीयो)। दियो (म्हे)। देख ई ढाण्ढी को पार ही कोनी पायो (हां पार को पायो हा नी कीयो)। अती दार तो कादा में लोटै ही (अर बूड़ी सी डांगरी बन रही)। देख पांच बरस की ढोरी बन गैइ (वाह वाह)। घोड़ा पर जीण

करो (हां गायां भागेली कीयो)। एक एक को पागड़ा में घाल लेयो (वाह वाह)। बो आतां ही ढाण्ढा का आडा तो फिरा लेयूं (हां आडा फिर जायूं)। अरै लेरै तो भाजां हो कीयो (वाह वाह)। और तो की कोनी दरबार का हुकमूं गाय जार नौसै निनानवै गाय के बीचै ऊबी रह गी (वाह वाह)। जाती गाय डिढाई (म्हे)। सगळी की सगळी गायां सागै के सागै (डिढाई जी कीयो)। कांई झमरी पर पूंछ मेलै (म्हे)। कांई गायां देखां अब दरबार का हुकमूं हिंवाड़ियां का खाळ लांघ जावै देखां (कीआवूं जाणज्यो देखां अब कीआवूं)। अबार कहवां देव का हुकमूं ले तूं (वाह वाह जी वाह वाह)। देवदाता तूं पार करी देखां।।

जाती गाय नाहरी बन गी बन देव की गाय।
काबर केलो साण्ड बैठ ग्यो डाय भुवानी लागी जाय।
रावजी का ई घोड़ा दपटिया दपटी ठाकर देव की गाय।
गायां लांघी ठाकरां हिंवाड़्यारो रो खाळ।
गुदलिया की पाळ से देव को नापो नीकलयो माथै मुकट बनाय।
धीरै रीज्यै दीया जोधका धरजै पांव।
काळू मीर दीयोजी पाछा फीर गुआल नै दाकले।
तूं तो गुआलिया रे अब के चोट समाय।।
(भलां जी भलां) किषन भलां

जाती गाय तो नाहरी बन गी (म्हे)। बनी देव की (गाय)। अरै गायां दपटी हेंर राव का अमराव दपटिया दपटी पारनमूनी (गाय)। अब गायां लांघ ही ठाकरां हिंवाड़ियां को (खाळ)। बांसां तक हिंवाड़ा को खाळ बहवो (म्हे)। गायां हो गी जी टैम बहवार देगो (हां बहवार देर सूख गियो)। हेंर रावजी का अमराव गिया नै (म्हे)। बी टैम पाछो (बांसां तक बहवण लाग गियो जी कीयो)। मीर बूझणा करी रे यार दीया गायां को दूध मीठो कोनी (हां जाण दे डूब अर मरणला कीयो)। गुदलिया से पाळ देव को से नापो नीकलयो अब (वाह वाह)। माथै मुकट (बना अर)। दरबार का हुकमूं रावजी साय का अमराव गुआल ने दाक लियो (म्हे)। गुआल देव का अब के चोट ही (समाय)। जीत तो देवजीआलां गायां की है (हां थै कठै जाओ)। मीर कीयो यार दीया जोधका आनै क्या दोष है गुआलो ऊबो है नी (हां आ नै पकड़ो कीयो)। गुआल कीयो रे भैइ थै लड़ो ही क्युं (हां गायां . . .)। गायां नै छोड़ी है तो माळा में मतै तो पड़ी कोनी मैं बाड़ी है (हां बाड़ी हूं कीयो)। मैं ऊबो हूं डर कांई है (हां थानै डर कांई बात को आवो सामे)। दरबार का हुकमूं दीयो बूझणा करी जरां समझ (हां अब समझ कीयो)। हेंर देख रे गुआल (म्हे)। मन में रह जायली बाह करणी है तो धाप अर कर ले (हां पहली कर ले कीयो)। गुआल कीयो ईंयां कींयां करी बात (हां ऊंधी बात कींयां करो कीयो)। अरै भैइ खेत को धणी गुआलिया नै कूटै गुआलियो खेत का धणी नै (हां कूटै कीयो)। तूं तो है खेत को (धणी)। अर मैं हूं (गायां को गुआल)। बाह करै तो दीया रे तूं ही (पहली कर कीयो)। दीयो बूझणा करी रे गुआल (म्हे)। मिनखा जूण पर बाह कोनी करूं (हां मैं बाह कोनी करूं कीयो)। कांई करै (हां हाको को हकाळ करूं ईयूं जीव नीकल जाय कीयो)। पीराण छुटै म्हारी हाक से (वाह वाह)। कीयो कीं कर भलां

पहली हक थारो है (हां हक थारो है पछ म्हां में करामात होय तो मैं कर (लेयां कीयो)। दरबार का हुकमूं दीयो छोड़ घोड़ा को आनो (म्हे)। के हाक मारी (वाह वाह)। गुआल नै बतलायो गुआल (कांई सला कीयो)। कीयो खांगो तो कोनी व्हियो ताणी हाकूं (इयां कांई हाक करी कांई कीयो मैं तो ऊबो बठै ही)। दरबार का हुकमूं मीर कीयो यार दीया जोधका क्युं आंतड़ा तोड़ै (म्हे)। हाक से मरबाली चीजां ए कोनी (हां ए कोय नै कीयो)। तीन तिलोकी का नाथ का देव का है गुआल (वाह वाह)। दीयोजी दरबार का हुकमूं तीर कमाण पर हाथ (मेलियो)। ले भैइ गुआल अब समजयी (अब सम कीयो)। कीयो आबा दियो (वाह वाह)। दरबार का हुकमूं दीया को जी टैम में बाण चाल्यो (म्हे)। गुआल घोड़ा को (हां फैरणी हो)। खोड़ला घोड़ा के नीचलै छेड़ै बड़ गो (वाह वाह)। तीर गियो अर पाछो असवार (हां हो ग्यो)। कांई सला (हां बठै ही हूं कीयो)। दो फरड़ा सागै छोड़ दियो (वाह वाह)। कठ जाय अब के देखां (हां अब के कठै जाय)। आवै के आवां दे (आण दे कीयो)। छप्पनजी भैरूंजी की कलां ई (म्हे)। छप्पनजी भैरूं लो टाल दिया (वाह वाह)। दीयो बतलायो कांई सला (हां कीयो बठै हूं कीयो)। दीयो मन में देखियो रे जलम की बात हो गी (म्हे)। थारी बहनचोद चोट बाहतिया आगै हाथी कोनी ठमै (हां आ मिनखा जूण है ई के की कोनी (बीगड़ियो बियां को बियां (खड़ियो है कीयो)। खांगो ही कोनी व्हियो (वाह वाह)। तीन फरड़ा सागै (मेलिया)। गुआल बोलै (म्हे)। कांई समचार दीया नै कहवै (हां कीआवूं जाणज्यो देखां अब कीआवूं)। अबार कहवूं देव का हुकमूं लियो थै।।

ए एक बाह तो जी सगळा नर करै रे माझी जोधका रे।
दीया भाई रे दूजी करै नै कोय।
तीजी बाह जको नर करै रे माझी जोधका।
बी को बाप तो रे गदा सामान होय।।
(भलां जी भलां) देव भलां

एक बाह तो सब नर करै (म्हे)। पछै दूजी करै नै (कोय)। अरै तीजी बाह तो जको नर करी (म्हे)। बी को बाप गदा सामान (होय)। सारा दिन बाहयां जाय (हां ठहर कीयो अब म्हांकाली ले तूं)। एक तो म्हानी ले अर (वाह वाह)। तीर कबाण के हाथ मेलियो (म्हे)। चरडाट बोल्यो के तोबा तोबा देव की दुहाई है भैइ (हां तीर छोड़ी मना)। तीर मत छोड़ी (वाह वाह)। तो गुआल का बहम से राव का अमराव डरता (डरता)। गायां हिंवाड़ियां को खाळ (लांघता)। देव की नौलाख अस्सीहजार गायां पाणी पी जातां जय बोलो श्री देव महाराज की (जय)। तो दरबार का हुकमूं अरै म्हारावूं झगड़ो कर ले भैइ नटियां ई कींयां करां की में (झगड़ो करो) हां हां (गुआल ही कहसी अब म्हांकाली टैम है कीयो)। तो दरबार का हुकमूं कीयो दीया गुआल बूझणा करी की झगड़ा म्हारा कन घणी भांत का है (म्हे)। किस्यो झगड़ो तूं थारावूं करूं (हां करणो चावै जको बताओ कीयो)। कीयो भैइ कती भांत का है के की तीन भांत का झगड़ो तो है म्हारै कन्नै (वाह वाह)। इसका नांव कीयो एक तो है सपरलोट हेंर एक दरबार का हुकमूं कांकड़ी बुरड़को है (म्हे)। हेंर गुड़बेद है (हां तीन भांत का झगड़ो है किस्यो करी कीयो)। मीर बूझणा करी नांव तीना का अच्छा (है पण आंका गुण ओगुण बूझो कीयो)। कीयो

भैइ गुआल सपरलोट तो किस्यो हुवै (म्हे)। गुड़बेद (किस्यो हुवे)। कीयो सुण भैइ मीर सपरलोट तो बो है के घोड़ा नै छोड़ द्यूं असवार नै मार द्यूं (असवार नै मार राळूं कीयो ओ तो सपरलोट है)। हेंर गुड़बेद के असवार नै छोड़ूं घोड़ा घोड़ा नै ही (हां मारूं कीयो)। कीयो कांकड़ी बुरड़को (घोड़ै को अर असवार को दोन्यां को सागै को सागै पापो काटां हां (कीयो)। कीयो तोबा तोबा तोबा तोबा दो ई तो नांव ही खोटा (हां दो नांव खोटा है कीयो)। आप नै तो आ गुड़बेद है (आ सीख लियो कीयो)। आ सीख लियो (वाह वाह)।।

चरक भवानी छोड़ो ठाकरां तोपां मेलो बाट।
बावड़ो गुआल गाय का कर लेयूं मूठ पर हाथ।
अती कहतां गुआल देव का बावड़िया दिया मूठ पर हाथ।
घोड़ो गांगला भाट के ठाकरां उजड़ चालतो बाट।
गायां को गुआल घोड़ा नै झाटक्यो ज्यूं पेट फुटै धोल पड़िया को गांगलो भाट।
घोड़ी दादा दायमा ठाकरां उजड़ चालती बाट।
गायां को गुआल घोड़ी नै झाटकी ठाकरां कर दियो खेत राजपालो।
घोड़ी दीया जोधका के ही बोर काळी रे।
गायां को गुआल नै गाय आ घोड़ी नै झाटकी दिया नै कर दियो खेत राजपालो रे।
घोड़ी काळू मीर के ठाकरां उजड़ चालती बाट।
मीर की फौजां में पड़ियो भजागड़ो।
फौजां में मीर गियो भाज।
गुआल देव महाराज को मीर के फीरयो अड़ावूं जाय।
म्हारा टटू छोड़ गुआल देव का देव का दळां में तेरा घणा बदावूं मान।
गलबल गलबल मत कर बैरी तूरकड़ा रे मती बजाज्यो घाल।
अब के फेगी खूंटै खेर के देखां हळ फाटै के हाल।
घोड़ा ही घोड़ा काटिया रे गुआल गाय के।
राव का अमरावां के माथै मेलिया पिलाण।
(भलां जी भलां) देव भलां

तोपवूं तोपां भवानी छोड़ो कीयो (म्हे)। हेंर तरक भवानी छोड़ दियो तोपां पर मेलो (बाट)। अरै बावड़ो म्हारा देलो (म्हे)। दियो मूठ पर अब (हाथ)। हकाळिया अर पाछा बावड़िया दिया मूठ पर (हाथ)। ए घोड़ी ऊठी गांगला भाट के (म्हे)। उजड़ चालती (बाट)। गायां को गुआल घोड़ी नै झाटकी गिरजा बी की रह गी (आंत)। घोड़ी ही दरबार का हुकमूं गांगा भाट के (म्हे)। हेंर ही ही भंवर घोड़ी हुती दादा दायमा के ऊजड़ चालती (बाट)। गायां को गुआल घोड़ी नै झाटकी पेट पुटै धोल पड़िया को गांगलो (भाट)। अरै घोड़ी ही दीया जोधका के ही बोर (काली)। गायां को गुआल घोड़ी नै झाटकी दीया नै कर दियो खेत राज (पाळो)। मीर की फौज में पड़ गो भजाड़ो (म्हे)। मीर गियो फौज में (भाज)। देव को गुआल ठाकरां फिरियो उडावो (जाय)। अरै मेरा टटू छोड़ गुआल गाय का (म्हे)।

देव का दळां में घणा राखूं (थारा मान)। कीयो गलबल गलबल मत कर गेली तूरकड़ा (म्हे)। मती बजाबो (घाल अर)। अरै अब के फेगी खूंटै खेर के देखां हळ फांटै की (हाल)। घोड़ा ई घोड़ काटिया गुआल देव को (म्हे)। ठाकरां राव का अमरावां के माथै मेल दिया (पिलाण)। काटियां तो बेचो (हेंर मजा करो)। मीर कीयो यार दीया कोय बिचार कोनी जान ने खतरा नैइ (म्हे)। टटू मरिया है (वाह वाह)। रावजी सा फैर दे गा (औरूं दे देय रावजी नै कीयो)। और कांई हुई जान देवती रह गी ने (वाह वाह)। अल्ला के नांव से पांच फकीर जिमावांगां जांतां ही (वाह वाह)। दीयो बूझणा करी तूं अल्ला के नांव जिमाई नै (म्हे)। मैं देबी का पांच भोपा (जिमा द्यूं जांवतां ही)। भली करी भगवान जिन्दा आयगा भैइ (वाह वाह)। जको कायदा रावजी का राखयोड़ा हा कीयो हारै जको सगस हार का चूंतरा पर जाओ (म्हे)। जीतै जको जीत का पर (हां जार बैठो)। ए तो हार का पर गिया बादरा ही (सीधो ही बठै जार बैठो हाराला चूंतरे)। दरबार का हुकमूं रावजी कीयो जलम हो गा (म्हे)। देवजीआला गुआलिया तो दात तो लाखां ही (हां नैइ देवे)। तो रावजी सा मन में बिचार करियो (म्हे)। अरै आपणै जुवाईं साय नै परवाणा दे देया (वाह वाह)। तो जी दिन गायां के घेरो लागायो नै देव औतार व्हियो जकै दिन (म्हे)। जकै दिन टोडा का सोलंकी को बाप हो जको बो गायां के मुण्डा के काम आयगो (हां बठै मरियो काम आयो कीयो)। जो बी का बाप का बैर भी नीकल जावै (म्हे)। हेंर आपणी की सारो (हां लाग जावै कीयो)। तो रावजी सा बोलै (म्हे)। कांई टोडेदे का परवणा अब देवै देखां (कीआवूं जाणज्यो देखां कीआवूं)।।

लिखिया परवाणा जी ए ई रावजी मोकळिया रे।
लिख दीना भाई रे सोलंकीयां के शहर।
बांचतै परवाणै बेगो चड़ी रे सोलंकीयां का डावड़ा।
ताणा पिता रे भीसमदास के बैर।।
(भलां जी भलां) देव भलां

लिखियार रावजी परवाणा टोडै ई मोकळिया (म्हे)। अरै लिख दिया सोलंकीयां के शहर (शहर)। ए बांचतै परवाणै बेगो आ सोलंकीयां का डावड़ा (म्हे)। थारा पिता भिसमदास के (बैर)। आ सिंग पद्दी अब हुई है सिंग पद्दी नी पहली जो बगड़ावतां का बारां में दास पद्दी रजपूत नै ई सिंग पद्दी नी ही दरबार का हुकमूं भीसमदास ने थारा बाप ने मारियो गुआल (म्हे)। बो बैर भी काढ ले हेंर दरबार का हुकमूं गाय नै अर गुआल नै पकड़ राताकोट में ही (हां ल्यायो)। रायका नै हुकम दियो जाओ रायका भाई (म्हे)। ओ परवाणो टोडै ले जार (हां देदेयो कीयो)। रायको चोखोसो टोरड़ियो पिलाण टोडा का मार गा टोरड़िया हांक दियो (वाह वाह)। दरबार का हुकमूं तारादे बाई ऊंची बैठी (म्हे)। मन में देखियो रे आज रायको भाई आपणा पीरालो कींयां आयो (हां कींयां आयो है कीयो)। तो बाई सा बोलै (म्हे)। कांई रायका नै बतलावै देखां (कीआवूं जाणज्यो देखां कीआवूं)।।

साण्डियो झैक द्यो जी रायका भाई रे चाण्दन चौक में औवूं रे।
पेड़ी ऊंचो आ पग दे आव।

तारादे करै रे तनै बूझणा।
म्हाना गढ में रे कांई पधारियो काम।।
(भलां जी भलां) देव भलां

साण्डियो झैक दे रायका भाई चाण्दन चौक में (म्हे)। ऊंचो महल में पेड़ी दे पग आव (आव)। अरै तारादे करै तनै बूझणा (म्हे)। म्हाना गढ में रायका भाई कांई पधारियो (तूं काम)। एक तो बाबोजी टोरड़ियां दिया जका लेरै रह गिया जका लेबै अर आयो (म्हे)। कोय चिठटी चिपाटी (हां ले अर आयो है कीयो)। कीयो बाई एकी कोनी ले आओ मैं (वाह वाह)। दरबार का हुकमूं मैं तो गाय गुआलां की पुकार ले अर (आयो हूं कीयो ई)। तो दरबार का हुकमूं टोडा की कछेड़ी के मांयनै परवाणै दरबार का हुकमूं कांई बंच जावै (म्हे)। कांई वारता बनै देखां (कीआवूं जाणज्यो देखां कीआवूं)।।

परवाणा बंचिया टोडा की कछेड़ी में तीसरा पोहर का जाय।
अब धेटा बांधो ठाकरां धाट का करो अमल असराळ।
सांमरी पेटी कस्सो नर बादरो कस लियो असल गैण्डा की ढाल।
आपणा दरबार में काढो भाई जूनी पाग सिरपाव।
पाणी रोको नंदी बनास को देवालो गुआलियो कठै बाही गाय।
थारै बांको गढ घणो सोलंकीयां का डावड़ा बांकै उज्जीनी धार।
आगै मिली गुआल देव का घणा बजायी भांलां केरा सार।
पाणी रोकियो रे नंदी बनास को।
डेरा दिया रे काळियादे पर जाय।।
(भलां जी भलां) देव भलां

परवाणो बंचियो टोडा की कछेड़ी में (म्हे)। तीसरा पोहर का (जा अर)। अब धेटा बांधो ठाकरां धाट का (म्हे)। अमल कर लेयो (असराळ)। आपणा दरबार मूं सिरदारां काढो जूनी पाग (सिरपाव)। अरै घोड़ा पिलाणो ताजी आरबी (म्हे)। धाटी घोड़ा (बोर)। रातड़ तो बोर मुआं धोळा घणा (सफेद)। सोलंकीयां को डावड़ो गाय गुआल पर नीकलयो चड़ अर (म्हे)। चड़ अर सावर को (राव)। दरबार का हुकमूं थारै तो गढ बांको घणो सोलंकीयां का डावड़ा (म्हे)। अरै बांकी उज्जीनी व्हिया (धार)। आगै मिली गुआल देव को (म्हे)। भालां का घणा बजाय (सार)। कीयो पाणी रोको नंदी बनास को (वाह वाह)। देवजीआलो गुआलियो को कठै बाही (गाय)। चड़ दरवाजा बाहरें सोलंकीयां को डावड़ो नीकल गो (म्हे)। ठाकरां बी कन्नै घोड़ो साडी पांच ही (हजार)। साडी पांच हजार घोड़ा लेय (म्हे)। हेंर दरबार का हुकमूं काळियादे पर जा डेरा (देदिया जी कीयो)। लियो भैइ अब कठै पाय गुआलियो गाय यो (हां अब . . .)। गुदलियो ही आगो रह गो (म्हे)। हेंर दरबार का हुकमूं काळियादे में ही पीबा द्यां कोय (नै)। रजपूतां का बेटा तंबूड़ा तो ताण लियो (वाह वाह)। हेंर रसोई पाणी की जुगत (हां होबा लगी)। तो दरबार का हुकमूं परभात की टैम गाय भगवान की अटेक गुदलिया आती नै (म्हे)। काळियादे पर ऊर (हां आंवती)। गोरम का भाखर से गुआल हेटा उतरिया (वाह वाह)। आ रावजी की बाईसी

गुआलां नै दीखी (वाह वाह)। बैरीबाज कीयो रे रावजी का बावन गढां सागा आयगा (हां चड़ अर आयग्या आज कीयो)। तो बैरीबाज आप की कहतो कोनी पहला की (सुणतो कोनी)। कांई टोडा का सोलंकीवूं पाधरो झगड़ो हो जावै देखां (वाह वाह)।।

जोड़ी पहरी गुआल बैरवीं ठाकरां सुरगनाथ मनायरा।
देव को नापो हाथां से ठाकरां ढाल तरवार समाया।
ऊठो भाई दुशमन पाणी रोकियो नंदी बनास को तिसाई ऊबी गाय।
जो गुआल ठाकरां तेग उजाटियो आभै करियो उजास।
टोडा की फौज नै झाटकी गुआल ठाकरां कर पूण्चा पाण।
घोड़ा अमराव काटिया रे गुआल गाय के।
जरां ठाकरां देव की रे पीयै तिसाई गाय।
घोड़ा अमराव कटार पाछो ही बावड़ियो।
रावजी जुवांईं की रे काना सुणी पुकार।।
(भलां जी भलां) देव भलां

जोड़ी गुआल खोली बैरवीं (म्हे)। सुरगनाथ मनाया (मनाया)। देव को नापो हाथां से ठाकरां ढाल तरवार (समाया)। बावड़ो देशो तो दरबार का हुकमूं टोडा का सोलंकी की फौज ऊबी ऊबी तिसाई (गाय)। तरवारियां ताळी उडी भांलां की बरसी (बाळ)। सूरां ठाकरां सांचां लड़िया काढ मतेई तज गा (पिराण)। गुआल देव को तेग उजाट्यो आभै करियो (उजास)। टोडा का सोलंअकी फौजां नै झाटकी ठाकरां कर कर पूण्चा (पाण)। पाणी छुट्यो नंदी बनास को (म्हे)। पाणी पीयै तिसाई देव की (गाय)। घोड़ा अमराव कटार सोलंकीयां को डावड़ो पाछो बावड़ गो (वाह वाह)। दरबार का हुकमूं पांच घोड़ावूं बंचर नीकलयो सावर गढ को (राव)। अब रावजी साय जुवांईं की काना ई सुणली (पुकार)। बी हाराला चूंतरा पर जा टोडा को सोलंकी (बैठ ग्या जी कीयो)। मीर बोल्यो ओ ले भैइ (म्हे)। आपां में हुई जकी की जकी ई में हुई बैरी में (हां जुवांईं में हुई है कीयो)। तो दरबार का हुकमूं टोडा का सोलंकी बोलै (म्हे)। हेंर कांई सुरां नै समचार कहवै देखां (कीआवूं जाणज्यो देखां कीआवूं)।।

कोय घोड़ो जी ए ई रावजी लाख को।
कोय म्हारो सुवा लखीणो टार।
बैरीबाज गुआल करां को बावड़ियो रे गुआल गाय को।
खाली कर दीना रावजी रे म्हारा पखरेतलां ठाण।।
(भलां जी भलां) देव भलां

कोय तो घोड़ो रावजी लाख को म्हारो (म्हे)। कोय सुवा लखीणी (हो टार)। बैरीबाज गुआल कर हाको बावड़ियो (म्हे)। खाली कर दियो रे रावजी म्हारा पखरेतालां (अब ठाण)। म्हारा घोड़ा अमराव मरा दिया तूं (वाह वाह)। मैं देखियो देवजीआला गुआल है जको आर पकड़ ल्यायो (म्हे)। कोय तो लाख को हो घोड़ो (वाह वाह)। कोय सुवा लाख को ही (हां हो टार कीयो)। मीर बोल्यो यार दीया

जोधका सांचो काम करियो तूं (वाह वाह)। अरै घोड़ा सब मर गा इसका (म्हे)। कोय बात कोय नी रावजी साय बोलै (म्हे)। कांई ओळमो दे देखां (कीआवूं जाणज्यो देखां कीआवूं)।।

ए बाई परणायीजी जो तनै रे सोलंकीयां का डावड़ा रे।
डायजै दियो रे सारो देश गुजरात।
घोड़ा अमराव मरा तूं पाछो बावड़ियो।
अब जुवांईं रे जिवेलो के काल।।
(भलां जी भलां) देव भलां

मैं तनै बाई परणायी कीयो (म्हे)। अरै डायजै दे दियो सारो देश (तनै गुजरात)। तूं घोड़ा अमराव कटार पाछो बावड़ गो रे सोलंकीयां का डावड़ा (म्हे)। अब जी कतरा (काल)। ए बेटी का बाप (हां जींवतो ही आयग्यो कीयो)। दरबार का हुकमूं थारो कायदो कत्तो राखियो मैं (म्हे)। बाई परणाई ए डायजै गुजरात देश सारो दे दियो (वाह वाह)। ओ समचार (रावजी कीयो)। तो टोडा को सोलंकी बोलै (म्हे)। कांई समचार पाछो रावजी नै कहवै देखां (कीआवूं जाणज्यो देखां कीआवूं)। अबार कह द्यां देव का हुकमूं ले तूं।।

ए ताणी बाई नै जी बेरां में राळ दे रे धणी राण का रे।
लगा द्यो देश डायजा के लाय।
मैं जींवतो पूगो रे जलम भोम का देश में।
मीणा के रावजी रे हाली रहूंलो जाय।।
(भलां जी भलां) देव भलां

ताणी बाई नै बेरां में राळ (म्हे)। ई डायजा के लगा देय तूं तो लाय (लाय)। अरै जींवतो पूगूं जलम भोम का देश में (वाह वाह)। मैं मीणा के रावजी हाली रहूं (जा अर)। ताणी बाई के खातर मरूं कोनी मैं (वाह वाह)। मीर बोल्यो रावजी साय (म्हे)। आपका जुवांईं अमखिया बोल मत बोलो (हां अमखिया बोल मत बोलो कठै)। आवघात कर लेला इस बाई का तारादे का छाती पर साल हो जायगा (वाह वाह आवघात कर मरेलो)। कांई राव कीयो इसका कांई कांई करो पाछा जिस्या सिरदार का कायदा बजावो (वाह वाह)। मीर कांई कायदो बजावां (म्हे)। कीयो इसनै घोड़ा द्यूं (वाह वाह)। अमराव द्यूं (म्हे)। दरबार का हुकमूं रावजी पांच से तो घोड़ा देदेया जुवांईं नै (वाह वाह)। पांच से अमराव (हां फौजां औरूं दे दीनी)। मीर को कीयोड़ो करियो (वाह वाह)।।

आखा खावो जी जो मीर जी तूं सांवता रे।
कींयां पी जावो उकलतो एराक।
गाय गुआलां पर अब के बीड़ो झेळ काळू मीरजी।
नीतर छोड़ दे म्हारी रे बांकी गढ सरवाड़ा।।
(भलां जी भलां) देव भलां

आखा खावै मीर सांवता कीयो (म्हे)। अर खाजावै भैंसां का (अधवाड़ा)। अब गाय गुआलां बीड़ो तूं झेळ (वाह वाह)। नीतर छोड़ो रे म्हारी बांकी गढ ई (सरवाड़ा)। ओ समचार रावजी साय (हां काळू मीरजी नै कीयो)। दरबार का हुकमूं मीर कीयो यार दिया जोधका (वाह वाह)। पट्टा बाज राखणा होवै तो सेंठी समालो भैइ (म्हे)। समचारां को पार कोनी रावजी साय सब अमरावां नै कहवै पण आपां गेला की बात कह रिया।।

कांकड़ में जाबा द्यो जी ए ई धणी राण का रे।
बाजो मीरां में मीर सुवायो रे।
गाय अर गुआल नै पकड़ लयावूं जी राताकोट में।
जरां जाणज्यो रे मीर मल्लां को जायो रे।।
(भलां जी भलां) देव भलां

म्हनै कांकड़ में जाबा देय (म्हे)। रावजी बाजो मीरां में मीर (सुवायो)। गाय अर गुआल नै पकड़ लियावूं तड़कै राताकोट में (म्हे)। जरां जाणज्यै रावजी मीर मल्लां को (ओ जायो)। तड़कै लियावूं (वाह वाह)। बाह वाह रे मीर वाह कीयो (म्हे)। दरबार का हुकमूं मीर की फौज तियारियां हो गी (वाह वाह)। टोडा को सोलंकी मन में बिचार करियो थारी तो हो गी हार (म्हे)। हेंर मीर की तड़कै हो जायी (हां जीत)। तूं तो मुण्डो दिखबालो रहवै कोनी अठै (वाह वाह)। थारो रहणो कींयां हुई भैइ (म्हे)। टोडा को सोलंकी बोलै (वाह वाह)। कांई समचार दरबार का हुकमूं मीर नै कहवै (हां कीआवूं जाणीज्यो देखां कींयां कहवे)। अबार कहवूं देव का हुकमूं (वाह वाह जी)।।

ए रूई बेचतो जी जो घोड़ी ल्यायो रे काळू मीर की रे।
ल्यायो भाई पीनण बेच पिलाणी रे।
आगै मिली रे गुआल गाय को।
महलां में घोर खोदे ताणी रे कूंकणदे पठाणी रे।।
(भलां जी भलां) देव भलां

तूं रूई बेचतो मीर घोड़ी ल्यायो है (म्हे)। अरै लेयायो पीनण बेच (पिलाणी)। आगै मिली गुआल देव का (म्हे)। महलां में घोर खोदे तेरी कूंकणदे (पठाणी)। महलां महलां में मीर दरबार का हुकमूं बीबी नै पहली नेप दिया (हां घोर को नेप दे रहा साडी तीन (फूट है ज्यादा ही है)। जको घोर खोदयोड़ी तियार (हां राखै कीयो)। मीर बूझणा करी रावजी साय (म्हे)। ए तमारा जुवांई बहुत मंगन गिंवार है (वाह वाह)। हमको अमखिया बोल बोल दीया (हां.)। हमारै फौज तो नैइ जाती है अब (वाह वाह)। मैला कपड़ा में मारिया जावै सिरदारां की बेगती नी होवै अगत जाय (हां अगत जाय कीयो)। रावजी सा कीयो रे मीर जावै की को पहेल के हार हियोड़ोयो थारी (म्हे)। कीयो श्री महाराज कपड़ा धुबा दे नै (हां जणा जांवां कीयो)। तो मीर का रावजी साय कांई धोबियां ने हुकम देवै (म्हे)। कांई कपड़ा धोबा की बता हो जावै (कीआवूं जाणज्यो देखां कीआवूं)। अबार कीआवूं भगवान देव का हुकमूं ले तूं।।

हलकारो फैरियो जी जो हिन्दवा रावजी रे।
ओ तो ठाकरां रे चिनकवार लगायां रे।
ए कताक धोबी रे राण के मांयने।
आ नै रावजी रे राजदरबार बेगा बेग बुलायी रे।।
(भलां जी भलां) देव भलां

हलकारो फैरियो हिन्दवा रावजी (म्हे)। ठाकरां बो चिनकवार (लगाई)। अरै कताक धोबी भाई थै शहर में (म्हे)। रावजी साया नै राजदरबारां नै बेगा बेगी (बुलायी)। बेगा आओ भैइ (वाह वाह)। क्युं की मीर का कपड़ा धोना है (वाह वाह)। तो धोबी तो आपांणी नांव उडीका लाय (हां तियार ही बैठिया)। तो रावजी सा हलकारा फैरतां हेंर दरबार का हुकमूं टोडा का सोलंकी का मुलायजा बदाता जय बोलो श्री देवनारायण भगवान की (जय)। दरबार का हुकमूं शहर का धोबी कहतां ही जेज लागी पण आतां जेज (हां नैइ लागी है)। रावजी साय की कपूरी धोबन ही (म्हे)। बी नै ठा (हां मोड़ो पड़ियो)। करै रावजी नै आपां तो आज (याद ही कोनी करिया)। दरबार का हुकमूं अरै सिरकार की धोबन तो ठेट की मैं हूं (म्हे)। बटवूं दरबार का हुकमूं घरांवूं चाली (वाह वाह)। कछेड़ी में पूगती (हुई है)। आंती कीयो श्री महाराज ईंयां कींयां करी (हां ईंयां कींयां करी आज थै कीयो)। कीयो धोबन कींयां करी क्युं नाचै (म्हे)। कीयो नाचै कांई बन्दी का कायदा मुलायजा जका हटा दिया थै (हां थै हटा दिया आज कीयो)। कीयो बन्दी का नांव शहर में तीन है (म्हे)। आधाक शहर में तो कपूर चन्दजी बाजूं (वाह वाह)। आधाक शहर में कपूर काकीजी बाजूं आधाक शहर में कपूरडी धोबनती (हां बाजूं कीयो)। श्री महाराज बन्दी का नांव तीन है नै (वाह वाह)। पण आपको म्हनै हुकम दियोड़ो जरां है (वाह वाह)। जो आज भूलिया कींयां म्हनै (हां म्हनै कींयां कोनी कुवायो भूल कींयां थे)। कीयो धोबन जा धोबियां के सागै जाती रह (म्हे)। थारै पिसाय आजाय पांती आया (वाह वाह)। कीयो ईंयां नी जावूं (हां ईंयां कींयां जावूं कीयो)। म्हारा मुलायजा कायदा होवै नै तो जावूं (हां बै का बै कायदा अर बै का बै का मुलायजा होवै जणा में (कपड़ा धोवनै जावूं कीयो)। जाय रे धोबन बै ई रही (हां बै का बै रही)। कांई कायदो है थारो (जकी बता)। श्री महाराज ए सब कपड़ा है जका म्हनै मिलता (म्हे)। तो मैं शहर का धोबियां कन्नु (हां धुआती)। पीसा सिरकार में सारा जका म्हारा हाथ में (हां आंवता)। मैं चुकाती लेरलां धोबियां नै (हां धोबियां नै चुकाती तो (मैं चुकाती सिरकारवूं कोनी चूकता)। सिरकार तो म्हनै देती (वाह वाह)। हेंर दरबार का हुकमूं सिरकार से म्हनै खच्चर मिलता (म्हे)। कपड़ो घालबा नै (हां बै कोनी)। कीयो जा धोबन थार बै का बै मुलायजार बै का बै कायदा तियार है (वाह वाह)। धोबन पाछी जाय कन्नै एक पांवणो रहतो (म्हे)। कमाली बेटी जको बी को जुवांईं बी को परणायोड़ो हो जको (म्हे)। कीयो पांवणा जावो कछेड़ी मूं साठ खच्चर लेयावो (वाह वाह)। म्हानी नांव भाज्यो नांव आवळ कावळ आयगो (हां भाज्यो)। श्री महाराज श्री महाराज म्हानी सासू आठ खच्चर मंगायां (हां आठ खच्चर दिरावो)। साठ को नांव भूल गो बापड़ो (वाह वाह)। रावजी साय कीयो रे धोबन तो घणा मांगै ई (म्हे)। ए जुवांईं सा है जका आठ ही मांगिया अब कोय बात नी दे द्यो (हां देदेवो कीयो)। आठ खच्चर ले अर धोबन कन्न पूगतो (व्हिया है)। धोबन कीयो पांवणा ईंयां कींयां करी

(इयां कींआ करी थांकन्नु खच्चर साठ मंगायां कीयो)। कीयो थारो बाप नांव कोनी आया म्हनै (हां आठ को ही नांव आयो कीयो)। कीयो दूजा तो सिरकार मूं मिलै कोनी (हां दूसरा गियावूं कोनी मिलै अब तो) इस्यो काम करो छै में तो कपड़ा घालो दोरा सोरा (म्हे)। हेंर एक पर पांवणा थै चड़ो (वाह वाह)। एक पर म्हनै (चड़ा लियो)। कपड़ा है सगळा जका छै में घालो (छै में घालियो अर शहर का धोबियां नै कह दियो पाळा (चालो)। राम मारिया थै पाळा चालो (वाह वाह)। तो छै में तो कांई करियो मीर का कपड़ा जका (घाल दिया)। एक खच्चर पर धोबनती (चड़ गी)। धोबन बोलै (म्हे)। कांई समचार धोबियां नै कहवै देखां (कीआवूं जाणज्यो देखां कीआवूं)। अबार कहवां देव का हुकमूं ले तूं (वाह वाह)।

सांठा रीज्यो जी ए ई म्हाना धोबनियां रे।
देवजीआला गुआलिया जायेला भाग।
गाय अर गुआल नै पकड़ ले चांलां रे राताकोट में।
जरां रावजी कन्नु रे घणी दिरावूं मोहताज।।
(भलां जी भलां) देव भलां

अब सांठा रीज्यो भैइ म्हारा धोबना (म्हे)। देवजीआला गुआलिया जायेला (भाग)। गाय नै गुआल नै पकड़ लेयावां राताकोट में (वाह वाह)। जरां रावजी कन्नु थानै घणी दिरादेवूं (मोहताज)। रावजी कन्नु मोहताज मोकळी दिरावूं (वाह वाह)। पण आप नै दरबार का हुकमूं गाय नै अर गुआल ने भाई धोबीड़ा रे पकड़ा ल्यानी है (वाह वाह)। कानियो धोबी जुवांई हो बी को (म्हे)। धोबन को (म्हे)। कानियो धोबी बोलै कांई समचार कहवै देखां (कीआवूं जाणज्यो देखां कीआवूं)।।

कानियो धोबी तो जी जो धोबियां में ऊबो चेरक्यो रे।
घालियो भाई रे आपका खच्चर का पूंछ नै हाथ।
बा गुआलां नै सासू ये ईंयां फैंक द्यूं।
फैंक द्यूं सासू ये भर भर दोन्यु बाथ।।
(भलां जी भलां) देव भलां

दरबार का हुकमूं कानियो धोबी धोबियां में चेरक्यो (म्हे)। घालियो आपका खच्चर का पूंछ नै (हाथ)। जो बा गुआलां नै ईंयां फैंकूं सासू (म्हे)। भर भर दोन्यु (बाथ)। खच्चर को पूंछ पकड़ (म्हे)। ए धोबीड़ो चारूंनेर फिर गो (वाह वाह)। कीयो ई खच्चर में करी नी (हां जकी की जकी जांवतो गुआलां में करूं कीयो)। धोबन कीयो बाह वाह जी पांवणा वाह जी पांवणा वाह जी पांवणा (ए तो थांका भरोसा ही है कीयो)। के पच्चास साठ नै थै एकला घणा (वाह वाह)। हेंर सौ खाण्ड नै मैं ही (हां साथ देयूं कीयो)। हेंर पछै राम मारिया शहर का धोबीड़ा है ई नै दूजोड़ा ए ई की तो करेला पछै कीयो (हां की ई तो ए करेला काम कीयो)। बा देवजीआला गुआलिया ने पकड़ा (वाह वाह)। तो दरबार का हुकमूं धोबन कांई करियो जाय (म्हे)। हेंर गुदलिया तलाब पर पूगती हु गी (वाह वाह)। धोबियां नै बूझणा (करी है)। अरै धोबीड़ा (म्हे)। दरबार का हुकमूं आधा कपड़ा धोबा लाग जाओ (वाह वाह)।

हेंर आधा कपड़ा का म्हारै कपड़कोट (हां बना द्यो)। डोड़ी परदा (हां लगा द्यो)। दरबार का हुकमूं डोड़ी परदा ल गा दिया हेंर धोबनती दीखै आपको महल बाना दियो आधा कपड़ावूं (वाह वाह)। आधा कपड़ा धोबीड़ा (हां धोवण लाग ग्या)। धोबन कांई करियो आपकी मांयनै बिराजमान (हो गैइ जी कीयो)। शहर का धोबियां नै हुकम दे दियो जाओ भाई कपड़ा धो (वाह वाह)। परभात की टैम में देव महाराज का गुआल अर गायां पूगती (व्हिया जी कीयो)। घोड़ां का पोड़ बोल्या (म्हे)। घोड़ा चड़ियोड़ा गुआल आया (वाह वाह)। तो धोबन बोलै (म्हे)। कांई गुआलां नै समचार (कहवै देखां)।।

जामरा कुत्ता तो जी ए ई कांवर सा डोर का रे।
थांकै कांवर जी ये मोती सोवै कान।
उणियारा दीखिया रे बीसळदे चुहाण का।
कींयां आया म्हारी रे मोटोड़ी गढ राण।।
(भलां जी भलां) देव भलां

जामरा कुत्ता भैइ कंवर सा डोर का (म्हे)। मोती सोवै (कान)। उणियारा दीखिया रे बीसळदे चुहाण का (म्हे)। कींयां पधारिया कंवरजी म्हारी मोटोड़ी गढ (राण)। कंवर साय (हां कींयां पधारिया हो कीयो)। देव महाराज का गुआल बोलै (म्हे)। कांई समचार धोबन नै (कहवै देखां कीआवूं जाणज्यो अब कीआवूं)। अबार कहवूं देव का हुकमूं ले तूं (वाह वाह जी वाह वाह)।।

ए जामरा कुत्ता तो जी जो धोबन म्हार कन्नै डोर का रे।
म्हांकै धोबन ये मोती सोवै कान।
गुआलिया बाजा ये नारायण देव का।
गायां चराताआया ये मोटोड़ी गढ राण।।
(भलां जी भलां) देव भलां

दरबार का हुकमूं जामरा कुत्ता तो डोर का है (म्हे)। हेंर मोती सोवै (कान)। के गुआल बाजा धोबन मां ठाकर देव (म्हे)। ए गायां चराता आयगा मोटोड़ी गढ (राण)। धोबन (म्हे)। मैं कंवर भंवर कोनी (हां मैं तो गायां का गुआल हां कीयो)। दरबार का हुकमूं गुआल बोल्या धोबन (म्हे)। कंवर भंवर मैं दरबार का हुकमूं कोय का ही (कोनी हां कीयो)। धोबन बोलै (म्हे)। कांई गुआलां नै दाकलै अब देखां (कीआवूं जाणज्यो देखां अब कीआवूं)।।

ए डोड़ियालां परदा तोड़िया जी ए ई जंगल का गुआलिया रे।
मैं हूं भाई रे राव के मरजीदान।
तड़कै पकड़ मंगावूं ये राताकोट में।
तड़कै मंगाल्यूं रे पूटियां मसकियां बांध।।
(भलां जी भलां) देव भलां

डोड़ियां का थै परदा तोड़ नाकिया (म्हे)। मैं हूं रावजी के मरजी (दान)। अरै तड़कै जावूं कछेड़ी के

मांयनै (म्हे)। थानै तड़कै मंगाल्यूं रे गुआलिया पूटियां मसकियां (बांध अर)। राम मारिया शरम ही कोनी आयी थानै (हां परदा के कन्नै ई आयग्या कीयो)। ले झूमरो (म्हे)। हेंर बाहरें नीकल गी (वाह वाह)। देवजीआली गायां पाणी पी अर कीयो रे धोबीड़ा (म्हे)। राम मारिया ऊबा ऊबा पाणी पीयै ढाण्ढियां (हां कपड़ा खराब करसी ठोको कीयो)। दरबार का हुकमूं ले ले मोगरा (म्हे)। हेंर देवजीआली गायां के धोबीड़ा (ठोकणो शुरू कर दिया जी कीयो)। सुरेमाता के धोबन एक मोगरा के (दीनी)। दोय मोगरा की (दीनी)। गुआल बोलै (म्हे)। कांई धोबन नै समचार कहवै (कीआवूं जाणज्यो देखां कीआवूं)। अबार कहवूं भगवान का हुकमूं ले तूं।।

मती बाहवै नै जी धोबन ये सुरै नै मोगरा रे।
लागी ये म्हारी ये कामधीण के डील।
ऊबा मत देखो रे गुआल गाय का।
धोबन दीखै रांड के रे लियो नै लीला पाड़।।
(भलां जी भलां) देव भलां

दरबार का हुकमूं मत मार धोबन म्हारी गाय नै मोगरा (म्हे)। ई ये लागै महारी कामधीण के डील (डील)। ऊबा कांई देखो रे गुआल देव का (म्हे)। रांड धोबनती के लियो नी लीला (पाड़)। रांड सुरै नै ठोक रे कीयो (म्हे)।।

मती बाहवो नै जी जो सुरै नै मोगरा रे।
लागे म्हारी रे कामधीण के टूंड।
ऊबो कांई देखै रे गुआल गाय का।
रांड धोबनती को आपां रे माथो ल्यो नै मुण्ड।।
(भलां जी भलां) देव भलां

दरबार का हुकमूं समचार गुआल देव को कीयो (म्हे)। कीयो मत बाह धोबनमां सुरै नै मोगरा (म्हे)। ई ये लागी म्हारी कामधेण के टूंड (टूंड)। ऊबो कांई देखै गुआल देव का रांड धोबनती को लियो नै माथो ई (मुण्ड)। ऊबा देखो गाय नै ठोकै (म्हे)। दरबार का हुकमूं बैरीबाज गुआल आप की कहतो कोनी पहला की (सुणतो कोनी)। तो धोबन को जार के चट्टो (पकड़ियो)। कड़ियां कड़ियां सुधा पाणी बड़तो (व्हिया जी कीयो)। दरबार का हुकमूं लेरली मूरी का गुआल पड़िया किरकाड़ (म्हे)। दरबार का हुकमूं कांई करियो के बैरीबाज गुआल के चट्टो पकड़ अर हिलोळा दिया (म्हे)। आव कपूरी जाव कपूरी आव कपूरी जाव कपूरी (जाय कपूरी लागा दीनी)। पाणीवूं भर नटां की ढोलकी भरै नै (म्हे)। जेसै भर गुदलिया की पाळ के उपरै (ले जार धोबन नै बैठा दीनी)। लेरली मोरी क गुआल (आयग्या)। बूझणा करी कांई बेधो करियो (हां कांई रोळो है कीयो)। कीयो बेधो कोनी (म्हे)। धोबनती का लाडकोड करां मैं तो (वाह वाह)। जरां म्हानै ही भैइ भुलावो कीयो पाणी तो अपरायोड़ी है (म्हे)। रूंगता थै चुग ल्यो (हां थै चुग ल्यो माथै का कीयो)। हेंसबाळा तो हेंसबाळा अर ख्यालां का खेलबाळा (वाह वाह)। कहतां ही जेज (लागी)। एक एक रूंगतो धोबन को पांती नी आयो (हां स का स उपाड़ लिया

कीयो)। लेरली मोरी का गुआल (औरूं आयग्या)। बैरीबाज गुआल गुदलिया का तळाव पर बेधो (क्यें को करियो कीयो)। नी भाई कोय बेधो कोनी धोबनती का लाडकोड (करां हां कीयो)। जरां भाई म्हां पर बेराजी हो जाय (हां म्हानै की भुलावो)। कीयो रूंगता तो मुण्डोयोड़ो है (म्हे)। चांचवा थै दे द्यो माथा (थोड़ा थोड़ा चांचवा दे द्यो)। चकूड़ा काढ चांचवा गुआल देव का (देदिया)। अताक पहली लेरली मोरी का गुआल (औरूं आयग्या)। बैरीबाज गुआल तळाव पर आज हाका बेधो (क्यें को कर मेलियो हो कीयो)। कीयो नी कोय बेधा कोय नी धोबनती आयी जको लाडकोडा करां (हां लाडकोड धोबनती का करां कीयो)। जरां म्हानै ही भुलावो (हां की मैं ही करां कीयो)। कीयो चांचवा दियोड़ा है (म्हे)। थोड़ोसो माथा में तपा देयो थै (वाह वाह)। छाना बाल लाल कर दियो (म्हे)। ए आकड़ो भर दियो (वाह वाह)। धोबन नै तो जियान गोर माण्डै है नै (हां जियान माण्ड अर पाळ के ऊपर बैठाण दीनी)। सिरायत गुआल लेरावूं (आयग्या)। बैरीबाज गुआल तळाव पर बेधो आज (कें को कर मेलियो हो कीयो)। कीयो बेधो नी करियो (म्हे)। मैं तो धोबनती का लाडकोड करिया है (वाह वाह)। कीयो जरां म्हां पर बेराजी होई (हां म्हानै की बताओ)। कीयो धोबनती कीयो कांई बताई दरबार का हुकमूं सिरायत गुआल के माथा के निंगै करी (म्हे)। अरै बेटी का बाप (जलम कर दिया कीयो)। ई जानवर नै क्युं मारियो रे बैरीबाज (म्हे)। दरबार का हुकमूं धोबन देखियो रे ओ गुआल सब मूं स्यानो है (हां ओ स्यानो है कीयो)। धोबन बोलै (म्हे)। कांई समचार देव का हुकमूं देखां गुआल नै सिरायत नै कहवै (कीआवूं जाणज्यो कीआवूं देखां कीआवूं)। अबार कहवां भगवान का हुकमूं देखां (वाह वाह सा)।।

ए जीभड़ली म्हानी तो जी गुआलजी लड़ बावळियां रे।
आ तो गुआलिया रे झक गी आळ झुंजाल।
चकूड़ा का चांचवा रे गुआल गाय का।
सहया म्हारी रे लाखीणी कपाळ।।
(भलां जी भलां) देव भलां

गुआल लेरलै जीभड़ली म्हारी लड़ बावळी (म्हे)। आ रांड झक गी आळ (झुंजाल)। चकूड़ा का चांचवा रे गुआल देव का (म्हे)। सहया म्हारै देख लाखीणै (कपाळ)। ई जीभूं बोलनी कोनी आयो (म्हे)। आ तो बोल रांड मांयनै बड़ गी (वाह वाह)। दरबार का हुकमूं देख ताणा गुआलिया म्हारा माथा में आ करी (हां ईंयां करी देख कीयो)। धोबन बोलै कांई समचार सिरायत गुआल नै कहवै (कीआवूं जाणीज्यो देखां कीआवूं)। अबार कहवूं भगवान का हुकमूं ले तूं (वाह वाह)।।

जीभड़ली म्हानी जी ए ई लड़ बावळियां रे।
गुआल देव का जै जाणै कोय बोल।
बिषकाळा को ही हेटो उतरे।
गुआल देव का रे जीभा के हिलोळ।।
(भलां जी भलां) देव भलां

गुआल जीभड़ली म्हारी लड़ बावळी (म्हे)। जै जीभ से कोय जाणै (बोल)। बिषकाला को रे गुआलिया हेटो ही उतरै (म्हे)। आ जीभ आयी तणै (हिलोळ)। गुआल (म्हे)। जीभ में ही तो जहर है (अर जीभ में ही अमरत है)। दरबार का हुकमूं म्हानी जीभ सावल कोनी री देख ले जरां म्हारो माथो ईंयां हु गो (वाह वाह)।।

कागा किसका जी धिन नी हरै गुआल गाय का रे।
गुआलिया देव का रे कोइयल किसको देत।
जीभड़लिया अमरत बसै रे गुआल गाय का।
गुआलिया भाई रे जुग अपना कर लेंत।।
(भलां जी भलां) देव भलां

दरबार का हुकमूं गुआल अरै कागा किसका धन नी हरै (म्हे)। अर कोयल किसको देत (देत)। जीभड़लिया अमरत बसै रे गुआल देव का जुग अपना (कर लेंत)। जी कागलो बोलै नै (म्हे)। जरां के भा2टां की देयो (हां उडावो कीयो)। कोयल बोलै (म्हे)। जरां कह देख फूटरी बोली (वाह वाह)। जीभ में रस होवै (म्हे)। जुग ही आपको हो जावै (वाह वाह)। धोबन दरबार का हुकमूं गुआल के मुण्डै के आय अर माथो दिखाळयो (म्हे)। हेंर कीयो देख गुआल लूगड़ी ई कन्नै जको ए लां फटकारो माण्डी (वाह वाह)। देख माथो करियो म्हारो (हां किस्यो करियो है सूगलो कीयो)। दरबार का हुकमूं सिरायत गुआल कन्नै ऊबो बैरीबाज धोबन है झोळी माण्डी नै (म्हे)। जरां ही मोटी सुवा मण की सिला (हां उठाई)। सिरायत गुआल बूझणा करी रे बैरीबाज (हां करियो ई को)। कीयो धोबनती माण्डी है नै झोळी (हां आ भरां नै)। कीयो सुण रे बैरीबाज (म्हे)। झोळी दुनिया में दोय है (वाह वाह)। के तो जोली है किरतार की (अर के झोळी है भरतार की)। पत्थर राळबा को जोली कोनी (वाह वाह)। तो सिरायत गुआल कांई करियो की और तो कन्नै हो कोनी (म्हे)। हेंर सुवा करोड़ को मूंदड़ो हो हाथ में (वाह वाह)। धोबनती के झोला में (हां मूंदड़ो खोल अर राळ दियो)। तो चौदाह सौ चम्मालीस सगळा गुआल सिरायत राळियो नै (म्हे)। लेरला सगळै तड़क तड़क धोबनती को भर दी झोळी काटी (हां मूंदड़ावूं मूंदड़ावूं भर देय)। धोबन मूंदड़ा पर हाथ फैरै जीव सोरो (हो जावे)। माथा पर हाथ फैरै रे जीवड़ा तो तड़कै मर जायी आ नै खाय कुण (हां खाय कुण कीयो अमरता नै)। दरबार का हुकमूं गुआल तो मतै मतै धोबन नै सीख दे अर जातां रियां (वाह वाह)। गिया पछै बा जी टैम में धोबन के निवतो पड़ियो नी (म्हे)। बी टैम में गुआल तो धोबीड़ा मतै मतै हा जका भाज छुट्या (वाह वाह)। कानियो धोबी भाजो (म्हे)। एकान बाहरा कोस की उजाड़ ही एकानै पाणी आयगो (पाणी आयग्यो)। जावै कुनै (जावै कठै)। तो धोबीआली बा सिला होवै नी बा ऊंचिया (हां घोड़ीसी करियोड़ी होवे)। बी के हेटै बड़ गो (वाह वाह)। दरबार का हुकमूं गुआल देव का गिया अर के बाहरें नीकलयो (म्हे)। धोबन कीयो रे जुवांईंजी थै कठै हा (हां थै कुनै गिया है कीयो)। मैं तो देखो गुआलां नै कूटती कूटती म्हारा बावळियां रहगिया (हां बोहळा कूटिया मूंदड़ा अता भेळा करियो कीयो (कूट कूट अर)। देवूं कामड़ी के सड़ाक मूंदड़ो राळै तड़ाक (वाह वाह)। देवूं कामड़ी की तड़ाक (म्हे)। मूंदड़ो डाल दियो तड़ाक (वाह वाह)। धोबीड़ो कीयो सासूजी बोल्या रहो (हां बोल्या रहो कीयो)। मूंदड़ा है जकी म्हनै

ठा है (हां थानै नीवतो पड़ितो जको ही म्हनै सगळो ठा है (मैं सगळी देखो)। कांई देखां थै (जकी बताओ कीयो)। कीयो देखो थानै गुआलिया पाणी में देखिज्यो ऊपराई (हां . . .)। हां हेंर रूंगता चुग्या (म्हे)। चांचवा दिया (वाह वाह)। आकड़ो दियो (अर पछै खोपड़ी बास्तै बाल तपाई)। पछै सिरायत गुआल आयो जरां थै बोबाया जरां मूंदड़ा दिया (हां बो दिन्या)। कीयो जुवांईंजी म्हनै कीया अबार (दूसरा नै मत कह दीज्यो)। शहर में जाय राण शहर में मत कैज्यो (वाह वाह)। ओ लियो एक मूंदड़ो (मत कैज्यो)। कीयो आज आज कोनी कहवूं (तड़कै कह द्यूं)। कीयो ओ लियो दोय (कीयो दो दिन कोनी कहवूं)। कीयो पांच ले लियो (कीयो पांच दिन तो पक्का ही कोनी कहवूं)। इयां कींयां करो (इयां कींयां करो कीयो)। कीयो जरां मूलो को बांटो कर (आधो आधा करो)। कदै कोनी कहवूं (कोनी कहवूं कीयो)। कीयो पांवणा ई जागां तो बांटूं जरां मूंदड़ा की से ऊठजाय (म्हे)। बठै चांलां आप नै घरां (अर बठै आधा आधा करल्यां कीयो)। म्हानी छोरी नै कमलूड़ी नै बुलालेवूं (म्हे)। बरोबर आधा देयूं (वाह वाह)। चालो कीयो (चालो कीयो)। चालणी कोनी आवै म्हारावूं कोय बै आपणा खच्चर हा नै (बै ल्यावो जको म्हनै चड़ार ले चालो)। कीयो थारा बाप गुआल गायां रळा ले गा (वाह वाह)। कीयो जरां पांवणा जरां चालणी कोनी आवै (हां म्हारावूं चालणी तो कोनी आवै कीयो)। तो दरबार का हुकमूं कानियो धोबी निंगै करियो (म्हे)। कुमहारांली घोड़ती निंगै (आयगी)। कीयो सासूजी कुमहारांली घोड़ी ऊबी है (हां बा कहवूं तो पकड़ ल्यावूं)। कीयो ल्यावो (हां ल्यावो पिराण राळ चांलां कीयो)। तो कुमहारांली घोड़ी पर धोबन नै छोड़ दी (म्हे)। धोबीड़ो लेरै (हां हुगियो)। आकड़ा की कामड़ी (तोड़ लीनी)। एक तो देवै टटू के (म्हे)। एक असवार के (हां सासूजी के ठोके)। धोबन कीयो जुवांईंजी कींयां करो म्हारै तो काल गुआल ही घणी ठोकी (हां थै क्युं ठोको कीयो)। कीयो सासूजी असवार नै ठोकिया बिनै ओ टटू बेराजी होवै (हां ओ चालणालो कोनी कीयो)। थोड़ो घणो दस्तूर थांकै करणो पड़ी (वाह वाह)। ईंयां कर घरां पूगता कर दिया (म्हे)। धोबन के आकड़ो चड़ गो जको घरां जार रात नै त्राह घाली (हां वाह रे)। सारै ही दरबार का हुकमूं नायियां को घर हो (म्हे)। परभात की टैम नायन आयी (वाह वाह)। कीयो काकीजी (म्हे)। भायां पाड़ोस में रात नै एकला रातीजोगो दे द्यो (हां म्हनै कीयो ई कोनी गीत गुवा देती कीयो)। कीयो नायन (म्हे)। की को रातीजोगो देय कमालिया तेली कन्नु काल के दिन में पत्थरणो (भरायो कीयो)। राम मारियो कोय कांकरो रह गियो मांयनै (कांकरां रह ग्या बै चुबा हा मैं तो त्राहि घाली ही)। नायन देखियो रे थारी मां जाणु देख कोमल शरीर की है आ (म्हे)। कीयो ईंयां मत कहो बात हुई जको कहो (हां कांकरो चुबियावूं अती त्राहि घालो कोनी)। जरां नायन नै कह माथो दिखाळयो देख नायन तूं है नायन (म्हे)। माथा घणा गूंथै म्हाना माथा को इलाज करै कांई (हां जकी बताय)। ओ बालियां काकीजी म्हनै रात कह दियो एनै (रात ई कर देती कीयो)। तो दरबार का हुकमूं पाणीवूं धोय माथा नै लगाय घी ठण्डो (म्हे)। लगा दवाई माथा के ठण्ड पटक दी (वाह वाह)। के मैण लगायो माथा के (म्हे)। नायां के घरां रूंगता को तो घाटो हो कोनी (हां घणा ई हा)। लेय बड़ा बड़ा रूंगता अर मैण के मांय चोब दिया (वाह वाह)। चोब (म्हे)। मौलीवूं माथो गूंथार धोबन को तियार कर दियो (हां चट्टो बना दियो)। कांई सला (कीयो अब हूं सेंठी)। हां चट्टा बिनै रांड नै चाल कोनी आवै रे नायनै (म्हे)। कीयो घाल दियो नै (हां अब घाल

दियो नै कीयो)। ओ ले जरां ए पांच मूंदड़ा (आ ले कीयो ओ हो)। दरबार का हुकमूं नायन देखियो रे थारी जाणु मां जाणु राणीजी को माथो रोजीना गूंथा आपां (हां कदै मूंदड़ो एक ही कोय नी दियो टको देवे)। देख धोबनती को माथो एक दिन गूंथियो (हां मूंदड़ा पांच देदिया कीयो)। नायन के तीन बरस को बच्च्यो हो गोदियां में (म्हे)। कीयो धोबनती काकीजी लियो थोड़ोसो म्हाना बच्च्या नै राखजियो मैं राणीजी को माथो गूंथयावूं (हां राणीजी को माथो गूंथर आवूं जतै बच्च्या नै राखो)। कीयो ल्या (बेगी ल्या बेटा मैं राखलूं)। दरबार का हुकमूं मूंदड़ा ने मूंज की जेवड़ीवूं पुवाया (म्हे)। की तो भी बच्च्या के घाल दिया (अर की आप के घाल दिया)। की आप पहर लिया (वाह वाह)। नायन कांई करियो छोड़ बच्चा नै (रावजी के महल में (हां पूगती हु गी)। बी के तो माथो गूंथो झट ही माथो ही गूंथ लियो (वाह वाह)। कीयो म्हारी ताकीदी है आज सा (म्हे)। गूंथ माथो कीयो सीख दिरावो (हां ल्यावो कीयो)। कीयो भैइ दासी नायन नै एक टको अर कांचळी ल्या द्यो (हां नायन नै एक टको अर कांचळी ले अर देदेयो)। नायन कीयो श्री महाराज ठीक है सिरकारवूं तो देयो थै (म्हे)। थै तो देश का धणी हो (वाह वाह)। थांकी धोबन को आज माथो गूंथ अर आयी हूं मैं (हां आज ही गूंथिया हूं पहली बार)। ए देखो पांच मूंदड़ा दिया है म्हनै (हां पांच मूंदड़ा दिन्या है कीयो)। टको देवो आप (अर आप टको ही देवो देश का धणी हो)। कीयो सुण ये धोबन (म्हे)। म्हांकै को तो मुलायजो कायदो बाताय पहली (हां कायदो बेसी कोनी दियां कीयो)। वाह तो भैइ जरां माथो म्हारावूं रोजीना गूंथीजै कोनी अब (म्हे)। नायन तो ले टको कांचळी आपकी ई गली आयगी (म्हे)। हेंर धोबन बच्च्या नै ले गला में बै मूंदड़ा घाल अर (हां . . .)। आपका पगां में घाल लियार गला में (की घाल लिया)। ई ई गली आयगी (वाह वाह)। दरबार का हुकमूं आ नायन नै गेला में सेंठी कोय नी (म्हे)। जार दरबार का हुकमूं राणीजीवूं रामा शामा (करिया जी कीयो)। आवो धोबनमा आवो काकीजी (आवो कीयो)। ओ टाबर (की को कीयो)। कीयो सा मैं भैरूंजी के जावूं गुदलिया का तळाव में (म्हे)। ओ तो काल म्हनै भैरूंनाथ दियो है (हां भैरूंजी बकसियो है कीयो)। कीयो भैरूंजी दिया है (म्हे)। ए मूंदड़ा कीयो ए मूंदड़ा तो देवजीआला गुआलिया आवै जको घणा ल्यावूं (हां बा नै ठोकूं अर मूंदड़ा ल्यावूं)। घर भर दियो (म्हे)। घरां ऊंधरा घणा रह गा राम मारिया टापरा पाड़ोसी नै न्याळ कर दिया (वाह वाह)। कांई के बीला के मांय के कर ले जा पाड़ोसिया के घर राळ दिया (हां बा नै और कर दिया न्याळ कीयो)। मन में देखियो रे थारी मां जाणु कीयो धोबन (म्हे)। म्हनै एक बच्च्यो तो म्हनै दिराय जरां (हां एक बच्च्यो म्हनै दिरावो नै जी)। श्री महाराज थानै कींयां लागी जी कीयो (हां थाने)। मैं तो कांकर में फिरबाळा आदमी हां तीन बारी जावा पाळा जातां रा (हां जचै जियान ऊठ जावां पण थै कींयां जावो)। देश का धणी हो थै (म्हे)। कीयो भाई धोबन एक तो डावड़ी मैं तो नापुत्रिया हां ए (हां बेटो तो म्हनै एक दिरावै जणा ही होवै कीयो)। कीयो श्री महाराज तड़कै दिरा द्यूं (हां दिरा तो मैं द्यूं पण (मैं कहवूं जियान करणो पड़े)। सुवा मण को तो परसाद करो गुलगुला को (वाह वाह)। कणकतीबंध नै खाड़ेती सुवाय दूजा नै लेयो मत मैं चालूं (हां सागै दूसरो सिरदार नै नैइ लेवोला)। तो दरबार का हुकमूं तड़कै के दिन दिरा द्यूं (वाह वाह)। तो चांलां कींयां कीयो मैं बतावूं सा (हां मैं बतावूं)। पेट दुखाओ (वाह वाह)। बैध भोपा हो जाय तो पेट राखजियो मत मैं आवूं अगराखां द्यूं भैरूंजी के नांव से (म्हे)। चुप बोल्या रह जाय (हां चुप रह जायज्यो)। तो धोबन

तो अती कह अर नीकल गी राणीजी तो आटी पाटी ले अर महल में (हां सोयगिया)। कीयो राणी के कांई हो भाई (हां राणीजी को कीयो पेट दुखन लाग रहियो है)। रावजी साय बैध भोपा करणा जका (कर लिया)। मिस को पेट क्युं रहवै (हां बो झूटो पेट क्यें को रहवै बा तो घणो घणै त्राहि त्राहि (करे)। दरबार का हुकमूं अताक पहली धोबन छोड़ भाव भैरूंजी को आयगी (वाह वाह)। कीयो कछेड़ी बेधा कांई है (क्यें को है कीयो)। कीयो धोबन राणीजी का पेट दुखै (म्हे)। कीयो धोबन मत कह तो (वाह वाह)। कीयो गुदलिया को भैरूंनाथ हूं (हां अबार धोबन कोय नै कीयो)। राणीजी को पेट मूठी बन्द मैं राखूं (हां बतावो)। पण ए एकली राणी की जात मांगूं (वाह वाह)। सुवा मण का गुलगुला (हां मांगूं कीयो)। कीयो धोबन राख तो सुरी थारा भैरूंजी ने कह दिरावां तड़कै (हां राख देय)। ओ ल्यो (वाह वाह)। अगराखां देता जेज लागी राणीजी कहतां अरै राम रे जीव सोरो हो म्हारो तो (बस टैम कांई लागो मिस के पेट में)। तड़कै लागेली जात (म्हे)। रावजी बोलै कांई समचार कहवै देखां (कीआवूं जाणज्यो कीआवूं देखां)। गुलगुला का सामान ल्यावो भैइ (वाह वाह)।।

रथड़ो जोत लियावो जी ए ई रथ का सागड़िया रे।
लियाजै भाई रे रथ के बेलिया जोत।
बांकड़ा बेटा बुकसै रे गुदलिया का भैरूंनाथजी।
नापुत्रिया रे रह गा रे मण्डोवरा पड़ीहार।।
(भलां जी भलां) देव भलां

बैलि जोत लिया भाई बैलिवान का (म्हे)। लियाजै रथ के बेलिया (जोत)। अरै बांकड़ा बेटा बुकसै गुदलिया का भैरूंनाथजी (म्हे)। मण्डोवरा रह गा मैं मण्डोवरा (पड़ीहार)। नापुत्रिया हां भैइ (म्हे)। जको म्हानै ई देखां एक टाबरियो दे देय तड़कै चोखो है राणीजी जाय मांयनै (वाह वाह)। सुवा मन का गुलगुला करां दिया हेंर बाकळा कराय (दिया)। दरबार का हुकमूं कीयो खाड़ेती एक चाहीज्यै सा (म्हे)। गांगा नै आ बूझणा करी गां गा (वाह वाह)। बैलि जोत ले भैइ (म्हे)। खाड़ेती जोय बेली अर कीयो ल्यायो साय की जागां ल्यावूं (म्हे)। कीयो महल के लेरै लगा देय (वाह वाह)। लेर महल की लेरली गली पर लगाय (दीनी)। धोबनती गुलगुला की पोट बोरी में बांध (म्हे)। रथ के मांयलै छेड़ै (मेलदी)। राणीजी नै कीयो आजावो साय (हां) मैं घरां चालूं जको तो जमाई धोक ले लेस्यूं (म्हे)। तो राणीजी लेरली बारी में आय कर बैठ (वाह वाह)। खाड़ेती नै बूझणा (करी)। खाड़ेती (म्हे)। दरबार का हुकमूं धोबनयाली गली के रथ नै चालबा देय भाई (वाह वाह)। कपूरडी रहवै बी गली में (हां चालण दे कीयो)। धोबनती तियार ही ऊबी (म्हे)। कीयो काकीजी तियार हो के हां करां की ऊबी हूं मैं (हां उडीकूं ही हूं आप नै)। कीयो आ जावो रथ में बैठो (वाह वाह)। ए श्री महाराज गांव का देख लेय (हां आपके बराबर मैं रथ में बैठूं कीयो)। ओळमो कोनी देवा (म्हे)। कीयो कुण देखै ई बड़ा आदमियां (हां आजावो काकीजी)। चालां झटकेन का आगा (हां बी नै तो बेटो चाहीज्यै कीयो)। कीयो देखो सा तीन बरस को म्हनै दिराज्यो कीयो कह दियो थानै (हां जातां ही दिरा द्यूं)। दरबार का हुकमूं धोबन आपांलां जुवांईं नै कीयो पांवणा (म्हे)। आज गुलगुला धपावूं हाथ आय (हां चालो कीयो काल बठै गुदलिया तळाव)। आप नै बी गुदलिया पाळ पर चालो (म्हे)। दरबार का हुकमूं बो

बड़लो हो नै (हां)। बी भैरूंजी है नै बड़लालो (वाह वाह)। बी का पुजारी बन जाओ (हां टीका टमका काढ बी पुजारी बन बैजावो)। के भाज्यो कानियो धोबी (म्हे)। जा टीका टमका काढ चूंतरा पर पुजारी बन (बैठग्या)। जागता बना लिया घूप ध्यान करै माठो (वाह वाह)। तो कीयो राणी सा (म्हे)। खाड़ेती नै भूख लागी जाय तो की और रसोई ल्यावो की (हां ल्यायूं कीयो)। कांई (कांदो अर बाटी)। ठीक है भैइ कांई ठी जोत मोड़ी बेगी आवै तो (वाह वाह)। क्युं भूखो रह जालाय (म्हे)। तो ईंयां करतां करतां कीयो राणीजी बैठो पण भैरूंजी नै याद करां (हां याद तो करां)। तो राणी बैठ रथ के मांय बरोबर धोबनती राणजी के जोड़ै (वाह वाह)। गींदूलो सुवाय शुरू कर देयो (म्हे)।

राजा की राणी जाय गुआलियां की गींदूलो बेटा की भूखी जाय गुआलिया गींदूलो।
रथ में रह बेटी जाय गुआलियां गींदूलो।
गुआलियां की कूटी जाय गींदूलो।
बेटा की भूखी जाय गुआलियां गींदूलो।।

राणीजी तो कहवै बेटा की भूखी जाय रे गुआलियां गुलगुल जाय गींदूलो (म्हे)। धोबनती कहवै गुआलियां की रांड गींदूलो थै ओ कूटी नांव कींयां लियो (हां ईंयां कींयां लियो नांव)। कीयो देखो थोड़ो लेनो पड़ै बिचै (हां बिचै ठरको लगानो पड़े)। दरबार का हुकमूं गाती बजाती गुदलियो को दरबार का हुकमूं ऐरियो आयो नै (म्हे)। ए कीयो राणी साहब अब चड़ियोड़ो नी जा सकै (हां अठै ही ई का रथ नै रोक द्यो)। हेंर खाड़ेती नै दोय तो डगलसा कांदा दे द्यो (म्हे)। हेंर बै बाटियां दे द्यो (हां खाड़ेती नै दे द्यो कीयो)। ओ आपकी जीम लेयी (वाह वाह)। धोबनती के मोहरा पर ऊंची पोट नै (म्हे)। दोहरी सोरी (हां भैरूंजी जिताईं ही पूगती करी)। कीयो लियो महाराज धोक दियो (धोक दियो कीयो)। बो जोत कर मेली आगै तियारी जोत कर धोक (म्हे)। हेंर के धोबीड़ा बी का कानिया का कांई पायचा भरिया धोतीआला (वाह वाह)। कीयो पायचा में तो गुलगुला धपावूं घाल लियो (वाह वाह)। ऊंचा चड़ो (हां बड़ पर ऊंचा चड़ो कीयो)। की ताणी कीयो कालाला निंगै राखणी है (हां गुआलियां आवै जरां थे)। म्हनै बता दीज्यो सैन कर दीज्यो (हां मैं तो भागूं ज्यूं)। तो बो जुवांई तो बड़ला के ऊपर बैठ गो (म्हे)। हेंर राणीजी अर धोबनती आपकी छप्पनजी भैरूंजी की लूरियां बोलै (अर भैरूंजी नै मनावे)। दोन्यु जणिया कीयो बेटो द्यो महाराज राणीजी नै बेटा द्यो (वाह वाह)। अताक पहली एकानै तो धोबीड़ा के आंख फूटियोड़ी (म्हे)। एकानै बड़लालो पाण आयगो (आडो)। आंतरावूं तो गुआल दीखिया कोनी (म्हे)। देखेण का घोड़ा का पोड़ बोल्या (अर के धोबीड़ो देखियो)। देख पोड़ बोल्या बी टैम में कानिया धोबी का हाथ छूट गा (वाह वाह ऊपरलो डाळा परूं)। पड़ियो किरकाड़ जको राणीजी के गोदियां में पड़ियो (म्हे)। राणीजी नीचै बैठां चूंतरा पर (वाह वाह)। धोबन कीयो श्री महाराज म्हनै दियो काल तीन को (आवो थै लेयो पच्चीस को)। डाढी मूंछियां ओ ल्यो (आ ल्यो समहालो)। ओ तो बेटो लेयो (म्हे)। हेंर आ म्हानी लेयो कामड़ी म्हारै कामड़ी काल बी केर में रह गी सुगंतरी बा बी ल्यावूं (बा मैं ल्यावूं)। गुआलियां कह दीज्यो कामड़ी के सड़ाक मूंदड़ो राळ देय तड़ाक (तड़ाक)। धोबनती तो भाज गी (वाह वाह)। राणीजी नै दे गी कामड़ी गुआल फट खायायी (म्हे)। आंतां ही दरबार का हुकमूं बैरीबाज गुआल कन्नै ऊबो रह आज भूणाली माता कींयां आयी अठै (कींयां आयी

है कीयो)। कीयो भूणाजी नै चूंगाई कोनी तो (म्हे)। तो दरबार का हुकमूं गुआल तो जाणयो अर माजी सावूं बात करां भूणा की मां जरां आपांणी मां ही ए लाण (म्हे)। राणीजी नेड़ो आतां ही कामड़ी की कह ऊंची होर सरकाई (वाह वाह)। तो गुआल देव को बोलै (म्हे)। बैरीबाज कांई राणीजी नै समचार कहवै देखां (कीआवूं जाणज्यो देखां कीआवूं)। अबार कहवूं भगवान का हुकमूं (वाह वाह सा)।।

ओछी राणीजी ए ई तूं राव की रे।
राणी राव की ये लांबी भर गी भीख।
भूणा की माता ये कुण की लागी सीख।
(भलां जी भलां) देव भलां

ओछी राणी राव की (म्हे)। लांबी भर गी (भीख)। ए भूणा की माता तूं कुण की लागी (अब सीख)। माताजी कुण की सीखवूं आयी तूं (म्हे)। देखै राम मारियो मूंदड़ो कोनी राळियो बोल्यो कीयां (वाह वाह)। दोन्यु हाथावूं कर जोड़ गुआल के (हां औरूं ठोकी)। ठोकतां ही जेज लागी (म्हे)। फट राणीजी को चट्टो पकड़ लियो (वाह वाह)। ठर जो घणा दुनिया तनै (हां बोहळा दुनिया मुलायजो राखियो माताजी से जकावूं कांई (कीयो)।।

ऊबो गुआल तो जी जो बो चेरक्यो रे।
घालियो राणी का चट्टा मांयनै हाथ।
राणी जै नै रे कादा में रोपदी।
राणी का चट्टावूं काटी रे मोतसरियां की लूम।।
(भलां जी भलां) देव भलां

ऊबो गुआल चेरक्यो (म्हे)। घालियो भाई राणीजी का चट्टा मांयनै (हाथ)। राणी नै तो कादा में रोप दी म्हे)। राणी का चट्टावूं काटी गुआलियो मोतसरियां की (लूम)। लाख रिप्या की लूम है जकी गुआल काढली (म्हे)। राणीजी नै कादा के मांय रोप दी (वाह वाह ओ डोल है कीयो)। थारो ओ डोल है तनै मां मां करियो ने जरां दो कामड़ी की दी म्हारै (म्हे)। राणीजी मन में देखियो आटै बेटा कठै है (हां अठै कठै बेटा अर कठै मूंदड़ा है)। रांड धोबनती देखी ल्यायी आपां नै (हां सूगली करायी कीयो)। गुआल कीयो भूणा की माता सिखायोड़ी आयगी (म्हे)। जाती रह तूं (हां ऊठ जा अब)। देव का सिरायत गुआल बूझणा करी बैरीबाज (म्हे)। कांई करै (वाह वाह)। अरै भूणा की मां है जकी आपणी मां है भाई (वाह वाह)। गुआल तो गुदलिया का तळाव पर आ घोड़ै असवार (हुई ग्या)। हेंर कुत्ता जका डोर के मांय छोड़ दिया (वाह वाह)। तो राणीजी कांई करियो खाड़ेती नै कीयो जरां खाड़ेती रीसा बळ गो (वाह वाह)। दोन्यु पेड़ा की एक एक पूठी रथ की (काड़ लीनी)। राणीजी गुलगुलै एक कोनी दियो आपां नै (हां पाछी जातां भाज राणीजी)। राणीजी देखेणी रथ में बैठी कीयो हां हांक (हांको कीयो गांगा कीयो)। गांगा झटकेन चाल बेगो (वाह वाह)। गांगो उजड़ घाल दी रथ नै (म्हे)। राणीजी के रैदा लागै अब (वाह वाह)।।

गैलै ले रे गैलै ले रे म्हारा गांगा हाली गैलै ले।
गैलै ले रे गैलै ले रे म्हारा रैदा लागै गैलै ले।
ए गैलै छै ए गैलै है मण्दड़ा की भूखी गैलै छे।
ए गैलै छै ए गैलै है राजा की राणी गैलै छे।
ए गैलै छै ए गैलै है म्हनै ठण्डी बाटी सालै छे।
गैलै ले रे गैलै ले रे म्हारा गांगलिया हाली गैलै ले।
ए गैलै ले ओ गैलै ले म्हारै रैदा लागै गैलै ले।
ए गैलै ले ए गैलै ले थारै पाग रंगा द्यूं गैलै ले।
ए गैलै ले रे गैलै ले रे थारी मुरकियां घड़ा द्यूं गैलै ले।
ए गैलै ले ओ गैलै ले तनै दोय परणाय द्यूं गैलै ले।
ए गैलै ले ओ गैलै ले तनै दोय परणाय द्यूं गैलै ले।
ए गैलै छै ए गैलै है मण्दड़ा की भूखी गैलै छे।
ए गैलै छै ए गैलै छै डावालो नारो जड़ो छे।
(भलां जी भलां) किषन भलां

गांगा नै मनायो नै (म्हे)। गांगो देखियो रे राणी राजा के रैदा लाग खराब हो जाय डील (वाह वाह)। पाछी पूठिया नै ठरकाली। राजा की राणी है दुख पावे। (. . .) दोय ब्याव करूं थारो (वाह वाह)। लाडकोड करूं भैइ (म्हे)। पाग रंगावूं (हां स काम कर द्यूं पण रैदाला मत लागन दे)। दरबार का हुकमूं पूठी नै ठरकाय (म्हे)। हेंर बिदा (व्हियो है)। कुत्ता कांई करियो गुआल कुत्ता नै छोड़िया नै (म्हे)। बै केर के मांयनै खिरगोश (नीकलयो)। खिरगोशिया के लेरै कुत्ता (भागिया)। राणी बा धोबनती कांई करियो की सारै झाड़कां की ऊंवार (हां.)। करपायी नै ऊंची (अर डीरा के नीचै बड़ गी)। मन में देखियो गुआलां नै दीखै कोनी (हां दीखा द्यो कोनी कीयो)। खिरगोशियो कांई करियो भाज्यो नै (म्हे)। बी वार में खिरगोशियो जार धोबनती के साहरै बैठ गो (वाह वाह)। कीयो राम मारिया जीव का कंस तूं कठवूं आयगो (म्हे)। कुत्ता बी के खिरगोश के लेरै भाज्योड़ा आया खिरगोश ऊंवार बड़ाय जको कुत्ता चारूंमेर घेरा दे दियो (हां चारूंमेर ऊंवार के फिरण लागग्या)। लेरेवूं गुआल आयग्या (म्हे)। कीयो कुत्ता आगा नै कोनी जाय भैइ (हां ई में है की)। दरबार का हुकमूं इस्यो काम करो चारूंमेर तो ऊबा रह जावो (म्हे)। हेंर ई नै लगा दियो (हां दीवांल लगा द्यो कीयो)। लगाबा को नांव लियो अर कह धोबनती ऊंची नीची (हां हुई)। गुआल कीयो रे गुंवार तो सगळी हालै खिरगोशियो कोनी जाजली बण बारा मण को सूर है भैइ (हां सूर लूंठो है ई के मांयनै कीयो)। बेगी बाहळो (म्हे)। धोबनती कीयो श्री महाराज कालाली हूं (कालाली)। कालाली हूं (कालाली)। कीयो कुण धोबन (हां कीयो बा ही हूं)। श्री महाराज अठै ही पड़ी हूं काल की (हां म्हारावूं चालणी कोनी आयो)। आकड़ो चड़ गो म्हारै (वाह वाह)। रह कीयो बळबा दे रे बा तो धोबनती रांड है अठै (हां जा)। पण बळ जायली मांयनै (हां बल जायली चालो कीयो)। गुआल तो मतै मतै बिदा (हु ग्या है)। धोबनती गुआलियां गिया के नीकल भाजी (म्हे)। तो गांव के गोरवें जातै राणीजी नै नावड़ गी (वाह वाह)। नावड़ी राणीजी

बोलै कांई धोबन नै समचार कह देखां (कीआवूं जाणीज्यो देखां कीआवूं)। अबार कहवां धणी देव का हुकमूं।।

दूरी दूरी जी ए ई रांड धोबनियां रे।
ए ई धोबन ये रथ सूं दूर खड़ी रे।
अब जावूं ये कछेड़ियां के मांयने।
करां द्यूं घोबन ये काल सूं आज बूरी रे।।
(भलां जी भलां) देव भलां

दूरी दूरी रांड धोबनी (म्हे)। ई ये रीज्यै म्हारा रथ से दूर (खड़ी)। अब जावूं कछेरियां के मांयनै (म्हे)। रांड करां द्यूं कालवूं आज (थारा में बूरी)। राणीजी ओ समचार (हां धोबन नै कीयो)। धोबन माथो उघाड़ राणीजी नै दीखायो के श्री महाराज (म्हे)। काल तो आ करी गुआलियां आज कांई करायी तूं बोल (जकी बताय कीयो)। कीयो रांड थारा में आ करी जर म्हनै क्युं लेगी बठै (हां म्हनै कींयां लेगी है कीयो)। कीयो श्री महाराज काल के दिन म्हनै गुआल कूटी अर मारी (हां कोझी घणी कीयो)। म्हारी कोय सुणाई (करी कोनी)। आज तनै गुआलियो कूटी है (म्हे)। बावन गढ काल चड़ जाय (हां काल चड़ जाय गुआलां पर कीयो)। तो राणीजी कांइ महल में जावै जाती कूकावै देखां (कीआवूं जाणज्यो देखां कीआवूं)।।

महलां चड़तां जी ए ई राणी बोल्या रे।
दे री राणी बूमा ऊपर बूम।
औरतां कां चट्टा कटा दिया रे काळू मीरजी।
अब तो मीर रे जीवेला के काल।।
(भलां जी भलां) देव भलां

महलां चड़ती राणी बोली (म्हे)। दे री बूमो ऊपर (बूम)। के औरतां का चट्टा काट दिया काळू मीरजी अब जीवेला के (काल)। ए बेटी का बाप कीयो औरतां का चट्टा कटा दिया कीयो (म्हे)। महलां चड़ती राणी बोली दे री बूमा ऊपर बूम के औरतां का चट्टा काट लिया हिन्दवा रावजी (म्हे)। गुआलियो बैरीबाज कटी रे माथा मूं मोतसरियां की (लूम)। रावजी रे देख ले (हां लूमां ही जकी सगळी बै काटली म्हारी (कीयो)। देवजीआला गुआलियां (वाह वाह)। दरबार का हुकमूं रावजी साय मीर नै दाक लियो (वाह वाह)। कीयो भैंसां खावै मीर सांवता (म्हे)। देख पीवै तूं उकलता (एराक)। काल का हां दरबार का हुकमूं औरतां का चट्टा कटा दिया मीर जीवेलो के (काल)। ए बेटी का बाप ओ जींवतो फिरै (वाह वाह)। जकी म्हारी अन्त्येवर राणीजी नै जकी के चट्टो काट लियो गुआल (हां आती कांई गुआलां की ऊठ ही कीयो)। दीयो आंतरै बैठो (म्हे)। रावजी बोलै अर कांई दिया नै समचार कहवै (कीआवूं जाणज्यो देखां कीआवूं)। अबार कहवां देव का हुकमूं।।

केर कट गा जी दीया भाई रे कूंडळ व्हिया रे।
दीया जोधका रातयूं कटक बिया ई रे।

रूशण की बेळियां रे दीयाजी कोय ने।
जावै बुलावै भाई रे आगो आव दिया रे।।
(भलां जी भलां) देव भलां

केर कटिया रे दीया कुण्डल हो गा (म्हे)। रातयूं कटक (बिया)। रूशण की बेळियां आज थोड़ी है दीया राव बुलावै आगो आव भाई (दिया)। औरतां का चट्टा कट गा बेटी का बाप कीयो (हां बेगी चड़ाई करो कीयो)। मीर कीयो देख ले दीया तोबा तोबा तोबा निवतो अब आयग्यो भैइ (म्हे)।।

दिया मीर की जी ए ई चड़ाई व्है ग्या रे।
ए तो ठाकरां जी हाथियां घणा बनाव।
ऊंधा तो सेला रे धुगता पाखरिया।
गाय गुआलां पर सज नीकल गो रे गढ टोडा को राव।।
(भलां जी भलां) देव भलां

कालू मीर के दीया के ठाकरां के सागत हो गा (म्हे)। हाथियां के घणो (बनाव)। गाय गुआल पर चड़ नीकलयो रे भाई दरबार का हुकमूं गढ सावर को (राव)। काळू मीरजी दीयोजी दरबार का हुकमूं रीस खाय (म्हे)। जार गुआलां पर चड़ तंबूड़ा ताण दिया (वाह वाह)। कठै गुदलिया पर पाछा बठै ही (वाह वाह)। परभात को टैम व्हियो देव की गायां तीन वारी दुशमन आडा फिर गा तीन वारी ई के मांय गायां हाथ कोनी आयी (म्हे)। तो गुआल उछेरबा गियो तो दरबार का हुकमूं सुरेमाता बोलै (वाह वाह)। कांई समचार गुआल नै कहवै (कीआवूं जाणज्यो देखां कीआवूं)। अबार कहवां देव का हुकमूं देखां (वाह वाह जी वाह वाह)।।

गायां के गंवळै रे जी ए ई गुआल आयगो रे।
उछेर म्हारी मना सुहानी माय।
तूं गाजरिया गहूं सरपटिया नितका खांवतां।
जाका नागली ये धणी रूस गा आज।।
(भलां जी भलां) देव भलां

गायां के गंवळी रे गुआल आयो (म्हे)। उछरी है म्हानी मनाई सुहानी (माय)। के गाजरिया गंवर सरपटिया जियान नितका तूं खांवती (म्हे)। जाका नागली ये धणी डेरा दे दिया (आज)। झटकेन चालो तूं ही कीयो (म्हे)। कीयो गुआल थारी उछेरी आज नी उछेरां (हां आज थारी उछेरी कोनी उछरूं कीयो)। थै माथो धूणै (गाय)। के तो थै आवां सवाई भोज को मेदू उछेरवै (म्हे)। जै पोववूं ठाकर देव उछेरै (आ अर)। के तो मेदूजी आवै तो उछेरां (म्हे)। नी जरां भगवान आयो तो (उछेरां कियो तो)। मेदू कंवर नै गुआल बोल्यो वाह साय आ गाय नट गी (हां उछेरै नैइ कीयो)। गुआल भुवा नै जाय अर कीयो (म्हे)। कीयो रे भुवाजी गायां कींयां नटी आज (वाह वाह)। गुआल देव को बोलै कांई भुवाजी नै समचार कह देय देखां (कीआवूं जाणज्यो कीआवूं)।।

उतर दियाड़ी जी भुवाजी ए सुर भरिया रे।
भैरूं कुरलिया मांझ गलंती रात।
रोजीना भुवाजी ए रोळा कूकूवा।
पड़ जायली भुवाजी ये पाखरिया परभात।।
(भलां जी भलां) देव भलां

दरबार का हुकमूं हेटी उतर भुवाजी दीयाजी सुर भरिया आज (म्हे)। ये भैरूं कुरल को मांझ गलंती (रात)। रोजीना तो होता ये भुवाजी रोळा ही कूकूवा (म्हे)। पड़ जायली परभातै पाखरिया (आज)। भुवाजी (म्हे)। परभातै गायां बन्ध हुई ताणी (वाह वाह)। थारा देव नै कह देय गायां उछेरज्यूं (हां अता दिन बाद दूसरी ही कीयो रोळा ईंयां होता)। भुवाजी तूं जाणै जकी बात अब कोनी आज (वाह वाह)। रोजीना तो हाका बेधा कर आ जाता मैं (म्हे)। आज आपै आवै जकी बात कोनी (हां आज आणाली बात कोनी कीयो)।।

गायां के गंवळी रहतो जी जो मेदूजी आप गा रे।
उछेरजै म्हारी मना सुहानी मांय ई।
तीन दिन चालै नै राता कोट में।
मैं आया नागली ये भालां अणी कढाय।।
(भलां जी भलां) देव भलां

दरबार का हुकमूं मेदूजी भोज को गायां की गंवळी ले अर आयो (म्हे)। उछेरजै आज मनाई सुहानी (मांय)। ए तीन चाल बैरी के पांवणी (म्हे)। मैं आया देखज्यै भांलां के अणी (कढाय)। तरवारियां के बाहर ही (दिरार)। भांलां की अणी कढा (म्हे)। तीन दिनूं बती कोनी रहबा द्यो (हां तीन दिन तो रहणो ही पड़ी कीयो)। थारी उछरी रे भोज का मेदू आज नैइ उछेरां (म्हे)। साथो धूणै (गाय)। के तो तेजा को मदनू उछेरवै (म्हे)। नी बालो देव उछेरै (आय)। थारी उछरी एकला की आज कोनी जावूं (हां एकेला के कहनो कोय नी चावूं कीयो)। तो ईंयां दरबार का हुकमूं सगळा भाई आयगा गायां के गंवळै (वाह वाह)। सगळा कह कह शुरू हो गा पण गाय तो हली कोनी (हां नट गी जकी नट ही गयी)। तीन तिलोकी को भगवान बोलै (म्हे)। कांई समचार गाय नै कहवै देखां (कीआवूं जाणज्यो देखां कीआवूं)।।

ए गायां रे गंवळिया तो जी ए ई दरबार आयगा रे।
उछेरजै म्हारी मना सुहानी माय।
तीन दिन चालै नी ये दुशमन के पांवणियां।
मैं आयो नागली ये लीला का सुम दिरार।।
(भलां जी भलां) देव भलां

गायां के गंवळिया रे भगवान आयगा (म्हे)। उछेरजै म्हारी मनाई सुहानी (माय)। तीन दिन चाल सुरेमाता बैरी के पांवणी (म्हे)। मैं आयो तीजै दिन लीला का सुम (दिरार)। घोड़ा का सुम दिरावूं

(म्हे)। अती ढील है (हां की टैम कोनी लगावूं लार को लार ई आवूं)। सुरेमाता बूझणा (करी है)। कांई भगवान नै सुरै नटै कांई समचार कहवै गाय नै (कीआवूं जाणज्यो कीआवूं)।।

थारी उछेरी तो जी ए ई दरबार नी उछेरां रे।
आ तो माथो धूण गी गाय ई ये।
के तो नेवा को रे भांगीजी उछेरवे।
नीतर बगड़ावतांलो रे भाट उछेरै आय।।
(भलां जी भलां) देव भलां

के थारी उछेरी भगवान आज कोनी उछेरां कीयो (म्हे)। माथो धूणै (गाय)। के तो नेवा को कंवर भांगी उछेरवै (म्हे)। नी बगड़ावतां को भाट उछेरै (म्हनै आर)। भाट आवै नै थांकाळो बैइ को (हां जणा उछरूं कीयो)। दरबार का हुकमूं देव महाराज जा अर भाट नै बूझणा (करी है)। अरै बाबा भाट (म्हे)। सुरेमाता नट गी भाई (हां उछेरो बी नै कीयो)। तो दरबार का हुकमूं कांई भाटजी आ जावै (म्हे)। कांई जरां सुरै नै समचार आतो ही कहवै देखां बैइ को भाट (कीआवूं जाणज्यो कीआवूं)।

ए गायां रे गंवळिया तो जी ए ई भाट आयगो रे।
नागलीमाता सुणज्यो भाट को।
लेरै नी चड़ै ये चुहाणां का डावड़ा।
कर द्यूं नागली ये कोड़ी सूंगो मोल।।
(भलां जी भलां) देव भलां

गायां के गंवळी रे भाट आयगो (म्हे)। नागलीमाता सुणज्यो भाट को (बोल)। लेरै नी चड़ै थांकै चुहाणां का डावड़ा (म्हे)। कर द्यूं ये नागली कोड़ी सूंगो (आंको मोल)। कोड़ीवूं सूंगा कर द्यूं (वाह वाह)। नी चड़ै तो (म्हे)। चालो (चालो कीयो अब)। तीन दिन बती कोनी रहवां द्यूं (वाह वाह)। तो बाबा भाट गाय नै समचार कहतां (म्हे)। सूरेमाता नै गुआल बाहरें काढता जय बोलै श्री देवनारायण भगवान की (जय)। दरबार का हुकमूं गाय नै गुआल बाहरें गंवळिया जा के काढी नै (म्हे)। जरां देव महाराज बूझणा करी रे भैइ गुआल (म्हे)। आव कीयो (वाह वाह)। कांई ठी रावजी का अमराव दरबार का हुकमूं रोजीना आवै (म्हे)। जको कांई ठी लोह की लाग जावै मारियो जावै तो आपां मन की मन में ही (रह जावै मिल लियां)। मिल लियां भैइ (वाह वाह)। तो देव महाराज अर गाय को गुआल मिल लिया (म्हे)। देव महाराज भगवान कांई करियो के गुआल को अंश खेंच लियो आप (हां करामात ही जकी सगळी की सगळी ले ली)। गुआल कीयो जरां श्री महाराज (अब मैं बठै जावूं ई क्यें नै) कांई करणो गाय के लेरै म्हारी देही तो बिरामणावूं बती हो गी (म्हे)। कीयो गुआल जा सोच मत कर म्हनै बगड़ावतां को बैर लेनो है थारी कळा खेंची है मैं (म्हे)। तीन चोट साबुत बही थारी (वाह वाह)। गुआल मन में देखियो पहली रावजी नै मारां (हां पहली चोट मैं रावजी नै द्यां)। पछै राजा नीमदे नै (हां मारल्या)। हेंर पछै दीयाजी नै (हां तीन्यो चोटां में तीन्या सिरदारां नै खतम कर द्यूं (कीयो)। देव महाराज कीयो रे गुआल तूं जाचै जकी कोनी होवै (हां ताणी जांचेड़ली कोनी होवेली कीयो)।

तूं आनै मारै जरां मैं बैर की मूं काढूं (हां की मूं काढां कीयो)। जा टोडो जगमालो (म्हे)। दरबार का हुकमूं सिरदार थारा हाथवूं काम आ जाय (वाह वाह)। उछरो भैइ (म्हे)। तो आज दरबार भगवान सुरेमाता के हाथ फैर डील पर कीयो माजीसा पधारो (वाह वाह)।।

जासरां से गुआल ठाकरां बिदा हु गो जाय उछेरी गाय।
अब उछेरतां गायां खेवान माच गो हुई नेवरियां झणकार।
सिर सोना की कोली ठाकरां नीकल चाली पार।
नेजो बांध्यो निरपाल खटाणो घालियो गायां को सींवली थानो।
गांगो तो गोरसी बादलो भड़ाणो पदमो पोसवाळ ऊबा करै बिचार।
भेळ द्यो बदशियां का माल।
गायां उछेर गी ठाकर देव की उछेरगी सेंई लुहार।
सिकराणी पर गुआलिया झण्डा रोपिया।
रोपिया दुशमन के रे छाती ऊपर साल।।
(भलां जी भलां) देव भलां

ठाकर देव महाराज को अब ठाकरां जाय उछेरी (गाय)। अरै उछेरता गायां खेवान माच गो (म्हे)। हुई नेवरियां (झणकार)। सिर सोना की खोली अब नीकल चाली (पार)। नेजो बांध्यो निरपाल खटाणो घाल दियो गाय को सिंग (थानो)। गांगो गरसी बादलो भड़ाणो ऊबा करै बिचार भेळो बदशियां का ई (माल)। गायां उछेरी रे ठाकर देव की उछेर गी सेंई (लुआर)। लुआरियां लेरै कर देयो भैइ तीन दिन गायां कोनी आवै भूखा मर जायला (वाह वाह)। सिकराणी पर गुआल झण्डा रोपिया दुशमन राव के छाती ऊपर ही (साल)। सिकराणी पर आगै तंबूड़ा ताण मेलिया (वाह वाह)। तो भगवान की गायां गी रावजी का अमराव सामनो कर लियो (वाह वाह)। देव को नापो बाहवै जका तीर को खाली पड़ै (वाह वाह)। हेंर काळू मीर दीयाजी की बठै जीत होबा लागी (म्हे)। तो नापो बाहवै जका तीर पाछा खाली पड़बा लागा (वाह वाह)। दरबार का हुकमूं मीर बूझणा (करी है)। अरै नापला (म्हे)। आज तीर मत गमा भैइ (हां आज तीर मत गमावा ना कीयो तूं)। कीयो सुण रे मीर गमावा तो कांई कोनी आज भगवान को म्हांकाला को हुकम कोनी (म्हे)। कीयो ताणा भगवान को हुकम एक तो म्हारा पर ही कोनी दूजा पर ही कोनी (वाह वाह)। कीयो थरो पार दीया पर कोनी (हां थां पर कोनि)।। दरबार का हुकमूं कीयो जरां देखां बो पत्थरवूं बोलै रे (हां बी पर देख)। सेनाणी होवै कोनी होवै देखां (वाह वाह)।। गुआल देव महाराज को ढाल घोडी हेंर के तीर ने (हां छोड़ियो)। पत्थर नै दरबार का हुकमूं कोकरियो काकरियो बिखेर दियो (वाह वाह)।। मीर बूझना करी दीया (म्हे)। आपां पर हुकम कोनी (हां आज देवजी को हुकम ही कोनी आपां पर)।। सैइ बात है नै जरां तो अबार पत्थर में करी जकी का जकी आपां (आपां में करै कीयो)। दरबार का हुकमूं दे घेरो गाय के (म्हे)।। अब कांई करां सोकळडा दरबार की गायां का घेरा ले लिया (वाह वाह)। घमसाय घोडो दीयोजी (म्हे)।। फट गुआल के कबाण घाल दी (आ लियो कीयो)। बन्द कर लियो (वाह वाह)।। दरबार का हुकमूं गुआल नै बन्ध कर लियो सिरायत नै तो (म्हे)। मांय घाल लियो (वाह वाह)।। हेंर गाय नै मुण्डा

के टोळ दी गाय को कीयोडो मतेई बहतो रवाना हो गी (हां मतेई जावै ही घरां जावै ज्यूं ही)। अब लेरल्1 गुआल ऊबा फिर फिका गायां नै ले गा (वाह वाह)।। तो चौदाह सौ चम्मालीस गुआल कांई पाछा बावडै (म्हे)। कांई बिसूवणो करै देखां (कीआवूं जाणीज्यो देखां कीआवूं)।। अबार कहवां भगवान को देखां हुकमूं गायां नै रातै कोट बाड़ दी लोग (वाह वाह)। फाटक उजड़ाया नी (हां नै बन्ध कर द्यो)।। जी हिसाब से (बन्ध कर दी)। ले भाई रावजी ओ ले कीयो ए गायां अर देखिज्यो ओ गुआल बो सिरायत है नै (हां ओ ले जस)।। तो गुआल नै ले जार बन्ध कर दियो अर गाय नै बन्ध कर दियो (वाह वाह)। रावजी कीयो वाह वाहरै कीयो सिरदारां जबरो काम करियो (वाह वाह)।। घणा दिन व्हिया गहूं खातियां गायां नै (म्हे)। तीन दिन हो गा (म्हे)।। रावजी साई कीयो रे मीर गायांवूं बेर कोनी आवै (वाह वाह)। बेर तो है बगड़ावतां का डावडावूं हे गायां नै छोड़ द्यो पाछी (हां गायां नै छोड़ द्यो जको चरै बापड़ियां)।। कीयो श्री महाराज नापलो दोहरो घणी दीनी (म्हे)। तो भाला के भचड़कै तो गायां नै दीनी अर भाला के भचड़कै पाछी (द्यां कीयो)।। थारावूं नी समै नै तो बावन गढ है थांकै (हां चौरासियां में सगहा में बांट द्यै कीयो)। पांच पांच गायां पांती आयी (वाह वाह)।। कीयो बांटां कोनी भायां (म्हे)।।

> गुआल आयो तो जी उछेरती गायां रे पदमा आपणियां रे।
> ए तो पदमाजी पाछी जांतां ही कुण बनी रे।।
> देख गायां नै लेगो रे धणी राण को।
> जरां आपां रे देखतां रियां धणी ये।।
> (भलां जी भलां) देव भलां

दरबार का हुकमूं देख गुआल उछेरती गायां आपणी ही भैइ (म्हे)। अर पाछी जाती कुण बनी (कुण बनी)।। अरै गायां नै लेगो देख राजा राण को (म्हे)। देखतां रह गा सगळा आपां ही (धणी)।। आपां धणी है देखतां रह गा कांई सत्ता हो गी अबार (हां देखो थै गायां तो ले गिया कीयो)। अरे रोजीना तो की करतां आज तो की व्हियो कोनी आपांवूं (म्हे)।। गुआल देव का ईकळ सिंगां की डूंगरी छोड़ै (म्हे)। कांई बिसूवणी करै देखां (कीआवूं जाणीज्यो देखां कीआवूं)।।

> सरगनै परवाणा जी ए ई गुआल मोकळा रे।
> पड़ गो भैइ साई कलमावालो टोट।।
> सवाई भोज नै कहतो जाईज्यो रे सुरै देवता।
> बांकाली गायां रे रूंद गी रातै कोट।।
> (भलां जी भलां) देव भलां

सरगनै परवाणा देवां आपां (म्हे)। पड़ गो आप नै साई कलमावालो (टोट)।। सवाई भोज नै कहतो जाज्यै सुर देवता (म्हे)। बांकी गायां रूंद गी आज रातै (कोट)।। सुर देवता (म्हे)। तूं भगवान के दरीखानै जावै नै (वाह वाह)।। जरां भैइ एक सवाई भोज नै पुकार सुणाई (हां थंकाळी गायां है के जकी आ . . .)। (रातै कोट पूगी कीयो)।। तो दरबार का हुकमूं ओ समचार गुआल कीयो (म्हे)।

कांई गुआल देव महाराज को ईकळ सिंगां से हेटो आ जावै (वाह वाह)।। कांई समचार कहवै देखां (कीआवूं जाणज्यो देखां कीआवूं)।।

ए ईकळ सिंगिया से जी जो गुआल देव को हेटो उतरिया रे।
आयगा ढाबा तळाव की पाळ।।
पाळ पर आतां रे गुआल गाय को।
दीनी ठाकरां रे सस्तरपाती राळ।।
(भलां जी भलां) देव भलां

गुआल आयो भैइ दरबार का ईकळ सिंगिया से हेटा आयगो (म्हे)। आयगो ढाब तळाव की (पाळ)।। अरै पाळ पर आतां गुआल देव को (म्हे)। दिया सस्तरपाती हेटा (सगळा राळ)।। सस्तर बांध चांलां गायां मुण्डा के थोडी हे भैइ (हां सस्तर हाथ में लिया चांलां कीयो)। गुआल सस्तर खोल दिया (वाह वाह)।। साज सिण्गार सारो खोल दियो (म्हे)। गुआल देव महाराज को कांई बिसूणो करै (म्हे)।। कांई फीको व्हियोड़ो समचार कहवै देखां (कीआवूं जाणज्यो देखां कीआवूं)। अबार कहवां देव का हुकमूं ले तूं।।

ईकळ सिंगिया सूं जी गुआल देव को रे हेटा उतरिया रे।
आयगो भवानी के शहर जुवाई।।
आया व्है तो मोकळ दीज्यो देबी चांवण्डा।
मितवाला हो भाला ये सुरजमल सोडियाल।।
(भलां जी भलां) देव भलां

ईकळ सिंगिया से गुआल हेटो आयगियो (म्हे)। आयो भवानी के शहर जुवाई (जुवाई)।। ए आया व्है तो मोकळ दीज्यै देबी चांवण्डा (म्हे)। मितवाला अब आया सुरजमल (सोडियाल)।। ले भैइ भवानी राणी (म्हे)। थारै मिन्दर बगड़ावत आजावै तो गायां की पुकार सुणा दीज्यै (हां पहली पोहर सुणा द्यो कीयो)।।

गोठां नै चांलां जी जो पदमा भाई रे आपां बिलखता रे।
गायां बिनै रे पाछा पड़ै आप नै खोज।।
गायां छुड़ाबाळा आज रे घरां कोनि।
घरां कोनी रे फूंफो सवाई भोज।।
(भलां जी भलां) देव भलां

गोठा नै चांलां रे पदमा भाई बिलखता (वाह वाह)। गायां बिनै पाछा पड़ै नी आपांणा (खोज)।। अरै गायां छुड़ावाला घरां कोनी रिया (म्हे)। घरां कोनी फूंफो सवाई (भोज)।। फूंफोजी होतां नै (म्हे)। आपणी पुकार (जरूर ही जांवतां ही सुणता कीयो)।। अरै पदमा कुण नै सुणा (हां क्यां की नै ओ गायां रूंद गी कीयो)। गायां तो राताकोट में रूक गी (म्हे)।। तीन तिलाकी को नाथ भगवान निन्दड़ां

को जाळ नाक दियो शहर पर (वाह वाह)। बसी को लोग (सगळो को सगळो सोय गियो)।। जानवर ही ई जाळ के बाहरें कोनी रियो (वाह वाह)। गुआल दुंगर पर निंगै करी (म्हे)।। बसी में तो कोई जागतो नर (कोनि)। कीयो आ कांई व्हियो भैइ (हां ईंयां कींयां हुई)।। अरै दरबार ही सुनो पड़ियो है (म्हे)। देव को गुआल बोलै (वाह वाह)।। कांई समचार कहवै देखां (कीआवूं जाणीज्यो देखां कीआवूं)।।

ए ये दड़ावट शहर तो जी पदमा भाई रे सुना व्है ग्या रे।
सुना पड़िया लीलागर का मेहन्दी भरणा केश।।
के तो बालो ठाकर धाम प्रापत व्हिया।।
नीतर पाछा ऊठ गा दीखै रे नानेराला देश।।
(भलां जी भलां) देव भलां

दड़ावट देश पदमा देख सुनो पड़ियो है (म्हे)। सुना पड़िया लीलागर का मेहन्दी भरणा (केश)।। के तो बालो ठाकर धाम प्रापत हो गा (म्हे)। नीतर पाछा ऊठ ग्या दीखै नानेराला ही (देश)।। नानेरा में सोरा रिया (हां नानेरा पाछा ऊठ गा दीखे)। आपणा तो गांव नै सुनू कर गा (वाह वाह)।। गुआल बोलै कांई बिसूणू करै (कीआवूं जाणज्यो देखां कीआवूं)।।

ए दड़ावट शहर तो जी जो धूणाजी सुना व्है ग्या रे।
सुना पड़िया देव का इन्द्र महला पोढणाला घोख।।
बालो ठाकर के धाम प्रापत व्है ग्यो।
नीतर दुशमन रावजी ले गो घाल गलै में थोक।।
(भलां जी भलां) देव भलां

दड़ावट शहर पदमा सुनो हो गो (म्हे)। अरै सुना पड़िया देव का इन्द्र महल का पोढणाला (घोख)।। के तो बालो ठाकर धाम प्रापत हो गो (म्हे)। नी जरां रावजी ले गो दीखै घाल गला में (थोक)।। आपां कन्नै चडर आया (म्हे)। गायां नै पकड़ (ले ग्या)।। हेंर अठै आया जका देवजी नै पकड़ ले गा (हां देव महाराज नै पकड़ ले गिया कीयो)। कुण नै सुणावां पुकार (वाह वाह)।। दरबार का हुकमूं गुआल बोलै कांई समचार कह देय देखां (कीआवूं जाणज्यो देखां कीआवूं)। अबार कहवां देव का हुकमूं ले तूं (वाह वाह)।।

ए गुआलियो आयो तो जी जो गोठा के गोरवें ओवूं रे।
आयग्यो कासा इन्द्र पोळ।।
गायां नै ले गो रे धरमराजा देवजी।
ले गो रावजी रे तांबा गला पर ठोर।।
(भलां जी भलां) देव भलां

गुआल आयगो भैइ गोठा के गोरवें (म्हे)। आयो कासा इन्द्र (पोळ)।। गाया नै देख ले गो बाळा हां हिन्दवा रावजी (म्हे)। ले गो धरमराजजी तांबा गला पर (ठोर)।। है भगवान गायां नै ले गा है (वाह

वाह)। ओ समचार गुआल देव को बडतो ही (कीयो है)।। तो जाळ के बाहरें जकै दिन कुण कुण रिया (म्हे)। के तो देव महाराज की धरम की धाय जकी जाल के बाहरें (हां साडूमाता रिया)।। हेंर देव महाराज की असत्री पीपळदे जाळ के बाहरें (रह गिय)। गोरम के भाखर बळाई को डावडो गियोड़ो हो। बो जाळ के बाहरें रह गो। ए तीन मानवी जाळ के बाहरें रह गा। और बसी के लोग सारी ही निन्दड़ा में सो ग्या। पीपळदे राणी गोखडै ऊंची आयी (म्हे)।। गुआलां की के आयोड़ा की सुरता देखी (वाह वाह)। कांई बूजी के रावळै (जावै है)।। जाती ही कांई देखां देव की मां नै जाय ओ समचार कहवै (कीआवूं जाणीज्यो देखां भोपाजी महाराज कीआवूं)। अबार कहवूं धणी का हुकमूं ले तूं (वाह वाह)।।

धूमाला धूमाला जी गुआलां का बूजी ये ढीला व्है ग्या रे।
गायां बिनै बूजी पाछा पड़ै नै खोज।।
गायां छुड़ाबाळा ये घरां कोई ने।
घरां कोनी म्हारै ये सुसरो सवाई भोज।।
(भलां जी भलां) देव भलां

दरबार का हुकमूं देख धूमाला धूमाला गुआलां का ढीला पड़ गा (वाह वाह)। बूजी गायां बिना का पाछा पड़ै (खोज)।। गायां तो छुड़ावाळा घरां कोनी रिया (म्हे)।। घरां कोनी म्हारै सुसर सवाई (भोज)। सवाई भोज होतां नै (म्हे)।। तो आ बिचारां की आयोड़ा पुकार (हां जरूरी सुण लेता)। रावजी को कांई मक़दूर जको आपांणै गायां नै (ले जाय कीयो)।। ताणो दूध का चूंगबालो बूजी महल में सोय गिया (हां पहल में चड कर सोय गा है कीयो)। दरबार का हुकमूं ए समचार राणी पीपळदे (हां साडूजी नी कीया है)।। दरबार का हुकमूं पीपळदे राणी बोलै (म्हे)। कांई बूजी नै समचार (हां औरूं कहवै देखां कीआवूं जाणीज्यो अब कीआवूं)।। अबार कहवूं भगवान देव का हुकमं ले तूं (वाह वाह सा)।।

नितका बिलावतां जी देख बूजी ये गमड़ बिलावणा रे।
परभातै बूजी ये कांई राज गमयोड़ ई रे।।
आया जेठ को ये साज ले आरतियो।
गायां गुमार गुआल ले अर बधाई धरां में आयो।।
(भलां जी भलां) देव भलां

नितका बिलावतां रे बूजी गमड़ बिलावणो (म्हे)! परभातै कांई राज (गमयोडो)।। आया नाप जेठजी को साजलै बूजी आरतियो (म्हे)। गायां गमार गुआल ले अर बधाई घरां नै (आयो)।। रोजीना आतो नै (म्हे)। आ कहतो बूजी रावजी का पांच से घोडा अर अमराव मार नाकिया मैं (वाह वाह)।। आज हजार (मारयाया)। पाण नी लांबा पागड़ाला असवार आज मिल लिया (हां देख मुण्डै पर झाटो सोक जमाय अर भेजै है कीयो)। गुआल की निंगै तो कर सुरता की (वाह वाह)। साडूमाता मन में देखियो (म्हे)।। अरै पीपळदे नै गुआल बोल बोलै जियान अबार आपां (हां बोलां)। आयोड़ा गुआल नै दो पगां नै ठौड़ (कोनी कीयो)।। साडूमाता बोलै आयोड़ा गुआल नै सेला सरी का (हां कीआवूं जाणीज्यो देखां कीआवूं)। अबार कहवां भगवान का हुकमूं देखां (वाह वाह जी)।।

आ भतीजा म्हारा रे बेठै रे गींदवै रे।
भतीजा म्हारा झारी ले मुख धोय।।
गायां तो रे आपणै गुआलिया मोकळी।
बालो ठाकर रे ऊद कटा से होय।।
(भलां जी भलां) देव भलां

आव भतीजा म्हारा बेठ गींदवै (म्हे)। झारी ले मुख धोय (धोय)।। अरै गायां तो भतीजा आपणै मोकळी (म्हे)। पण बालो ठाकर ऊद कठै से (होय)।। सुण रे लाल (म्हे)। अरै भगवान तो मोल लेबा की चीजां (कोनी है)।। दरबार का हुकमूं साडूमाता बोलै कांई समचार गुआल नै कहवै देखां (कीआवूं जाणीज्यो देखां कीआवूं)।।

ओर खरीदूं जी जो भायां रे गायां मोकळियां रे।
खरीदूं सुरै सारसी गाय।।
ठा मत कर दीज्यै रे कुबदिया भाट ने।
चड़ चौबारै देलो रे बाहरूं का ढोल बजाय।।
(भलां जी भलां) देव भलां

गायां तो और खरीदूं (म्हे)। दरबार का हुकमूं खर लेयूं सुरै सारसी (गाय)।। अरै ठा मत कर देय कुबदिया भाट नै (म्हे)। चड चौबारै दळो रे भैइ बाहरूं का ढोल (बजाय)।। भतीजा (म्हे)। कह तो गाय की बात तूं सुणी कह मैं सुणी अब (हां तीजो आदमी कोई नै सुणै है)।। आ नी होवै तूं दूजा नै ठा कर देय (वाह वाह)। बगड़ावतां की बारां की मोहरां म्हारा कन्नै (मोकळी है कीयो)।। देवजी जागी (हां जतै नै बतो को बतो चोपो कर तनै लारै उछेर द्यूं कीयो)। साडूमाता बोलै (म्हे)। कांई समचार गुआल नै कहवै (कीआवूं जाणज्यो कीआवूं)।। दरबार का हुकमूं साडूमाता बोलै (म्हे)। कांई देव का गुआल नै आयोड़ा नै समचार कहवै देखां (कीआवूं जाणज्यो देखां कीआवूं)। अबार कह द्यूं देव का हुकमूं देखां।।

ए निंदा में ओज ग्यो जी ए ई गुआल गाय का रे।
थारै भई छाती आयो हाथ।
गायां तो चड़ गी रे भतीजा गोरम का भाखरां।
देखियायो भतीजा रे पोखर जाती जात।।
(भलां जी भलां) देव भलां

तूं निंदा में ओज ग्यो (म्हे)। गुआल छाती आयो (हाथ)। अरै गायां तो चड़ गी रे भतीजा गोरम का भाखरां (वाह वाह)। देखयायो तूं भाई पोखर जाती (जांत)। कात्तिक को महीनो है (हां नंगारबंद सिरदार पुष्करराज के मेलै (जांवां हा)। थै तो भाई रे भाखर पर सोय गा (म्हे)। गायां भाखर के हेटै (ढळ गी कीयो)। दरबार का हुकमूं नंगारबंद सिरदार बेह रियो थै नंगारो सुण जाग अर म्हार कन्नै (हां भाग्याया कीयो)। रावजी को कांई मकदूर जको आपणी गायां नै (हां ले जावै कीयो जावो ल्यावो

कीयो)। गुआल मन में देखियो रे भुवाजी देख आपां नै झोलावै है (म्हे)। गुआल बोलै कांई समचार साडू नै कहवै देखां (कीआवूं जाणज्यो कीआवूं देखां)। अबार कहवूं देव का हुकमं ले तूं (वाह वाह सा)।।

ए निंदा में तो जी नी ओज ग्यो ये भुवाजी राजवन ने।
टोडो जगमालो मारिया चौगांवां की सान।
दापट घोड़ो दीयोजी म्हानै दाकलिया।
म्हारै मुण्डा के लियो ये गुआल बगूलो बांध।।
(भलां जी भलां) देव भलां

निंदा में भुवाजी कोनी ओज ग्यो (म्हे)। नी छाती आयो (म्हारै हाथ)। दरबार का हुकमूं निंदा में नी ओज ग्यो भुवा राज में टोडो जगमालो मारिया चौगांवां की (सान)। एक दापट घोड़ो दीयोजी म्हानै ही दाकलियां (म्हे)। म्हारै मुण्डा के लियो ए है बगूल सिंग नै (बांध)। ताणा बगूलिया गुआल की तो बन्ध हो गी (म्हे)। अर गायां राताकोट नै हंकती (हां हो गी)। साडूमाता कांई करियो गुआलां के मांयनै ऊबी व्हियोड़ो निंगै (करी ही)। तो बगूल सिंग गुआल गुआल गायां में (कोनी)। मन में देखियो (म्हे)। आज बगूलियो घरां कोनी जरां गायां ही (हां घरां कोनी कीयो)। अब साडूमाता बोलै (वाह वाह)। कांई समचार कहवै देखां (कीआवूं जाणज्यो देखां कीआवूं)। अबार कहवां देव का हुकमूं देखां।।

दूध कटोरा जी तनै पाती रे गुआल गाय का रे।
भतीजा म्हारा रे घी भर देती थाळ।
गायां के मुण्डै कीयो मर गो नै रे गुआल गाय का।
हु गो भाई रे लूण हरामी गुआल।।
(भलां जी भलां) देव भलां

दरबार का हुकमूं दूध कटोरा पायो तनै (म्हे)। घी भर देती (थाळ)। अरै गायां के मुण्डै क्यु मर गो नै रे म्हारा लूण हरामी (गुआल)। औरूं मुण्डो दिखाळबा नै आयगो (वाह वाह)। ओ समचार कुण कीयो की साडूमाता (हां गुआल नै कीयो)। गुआल बोलै कांई समचार भुवाजी नै (कहवै देखां)। गुआलियो मन में बिचार करियो (म्हे)। के पोछड़ी को समचार हो जको तो भुवाजी (हां कह दियो)। अब तूं ही कह आगी (हां अब क्यु बाकी राखो)।।

ए मरण मरण तो जी जो कींयां करियो ये भुवाजी राजवन ने।
भुवाजी म्हाना जी मरण देयी के हाथ।
फूंफोजी पड़ गा ये बीर खेत में।
सती व्है गी ये की नै फूंफा भोज की साथ।।
(भलां जी भलां) देव भलां

मरण मरण कींयां करियो (म्हे)। बूजी मरण देयी के (हाथ)। फूंफोजी पड़ गा बीर खेत में (म्हे)। जरां सती हो गी की नै फूंफा भोज की (साथ)। सब गूजरियां बळी तूं तो कोनी बळी नै (हां तूं कोनी बळी नै जकै दिन कीयो)। दरबार का हुकमूं ओ समचार गुआल कीयो (वाह वाह)। तो साडूमाता नै कहतां जेज लागी (म्हे)। डील में सतीवाड़ो बापण होतां जेज (नैइ लागी)।।

ए चन्दन कटावो जी सल रचो रे पीथाजी भाण का रे।
गोठां में घुरावो जंगीड़ासा ढोल।
ग्यारह बरसावूं रे साडू नै सत चड़ ग्या।
जरां हो गा रे भुवा अर भतीजा बोल।।
(भलां जी भलां) देव भलां

चन्दन कटावो सल रचो पीथाजी भाण का (म्हे)। अरै गोठां में धुरावो भाई जंगीड़ासा (ढोल)। ग्यारहा बरसावूं साडूमाता नै सत चड़ गा (म्हे)। अब हो गा भैइ रे भुवा ई भतीजा (बोल)। भतीजा के बोल के साठै भुवाजी बळबा नै तियारियां हो गी (वाह वाह)।।

ए भैरूं नै चड़ावो जी ए ई बाटी बाकळा रे।
बगड़ावतालां भाट छोछू नै दिरावो छाळी रे।
ग्यारह बरसावूं साडू नै रे सत चड़ ग्या।
जरां धरती में रे हु गी बात अचाळी रे।।
(भलां जी भलां) देव भलां

भैरूं के चड़ावो भाई बाटी बाकळा (वाह वाह)। बगड़ावतालां भाट छोछू नै दिरावो (अब छाळी)। अरै ग्यारहा बरसावूं साडू नै सत चड़ गा (म्हे)। हु गा रे भैइ धरती पर बात ही (अचाळी)। गुआल मन में देखियो (म्हे)। थारावूं तो थाकड़ो ही (अब कोनी लागे)। दरबार का हुकमूं देव महाराज जागी जरां दोय ओळमा (सागै देसी ही)। देख तूं सुरेमाता नै तूं बैरियां के मुण्डा के (हां करियायो)। हेंर धरम की दाय (जकी नै बोल बोल)। ए बाळ दी (बाळ दीनी)। पण आपांवूं थाकड़ो कोनी लागै (हां अब आपांवूं थाकड़ो लागनो को कोनी)। बगड़ावतांलां भाट कन्नै चालां (म्हे)। तूं जरूर थाकड़ो लगावै (वाह वाह)। कांई बगड़ावतांलां भाट कन्नै जावै (वाह वाह)। कांई भाटबाबो साडूमाता सत हेटा उतारै देखां (कीआवूं जाणज्यो देखां कीआवूं)।।

पीलै घोड़ै राज पदमो चड़ियो चड़ियो राज निरपाल।
ऊठ भाट ठाकरां फूलरिया पीला घोड़ा पर असवार।
ऊठ बैइ का भाटजी साडूमाता का चड़ियोड़ा सत हेटा उतार।
झटकाय अर पछेवड़ी ठाकरां ऊठ गो भाट बंगाल।
बळ बिनै कोनी जेवड़ी नी घोसा बिना कबाण।
भायां बिनै गाहड़ कोनी नी पूता बिनै पिरवार।

मेह गाजिया बिनै फीकी लागै माजी मोरिया तणी मलहार।
बिनै पीव फीको लागै गोरी को सिण्गार।
गहूंवां को घी बिनै सरब अलूणो खाण।
भुवा अर भतीजा दोन्यो ओसाण चूकगा।
अब तो माजी ये रुळिया तजो पिराण।।
(भलां जी भलां) देव भलां

पीलै घोड़ै तो पदमो चड़ियो (म्हे)। चड़ियो राज (निरपाल)। ऊठ रे बगड़ावतालां भाट साडूमाता का चड़योड़ो सत हेटा (उतार)। झटकाय पछेवड़ी ऊठ गो भाट (बंगाल)। बळ बिनै माजी नी जेवड़ी नी घोसा बिनै (कबाण)। भायां तो बिनै गाहड़ नी (म्हे)। अर पूता बिनै कोनी (पिरवार)। मेह गाजिया बिनै फीकी लागै माजी मोरा तणी (मलहार)। बिनै पीव फीको लागै गोरी को (सिण्गार)। ए घी बिनै माता गहूंवां को सरब अलूणो (खाण)। अब तो भुवा अर भतीजो दोन्यो ओसाण चूक गा (म्हे)। अब भला रुळयायी तजो (पिराण)। ओ गुआल तो गायां के मुण्डै मरतो (जणा चोखो लागतो)। हेंर तूं भोज के लेरै सतीवाड़ै जाती नै (वाह वाह)। जरां चोखी (लागती)। अब तो बळजा भलै ही सतीवाड़ा नैइ बाजै जंवर बाजै (हां जंवर बाजी कीयो)। बगड़ावतां के लेरै गायां छोड़ गा (म्हे)। बी गायां के पाछै मुलक माळवा (सगळा फिरयाया)। रावजी का अमराव आया गायां नै पकड़ (ले ग्या)। लेरेवूं बांकी लुगाइयां ही नै (म्हे)। जंवर कर कर बळ गी (बळ गी जी कीयो)। गुआल देव महाराज संपाड़ो करै बी लेयार कूण्डी को छांटो दे देय (वाह वाह)। गुआल देव महाराज संपाड़ो करतां बी कूण्डी को (वाह वाह)। गुआल देव महाराज संपाड़ो करतां बी कूण्डी को लेयार साडू के छांटो (दियो)। तो साडूमाता का सत हेटा उतर (गिया जी कीयो)। बगड़ावतां को भाट साडू का सत हेटा उताराता हेंर दरबार का हुकमूं गुआल गोठां में आतां (आंवतां)। जय बोलो भैइ श्री देवनारायण की (जय)। बोलज्यो भैइ छोटा अर मोटा (स)। गुआल आया जका निंदड़ा का जाळ में बठै ही सोय ग्या (वाह वाह)। हेंर देव महाराज जाग्या कोनी (म्हे)। रावजी का अमराव गाय नै राताकोट में बाड़ रावजी साय नै बूझणा (करी ही)। के श्री महाराज (म्हे)। मैं गायां नै लियाया (वाह वाह)। अकल मीर कीयो एक अकल म्हनै उपज्यै म्हारा कीया करो (वाह वाह)। मीर भैइ कांइ करां (कांई करणो कीयो)। कीयो मैं अर दीयो चड़ ग्या तो गायां नै अर गुआलां नै पकड़ (लियाया)। अब दूजा मैं चड़ाई (करां)। तो धोळा दोपारां तो दड़ावट नै (लूट ल्यावां)। हेंर देवजी का अर मेदूजी का शीश उतार ल्यावां (वाह वाह)। रावजी कीयो वाह वाह रे मीर वाह रे मीर ए तो थारा (भरोसा ही है)। तो दूजा चड़ाई करां अर गोठां पर आयगा (वाह वाह)। गोठां में आया तो गोठां में कोय चनक नै (हां भणक)। भगवान इन्द्र को जाळ नाक दियो बसी को लोग सारो ही नींद में सोय ग्यो (वाह वाह)। तो दरबार का हुकमूं मीर बूझणा करी रे यार दिया (वाह वाह)। आपां जीत का नंगारा बजाया नै (म्हे)। बी टैम लोगां का पिराण छूट गा (वाह वाह मर ग्या सब)। इस में घोर शीलावाला नैइ मिलिया यहीं पड़िया रह गा (म्हे)। भूणा जियान का अमराव होबा का कोनी अर अब होवेला ही (हां कोनी)। जका की मौत आयी तो याहां पर आम मर गा देख इस पड़िया इस में धोर शिलावाला नी मिलिया (वाह वाह)।

दीयोजी कीयो रे मीर (म्हे)। सारो दिन घोर को नांव नी लेनो (हां सारो दिन घोर ही घोर को नांव नैइ लेनो कीयो)। म्हांकै हिन्दवा भैइ घोर नी होवै (वाह वाह)। तो जरां दीया आया जियान पाछा चालां (हां पाछा चालां कांई कीयो)। मीर कीयो हमारा कीया एक और कर लेयो (म्हे)। कांई देवजीआला गढ है नै (वाह वाह)। इसकै एक सैनाणी कर देयो (हां भालै की दे तूं कीयो)। तो दीयोजी कंस के औतार हो (वाह वाह)। डाल घोड़ी हेंर के तीर भांलां के ठोकी गढ के (वाह वाह)। देव महाराज का गढ को कोकरियो कोकरियो (हुगियो)। पीपळदे राणी गोखड़ो आयी (म्हे)। बैरी दरबार का हुकमूं भाला की तो जोर की दीनी भैइ चौट कीयो (वाह वाह)। देव की अस्त्री बोलै कांई समचार दीया नै कह देय देखां (कीआवूं जाणज्यो देखां कीआवूं)। अबार कहवूं भगवान का हुकमूं ले तूं

ए धौळहर गढ नै तो जी जो भालो मत बाहवै रे माझी जोधका रे।
धूज गी म्हारा रे धोळहर गढ की नीव।
मुशकल में लेवो रे सावर गढाली कोटड़ियां रे।
गोठां में जागै रे भोज सतनगज भीवै।
(भलां जी भलां) देव भलां

धौळहर गए नै तो दीया रे भालो मत बाह (म्हे)। अरै धूजै अब धौळहर गढ की देख नीव (नीव)। मुशकल होवै लेबो तनै साबर गढ की कोटड़ियां (वाह वाह)। गोठां में जागी भोज सतनगज (भीव)। भीमजी महाराज जागी अबार (हां जाग गिया)। मुशकल हुई मीर बोल्यो तोबा तोबा तोबा तोबा तोबा तोबा इस महल में देख औरत बोली (वाह वाह)। एक और दे (हां एक और दे ठा पड़ै ज्यूं कीयो)। दीयोजी कंस के औतार हो ढाल धोड़ी अर के भांलां की (हां एक और दीनी जी गढ के)। देव महाराज का गढ को तो कोकरियो कोकरियो धूजबा लागो औरूं (वाह वाह)।।

ए धौळहर गढ पर तो जी जो भालो मत बाहवै माझी जोधका रे।
धूजै भाई धौळहर गढ को लेव।
मुशकल होवै लेबो रे सावर गढाली कोटड़ियां।
गोठां में जागै रे बालो ठाकर देव।।
(भलां जी भलां) देव भलां

धौल गढ में भालो मत बाह भैइ (म्हे)। अरै धूजै देख धौला गढ (लेव)। मुशकल होवै लेवो तनै सावर गढ की कोटड़ियां (म्हे)। गोठां में जागी बालो ही ठाकर (देव)। ओ देव महाराज जाग जायी नै (म्हे)। अबार भागतां नै मारग कोनी लाधै भैइ (हां मारग नैइ लाधेलो कीया)। मीर कीयो तोबा तोबा तोबा तोबा तोबा औरत नै बड़ो जोर है ई कन्नै (म्हे)। पीपळदे राणी मन में बिचार (करियो है)। साडा सात बीसी राव की कछेड़ी में दीया सिरदार नौकरी (करै है)। पण ताणा गढ पर ओ भालो बाहवै (म्हे)। जको दीयो कांई ठी किस्यो है (किस्यो है ई को पत्तो पाड़ा)। देव की पदमणी बोलै (म्हे)। कांई दीया नै बतलावै देखां (कीआवूं जाणज्यो देखां कीआवूं)।।

ए किस्यो दीयोजी तो जी जो थामालो रे मंगल थोगलै औवूं रे।
किस्या दीया की चालै कालै ऊंठ कबाण।
किस्यो दीयो बाजै जोधको जायो डीकरो।
बी दीया का ठाकरां रे धक्का पड़ै गढ राण।।
(भलां जी भलां) देव भलां

किस्या दीयोजी भाई थामालो मंगल थोगलै (म्हे)। हेंर किस्या दीया की चालै कालै ऊंठ (कबाण)। अरै किस्यो दीयो बाजै जोधको जायो डीकरो (म्हे)। बी का धक्का पड़ै मोटोड़ी गढ (राण)। रावजी साय धड़को मानै बो दीयो कुण है (हां थामालो किस्यो हो भाई कीयो)। मीर कीयो तोबा तोबा देख तमार नाम महलां की औरत जाणती है (म्है है तो जोर को ही दीया कीयो)। दीया बड़ो जोर को व्हियो (वाह वाह)। दीया नै आंजस आयगो (म्हे)। दरबार का हुकमूं राव की फौज के मांय हाथी ऊबो (म्हे)। हेटै पर हथैली उठा लियो (हां अधर घुमा दियो हथेलीवूं)। दीयोजी बोलै कांई समचार राणी पीपळदे नै कहवै (कीआवूं जाणज्यो देखां कीआवूं)। अबार कह द्यूं देव का हुकमूं ले तूं।।

इयां हाथावूं जी ए ई मंगल नै थोगला रे।
म्हारी चालै कालै ऊंठ कबाण।
मैं बाजूं ये जोधको जायो डीकरो।
म्हारां पदमणी ये धक्का पड़ी गढ राण।।
(भलां जी भलां) देव भलां

इयां हाथावूं देख मंगल थोगला मैं (म्हे)। म्हारी चालै कालै ऊंठ (कबाण)। मैं ही बाजूं जोधको जायो डीकरो (वाह वाह)। म्हारा धक्का पड़ै मोटोड़ी गढ ई (राण)। बो रावजी सा धड़को मानै जको दीयो मैं हूं (मैं हूं कीयो आछी में बडी)। मह तो बडी जावै ईमें कांई बात है पीपळदे राणी मन में देखियो (म्हे)। अरै सेजाय दड़ावट दीयोजी ताणै दड़ावट को पर आय गियो दौड़ो (हां आयग्यो)। ई को माजनो तीन कोड़ी (हां कर देवां कीयो)।।

ए अतरा दिन ताणी तो जी तणै दीया रे सुरग्याणी जाणता रे।
नीकल गो दीया रे व्हिया बड़ो अग्याण।
दान्त तोड़ दाकल कर छोड़ियो दरबार गाड़ां की गढार में।
बी धणी के दीया रे कींयां पधारियो गांव।।
(भलां जी भलां) देव भलां

अता दिन दीया सुरग्याणी घणो जाणती (म्हे)। अरै नीकल गो आज व्हिया बड़ो (अग्याण)। दान्त तोड़ दाकल कर छोड़ियो गाड़ां की गढार में (म्हे)। अरै बी धणी के दीया पाछो तूं कींयां आयो (गांव)। तनै ठा है ओ गढ कुण को है (वाह वाह)। दरबार चारूं तो दान्त तोड़िया थारा (म्हे)। हेंर दरबार का हुकमूं बंवळी घोड़ी कोसी (वाह वाह)। बी धणी को गांव है (हां बी को है ओ गांव कीयो)। मीर बोल्या यार दीया तमारा माजना तो महलां की औरत (हां तीन कोड़ी का कर दिया)।।

अतरा दिन ताणी जी जो सुरग्याणी जाणता रे।
नीकल गो दीया व्हिया बड़ो अग्याण।
उतम राई नै मारियो दरबार घाटी सांखळी।
जकै दिन टणकाई नै रे किस्यै तेल दी गांव।।
(भलां जी भलां) देव भलां

अता दिन भाई दीया सुरग्याणी घणो जाणती (म्हे)। अरै नीकल गो व्हिया बड़ो (अग्याण)। उतम राई नै मारियो कंवर दरबार घाटी सांखळी (म्हे)। जकै दिन दीया टणकाई नै किसै मेली तूं (गांव)। टणकाई नै गांव गोठ भेजी की जकै दिन (हां आ बता कीयो)। उतम राई कंवर नै मारियो (म्हे)। बंवळी घोड़ी की बन्ध कटाई भगवान (वाह वाह)। मीर बोल्यो तोबा तोबा तोबा तोबा तोबा ओ तो ऊमरताण को साल है थारो पदमणी को (हां भूल गियो कींयां तूं ई आ बांतां नै कीयो)। उतम राई की कंवराणी धौला जकै दिन ओड़ मेलिया (वाह वाह)। अब दीयोजी बोलै देखां (म्हे)। कांई समचार पीपळदे नै कहवै (कीआवूं जाणज्यो देखां कीआवूं)।।

ए नानरिया स्याम नै जी जो जगां लियो ये महलां की पदमणियां रे।
नी तो मारूं ये महलां भीतर आय।
उतम राई दांता को बैर काढबा आयगो।
ताणी धरती पर जी पाछा पड़ सी न्याव।।
(भलां जी भलां) देव भलां

दरबार का हुकमूं नानरिया स्याम नै अब जगा (म्हे)। नीतर मारूं महलां ही भीतर (आ अर)। उतम राई को ताणो दांता म्हाना दांता को बैर काड़बा आयगो (वाह वाह)। धरती पर पदमणी पाछा पड़ी (न्याव)। तणै ठा आयो कीताणू (वाह वाह)। ई बातै आयूं हूं (हां ई के वास्तै आयूं हूं)। दांता को बैर काढबा अर उतम राई को बैर काढबा आयो हूं (वाह वाह)। पीपळदे राणी बोलै कांई समचार कहवै देखां (कीआवूं जाणज्यो कीआवूं देखां)।।

नानरियो मत कहवै नै जी जो माझी जोधका रे।
नानरियो सुतो धीण तमारै मांयने।
मुशकल होवै लेबो सावर गढ वाली कोटड़ियां।
गोठां में जागी रे काळकनाथन कान।।
(भलां जी भलां) देव भलां

नानरियो मत कह भैइ दीया (म्हे)। नानरियो सुतो महलां में धीण तमारै (मान)। मुशकल होवै लेबो सावर गढ की कोटड़ियां (म्हे)। अरै गोठां में जागी काळकनाथन (कान)। कानजी महाराज जाग जायला तो भागतां नै मारग (नी लाधेलो कीयो)। मीर कीयो तोबा तोबा तोबा तोबा तोबा इस औरत कन्नै (हां) हजार पंद्रा सौ रजपूतां का गेबावूं फेटा है (हां जोरूं घणी बोलै है कीयो)। दीयोजी दरबार का हुकमूं मीर बूझणा करी दीया (म्हे)। थारा तो गांव बूझ लिया अर नांव (बूझ लिया)। तूं ई तो बूझ

देखां कुण की तो लुगाई है अर कुण की बेटी है देखां (हां कुण की बेटी है आ तो बूझ तो ले कीयो)।।

किस्या राजा की जी ए ई तूं डीकरियां रे।
गोठां में पदमणी किस्या बड़ की नार।
म्हारावूं करै करां की सामना।
ऊबी पदमणी ये धौला गढ के मांय।।
(भलां जी भलां) देव भलां

किस्या राजा की बाई डीकरी है (म्हे)। गोठां में तूं किस्या बड़ की (तूं नार)। म्हारावूं करै पदमणी करां की सामना (म्हे)। ऊबी दरबार का हुकमूं धौला गढ के (थारै मांय)। कुण की है तूं (हां कुण की है कीयो)। दरबार का हुकमूं पीपळदे राणी बोलै कांई समचार कहवै देखां (कीआवूं जाणज्यो कीआवूं देखा)।।

ए धार का धणी की जी दीया भाई रे मैं डीकरिया रे।
गोठां में ऊद करण घर नार।
थारावूं करूं दीयाजी करां की सामना।
ऊबी दीया रे म्हाना गढ के मांय।।
(भलां जी भलां) देव भलां

धार का धणी की डीकरी हूं (म्हे)। गोठां में ऊद करण घर (नार)। थारावूं करूं दीया ऊबी करां की सामना (म्हे)। ऊबी मैं म्हारा गढ (के मांय)। म्हारा घर में हूं मैं (वाह वाह)। चलार आया दीया म्हाना घर पर तूं (तूं आयो है कीयो)। मैं तो म्हारी ठौड़ा ही (हां हूं कीयो)। मीर बूझणा करी तमारा माजना तो दीया तीन कोड़ी का (कर दिन्या) अब हमारा कीया कर लियो (म्हे)। कांई कीयो दोय हाथी ऊबा है कछेड़ी में (वाह वाह)। आंका तो पेंकड़ा काट ल्यो (म्हे)। आपणी जीत का नंगार बजा दियो (अर भाग चालो पाछा)। तो अच्छी बात हो जावै (वाह वाह)। बाह वाह मीर जादी काट पेंकड़ा काट ले (म्हे)। तो एक तो हाथी हो जको मेदू का डायजा को (हां हो कीयो)। एक धणी धार का धणी की दियोड़ी देव का डायजा की ही (वाह वाह)। हाथियां पर काळू मीरजी सम गो (म्हे)। पीपळदे राणी मन में देखियो इती दार तो दाद (हां कोनी दियो)। अब थारावूं थागलो (हां लागै कोनी)। फौज में निंगै कर सैन्धो-मैन्धो कोय सिरदार (हां हुवे)। शरम घाला (वाह वाह)। हाथी खुलता जरूर रह जावै (हां रहवा कदै होवे)। ध्वाया को करण सिंगजी पूंवार निंगै आयगो (वाह वाह)। अरै काकोजी है नी करण सिंगजी डर कांई हो (हां डर की बात को है)। करण सिंगजी मन में देखियो ऊटै धार की बाई है राजा की (म्हे)। आपां नै ओळख लेय तो बड़ो ओळमो (देयी कीयो)। उतर घोड़ावूं नीचो (म्हे)। धोती को धाटो मारबा लागो (वाह वाह)। बाई ओळख ले नी (हां ओळख ले नी)। पीपळदे राणी बोलै कांई करण सिंगजी नै समचार कहवै देखां (कीआवूं जाणज्यो देखां कीआवूं)।।

ए धोती को धाटो तो जी मत मारो जी काका करण सिंगजी रे।
मत बनो जाण का अन्जाण।

ए हाथीड़ा सुलता रखा देय काका करण सिंगजी।
धार का धणी कन्नु रे घणा रखास्यूं मान।।
(भलां जी भलां) देव भलां

दरबार का हुकमूं धोती को धाटो मत मारो (म्हे)। काका करण सिंगजी मत बनो जान्अ का (अन्जान्अ)। आज हाथीड़ा म्हाना सुलता रखा दियो (म्हे)। धार का धणी कन्नु आप का घणा राखस्यूं (मान)। धार जावूं नै मैं (म्हे)। जी दिन आप को मान (घणो ही बड़ावूं कीयो)। दरबार का हुकमूं ओ समचार राणी पीपळदे (हां कीया जी कीयो)। ध्यावा को करण सिंगजी बोलै (म्हे)। कांई बाई नै जवाब देय देखां (कीआवूं जाणज्यो देखां कीआवूं)।।

ए आबा पर तो जी लाय लागी ये बाई राजवन।
कोनी बुझै बुझाय बाई पाणी का घड़ा।
के तो बुझावै बालो देवजी।
नीतर बुझै ये दूजार भिड़यां।।
(भलां जी भलां) देव भलां

आबा पर लाय लागी आज (म्हे)। कोनी बुझै बुझाय पाणी का (घड़ा)। के तो बुझाय बालो देवजी (वाह वाह)। नी तो बुझै दूजा जोध (औरूं भिड़या)। थारावूं म्हारावूं लाय (हां बुझनाली कोनी कीयो)। कीयो काकाजी कोय बात कोनी जाओ जरां (जावो कीयो)। तो दरबार का हुकमूं मीर कांई करियो (म्हे)। मांयनू दरवाजा के बड़ (वाह वाह)। हाथियां का पेंकड़ा दोन्यां का (हां काट राळिया जी कीयो)। पीपळदे राणी कांई बूजी के रावळै (जावे)। जांती सासू नै बतलावै देखां (कीआवूं जाणज्यो कीआवूं देखा)।।

ए पटमर हाथी नै जी बूजी म्हारावूं तो कायदा खोलियो रे।
लेरै करया म्हारी काबरड़ी का खोज।
हाथयां नै छुड़ाबाळा बूजी ये घरां कोय नी।
घरां कोनी ये सुसरो सवाई भोज।।
(भलां जी भलां) देव भलां

पटमरा हाथी नै बूजी जो कायदा खोलियो (म्हे)। लेरै कर दिया म्हारी काबरड़ी का (खोज)। हाथी छुड़ाबाळा बूजी रिया कोनी (म्हे)। घरां कोनी ये सुसरा सुसरो सवाई (भोज)। सवाई भोज होतां नै (म्हे)। तो हाथियां का पेंकड़ा लाखां कोनी कटतां (हां पेंकड़ा घरांवूं कोनी कटतां कीयो)। पण नी ताणो दूध को चूंगबालो महल में सोय गियो जागै कोनी अब (हां जागै नैइ कीयो)। पीपळदे बोलै कांई साडू नै बतलावै देखां (कीआवूं जाणज्यो कीआवूं देखा)।।

ए मछी जिनावरां जी जो रातै बूजी ये अच्छियो मोकळो रे।
रातियो बोल्यो बिरखै वाला मोर।
पण हिलगत पड़ गी ये कूबदियां राव ने।

म्हानी गोठां पर जी दो बर लेवै दौड़।।
(भलां जी भलां) देव भलां

मछी दरबार का हुकमूं मछी जिनावर अच्छियो मोकळो व्हियो (म्हे)। रात्यूं बूजी बोल्या बिरखै केरा (मोर)। ई ये हिलगत पड़ गी देख कुबदिया राव नै (म्हे)। म्हारी गोठां पर दो बर देवै (दौड़)। पहली चड़ आया म्हानी गायां नै पकड़ अर (ले ग्या)। अब दूजा आया है नै (म्हे)। म्हारा हाथियां का पेंकड़ा (हां काट अर ले ग्या कीयो)। पण भाई हिलगत आयगैइ (वाह वाह)। दरबार का हुकमूं हिलगत नी आवै जरां कांई मकदूर नै गोतो दो बारी दौड़ दे दियो (हां दो बारी दौड़ो दे दिया)। मीर बूझणा करी दीया (म्हे)। बजावो जीत का नंगारा (वाह वाह)। दरबार का हुकमूं ए तो हाथियां का पेंकड़ा काट अर (म्हे)। बाहरलै छेड़ै नीकल गा (वाह वाह)। तो दरबार का हुकमूं बी के मांयनै गांगो भाट हो (म्हे)। बी रावजी की फौज में (वाह वाह)। गांगो भाट बोलै कांई समचार कहवै देखां (कीआवूं जाणीज्यो कीआवूं देखां)। मीर बूझणा करी यार दिया अरै गांगलो भाट देव की सरावणा रोजीना करतो (म्हे)। इसका देव आज कहां गिया (आज कठै गियो)।।

ऊदिया ऊदिया करतो भाट गांगला कठै गिया ऊदिया बाण।
सैना में दड़ावट शहर लूटली अर कांई हुई ऊदिया बाण की जाण और पिछाण।
फौज में ऊठियो भाट गांगलो देव नै हाजर जोड़ियां हाथ।
जो हेलो सुणानै गोठालां राजवियां भाट गांगला नै कोनी बोलवा दे काळू
 मीर दिन रात।
गांगला भाट को हेलो सुणयो बालो ठाकर देवजी राज सिंग घोड़ो बळाई
भरतो आयो मिरगा कासा डाण।
धीरो रीज्यै दीया जोधका धीरो धरजै पांव।
धौलासा देवळ बीर खेत में बाळा पड़ता कांई बिका द्यूं भाव।
गोरम का भाखर से बाळाई को डावड़ो उतरियो उतरियो बड़ो मजबूत।
काळिसी घोड़ी हल्लायी रे।
दीयो करै बूझाना भलो लड़ै गोठां को राज सिंग बळाई रे।
बळाई मत कह रे दीया जोधका बळाई बताई आयी जान ने डेरो।
पाखरियो बाजू नारायण देव को ताणी फौजां में घाल द्यूं अबार बिखेरो रे।
बळाई मत कह माझी जोधका कदै नै कुण्डै पाण सळाई रे।
पाखरियो बाजू नारायाण देव को ताणी फौजां में घाल द्यूं बीचा बीच हळाई रे।
बळाई मत कह माझी जोधका बळाई बैठ खाड़ा में बेजो रे।
पाखरियो बालो ठाकर देव को तणी फौजां का उतार द्यूं फरगन्ता नेजो रे।
दो हाथी कोसिया रे बळाई डावड़ो ठाकर देव का।
दो हाथी रावजी फौजां में औरूं ल्यायो तोल।।
(भलां जी भलां) देव भलां

ऊदिया ऊदिया करतो भाट गांगला (म्हे)। तेरा आज कहां गिया ऊदिया (बाण)। सैना में दड़ावट शहर लूटली (म्हे)। कांई री तेरा उदिया बाण की जाण (औरूं पिछाण)। जाण पिछाण कोनी री (कांई री कीयो)। फौज में ऊठियो भाट गांगलो ठाकर देव नै हाजर जोड़ियां (अब हाथ)। हेलो सुणो जी गोठां का राजवी (म्हे)। भाट गांगला नै काळू मीर दीयोजी कोनी बोलबा देय दिन (रात)। गांगला भाट को हेलो सुणयो बालो देवजी (म्हे)। राज सिंग बळाई को घोड़ो भरतो आयो मिरगा कासा (डाण)। धीरो रीज्यै माझी जोधका धीरै धरज्यै (पाव)। गोरम का भाखर से उतरियो बळाई को डावड़ो (म्हे)। ठाकरां उतरियो बड़ो (मजबूत)। अर काळिसी घोड़ी हल्लायी (हल्लायी)। दीयो करै बूझणा भलो लड़ै आज गोठां को राज सिंग (बळाई)। बळाई मत कह माझी जोधका कदै पाण (सळाई)। पाखरियो ठाकर देव को थारी फौजां में घालूं बीचा बीच (हळाई)। बळाई मत कह माझी जोधका (म्हे)। बळाई बनै बैठ खाड़ा में (बेजो)। पाखरियो हूं देव को (म्हे)। थारी फौजां का उतारूं फरगन्ता (नेजा)। बळाई मत कह माझी जोधका (म्हे)। अरै बळाई बतावै आयी जान नै (डेरो)। पाखरियो ठाकर ठाकर देव को ताणी फौजां में अबार घालूं (बखेरो)। दोय हाथी कोसिया बळाई को डावड़ो ठाकर देव का (म्हे)। दो हाथी फौजां में औरूं ल्यायो (टोळ)। किरकाड़ पड़ियो (म्हे)। पांच टारड़ा कठै गिया अर पांच कठै की रह (हां गिया कीयो)। सिकराणी का छापरा जाय सात कोस तंबूड़ा ताण दिया (वाह वाह)। बाळा भांबी की जीत होतां (म्हे)। हाथियां का पाछा दरबार का हुकमूं हाथी कोसतां (कोसतां)। दड़ावट में ल्यातां जय बोलो श्री देव महाराज की (जय)। तो दरबार का हुकमूं बगड़ावतां के दड़ावट पर पाछा हाथी ल्यायो नी ओ भांबी (म्हे)। बूझणा करी ये माजी साय (वाह वाह)। ईंया कींयां बात करी (हां ईंयां कींयां करियो कीयो)। धोळा दोपारां दड़ावट शहर की लूट हुई देव कोनी गिया (हां देव कुनै ऊठ गिया कीयो)। कीयो रे भाई देव तो पोढी लगाली जको जाग्या कोनी (जाग्या कोनी)। कीयो माजी साय तूं देव नै जगायो कोनी (हां जगायां कोनी कीयो)। कीयो रे भाईड़ा में हेला घणा ही मारिया (पण कोनी जाग्या)। बाळो भांबी बूझणा (करी ही)। सुण ये माता (म्हे)। हेलावूं जागै मिनखियो मळाधारी (ए ठाकर देव महाराज कळाधा)। हेलावूं जागबाळा जिनस ए कोनी (हां नैइ है कीयो)। देव को जगानो याद कोनी रियो तनै (हां कोनी रही भूल गी कीयो)। कीयो लाल माळवा में भगवान सोय जातां नै (म्हे)। मैं जगा लेती (वाह वाह)। अठै आया पछै ओ नापलियो अर भाटड़ियो म्हारै जीव नै कळह राखी (हां मैं तो देव महाराज का जगावणा भूल गी कीयो)। लाल रे दुबध्या के मांयनै जगानो भूल गी (वाह वाह)। ले माजी मैं बतावूं आज (म्हे)। दरबार पोड़ मेलया जकी ढोलनी पर चार पायां पर धूपेड़ा रख दियो (म्हे)। हेंर एक धूपेड़ा राणी पीपळदे का हाथ में (दे देयो)। देव नै गूगळ धूप खेवो (म्हे)। गूगळ की बासनावूं भगवान मतै जाग जायी (अबार ऊठ जायी कीयो)। तो कांई बताई थोक बनावै (म्हे)। कांई भगवान देव नै जगावै देखां अब (कीआवूं जाणज्यो देखां कीआवूं)। अबार कहवां देव का हुकमूं ल्यो तूं।।

आंगन में राणी फिर गी ठाकरां राणी के बीचिया ढळ गा पाव।
जो रिमझिम कर राणी महलां चड़ गी मद पीता गजराज।
तांबै बाही राणी थाप की ताला खुल गा बीजळसार का रे।

हाथी खुल गा दरबार ताणी मान साळ का।
हाथियां की पुकार देव नै पहली सुणाई।
ऊठो मुख चांटो कुल्ला करो पियो सुरेमाता का सुखड़िया दूध।
छोत छोत कर ऊठिया देव मांगिया पाणी झारी भर ल्या पीपळदे राणी रे।
सोना को कळसियो रूपा की झारी हजार ऊबी देव की पीपळदे राणी।
ऊठता ठाकर देव महाराज मूंछ तामी रे।
तंबू तंबू में घणी लाय लगादी।
लगा दी भगवान रे सात कोस सिकराणी रे।
(भलां जी भलां) देव भलां

आंगन मैं तो राणी फिर गी (म्हे)। राणी के बीचया ढळ गा (पाव)। अरै रिमझिम कर राणी महलां चड़ गी मद पीतो (गजराज)। थामै भाई राणी जातै थाप की (म्हे)। ताला खुल गा बीजळ (सार का)। हाथी खुल गा रे दरबार थारी मानै (साळ का)। हाथियां की पुकार भगवान नै पहली सुणाई (म्हे)। ऊठो अब (वाह वाह)। मुख छांटो अर कुल्ला करो सुरेमाता का पीवो सुखड़िया (दूध)। रोजीना पिता जका आज पीवो (हां आज ही पीवो थे)। छोत छोत कर ऊठिया देव मांगिया पाणी (पाणी)। झारी भर ल्याया थारा देव की पीपळदे (राणी)। सोना को कळसियो रूपा की झारी (म्हे)। हाजर ऊबी ठाकर देव महाराज की पीपळदे (राणी)। ऊठता ठाकर देव महाराज मूंछ (ताणी)। तंबू तंबू मैं लाय लगा दी म्हारा सात कोस ही (सिकराणी)। ऊठता देव महाराज जहर की नजर (झांकिया)। काळू मीर का तंबूड़ा तण मेलिया नै सात कोस पर (म्हे)। सागै झूप गा (वाह वाह)। मीर बूझणा करी दीया तमारा तंबू में क्या हुया (हां तमहारा तंबू में देख क्या हुआ कीयो)। कीयो हुया कांई बळै ताणो है बळै म्हानै है (म्हानो ही है कीयो)। कीयो जणा देवजी जाग ग्या (हां जाग ग्या अब आवणाला ही है)। चालो (हां भागो कीयो बेगा)। उतावल में घोड़ के लेरै कांई बोलै बै (पछाड़ियां)। अगाड़ियां पछाड़ियां कोय उतावल में सिरदार पाड़ी कोय (कोनी पाड़ी)। ईंयां चड़ ऊबा रिया (वाह वाह)। घोड़ा नै झेळ दिया (म्हे)। दरबार का हुकमूं घणा का तो फूलडोल बाळो भांबी (फोड़ आया)। घणकरां लेरै रिया जका का गुल मेखावूं मतै फूट गा (हां लागै पटकारो पछाड़ी के देय कांई)। पिलाण खाली हो जावै (खाली हो जाय)। दरबार का हुकमूं पांच घोड़ा से बच अर (म्हे)। दीया की काळू मीर की हार हुई अर बी हारालै चूंतरै गिया (हां जार बैठ ग्या)। रावजी कीयो बै ल्याया देवजी का माथा देख लियो (देव मेदू का माथा लियाया अब कांई हाथै ही लियाया (दीखे)। दीया की हार होतां देव तीन तिलोकी को नाथ भगवान जागता जय बोलो श्री देवनारायण की (जय)। देव महाराज जाग्या (म्हे)। बसी को लोग सारो जग गो (हां सगळो को सगळो जाग गियो जी कीयो)। तो ए भाई मेदूजी मदन सिंगजी भूणोजी ए ई जाग्या (वाह वाह)। गायां दीखी कोनी (म्हे)। कीयो माजी गायां (म्हे)। कीयो गायां गिया दिन तीन व्हिया लाल (हां राताकोट में बन्ध व्हिया नैइ कीयो)। तो पहली गायां के बारूं कुण चड़िया (म्हे)। सवाई भोज को मेदूजी बिदा हु गो (वाह वाह)। दरबार का हुकमूं मदन सिंगजी (बीर हु ग्या)। दोन्यु भाई जाय (म्हे)। तीन कोस के आगलै छेड़ै बाघजी को खुदायोड़ो तळाव

को एक (वाह वाह)। बी जागां डेरा देदिया (म्हे)। आगै कोनी चालां भैइ भाई सब भेळा हो जायां अटवूं जरां चालां (जरां चालां बै ई आजावै लरवूं)। आबा देयो लेरावूं (वाह वाह)। तो दरबार का हुकमूं तीन तिलोकी को नाथ कांई पाला कुमहार नै बतलावै (म्हे)। कांई लीला घोड़ा नै अब पिलाणै देखां (कीआवूं जाणज्यो देखां कीआवूं)।।

पालासानी पूंग पिलाण लियो अर के लीला के बाहरें बेगो आण।
लीलो चाल्या धरतीमाता धर हरै बासक डरै पियांळ।
लीलो मकेरै गियो धरमराजा देवजी लीलै हला दी बाग।
जो हुकम करो गोठां का राजवी औरूं पिलाणूं दूधां धायां काबरिया टार।
मकेरिया नै माथा मार पालासानी पाड़ी चरण दियो लाप।
पिलाण लियो काळी जायो लीलड़ो बैरियां में घालूं अंवळी संवळी जाप।
लीला पर नारायण को बैसणो देव बिराजा आय।
नौसर खरां पर पाखर पड़िया रे।
चड़िया लटधारी चड़िया जटधारी चड़िया रूपनाथ की प्यारी।
बगड़ावतां का बैर पर शंकर महादेव थोड़ी सला बिचारी रे।
अंटेळाव से चड़िया नौसर करिया पाखर पड़ियार।
काळका देबी करै भैरूं नै सेडल।
आज देव की ताणा की रे कुण हुई चड़ाया रे।।
(भलां जी भलां) देव भलां

पाला भाई पूंग पिलाण ले अर कस लीलागर बाहरें बेगो (आण)। अरै लीलो चालयावूं धरतीमाता धर हरै बासक डरै (पियांळ)। लीलो तो परणालिया गी परो धरमराजा देवजी लीलै हिला दी (बाग)। हुकम करो गोठां का राजवी औरूं पिलाणूं दूधां का धायां काबरिया (टार)। मकेरिया नै माथै मार पालासानी पड़ी चरण दे (लांप)। पिलाण काळी जायो लीलड़ो बैरियां में घालूं अंवळी संवळी (जांप)। लीला पर नारायण को बैसणो देव बिराज्यो (आन)। नौ से खरां पर पाखर (पड़िया)। चड़िया लटधारी चड़िया जटधारी (म्हे)। अरै चड़िया रूपनाथ की (प्यारी)। बगड़ावतां का बैर में शंकर महादेव थोड़ी सला (बिचारी)। चेला को बैर काढा भैइ (वाह वाह)। अंटेळावसूं सेडल चड़ गी (म्हे)। नौ से खरां पर पाखर पड़ी (पड़ी)। काळका देबी करै भैरूं नै बूझणा (म्हे)। आसांगांवूं आज देव की ताणा की कुण हुई (चड़ायां)। अरै भैरवानाथ आज तो खप्पर भरीजीक (हां भरीजी)। कीयो अब धपावो भर लियो (वाह वाह)। बगड़ावतां का डावड़ा बगड़ावतां का बैर काड़बा नै जाय (म्हे)। धपावूं रंगी चंगी हो जायो (वाह वाह)। चौसट जोगणियां अठोतर खेतरपाल (म्हे)। जोगणियां लोही पीबा नै सागै हो गैइ बीर (वाह वाह)। धाप धाप बठै ही पियां भैइ (हां आज पियां कीयो)। दरबार का हुकमूं घोड़ा नै भगवान पिलाण बाहरलै छेड़ै मांगायो है नै (म्हे)। देव महाराज लीला के ऊपर असवार व्हिया (वाह वाह)। माजी आर घोड़ा के बाग नै (हां पकड़ लीनी)। मात खटाणी बोलै (म्हे)। कांई भगवान नै समचार कहवै देखां (कीआवूं जाणज्यो देखां कीआवूं)।।

गायां रे गी तो जी आगड़ी जाणदे रे कंवर लागला रे।
नान्या म्हाना जी औरै मंगां द्यूं तूं मोल।
थै मारया जावेला राताकोट की राड़ में।
मात खटाणी नै ऊद कठै से होय।।
(भलां जी भलां) देव भलां

साडूजी घोड़ा की लगाम पकड़िया ऊबी है (म्हे)। गायां गी तो लाल आगड़ी जाणज्यै (वाह वाह)। और मंगा द्यूं (मोल)। थै मारिया जावो राताकोटा का झगड़ा में (म्हे)। तो मात खटाणी पछै ऊद कठै से (होय)। गायां तो लाल मोल ले ल्यो (हां घणी ले ल्यां)। थारै जियां की चीजां लाल रे मोल आबा की कोनी है (हां कोनी कीयो)। ढाण्ढियां नै जाबा दे आगी (जान्9अ दिया)। कीयो माजी साय (म्हे)। बाग नै अब छोड़ दे कीयो (वाह वाह)। माजी साय काटी पकड़ै (म्हे)। देव तीन तिलोकी को नाथ अब बोलै (म्हे)। माजी साय नै कांई समचार कहवै (कीआवूं जाणीज्यो देखां कीआवूं)।।

ए लीला री बाग नै तो जी ए ई परी छोड़ द्यो रे।
लीलड़ो माजी ये दाबै आपका पाव।
मेदू मदनो मारिया जाय राताकोट की राड़ में।
झगड़ो जीतै ये राणा गढ को राव।।
(भलां जी भलां) देव भलां

दरबार का हुकमूं लीला की बाग नै परी छोड़ (म्हे)। माजी लीलो दाबै आपका (पाव)। मेदू अर मदनू भेइ मारिया जाय राताकोट की राड़ में (म्हे)। दरबार का हुकमूं झगड़ो जीती राणा ई गढ को (राव)। झगड़ो जीत जायलो (म्हे)। हेंर भाई मारिया जाय म्हारा (वाह वाह)। लीला की बाग नै छोड़ (हां छोड़ो कीयो)। साडूमाता काटी पकड़ै (म्हे)।।

ए लीला री बाग नै तो जी ए ई परी छोड़ द्यो रे।
लीलड़ो अब जायी बाग उजाट।
गायां रूकयोड़ी ऊबी है राताकोट में।
दुशमन रावजी देवै न्यारी न्यारी ये चौरासियां नै बांट।।
(भलां जी भलां) देव भलां

दरबार का हुकमूं समचार कीयो (म्हे)। लीला की बाग नै माजी परी छोड़ दियो (वाह वाह)। अब जावेलो लीलड़ो बाग नै (उजाट)। गायां रूकयोड़ी ऊबी माता राताकोट में (म्हे)। दुशमन रावजी दे न्यारी न्यारी म्हारी चौरसियां नै (बांट)। अबार तो एक जागां (म्हे)। हेंर रावजी साय न्यारी न्यारी बांट दी तो (हां चौरासी गढां का कणा झगढा करूंला अर कणा गायां (नै भेळी कर ल्यावूंला)। अता म्हांका तो वादा कोनी रिया (वाह वाह)। छोड़ देय (म्हे)। साडूमाता काटी पकड़ै (वाह वाह)।।

ए लीला री बाग नै तो जी जो परी छोड़ दियो रे।

लीलड़ो दाबै आपका सुम।
मेदू अर मदनू ये मारिया जासियां।
बै भाई म्हारै ये मोतसरियां की लूम।।
(भलां जी भलां) देव भलां

लीला के बाग नै अब छोड़ (म्हे)। लीलो दाबै रे आपका (सुम)। ए मेदू अर मदनू मरिया जाय राताकोट की राड़ में (म्हे)। बै भाई म्हारै माथा मोतसरियां की (लूम)। माता दुशमन लूम काट लेयी म्हारी (वाह वाह)। हेंर तीन दिना को सुरै गायूं कौल हो म्हारो (म्हे)। छोड़ देय माता ये (जान्9अ द्यो कीयो)। कीयो लाल रे तनै तो कोय नी जान्9अ द्यूं (हां बा नै जाण द्यै भायां नै)। बै गी परा (म्हे)। तनै की की जान्9अ द्यूं मैं (वाह वाह)। कीयो माजी देख घोड़ो बाग नै उजाड़ देलो तो म्हनै ठा कोनी है (म्हे)।।

ए आगला नै घणा बरजा तो जी ए ई कंवर लाडला रे।
दिरायी राजा अजयपाल की आण।
पण कंकाळी देबी ल्याय रे बेटा बाग का।
घोड़ा खिलाया नान्याजी दुरजनसाल की राण।।
(भलां जी भलां) देव भलां

मैं लाल आगला नै बगड़ावतां नै घणा ही बरज्या (हां बा नै ही बोहळा बरज्या कीयो)। दिरायी राजा अजयपाल की (आण)। कंकाळी देबी ल्याया बेटा बाग का (म्हे)। घोड़ा खिलाया लाल दुरजनसाल की (राण)। अरै मैं बगड़ावतां नै घणा ही बरज्या (हां बै ही थांकाळी जियान जीद चड़ ग्या)। बरजता बगड़ावतां गिया नै (म्हे)। बता थोक बगड़ावतां नै (व्हिया कीयो)। देव महाराज मन में देखियो (म्हे)। माजी है तो ठेट की कळजीभी (हां कळजीभी है)। आ माजी कहवै जकी बात होवै बिन तो (लाखां ही नैइ रहवे)। माजी का हुकम ले अर चांलां अच्छी बात हां (बन जावे)।।

नौआ खालड़ी कटावूं जी माता म्हारी ये हिन्दवा राव की रे।
माजी छुरियावूं फाडूं मोर।
रावजी का मारयोड़ा ये मर गा है बेटा बाघ का।
माता म्हारी ये बै मितवालां और।।
(भलां जी भलां) देव भलां

(मैं लाल आगला नै बगड़ावतां नै हां) नौआ खालड़ी अब के काडूं ये माजी दुशमन राव की (म्हे)। छुरियावूं फाड़ द्यूं (मोर)। ए राव का मरिया मर गा बेटा बाघ का (म्हे)। बै मितवालां हा (और)। दरबार का हुकमूं रावजी मारिया जका मानवी दूजा (हां दूसरा हां कीयो माजी)। तूं जाणै जकी बात कोनी लाल भलाई की हो भैइ (म्हे)। मैं तनै कोनी जाबा द्यूं (तनै तो कोनी जान्9अ द्यूं)। तीन तिलोकी को नाथ मन में देखियो (म्हे)। अरै माजी का हुकम बिन तो कोनी चांलां (हां हुकम ले अर ही चांलां कीयो)। तो दरबार का हुकमूं लीला घोड़ा पर भगवान चड़ियोड़ा हा (म्हे)। लीला का ताजणा नै के हेटो (नाक

दियो)। दरबार उनै की उनै निंगै (करबा लागग्या)। दरबार का हुकमूं साडूमाता बूझणा (करी है)। अरै लाल (कांई देखो)। कीयो माजी सा घोड़ा को देख ताजणो नीचो पड़ गो (हां)। ताजणो हाथ मूं छूट अर नीचो पड़ गियो कोय सिरदार (आजाय म्हानै ताजणो जिला देवै कीयो)। कीयो लाल मैं ऊबी हूं ने (हां मैं जिला द्यूं)। कीयो नैइ नैइ नैइ (म्हे)। कीयो माता थारी जीभ से मैं दूध चूंग लियो (म्हे)। तनै ई जीभूं काम कोनी उडावूं (हां काम उडाणो को धरम कोनी म्हारो कीयो)। कीयो लाल म्हारो छिरो नी लागै (म्हे)। तो एक हाथवूं माजी साय घोड़ा की बाग नै काटी पकड़ली (म्हे)। एक हाथ से ताजणो उठावा नीचै लुळी (लुळगी)। अताक पहली (ताजणो हाथ मूं लगाम छूट गी जी कीयो)। देव होंकारा करियो (म्हे)। होंकारा का समचै से सेस लीला हो गा सेस देवजी हो गा (वाह वाह)। माजी की फटकारो लाग गियो तो लगाम हाथ मूं (छूट गी)। बो ही कह लिया माजी देय ताजणो बो ही कह लिया माजी देय म्हनै (ताजणो)। थारो देवजी है जका नै अब ले जा (हां म्हारै कन्नै जरूरत कोनी मैं तो जास्या)। लेरला देवजी रातेकोट में जाय थारो देवजी है जका नै पकड़ पाछो ले जा (पाछो ले जा)। माजी मन में देखियो एक सौ ही तो घोड़ो अर एक सौ ही (असवार)। ताणो देवजी कांई आ में किस्यो है अब ठा कोनी (हां किस्यो है किस्यो नै पकड़ा)। तूं अबार ई नै पकड़यो ओ कह दियो मैं थारो देवजी कोनी (हां)। आ तो कबज बात बैठै कोनी अब (म्हे)। कीयो लाल मैं थारी करामात में अब समझ गी (हां अब समझ गी कीयो)। रावजी को कांई मकदूर जको तनै (मारै कीयो)। ताजणो द्यूं जरां ही (म्हे)। बो ही घोड़ो अर बो ही असवार पाछो होवै (जणा द्यूं कीयो)। ईंयां ताजणो कोनी द्यूं (कोनी द्यूं)। तो दरबार कीयो माजी सा अपूठा फिरो (म्हे)। माजी सा उनै देखियो जिता नै देव महाराज तो एकला घोड़ा पर चड़योड़ा ऊबा (वाह वाह)। लिया माजी (लिरावो कीयो)। तो कांई भगवान नै माजी सा ताजणा बकसै (म्हे)। कांई दरबार का हुकमूं राताकोट का हुकम देवै देखां (कीआवूं जाणज्यो कीआवूं देखां)।।

अब जावो तो जी नान्या म्हारा रे सीधा जावज्यो रे।
जाज्यो नान्या जी राण शहर के डाण्डै औवूं रे।
राव पड़ीहार नै रे हाथावूं मारज्यो।
नीतर बगड़ावतां का रे गलयोड़ा बैर मत भाणडो रे।।
(भलां जी भलां) देव भलां

अब जावै लाल तो सीधो जा (म्हे)। जाज्यै राण शहर के (डाण्डे)। तूं रावजी नै तो हाथावूं मारज्यै (म्हे)। नीतर बगड़ावतां के गलयोड़ा बैर मत (भाणडो)। पुराणा पड़ गा (म्हे)। आ नी होवै तूं पाछा नूवा कर ले (हां नया कर आ जाय कीयो)। कांई राताकोट की भोलावणी देय देखां (कीआवूं जाणज्यो कीआवूं देखां)।।

ए नौकरी करै जका सिरदार नै तो जी नान्या म्हाना जी हाथावूं मती मारज्यो रे।
पेट की खातर करै परायी चाकरियां रे।
राव पड़ीहार नै लाल रे हाथावूं मारज्ये।

नीतर मरयायो रावजी को छोटक्यो नीमदे भाई।।
(भलां जी भलां) देव भलां

दरबार का हुकमूं के नौकरी करै जका सिरदार नै जार मात मारज्यो (म्हे)। बो पेट की खातर करै परायी चाकरी (चाकरियां)। राव पड़ीहार नै तो लाल हाथावूं मार नाकियो (म्हे)। नी जरां मारयायो राव को छोटक्यो नीमदे (भाई)। नीमदे नै मारयाज्यो रावजी नी भाज जाय तो (वाह वाह)। आंपां देखां (म्हे)। छोटक्यां का बैर नीकल गा बड़योड़ा का ही (हां नी नीकलै लागो)। नीमदे राजा सितर बाळक हा बगड़ावतां के (वाह वाह)। जका नै शिला पर पछाड़ पछाड़ बाळकां नै मार गो (म्हे)। आंपां देखां भैइ छोटक्यां का ही बैर (हां नीकला लागो)। देव महाराज कीयो माजी सा बीजो महतो किस्यो हो (हां किस्यो है कीयो)। ओ दादो भांगीजी ल्यायो अर घोड़ा के पायगा में बांध्यो बो नी होवै (बो ही है कीयो)। कीयो सागै को सागै है (बो ही है कीयो)। कीयो जाणु बी नै (जाणु कीयो कोनी मरूं)। जरां लाल चोखी तरह पधारो (जावो कीयो)। देव महाराज नै माजी सीख दे दी (म्हे)। माळो जीव हो बस में कोनी रियो (वाह वाह)। अब मुण्डा के पारस पींपळी आयगी (म्हे)। कांई पारस पींपळी नै समचार कहवै देखां (कीआवूं जाणीज्यो देखां कीआवूं)। अबार कहवूं देव का हुकमूं देखां।।

ए गोठां आगली जी ए ई पारस पींपळियां रे।
ताणा भायां ये पात घणा सुपात।
बाळक ठाकर नै लेयाज्यै पीपळी तूं जीवतो।
पाछा आतां दिरावूं ये गल जोड़ा की दोवड़ी जात।
(भलां जी भलां) देव भलां

गोठां आगली पारस पींपळी (म्हे)। थारा बीरा पात घणा (सुपात)। बाळक ठाकर नै ल्याज्यै पाछो पीपळी जीवतो (म्हे)। पाछा आंतां ही दिरावूं गुल जोड़ा की दोवड़ी (जात)। थारै परिकरमा जात दिरावूं भायां (हां जींवतां ल्यायो)। देव नै जींवतो ल्यायी (वाह वाह)। पीपळी भलां बुरा कुण का करै (म्हे)। माळो जीव (हां रियो कोनी)। कीयो गोठां आगली बीरा पारस पींपळी (म्हे)। मत लागो रजपूतां की भालां के ई (खेव)। चुहाणा का भालां पीपळी है पड़ीहारां के लागज्यो (म्हे)। जाणै पैह छक्रियां का (म्हे)। मेह बरसै नै (म्हे)। जियान रावजी के दुशमन के भाला की लागज्यो (वाह वाह)।।

ए गोठां आगली तो जी ए ई पारस पींपळियां रे।
थारा पीपळी पात घणा सुपात।
बाळक देव नै लेयायज्यै तूं जींवतो।
म्हानो नान्यो ये भूल पधारज्यो जान।।
(भलां जी भलां) देव भलां

दडावट आगली बीरां पीपळी की (म्हे)। केसरूं सिंदुरूं चिरचूं थारा (पान)। बाळक देव नै ल्या पीपळी जींवतो (म्हे)। दरबार का हुकमूं म्हानो नान्यो ऊदल भूल पधारियो (जान)। आ राण शहर है नै (म्हे)। ठेट की कुंवारी (हां रह गी)। आज भगवान गिया है (परणीजाज्यो कीयो)। दरबार का हुकमूं पीपळी

भलां बुरा कुण का करै (म्हे)। माळो जीव हो (हां रियो कोनी)। तो दरबार का हुकमूं साडूमाता पीपळी की कन्नै बात होतां (म्हे)। कांई देव नै सीख देतां (देवतां)। जय बोलो श्री देवनारायण भगवान की (जय)। बोलो भैइ छोटा अर मोटा (स)। तो दरबार का हुकमूं साडूमाता देव नै सीख देय (म्हे)। हेंर पाछी (हां बावड़िया जी कीयो)। तो भूणोजी कलवन्ता बुला रियो (म्हे)। हेंर दुगाणी बांट रियो (वाह वाह)। साडूमाता मन में देखियो रे जलम की बांतां हो गी (म्हे)। भूणोजी तो भायां के सामिल कोनी दीखियो माठो (हां . . .)। गियो कोनी (हां गिया कोनी रावजी के सामिल ही है कीयो)। साडूमाता बोलै कांई कंवर भूणा नै बतलावै देखां (कीआवूं जाणज्यो कीआवूं)।।

भला गुवाया जी नान्यो भूणाजी तूं जांगड़िया रे।
नान्या भूणा रे भलां घुराया ढोल।
बाळक भाई पहुंच गो रे राताकोट की राड़ में।
सुणीज्यै नान्या रे माताजी का बोल।।
(भलां जी भलां) देव भलां

भला गुवाया भूणा बेटा जांगड़िया (म्हे)। भलां घुराया (ढोल)। अरै बाळक भाई पहुंच गो राताकोट की राड़ में (म्हे)। लेरावूं सुणज्यै माताजी को ई (बोल)। थारावूं बाळक हा जका तो राड़ में गिया तूं अठै बैठो हाल (हां अठै ही बैठो है कीयो)। ओ समचार कुण कीयो साडूमाता कीयो (वाह वाह)। पीपळदे राणी बोलै कांई भूणाजी नै समचार कहवै देखां (कीआवूं जाणज्यो कीआवूं)।।

ए दरवाजा गाड़ा जड़ ल्यो जी ए ई म्हाना जेठ सा रे।
आप तो सेठजी हो खुली राखी झांकी रे।
भायां के सामिल कोनी लाग्या जी म्हानो जेठ सा।
थै तो जेठ जी रे रूं पड़ीहारां की राखी।।
(भलां जी भलां) देव भलां

दरवाजा तो गाड़ा जड़ ल्यो (म्हे)। जेठ सा खुली राखी (झांकी)। थै भायां के सामिल कोनी रह गिया (म्हे)। रूं पड़ीहारां की (अब राखी)। ठा पड़ गी महानै भायां के सामिल कोनी थै (म्हे)। दरबार का हुकमूं रावजी का लूण पाणी खायोड़ा हो नै (म्हे)। रावजी की (हां राखो बात थै तो)। दरबार का हुकमूं ए समचार राणी पीपळदे (कीया है)। भूणोजी बोलै अर कांई समचार पीपळदे नै कहवै देखां (कीआवूं जाणीज्यो कीआवूं)। अबार कहवूं देव का हुकमूं ले तूं।।

ए बड़बड़ बोल्या तो जी तूं पीपळदे भूणा नै बोलड़ा रे।
पदमणी बाळा ये नैना सुरमो सार।
पीपळदे नै ये कर द्यो ये पीर नै पूगता।
भूणोजी बोलै ये राळां जीव से मार।।
(भलां जी भलां) देव भलां

बड़बड़ बोल्या भैइ पीपळदे बोलड़ा (म्हे)। नैना सुरमो (सार)। पीपळदे नै माजी कर देयो पीर नै पूगता (म्हे)। भूणोजी कहवै राळो जीव से (मार)। करां तो आयी करां की जकी बोल बोलै (म्हे)। दरबार का हुकमूं ओ समचार कंवर भूणोजी (कीया है)। पीपळदे बूझणा (करी)। मारबो तोड़बो जेठजी कदूं सीखया (म्हे)। कहतां आयी कोनी थानै (लाज)। राठोड़ां का बीर खेत में भोज नै रावजी सा मरियो नै (म्हे)। जकै दिन जेठ सा थै क्युं घाली नै (बाथ)। म्हनै मारबा नै सज गा तो जकै दिन दुशमन नै तो कोनी मारियो (वाह वाह)। भूणोजी मन में देखियो (म्हे)। जाणा लुगाइयां के दगो हो गो (हां दगो हो गियो)।।

अबकाळै सुणीज्यो जी ए ई काकीयाईं मावसियां रे।
सुण लीज्यो माण्डल की कुळ राज भुवा ई रे।
भला बुरा को पीपळदे ठा पड़ियो कोय ने।
ठा पड़ेलो भूणो ये रातै कोट गियां।।
(भलां जी भलां) देव भलां

अब कालै सुणज्यो काकी मावसियां (म्हे)। सुणज्यो माण्डल की कुळ राज (भुवा)। भला बूरा को हाल ठा कोनी पड़ै तनै (म्हे)। भला बूरा को ठा पड़ी भूणोजी रातेकोट ही (गियां)। मैं रातै कोट मैं जावूं (म्हे)। जरां थानै (बठै भला बुरा का ठा थानै पड़ी कीयो)। दरबार का हुकमूं मैं तो देखियो ये माता (म्हे)। के लाख को दान करियो मैं दातण फाडूं कोनी मैं (हां दातण फाड़ूं कोनी)। झगड़ा में दो तीन दिन लागी (हां)। दो तीन दिन को सामिल ई जागां भेळै कर द्यूं नै (हां तो म्हारै अड़ास कोनी लागै कीयो)। मैं तो बी की खातर कबसरियां नै दान बांटो (वाह वाह)। कंवर भूणोजी अठारा हजार की सायबी लेय (वाह वाह)। भायां के सामिल हो गा (जाय लिया)। दरबार का हुकमूं माजी सा चाण्दन चौक में पूगती हो गी (म्हे)। तो आगै नेवाजी को कंवर भांगीजी हो नै (वाह वाह)। चाण्दन चौक में सुतो रह गो लेरै (हां सुतिया ही रह गिया)। मन में देखियो रे सब भायां नै सीख दिरा दी (म्हे)। गायां को छुड़ाबालो हो जको अठै रह गो हाल (हां ओ तो अठै सुतो ही रह गियो कीयो)। क्युं की ई का माता का वचन है (म्हे)। बांवल्यो पकड़ कर बैठो (करियो हो)। भांगीजी होय बैठ उनै के उनै निंगै (हां करी है)। ए माता (म्हे)। थारो देवजी कोनी दीखियो अर भाई कोनी दीखिया (हां कांई बात है कीयो)। कीयो लाल तनै ठा कोनी (हां बै तो गायां छुड़ान नै राताकोट गिया कीयो)। गायां बन्ध कर ली दुशमन (वाह वाह)। कीयो माजी साय (म्हे)। भायां जिस्या ब्यहवारी कोनी अर भायां जिस्या बैरी (हां कोनी कीयो)। मैं किस्या म्हाना बाप को बैर कोनी काढतो कांई (हां काढतो कोनी कांई कीयो)। म्हनै जगायो कोनी म्हारै लेरै छोड़ गा (म्हे)। जबरो काम करियो भैइ ओ (वाह वाह)। कीयो लाल हाल तो तीन कोस पर भैइ भेळा हो मिलिया तूं ही जातो रह (हां जातो रह)। कीयो माजी साय सब भायां कन्नै टटू है (वाह वाह)। म्हारै कन्नै घोड़ो ही कोनी मैं कींयां जावूं पाळो जावूं (हां पाळो जावूं भूंडो कोनी लागो कांई कीयो)। माजी साय कहनी आयगो लाल पाळो क्युं जाय म्हारी घोड़ी ऊबी है काळवी (आ रही ई पर चड़ जाओ कीयो)। कीयो ठीक है (हां अब ठीक है माजी कीयो)। भांगीजी कंवर घोड़ी कानै चाल्यो नै (म्हे)। माजीवूं कहनी तो आयगो (वाह वाह)। मन में

देखियो रे कावळ बात हो गी (म्हे)। ओ है भंगेरियो (हां घोड़ी नै कठै ही गेलावूं मेल अर आवेलो)। टरड़ी नै गमाव अर आयो (वाह वाह)। माजी बोलै कांई समचार भांगी नै कहवै देखां (कीआवूं जाणीज्यो कीआवूं देखां)। अबार कहवूं देव का हुकमूं देखां (वाह वाह जी वाह वाह)।।

ए अंवळी की बंवळी होती जी ए ई कंवर भांगड़ा रे।
नान्या घोड़ी बा घोड़ियां की खान।
घोड़ी नै घणावूं मत मेली रे कंवर भांगड़ा।
घोड़ी म्हारी जी औरूं देयली ठाण।।
(भलां जी भलां) देव भलां

अंवळी की लाल बंवळी हुई (म्हे)। घोड़ी म्हारी बा घोड़ियां की (खान)। घोड़ी नै घणावूं मत मेली कंवर भांगड़ा घोड़ी म्हारी औरूं देयी (ठाण)। देवजीआलो घोड़ो है ई को दूध पियो (हां ई को ही दूध पियोड़ो है कीयो)। हेंर लाल रे बिस्यो को बिस्यो ई का पेट में औरूं (औरूं है कीयो)। आ नी होवै तूं टारड़ी नै कठै घणावूं (मेल आवेलो)। कीयो माता बेचूं कोनी (हां बेचूं कोनी घणावूं तो मेल लेवूंला भांग निवट (जायली तो)। पिसिया देयायी थारी नै छुड़ार लेयाई (वाह वाह)। भांग निवट जाय जरां टारड़ी मेल द्यूं माताजी भला की बात हो (हां की हो)। साडूमाता कीयो रे लाल पिसिया क्युं निवट जायी मोहरां घणी है बगड़ावतां की बारां की म्हारै कन्नै (हां ले आ सागै कीयो मोकळी)। ओ ले ओ कूंची ले जार भैंस ऊबरै घणो मोहरांवूं भरियो है (म्हे)। दरबार का हुकमूं भांगीजी कूंची लेय तोसाखानै पूगतो हु गो (वाह वाह)। चौमट चार पोटां मोहरां की (बांधी)। हमालां के माथै (मेलदी)। बजार में पूगती (हां व्हिया है)। जी टैम भांगीजी की मोहरां बजार में गी ने (म्हे)। बी टैम तीन से पोट भांग का आयगा (हां बाळदाला ले अर आयगा)। गाड़ियां कठै ही बी टैम (वाह वाह)। बाळदवूं बिणजारा ल्यातां (म्हे)। कीयो भैइ हां बाळद में कांई (कांई हो भैइ कीयो)। कीयो भांग है श्री महाराज (भांग है)। सेठां नै कीयो सेठां साहूकारां (म्हे)। मैं तो लेख को हिसाब (जाणा कोनी)। लेख को हिसाब कर द्यो (म्हे)। ई जागावूं राण शहर चौईस कोस है (हां चौईस कोस है कीयो)। जको भाड़ो भेळै ही चुका द्यूं (हां भेळो औरूं कर द्यो भाड़ो ही)। तो चौईस कोस को तो भाड़ो दे दियो लेख को हिसाब कर तीन से पोट को (म्हे)। दाम देदिया (हां आ ल्यो कीयो भायां)। बाकी की पाछी रकम ही तोसाखानै पूगती कर दी (म्हे)। बाळदाला आर कीयो ल्यो भैइ चालो (चालो)। आगै म्हारावूं औतारी पुरुष गियोड़ो है (म्हे)। बी को थानै तंबू निंगै (आ जावे)। बी के भैइ रे उरै ही ठम जाज्यो आगै मत काढज्यो (हां आगै मत काढज्यो भांग को नशो खतम कर देलो कीयो)। आगै नीकल जायली औतार के तो म्हारै तो कोयला हो जाय ऊगेली कोनी (हां ऊगेली कोनी कीयो)। तो दरबार का हुकमूं भांगीजी सुवा मण भांग को नशो कर (म्हे)। हेंर बूझणा करी माजी साय (वाह वाह)। अब थांकै टारड़ी नै घणावूं कोनी मेलूं (हां अब कोनी मेलूं कीयो)। बहम मत करियो (वाह वाह)। ए चड़ूं ही कोनी घणो म्हारै सोक कोय नै चड़बा को (हां चाहीज्यै सिरदार कन्नै कीयो)। दरबार का हुकमूं काळवी घोड़ी नै खोल भांगीजी (म्हे)। हेंर माजी देखियो जर घोड़ी पर कोनी चड़ियो (हां खेंचावूं राखी)। मन में देखियो डोकरी को जीव तो दुख पाय (हां दुख पाय डोकळडी को)। माजी साय देखबा में रियो

नै (म्हे)। ठेकेन का ऊबीरा घोड़ी पर चड़ गा (हां चड़ ऊबा रिया)। दरबार का हुकमूं मन में बिचार करियो के सब भायां कन्नै सस्तर है (म्हे)। हेंर आपां के सस्तर ही कोनी (हां सस्तर ही की कोनी कीयो)। तेलीड़ो एक घाणी फैरो (म्हे)। मन में देखियो रे दरबार का हुकमूं ए लाठियावूं तो कर लेवां झगड़ो (म्हे)। हेंर दोन्यु काम आजायी भांग की घोठ ल्याया (अर टोप भी साज ल्याया)। तेलीड़ा के लपेड़ की दीनी तेलीड़ा परै जार पड़िया नारां नै खोल तो घेर दियो आंतरै (म्हे)। दे मठोठी (वाह वाह)। हेंर लाठ नै खुंवा पर मेली घाणी नै पाड़ (म्हे)। माथा पर ठोर जचा लियो (वाह वाह)। लोह की लागै नै कोय लकड़ की (हां लगै कीयो)। जबरो काम व्हियो (म्हे)। ईवूं तो भांग घोठल्यां आपणी (अर ईवूं ही)। पील्यां (पील्यां)। सस्तर कोनी हो जको सस्तर हु गो कन्नै (वाह वाह)। भांगीजी काळवी पर चड़ियोड़ा (म्हे)। देव महाराज नै के आंतां दीखिया (वाह वाह)। कीयो बाबा भाट अबकाळो भैइ किस्यो आवै ओ (हां किस्यो आवै है कीयो)। कीयो बगड़ावत मरिया पछै कम दीखै म्हनै तो (म्हे)। कीयो दरबार का हुकमूं लकड़ा अर मुसळा तो ले मेलिया है (म्हे)। काळवी घोड़ी है चड़बा नै (हां माताजीआली)। कीयो बाबा भाट कीयो भंगेरियो आय गियो भैइ (म्हे)। हेंर आगै बाळद बहवै (वाह वाह)। कीयो रे बाबा भाट जलम की बात हो गी (म्हे)। के ओ भाई है जको सुवा मण भांग को नशो तो रोज का ही (करै है)। झगड़ा मैं जायी नै (म्हे)। बी टैम ढाई मन को (हां करी कीयो)। अता नशा में आगलो को आप को अर पराया को होश तो (हां रहवै कोनी)। ओ रावजी के अमरावां नै मारतो ही मारी आंपां मुण्डा के आजायी तो आंपां नै ही (पहली मारी ओ)। ई भाई नै सीख दे द्यो पाछी (वाह वाह)। जको आप को आपणै गढ की रूखाली राख ले (वाह वाह)। कीयो मैं कोनी द्यूं सीख आज के दिन (हां आज के दिन सीख देयो तो श्री महाराज आप दिरावो)। देव बोलै (वाह वाह)। कांई भाई भंगेरिया नै पाछो भेजे देखां (कीआवूं जाणज्यो देखां कीआवूं)। अबार कहवूं देव का हुकमूं ले तूं।।

भंग होवै तो जी दादा भाई रे भिड़कणी रे।
झगड़ो देखिया रे अमल हुवै अचराळ।
बाळक भाई करे तनै बूझणा।
तूं तो भांगीजी दड़ावट पाछो चाल।।
(भलां जी भलां) देव भलां

भांग तो होवै दादा भाई भिड़कणी (म्हे)। झगड़ो देखिया अमल चड़ जावै (अचराळ)। देव करै बूझणा भांगी तूं दड़ावट पाछो (अब चाल)। दड़ावट शहर सुनो है भैइ (हां थै बठै चालो कीयो)। कोय भाई कोनी रिया सगळा आयगा (वाह वाह)। भांगीजी मन में देखिया माठा पहली लेरां छोड़ां आया (हां अब सगळा में हळको ही औरूं तनै ही बरतै है कीयो)। औरूं तनै ही कह पाछो चाल (वाह वाह)। भांगीजी बोलै (म्हे)। कांई समचार कहवै देखां (कीआवूं जाणज्यो कीआवूं)।।

ए भांग होवै तो जी बाळक भाई रे बा भिड़कणा रे।
झगड़ो देखिया रे अमल होवै अचराळ।

ताणा बाप का काटिया भवानी बै पापड़ा।
म्हानो बाप माथो दिया पछै भाई रे असी पहर तरवार।।
(भलां जी भलां) देव भलां

भांग जरूर होवै भिड़कणी (म्हे)। झगड़ो देखिया अमल चड़ै (अचराळ)। भोज का काटिया भाजतां का भवानी पापड़ा (म्हे)। म्हानो बाबोजी शक्ती नै माथो दिया पछै महाभारत में असी पहर बाही (तरवार)। म्हारो बाप तो असी पहर माथो दिया पछै ही बाही (म्हे)। ए ताणो बाप है जको झगड़ो बता कत्तो करियो कीयो (कत्तो करियो कीयो भाग गिया जर लारावूं भवानी नावड़ी)। देव महाराज बूझणा करी रे बाबा भाट (म्हे)। भाई बड़ो बीर खान है ओ (वाह वाह)। पाछो कोनी जावो ओ (ओ जाणालो कोनी)। दरबार का हुकमूं भूणाजी को विश्वास ही कोनी तेजाजी को कंवर है नै (म्हे)। तो बाबोजी तेजोजी कह बातावै भाग जातां भैइ (हां भाग जातां)। ओ ई भाग जाय नै (हां तोई भाग्या भाग्या हो जावेला)। ई नै पाछो खिना दियो (ई नै खिना दियो)। कीयो श्री महाराज तूं ही भेज (मैं कोनी भेजूं कीयो)। देव बोलै कांई तेजाजी का कंवर नै समचार कहवै (कीआवूं जाणज्यो देखां कीआवूं)। अबार कहवूं भगवान का हुकमूं ले (वाह वाह)।।

ए भाजना नरां के तो जी जो नर जलमै भाजना रे।
जलमै भाई रे झूंझारां के झूंझार।
बाळक भैइ करै तनै बूझणा।
तेजा का मदना रे दड़ावट पाछो चाल।।
(भलां जी भलां) देव भलां

भाजना नरां के नर जलमै भाजना (म्है जलमै सुरां के झूंझार)। अरे दरबार का हुकमूं देव करै बूझणा (म्हे)। तूं तेजा का कंवर अब दड़ावट ही पाछो (अब चाल)। कह बातावै भैइ तेजोजी भाज जातां (म्हे)। तूं ही भाज जाय तो मैं तो भाई भाज्या भाज्या (भाज्या भाज्या हो जावां कीयो)। मदन सिंग (हां पाछा चालो कीया)। के रीस करी बटूं जोरूं (वाह वाह)। अरै भाई देखियो के (हां आपां नै सीख देवै नै)। हळको तनै कांई जाणयो ओ तो (म्हे)। तो बोलै कांई समचार देव नै पाछो कहवै देखां (कीआवूं जाणीज्यो कीआवूं)। अबार कह देयां सा देव का हुकमूं (वाह वाह)।।

ए भाजना नरां के तो जी जो नर जलमै बै भाजना रे।
जलम जावै दरबार ये झूंझारां झूंझार रे।
भोज का काटिया रे शक्ती पापड़ा।
म्हानो बाबोजी बावन रोळा रे बारा करी जी राड़।।
(भलां जी भलां) देव भलां

भाजना नरां के नर जलमै जरूर भाजना (म्हे)। जलम जावै दरबार झूंझारां के ही (झूंझार)। भोज का काटिया भवानी भाजतां का पापड़ा (म्हे)। म्हानो बाबोजी बावन तो रोळा अर बारा करी (राड़)। बावन तो छोटा मोटा रोळा कर लिया (म्हे)। बारा भारत बड़ा (करिया कीयो)। थानै ठा है सतीवाड़ै

कुण कराया (वाह वाह)। म्हारो बाप कराया लेरला का (म्हे)। म्हारो तो बाप को बचन कोनी हो शक्तीवूं (वाह वाह)। जरां माथो कोनी दियो (म्हे)। म्हारै बाप तो बगड़ावतां में कोय भारत नैइ करियो (वाह वाह)। अरै सवाई भोज कह बताय भाज गो भैइ (म्हे)। माथावूं डरतो (वाह वाह)। जको तूं सवाई भोज को लड़को है (हां तूं भागेलो कठै ही)। तूं पाछो जा (वाह वाह)। गायां नै मैं छुड़ा ल्यां भैइ (हां छुड़ा ल्यां कीयो)। देव महाराज म्हारो धणी बक बक हेंसिया बाबा भाट भाई बड़ो बीर खान है (म्हे)। ए कोनी जावै पाछा (पाछा जाणाला कोनी)। अब ईंयां करो के भूणाजी है जको रावजी कन्नै मोटो छोटो हु गो (म्हे)। पाळ पोस रावजी करी है (वाह वाह)। अरै तो भैइ कांई ठी बी जागां आपणै बाणो होवै कांई ठी रावजी के सामिल हो जाय तो कांई ठा (कांई ठा पड़ै कीयो)। ई भाई नै पाछो भेजो (वाह वाह)। तो दरबार का हुकमूं देव बोलै कांई भूणा नै बतलावै देखां (कीआवूं जाणज्यो भोपाजी महाराज कीआवूं)। कीआवूं देखां कीआवूं अबार कहवूं देव का हुकमूं (वाह वाह)।।

ताणा रजपूतां नै जी सोवै भूणा रे सेला बाफता रे।
सोवै तनै जी बावन फूल की ढाल।
दरबार करै रे तनै बूझणा।
दादा भूणा रे गोठां में पाछो चाल।।
(भलां जी भलां) देव भलां

ताणा रजपूतां नै सोवै रे भूणा सेला बाफाता (वाह वाह)। सोवै बावन फूल की (ढाल)। दरबार भगवान करै बूझणा (म्हे)। दादा भूणा दड़ावट पाछो (अब चाल)। दादा भूणा (म्हे)। दड़ावट चालो सुनी है (वाह वाह)। भूणोजी मन में देखियो माठो भाई तो तनै हलको मानियो दीखै (म्हे)। भूणोजी बोलै (वाह वाह)। कांई समचार देव नै कहवै देखां (कीआवूं जाणीज्यो देखां कीआवूं)। अबार कहवूं देव का हुकमूं ले तूं (वाह वाह)।।

ए म्हाना रजपूतां नै जी सोवै दरबार ए सेला बाफता रे।
सौवै अन्नदाता रे बावन फूल की ढाल।
म्हनै पाछो खिनावै तो बाळक भैइ रे ई तूं पाछो चाल।।
(भलां जी भलां) देव भलां

म्हाना रजपूतां नै सोवै भैइ सेला बाफता (म्हे)। सोवै बावन फूल की (ढाल)। तूं म्हनै पाछो खिनायो रे बाळक भाई (म्हे)। तूं ई गोठां पाछो (चाल)। मैं चड़िया जरां कोय लेरै कोनी चड़िया म्हांकै (म्हे)। अर तूं चड़ियो नै (वाह वाह)। ताणी माजी कोस एक तो लेरै भाजतां लेरै आयी (हां लेरै आयी)। पछै (झाड़ के झाड़ के बांट बांट बोलती गयी जात)। तूं तो आपणै जातां ही देर तियार हो जा (हां मैं तो गायां नै छुड़ा नै जावां तूं जातां रह)। जो गायां छुड़ा ल्यां अर बैर ई काढ ल्यां मैं तो (वाह वाह)। तूं जाता रह (हां जाता देबो कर कीयो)। देव महाराज बक बक हेंसिया बाबा भाट (म्हे)। भाई तो बड़ो बीर खान है (वाह वाह)। ओ कोनी जाय कीयो श्री महाराज ए तूं कीयो बतलाया आज (म्हे)। मैं बतला ल्यूं तो फूलडोल फोड़ नाकै म्हारा (हां म्हारा बंस नै अठै मारै ये)। तो बाबा भाट इस्यो

काम करां भैइ (म्हे)। कह सिरदारां नै सब नै कह देय घोड़ा को कोतल खिंचावो (म्हे)। गोठां सामा सस्तर पाती (मेल दियो)। हेंर जय देवजी की करां देयो तीन बारी (हां जय देव जय देव कहवां देयो कीयो)। पीठ पाकी कर द्यूं सारां की (वाह वाह)। कोय लोह की लागै न लकड़ की (हां लागै कीयो)। भाट कह हलकारो करियो (म्हे)। फौज में सगळै फिर गो (वाह वाह)। कीयो सिरदारां गोठां सामा सस्तर मेल दियो अर घोड़ा खिंचावो ल्यायो (म्हे)। हेंर जय देवजी की तीन बारी करो (तीन बारी कह द्यो)। तो थांकी पीठ पाकी हो जायी सारां की (वाह वाह)। सब सिरदार गोठां सामा सस्तर मेल दिया (म्हे)। हेटा उतर सलामी कर ली की जय देव की जय देव की जय देव की (जय देव की)। भांगीजी लकड़ा मुसला लिया बठै हो (वाह वाह)। कीयो श्री महाराज देव को हुकम है जय देवजी करो (म्हे)। भांगीजी कीयो रे भाट तीन ही कोस आया हाल (वाह वाह)। तीन कोस में थारो देवजी जय देवजी करां म्हावूं कोनी होवै (म्हावूं कोनी होवै कीयो)। राताकोट का भारत पर जावूं नै (हां जरां बठै कह द्यां एकर)। एकर ही भेळै कर लीज्यै म्हार कन्नै तूं (वाह वाह)। के सारै दिन जय देवजी की कोनी होवै (म्हारावूं कोनी होवै कीयो)। भाट आर कीयो श्री महाराज सब सिरदार जय देवजी की कर ली (म्हे)। ओ भांगीजी थारो (नट गियो)। कीयो बाबा भाट भाई भंगेरिया नै तो जकै दिन जोगियाली जमातवूं ल्यायो नै मैं (म्हे)। जकै दिन पीठ नै पाकी (करयोड़ी है)। ई माजीआली घोड़ी की पीठ काची है (हां ई टारड़ी की काची रह गी)। दुशमन दीया को बाण लागी घोड़ी के रे बाबा भाट (वाह वाह)। चालबा द्यो असवारी (चालण दियो कीयो अब)। तो बगड़ावतां का बैर में बगड़ावतां का डावड़ा तळाव परूं बिदा हो गा (वाह वाह)। दरबार का हुकमूं भूणोजी के भंवर नै आडी फैरी (म्हे)। फैर आडी बूझणा करी री महाराज (म्हे)। राण शहर में बड़ो तो जुगतवूं (बड़ीज्यो) म्हारा हाथ से (म्हे)। एक एक बुरज पर सितर सितर नाळ है सागै (हां चड़ायोड़ी है कीयो)। सितर तोपां का सागै पलीता लागी (वाह वाह)। तो सांखळी घाटी आयगी आगै (हां आगै सांखळी घाटी ही)। एक घोड़ो अर एक असवार मावै बी में (हां दो मावै ही कोनी सागै)। तो जियान आपां जाय नै जियां तो रावजी साय तोपां का पलीता देय जको चन्ना नै भूनै हे नै (म्हे)। जैसा आपां नै (भून देय कीयो)। तो जरां भैइ अब कांई करां (कींयां करनो)। कीयो श्री महाराज थाट की थाट फौजां पड़ जाय मांयनै (म्हे)। तो की जुगत बैठै (वाह वाह)। भांगीजी लेरै हा के आगा आया (म्हे)। कीयो भाटड़ा फौजां नै कींयां ऊबी राखी (हां ऊबा कींयां रिया हो कीयो)। कीयो श्री महाराज घाटी आयगी सांखळी (म्हे)। तो जरां कीयो जरां कांई मावा कोनी (मावा कोनी कीयो)। कीयो रे भाटड़िया तूं तो जीभवूं झगड़ा करिया ऊमर में (म्हे)। थारा देव नै आ झगड़ा को ठा ही कोनी (हां ई नै ठा कोनी)। किस्यो गांव में गियो झगड़ा करबा नै (वाह वाह)। एकानै हो जावो (छेड़ो हो जावो कीयो)। शंकर को बरदान हो भांगीजी नै (म्हे)। तो लाठ लेय एक उनै दीनी एक उनै दीनी जता नै घाटी जकी डूंगर की (हां फोड़ राळी सगळी ही)। बी टैम में देव भांगीजी तो घाटी नै तोड़ी (म्हे)। हेंर देव महाराज के मुखारबिन्द नै फाड़ियो (वाह वाह)। धूंर राळ दी धूंर पैदा कर दी उबासीवूं (हां कीं आगी नै सुजै ही कोनी)। राताकोट पर सायीवान बैठा (म्हे)। जकां के धूंर आयगी जको बा नै तो दर में ही कोनी दीखियो (आगै दीखै ही कठवूं)। ए सांखळी घाटी टूटगी (वाह वाह)। देव महाराज म्हारो धणी बक बक हेंसियो (वाह वाह)। अरै बाबा भाट (म्हे)। ई भाई नै आपां पाछो खिनावा (हां ई बिनै आ घाटी

कुण तोड़तो कीयो)। आप नै तो अठै ही अड़ गी (वाह वाह)। ओ भाई हो जरां घाटी नै तोड़ नाकी (म्हे)। घाटीवूं नीकलता ही भाट नै कीयो रे भैइ औरूं भूणा को विश्वास नैइ है (वाह वाह)। तो ए अटकलो कींयां के भाट भूणाजी नै बूझो एक तो राण शहर नै भेळो पहली के राताकोट नै (हां भेळो कीयो)। भूणाजी कीयो श्री महाराज राण शहर तो लुगाई के नांव है रांड के नांव (म्हे)। ई नै कांई भेळां (ई नै कोनी भेळां)। रातो कोट मोटियार के नांव जावो पहली बो नै तोड़ो (बी नै भेळो कीयो)। तो गायां तो गायां छूट जायी (म्हे)। हेंर बी जागां सज जरां बैर काढ लेयायां (वाह वाह)। वाह राताकोट का मोरचा पर जा रजपूतां का बेटा तंबूड़ा (ताण दिन्या)। दरबार का हुकमूं रसोई पाणी की जुगतां (होबा लागी)। तरवारियां के बाड़ दिरावां लागा अर भालां के (हणी कढाबा लाग गिया जी कीयो)। तीन तिलोकी को नाथ अम्मी की नजर झांकिया (म्हे)। गैबावूं फौजां देख पैदा कर दियो (वाह वाह)। ए तो पांच ही भायां घणी फौज कोनी (हां फौजां कठवूं आवे)। दरबार अम्मी की नजर से गैबावूं फौज कर दी (वाह वाह)। देखै जटै घोड़ावूं तो घोड़ो अड़ मेल लियो (म्हे)। असवारूं (असवार अड़ मेलिया)। ए तंबू से तंबू (अड़ मेलिया जी कीयो)। घेरो दे लियो गांव के (म्हे)। राताकोट के (वाह वाह)। सुवा पहर दिन चड़ियो (म्हे)। जरां धूंर एकानै (हुई)। सयाईवान के निंगै (आया करी है)। देखेण जटै तो तंबू तण मेलियो अर देखै जटै घोड़ा अर असवार ऊबा (वाह वाह)। अरै थारी मां जाणु रे जलम हो गा! (जलम हो गिया कीयो मौत आयगी)। सयाईवान राताकोट को रावजी कछेड़ी (जावे)। जांतो ही कांई समचार अब धणी नै आपका नै कहवै (कीआवूं जाणज्यो देखां कीआवूं)। अबार कहवां रे भगवान का हुकमूं भैइ (वाह वाह)।।

साही पुकारै जी ए ई राताकोट को रे।
रावजी सुणा नै म्हारी बात।
चड़ अर आयगा रे चुहाणां का डावड़ा।
सागै आयो रे मितवालां को साथ।।
(भलां जी भलां) देव भलां

साही पुकारै आज राताकोट में (म्हे)। रावजी अब सुणज्यो म्हारी (बात)। चड़र आया मितवालां का डावड़ा (म्हे)। सागै आयगा दरबारा का हुकमूं मितवालां का (साथ)। दरबार का हुकमूं बगड़ावत चड़याया (म्हे)। बगड़ावतां का चुहाणां का डावड़ा आयगा बैर पर (वाह वाह)। तो दरबार का हुकमूं सायीवान समचार कीयो (म्हे)। कीयो दरबार का हुकमूं साही पुकारै राताकोट को (वाह वाह)। रावजी सुणज्यो म्हारी (बात)। अरै चड़ अर आयगा मितवालां का डावड़ा (म्हे)। सागै आयगो मितवालां को ही (साथ)। रावजी निंगै करो (हां निंगै तो करो)। दरबार का हुकमूं रावजी सा बोलै सायीवान नै समचार कहवै (कीआवूं जाणीज्यो कीआवूं देखां)। अबार कहवूं भगवान का हुकमूं कहवूं मैं तो (वाह वाह)।।

खाळड़ी फोड़ावूं जी साही म्हारा रे राताकोट का रे।
खाल में भरां द्यूं रे जहरी कालर लूण।
तनै आतं नी दीखिया रे चुहाणां का डावड़ा।

बा फौजां में आयो रे बळवन्तकारी भूण।।
(भलां जी भलां) देव भलां

खाळड़ी फोड़ावूं भैइ सायीवान राताकोट का (म्हे)। अरै खाल में भरां द्यूं थारै जहरी कालर (लूण)। तनै आतां नी दीखिया भैइ चुहाणां का डावड़ा (म्हे)। बा फौजां में आयग्यो रे बळवन्तकारी (भूण)। तूं औरां नै कोनी जाणया (म्हे)। भूणोजी तो काल ही गियो (हां जाणै कोनी हो कांई कीयो)। कीयो श्री महाराज की को भलाई मैं तो की कोनी देखिया (वाह वाह)।।

खाळड़ी फोड़ावूं जी साही रे राताकोट का रे।
लगा द्यूं नैना में धोबा धोबा रेत।
चड़ अर आया रे चुहाणां का डावड़ा।
बा फौजां में भैइ रे माच रियो रण खेत।।
(भलां जी भलां) देव भलां

खाळड़ी फोडूं थारी (म्हे)। अरै नैना में नेका द्यूं धोबा धोबा (रेत)। तनै आतां नी दीखिया भैइ चुहाणां का डावड़ा (म्हे)। बा फौजां में माच रियो रण (खेत)। बै ही छानै रह ग्या कांई (हां छानै थोड़ा ही आया कीयो)। कीयो भैइ रावजी की कह भलाई (हां म्हानै तो कोनी दीखिया)। म्हनै तो ठा ही नी पड़ी (वाह वाह)। दरबार का हुकमूं अताक पहली रावजी साय को गांगो भाट आयगो (वाह वाह)।।

ए फौजां आयी तो जी रावजी ये बाळा देव की रे।
सागै आयगा रावजी देव तणा बियाण।
तेजाजी का मदना नै बाई परणा दे धणी राण का।
तनै देव नै रे बैठाणू एक दियाण।।
(भलां जी भलां) देव भलां

फौजां आयी बाळा देव की (म्हे)। अरै सागै आयगा भैइ देवतणा बियाण (बियाण)। तेजा रावत का मदना नै ताणी बाई परणा द्यो (म्हे)। तनै देव नै दोन्यां नै बैठाणो एक दियाण (दिवाण)। एक जागां बैठा अर अबार थानै बांतां कर द्यूं (वाह वाह)। बैर बना द्यूं (म्हे)। पण बाई परणा भैइ (वाह वाह)। थारी बड कंवर बाई है नै (म्हे)। बी नै परणा दे (वाह वाह)। रावजी सा बोलै (म्हे)। कांई समचार कहवै देखां (कीआवूं जाणज्यो कीआवूं देखां)। अबार कहवां धणी देव का हुकमूं कीआवूं कहवूं (वाह वाह सा)।।

बाई के मदनो जी भाई कैज्यै रे भाट गांगला रे।
भाट गांगलिया रे भोज धरम को बाप।
आ मरबा की घाटी आयी रे भाट सांखळी।
घड़ी पलक के कारण काया पर क्युं छोड़ै मोटो पाप।।
(भलां जी भलां) देव भलां

दरबार का हुकमूं समचार रावजी कीयो है (म्हे)। कीयो मदना के तो भाट बाई धरम की बहन है (म्हे)। हेंर भोज धरम को (बाप)। आ म्हारै मरबा की घाटी आयगी सांखळी (म्हे)। घड़ी सात के कारण रे भाट काया पर मत छोड़ै मोटो (पाप)। पाप मत बोल भैइ (हां ईंयां की बात मत कर कीयो)। म्हांकी बीगड़ी है तो बै बीगड़ी है (म्हे)। रावजी कीयो के म्हारै अर बगड़ावतां में पाग बदल भैइ व्हियोड़ा धरम का भाई है म्हारा (वाह वाह)। तो भाई के भैइ भाई लागै (म्हे)। ए बेटी का बाप बाई नै कींयां परणावूं रे (म्हे)। गांगो भाट बोलै अर कांई रावजी नै समचार कहवै अब (कीआवूं जाणज्यो कीआवूं देखां)। अबार कहवूं भगवान का हुकमूं।।

बाळक मारयायो जी जो बगड़ावतालां पाळनै रे।
मारायो रावजी ये पीतल कासा तूं देव।
बा बाळां के रावजी कारण।
दरबार दिन्यो रे राताकोट के घेर।।
(भलां जी भलां) देव भलां

बाळक मार नाकिया रे रावजी तूं बगड़ावतां का पाळनै (म्हे)। मारायायो भैइ तूं पीतल कासा (तूं देव)। बा बांलां के कारण रावजी (म्हे)। ओ देवजी दियो थारा राताकोट के (घेर)। लेरली बातां भूल गो की तूं (हां भूल ग्यो थोड़ी याद कोनी तनै कीयो)। सितर बाळकां पाळणा में ले रे (म्हे)। बै जका पछाड़ पछाड़ मारियायो तूं (वाह वाह)। बा के कारण देख आ फौजां आयगी (वाह वाह)। दरबार का हुकमूं ओ समचार रावजी साय को गांगो भाट (कीया है)। रावजी साय बोलै (म्हे)। कांई समचार पाछो कहवै (कीआवूं जाणीज्यो देखां कीआवूं)।।

ए बाळक मारिया तो जी जो बगड़ावतां का पाळणै औवूं रे।
भाट गांगला रे अब किसी द्यूं नाय।
सितर हजार घोड़ा की सायबी।
देवूंला भाट रे राण शहर के मांय।।
(भलां जी भलां) देव भलां

के बाळक मारियायो भाट गांगला बगड़ावतां का पाळणै (म्हे)। हेंर मैं अब किसी देयूं भैइ (नाय)। नाय कोनी द्यूं मारिया मैं (म्हे)। के अठारा हजार घोड़ा की सायबी (म्हे)। द्यूं भई राण शहर के (माई)। अठारा हजार घोड़ा असवार अबार मैजूद है म्हारै कन्नै (वाह वाह)। बै काम आया पहली तो म्हारा पर हाथ पड़ै कोनी (म्हे)। बै मर जायी (जणा कोय देखी जाय)। जरां बारी म्हानै आयी (वाह वाह)। गांगो भाट बोलै कांई समचार कहवै देखां (कीआवूं जाणज्यो कीआवूं देखां)।। तूं तो म्हारा निरजन तूं तूं तो म्हारा दाता तूं म्हारा दाता तूं म्हारा दाता तूं म्हारा दाता तूं म्हारा दाता तूं देव के निरजन तूं

छीलै छीलै तो जी जो बाजै बगड़ावतां के गमड़ बिलावणा रे।
जियान भैइ रे नाड़ी खाबड़ै पाणी की पणियार।

पहल का भारत में कुलायी रे मितवालां की कामणियां।
अबकाळा भारत में कुलावै रे दिया पड़ीहारां की नार।।
(भलां जी भलां) देव भलां

देव आज छीलै छीलै बाजै गमड़ बिलावणा (म्हे)। नाड़ी खाबड़ै पाणी की (पणियार)। अर पहलकाला तो भारत में कुलायी मितवालां की गूजरिया (म्हे)। कामणियां अबकाळा भारत में कुलायी दीया पड़ीहारां की (नार)। रावजी साय ले सज बारी आयगी (हां बारी आयगी अब कीयो)। कीयो आयगी गांगा अब कांई है डर कांई है कीयो (वाह वाह)। मरणो कबूल है (म्हे)।।

अब आबां पर जी चमकै रे बै बीजलियां रे।
लाग री उतर घर दिखण घर में मोक।
खड़क मेल बदरस जपो पड़ीहारां को ठाकरो।
ठाकर देव से रे नी लड़बा का जोग।।
(भलां जी भलां) देव भलां

दरबार का हुकमूं ओ समचार कुण कीयो गांगो भाट (कीया है)। कीयो आबा आबा में चिम्कै रावजी देख बीजलियां (म्हे)। अरै लाग री उत्तर घर दिखण घर में (मोक)। खड़क मेल बदरसै जमो (म्हे)। ठाकर देव से थांका कोनी लड़बा का (जोग)। खड़क मेल दियो भैइ (वाह वाह)। बदरसो को नांव कुण को है सा बोलो बदरस कुण ने कहतां खड़क मेल बदरस पड़ीहारां को ठाकरो बदरस कुण हो भगवान का नांव है के भगवान नै जपो अब देवूं थै झगड़ो नी जीतां रावजी साय के गांगा भाट की बांतां हुई (म्हे)। देव महाराज की फौज के मांयनै कीयो सिरदारां देव महाराज बूझणा करी (म्हे)। कीयो रे बाबा भाट (वाह वाह)। हां श्री महाराज (म्हे)। कीयो हां अब लियो भैइ कड़ाव मंगावो रंग गुलावो (हां रंग गुलावो कीयो)। रजपूत को बेटो भारत करै नै (हां केसरिया कसूमल पहली करो कीयो)। रंग का कड़ाव गुलावो (वाह वाह)। तीन तिलोकी को नाथ भगवान की फौज में (म्हे)। रंग गुलबा लागा केसरिया कसूमल का कड़ाव चड़ गा (वाह वाह)। तो रंग दरबार का हुकमूं गुलता (म्हे)। भाट रावजी नै समझातां (समझांवतां)। जय बोलो श्री देव नारायण की (जय)। बोलीज्यो छोटा मोटा (स)। तो दरबार का हुकमूं भांगीजी बूझणा करी भाट नै (म्हे)। अरै बाबा भाट (आज कांई रसोई बनै है कीयो)। कीयो कठै श्री महाराज (हां कड़ाव चड़ मेलिया नै)। ताणा देवजी कड़ाव मंगायां भैइ (म्हे)। कीयो श्री महाराज रसोई कठै अठै (हां रसोई कोय नै कीयो)। तो कीयो जटै झगड़ा हो जटै रसोयां कठै ही (वाह वाह)। कीयो श्री महाराज रजपूत को बेटो भारत करबा जावै (म्हे)। केसरियां कसूमल रंग कर जावै केसरियां कसूमल गुलै रंग गुलै (हां रंग गुल रिया है कीयो)। अरै भाट (म्हे)। थारा धणी देव नै कह (वाह वाह)। म्हारै पहली कोय केसरिया कसूमल कर ले तो मैं मारूंलां (हां मैं मारूंलां पहली केसरियां कसूमल मै करूंला (कीयो)। तो जकै दिन बगड़ावतां का बैर काढबा नै गिया नै (म्हे)। जकै दिन सारा पहली नेवाजी को कंवर केसरिया कसूमल कर लिया (वाह वाह)। दरबार का हुकमूं केसरियां कसूमल करिया नै (म्हे)। भगवान बोलै (वाह वाह)। देव बोलै कांई भांगीजी

नै समचार कहवै देखां (कीआवूं जाणज्यो कीआवूं देखां)। अबार कहवूं भगवान का हुकमूं (वाह वाह जी)।।

> दोवड़ा कोट तेवड़ा खायी सुण भांगड़ा भाई रे।
> जो के तो रातै कोट जायी मती जै जावै तो देव की रूधी गाय छुड़ाय।
> गियो राताकोट के मोरचै चिनक वार लगायी।
> अठारा मन की गुरज भांगीजी हाथावूं समायी रे।
> गियो राताकोट के मोरचै ठाकरां चिनक वार लागायी रे।
> रावजी दीया नै दाकलियो दाकलियो दुरजनसाल पड़ीहार रे।
> ऊठ दीया जोधका आयग्यो भंवर काळवी घोड़ी को असवार।
> दीयोजी ठाकरां पेल उजाटियो आभै करियो उजास।
> जो भारत नै बैठ ग्यो अरड़ के गोड़ी ढाल।
> दियो भाल बाही गो दरबार का हुकमूं घणी छोड़ दी लाड़।
> इसी झाटकी दुश्मन घोड़ी के ऊपरे।
> दीया की भाल घोड़ी को लेगी रे हियो कीरोयी काढ।
> (भलां जी भलां) देव भलां

दरबार का हुकमूं दोवड़ा कोट तेवड़ा खायी सुण भांगड़ा (भाई)। के तो रातै कोट जाज्यै मत (म्हे)। जै जावै तो देव की रूधी गाय (छुटाई)। अरै अती कहतां सजियो नेवा को सुतन सायबो (म्हे)। अठारा मन की गुरज हाथावूं (समायी)। गियो राताकोट के मोरचै बो चिनक वार (लागायी)। रावजी साय दीया नै दाकलियो (म्हे)। दाकळियो दुरजनसाल (पड़ीहार)। ऊठ दीया जोधका (म्हे)। देख बो आवै काळी घोड़ी को (एकलड़ो असवार)। अतीक कहतां दीयाजी ऊठ गो (म्हे)। दरबार का हुकमूं बैठ अरड़ के गोड़ी (ढाल अर)। तरवारियां की ताली उडी भालां की मतेई बरसी (भाल)। अरै सुरा तो पहली मतेई दरबार का हुकमूं मर गा (म्हे)। कायर रे मतेई तज गा (पिराण)। दीयोजी भाल बाही (वाह वाह)। भाल नै घणी छोड़ दी (लाड़)। इसी झाटकी घोड़ी के ऊपरै (म्हे)। दीया की भाल घोड़ी की ले गो घोड़ी की हियो किरोयी (काड़)। दीयोजी घोड़ी के बाण की दी छिड़कायी (वाह वाह)। तो घोड़ी तो एकानै पड़ गी (म्हे)। हेंर भांगीजी एकानै पड़ ग्या धुंआ का धकरोल में तोपां का अळड़ाट में (म्हे)। दरबार का हुकमूं सितर तोप का सागै पलीता जगायां (वाह वाह)। तो भगवान की सता ही ऊपरा कर नीकल गा (म्हे)। धुंआड़ो धुंआड़ो लागियो (हां खाली धुंआ ही नीसरयो)। भांगीजी मन में देखियो ई धुंआ में अरै टारड़ी तो बैरी हो गी चापली झेळ गी (हां माताजी की चड़बा की (ही ई नै ठा ही कांई है झगड़ो को)। क्युं धुंआ धकरोल देखियोड़ी कोनी हा (वाह वाह)। खाख में घाल (म्हे)। हेंर देव महाराज हा तंबू का जटै ल्यायो (वाह वाह)। तंबू नै आती के तो भगायो घोड़ी नै (हां जोरूं फैंकी तंबू के सारे)। तो धेड़ो बोल्यो (म्हे)। बैइ को भाट म्हानी नांव गला में तूंबा घाल मेलिया अर बैठो (हां देव महाराज के कन्नै ही बैठियो हो)। कीयो बाबा भाट (म्हे)। धेड़ा कीं का बोल्या (हां बाहरें धेड़ा कें का बोलो तंबू कन्ने)। भाट बाहरें नीकल गियो श्री महाराज (म्हे)। भांगीजी तो

टारड़ी नै मरायो (वाह वाह)। कीयो मैं कीयो नै पहली (हां घोड़ी की पीठ कच्ची रह गी कीयो)। दुशमन दीया को बाण लागी (वाह वाह)। देव महाराज बूझणा करी बाबा भाट (म्हे)। हां खाड़ा तो खुलावो (हां) घोड़ी नै जमी दाग द्यो (जमी दाग दे द्यो)। म्हानी नांव घाल गला में तूंबा (म्हे)। भाट तो बीर हु गो (हां बीर हु ग्यो)। क्युं भाट (कुनै जाय कीयो)। कीयो नी श्री महाराज थै काढ लिया बगड़ावतां का बैर नीकल ग्या नै (हां नीकल ग्या कीयो जाण ग्यो थानै मैं)। क्युं (म्हे)। कीयो आगै नै दीयोजी है बठै अमराव (वाह वाह)। कंस के औतार है दरबार का हुकमूं (कताक घोड़ा नै खुदाय खुदाय अर बुरासी तूं)। तो जरां बाबा भाट कांई करां (कांई करूं कीयो)। कीयो आयी तो घोड़ी (अर ओ ई असवार)। पाछो जावै नै मोरचा पर (म्हे)। जरां दुशमन दीयोजी धड़को मानेलो (हां धोकालो मानै नैइ तो बिलकुल ही कोनी मानेलो)। तीन तिलोकी को नाथ भगवान बाहरें नीकलया (म्हे)। घोड़ी नै आर देखी (वाह वाह)। भगवान नै कीयो हां देव महाराज बोलै (म्हे)। कांई समचार कहवै देखां (कीआवूं जाणीज्यो देखां कीआवूं)।। तूं तो तूं . . .

एक चोट तो जी दोय नारदा रे बैइ का भाट जी रे।
घोड़ी के भाटजी रे बहवै रकत की खाळी रे।
धिन है रे दीयाजी जोधका।
धिन है भैइ चोट का बावण रे दिया जोधका भाणावली रे।।
(भलां जी भलां) देव भलां

देख एक चोट है घोड़ी के दोय नारदा (म्हे)। बाबा भाट देख घोड़ी ले रकत की (खाळी)। धिन है चोट की बावणी दीया जोधका (भाणावली)। बाह वाह रे दुशमन देख घोड़ी के दीनी (हां है तो जोर को ही)। एक ही चोट दीनी दुशमन (पण देख?) घोड़ी को काळज्यो कोनी छोड़यो (वाह वाह)। भाट बूझणा करी श्री महाराज दुशमन नै सरावै बैरी नै (हां सरावै कीयो)। कीयो सुण रे भाट (म्हे)। बैरी को तो घाव सराणो (वाह वाह)। देख दुशमन कींयां की घोड़ी की दी ही है म्हारी के (म्हे)। जा दरबार का हुकमूं कूण्डी को छांटो राळ (हां कूण्डीआलो संपाड़ो नै छांटो द्यो ई के कीयो)। देव महाराज संपाड़ो करतां (म्हे)। बी कूण्डी को ल्यार के घोड़ी को छांटो (दीन्यो)। तो घोड़ी उछळ (वाह वाह)। तीन कदम ऊंची जार एकानै पड़ी (ऊबी रहणी)। भांगीजी कीयो देखो दादा भैइ टारड़ी बठै चापली झेळ गी (हां अठै देखो कूदण लाग गी कीयो)। अठै आयी उजाड़ में जरां अब कूदै (वाह वाह)। मैं देखियो देवजीआला घोड़ा ले जा अब के (म्हे)। पण ओ घोड़ो लड़ंगो दे भैइ (हां कांई ठा पटक देवै कीयो)। भारत में पटक दे लोग मार नाक बठै ही (म्हे)। आ घोड़ी माजीआली सोरी है पीठ की (हां ई नै ही ले जावां जणा होवै कीयो)। ई नै ले जाओ (वाह वाह)। तो घोड़ी नै भगवान जिन्दी करतां (करतां)। भांगीजी पाछो सजतां (सजतां)। जय बोलो श्री देवनारायण भगवान जी (जय)। तूं तो तूं म्हारा दाता तूं तूं तो देव के निरजन तूं तूं तो म्हारा दाता तूं म्हारा दाता तूं भांगीजी काळी घोड़ी पर चढ़ (वाह वाह)। पछो तियारी हु गो (म्हे)। देव महाराजा बोलै अर कांई सावल भुलावणी अब दे (कीआवूं जाणज्यो देखां कीआवूं)।।

दोवड़ा कोट तेवड़ा खायी अब सावल सुण रे भांगड़ा भैइ रे।
के तो राताकोट के मोरचै जायी मत जै जावै तो रूधी गाय छुटाई रे।
गियो राताकोट के मोरचै भांगीजी चिनक वार लगायी रे।
अठारा मण की गुरजा हाथावूं समायी रे।
साजियो नेवा को सुतन सायबो चिनक वार लागायी रे।
रावजी दीया नै दाकलियो दाकलियो साल पड़ीहार रे।
ऊठ दीया जोधका बोर काळवी घोड़ी को असवार।
अती कहतां दीयोजी ऊठ गियो अर घालियो भाल नै हाथ।
झगड़ो नैइ जीतां राणाजी सुणज्यै म्हारी बात।
बाळो ठाकर देव मुई घोड़ी फैर जिवायी रे।
अती कहतां राव का पग छूट गा भाज गो दुरजनसाल पड़ीहार।
पाळ चड़ गो तळाव पिछोदा की पाळ रे।
दीयोजी सस्तर पाती हेटा राळ दीयोजी बैठ गो हट के गोड़ी ढाल।
भांगीजी बाही गुरजा जोधारो बारा व्है ग्या।
रूंधी छूटी रे पारब्रिम की गाय।
बाही गुरज जोधारो बारा व्है ग्या।
तीन दिन की रूकयोड़ी ये रूंधी छूटी गाय।।
(भलां जी भलां) देव भलां

दोवड़ा कोट तेवड़ा खाय सावल सुण भांगड़ा भाई (भाई)। अब सावल सुणज्यै (म्हे)। के तो राताकोट के मोरचै तूं अब जाज्यै मत (म्हे)। जै जावै तो अबकाळै रूंधी गाय छुड़ायी (वाह वाह)। पहल कानी ना मत आजाय (हां अब के ईंयां मत आयी खाली)। अती कहतां सजियो नेवा को सुतन सायबो (म्हे)। अठारा मण की गल हाथावूं समायी दरबार का हुकमूं अठारा मण की गुरज ही (म्हे)। हाथ में समाली (वाह वाह)। अरै गियो राताकोट के मोरचै बो चिनक वार लगायी (लगायी)। रावजी सा दीया नै दाकलियो दाकलियो दुर्जनसाल (पड़ीहार)। ऊठ दीया जोधका आयगो भंवर काळवी घोड़ी को (सागै बो असवार)। अरै बो को आयो है बेटी का बाप (वाह वाह)। घोड़ी नै देखतां दीयो जोधका ठाकरां दिया अरड़ के सस्तर पाती हेटा (राळ)। हेटा नाक दिया (वाह वाह)। कीयो दीया ईंयां कांई करै (म्हे)। कीयो झगड़ो नैइ जीतां गेलिया रावजी (वाह वाह)। निंगै कर बालो ठाकर मुई घोड़ी फैर जिवायी (जिवायी)। अरै अबार मारी मैं ई नै (म्हे)। अबार की अबार (हां पछी आकी आयगी कीयो)। अब कांई सस्तर कांई घुमाणा खराब करणा है ही बाह (हां) बाह आ तीरां नै (म्हे)। तीर हेटा राळिया नै दीयोजी (वाह वाह)। रावजी साय को काळजो जागां छोड़ दियो नै थारी मां जाणु बाणावळियो जको है सस्तर राळ दिया (अब मौत आयगी कीयो)। पग छूट गा पाट छूट गी बी जागावूं (म्हे)। रावजी साय तो दरबार का हुकमूं भाज्यो भाज्यो जावै बण में (वाह वाह)। तळाव हो पिछोदो (म्हे)। बण में बनबास घणी ही दरबार का हुकमूं पौध हा जका ज्यादा हा बी जागां (वाह वाह)। पौधै के पौधै में दीखा

तो आत कोनी (म्हे)। आगा भाजां (भाग ज्यां कीयो)। रावजी चड़ गो भाज तळाव पिछोदा की पाळ (पाळ)। पाळ पाळ पर जार केर में बड़ गो (वाह वाह)। भांगीजी बाही गुरज जोधारा बारा हो गा अर ऊनी छूट गी पार नमूनी (गाय)। तीन दिना की रूकयोड़ी गायां ही जकी मतै मतै आपकी छूट गी (वाह वाह)। बाही गुरज खलियो नौगज रातो (कोट)। अरै खेलियो बारा हो गार ऊनी छूट गी आ पार नमूनी (गाय)। गायां नै भांगीजी छुड़ाता (म्हे)। दीया की हार होतां (वाह वाह)। रावजी भाजतां (भागतां)। जय बोलो भैइ श्री देवनारायण भगवान की (जय)। के अमरावां नै जका नै भांगीजी लाठवूं बठै ही मार नाकिया बी फैरी लाठवूं (म्हे)। अरै राम मोटा मोटा अमराव जका भाज छूटियो (वाह वाह)। भांगीजी टोळा का तो टोळा अर छांगा की छांगा देव के सारो तंबू काढी (हां गायां नै काढी जी कीयो)। लो श्री महाराज समालो आप की (हां समालो कीयो से नै छुटा ल्याया हूं)। अरै समाला तो सरी पण बगड़ावतां को बैर कठै बै (म्हे)। रह गा कुण में है (वाह वाह)। कीयो म्हनै कांई म्हनै रावजी दीखियो कोनी (हां म्हनै रावजी तो कोनी दीखियो कीयो)। भाजतो दीखियो (वाह वाह)। मेदूजी मदन सिंगजी कीयो बेगा भाजो भाजो (हां बेगा चड़ो कीयो)। चड़ चड़ घोड़ा पर भाज छुट्या देव नै कीयो तूं ही भाज (म्हे)। कीयो मैं कोनी भाजूं (हां भाग्योड़ो के लेरै मैं तो कोनी भागूं)। भूणोजी बूझणा करी ओ कोनी भाजै ई को बाप थोड़ो है भैइ (हां ई के बाप थोड़ो ही हो)। आपणै बड़कां को बैर आपां भाजां (आपां भागां नावड़सिया अबार)। चारूं भाई रावजी के लेरै दबाया (वाह वाह)। घोड़ा का कोड़ बोल्या नै (म्हे)। मन में देखियो आपां ही घोड़ा असवार हो (वाह वाह)। रावजी ठेकेन के केर मूं नीकल घोड़ा असवार हु गो (वाह वाह)। लूकियोड़ो रियो तो कोनी (म्हे)। तो देव महाराज तीन तिलोकी को नाथ भगवान बी जागावूं घोड़ा की बाग नै नीचै राळ दी (हां पताल में राळी)। घोड़ो दरबार का हुकमूं रावजी के सामू जार नीकल गियो (वाह वाह)। रावजी को मुण्डो हो नै (म्हे)। बी जागां सामू नीकलयो (वाह वाह)। सामू नीकलयो अर कह धड़को मानियो रावजी फट ठमिया (हां ठमिया)। ठमता ही भूणोजी हो आगै ही आगै (म्हे)। कबाण घाल दी रावजी साय के (लारूं गलै में घाली अठै)। बैरी नै आगो राळो नै (राळो कीयो)। भूणाजी की तो कबाण घालनी हुई (म्हे)। हेंर देव को बूड़ी बाही हुई (वाह वाह)। दोन्यो भाई सामिल हो लेरला भाई तो लेरै ऊबा (म्हे)। रावजी नै दे हेटै पटक दी (हां ठेकै मर गियो रावजी)। दरबार का हुकमूं रावजी मरिया नै (म्हे)। भाट बगड़ावतां को लेरै भाज अर आयो के बी नै पेट फाड़बा लाग्यो (हां पेट नै फाड़ियो)। अरै कीयो भाट पेट मत फाड़ (वाह वाह)। कीयो तनै ठा ही कोनी (म्हे)। बगड़ावतां का बैर ही जका ई का पेट में हा (वाह वाह)। पेट तो फाड़ा भाटां भरां मांयनै (भाटां भरस्यूं ई में)। तो भूणोजी कन्नै ऊबा के भूणा का आंखियां में चौसरा चाल्या (हां आंखियां में पाणी चालगियो)। देव महाराज निंगै राखी सामू ऊबा के निंगै करी के भूणा (म्हे)। मैं तो दुशमन नै बैरी नै मारियो राजी हु गा सारा ही (अर तूं रोयियो कींयां कीयो)। कीयो श्री महाराज हो तो बैरी (ब्यहवारी तो कोय नै)। पण म्हारी पाळ पोस म्हनै मोटो ओ ई करियो (हां सोरो घणो राखियो)। म्हारै तो बाप हो (म्हे)। जी की खातर रोज आयो म्हनै और कोय बात (और कोय बात कोय नै)। ब्यहवारी कोनी हो (म्हे)। बैरी हो (वाह वाह)। कीयो भूणा अतो सोरो राखियो कीयो हां महाराज (सोरो राखियो)। कीयो भाई जरां ईंयां कर के बैर तो म्हांकै तो बगड़ावतां का नीकल गा (हां काढ लियां आपां)। कीयो मर गो नीकलयोड़ा है (म्हे)। हेंर शीश जोड़

दे थारा को (वाह वाह)। बैठो मैं कर देवूं (बैठो पाछो कर देवूं)। तो भूणोजी बाबा रावजी को झड़का रेतवूं शीश नै (म्हे)। कर सळियो (वाह वाह)। पाछो चेप्यो (म्हे)। कीयो ओ लियो श्री महाराज चेप तो मैं दियो (चेप दियो)। देव महाराज अम्मी की नजर झांकी (म्हे)। रावजी सा अरदररररर कानी बैठो (पाछो हो ग्या)। देव महाराज बूझणा (करी ही)। कीयो भैइ राण शहर को राव तो आजवूं जावेलो (हां गियो थारो)। हेंर बा पद्दी ही नै रावजी की (हां बा ही गयी)। भाई समझो के अता दिन बाजता मण्डोवरा (म्हे)। हेंर पड़ीहार किस्या मण्डोवरा नै (मण्डोवरा नै)। आजवूं मण्डोवरी पद्दी तो खतम है (म्हे)। हेंर दरबार का हुकमूं राणोजी बसावै जटै म्हारै नांव से उदयपूर है (हां उदयपूर बसावै होवे)। हेंर शीसोदिया राणा बाजोला भैइ (वाह वाह)। शीश जोड़ बैठा करिया मैं (म्हे)। तो जकै दिनवूं भगवान शीश जोड़ बैठा करिया नै (वाह वाह)। जकै दिनवूं पद्दी हुई शीसोदिया राणा की (म्हे)। हेंर राणोजी बसायी जटै देव का नांव उदयपूर जा अर बसायी (हां म्हारै नांव बसा ले नांव थारो है अर गांव को नांव म्हारो (है)। म्हारो है भैइ (वाह वाह)। तो राणाजी की पद्दी शीसोदिया की देतां (देवतां)। राणोजी दरबार का हुकमूं उदयपूर आतां (बसावतां)। बगड़ावतां का बैर नीकलता सारा (वाह वाह)। देव महाराज की गायां छूटता जय बोलो श्री देव की जय हो जय हो जय हो भैइ। तो तीन तिलोकी को नाथ गायां नै छुड़ाय (म्हे)। हेंर पाछा भाई भाई पूगता हु गा (वाह वाह)।।

थै तो आण बिराजा जी बापजी भलां बिराजा जी।
बतवन्त बाईका बीर समंदर की तीर बिराजा जी।
चोका चोका राण्धू रे चावलिया हरी नै जिमावां।
चोका रे चोका राण्धू चावलिया हरी नै जिमावनां।
थै भलां बिराज्यो बापजी आण बिराजा जी।
छोटीसी मथरा सारी देव बिराजा जी।
ए काळी मुण्डी को आदमी रे बी की लांबी चोटी।
काळी मुण्डी को आदमी बी की लांबी चोटी।
थै तो भलां बिराज्यो बापजी आण बिराजा जी।
ए छोटीजी मलासरी में देव बिराज्यो जी।

दरबार का हुकमूं साडूमाता भगवान नै चोखी तरहवूं धोलिया धोलिया चावल राण्ध (म्हे)। हेंर भगवान नै गायां की खीर बनाय चोखी तरह भोजन जिमाया आवो पधारो महाराज (वाह वाह जीमो कीयो)। अरै मालासरी में भगवान छोटीसी मथरासरी जकी ए भगवान को बैसणो व्हियो जरां देखो इन्द्रासन जावै (वाह वाह)। चोखी तरह भगवान नै चावल भात जिमाया है (वाह वाह)। हेंर भगवान को आरतियो करियो (म्हे)। राणी नै बूझणा करी पीपळदे नै कीयो ले भैइ पीपळदे राणी मैं म्हांकै तो अब वादा अब नी है (हां इन्द्रासन जांवसिया कीयो टैम हुगियो)। कीयो श्री महाराज (म्हे)। आप तो इन्द्रासन जावो म्हांकै कांई म्हांको आधार होवेलो लेरेवूं (हां म्हांको कांई हूसी कीयो)। आपणै सेंसारी दुनिया जाणी (हां मैं थांकै लारै आयी म्हनै कुण जाणियो कीयो)। कीयो राणी पीपळदे (म्हे)। दरबार का हुकमूं देख नांव तो म्हारो (वाह वाह)। पूजा रही थारी जोड़ो रही आपणो (हां जोड़ो ही रहसी सदा

ही)। कीयो देवरो बनी कीयो देव महाराज को देवरो है सा (म्हे)। तो बी जागां पूजा ईंठ की रही (हां ईंठां की रहसी ही)। देवरा में बडी के ईंठां ए ईंठां का स्याम तो पूजा तो थारी लुगाई के नांव है ईंठ पूजा तो हे पीपळदे राणी की हेंर आपां के देवरो कुण को हो देवजी को हो (देवजी को)। तो बठै बठै देवजी की पूजा कोनी बठै पीपळदे का है कीयो नी महाराज म्हानै आवड़ै कोनी है (म्हे)। आलम कीवूं कराय तो भगवान दरबार का हुकमूं दोय फल तोड़ पीपळदे राणी नै (देदिया)। ओ ले थारै आलम हो जाय आंका (आंका आलम हो जायसी)। तो भगवान तो रात की लेरली चार बाजै जर पीपळदेवूं चौपड़ पासा खेल (म्हे)। धाम प्रापत हो गा (वाह वाह)। हेंर भगवान कीयो रोज का दो मिनट चार मिनट जा तनै समाल लेवूं थारै मेल चौपड़ को डांव खेला एक (वाह वाह)। पण नीती आ राखणी (म्हे)। गाय को कुंवारी को पोटो ल्यार एक चोखो देदेनो (हां चोखो देदेज्यो)। बो जतै सूखी (हां जतै थारै कन्नै ठहर जासी)। अतो ही कौल बचन हो (वाह वाह)। पीपळदे राणी स्याम का ही एक आपको कुंवारी केरड़ी को तो गोबर लेय ढोलिया के हेटै पोतारो दे द्यो (वाह वाह)। देव महाराज आजातां दो बात कर लेता चौपड़ को डांव खेल लेता (म्हे)। छै महीना तक ईंयां ही चाल्या तो साडूमाता धरम की धाय भगवान पीपळदे नै बूझणा करी (म्हे)। की पीपळदे राणी म्हारा देव नै छै महीना हो गा इनद्रासनवूं मालम व्हिया नै (वाह वाह)। थारा हाथ को जो सिण्गार है जका मैजूद है (हां)। हेंर महल में चाण्दन पील सोत रातूं जगै थारै (हां बियां की बियां जगै है कीयो)। एक दो दिन तो बूझणा हां कीयो कोनी (म्हे)। पीपळदे नै पूरी अगताई जरां कीयो श्री महाराज देव महाराज देव महाराज म्हारै महल रोजीना आवै (हां रोजीना ही आवै थांको बेटो कीयो)। कीयो कींयां मानो मैं बोबा चूंगायां जको म्हनै दरसाव कोनी देय (म्हारो मिलै ही कोनी थारै कन्नै आवे)। कीयो बोल कांई रीति से आवै (जकी बता)। कीयो सा एक पोतियारो देवूं ढोलिया के नीचै जितै बो करड़ो रहवै नै (म्हे)। जिती ही जार दो चार मिनट बात करै (हां पछै ऊठ जाय)। तो इस्यो काम करणो बेटा काल (म्हे)। गाय का घी घणा पड़िया आपां कन्नै घी के मांय मिलाकर (हां पोतो दे द्यो)। ओ सुखै ही नै पाछा भगवान (हां जावै कीयो)। पीपळदे राणी दूजै दिन घी में घारो कर ढोलिया के हेटै आपको नीप द्यो (वाह वाह)। देव महाराज की टैम हुई बियाण आयो (म्हे)। अब बी टैम का जाबा लाग्या तो बियाण हिल्यो ही कोनी बी जागां देखो (बठै ही ठहर ग्यो)। कीयो पीपळदे बात कांई (हुई कीयो)। कीयो महाराज म्हनै कांई ठी आप जाणो (आप जाणो कीयो)। कीयो नैइ की दूजी रचना बन गी ए तो (म्हे)। कौल इस्या के जतै चोखो सूखी जरां निंगै करी नीचा ने तो आगो कादो पड़ियो (हां आलो को आलो रियो)। कीयो पीपळदे राणी (म्हे)। ओ आज चोखो कुण दियो (हां कुण दियो कीयो)। कीयो आपकी मां दिरायो सा (मां दिरायो)। वाह भैइ जरां कीयो (वाह वाह)। परभात को टैम व्हियो पीपळदे जार सासू नै बूझणा (करी)। लियो साय समालो आपको बो बेटो रियो लियो मीलो (हां बो ही है दूसरो है)। साडूमाता आयी भगवान पगां पड़िया (वाह वाह)। आवो माताजी कीयो (आवो कीयो)। कीयो तूं चोखी कर गो रे भैइ (म्हे)। मैं बोबा दिया जकै नै दरसाव नैइ दियो हेंर थारी लुगायी है जकी नै बांतां रोजीना करै (हां रोजीना मिल अर जाय कीयो)। कीयो भैइ माजी साय अतरा दिन तो म्हारी गलती हो गी (म्हे)। अब आज फैर जा थानै छोड़ कठै कोनी जावूं (वाह वाह)। तो भगवान दरबार का हुकमूं पछै साडू नै (म्हे)। हेंर आपका चारां भायां नै (भायां नै)। हेंर दरबार का हुकमूं

देव महाराज बा का ही पीपळदे सेवना करी देव महाराज (म्हे)। दो बच्चा बच्ची पैदा हो गा (वाह वाह)। कीयो ले भैइ पीपळदे आलम राखै जरै तो ए बच्चा बच्ची थारा है (है)। जका नै समाल ले (वाह वाह)। हेंर भगवान को ही बियाण पकड़ै (म्हे)। जरां बियाण में बैठ जावो (हां सागै हो जावो)। इन्द्र की परियां आयी पड़ै में लेख है ई को (हां है कीयो)। इन्द्र की परियां जूत मेली है बियाण के हेंर आकाश में उड रही है तो लेख परवाणू पीपळदे राणी कीयो महाराज ए बच्चा बच्ची जाणै अर आप जाणो (आप जाणो)। तो तीन तिलोकी को नाथ बियाण उडायो (म्हे)। कांई देही बैकुण्ठ गायां नै साडू नै भायां नै (ले ग्या जी कीयो)। तो इन्द्रासन मालम होतां भगवान बीला नै अर बीली नै पैदा करतां (करतां)। बगड़ावतां का बैर काढता सब काम कारया सुधारती बगड़ावतां की (वाह वाह)। जकै दिन कौल बचन करियो के थांका पछेबा सगळा सुधार द्यूं (वाह वाह)। तो बगड़ावतां का चौईसी भायां का पछेबा सकलप होतां जय बोलो भैइ श्री देवनारायण भगवान की (जय)। ई जागावूं बीलो भगवान की सेवा पर बाईजी कहबा लागी हेंर बीला के अर बाई के युध होबा लागो (वाह वाह)। तो आगै सेवा समाय दी बीला नै अबार गायी तो बाई के अर बीली के बांतां होतां जय बोलो श्री देवनारायण भगवान की (जय)।।

ए सेव हो गी तो जी गोठां का राजवियां रे।
बाळा देव के जी चड़ी भाट की दीवां।।
सिंवरिया सिंज्या का जी पाठ पधारियो।
बाळा देव का जी लिया नांव जीवां।।
(भलां जी भलां) देव भलां

सेवा हो गी भैइ भगवान का दीवां (म्हे)। देव के चड़ी भाट की (जीवां)।। सिंवरिया सिंज्या का पाठ पधारो धणी का आपां लिया ही नांव (अब जीवां)।।

ए सेवा हो गी तो जी जो गोठालां राजवियां रे।
पिण्डा पुजारी लाग्या देव की सेंव।।
सिंवरिया सिंज्या का जी पाठ पधारज्यो।
पधारो धणी रे ई अलख निरजन देव।।
(भलां जी भलां) देव भलां

सिंज्या हो गी भैइ भगवान का देवरा में (म्हे)। पिण्डा पुजारी लाग्या देव की (सेंव)।। सिंवरिया सिंज्या रा पाठ पधारो अलख निरजन ही (देव)।।

ए सिंज्या पूल गी तो जी जो गोठालां राजवियां रे।
पिण्डा पुजारी घालिया घेरा गूगळ धूप।।
सिंवरिया सिंज्या का जी पाठ पधारज्यो।
पधारी भगवान रे सदै ही सैन सरूप।।
(भलां जी भलां) देव भलां

सेवा होयी भगवान का देवरा में (म्हे)। पिण्डा पुजारी घालै घेरा गूगळ ही (धूप)।। के सिंवरिया सिंज्या का भगवान बेगा आजावो (म्हे)। पधारो भगवान सदै ही सैन ही (सरूप)।। है दाता तूं सरूप ही (पधारज्यो)।।

शंख पचाईण जी जो सेवा में बाज गा रे।
बाज गा देव के घेरा नाद गंभीर।।
सिंवरिया सिंज्या का जी पाठ पाधारज्यो।
बड भूणा भांगी मेदू रे मदन सिंग का बीर।।
(भलां जी भलां) देव भलां

शंख पचाईण भगवान की सेवा में बाजिया (म्हे)। बाजिया देव के घेरा नाद (गंभीर)।। सिंवरिया सिंज्या रा पाठ पाधारज्यो बड भूणा भांगी मेदू मदन सिंग का (बीर)। पांचू भाई सागै ही (पधारज्यो)।। सेवा हुई देव का देवरा हो गा मण्दिरिया झालरिया (झणकार)। क सिंवरिया का बेगा पधारो (म्हे)।। दरबार होय लीला पर (असवार)।।

ए सिंज्या हो गी तो जी ए गोठालां राजवियां रे।
देव के पड़ै असल नंगारा ठोर।।
परदेशा ऊदाजी पुराणी भोम मेम्।
देव बिन म्हारै जी धणी कोय न और।।
(भलां जी भलां) देव भलां

सेवा हो गी भैइ देव का देवरा में (म्हे)। भगवान के पड़ै असल नंगार (ठोर)।। परदेशा पर भूमी में भगवान आप बिन धणी कोनी दूजा ही (म्हारै और)। आप बिन कोई धणी (हां कोई नी जी कीयो)।। सेवा हो गी देव का देवरा मालन मनावै (केळ)। सिंवरिया सिंज्या का बेगा पधारो (म्हे)।। करो भगवान गौ बाच्छरा का ही (मेल)।।

ए सिंज्या हो गी तो जी जो गोठालां राजवियां रे।
गाय का देव के जी रथा रावळा बैल।।
सिंवरिया सिंज्या का जी पाठ पाधारज्यो।
काशीवूं भैरूं लेयावो रे ई काळा रे गोरा घेळ।।
(भलां जी भलां) देव भलां

सेवा हो गी भैइ देव का देवरा (वाह वाह)। आया देव के रथा ही रावळा (बैल)।। सिंवरिया सिंज्या का बेगा आयज्यो (म्हे)। काशीवूं आतां भैरूं लेयावो भगवान काळा गोर (घेळ)।। काशीवूं भैरवानाथा नै सागै ले री (हां पाधारज्यो)। सेवा होयी देव का देवरा ठाणा पर आया लीलागर (घोडा)।। सिंवरिया सिंज्या का बेगा पधारो (म्हे)। कैज्यो गढ सावर थै पीलोदा का (दौड़ा जी दौड़ा)।।

कांई पधार गा जी जो दाता रा गढ गाज नै ओवूं रे।
कांई ऊठ गा ऊदाजी रे मीठै देश मेवाड़।।
कांई सेंस के दरवाजै बासकवूं बांतां लाग ग्या।
कांई चौपड़ की स्यारां जी रम गा जी तेंहरवीं पियांळ।।
(भलां जी भलां) देव भलां

कांई कीया दरबार दाता के गढ गाज नै (म्हे)। कांई ऊठ गा मीठी देश (आप मेवाड़)।। अरै कांई सेंस के दरवाजै बासकवूं बांतां लाग्या (वाह वाह)। कांई चौपड़ की स्यारां रम गा तेंहरवीं (पियाल)।। है भगवान अतो मोडो (हां आप कीयां करो कीयो)। सेवा हो गी देव का देवरा (म्हे)।। दीया पर चड़ गी (पाठ)। ए देळू भाटणी बोलै भगवान की छावरिया (वाह वाह)।। भलो बिरदावै लागो देव नै छोछू बंगाली (भाट)। सेवा हुई देव का देवरा दीया पर चड़ गी (लोया)।। सिंवरिया सिंज्या का बेगा पधारो (म्हे)। आप की भगवान अपचल सेवा (होय)।। अपचल सेवा भाई बीलाजी (वाह वाह)। अर खास ईड राजा (हरचन होय)।। अरै दीगता नरां नै ठामै (म्हे)। मछियां ने ढाबै (समन्द)।।

सेवा साजी तो जी बीलो नारायण देव की रे।
ए साजी बीलजती रे।।
बीली के मनाया बेगा बावडो।
दफ्तरखानै म्हानै रे भूलो मती एक ही रती।।
(भलां जी भलां) देव भलां

अब सेवा साजी बीलो नारायण देव की (वाह वाह)। साजी बीला (जती)।। अरै बाई के मनाया बेगा बावडज्यो (वाह वाह)। दफ्तरखानै म्हानै भूलै मतै एक ही (रती)।। ए भगवान (म्हे)। तूं ही भूलिया (कठै ही धर कोय नै)।। सेवा हो गी देव का देवरा (वाह वाह)। जोकां काळियां का (ऊंठ)।। सिंवरिया सिंज्या का पाठ पाधारो सेवा भगवान की हो गी इन्द्रासन (बैकुण्ठ)।।

ए रीस करतां तो जी जो रावण नै आत लियो रे।
जी दिन रावण की जी भुजा भिखेरी बीस।।
सतमाता साडू के कारण।
झोळिया में रस गो रे जोतकलां जगदीश।।
(भलां जी भलां) देव भलां

कीयो रीस कर रावण नै आत लियो (वाह वाह)। जिण दिन रावण की भुजा भिखेर दी (बीस)।। अरै सतमाता साडू गूजरी के कारण (वाह वाह)। झोळिया में तूं रम गो तूं जोतकलां (अब जगदीश)।। सत के पाछै भगवान साडूमाता की झोळिया में (खेलिया जी कीयो)। सेवा हो गी देव का देवरा गोरियां आयो काबर केर (डोर)।। कांई बगड़ावतां का बैर भगवान नै याद आया (वाह वाह)। कांई हिरद में बेगा (कठोर)।।

सेवा ही पूल गी जी जो गोठां का राजवियां रे।
देमाली में देव के जी छायरी दीखै कहना।।
भर नीजर दुर्बल कानी नै सामा नाळज्यो।
नाळी देव तूं रे अम्मी भरिया नैना रे।।
(भलां जी भलां) देव भलां

सेवा हो गी भाई देव का देवरा (म्हे)। देमाली में छायरी (अब कहना)।। कीयो भर नीजर दुर्बल कानी देखज्यो (वाह वाह)। खांव म्हारा अम्मी भरिया (आप नैना)।। है भगवान (अम्मी का नैनवूं म्हां कानी झांकीज्यो)। सेवा हो ही गी देव का देवरा तारां छायां (गेन)।। सिंवरिया सिंज्या का बेगा पधारी भगवान तूं गरड चड़ियो (गोबिन्द)। सेवा हो गी देव का देवरा बिल पर आयी पशू जिनावर (कीड़ी)।। तूं सबळां को साल कीज्यै गोठां क़ा राजवी ओ बाजै दुर्बल को (भीडी जी भीडी)।।

ए सिंज्या हो गी तो जी ए गोठालां राजवियां रे।
बागां फूलिया सोहवणी फूल।।
मिनखी मळधारी देव नै भूलवे।
तूं मत भूलै म्हनै जी जलम सुधारै नै ऊद।।
(भलां जी भलां) देव भलां

सेवा हो गी भगवान का देवरा (म्हे)। बागां फूल गा सोहवणी (फूल)।। अरै मिनख मळधारी जरूर भूली (वाह वाह)। तूं मत भूलै म्हनै जलम सुधारण (ऊद)।। है दरबार आपके तो भूलिया कठै धरै कीयो (हां कोनी है कीयो)। सेवा हो गी देव का देवरा गुवाडै ऊबी ईंडळ भींडळ (गाय)।। सिंवरिया सिंज्या का बेगा पधारो (वाह वाह)। हां आप नै बाई बीली देव की बेटी घणी रिया (मनाय)।।

ए सिंज्या हो गी तो जी जो गोठालां राजवियां रे।
देव के दर्शन जी नापो ल्यायो गाय।।
सिंवरिया सिंज्या का जी पाठ पधारज्यो।
देव की आरती रे सजै साडू माय।।
(भलां जी भलां) देव भलां

सेवा हो गी देव का देवरा में (वाह वाह)। दरबार के दर्शन दे नापोजी ल्यायो (गाय)।। सिंवरिया सिंज्या का पाठ पधारो (वाह वाह)। आपकी आरती सजै साडू खटाणी (माय)।। आरती जुगत तियारणी सब दुख निवारणी (म्हे)। पांच नांव देव का ले लिया तो ई का नांव लेवूंला भूखा कदै नी (रहवां जी कीयो)।। भगवान का नांव लेतां जय बोलो श्री देव महाराज की (जय)।।

देव नै पूज लियो जी ए ई बीला कंवरजी रे।
ले ले बीला पंखा पंछी हाथ।।
परदेशा बिलाजी पुराणी भूमी में।

रहवैलां बाबोजी रे सदा बलावूं साथ।।
(भलां जी भलां) देव भलां

देव नै पूज रे बीला कंवरजी (म्हे)। बीला ले ले पंखा पंछी (हाथ)।। अरै परदेशा पर भूमी में (म्हे)। बाबोजी बीला रह जय आपणै सदा ही बलावूं (साथ)।। बीला (म्हे)। देव नै पूज अब (वाह वाह)।। भगवान दरबार का हुकमूं देव नै पूजबो करो (म्हे)। जब दोन्यु बहन भाई आपां आराम पावां (हां सुख पावांलां कीयो)।।

ए देव नै पूज ल्यो जी जो बीला कंवरजी रे।
कर ले देव की जर हरत तोड़ी जोत।।
बिन धायो बिन सहयो अर बिनै बावडै कोय ने।
बाबोजी आपणा रे घणा बदावै गोत।।
(भलां जी भलां) देव भलां

देव नै ई पूज बीला भाई (म्हे)। कर ले रे भगवान की जर हरत तोड़ी (जोत)।। बिनै धायो रे अर बिनै सहयो रे बीला बावडै कोनी (म्हे)। बाबोजी आपणा घणा बदारी (गोत)।। बीला देव नै पूज भाई (वाह वाह)। कीयो बाई किसी बांतां कर गी तूं कांई पूजै (म्हे)।। दरबार का हुकमूं राजावां का बेटा हां (म्हे)। राज करै बीली कीयो (हां पूजा पूजी म्हावूं तो को होवै नै कीयो)।।

ए देव नै पूज लियो जी ए ई बीला कंवरजी रे।
पूज ले बीला तुलसी का पाना ई रे।।
बांकै बीला टोटो बीला कदै नै बापरे।
नी आवै बीला रे धीणा और धाना रे।।
(भलां जी भलां) देव भलां

देव नै पूज बीला कंवरजी (म्हे)। बीर पूज ले तुलसी का (पाना)।। अरे कदै थारै तोटो नै बापरै बीला धिना और ही (धाना)। भगवान नै पूजै नै (म्हे)।। जकां के धान को अर धीणा को कदै टोटो (नै आवै कीयो)। बाई बोलै बीला नै समझावै देखां (कीआवूं जाणज्यो कीआवूं देखां)।। अबार कहवूं देव का हुकमूं देखां।।

जक नर पूज्या जी बीला भाई रे नारायण देव नै ओवूं रे।
कर ली देव की जर धोळी जोत।।
बिनै उगयायो बिनै सहयो बीला जीव बावडै कोय ने।
बाबोजी आपांणा रे घणा भादाय गोत रे।।
(भलां जी भलां) देव भलां

अब देव नै पूज ले कीयो (म्हे)। बीला कंवरजी कर ले देव की जर धोळी (जोत)।। अरै बिनै धयायो बिनै सहयो कोनी बावडै (म्हे)। बाबोजी घणा पधारी (गोत)।। गोत का पूजन कर भैइ (वाह वाह)।

दरबार का हुकमूं बीली के बीला के कांई बांतां होवै देखां (कीआवूं जाणज्यो देखां कीआवूं)।।

जका नर कोनी पूज्या तो जी ए ई नारायण देव नै ओवूं रे।
बीला पूजता मन में घणी मरोड।।
बा नै भगवान नै चूडा कर दिया।
बै तो बीला रे बसै गांव की ओड।।
(भलां जी भलां) देव भलां

नारायण देव नै जका कोनी पूजै (म्हे)। पूजता मन में करी (मरोड)।। बा नै भगवान बीला चूडा कर दिया (म्हे)। बै बसै गांव की (ओड)।। भगवान नै नी पूजै नै जका बीला बस्ती में कोनी बसै (वाह वाह)। देव नै पूज (म्हे)।।

जका नर तो जी जो कोनी पूज्या रे जरवा देव नै ओवूं रे।
पूजा व्हिया ऊपर हेत।।
बै नर धीरै धीरै ईंयां गिया रे बीला कंवरजी।
गिया परा बीला रे रायी मुला को खेत।।
(भलां जी भलां) देव भलां

जका ही नर बीला नी पुज्या नारायण देव नै (म्हे)। पूज्या व्हिया ऊपर (हेत)।। बै नर धीरै धीरै गी परा (म्हे)। रायी मुला के (खेत)।। रायी मुला को खेत जावै (म्हे)। जियान बै नर भगवान नै नी पूजै जका जावै (वाह वाह)।।

जका नर पूज्या जी बीला भाई रे नारायण देव नै ओवूं रे।
बीला भाई जका घरां नै नाळ।।
छाछ कूवांड़ा रे बा के घी घणा।
बा के बीला जी आंग खेलै बाळ।।
(भलां जी भलां) देव भलां

देव नै जका नर पूज्यो बीला कंवरजी (म्हे)। अरै जकां के घरां नै (नाळ)।। छाछ कूंवाड़ा बीला बा के घी घणा (म्हे)। आंग खेलै (बाळ)।। भगवान नै पूजै नै जका के बाळां को छाछ को घी को टोटो कदै नी (रहवे)। बैइ बोलै (वाह वाह)।। बीली कांई बीला नै समझावै देखां (कीआवूं जाणज्यो देखां कीआवूं)।।

ए देव नै पूज लियो जी बीला कंवरजी रे।
बीला भाई मान बडा की सीख।।
बीण बजा ले रे नारायण देव की।
बीला भाई रे थावर मांगो भीख।।
(भलां जी भलां) देव भलां

देव नै पूज्यै रे बीला कंवरजी (म्हे)। मान बडा की (सीख)।। बीण बजा ले बीला अब नारायण देव की (म्हे)। थावर के दिन मांगो (अब भीख)।। तूं देव के नांव थावर के दिन भीख मांग खाय ले (म्हे)। तो सुख पावां दोन्यु बहन भाई (वाह वाह)।। दरबार का हुकमूं ओ समचार कुण कीयो (बीली बाई कीयो)। बीलो अब के बोलै (म्हे)।। कांई बाई नै समचार कहवै देखां (कीआवूं जाणज्यो देखां कीआवूं)। अबार कहवूं भैइ भगवान का हुकमूं देखां (वाह वाह सा)।।

ए भीकडली मांगिया तो जी रे जो बीली बाई ये जुग हेंसवै रे।
बीली नी मांगण को जोग।।
घर घर का बहनड़ी ये कुत्ता काटना।
अबडो बोलै ये भाई ये देमाली को लोग।।
(भलां जी भलां) देव भलां

भीकडली मांगियावूं भाई जुग हेंसै (म्हे)। नी मांगण को (अब जोग)।। ए घर घर का बहनड़ी कुत्ता काटना अबडो घणो बोलै ये म्हनै देमाली को (लोग)। बीली राजावां का बेटा राज करै गेली भीख मांगै कीयो (म्हे)।।

ए म्हाना नाना के तो जी जो लख घोडै काटी पड़े ये भोली राजवन ओवूं रे।
धन लच्छमी को अन्त न पार।।
धर ठुकरायी रण धोल की।
नानोजी लाजै ये जयसंगदे पूंवार।।
(भलां जी भलां) देव भलां

दरबार का हुकमूं म्हानै नाना के लख घोडै रोजीना काटी पड़े (वाह वाह)। बाई धन लच्छमी को अन्त नी (पार)।। धूर ठुकराय लाज जाय रे रण धोल की (म्हे)। नानोजी लाजाय जयसंगदे (पूंवार)।। मैं भीख मांगूं नै (म्हे)। अत थोक पहली होवै (वाह वाह)।। बाई राजावां का बेटा भीख कोनी मांगै गेली कीयो (म्हे)।।

अतरी कहतां तो जी जो बीला के देही बिगड़ी रे।
ढळ आयगी आंगलियां को गोल।।
पण डील पर बैठै रे माखी बीला कंवरजी।
ई मुण्डा से चाबतो रे नागर पान तमोळ।।
(भलां जी भलां) देव भलां

अतरी कहतां तो बीला की देही बिगड़ गैइ (म्हे)। ढळर आयगी आंगलियां की (गोल)।। डील पर माखी बैठबा लागी बीला कंवरजी (वाह वाह)। ई मुण्डा से चाबतो रे बीरा नागर पान (तमोळ)।। देखिया देव का तमाशा (म्हे)।।

आम्बो कर कर तो जी बीला भाई रे तनै पूजिया रे।
बीला भाई नीकल गयो बंबूल।।
मैं बैठबा लागी रे ताणी छावलिया।
जरां म्हारै रे भाजन लागी सूल।।
(भलां जी भलां) देव भलां

बीला तनै आम्बो जाण पूजिया भैइ (म्हे)। अरै नीकल गो बंबूल (वाह वाह)।। बैठबा लागी थारी छावलिया (म्हे)। बीला म्हारै भाजन लागी (सूल)।। ए भरोसा थारा बीरा कोनी जाणया मैं (वाह वाह)। देव नै देख पूजेलो जर सुख पावेलो देख देव का तमाशा देखिया (म्हे)।। कीयो ताणो देवजी कांई करै भाई (हां कांई करै कीयो)। दरबार का हुकमूं बीलो बोलै (म्हे)।। कांई समचार बाई नै कहवै देखां (कीआवूं जाणज्यो देखां अब कीआवूं)। अबार कहवां भगवान का हुकमूं देखां (वाह वाह सा)।।

सेवा करतां जी बीली बाई ये नारायण देव की रे।
बाबोजी म्हाना जी मन में मानियो रोष।।
लेरली ये करणी का फल उगड़िया।
ठाकर देव नै ये कांई बात को दोष।।
(भलां जी भलां) देव भलां

सेवा करज्यै तूं म्हारै ठाकर देव की (म्हे)। ए बाबोजी म्हाना मन में मानियो (रोष)।। लेरली करणी का बीली फल उगड़िया (वाह वाह)। ठाकर देव नै कांई बात को (अब देवां दोष)।। भगवान नै कांई दोष है भैइ (म्हे)। म्हारी करणी है नै (जकी का फल उगड़िया है कीयो)।। ईसी करियोडी म्हारी (वाह वाह)। बाई राजावां का बेटा राज करै भीख तो कोनी मांगै (म्हे)।।

गर्बियोडो मत बोलै नै जी जो बीला कंवरजी रे।
बीला भाई गर्ब करियो नर हरियो।।
गर्ब करियो रतनागर सागरा।
बी को भगवान रे नीर खारो कर राळियो रे।।
(भलां जी भलां) देव भलां

गर्बियाडो मत बोल बीला भाई (देव)। गर्ब करै सो नर (हारियो)।। गर्ब करियो रे रतनागर सागरा (वाह वाह)। जिको भगवान नीर खारो (कर राळियो)।। रतनागर सागर समंद बोल्यो (म्हे)। की म्हारै जिस्यो नीर उगिया दीप में मीठो कोनी (हां म्हारै सरी तो मीठो होवै नी कीयो)।। पण नी गर्ब कोनी चालबा दियो भगवान खारो जहर कर दियो (वाह वाह)।।

ए गर्बियोडो मत बोलै नै जी ए ई बीला कंवरजी रे।
बीला भाई गर्ब करियो नर हरियो ई रे।।
गर्ब करियो रे डूंगरी की लाल चिरमियां।

जिको बाबोजी रे मुखा काळो राळियो रे।।
(भलां जी भलां) देव भलां

गर्बियोडो मत बीला कंवरजी (म्हे)। के गर्ब करियो सो नर (हारियो)।। अरै गर्ब करियो बीरा डूंगर की लाल चिरमी (म्हे)। जिको भगवान मुंह काळो (आगेवूं कर राळियो)।। डूंगर की चिरमी कीयो (म्हे)। म्हारै जिसी सरूप लाल तो ऊदिया दीप में (हां नै है कीयो)।। पण नी भगवान गर्ब कोनी चालबा दियो (म्हे)। मुण्डा पर काळी टीकी दे दी (वाह वाह)।। दरबार का हुकमूं कीयो भैइ काळा मत जिक तूं (म्हे)। कीयो गर्बियोडो मत बोल बीला कंवरजी गर्ब करियो सो नर (हारियो)।। अरै गर्ब तो करियो चकवा और चकवी (म्हे)। बी के भगवान रैण बीचेरो ही (राळियो)।। चकवा और चकवी बोल्या (म्हे)। के आपणै जियान को समध तो उदिया दीप में ही (हां कोनी कीयो)।। पण नी रात का बिका में एक डाळी पर दोनी जानवर कोनी बैठै अब (हां दो पर बैठै जी कीयो)। बीला गर्बा नी करणो (म्हे)।। कीयो बाई देख दरबार का हुकमूं कठै म्हारा दुवा दारू लागै जटै ले चाल (हां काळा मत जगणा कीयो)। तो बीली कीयो बीला बस्ती में जावूं जरां (म्हे)।। तो बाई बस्ती में पूगती (हुई है)। जार पटेल पांचिया बैठां हा जका नै बूझणा (करी)।। अरै पटेलां (म्हे)। बीला की देही बिगड़ी रे कठै दुवा दारू लागै तो बतावो रे भैइ (हां बठै बतावो नै कठै जावूं कीयो)।। कीयो बाई सा (वाह वाह)। दरबार का हुकमूं आ तीन कोस पर बैधनाथ बाबा की झूंपड़ी है (म्हे)।। सेंकड़ी कोढियां की कोढ झड़ै (वाह वाह)। सेंकड़ी बठै झूंपड़ियां बांध मेली है (म्हे)।। ले जावो (बठै झड़ जाई कीयो)। बैध का जोरूं भाई देवै (म्हे)।। जड़ी बूंटी की है (वाह वाह)। कीयो पटेलां बठै दूर बिलावूं तो कोनी चालणी आवै (हां पैदलवूं तो चालणी आवै ही कोनी कीयो)। टांग लियो कर द्यूं बीरा (म्हे)। दरबार का हुकमूं टांगालो जाय बूझणा करी रे भाई देव का बेटी बेटा है जका नै बैधनाथ बाबाली झूंपड़ी छोड़िया (हां छोड़िया ले जा अर)।। बाई कीयो भैइ चोना को मूंदड़ो द्यूं (हां मूंदड़ो है म्हां कन्न ओ तनै दे द्यूं)। तो बाई मूंदड़ो बोथ (म्हे)।। हेंर टा9गो भाड़ै कर लेयायी (वाह वाह)। बीला के कन्नै आर बूझणा (करी है)।। ले भैइ बीला अठै बैधनाथ बाबा की झूंपड़ी हे बठै कोढ झड़ै जको टां गा पर बैठ चालां (हां बठै चालां कीयो)। तो बीलो बैठ गो अर बाई बीली (बैठ गी)।। बैधनाथ बाबालै झो1पड़ी कानै गैलै हां बैली हांक दी (वाह वाह)। दरबार मन में देखियो अता थोक कर दिया तो ही बीलो नुवै कोनी (हां मानियो कोनी कीयो)। बिरामण को रूप धार (म्हे)।। डोर लोटियो ले अर गेला में आडा फिर गा (हां आगै बैठ गिया बांध पगां के पाटा अर)। ए कुण का को रे भाई थें कीयो (म्हे)।। तो बिरामण रूप छानो कांई रो (वाह वाह)। बिरामण दादा मैं तो देव का बेटी बेटा हां भैइ कीयो उनै (उनै जाओ कीयो)।। कीयो बैधनाथ बाबा की झो।पड़ी (जासियां)। बीला की देख देही बिगड़ गैइ (म्हे)।। कीयो बीली मैं ही भिखारथ बिरामण हूं (म्हे)। बठै देख प गां के म्हारै दुखना हो गा चालणी कोनी आवै (हां टांग लियो में बैठाय)।। नण्दवाड़ै बस्ती ताण बाई म्हनै ई पूगतो करो (करो कीयो)। बिरामण हूं (म्हे)।। बाई बूझणा करी रे बीला (वाह वाह)। पछवाड़ो फैर जको बिरामण दादा ने बैठना (हां अठै बैठां लिया आपणै कन्नै ई)।। कीयो थारा बिरामण बाबा का बाप का लाग्या है कांई पिसिया (म्हे)। पिसिया तो मैं दिया हूं (वाह वाह)।। मैं कोनी बैठाणू (हां कोनी बैठाणू छेड़ै राख)।

अरै बीला बिरामण है (हां बैठां ले कीयो)।। कीयो बैठावूं तो बाई पगां के दूखणा है (हां ई के बास आवै कीयो)। कीयो बीला थारै कीयो म्हानी देही की बास कोनी आवै म्हनै (हां म्हनै आवै कोनी)।। तो बीली कीयो रे बिरामण दादा (म्हे)। म्हानी जागां बैजा (हां ओ भाई तो सदा ही को सबळबा दी है कीयो)।। बाईजी हेटा उतर गा (म्हे)। ले बिरामण दादा म्हानी जागां बैठ भैइ (हां अठै बैठो आवो कीयो)।। तीन तिलोकी को नाथ पेड़ा पर पग दियो (म्हे)। देतां ही मसरको दियो (वाह वाह)।। बैली नै तो तेंहरवीं पिताल (नीचै मेलै दिनी)। हेंर बैलियां नै बण का रोजड़ा कर (भिड़काय दिया)।। बालो ठाकर तीन तिलोकी को नाथ बिलाय गा (वाह वाह)। बाई कीयो बीला (म्हे)।। देखिया देव का तमाशा (देख कीयो)।

बिन मेवा तो जी देख गाड़ी गिळ गी ये बीला कंवरजी रे।
बीला भाई रे पेड़ा गिया पियांळ।।
बैलियां नै कर दिया बाबो जी रे बण का रोजड़ा।
आ नै बीला रे दिया जंगल भिड़काय।।
(भलां जी भलां) देव भलां

बिनै मेवा देख बीला गाड़ी गिळ गी (म्हे)। पेड़ा गिया (पताल)।। अरै बैलियां नै कर दिया बाबोजी बण का रोजड़ा दिया जंगल में (भिड़काय)। देव का ही तमाशा है (म्हे)।। कीयो की का देव का तमाशा है बो बिरामण दादा नै मैं कीयो मत बैठाण (म्हे)। खोड़ोलो हो बो (खोड़ीलो हो कीयो)।। जको बो ही तो गिळ गो (अर गाड़ी गिळ गी)। आपां तीना का तकदीर चोका हां जको ऊबर गा (हां आपां ऊबरिया देख बीली कीयो)।। कीयो तो दरबारा का हुकमूं खाड़ेती की तो बीला की तो बाई के तो बाई के जीव नै (सहनी ही)। खाड़ेती औरूं हो गी (वाह वाह)।। कीयो बाई साय (म्हे)। मैं म्हारा टांगलियावूं टाबरां नै कमार घालो (हां म्हारा गाड़ी)।। टांगो कर दे (हेंर बै नारां दे)। अब बाई के बीला के सहनी ही पण ओ खाड़ेती घणी हो गी (वाह वाह)।।

दो पाना की जी जो बनाई तो बोरड़ियां रे।
अन्नदाता काटियावूं कतरो होय।।
बिनै भायां की कर दी रे तूं बहनड़ियां।
पीर सासर अन्नदाता रे आदर थोड़ा होय।।
(भलां जी भलां) देव भलां

दरबार का हुकमूं दो पाना की बना दी बोरड़ी (म्हे)। काटियावूं बी के पालो कत्तो (होय)।। बिनै भायां की बानायी रे भगवान बहनड़ी (वाह वाह)। पीर सासर बिना आदर थोड़ा (होय)।। है श्री महाराज ओ एक तो दियो म्हनै भाई (म्हे)। जका नै ईंयां कींयां मारो (वाह वाह)।। है भगवान ई की तो जीव नै सहनै ही पण ए खाड़ेती की क्युं करी (हां ई की म्हारै औरूं कींयां करी आप)। बाई हेलो मारै नै देव नै (म्हे)।। कन्नै ऊबा रे (वाह वाह)। दरबार का हुकमूं बाई नै पाछो बस्तीआलै गैलै टांग लियो जातो (दीखियो)।। कीयो रे खाड़ेती भाई (बो जाय टांगो थारै नावड़गियो)। खाड़ेती की चिटली में

मूंदड़ो बाई आलो हो (म्हे)।। काढ पाछो फैंक दियो (आ लियो बाईजी ये थारो मूंदड़ो बा राख कीयो म्हारै कोनी (चाहीज्ये)। म्हनै ईंयां की धैग की ठा कोनी पड़ियो (म्हे)।। मैं आतो ही कोनी (वाह वाह)। अब खाड़ेती आयगो देमाली के उजाड़ में (म्हे)।। बीलो अर बीली दोन्यो बहन भाई एकला रह गा (वाह वाह)। दरबार का हुकमूं देव मेह अर आंधी बी जागां इतारां को टैम हो जको बना दी (हां चला दिनी)।। पहली तो आंधी (म्हे)। बा डूंगर की चांवलियां की बीला के डील के (हां लागी)।। बीलो त्राहि (घाली)। पछै मोती मोटी छांटां (हां पड़ण लागी)।। बीलो कीयो बाई साय (मरज्यायां कीयो)। ले लेनो देनो कर भैइ (वाह वाह)।। धरम पुण कर देय (म्हे)। म्हारो जीव जाय अब (हां रुकै कोनी)।। बाई छती हेटै घणो ही बाड़ै पण भगवान की आंधी चलायोड़ी ही (हां सारै स तो क्यें की रहवे)। बीलो को काळजो जागां छोड़ियो भगवान दरबार बेगावूं गेबावूं एक मिन्दर पैदा कर दियो (वाह वाह)।। बाई नै मिन्दर का सळाकूं (मिन्दर दीखियो)। कीयो बीला एक सारै मिन्दर दीखै भैइ आ ले चांलां (हां चाल बी में बड़ जावां कीयो)।। पकड़ बीला को बांवल्यो (वाह वाह)। बाई मिण्दिर के सांकड़ो (लेगी)।। बीलो कीयो बाई आयगो मिण्दिर (हां आयग्यो कीयो)। बांवल्यो छोड़ (हां छोड़ कीयो म्हारै पग हाथ अब)।। क्युं (मैं सामनै मुण्डो कर बड़ूं कोनी)। देवातण होवै तो म्हारी निवण मान ले (वाह वाह)।। बीलो देव को बेटो कांई करियो के मिन्दर में (अपूठो बड़ गियो)। तो भगवान की बेमरजी हुई (म्हे)।। चारो पट्टियां मिन्दर के सगै टूट गी (वाह वाह)। बाई बीली ऊबी री जको बा पट्टी एक री (म्हे)।। दरबार का हुकमूं बीली बोलै (वाह वाह)। कांई समचार कहवै देखां (कीआवूं जाणज्यो देखां कीआवूं)।।

मेह बरसै तो जी मिन्दर छूवै रे बीला कंवरजी रे।
बीला भाई भींतयां छोड़ियो लेव।।
बीला को ऊपराड़ो करज्यो नारायण देव की।
बीला के कारण रे रात्यूं सिंवरिया देव।।
(भलां जी भलां) देव भलां

दरबार का हुकमूं मेह तो बरसै देख मिन्दर छुवै (म्हे)। भींतयां छोड़ियो (लेव)।। बीला पर ऊपराड़ो करज्यो ओ बाळा ठाकर देवजी (म्हे)। बीला के कारण बाई रे रात्यूं सिंवरियां (देव)।। सारी रात बाई देव देव करियो जर एक पट्टी रही (म्हे)। तो परभात की टैम सुरजी उगियो नै (वाह वाह)।। जरै बाईजी सुरजी नै ओळमो दियो (म्हे)। कीयो सुरज के साथै संदेसो मोकळूं (वाह वाह)।। लिख द्यूं परवण वालै (पाण)। हरकी का बाबाजी नै कह दिय सुरज देवता (म्हे)।। ताणी बाई रे बीली दर्शन करै पहरै (कान)। सुरज देवता रे भगवान के दरी खानै जावै तो तूं म्हारियो तूं कागदियो दे दीयै भगवान नै (हां अब दर्शन)।। जोगण हूं मैं (वाह वाह)। अगती हो गी मैं तो (वाह वाह)।। दरबार का हुकमूं भगवान देखियो सुरजी उगियो नै (म्हे)। तो बीला नै भूख लगा दी (वाह वाह)।। कीयो बाई भूखा मरूं अब (म्हे)। तो बाई बीला नै दासनियां तोड़ तोड़ मोकळी (हां राळ दीनी)।। कीयो ये बाई आवूं भूख कोनी मिटै (हां जाण जाय कीयो)। अन्न को तो एक घास होवै के (हां तो ही म्हारी भूख है जकी मिट जावे)।। तो दरबार का हुकमूं बाई ऊंची चड़ निंगै करी (वाह वाह)। नण्दवाड़ो

शहर सारै दीखी (म्हे)।। कीयो बीला नण्दवाड़ो सारै दीखै भीख मांग लेयावूं (हां भीख मांग अर लेयावूं खायी कोनी खायी कीयो)। कीयो ये भाई देव का नांव लेयायी तो मैं कोनी खावूं (हां म्हारै नांव मांग अर लेयावे)।। तो खालेवूं (खालेसूं)। कीयो कींयां मांगूं (म्हे)।। कीयो बस्ती में जाती कह देय के (जय बीलजती की)। ईंयां कर मांगी (वाह वाह)।। भाई के कपड़ा भिखा में फाट गा (म्हे)। हेंर दरबार का हुकमूं गरीबी हालत हो गी (हां काटी)।। ठांव बाई कन्नै हो कोनी (हां ठांव तो कठवूं आवे)। बस्ती में बडी जरां कुमहार का घर आयगो न्याव आयगो मुण्डा के (म्हे)।। एक मोटो सो ठीकरो उठा लियो (हां न्यावड़ै मूं)। देखियो भाई की कोई घाली बस्ती का लोग तो लेयावां किनै (हां लेयास्यां क्यां में इयां)।। तो ठीकरो लेयाय अर बिदा (व्हिया है)। भगवान देव महाराज अम्मी की नजर (झांकिया जी कीयो)।। तो बरी बेदड़ा का तो बाई के बेस बन गा (म्हे)। बै ठीकरां के सोना को बाटगो बन गो (वाह वाह)।। तीन तिलोकी को नाथ बस्ती में जार घर घर फिर गो (म्हे)। कीयो एक छलावा आवै भैइ (वाह वाह)।। सोना को बाटको है (बरी का पहरनै बेस है)। कोई बी नै मुण्डा लगाली तो आगै जावूंला (हां अगत मारिया जावूंला जी कीयो)।। अबार आबाली है (वाह वाह)। अती के औतारी पुरुष हो तो बो बिलाय गो (वाह वाह)।। अताक पहली बाईजी अवाज कर दी (म्हे)। जय बिलजती के अन्न घालो भैइ (वाह वाह)।। कीयो देख बिरामण दादो कहवो जको (आ आयगी सागे)। सब मोड़ा जड़ दिया (म्हे)।। बाई सगळी बस्ती में फिरली पण अन्न तो कोई कोनी घालियो (हां बारिया मांय देखै से)। बाई के मुण्डा के कोनी आयो कोई (वाह वाह)।। बाई अगती हो गी मन में देखियो अब एक एक घर नायी को रह गो (हां बठै चालां देखां)। बीलो किस्यो देखबा नै थोड़ो आवै (हां बठै जय देवनारायण की कह देयां)।। देखां देव को नांव ले लेयां (वाह वाह)। तो नायां के घरां बड़ती बाई कीयो नायी बाबा जय देवनारायण की बाई (हां जय देवनारायण की आयो बाई सा)।। आयो बाई सा नायी सा का घर का सारा ही भाज भाज पगां में पड़ गा (वाह वाह)। धिन घड़ी धिन भाग देव की बाई म्हांकै घरां आया (हां घरां आया कीयो)।। बाई सा बोलो किनै पधाराया (फरमावो कीयो)। अरै भाई नायी बाबा भगवान की दिया हो गी जिको बीला के कोढ नीकल गी (हां देही बीला भाया की बिगड़ गी)।। जको बैधनाथ की झूंपड़ी जावै गेला में भूख लागी (हां भूख लागी जी वास्तै आयी)। कीयो बाईजी चावल मोकळा आयोड़ा पड़ियोड़ा तिजा का (वाह वाह)।। आप ही जीम जावो (म्हे)। हेंर बीला ताणी धपावो (हां ले जावो)।। कीयो नायी बाबा जलमिया पछै तो हाल भेळै जीमिया (हां दोन्यु बहन भाई सगै ही जीमिया न्यारा न्यारा कोनी (जीमिया)। ई कछोरा में घाल दियो (वाह वाह)।। तो धपावो तो मूंग अर चावल घाल दिया मोकळो घी (हां ऊपर घाल दिन्यो)। बाईजी सा ले पधारो (हां की शक्कर ही घाली)।। घाली सा (वाह वाह)। बाईजी ले जीमन गांव के बाहरलै छेड़ै (नीकली)।। तो बो ही तो बाई के फाटयोड़ो बेस हो गो (म्हे)। बो ही कुमहारालो ठीकरो (हाथ में व्हियो)।। भैरूंजी नै कीयो भैरूंजी (म्हे)। नायां को घर को बीलो खा लेजर म्हारी सोवै जोगो तो (हां रहवै कोनी)।। क्युं के नायी के तीजा के बापरियोड़ो है (वाह वाह)। तीजा को खार सेव करै तो मैं मानू कोनी (हां म्हारै तो अगती जायी)।। गोरो कलो महाराज बन कागला आया (म्हे)। दे फटकारो ठीकरां नै पटक दियो (हां जावो उछाळ दियो)।। ठीकरो फूट गो (वाह वाह)। चावल मूंग मूंग मतै ही भिखर गा (म्हे)।। बाई देखियो रे दिखाळां कांई (हां ले जाणा)। ले चालां (हां तो दिखा तो दियां मूंग नै)।। बाई सोदबा

लागी जटै दरबार जहर की नजर झांकिया (म्हे)। चांवलां का तो कीड़ा कर दिया (वाह वाह)।। हेंर मूंगा का मकोड़ा (बना दिया)। शक्कर का मुड़िया कांकरां (कर दिन्या)।। घी को राद अर लोही (बना दियो)। मन में देखियो देख देव का तमाशा (वाह वाह)।। पण बैरी नै दिखाळी कांई चिन्योसो ले तो चांलां (हां थोड़ो घणो ले चालां)। ठीकरी में घाल बाई बिदा हो गी लेरावूं डूंगर लागो (म्हे)।। लाय लागी (वाह वाह)। बाईजी मन में देखियो ओ ले भैइ (भायो तो मांय बळ गो)।। दाग हो गो (वाह वाह)। कांई भगवान नै अरदास करै कांई समचार कहवै देखां (कीआवूं जाणज्यो देखां कीआवूं)।।

दूण लागी जी बांसां पर जली रे गोठालां राजवियां रे।
आ तो भाईजी डूंगर भभकी लाय।।
एक पड़ालो ऊबा रियो गोठालां राजवियां।
ताणी भाई रे बील कंवर के भाग।।
(भलां जी भलां) देव भलां

दूण लागी (म्हे)। बांसां जली डूंगर भभकै (लाय)।। एक पड़ालो ऊबा रियै गोठां का राजवी बाई थारी बील कंवर के (भाग)। है श्री महाराज म्हारै कान देखो (हां भाई नै ऊबा रीज्यो)।। बाई देव ने हेलो मारै कन्नै ऊबा रह (वाह वाह)। बीलो जकी क्यारी में सुतो है नै (म्हे)।। जकै के लाय तो नेड़ी ही कोनी गी आंटा देय अर बाहरवूं नीकल गी (हां छेड़ै छेड़ै निसर गी)। काळ गोरा भैरूंनाथ नै बना नार दरबार नै खिना दिया कोई देख बीला की देही नी गमा देय भैइ (वाह वाह)।। नार रूखालै बैठां (म्हे)। बाई देखियो लाय तो बच गो (पण ए नारडिया खासी)।। दरबार का हुकमूं बाई के नजर नारां की मिली नै (म्हे)। नार ऊठ ऊठ मतै बीर (हो ग्या)।। आती बीली समचार (कीयो)। कीयो तूं सुतो रह बीला देमाली की उजाड़ में (म्हे)।। अर सुतो (डासा अनी?) की (छांय)। देख चोर नार दूरा दूरा फिरै (म्हे)।। अरै सुतो सबळ धणी की (बांय)। भगवान की बांय सुतो है (म्हे)।। जण ए आंतरै आंतरै (हां ए फिरै कीयो)। तो दरबार का हुकमूं कांई बीलो कीयो ये बाई बीली हांका क्युं करै (म्हे)।। अन्न लेयायी कोनी लेयायी (हां जकी बता कीयो)। बा ठीकरी बीला के मुण्डा के (मेल दीनी)।। कीयो ए बाई (म्हे)। अताक दिन तूं म्हारी अर म्हारावूं मजाक कोनी करती (हां आजवूं तूं म्हारी मजाका उडावण लागी कीयो)।। आ राद लोय तो म्हारै कन्नै घणी (हां अठै ही घणी है बाई अती बार बाहरें क्युं फिरी तूं (गांव में) बाई कह रही है बीलो सुणै

ए शहर नण्दवाड़ै तो जी जो मैं भिड़ गी रे बीला कंवरजी रे।
बीला ओड़बा नै झिनी झिनी लोय।।
सोना के बाटकै रे बीला कंवरजी।
थारै नांव सूं बीला रे भीख नै घाली कोय।।
(भलां जी भलां) देव भलां

शहर नण्दवाड़ै बीला मैं फिरी (म्हे)। ओड़बा नै झिनी झिनी (लोय)।। सोना के बाटकै बीला थारै नांववूं म्हनै भीख न लागी घाली (कोय)। बीला कोय भीख कोय नी घाली (वाह वाह)।। देव की

लगायोड़ी भूख ही बीला की भूख तो (मिटगी)। भगवान तिस लगा दी (वाह वाह)।। कीयो बाई जळ है तो लेया नी तो जाण जाय (म्हे)। बाई कीयो रात बीला बरस्यो मेह जको निंगै करां भैइ (हां)। निंगै करूं देखां कठै ई तो कोई (भेळो व्हियोड़ो है तो पाणी)।। तो बाई निंगै करी तो भगवान एक गेबावूं नाड़ी बना दी (वाह वाह)। दरबार का हुकमूं कीयो बीला ऊठ भैइ (हां चाल कीयो नाड़ी सरै है)।। एक छोटीसी तलाई है (म्हे)। बाई बीला को पकड़ बांवल्यो तलाई पर लेगी (वाह वाह)।। कीयो रे बीला बाई को कहनी आयगो (म्हे)। कीयो देव देव करतो जार ई तलाई में सिनान करै तो काया कंचन की हो जावै (हां थारी काया कंचन की होवै कीयो)।। कीयो ए बाई तमाशा करै म्हारावूं सांचा नी हो जावै (हां सांचा नी हो जाय कीयो)। बीलो आगतो व्हियोड़ो पूरो हो (वाह वाह)।। तो देव को नांव लेय बीलो तलाई में सिनान करबा लागो देव देव देव देव (वाह वाह)। तो बीला की काया भगवान कंचन की कर दी बी जागां (हां कंचन की बनादी)।। तो पहली कोढ झड़तां (म्हे)। भगवान नाड़ी में बीला की काया सुधारतां (सुधारतां)।। जय बोलो भैइ श्री देवनारायण भगवान की (जय)।। तो बीला की भगवान बी टैम बाई कीयो रे देख बीला के भगवान नै पूजै बी का नांव से सिनान करै जळ में तो देख थारी काया कंचन की कर दी भगवान (म्हे)। बीलो कीयो ए बाई भगवान ताणो नी करी है के रात के टैम में ओ जळ है जको ई तजबीज को बरस्यो (हां चोखो अमरत बरस्यो)।। तो ई जळ से म्हारी काया है जकी कंचन की हो गी (हां कंचन की हो गयी कीयो)। बाई ने आ रीस आयगी बीला में अता थोक होवै तो ही पूजा देव की भगवान की करै कोनी (म्हे)।। कीयो बीला ई जळ में ही तो अमरत है जरां ले (अब के नाह कीयो)। पाछो नाह (वाह वाह)।। तो बी जळ के मांयनै पाछो बीलो सिनान करियो है तो जैसै बीला की दूणी बी में कोढ पाछी पैदा हो गी (वाह वाह)। कांई सला बीला (हां अब देख कांई)।। देव का तमाशा देख (म्हे)। कीयो बाई दरबार का हुकमूं ओ तो भगवान की कर दी पण सेवा पूजा तो बाई म्हारावूं नी सज आवै (हां कोनी करूं कीयो)।। देव महाराज मन में देखियो अता थोक कर दिया बीलो में तो (पिला?) अता थोक निवण तो नी करै (वाह वाह)। बीला की बी टैम में नौ गज लांबी देही बना दी (वाह वाह)।। भैरवानाथा नै कागला बनार खिना दिया जाओ बीला नै अगता दियो (हां टांचा की दियो कीयो)। तो कांई करै के कागला बन भैरूंजी आयगा बीला के पगतळी के देवै कीयो बाई बीली म्हारी कागलो पगतळी फोड़ै (म्हे)।। बाई पगतळी कन्नै आवै तो कागलो माथो के टांच की दे पाड़ै (वाह वाह)। बाई बोलै कांई समचार कहवै देखां।।

ए सार का बनाया तो जी बीला रे बाबोजी कगला रे।
आंकी बिलाजी लोहा जड़ दी चांच।।
ए म्हारै उडायोड़ा जी उडै कोई ने।
कोई नी उडै रे ई सबळ धणी का काग।।
(भलां जी भलां) देव भलां

सार का बना दिया देख बीला बाबोजी कागला (म्हे)। अरै लोहवूं जड़ दी (चांच)।। ए म्हारै उडयोड़ा बीला नी उडै (म्हे)। अरै सबळ धणी का (काग)।। भगवान का बनायोड़ा है म्हारावूं बीला उडै कोनी

(वाह वाह)। अताक पहली बीलो कीयो बाई जरां म्हारी तो देख पगतळी फोड़ नाकी कागलो (वाह वाह)।। बाई भाजी पगतळी कानै गैइ कागलो कांई बी सिराणै जार बैठ गो (वाह वाह)। बाई बोलै कांई समचार बीला नै कहवै देखां (कीआवूं जणीज्यो कीआवूं)।।

ए सार का बनाया तो जी बिलाजी बाबोजी कागला रे।
आंकी बिलाजी लोहा झड़ दी चांच।।
ए म्हारै उडायोड़ा बिलाजी उडै कोई ने।
मैं तो बीला रे ई सिराणै आवूं क पगात।।
(भलां जी भलां) देव भलां

सार का तो बनाया बीला बाबोजी कागला (म्हे)। अरै लोहावूं झड़ दी (चांच)।। ए म्हारै उडयोड़ा बीला नी उडै (म्हे)। मैं सिराणै आवूं के (पगात)।। बीला कोनै कोनै आवूं रे भैइ (वाह वाह)। कतीक लांबी देही है थारी (म्हे)।। तो बीली कह भगवान ई बीला नै दुख दियो जको दियो पर म्हनै क्युं दियो (वाह वाह)। बाई भगवान नै सिंवरै जरां बाई के तो भगवान नजीक ही (हां खड़ायी रहवे)।। बीला के देही पाछी मिनख की ही जती कर दी (वाह वाह)। पण कोढ कोनी झड़ी (म्हे)।। बीलो कीयो ए बाई ई बैधनाथ बाबा कन्नै चालो (वाह वाह)। जो दवाई पाणी तो म्हारै लागावां कठै ही (हां दुखै कीयो सगळ शरीर ही)।। तो बीलो रे बाई बीली दोन्यु जणा बैधनाथ बाबा की झूंपड़ी की गैलै बिदा हो गा (वाह वाह)। देव महाराज बिरामण को रूप धार (म्हे)।। हेंर बैधनाथ बाबा के पहली पूगिया (वाह वाह)। कीयो रे बैधनाथ बाबा कता कोढियां की कोढ झाड़ दी कीयो महाराज सेंकड़ी की तो झड़ गी सेंकड़ी औरूं पड़िया है (हां औरूं पड़िया है कीयो)।। दवा दारू लगावूं जड़ी बूंटी की दवाई है देशी दवाई है म्हारै कन्नै (वाह वाह)। जको कताक दिना में झाड़ै कीयो श्री महाराज कोई की छै महीनावूं झड़ जाय कोई की बरी महीनावूं झड़ जाय अर कोई की महीना में झड़ जाय चोखो तकदीर हो तो (वाह वाह)।। कीयो रे भैइ एक ईंयां को कोढियो आवै तो एकेदम बी की कोढ झाड़ (हां एकदम झाड़ै जियान को काम है की थारै कन्नै)। कीयो श्री महाराज ईंयां की दवाई कोनी म्हारै कन्नै (हां कोनी कीयो)।। एकेदम तो नी झड़ै (वाह वाह)। कीयो एकेदम झड़ जाय जरां कीयो श्री महाराज एकेदम कोई झाड़बालो होवै (म्हे)।। तो ओ बैध आजवूं छोड़ दूं मैं (हां आजवूं ही छोड़ दूं)। तो दरबार का हुकमूं देव महाराज कीयो रे भैइ एकेदम झाड़बालै लाध जाय (हां लाधै कीयो)।। तीन तिलोकी को नाथ जहर की नजर झांक दी (म्हे)। तो कोढियां कांई बै धूणी के चारूंमेर झूंपड़ियां बांध मेली आपणी (हां बैठया हा)।। एकेदम झूपड़ियां ही जकी जूप गी (हां सागै के सागै जूपी है)। कोढियां नीकल नीकल (भाज्या)।। कीयो भागो मत (म्हे)। आप आप की झूंपड़ी तपता जाओ भाई रे देव देव करतां ही (जाओ)।। काया थांकी कंचन की हो जायी (वाह वाह)। कोढियां तो आप आप की झूंपड़ी तपता ग्या देव देव देव देव देव करतां ही (हां गिया परा)।। तो काया भगवान बा की सेंकड़ी कोढियां की कंचन की कर दी (वाह वाह)। सेंकड़ियां की कोढ भगवान झाड़ता जय बोलो श्री देवनारायण भगवान की (जय)।। कीयो ले भैइ बैधनाथ बाबा (म्हे)। सेंकड़ी कोढियां की मैं एकेदम झाड़ी है कोढ (वाह वाह)।। एक कोढियो तूं आवै जो बी की तूं झाड़ दे (हां बी की अब तूं झाड़)।

कीयो श्री महाराज म्हारावूं तो नी झड़ै (हां कोनी झड़ै कीयो)।। क्युं के म्हारा बैध में कोनी ईंयां की बात (म्हे)। तो भैइ नी झड़ै कीयो ओ लियो श्री महाराज आजवूं झोली झण्डा बैध पोथी ओ लियो मैं थानै दीनी (हां थानै दीनी)।। बैधनाथ बाबो तो देव नै भुलाय आप को तो धूणी छोड़ दी (वाह वाह)। तो बै आज दिन मिन्दर के मांय टोपलिया भोपा करै ने देव नै सेवा (म्हे)।। ओ बाहनो बी को है किस्या को (बैधनाथ को)। बैधनाथ को झोळी झण्डा ए राखै झोळी राखै सेली राखै बो टोप राखै तो बी टोपवूं सैनाण है बैधनाथ बाबा को बी का पंथ का तो ये नागा भोपा व्हिया (वाह वाह)।। अब बीलो रह गो (म्हे)। कीयो भाई देख सेंकड़ी कोढियां की कोढ तो मतै झड़ गी पण आपणा भैइ तकदीर ई कोनी ईंयां का (हां आपां तकदीर कोनी आपां की झड़ी)।। अब बाई रे बीलो कांई करै के देमाली की उजाड़ मैं आयगा (म्हे)। हेंर बीलो कह बाई अब जीव म्हारो दुख पावै घबरावै (वाह वाह)।। तो दरबार का हुकमूं बाई भी आगती हो गी बाई बोलै कांई देखां समचार एक मोर बैठो जका मोर नै कहवै देखां (कीआवूं जाणीज्यो देखां कीआवूं)।।

ए सुहावनो बोली जी बीरा रे डूंगर का मोरला रे।
मोरिया भाईजी लीलै नीम चड़ियो रे।।
बाईजी का जीमी जी मोरिया दीखै तनै आंवतां।
मोरिया भाई रे लीलै हिंवर चड़ियो रे।।
(भलां जी भलां) देव भलां

सुहावनो बोल भैइ डूंगर का मोहरला (म्हे)। हेंर लीलै ही नीम (चड़ियो)।। अरै बाईजी का जामी दीखै मोरिया तनै आंवतां (म्हे)। लीले हिंवर (चड़िया)।। लीलो घोड़ो है म्हारा बाबाजी कन्न (वाह वाह)। मोरिया दीखै तो बोल रे भैइ (हां बोल जो आवै कीयो)।। बाई बोलै कांई मोरिया नै बतलावै देखां (कीआवूं जाणज्यो देखां कीआवूं)।।

ए सुहावनो बोली जी ए ई डूंगर का मोरला ओवूं रे।
मोरिया भाई रे बैठ डूंगर की खियां।।
बाईजी का जामी दीखै रे तनै आंवतां।
मोरिया भारे रे ताणा मीठा अर बहन कीआवूं रे।।
(भलां जी भलां) देव भलां

सुहावनो बोल रे डूंगर का मोरला (म्हे)। दरबार का हुकमूं बोलज्यै बैठ डूंगर की (खियां)।। अरै बाईजी का जामी दीखै मोरिया भाई तनै आंवता (म्हे)। मोरला रे थारा मीठा बहन ही (कीआवूं)।। दरबार का हुकमूं निंगै कर भगवान आवै कोनी आवै देखां (म्हे)। दरबार का हुकमूं अब के मोरियो बोलै (वाह वाह)।। कांई बाई नै जवाब देवै देखां (कीआवूं जाणज्यो देखां कीआवूं)।।

ए मैं डूंगर का जी बीली बाई ये मैं मोहरला रे।
मैं तो बीली ये चुग पत्थरावूं पेट भरां रे।।

बिनै रुत आया बिन ये बहनड़ी बोलां कोय ने।
जै बोलां तो बीली जी तो हिंवड़ो (पांच?)मरां रे।।
(भलां जी भलां) देव भलां

बाई मैं डूंगर का मोरिया हां (म्हे)। देख चूग अर पत्थरां से पेट (भरां)।। बिनै रुत आया बिनै ये बीली कोनी बोलां (म्हे)। जै बोल जावां तो हिंवड़ो (पांच?) (मरां)।। झूटा कींयां बोला ये बाई कीयो (वाह वाह)। तो बाई रुदन करबा लागी (म्हे)।। बाई रुदन करियो बी टैम में भगवान दुवारकाजी में हा (वाह वाह)। दरबार का हुकमूं दुवारकाजीवूं भगवान देखियो रे बाई में बीको पड़ गो चालो भैइ (हां चालां कीयो)।। दुवारकाजी से देव पधार गा हुई लीलै (असवार)। अरै रूंखा रूंखा रली बधावा अरै भगवान नै पत्थर लिया (जुंवार)।। (अळड़ाट?) बोल्यो (वाह वाह)। पत्थर तो दरबार का हुकमूं दुल देमाली को कांकड़ सारो ही भगवान नै सलाम (करी ही)।। हेंर रूंख है नै (म्हे)। सगळा ही बधावा गाबा लागा (वाह वाह)।। बाईजी देखियो रे भगवान अब आया (हां अब आया)। तीन तिलोकी को नाथ आंतां ही बूझणा करी है बाई (म्हे)।। दुशमन (निवे?) तो कोनी (हां कोनी निवै कीयो)। हां श्री महाराज नी निवै (वाह वाह)।। पण म्हनै तो दुख नी देनो (हो?) तनै (म्हे)। तीन तिलोकी को नाथ सुवा को सेस मण की शिला पड़ी ही (म्हे)।। के ठोकर पायी (वाह वाह)। तो जी टैम बीला पर शिला छोड़ी तो बाई कांई करियो के आंगली को सामै हाथ दे दियो (हां आडो हाथ दियो)।। कीयो बाई हाथ में देय (म्हे)। दुशमन नै मारबा देयो देश छुट जाय (हां थारो तो कीयो)।। कीयो श्री महाराज एक तो भाई दियो इयां तो मत मारो ईनै (वाह वाह)। भगवान कीयो सेवा समा भाई (म्हे)।। कीयो कांई होवै सेवा (कांई करो सेवा किसी होवै म्हनै ठा कोनी)। कीयो बतायावूं हा श्री महाराज बतायावूं तो समझ आवै तो कांई ठी (हां कर लेवां)।। बी शीला के हेटै बीला ऊबो हेंर बीली ऊबी है (म्हे)। बीली तो हाथ दे मेलियो है (वाह वाह)।। दरबार का हुकमूं भगवान गेबावूं एक पाट बनाय हेंर अती की ईंठा पैदा करी (वाह वाह)। बै भी है भगवान की करियोड़ी है मिनख की बनयोड़ी नी है बी जागां तो दरबार का हुकमूं जागता बनाय अर भगवान बी जागां सेवा करी (हां आपो आप सेवा करी जी कीयो)।। सेवा करी की बीलो हाथमूं भगवान कावूं (कोसी)। श्री महाराज मैं झूटो दुख पायो (हां अता दिन झूटो ही दुख पायो म्हनै ठा कोई नी सेवा (कांई होवै आ होवै जर कर लेवो)।। थै म्हारा पिताजी हो जको ओ काम कर लेवो (म्हे)। अब म्हनै शरम ही (हां कोनी कीयो)।। जाओ श्री महाराज मैं करूं (हां अब लेयायो मैं करू)। तो बीलो सेवा समायी देव महाराज अम्मी की नजर (झांकिया)।। तो बीला की काया भगवान की बी जागां कंचन की (कर दीनी)। देमाली से तो देवरा हो गा (म्हे)।। बीला से भोपा हो गा (भोपा व्हिया)। पहली कोई देवरा मसीद कुछ नी होवै (हां कोनी हां)।। नी भोपा अर कोई भगत नी न पुजारी हां (वाह वाह)। तो भगवान बीला की काया सुधारतां (म्हे)।। देमाली को देवरो होतां (होंवतां)। बीला से भोपा होतां (वाह वाह)।। जय बोलो भैइ श्री देवनारायण भगवान की (जय)।।

Glossary

Ād: Name of king who is first in a genealogy of Cauhān kings, at the end of which Savāī Bhoj and Devnārāyaṇ appear. The genealogy is recited on different occasions by Chochū Bhāṭ.

Ād Sagat: Great or first Goddess.

Aḍadū: Main market place or bazaar.

Agra: City in which the Tāj Mahal is built.

Ajaypāl: Legendary ancestor of equally legendary Cauhān king Bīsaldev. Ajaypāl supposedly founded the city of Ajmer.

Ajmer: Famous Sūfī pilgrimage centre near Pushkar.

Ākhā Tīj: Festival of swings celebrated in the month of Baisākh (April-May) on the third day of the bright half of the lunar cycle.

Āḷā Rāvat: One of the twenty-four Bagaḍāvats.

Amarāv: King, general, high ranking person.

Āmbesar: Name of a well located near Daḍāvaṭ.

Āmo-Nīmo: Sāḍū Mātā's brothers who accompany her on the way to Mālwā.

Amṛt: Nectar or ambrosia of the gods.

Āṇandrāmjī: Gate-keeper at Pātū Kaḷālī's mansion.

Ann/Anndev: Nourishment, grain, food; Lord of nourishment or food.

Āratī: A prayer or hymn of praise performed with lamps in

front of a deity or person.

Arjan: Arjun, younger brother of Bhīma, the strongest of the five Pāṇḍava brothers.

Āsīn: Township *Āsīnd* in the vicinity of Bhīlwārā city in Bhīlwārā district on the banks of the Khārī river.

Avadhūt: *Yogī*, ascetic, renouncer; especially an ascetic of the Nāth Panth.

Āvar-Sāvar: Terrirtory under the jurisdiction of Dīyājī Jodhkā.

Avatār: Incarnation, especially of Lord Viṣṇu.

Badnor: Capital of the Bagaḍāvats.

Bagaḍāvat: Twenty-four brothers who are the heroes of the narrative called the Bagaḍāvat Bhārat. The most famous are Savāī Bhoj and Nevājī.

Bāgh Siṅg: Father of the twenty-four Bagaḍāvats, man-lion with head of a lion and body of a man.

Bāgoṭ: Territory belonging to Bhūṇājī's father Bārāvat.

Bāījī: Term of endearment used for 'sister'.

Baikuṇṭh: Lord Viṣṇu's heavenly abode.

Bālā Dev: Infant or child Devnārāyaṇ.

Bāndarvāḍā: Territory belonging to Rāvji's younger brother, Nīmde.

Bandrāban: Vr̥ndāvan, the forest in which Kr̥ṣṇa lived. Devnārāyaṇ is often referred to as the king of Bandrāban.

Banīyā: Shopkeeper, merchant, trader.

Banjārā/Binjarā: Cattle-keeping pastoralist

Bārāvat: Bhūṇājī's father; one of the twenty-four Bagaḍāvats.

Bārahaṭh: A title given to a *cāraṇ* or royal bard.

Bāsak: Serpent king of the underworld.

Baṭūṭ: Territory in the district of Ajmer held under the

jurisdiction of Devnārāyaṇ's brother Medu.

Bā̃vlī Ghoḍī: Savāī Bhoj's mare.

Berībaj Bagūl Siṅg: Cowherd who defends the capture of Devnārāyaṇ's cows.

Bhā̃bhī: A person belonging to the community of leather workers and weavers.

Bhādvā: Lunar month from mid-August to mid-September.

Bhagavān: Lord/God; frequent address for Devnārāyaṇ.

Bhairū̃jī/Bhairavanāth: Kālā and Gorā Bhairū̃, assistants/guardians of Devnārāyaṇ.

Bhāṅg: Narcotic drink made from hemp leaves.

Bhāṅgījī: Devnārāyaṇ's elder brother, the son of Nevājī. He compares with Bhīmā in having enourmous strength as well as gargantuan appetite especially, for opium and *bhāṅg*.

Bhārat: Lengthy martial narrative.

Bhāṭ: Individual belonging to the community of bards and genealogists.

Bhāṭaṇī: A female member of community of bards and genealogists; A *bhāṭ*'s wife.

Bhāṭṭī: Rājpūt clan ruling over Jaisalmer.

Bhavānī: The goddess of battle; the Goddess Durgā.

Bhīl: A 'tribal' community living in southern Rajasthan and Mālwā.

Bhīlmal: Capital of the Bhīl king.

Bhojī/Bhojāi: Elder brother's wife; sister-in-law.

Bholānāth: Address for Lord Śiva.

Bhopā: Generic term for singer or priest in Rajasthan.

Bhū̃āl: Kingdom belonging to Queen Jaimatī's father.

Bhūṇājī: Bārāvat's son; Bhūṇājī was adopted by Rāvjī and

brought up under the the name of Khāṇḍerāv.

Bhuvāijī: Father's sister, paternal aunt.

Bhuvānī: Owl like bird associated with omens.

Bījā Mehtā: A village headman in the service of Rāvjī.

Bīlā-Bīlī: Devnārāyaṇ's son and daughter.

Bīṇ: Double gourd string instrument used by Bhopās.

Bijorī Kā̃jarī: Clan goddess of the Bagaḍāvats.

Bīsaldev: Legendary ruler of Ajmer.

Bor Ghoḍī: Bārāvat's mare.

Cā̃dan: 'Silver' square; a particularly fine market place.

Chochū Bhāṭ: The Bagaḍāvat's genealogist and bard.

Cāmal: Name of a stretch of ravines in Madhya Pradesh famous for being the hide-out of many dreaded dacoits.

Cāmpānehrī: Name of a village in the district of Bhīlwārā.

Cāṇdārūṇ: Territory ruled over by Sāṇkhlā Sirdār who cut off Bhūṇājī's little finger when he was adopted by Rāvjī.

Caṇḍī: The Goddess Pārvatī, Lord Śiva's wife.

Cāraṇ: Person belonging to the community of bards, singers and genealogists.

Caudharī: Village headman; a person belonginng to the Jāṭ community.

Cauhān: Rājpūt (and Gūjar) ruling clan to which Devnārāyaṇ and his brothers belong.

Caupaḍ: A game of dice played on a cross-shaped piece of cloth or board.

Causle Kheḍā: Capital of Devnārāyaṇ's kingdom.

Cāvaṇḍā: The Goddess Cāmuṇḍā.

Cā̃vṭī: Devnārāyaṇ's second wife, daughter of demon of Fort Gājanā.

Crore: A number of equalling 10 millions (10,000,000).

Daḍāvaṭ: Place of Devnārāyaṇ's childhood.

Deḷū Bhāṭanī: Cocū Bhāṭ's mother.

Demālī: Hillside shrine making first place of Devnārāyaṇ's worship.

Devlī: Memorial stone, small shrine.

Dharamrājā Devjī: An epithet of Devnārāyaṇ.

Dhobī/Dhoban: A man or a woman belonging to the community of clothes-washers.

Diyājī Jodhkā: A general in the service of Rāvjī.

Dūdiyā Talāv: A pond on the way of Mālwā. Devnārāyaṇ is supposed to have stopped drinking his mother's milk at this place.

Durjan Sāl: Seldom used address for Rāvjī.

Dūtī: Messenger woman or sorceress.

Dvārkā: Lord Kṛṣṇa's capital in Saurashtra.

Gajmaṅgalā: An elephant belonging to the Bagaḍāvat's that was captured by Rāvjī.

Gaṇeś/Guṇeś: Lord Gaṇeś; term for elephants in general.

Goḍī Mālāgarī Rāg: A particular *rāga* or Indian musical melody.

Goṭhā: Place of Devnārāyaṇ's childhood (see Daḍāvaṭ).

Guāl: A cowherd.

Gudaliyā: Name of pond on the borders of Rāvjī's kingdom.

Gūjar: Pastoral and farming community into which Devnārāyaṇ was born.

Gūjrī: A woman belonging to the Gūjar community.

Harirāmjī: Bāgh Siṅg's father; Devnārāyaṇ's great grandfather.

Hīrāgar: A maidservant.

Ind: Indra, king of the gods.

Jagīśyo: A fictional name given by Chochū Bhāṭ to himself.

Jaldev: Lord of water.

Jam: Yama, the god of death; a demon or giant.

Jāsā: Father of Nirpāl, cowherd in the service of Devnārāyaṇ.

Jāṭ: A farming and cattle-breeding community.

Jaymaṅgalā: Name of an elephant belonging to the Bagaḍāvat's which was captured Rāvjī.

Jogīṇī: Lower ranked demonic female deities or witches.

Kacchāvā: Kacchavāhā Rājpūts; name of a clan that ruled over the kingdom of Jaipur.

Kālīyode: Name of a pond frequented by Devnārāyaṇ's cows.

Kālū Mīr: A Paṭhān general in the service of Rāvjī.

Kāḷvī: Sāḍū Mātā's mare.

Kapurḍī/Kapurī Dhoban: Washerwoman in the service of Rāvjī.

Kārttik: Auspicious lunar month in October-November during which a number of festivals are held.

Kā̃s: Kaṁsa — Kr̥ṣṇa's maternal uncle who tries killing the latter while he is an infant; a particularly evil or wicked person.

Khanār: A territory in Afghanistan whose king kept Rāvjī in captivity.

Khāṇḍerāv: Name given to Bhūṇājī after his adoption by Rāvjī.

Khārī: A river that flows past Āsīnd in the district of Bhīlwārā.

Khejaḍā: The *sāmī* tree.

Kos: A distance of about 3.2 km.

Koṭ: A fort or citadel.

Kuldevī: Family or clan goddess.

Kuldevī Āsāvarī: Clan goddess of Bagaḍāvats.

Kumhār: A person belonging to the community of potters.

Lakh: A number of equalling one-hundred-thousand (100,000).

Lenuḍī Kumahārī: An acquaintance of Chochū Bhāṭ's belonging to the potter community.

Līla/Līlāgar: Devnārāyaṇ's horse.

Madnā/Madan Siṅg: Tejājī's son; Devnārāyaṇ's eldest brother.

Mahābhārat: A story of epic dimensions; a great battle.

Mā̃h: The lunar month of *Māgh* (January-February).

Mahājan: A person of the trader or merchant community.

Mālāgar: The region of Mālwā.

Mālāsarī: The hilltop where Devnārāyaṇ arises from the underworld to take incarnation.

Malhār: Name of a *rāga* or Indian musical melody.

Maṇ: A weight equalling about 40 kg.

Maṇḍal: A lake situated halfway between Āsīnd and Bhīlwārā.

Maṇḍovar: Name of a city ruled over by a Paḍihār king.

Maṅgānā: An elephant belonging to Rāvjī which is slain by Bhūṇājī.

Medu: Devnārāyaṇ's elder brother who was adopted by the king of Ajmer.

Nāg: A serpent deity; snake, cobra.

Nāgaur: Capital of the district of Nāgaur in Rajasthan.

Nāgkanyā: Devnārāyaṇ's wife; daughter of serpent king of the underworld.

Nāglī: Name of Nevājī's cow.

Nāpā: Cowherd chieftain in the service of Devnārāyaṇ.

Nāradī Bhāṭ: Address for Chochū Bhāṭ associating him with

Nārada Muni.

Nāth: An ascetic belonging to the Nāth *Panth*.

Nausar: A pass on the Arāvallī hill range between Ajmer and Pushkar.

Netūjī: Nevājī's wife and Bhāṅgījī's mother.

Nevājī: The bravest and most impetuous of the Bagaḍāvats.

Nīm: The Margosa tree.

Nīmde: Rāvjī's younger brother.

Nolke Bāg: Garden located on the outskirts of Rāṇ City.

Pālāsānī: Stable-boy.

Pālī: Capital of the district of Pālī.

Pāras Pīplī: Name of a particular *pīpal* tree (*ficus religiosa*).

Paṭel: Village headman.

Pātū Kaḷālī: Name of the owner of the liquor shop frequented by the Bagaḍāvats.

Paḍ: 'Cloth'; cloth scroll from Rajasthan upon which a narrative is depicted.

Pavan: Lord of air/wind.

Phep: A mythic flower.

Phūlrīyo: Chochū Bhāṭ's horse.

Pilodā: Fort belonging to the Dhārapatī king.

Pīpalde: Devnārāyaṇ's wife; daughter of the king of Dhār.

Pushkar: Pilgrimage town and sacred lake situated near Ajmer; 'Old Puskar': another lake on the vicinity of the town.

Puṭiyā: A bird that sleeps with its feet pointing upwards.

Rābaḍī: A meal prepared with millet or wheat flour and buttermilk.

Rākhī: A protective talisman consisting of a rosette tied around the wrist with a thread.

Rāṭhor: A Rājpūt ruling clan.

Rāṇ Śahar: Name of Rāvjī's city.

Rāv/Rāṇā: Title of Rājpūt ruler; the ruler of Rātākoṭ; enemy of the Bagaḍāvats and Devnārāyaṇ.

Rūpnāth: The Bagaḍāvat's *guru* who adopted Bhāṅgījī after their deaths.

Sāḍū Mātā/Māt Khaṭānī: Devnārāyaṇ's mother and Savāī Bhoj's wife.

Sālagrām: An aniconical image of Viṣṇu in the form of naturally found smooth, rounded black stone containing anmonites.

Sāṅkhlī: Name of a hill pass.

Salūṇ: Bhūṇājī's mother name; Sāḍū Mātā's sister.

Saprā: A river flowing through Rajasthan and Madhya Pradesh.

Sarvāḍ: Territory given to Kālū Mīr to oversee by Rāvjī.

Sat: Truth, honour, virtue; the force of virtue that enters a woman about to commit the act of *satī*.

Satī: Act of self-immolation by women; a woman who has committed the act of self-immolation.

Satīvaḍā: Place where a women commits *satī*.

Savāī Bhoj: One of the principal characters of the narrative; Devnārāyaṇ's father, Saḍū Mātā's husband, and Queen Jaimatī's lover.

Savāmaṇi: A feast consisting of one-and-a quarter *maṇ* of foods celebrated in honour of Devnārāyaṇ usually as a consequence of a vow being fulfilled.

Sāvan: The lunar month falling between July-August.

Siddhi: Mystical or magical powers obtained through yogic meditational practices; supernatural powers of a *yogī*.

Sikarānī: Name of a place near Bhīlwārā.

Sindhbāḍā: Location inhabited by *jogīṇīs* who devour Chochū Bhāṭ.

Sisodiyā: A Rājpūt clan whose rulers established the city of Udaipur.

Sudābāī: A sacred pool within the boundaries of Pushkar which has healing properties for people suffering from spirit possession.

Surbīṇ: See Bīṇ.

Suremātā: The divine or celestial cow.

Tārāde: Rāvjī's daughter; Bhūṇājī's foster-sister.

Tejājī: The eldest of the twenty-four Bagaḍāvats.

Ṭīm Talāv: Name of a pond where Dīyājī and Devnārāyaṇ confront each other during the latter's recovery of Bāvlī Ghoḍī.

Tī̃ṭodī: Sandpiper or lapwing.

Ṭoḍā Solaṅkī: Rāvjī's son-in-law who belongs to the Solaṅkī Rājpūt ruling clan.

Ṭhumrī: A kind of song sung with two voices.

Toraṇ: An emblem struck down by the bridegroom before entering the bride's home.

Ūd, Ūdkaraṇ, Ūdojī: Epithets of Devnārāyaṇ's that associate him with the rising sun, auspiciousness, and prosperity.

Ūsrī Talāv: Name of pond where Devnārāyaṇ beheads King Bīsaldev's buffaloes.

Wazir: Vizier; a minister.

Yogī: An ascetic or renouncer; a member of the Nāth *Panth*.

पारिभाषिक शब्द-कोश

अड़दू: मुख्य मण्डी या बाजार।

अजमेर: पुष्कर के निकट प्रसिद्ध सूफी तीर्थयात्री केन्द्र।

अजयपाल: चौहान राजा बीसलदेव के समान पौराणिक। उनका पौराणिक पुरखा। माना जाता है कि अजयपाल ने अजमेर नगर की स्थापना की।

अन्न/अन्नदेव: पोषण, अनाज, भोजन, पोषण या भोजन का स्वामी।

अमराव: राजा, सेनापति, उच्च दर्जे का व्यक्ति।

अमृत: देवताओं का पेय या आहार।

अर्जन: पांच पाण्डव भाईयों में सबसे शक्तिशाली भीम से छोटा भाई अर्जुन।

अवतार: देह-धारण, विशेषकर भगवान विष्णु का देह-धारण।

अवधूत: योगी, संन्यासी, विरक्त; विशेषकर नाथ पंथ का संन्यासी।

आखा तीज: वैसाख (अप्रैल-मई) के मास में शुक्ल पक्ष के तीसरे दिन मनाया जाने वाला झूलों का त्यौहार।

आगरा: वह नगर जिसमें ताजमहल बनाया गया है।

आद: एक राजा का नाम, जो चौहान राजाओं की वंशावली में प्रथम राजा है। इस वंशावली के अंत में सवाई भोज और देवनारायण हुए। इस वंशावली को विभिन्न अवसरों पर छोछू भाट ने सुनाया है।

आद सगत: महान् या प्रथम देवी।

आनन्दरामजी: पातू कलाली के महल का द्वारपाल।

आम्बेसर: दड़ावट के पास स्थित एक कुएं का नाम।

आमो-नीमो: साडूमाता के दो भाई, जो मालवा तक के रास्ते में उसके साथ गए।

आरती: देवता या व्यक्ति के सामने दीये जलाकर उसकी स्तुति में प्रार्थना या भजन गाना।

आला रावत: चौबीस बगड़ावतों में से एक।

आवस-सावर: दीयाजी जोधका के न्यायाधिकार के अन्तर्गत प्रदेश।

आसीन: आसीन्द नगर, जो भीलवाड़ा जिले में खारी नदी के किनारे भीलवाड़ा नगर के पास स्थित है।

इन्ड: इन्द्र, देवताओं का राजा।

ऊद, ऊदकरण, ऊदोजी: देवनारायण की उपाधियां जो उसे उगते सूर्य, सौभाग्य और समृद्धि का प्रतीक बताती हैं।

ऊसरी तालाब: तालाब का नाम जहां देवनारायण ने राजा बीसलदेव की भैसों के सिर काट डाले थे।

कछावा: कछवाहा राजपूत; एक वंश का नाम जिसने जयपुर राज्य पर शासन किया।

कपुड़ी/कपुरी धोबन: रावजी की सेवा में नियुक्त कपड़े धोने वाली महिला।

कंस: कृष्ण का मामा, जिसने उसे मारने की कोशिश की; एक विशेष बुराई या दुष्ट व्यक्ति।

करोड़: 10 मिलियन या 100 लाख के बराबर संख्या।

कात्तिक: अक्तूबर-नवम्बर के दौरान मांगलिक चन्द्रमास, जिसमें कई त्यौहार मनाए जाते है।

कालवी: साडूमाता की घोड़ी।

कालीयोदे: एक तालाब का नाम, जिस पर देवनारायण की गायें बार-बार जाती थीं।

कालू मीर: रावजी की सेना में एक पठान सेनापति।

कुम्हार: मिट्टी के बर्तन बनाने वाले समुदाय का व्यक्ति।

कुलदेवी: परिवार या कुल की देवी।

कुलदेवी आसावरी: बगड़ावतों की कुल देवी।

कोट: किला या दुर्ग।

कोस: लगभग 3.2 कि॰मी॰ लम्बी दूरी।

खनार: अफगानिस्तान में एक राज्य, जिसके राजा ने रावजी को कैद करके रखा।

खाण्डेराव: रावजी द्वारा भूणाजी को गोद लेने के बाद, भूणाजी को दिया गया नाम।

खारी: एक नदी जो भीलवाड़ा जिले में पुराने आसीन्द में बहती है।

खेजड़ा: सामी वृक्ष।

गजमंगला: बगड़ावतों से सम्बन्धित एक हाथी जिसे रावजी ने पकड़ लिया था।

गुआल: ग्वाला।

गुदलिया: रावजी के राज्य की सीमा पर स्थित तालाब का नाम।

गूजर: चरागाही और खेती करने वाला समुदाय, जिसमें देवनारायण ने जन्म लिया था।

गूजरी: गूजर समुदाय की महिला।

गणेश/गुणेश : भगवान गणेश; सामान्य रूप से हाथियों के लिए उपयोग किया जाने वाला शब्द।

गोड़ी मालागरी राग : भारतीय संगीत की एक विशेष लय या राग।

गोठा: देवनारायण के बचपन का स्थान (देखिए दड़ावट)।

चण्डी : देवी पार्वती, भगवान शिव की पत्नी।

चंदन : "चांदी" का वर्ग; विशेष रूप से आकर्षक मण्डी स्थल।

चाम्पानेहरी: भीलवाड़ा जिले में एक गांव का नाम।

चामल: मध्यप्रदेश में विस्तृत घाटियों का नाम जो अनेक भयंकर डाकुओं के छिपने के स्थान के रूप में विख्यात है।

चाण्दारूण: साण्खला सिरदार द्वारा शासित प्रदेश। साण्खला सिरदार ने उस समय भूणाजी की तर्जनी अंगुली काट दी थी जब उसे रावजी ने गोद लिया था।

चारण : कवियों, गायकों और वंश परम्परा रखने वालों के समुदाय से सम्बन्धित व्यक्ति।

चांवटी: देवनारायण की दूसरी पत्नी, किला गाजना के दैत्य की पुत्री।

चावण्डा: देवी चामुण्डा।

चौधरी: गांव का मुखिया; जाट समुदाय का व्यक्ति।

चौपड़: पासे का खेल, जो कपड़े या बोर्ड के क्रॉस आकार के टुकड़े पर खेला जाता है।

चौस्ले खेड़ा: देवनारायण के राज्य की राजधानी।

चौहान: राजपूत (और गूजर) शासकों का वंश जिसमें देवनारायण और उसके भाईयों ने जन्म लिया था।

छोछू भाट : बगड़ावतों की वंश परम्परा रखने वाला और कवि।

जगीशयो : छोछू भाट द्वारा स्वयं के लिए कल्पित नाम।

जम : यम, मृत्यु का देवता; दैत्य या राक्षस।

जयमंगला: बगड़ावतों के एक हाथी का नाम जिसे रावजी ने पकड़ लिया था।

जलदेव: जल का देवता।

जाट : खेती करने वाली तथा पशु पालने वाली जाति।

जासा: निरपाल का पिता, देवनारायण का ग्वाला।

जोगिणी: निचले दर्जे की पिशाच महिला या जादूगरनी।

टींटोड़ी: टिटिहरी।

टीम तालाब: एक तालाब का नाम जहां दियाजी और देवनारायण का मुकाबला बंवली घोड़ी के स्वास्थ्य लाभ के दौरान हुआ था।

टोडा सोलंकी: रावजी का दामाद जो सोलंकी राजपूत शासक वंश से है।

ठुमरी: दो आवाजों में गाया जाने वाला एक किस्म का गाना।

तारादे: रावजी की बेटी; भूणाजी की दूध-बहन।

तेजाजी: चौबीस बगड़ावतों में सबसे बड़ा भाई।

तोरण: दुल्हन के घर में प्रवेश करने से पहले दूल्हे द्वारा तोड़ा जाने वाला चिह्न।

दड़ावट: देवनारायण के बचपन का स्थान।

द्वारका: सौराष्ट्र में भगवान कृष्ण की राजधानी।

दियाजी जोधका: रावजी का एक सेनापति।

दुर्जन साल: रावजी को सम्बोधित करने के लिए कभी-कभी उपयोग किया जाने वाला शब्द।

दूती: संदेशवाहक महिला या जादूगरनी।

दूदिया तालाब: मालवा के मार्ग में स्थित एक तालाब। माना जाता है कि इस स्थान पर देवनारायण अपनी माता का दूध पीने के लिए रुके थे।

देमाली: देवनारायण की पूजा के लिए पहाड़ के भीतर बनाई गई समाधि।

देलू भाटनी: छोछू भाट की माता।

देवली: स्मृति शिला, छोटी समाधि।

धर्मराजा देवजी: देवनारायण की एक उपाधि।

धोबी / धोबन: कपड़े धोने वाली जाति का पुरुष / महिला।

नाग: सर्प देवता; सांप, कोबरा।

नागकन्या: देवनारायण की पत्नी, पाताल-लोक के सर्प राजा की पुत्री।

नागली: नेवाजी की गाय का नाम।

नागौर: राजस्थान में नागौर जिले का मुख्यालय।

नाथ: नाथ पंथ का संन्यासी।

नापा: देवनारायण की सेवा में नियुक्त ग्वालों का मुखिया।

नारदी भाट: छोछू भाट के लिए सम्बोधन, जिसमें उसे नारद मुनि के समान माना गया है।

नीम: नीम का वृक्ष।

नीमदे: रावजी का छोटा भाई।

नुसर: अजमेर और पुष्कर के बीच अरावली पर्वत-माला पर एक दर्रा।

नेतूजी: नेवाजी की पत्नी और भांगीजी की माता।

नेवाजी: बगड़ावतों में सबसे वीर और तेज।

नोल्के बाग: राणनगर की सरहद पर स्थित बाग।

पटेल: गांव का मुखिया।

पवन: वायु / हवा का देवता।

पातू कलाली: मदिरालय के मालिक का नाम जिस पर बगड़ावत प्रायः जाते थे।

पारस पीपली: पीपल के विशेष वृक्ष का नाम।

पालासानी: अस्तबल में काम करने वाला लड़का।

पाली: पालि जिले की राजधानी।

पिलोदा: धारापती राजा का किला।

पीपलदे: देवनारायण की पत्नी, धार के राजा की पुत्री।

पुटिया: एक पक्षी जो अपने पैर आगे करके सोता है।

पुराना पुष्कर: नगर के निकट स्थित अन्य झील।

पुष्कर: तीर्थयात्रियों का नगर और अजमेर के निकट स्थित पवित्र झील।

फड़: "कपड़ा", राजस्थान में लिपटा हुआ कपड़ा जिस पर कथा लिखी / चित्रित की जाती है।

फूलरीयो: छोछू भाट का घोड़ा।

फेप: एक पौराणिक फूल।

बगड़ावत: चौबीस भाई, जो बगड़ावत भारत कथा के नायक हैं। इनमें सर्वाधिक विख्यात सवाई भोज और नेवाजी हैं।

बटूट: अजमेर जिले में एक प्रदेश, जो देवनारायण के भाई मेदु के अधिकार क्षेत्र के अन्तर्गत आता था।

बदनोर: बगड़ावतों की राजधानी।

बन्द्राबन: वृन्दावन वह वन जिसमें कृष्ण रहते थे। देवनारायण का उल्लेख प्रायः बन्द्राबन के राजा के रूप में किया गया है।

बनजारा / बिनजारा: पशु रखने वाला चरवाहा।

बनिया: दुकानदार, सौदागर, व्यापारी।

बंवली घोड़ी: सवाई भोज की घोड़ी।

बाईजी: बहन के लिए प्यार से बोला जाने वाला शब्द।

बागोट: भूणाजी के पिता बारावत से सम्बन्धित प्रदेश।

बाघ सिंह: चौबीस बगड़ावतों का पिता, नर-सिंह जिसका सिर सिंह का और शेष शरीर मानव का था।

बान्दरवाड़ा: रावजी के छोटे भाई नीमदे से सम्बन्धित प्रदेश।

बारहठ: चारण या राजकवि को दी जाने वाली उपाधि।

बारावत: भूणाजी का पिता; चौबीस बगड़ावतों में से एक।

बाला देव: शिशु या बालक देवनारायण।

बासक: पाताल-लोक का सर्प राजा।

बिजोरी कांजरी: बगड़ावतों की कुलदेवी।

बीजा मेहता: रावजी की सेवा में लगा एक गांव का मुखिया।

बीन: भोपाओं द्वारा बजाया जाने वाला दोहरे तुम्बे (कद्दू के आकार का थोथा खोल) और तार वाला वाद्ययन्त्र।

बीला-बीली: देवनारायण का पुत्र और पुत्री।

बीसलदेव: अजमेर का पौराणिक शासक।

बेरीबाज बगूल सिंह: ग्वाला, जिसने देवनारायण की गायों को पकड़े जाने से बचाया।

बैकुण्ठ: भगवान विष्णु का स्वर्ग का निवास।

बोर घोड़ी: बारावत की घोड़ी।

भगवान: देवनारायण का नित्य सम्बोधन।

भवानी: युद्ध की देवी: देवी दुर्गा।

भांग: भांग के पत्तों से बना मादक पेय।

भांगीजी: देवनारायण का बड़ा भाई, नेवाजी का बेटा, अतुल बल और अत्यधिक पेटू, विशेषकर अफीम और भांग के लिए, होने के कारण उसकी तुलना भीम से की जाती है।

भाट्टी: जैसलमेर पर शासन करने वाला राजपूत वंश।

भाट: कवियों और वंश परम्परा का अन्वेषण करने वाले समुदाय से सम्बन्धित व्यक्ति।

भाटणी: कवियों और वंश परम्परा अन्वेषकों के समुदाय की सदस्या स्त्री; भाट की पत्नी।

भादवा: मध्य अगस्त से मध्य सितम्बर तक चन्द्रमास।

भांभी: चमड़े का काम करने वालों (चमारों) और बुनाई करने वालों के समुदाय से सम्बन्धित एक व्यक्ति।

भारत: लम्बी युद्ध कथा।

भील: दक्षिणी राजस्थान और मालवा में रहने वाला "क़बीलाइ" समुदाय।

भीलमल: भील राजा की राजधानी।

भुवाजी: पिता की बहन।

भुवानी: उल्लू जैसा पक्षी, पूर्वाभास में सहायक।

भूंआल: रानी जैमती के पिता से सम्बन्धित राजधानी।

भूणाजी: बारावत का पुत्र, भूणाजी को रावजी ने गोद लिया था और उसका नाम खाण्डेराव रख दिया था।

भैरूंजी / भैरवनाथ: काला और गौरा भैरूं, देवनारायण के सहायक / अभिभावक।

भोजी / भोजाई: बड़े भाई की पत्नी, भाभी।

भोपा: राजस्थान में गायक या पुजारी के लिए जातिगत शब्द।

भोलानाथ: भगवान शिव के लिए सम्बोधन।

मंगाना: रावजी का एक हाथी, जिसका वध भूणाजी ने कर दिया।

मण: लगभग 40 कि॰ग्रा॰ के बराबर वजन।

मदना / मदन सिंह: तेजाजी का पुत्र, देवनारायण का बड़ा भाई।

मल्हार: एक राग या भारतीय संगीत की लय का नाम।

महाजन: व्यापारी या सौदागर समुदाय का व्यक्ति।

महाभारत: महाकाव्य के आकार की कहानी; एक महायुद्ध।

माण्डल: आसीन्द और भीलवाड़ा के बीच आधी दूरी पर स्थित झील।

मान्डोवर: पडिहार राजा द्वारा शासित एक नगर का नाम।

मालागर: मालवा का प्रदेश।

मालासरी: पर्वत-शिखर, जहां देवनारायण देह-धारण करने के लिए प्रकट हुए।

मांह: माघ (जनवरी-फरवरी) का चन्द्रमास।

मेदु: देवनारायण का बड़ा भाई, जिसे अजमेर के राजा ने गोद लिया था।

योगी: एक संन्यासी या विरक्त; नाथ पंथ का सदस्य।

राखी: एक सुरक्षात्मक रक्षा-कवच जिसमें फीते का बना हुआ कृत्रिम गुलाब कलाई पर धागे से बांधा जाता है।

राण शहर: रावजी के नगर का नाम।

राठोर: राजपूत शासकों का एक वंश।

राबड़ी: एक भोजन जिसे बाजरे या गेहूं के आटे और मक्खन-दूध से तैयार किया जाता है।

राव/राणा: राजपूत शासक की उपाधि, राताकोट का शासक; बगड़ावतों और देवनारायण का शत्रु।

रूपनाथ: बगड़ावतों का गुरु जिसने उनकी मृत्यु के बाद भांगीजी को गोद लिया।

लाख: एक सौ हजार के समान संख्या (1,00,000)।

लीला/लीलागर: देवनारायण का घोड़ा।

लेनुड़ी कुम्हारी: छोछू भाट की परिचित जो कुम्हार जाति की थी।

वजीर: विजिर; मंत्री।

सत: सत्य, सम्मान, सतीत्व; सतीत्व की शक्ति जो उस महिला में प्रवेश करती है जो सती होने वाली है।

सती: महिला द्वारा आत्मबलिदान का कार्य; एक महिला जिसने आत्मबलिदान कर दिया है।

सतीवाड़ा: वह स्थान जहां कोई महिला सती हुई है।

सपरा: राजस्थान और मध्यप्रदेश में बहने वाली एक नदी।

सलूण: भूणाजी की माता का नाम, साडूमाता की बहन।

सर्वाड़: रावजी द्वारा कालू मीर को देख-रेख के लिए दिया गया राज्य।

सवाई भोज: कथा के प्रमुख चरित्रों में से एक; देवनारायण का पिता, साडूमाता का पति और रानी जैमती का प्रेमी।

सवामणि: देवनारायण के सम्मान में सवा मण भोजन का प्रीतिभोज कराना जो प्रायः किसी व्रत के पूर्ण होने पर कराया जाता है।

सांखली: पहाड़ी दर्रे का नाम।

साडूमाता/मात खटानी: देवनारायण की माता और सवाई भोज की पत्नी।

सालग्राम: विष्णु की आकृति जो प्राकृतिक रूप से चिकने, गोल, काले पत्थर के रूप में मिलता है।

सावन: जुलाई-अगस्त के बीच पड़ने वाला चन्द्रमास।

सिकरानी: भीलवाड़ा के निकट एक महल।

सिद्धि: रहस्यमयी या मायावी शक्तियां जो योग की ध्यान क्रियाओं के माध्यम से प्राप्त होती हैं; योगी की अलौकिक शक्तियां।

सिन्धबाड़ा: जोगिणियों के रहने का स्थान जिन्होंने छोछू भाट को निगल लिया था।

सिसोदीया: राजपूत वंश, जिसके शासकों ने उदयपुर नगर बसाया।

सुदाबाई: पुष्कर की सीमाओं के भीतर एक पवित्र जलाशय जिसमें आत्मा द्वारा पकड़े जाने से पीड़ित लोगों को स्वस्थ करने की शक्तियां हैं।

सुरबीण: देखिए बीण।

सुरेमाता: दिव्य या दैवी गाय।

हरिरामजी: बाघ सिंह के पिता; देवनारायण के पर-पितामह।

हीरागर: नौकरानी।

Bibliography

Allen, W.S., 1957, 'Some phonological characteristics of Rājasthānī', In *Bulletin of the School of Oriental and African Studies*. 20: 5-11.

Allen, W.S., 1960, 'Notes on the Rājasthānī verb', In *Indian Linguistics*. 21: 4-13

Bakhin, M.M., 1986, 'The problem of speech genres', In *speech genres and other late essays*, trans. V.W. McGee, Austin: University of Austin Press.

Behl, K.C., 1980, *Ādhunik rājasthānī kā saṁracanātmak vyākaraṇ,* Jodhpur: Rājasthānī Śodh Saṁsthān Caupāsanī.

Binford, M.R., 1976, 'Mixing in the colour of Ram of Ranuja', In *Hinduism: New essay in the history of religions*, B.L. Smith (ed.), Leiden: E.J. Brill.

Blackburn, S.H., *et al* (eds.) 1989, *Oral epics in India,* Berkeley: University of California Press.

Brückner, H., L. Lutze, A. Malik (eds.) 1993, *Flags of Fame: Studies in South Asian folk culture*, Delhi: Manohar Publishers.

Finnegan, R., 1992, *Oral traditions and the verbal arts*, London: Routledge.

Fuimara, G.C., 1990, *The other side of language: A philosophy of listening,* London: Routledge.

Gold, A.G., 1992, *A carnival of parting,* Berkeley: University of California Press.

Goodwin, C., 1981, *Conversational organization*, New York: Academic Press.

Grierson, G.A., 1908/1968, 'Rājasthānī'. In *Linguistic Survey of India,* vol. 9, Part 2, Delhi: Motilal Banarsidass.

Gumperz, J., 1982, *Discourse strategies*, Cambridge: University of Cambridge Press.

Kersenboom, S., 1995, *Word, sound, image*, Oxford: Berg Publishers.

Lapoint, E.C., 1978, 'The epic of Guga: A north Indian oral tradition', In *American Studies in the anthropology of India*, S. Vatuk (ed.), Delhi: Manohar Publishers.

Lodrick, D.C., 1994, 'Rajasthan as a region: Myth or reality?', In *The idea of Rajasthan*, Vol. I, K. Schomer *et al*. (eds.), Delhi: Manohar Publishers.

Magier, D., 1992, 'The language of the bard', Appendix in A.G. Gold.

Malik, A., 1993a, '*Das Puṣkara-Māhātmya*', In *religionswissenschaftlicher Beitrag zum Wallfahrtsbegriff in India,* Stuttgart: Franz Steiner.

Malik A., 1993b, 'Avatāra, avenger, and king: Narrative themes in the oral epic of Devnārāyaṇ', In H. Brückner, L. Lutze, A. Malik (eds.).

Malik, S.C., 1995, *Reconceptualizing the sciences and the humanities: An integral approach,* Delhi: Manohar Publishers.

Miller, J.C., 1980, 'Current investigations in the genre of Rajasthani *Paḍ* painting recitations', In *Early Hindi devotional literature in current research,* W.M. Callewaert (ed.), New Delhi: Impex India.

Miller, J.C., 1994, *The twenty-four brothers and Lord Devnārāyaṇ: The story and performance of a folk epic of Rajasthan,* Ph.D. dissertation, University of Pennsylvania.

Singh, B., 1993, 'The episode of the golden Śiva image', In H. Brückner, L. Lutze, A. Malik. (eds.).

Smith, J.D., 1976, *The Vīsaldevarāsa: A restoration of the text*, Cambridge: Cambridge University Press.

Smith, J. D., 1991, *The epic of Pābūjī*, Cambridge: Cambrige University Press.

Smith, J.D., 1992, 'Epic Rajasthani', In *Indo-Iranian Journal* 35: 251-269.

Tannen, D., 1994, *Talking voices: Repetition, dialogue, and imagery in conversational discourse,* Cambridge: Cambridge University Press.

Thiel-Horstmann, M., 1985, *Nächtliches Wachen*, Bonn: Indica et Tibetica Verlag.

Wardough, R., 1985, *How conversation works*, Oxford: Basil Blakwell.

सन्दर्भ ग्रन्थ-सूची

एलेन, डब्ल्यू. एस., 1957, राजस्थानी की कुछ ध्वनि विज्ञान सम्बन्धी विशेषताएं, *बुलेटिन ऑफ द स्कूल ऑफ ओरिएन्टल एंड अफ्रीकन स्टडीज* में 20:5-11।

एलेन, डब्ल्यू. एस., 1960, राजस्थानी क्रिया पर टिप्पणियां, *इंडियन लिंग्विस्टिक्स* में 21:4-13।

भक्तिन, एम.एम., 1986, भाषण शैलियों की समस्या, *स्पीच जनरस एंड अदर लेट एस्सेज* में, अनुवाद वी. डब्ल्यू. मक्गी, आस्टिन, आस्टिन विश्वविद्यालय मुद्रणालय।

बहल, के.सी., 1980, *आधुनिक राजस्थानी का संरचनात्मक व्याकरण*, जोधपुर, राजस्थानी शोध संस्थान चौपासनी।

बिनफोर्ड, एम.आर., 1976, रनुज के राम के रंग में रंगना, *हिन्दुइज्म : न्यू एस्से इन द हिस्ट्री ऑफ रीलिजन्स* में, बी.एल. स्मिथ (संपादक), लीडेन, ई.जे. ब्रिल।

ब्लैकबर्न, एस.एच., आदि (संपादक), 1989, *ओरल एपिक्स इन इण्डिया*, बर्कले, कैलिफोर्निया विश्वविद्यालय मुद्रणालय।

ब्रूकनर, एच., एल. लुत्से, ए. मलिक (संपादक), 1993, *फ्लैग्स ऑफ फेम : स्टडीज इन साउथ एशियन फोक कल्चर*, दिल्ली, मनोहर प्रकाशन।

फिन्नेगन, आर, 1992, *ओरल ट्रेडिशन्स एंड द वर्बल आर्टस*, लंदन, रूटलेज।

फुइमारा, जी.सी., 1990, *दी अदर साइड ऑफ लेंग्वेज : ए फिलास्पी ऑफ लिसनिंग*, लंदन, रूटलेज।

गोल्ड, ए.जी., 1992, *ए कार्निवल ऑफ पार्टिंग*, बर्कले, कैलिफोर्निया विश्वविद्यालय मुद्रणालय।

गुडविन, सी., 1981, *कन्वर्सेशनल ऑर्गेनाइजेशन*, न्यूयार्क, अकेडेमिक प्रेस।

ग्रीसन, जी.ए., 1908/1968, राजस्थानी, *लिंग्विस्टिक सर्वे ऑफ इंडिया* में वाल्यूम-9, भाग-2, दिल्ली, मोतीलाल बनारसीदास।

गुम्पेर्ज, जे., 1982, *डिस्कोर्स स्ट्रेटिजीज*, कैम्ब्रिज, कैम्बिज विश्वविद्यालय मुद्रणालय।

कर्सेनबूम, एस., 1995, *वर्ड, साउंड, इमेज*, ऑक्सफोर्ड, बेर्ग पब्लिशर्स।

लापॉइन्ट, ई.सी., 1978, गूगा की कथा : उत्तर भारतीय मौखिक परम्परा, *अमेरिकन स्टडीज इन दी अन्थ्रोपॉलोजी ऑफ इण्डिया*, एस. वतुक (संपादक), दिल्ली, मनोहर प्रकाशन।

लोड्रिक, डी.सी., 1994, राजस्थान एज ए रिजन : मिथ ओर रीयलिटि, *दी आईडया ऑफ राजस्थान*, भाग–एक में, के. शोमर और अन्य (संपादक), दिल्ली, मनोहर प्रकाशन।

मागीर, डी., 1992, कवि का भाषा, *ए.जी. गोल्ड* में परिशिष्ट।

मलिक, ए॰, 1993a, *दास पुष्कर-माहात्म्य : इन रिलीजनस्वीसइन्साफ्टलिचर बैटर्ग जुम वालफार्टस-बेग्रिफ इन इण्डियन,* स्टुटगर्ट, फ्रांज स्टेइनर।

मलिक, ए॰, 1993b, अवतार, प्रतिशोधी और राजा : देवनारायण के मौखिक महाकाव्य में कथा के उद्देश्य, इन एच॰ ब्रूकनर, एल॰ लुटजे, ए॰ मलिक (संपादक)।

मलिक, एस॰सी॰, 1995, *रिकान्सेप्टुअलिजिंग द साईंसिज एंड द ह्यूमनटीज : एन इन्टिग्रल अप्रोच,* दिल्ली, मनोहर प्रकाशन।

मिल्लेर, जे॰सी॰, 1980, राजस्थनी फड़ के चित्रित सस्वर पाठ की शैली में ताजा अनुसंधान, *अरली हिन्दी डिवोसनल लिटरेचर इन करंट रिसर्च में,* डब्ल्यू॰एस॰ कालेवर्ट (संपादक), नई दिल्ली, इम्पेक्स इण्डिया।

मिल्लेर, जे॰सी॰ 1994, द टवन्टी फोर ब्रदर्स एंड लॉर्ड देवनारायण : द स्टोरी एंड परफारमेंस ऑफ ए फोक एपिक ऑफ राजस्थान, Ph. D डिसर्टेशन, पेनस्यलवानिया विश्वविद्यालय।

सिंह, बी॰, 1993, सुनहरी शिव आकृति का उपाख्यान, इन एच॰ ब्रूकनर, एल॰ लुटजे, ए॰ मलिक (संपादक)।

स्मिथ, जे॰डी॰, 1976, *द बीसलदेवरास : ए रेस्टोरेशन ऑफ द टेक्सट* , कैम्बिज, कैम्ब्रिज विश्वविद्यालय मुद्रणालय।

स्मिथ जे॰डी॰ 1991, *द एपिक ऑफ पाबूजी,* कैम्ब्रिज, कैम्ब्रिज विश्वविद्यालय मुद्रणालय।

स्मिथ, जे॰डी॰ 1992, एपिक राजस्थानी, *इण्डोईरानियन जरनल* में 35:251-69.

टन्नेन, डी॰, 1994, *टाकिंग वाइसिज : रिपिटिशन, डायलॉग एंड इमेजरी इन कन्वर्सेशनल डिसकोर्स,* कैम्ब्रिज, कैम्ब्रिज विश्वविद्यालय मुद्रणालय।

थील हॉर्टस्टमन, एम॰, 1985, *नेक्टलिशेस वाखन,* बोन्न, इण्डिका एट तिब्बेतिक वर्लाग।

टर्नर, जी॰डब्ल्यू॰, 1987, स्टाईलिस्टिक्स, हारमोन्डसवर्थ, पेंग्विन बुक्स।

वारडॉग, आर॰ 1985, *हाऊ कन्वर्सेशन वर्क्स,* ऑक्सफोर्ड, बेसिल ब्लैकवैल।

The altar in front of Devnārāyaṇ's image on the *paḍ*
फड़ पर देवनारायण के चित्र के सामने वेदी

Devnārāyaṇ's birth on Mālāsarī Hill
मालासरी पर्वत पर श्री देवनारायण के जन्म का फड़ में चित्रण

Devnārāyaṇ in his court together with his four brothers
अपने चार भाईयों के साथ देवनारायण अपने दरबार में

Bhuṅājī speaks with his mother's memorial stone
अपनी माता की स्मृति.शिला से बात करते हुए भूणाजी

Row of bricks representing Devnārāyaṇ
देवनारायण को प्रदर्शित करती ईंटों की पंक्ति

The temple on Mālāsarī Hill where Devnārāyaṇ was born
मालासरी पर्वत पर स्थित मन्दिर जहां देवनारायण ने जन्म लिया था

Śrī Śrīlāl Jośī (3rd from left), his son (2nd from left) along with singers of the narrative
श्री श्रीलाल जोशी (बाएं से तीसरे), उनका पुत्र (बाएं से दूसरे) कथा के गायकों के साथ

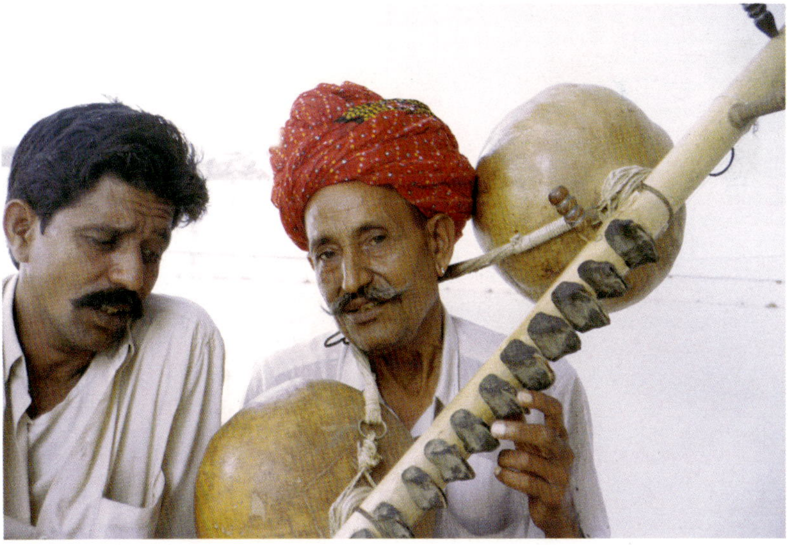

Śrī Hukmārām Bhopā with his nephew Śrī Kiṣnārām
श्री हुक्माराम भोपा अपने भतीजे श्री किसनाराम के साथ

Śrī Hukmārām Bhopā's youngest son (2nd from left) and younger daughter
श्री हुक्माराम भोपा का सबसे छोटा पुत्र (बाएं से दूसरे) और छोटी बेटी

The image of the goddess Bhavānī at the temple of Savāī Bhoj
सवाई भोज के मन्दिर में देवी भवानी की प्रतिमा